Essential Criminal Law

2nd Edition

For NBB

Essential Criminal Law

2nd Edition

Matthew Lippman
University of Illinois at Chicago

$SAGE

Los Angeles | London | New Delhi
Singapore | Washington DC | Melbourne

FOR INFORMATION:

SAGE Publications, Inc.
2455 Teller Road
Thousand Oaks, California 91320
E-mail: order@sagepub.com

SAGE Publications Ltd.
1 Oliver's Yard
55 City Road
London EC1Y 1SP
United Kingdom

SAGE Publications India Pvt. Ltd.
B 1/I 1 Mohan Cooperative Industrial Area
Mathura Road, New Delhi 110 044
India

SAGE Publications Asia-Pacific Pte. Ltd.
3 Church Street
#10-04 Samsung Hub
Singapore 049483

Printed in the United States of America

Library of Congress Cataloging-in-Publication Data

Names: Lippman, Matthew Ross, 1948- author.

Title: Essential criminal law / Matthew Lippman, University of Illinois at Chicago.

Description: Second edition. | Thousand Oaks, California : SAGE Publications, [2016] | Includes bibliographical references and index.

Identifiers: LCCN 2016017162 | ISBN 9781506349039 (pbk.: alk. paper)

Subjects: LCSH: Criminal law--United States.

Classification: LCC KF9219.85 .L57 2016 | DDC 345.73—dc23
LC record available at https://lccn.loc.gov/2016017162

This book is printed on acid-free paper.

Acquisitions Editor: Jerry Westby
Editorial Assistant: Laura Kirkhuff
eLearning Editor: Allison Hughes
Production Editor: Tracy Buyan
Copy Editor: Melinda Masson
Typesetter: C&M Digitals (P) Ltd.
Proofreader: Bonnie Moore
Indexer: Michael Ferreira
Cover Designer: Candice Harman
Marketing Manager: Amy Lammers

16 17 18 19 20 10 9 8 7 6 5 4 3 2 1

Brief Contents

SAGE was founded in 1965 by Sara Miller McCune to support the dissemination of usable knowledge by publishing innovative and high-quality research and teaching content. Today, we publish over 900 journals, including those of more than 400 learned societies, more than 800 new books per year, and a growing range of library products including archives, data, case studies, reports, and video. SAGE remains majority-owned by our founder, and after Sara's lifetime will become owned by a charitable trust that secures our continued independence.

Los Angeles | London | New Delhi | Singapore | Washington DC | Melbourne

Detailed Contents

Preface

Essential Criminal Law discusses the central elements of common law and statutory crimes. The text provides a book for faculty who find that cases are challenging for students to read and to understand and are an ineffective and inefficient tool for learning. The aim of this book is to combine a brief definition of crimes with illustrative examples and with a discussion of larger public policy concerns. The text is comprehensive in coverage and includes important topics that often are not included in undergraduate criminal law texts. I hope that nonlawyers as well as lawyers will find that the book achieves the goal of enhancing teaching and learning in the classroom.

CHAPTER ORGANIZATION

Each chapter is introduced by a **vignette** that raises a significant issue discussed in the text. The learning objectives and chapter introductions help students focus on key points in the chapter. In many instances, following the discussion of a particular crime, the text features a **legal equation** that summarizes the law. In many instances, the relevant portion of the **Model Penal Code** is reprinted and analyzed. A number of the topics covered in each chapter are followed by a **You Decide** section that asks students to apply the material to a new and novel factual scenario. The answer is available on the book's **study site** at study.sagepub.com/lippmaness2e. The book relates the law to current developments by including **Criminal Law in the News** and **Criminal Law and Public Policy** features. Various chapters also offer **charts** listing the frequency that crimes are committed in the fifty states. At the end of each chapter, there is a **Case Analysis**, which is an edited version of a case that is relevant to the material discussed in the chapter. The chapters conclude with a **chapter summary** and with **chapter review questions** that are designed to help students review the material. **Legal terminology** is listed at the end of each chapter, and the book also includes a **glossary**. Cases, statutes, and various learning tools are included on the **study site** accompanying the book.

ORGANIZATION OF THE TEXT

Criminal law is one of the most dynamic areas of American law. You only need look at a newspaper to read about controversies regarding the law of self-defense, marijuana legalization, and sexual offenses. I have taught criminal law for more than twenty years and have the same excitement in teaching the topic that I had when I started.

The textbook provides comprehensive coverage of criminal law. It begins with the nature, purpose, function, and constitutional context of criminal law and then covers the basic elements of criminal responsibility and offenses. The next parts of the textbook discuss crimes against the person and crimes against property and business. The book concludes with discussions of crimes against public order and morality, crimes against the administration of justice, and crimes against the state.

- *Nature, Purpose, Function, and Constitutional Context of Criminal Law.* Chapter 1 discusses the nature, purpose, and function of criminal law. This is followed by Chapter 2 that covers the constitutional limits on criminal law, including due process, equal protection, freedom of speech, and the right to privacy.

- *Principles of Criminal Responsibility.* This section of the book covers the foundational elements of a crime. Chapter 3 discusses criminal acts and criminal intent, concurrence, and causation.
- *Parties, Vicarious Liability, and Inchoate Crimes.* The next part of the text discusses the scope of criminal responsibility. Chapter 4 discusses parties to crime and vicarious liability. Chapter 5 covers the inchoate crimes of attempt, solicitation, and conspiracy.
- *Criminal Defenses.* The next section of the text in Chapter 6 discusses defenses to criminal liability.
- *Crimes Against the Person.* This part of the book focuses on crimes against the person. Chapter 7 covers homicide. Chapter 8 discusses assault and battery, criminal sexual conduct, kidnapping, and false imprisonment.
- *Crimes Against Habitation and Property, and White-Collar Crime.* Chapter 9 covers crimes against property, including larceny, embezzlement, and robbery. Chapter 10 discusses white-collar crime.
- *Crimes Against Public and Social Order and Morality.* Chapter 11 focuses on crimes against public order and morality that threaten the order and stability of the community, including disorderly conduct, rioting, and vagrancy, and efforts to combat homelessness, gangs, and prostitution. Chapter 12 covers three other crimes against social order and morality: alcoholism, gambling, and narcotics.
- *Crimes Against the Administration of Justice.* Chapter 13 discusses crimes against the administration of justice, including bribery, perjury, obstruction of justice, resisting arrest, compounding a crime, and escape.
- *Crimes Against the State.* The text concludes in Chapter 14 by discussing treason, sedition, espionage, and counterterrorism.

ANCILLARIES

Instructor Teaching Site

A password-protected site, available at study.sagepub.com/lippmaness2e, features resources that have been designed to help instructors plan and teach their courses. These resources include suggested answers to the You Decide questions, reprints of cases and statutes, online appendices, downloadable tables and figures, and more.

Student Study Site

An open-access study site is available at study.sagepub.com/lippmaness2e. This site includes eFlashcards, suggested answers to the You Decide questions, reprints of cases and statutes, and online appendices.

SECOND EDITION

A number of modifications have been made to the second edition.

Text. Material has been included in the text that discusses new developments and that provides additional illustrative examples.

Opening vignettes. Most chapters include new opening vignettes.

You Decide features. A number of new You Decide boxes have been incorporated into the text.

Features. Most chapters include new Criminal Law in the News, Criminal Law and Public Policy, and tables.

Cases. New cases have been included in the Case Analysis at the end of most chapters.

Study site. New material has been included on the student study site at study.sagepub.com/lippmaness2e.

Acknowledgments

I hope that the textbook conveys my passion and enthusiasm for the teaching of criminal law and contributes to the teaching and learning of this fascinating and vital topic. The book has been the product of the efforts and commitment of countless individuals who deserve much of the credit.

I have benefited from the comments and suggestions of colleagues who reviewed the text. They took the task seriously and greatly improved the text. I owe them a great debt of gratitude.

Stephen A. Brundage	College of DuPage
Brian E. Cranny	Greenville Technical College
Valencia Davis	University of West Florida
Mary Pyle	Tyler Junior College
Sheldon H. Rifkin	Kennesaw State University
Stephen M. Sherlock	California State University, Chico
Kurt D. Siedschlaw	University of Nebraska at Kearney
Frank Zotter Jr.	School and College Legal Services of California

The people at SAGE are among the most skilled professionals that an author is likely to encounter. An author is fortunate to publish with SAGE, a publisher that is committed to quality books. Publisher and Acquisitions Editor Jerry Westby took an active and intense interest in the book and throughout the writing provided intelligent suggestions and expert direction. In my opinion, Jerry is unmatched in the field. Laura Kirkhuff as always provided invaluable assistance. Nicole Mangona deserves full credit for her efficient and effective work on the study site. I would also like to thank all the expert professionals at SAGE in production and design who contributed their talents, particularly Production Editor Tracy Buyan, who expertly coordinated the preparation and publication of this lengthy manuscript. A special thanks as well to Marketing Manager Amy Lammers. The text was immensely improved by the meticulous, intelligent, and insightful copy-editing of Melinda Masson.

At the University of Illinois at Chicago, I must mention colleagues Greg Matoesian, John Hagedorn, Lisa Frohmann, Dennis Judd, Beth Richie, the late Gordon Misner, Laurie Schaffner, Dagmar Lorenz, Evan McKenzie, Dick Simpson, Amie Schuck, the late Gene Scaramella, Nancy Cirillo, Natasha Barnes, Bette Bottoms, Dean Astrida Tantillo, and Dennis Rosenbaum. A great debt of gratitude, of course, is owed to my students, who constantly provide new and creative insights.

I am fortunate to have loyal friends who have provided inspiration and encouragement. These include my dear friends Wayne Kerstetter, Deborah Allen-Baber, Agata Fijalkowski, Sharon Savinski, Mindie Lazarus-Black, Kris Clark, Donna Dorney, the late Leanne Lobravico, Sean McConville, Sheldon Rosing, Bryan Burke, Maeve Barrett Burke, Bill Lane, Kerry Peterson, Ken Janda, Annamarie Pastore, Jess Maghan, Oneida Meranto, Robin Wagner, Jennifer Woodard, Tom Morante, and Marianne Splitter. I also must thank the late Ralph Semsker and Isadora Semsker and their entire family. Dr. Mary Hallberg has continued to be an important source of support in my life, and the late Lidia Janus remains my true north and inspiration.

I have two members of my family living in Chicago. My sister, Dr. Jessica Lippman, and niece, Professor Amelia Barrett, remain a source of encouragement and generous assistance. Finally, the book is dedicated to my parents, Mr. and Mrs. S. G. Lippman, who provided me with a love of learning. My late father, S. G. Lippman, practiced law for seventy years in the service of the most vulnerable members of society. He believed that law was the highest calling and never turned away a person in need. Law, for him, was a passionate calling to pursue justice and an endless source of discussion, debate, and fascination.

THE NATURE, PURPOSE, AND FUNCTION OF CRIMINAL LAW

Learning Objectives

1. Define a crime and distinguish between civil and criminal law.

2. Appreciate the difference between criminal law and criminal procedure.

3. Know the difference between felonies and misdemeanors and the difference between *mala in se* and *mala prohibita*.

4. Appreciate the various sources of criminal law.

5. Understand the stages of the federal criminal justice process.

6. Know the structure of the federal judicial system.

7. Understand the general structure of state court systems.

INTRODUCTION

The criminal law is the foundation of the criminal justice system. The law defines the conduct that may lead to an arrest by the police, trial before the courts, and incarceration in prison. When we think about criminal law, we typically focus on offenses such as rape, robbery, and murder. States, however, condemn a range of acts in their criminal codes, some of which may surprise you. In Alabama, it is a criminal offense to promote or engage in a wrestling match with a bear or to train a bear to fight in such a match. A Florida law states that it is unlawful to possess "any ignited tobacco product" in an elevator. Rhode Island declares that an individual shall be imprisoned for seven years who voluntarily engages in a duel with a dangerous weapon or who challenges an individual to a duel. In Wyoming, you can be arrested for skiing while being impaired by alcohol or for opening and failing to close a gate in a fence that "crosses a private road or river." You can find criminal laws on the books in various states punishing activities such as playing dominos on Sunday, feeding an alcoholic beverage to a moose, cursing on a miniature golf course, making love in a car, or performing a wedding ceremony when either the bride or groom is drunk. In Louisiana, you risk being sentenced to ten years in prison for stealing an alligator, whether dead or alive, valued at $1,000.[1]

THE NATURE OF CRIMINAL LAW

Are there common characteristics of acts that are labeled as crimes? How do we define a crime? The easy answer is that a **crime** is whatever the law declares to be a criminal offense and punishes with a penalty. The difficulty with this approach is that not all criminal convictions result in a fine or imprisonment. Rather than punishing a **defendant**, the judge may merely warn him or her not to repeat the criminal act. Most commentators stress that the important feature of a crime is that it is an act that is officially condemned by the community and carries a sense of shame and humiliation. Professor Henry M. Hart Jr. defines crime as "conduct which, if . . . shown to have taken place," will result in the "formal and solemn pronouncement of the moral condemnation of the community."[2]

The central point of Professor Hart's definition is that a crime is subject to formal condemnation by a judge and jury representing the people in a court of law. This distinguishes a crime from acts most people would find objectionable that typically are not subject to state prosecution and official punishment. We might, for instance, criticize someone who cheats on his or her spouse, but we generally leave the solution to the *individuals involved*. Other matters are left to *institutions* to settle; schools generally discipline students who cheat or disrupt classes, but this rarely results in a criminal charge. Professional baseball, basketball, and football leagues have their own private procedures for disciplining players. Most states leave the decision whether to recycle trash to the *individual* and look to *peer pressure* to enforce this obligation.

CRIMINAL AND CIVIL LAW

How does the criminal law differ from the **civil law**? The civil law is that branch of the law that protects the individual rather than the public interest. A legal action for a civil wrong is brought by an individual rather than by a state prosecutor. You may sue a mechanic who breaches a contract to repair your car, or bring an action against a landlord who fails to adequately heat your apartment. The injury is primarily to you as an individual, and there is relatively little harm to society. A mechanic who intentionally misleads and harms a number of innocent consumers, however, may find himself or herself charged with criminal fraud.

Civil and criminal actions are characterized by different legal procedures. For instance, conviction of a crime requires the high standard of proof beyond a reasonable doubt, although responsibility for a civil wrong is established by the much lower standard of proof by a preponderance of the evidence or roughly 51 percent certainty. The high standard of proof in criminal cases reflects the fact that a criminal conviction may result in a loss of liberty and significant damage to an individual's reputation and standing in the community.[3]

The famous eighteenth-century English jurist William Blackstone summarizes the distinction between civil and criminal law by observing that civil injuries are "an infringement . . . of the civil rights which belong to individuals . . . public wrongs, or crimes . . . are a breach and violation of the public rights and duties, due to the whole community . . . in its social aggregate capacity." Blackstone illustrates this difference by pointing out that society has little interest in whether an individual sues a neighbor or emerges victorious in a land dispute. On the other hand, society has a substantial investment in the arrest, prosecution, and conviction of individuals responsible for espionage, murder, and robbery.[4]

The difference between a civil and criminal action is not always clear, particularly with regard to an action for a **tort**, which is an injury to a person or to his or her property. Consider the drunken driver who runs a red light and hits your car. The driver may be sued in tort for negligently damaging you and your property as well as criminally prosecuted for reckless driving. The purpose of the civil action is to compensate you with money for the damage to your car and for the physical and emotional injuries you have suffered. In contrast, the criminal action punishes the driver for endangering society. Civil liability is based on a preponderance of the evidence standard, while a criminal conviction carries a possible loss of liberty and is based on the higher standard of guilt beyond a reasonable doubt. You may recall that former football star O. J. Simpson was acquitted of murdering Nicole Brown Simpson and Ron Goldman but was later found guilty of wrongful death in a civil court and ordered to compensate the victims' families in the amount of $33.5 million.

The distinction between criminal and civil law proved immensely significant for Kansas inmate Leroy Hendricks. Hendricks was about to be released after serving ten years in prison for molesting two thirteen-year-old boys. This was only the latest episode in Hendricks's almost thirty-year history of indecent exposure and molestation of young children. Hendricks freely conceded that when not confined, the only way to control his sexual urge was to "die."

Upon learning that Hendricks was about to be released, Kansas authorities invoked the Sexually Violent Predator Act of 1994, which authorized the institutional confinement of individuals who, due to a "mental abnormality" or a "personality disorder," are likely to engage in "predatory acts of sexual violence." Following a hearing, a jury found Hendricks to be a "sexual predator." The U.S. Supreme Court ruled that Hendricks's continued commitment was a civil rather than criminal penalty, and that Hendricks was not being unconstitutionally punished twice for the same criminal act of molestation. The Court explained that the purpose of the commitment procedure was to detain and to treat Hendricks in order to prevent him from harming others in the future rather than to punish him.[5] Do you think that the decision of the U.S. Supreme Court makes sense?

THE PURPOSE OF CRIMINAL LAW

We have seen that the criminal law primarily protects the interests of society, and the civil law protects the interests of the individual. The primary purpose or function of the criminal law is to help maintain social order and stability. The Texas criminal code proclaims that the purpose of criminal law is to "establish a system of prohibitions, penalties, and correctional measures to deal with conduct that unjustifiably and inexcusably causes or threatens harm to those individual or public interests for which state protection is appropriate."[6] The New York criminal code sets out the basic purposes of criminal law as follows.[7]

- *Harm.* To prohibit conduct that unjustifiably or inexcusably causes or threatens substantial harm to individuals as well as to society
- *Warning.* To warn people both of conduct that is subject to criminal punishment and of the severity of the punishment
- *Definition.* To define the act and intent that is required for each offense
- *Seriousness.* To distinguish between serious and minor offenses and to assign the appropriate punishments
- *Punishment.* To impose punishments that satisfy the demands for revenge, rehabilitation, and deterrence of future crimes
- *Victims.* To ensure that the victim, the victim's family, and the community interests are represented at trial and in imposing punishments

The next step is to understand the characteristics of a criminal act.

THE PRINCIPLES OF CRIMINAL LAW

The study of **substantive criminal law** involves an analysis of the definition of specific crimes (specific part) and of the general principles that apply to all crimes (general part), such as the defense of insanity. In our study, we will first review the general part of criminal law and then look at specific offenses. Substantive criminal law is distinguished from **criminal procedure**. Criminal procedure involves a study of the legal standards governing the detection, investigation, and prosecution of crime and includes areas such as interrogations, search and seizure, wiretapping, and the trial process. Criminal procedure is concerned with "how the law is enforced"; criminal law involves "what law is enforced."

Professors Jerome Hall[8] and Wayne R. LaFave[9] identify the basic principles that compose the general part of the criminal law. Think of the general part of the criminal law as the building blocks that are used to construct specific offenses such as rape, murder, and robbery.

- *Criminal Act.* A crime involves an act or failure to act. You cannot be punished for bad thoughts. A criminal act is called *actus reus*.
- *Criminal Intent.* A crime requires a criminal intent or *mens rea*. Criminal punishment is ordinarily directed at individuals who intentionally, knowingly, recklessly, or negligently harm other individuals or property.

- *Concurrence.* The criminal act and criminal intent must coexist or accompany one another.
- *Causation.* The defendant's act must cause the harm required for criminal guilt, death in the case of homicide, and the burning of a home or other structure in the case of arson.
- *Responsibility.* Individuals must receive reasonable notice of the acts that are criminal so as to make a decision to obey or to violate the law. In other words, the required criminal act and criminal intent must be clearly stated in a statute. This concept is captured by the Latin phrase *nullum crimen sine lege, nulla poena sine lege* (no crime without law, no punishment without law).
- *Defenses.* Criminal guilt is not imposed on an individual who is able to demonstrate that his or her criminal act is justified (benefits society) or excused (the individual suffered from a disability that prevented him or her from forming a criminal intent).

We now turn to a specific part of the criminal law to understand the various types of acts that are punished as crimes.

CATEGORIES OF CRIME

Felonies and Misdemeanors

There are a number of approaches to categorizing crimes. The most significant distinction is between a **felony** and a **misdemeanor**. A crime punishable by death or by imprisonment for more than one year is a felony. Misdemeanors are crimes punishable by less than a year in prison. Note that whether a conviction is for a felony or a misdemeanor is determined by the punishment provided in the statute under which an individual is convicted rather than by the actual punishment imposed. Many states subdivide felonies and misdemeanors into several classes or degrees to distinguish between the seriousness of criminal acts. **Capital felonies** are crimes subject either to the death penalty or to life in prison in states that do not have the death penalty. The term **gross misdemeanor** is used in some states to refer to crimes subject to between six and twelve months in prison, whereas other misdemeanors are termed **petty misdemeanors**. Several states designate a third category of crimes that are termed **violations** or **infractions**. These tend to be acts that cause only modest social harm and carry fines. These offenses are considered so minor that imprisonment is prohibited. This includes the violation of traffic regulations.

Florida classifies offenses as felonies, misdemeanors, or noncriminal violations. Noncriminal violations are primarily punishable by a fine or forfeiture of property. The following list shows the categories of felonies and misdemeanors and the maximum punishment generally allowable under Florida law:

- *Capital Felony.* Death or life imprisonment without parole
- *Life Felony.* Life in prison and a $15,000 fine
- *Felony in the First Degree.* Thirty years in prison and a $10,000 fine
- *Felony in the Second Degree.* Fifteen years in prison and a $10,000 fine
- *Felony in the Third Degree.* Five years in prison and a $5,000 fine
- *Misdemeanor in the First Degree.* One year in prison and a $1,000 fine
- *Misdemeanor in the Second Degree.* Sixty days in prison and a $500 fine

The severity of the punishment imposed is based on the seriousness of the particular offense. Florida, for example, punishes as a second-degree felony the recruitment of an individual for prostitution knowing that force, fraud, or coercion will be used to cause the person to engage in prostitution. This same act is punished as a first-degree felony in the event that the person recruited is under fourteen years old or if death results.[10]

Mala in Se and Mala Prohibita

Another approach is to classify crime by "moral turpitude" (evil). **Mala in se** crimes are considered "inherently evil" and would be evil even if not prohibited by law. This includes murder, rape, robbery, burglary, larceny, and arson. **Mala prohibita** offenses are not "inherently evil" and are only considered wrong because they are prohibited by a statute. This includes offenses ranging from tax evasion to carrying a concealed weapon, leaving the scene of an accident, and being drunk and disorderly in public.

Why should we be concerned with classification schemes? A felony conviction can prevent you from being licensed to practice various professions, prohibit you from being admitted to the armed forces or joining the police, and prevent you from adopting a child or receiving various forms of federal assistance. In some states, a convicted felon is still prohibited from voting, even following release. The distinction between *mala in se* and *mala prohibita* is also important. For instance, the law provides that individuals convicted of a "crime of moral turpitude" may be deported from the United States.

There are a number of other classification schemes. The law originally categorized crimes that were considered to be deserving of shame or disgrace as **infamous crimes**. Individuals convicted of infamous offenses such as treason (betrayal of the nation) or offenses involving dishonesty were historically prohibited from appearing as witnesses at a trial.

Subject Matter

This textbook is organized in accordance with the subject matter of crimes, the scheme that is followed in most state criminal codes. There is disagreement, however, concerning the classification of some crimes. Robbery, for instance, involves the theft of property as well as the threat or infliction of harm to the victim, and there is a debate about whether it should be considered a crime against property or against the person. Similar issues arise in regard to burglary. Subject matter offenses are as follows:

- *Crimes Against the State.* Treason, sedition, espionage, terrorism (Chapter 14)
- *Crimes Against the Person: Homicide.* Homicide, murder, manslaughter (Chapter 7)
- *Crimes Against the Person: Sexual Offenses, and Other Crimes.* Rape, assault and battery, false imprisonment, kidnapping (Chapter 8)
- *Crimes Against Property and Habitation.* Larceny, embezzlement, false pretenses, receiving stolen property, robbery, burglary, trespassing, arson (Chapter 9)
- *White-Collar Crimes.* Corporate and environmental fraud, identity theft, computer crime (Chapter 10)
- *Crimes Against Public and Social Order and Morality.* Disorderly conduct, riot, prostitution, alcoholism, gambling, narcotics (Chapters 11 and 12)
- *Crimes Against the Administration of Justice.* Obstruction of justice, perjury, bribery (Chapter 13)

The book also covers the general part of criminal law, including the constitutional limits on criminal law (Chapter 2), criminal acts (Chapter 3), criminal intent (Chapter 3), the scope of criminal liability (Chapters 4 and 5), and defenses to criminal liability (Chapter 6).

SOURCES OF CRIMINAL LAW

We now have covered the various categories of criminal law. The next question to consider is this: What are the sources of the criminal law? How do we find the requirements of the criminal law? There are a number of sources of the criminal law in the United States:

- *English and American Common Law.* These are English and American judge-made laws and English acts of Parliament.
- *State Criminal Codes.* Every state has a comprehensive written set of laws on crime and punishment.
- *Municipal Ordinances.* Cities, towns, and counties are typically authorized to enact local criminal laws, generally of a minor nature. These laws regulate the city streets, sidewalks, and buildings and concern areas such as traffic, littering, disorderly conduct, and domestic animals.

- *Federal Criminal Code.* The U.S. government has jurisdiction to enact criminal laws that are based on the federal government's constitutional powers, such as the regulation of interstate commerce.
- *State and Federal Constitutions.* The U.S. Constitution defines treason and together with state constitutions establishes limits on the power of government to enact criminal laws. A criminal statute, for instance, may not interfere with freedom of expression or religion.
- *International Treaties.* International treaties signed by the United States establish crimes such as genocide, torture, and war crimes. These treaties, in turn, form the basis of federal criminal laws punishing acts such as genocide and war crimes. These cases are prosecuted in U.S. courts.
- *Judicial Decisions.* Judges write decisions explaining the meaning of criminal laws and determining whether criminal laws meet the requirements of state and federal constitutions.

At this point, we turn our attention to the common law origins of American criminal law and to state criminal codes.

The Common Law

The English *common law* is the foundation of American criminal law. The origins of the common law can be traced to the Norman conquest of England in 1066. The Norman king, William the Conqueror, was determined to provide a uniform law for England and sent royal judges throughout the country to settle disputes in accordance with the common customs and practices of the country. The principles that composed this common law began to be written down in 1300 in an effort to record the judge-made rules that should be used to decide future cases.

By 1600, a number of **common law crimes** had been developed, including arson, burglary, larceny, manslaughter, mayhem, rape, robbery, sodomy, and suicide. These were followed by criminal attempt, conspiracy, blasphemy, forgery, sedition, and solicitation. On occasion, the king and Parliament issued decrees that filled the gaps in the common law, resulting in the development of the crimes of false pretenses and embezzlement. The distinctive characteristic of the common law is that it is, for the most part, the product of the decisions of judges in actual cases.

The English civil and criminal common law was transported to the new American colonies and formed the foundation of the colonial legal system that in turn was adopted by the thirteen original states following the American Revolution. The English common law was also recognized by each state subsequently admitted to the Union; the only exception was Louisiana, which followed the French Napoleonic Code until 1805 when it embraced the common law.[11]

State Criminal Codes

States in the nineteenth century began to adopt comprehensive written criminal codes. This movement was based on the belief that in a democracy the people should have the opportunity to know the law. Judges in the common law occasionally punished an individual for an act that had never before been subjected to prosecution. A defendant in a Pennsylvania case was convicted of making obscene phone calls despite the absence of a previous prosecution for this offense. The court explained that the "common law is sufficiently broad to punish . . . although there may be no exact precedent, any act which directly injures or tends to injure the public."[12] There was the additional argument that the power to make laws should reside in the elected legislative representatives of the people rather than in unelected judges. As Americans began to express a sense of independence, there was also a strong reaction against being so clearly connected to the English common law tradition, which was thought to have limited relevance to the challenges facing America. As early as 1812, the U.S. Supreme Court proclaimed that federal courts were required to follow the law established by Congress and were not authorized to apply the common law.

States were somewhat slower than the federal government to abandon the common law. In a Maine case in 1821, the accused was found guilty of dropping the dead body of a child into a river. The defendant was convicted even though there was no statute making this a crime. The court explained that "good morals" and "decency" all forbid this act. State legislatures reacted against these types of decisions and began to abandon the common law in the mid-nineteenth century.

The Indiana Revised Statutes of 1852, for example, proclaim that "[c]rimes and misdemeanors shall be defined, and punishment fixed by statutes of this State, and not otherwise."[13]

Some states remain **common law states**, meaning that the common law may be applied where the state legislature has not adopted a law in a particular area. The Florida criminal code states that the "common law of England in relation to crimes, except so far as the same relates to the mode and degrees of punishment, shall be of full force in this state where there is no existing provision by statute on the subject." Florida law further provides that where there is no statute, an offense shall be punished by fine or imprisonment but that the "fine shall not exceed $500, nor the term of imprisonment 12 months."[14] Missouri and Arizona are also examples of common law states. These states' criminal codes, like that of Florida, contain a **reception statute** that provides that the states "receive" the common law as an unwritten part of their criminal law. California, on the other hand, is an example of a **code jurisdiction**. The California criminal code provides that "no act or omission . . . is criminal or punishable, except as prescribed or authorized by this code."[15] Ohio and Utah are also code jurisdiction states. The Utah criminal code states that common law crimes "are abolished and no conduct is a crime unless made so by this code . . . or ordinance."[16]

Professor LaFave observes that courts in common law states have recognized a number of crimes that are not part of their criminal codes, including conspiracy, attempt, solicitation, uttering gross obscenities in public, keeping a house of prostitution, cruelly killing a horse, public inebriation, and false imprisonment.[17]

You also should keep in mind that the common law continues to play a role in the law of code jurisdiction states. Most state statutes are based on the common law, and courts frequently consult the common law to determine the meaning of terms in statutes. In the well-known California case of *Keeler v. Superior Court*, the California Supreme Court looked to the common law and determined that an 1850 state law prohibiting the killing of a "human being" did not cover the "murder of a fetus." The California state legislature subsequently amended the murder statute to punish "the unlawful killing of a human being, or a fetus."[18] Most important, our entire approach to criminal trials reflects the common law's commitment to protecting the rights of the individual in the criminal justice process.

State Police Power

Are there limits on a state's authority to pass criminal laws? Could a state declare that it is a crime to possess fireworks on July 4? State governments possess the broad power to promote the public health, safety, and welfare of the residents of the state. This wide-ranging **police power** includes the "duty . . . to protect the well-being and tranquility of a community" and to "prohibit acts or things reasonably thought to bring evil or harm to its people."[19] An example of the far-reaching nature of the state police power is the U.S. Supreme Court's upholding of the right of a village to prohibit more than two unrelated people from occupying a single home. The Supreme Court proclaimed that the police power includes the right to "lay out zones where family values, youth values, the blessings of quiet seclusion, and clean air make the area a sanctuary for people."[20]

State legislatures in formulating the content of criminal codes have been profoundly influenced by the Model Penal Code.

The Model Penal Code

People from other countries often ask how students can study the criminal law of the United States, a country with fifty states and a federal government. The fact that there is a significant degree of agreement in the definition of crimes in state codes is due to a large extent to the **Model Penal Code**.

In 1962, the American Law Institute (ALI), a private group of lawyers, judges, and scholars, concluded after several years of study that despite our common law heritage, state criminal statutes radically varied in their definition of crimes and were difficult to understand and poorly organized. The ALI argued that the quality of justice should not depend on the state in which an individual is facing trial and issued a multivolume set of model criminal laws, *The Proposed Official Draft of the Model Penal Code*. The Model Penal Code is purely advisory and is intended to encourage all fifty states to adopt a single uniform approach to the criminal law. The statutes are accompanied by a commentary that explains how the Model Penal Code differs from various existing state statutes. Roughly thirty-seven states have adopted some of the provisions of the Model Penal Code, although no state has adopted every single model law. The states that most closely follow the code are New Jersey, New York, Pennsylvania, and Oregon. As you read this book, you may find it interesting to compare the Model Penal Code to the common law and to state statutes.[21]

This book primarily discusses state criminal law. It is important to remember that we also have a federal system of criminal law in the United States.

Federal Statutes

The United States has a federal system of government. The states granted various powers to the federal government that are set forth in the U.S. Constitution. This includes the power to regulate interstate commerce, to declare war, to provide for the national defense, to coin money, to collect taxes, to operate the post office, and to regulate immigration. The Congress is entitled to make "all Laws which shall be necessary and proper" for fulfilling these responsibilities. The states retain those powers that are not specifically granted to the federal government. The Tenth Amendment to the Constitution states that the powers "not delegated to the United States by the Constitution, nor prohibited by it to the states, are reserved to the states respectively, or to the people."

The Constitution specifically authorizes Congress to punish the counterfeiting of U.S. currency, piracy and felonies committed on the high seas, and crimes against the "Law of Nations" as well as to make rules concerning the conduct of warfare. These criminal provisions are to be enforced by a single Supreme Court and by additional courts established by Congress.

The **federal criminal code** compiles the criminal laws adopted by the U.S. Congress. This includes laws punishing acts such as tax evasion, mail and immigration fraud, bribery in obtaining a government contract, and the knowing manufacture of defective military equipment. The **Supremacy Clause** of the U.S. Constitution provides that federal law is superior to a state law within those areas that are the preserve of the national government. This is termed the **preemption doctrine**. In 2012, in *Arizona v. United States*, the Supreme Court held that federal immigration law preempted several sections of an Arizona statute directed at undocumented individuals.[22]

Several recent court decisions have held that federal criminal laws have unconstitutionally encroached on areas reserved for state governments. This reflects a trend toward limiting the federal power to enact criminal laws. For instance, the U.S. government has interpreted its power to regulate interstate commerce under the **Interstate Commerce Clause** as providing the authority to criminally punish harmful acts that involve the movement of goods or individuals across state lines. An obvious example is the interstate transportation of stolen automobiles.

In the past few years, the U.S. Supreme Court has ruled several of these federal laws unconstitutional based on the fact that the activities did not clearly affect interstate commerce or involve the use of interstate commerce. In 1995, the Supreme Court ruled in *United States v. Lopez* that Congress violated the Constitution by adopting the Gun-Free School Zones Act of 1990, which made it a crime to have a gun in a local school zone. The fact that the gun may have been transported across state lines was too indirect a connection with interstate commerce on which to base federal jurisdiction.[23]

In 2000, the Supreme Court also ruled unconstitutional the U.S. government's prosecution of an individual in Indiana who was alleged to have set fire to a private residence. The federal law made it a crime to maliciously damage or destroy, by means of fire or an explosive, any building used in interstate or foreign commerce or in any activity affecting interstate or foreign commerce. The Supreme Court ruled that there must be a direct connection between a building and interstate commerce and rejected the government's contention that it is sufficient that a building is constructed of supplies or serviced by electricity that moved across state lines or that the owner's insurance payments are mailed to a company located in another state. Justice Ruth Bader Ginsburg explained that this would mean that "every building in the land" would fall within the reach of federal laws on arson, trespass, and burglary.[24]

In 2006, in *Oregon v. Gonzalez*, the Supreme Court held that U.S. Attorney General John Ashcroft lacked the authority to prevent Oregon physicians acting under the state's Death With Dignity Act from prescribing lethal drugs to terminally ill patients who are within six months of dying.[25]

The sharing of power between the federal and state governments is termed **dual sovereignty**. An interesting aspect of dual sovereignty is that it is constitutionally permissible to prosecute a defendant for the same act at both the state and federal levels so long as the criminal charges slightly differ. You might recall in 1991 that Rodney King, an African American, was stopped by the Los Angeles police. King resisted and eventually was subdued, wrestled to the ground, beaten, and handcuffed by four officers. The officers were acquitted by an all-Caucasian jury in a state court in Simi Valley, California, leading to widespread protest and disorder in Los Angeles. The federal government responded by bringing the four officers to trial for violating King's civil right to be arrested in a reasonable fashion. Two officers were convicted and sentenced to thirty months in federal prison, and two were acquitted.

We have seen that the state and federal governments possess the power to enact criminal laws. The federal power is restricted by the provisions of the U.S. Constitution that define the limits on governmental power.

Constitutional Limitations

The U.S. Constitution and individual state constitutions establish limits and standards for the criminal law. The U.S. Constitution, as we shall see in Chapter 2, requires that

- a state or local law may not regulate an area that is reserved to the federal government. A federal law may not encroach upon state power.
- a law may infringe upon the fundamental civil and political rights of individuals only in compelling circumstances.
- a law must be clearly written and provide notice to citizens and to the police of the conduct that is prohibited.
- a law must be nondiscriminatory and may not impose cruel and unusual punishment. A law also may not be retroactive and punish acts that were not crimes at the time that they were committed.

The ability of legislators to enact criminal laws is also limited by public opinion. The American constitutional system is a democracy. Politicians are fully aware that they must face elections and that they may be removed from office in the event that they support an unpopular law. As we learned during the unsuccessful effort to ban the sale of alcohol during the Prohibition era in the early twentieth century, the government will experience difficulties in imposing an unpopular law on the public.

Of course, the democratic will of the majority is subject to constitutional limitations. A classic example is the Supreme Court's rulings that popular federal statutes prohibiting and punishing flag burning and desecration compose an unconstitutional violation of freedom of speech.[26]

THE CRIMINAL JUSTICE PROCESS

A person accused of a felony in the federal criminal justice system progresses through a number of stages that are outlined below. Keep in mind that this process is somewhat different in the federal criminal justice system than it is in state systems (see Figure 1.1). The striking feature of the criminal justice process is the number of procedures that exist to protect individuals against an unjustified detention, arrest, prosecution, or conviction. Individuals may be weeded out of the system because there is a lack of evidence that they committed a crime, or because a police officer, prosecutor, or judge or jury exercises discretion and decides that there is little social interest in continuing to subject an individual to the criminal justice process. The police may decide not to arrest an individual; a prosecutor may decide not to file a charge, to file a less serious charge, or to enter into a plea bargain; the jury may acquit a defendant; or a judge may determine that the offender merits a lenient sentence.

Criminal investigation. The criminal investigation phase involves detecting and investigating criminal offenses. The questions for the police are, first, to determine whether a crime has been committed and, second, to identify who committed the crime. The police may receive reports of a crime from a victim or from an informant, or they may discover ongoing criminal activity and arrest an alleged offender at the scene of the crime.

Arrest. Once the police have established that there is probable cause to believe that a crime has been committed and that there is probable cause to believe that a suspect has committed a crime, they are authorized to execute an arrest of an individual and to place him or her in custody. The police may seize a suspect without a warrant or obtain an arrest warrant from a judicial official. A suspect may be searched at the time of his or her arrest.

Postarrest. An individual who has been subjected to a custodial arrest will be booked at the police station or jail. This phase involves recording information regarding the arrestee and taking a mug shot and fingerprints. An individual may be subjected to an inventory of his or her possessions.

Postarrest investigation. Following an individual's arrest, the police may continue to engage in investigative activities designed to gather evidence of the suspect's guilt.

The criminal charge. Prosecutors have the discretion to formally charge suspects with criminal offenses or to decide not to file formal charges and release suspects from custody. Prosecutors who decide to pursue cases file complaints that describe the alleged crimes and the relevant sections of the criminal code. Suspects are then brought for their first appearance before a **magistrate** (a lawyer appointed by a district court judge for an eight-year term) and are informed of the charges against them and of their rights to silence and counsel. Lawyers are appointed for indigents, and bail is fixed. In the case of a warrantless arrest, the first appearance often is combined with a ***Gerstein hearing*** to determine whether there was probable cause to arrest and to detain the suspect.

Pretrial. The next step in some jurisdictions is a preliminary hearing at which a magistrate determines whether there is probable cause to believe that the defendant committed the crime charged in the complaint. The prosecutor presents witnesses who may be cross-examined by the defense. This allows the defense to learn what some of the evidence is that will be relied on by the prosecution. The defense also may file a motion for discovery, which is a court order requiring the prosecution to turn over information, such as the results of physical examinations or scientific tests, to the defense. A determination that probable cause is lacking results in the magistrate dismissing the case. In the majority of states, a determination of probable cause to support the charge results in the prosecutor filing an **information** with the clerk of the court and the case being bound over for trial. In the federal system and in a minority of states, the case is bound over from the preliminary hearing to a grand jury. A finding of probable cause by the grand jury results in the issuance of an **indictment** against the defendant. Keep in mind that a prosecutor may decide to dismiss the complaint by filing a motion of *nolle prosequi*.

The next step is the arraignment, at which individuals are informed of the charges against them, advised of their rights, and asked to enter a plea. At this point, plea negotiations between the defense attorney and prosecution may become more heated, as both sides recognize that the case is headed for trial.

Pretrial motions. The defense attorney may file various pretrial motions. These include a motion to dismiss the charges on the grounds that the defendant already has been prosecuted for the crime or has been denied a speedy trial, a motion to change the location of the trial, or a motion to exclude unlawfully seized evidence from the trial.

Trial. The accused is guaranteed a trial before a jury in the case of serious offenses. A jury trial may be waived where the defendant pleads guilty or would prefer to stand trial before a judge. A jury generally is composed of twelve persons, although six-person juries are used in some states for less serious felonies and for misdemeanors. Most states require unanimous verdicts despite the fact that nonunanimous verdicts are permitted under the U.S. Constitution.

Sentencing. Following a criminal conviction, the judge holds a sentencing hearing and establishes the defendant's punishment. There are various types of punishments available to the judge, including incarceration, fines, and probation. States have adopted a variety of approaches to sentencing that provide trial court judges with varying degrees of discretion or flexibility.

Appeal. A defendant has the right to file an appeal to a higher court. The U.S. Supreme Court and state supreme courts generally possess the discretion to hear a second appeal.

Postconviction. Individuals who have been convicted and have exhausted their appeals may file a motion for postconviction relief in the form of a writ of habeas corpus, claiming that the appeals courts committed an error.

Figure 1.1 Criminal Justice Flow Chart

What is the sequence of events in the criminal justice system?

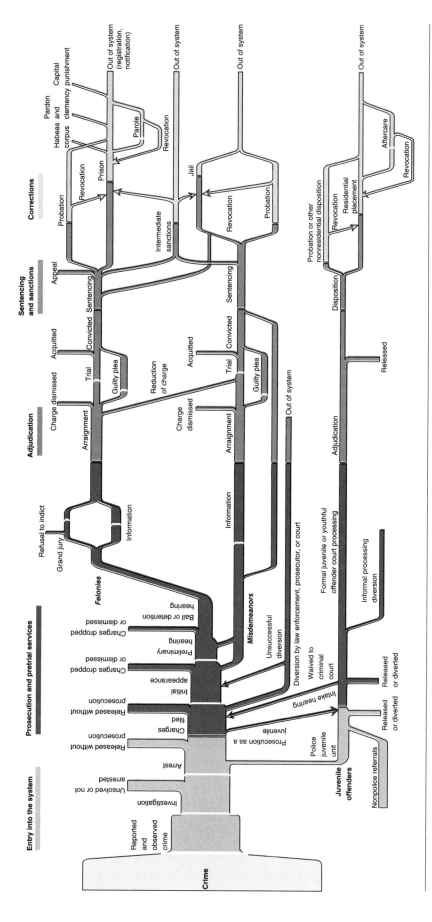

Source: Department of Justice.

Note: This chart gives a simplified view of caseflow through the criminal justice system. Procedures vary among jurisdictions. The weights of the lines are not intended to show actual size of caseloads.

THE STRUCTURE OF THE FEDERAL AND STATE COURT SYSTEMS

The United States has a federal system of government in which the Constitution divides powers between the federal government and the fifty state governments. As a result, there are parallel judicial systems. Federal courts address those issues that the U.S. Constitution reserves to the federal government, while state courts address issues that are reserved to the states. Federal courts, for example, have exclusive jurisdiction over prosecutions for treason, piracy, and counterfeiting. Most common law crimes are matters of state jurisdiction. These include murder, robbery, rape, and most property offenses. A state supreme court has the final word on the meaning of a state constitution or state statutes, and the U.S. Supreme Court has no authority to tell a state how to interpret matters of state concern.

The U.S. Supreme Court has recognized the **concurrent jurisdiction** or joint authority of federal and state courts over certain areas, such as claims under federal civil rights law that a law enforcement official has violated an individual's civil rights. This means that an action may be filed in either a state or a federal court.

The federal government and a state government are separate sovereign entities, and an individual may be prosecuted for the same crime in both a federal and a state court. For example, Terry Nichols was convicted in federal court of involvement in the bombing of the federal building in Oklahoma City and was given life imprisonment. He later was tried in an Oklahoma state court for the same offense and was convicted of 161 counts of murder and was sentenced to 161 life sentences. An individual also can be prosecuted in two states so long as some part of the crime was committed in each state jurisdiction.

The Federal Judicial System

Article III, Section 1 of the U.S. Constitution provides that the judicial power of the United States shall be vested in one Supreme Court and in such "inferior Courts as the Congress may establish."

The federal judicial system is based on a pyramid (see Figure 1.2). At the lowest level are ninety-four district courts. These are federal trial courts of general jurisdiction that hear every type of case. District courts are the workhorses of the federal system and are the venue for prosecutions of federal crimes. A single judge presides over the trial. There is at least one judicial district in each state. In larger states with multiple districts, the district courts are divided into geographic divisions (e.g., Eastern District and Western District). There also are judicial districts in the District of Columbia, in the Commonwealth of Puerto Rico, and for the territories of the Virgin Islands, Guam, and the Northern Mariana Islands. Appeals to district courts may be taken from the U.S. Tax Court and from various federal agencies, such as the Federal Communications Commission.

One or more U.S. magistrate judges are assigned to each district court. A magistrate judge is authorized to issue search warrants, conduct preliminary hearings, and rule on pretrial motions submitted by lawyers. Magistrates also may conduct trials for misdemeanors (crimes carrying criminal penalties of less than a year in prison) with the approval of the defendant.

The ninety-four district courts, in turn, are organized into eleven regional circuits (see Figure 1.3) and the District of Columbia. Appeals may be taken from district courts to the court of appeals in each circuit. The eleven regional circuit courts of appeals have jurisdiction over district courts in a geographical region. The U.S. Court of Appeals for the Fifth Circuit, for example, covers Texas, Mississippi, and Louisiana. The U.S. Court of Appeals for the Tenth Circuit encompasses Colorado, Kansas, New Mexico, Oklahoma, Utah, and Wyoming. The U.S. Court of Appeals for the District of Columbia hears appeals from cases involving federal agencies. A thirteenth federal circuit court of appeals has jurisdiction over the Federal Circuit in Washington, D.C., and has nationwide jurisdiction over patent and copyright cases and other specialized appeals involving federal law.

Circuit courts of appeals sit in three-judge panels. In certain important cases, all of the judges in the circuit will sit **en banc**. The decisions of a court of appeals are binding on district courts within the court's circuit. In the event that an appeal is not taken from a district court decision, the district court decision will be final. The number of judges in each circuit varies depending on the size of the circuit. The Ninth Circuit, which includes California, has twenty-eight judges, while the First Circuit in New England has six. Courts of appeals tend to have differing levels of

Figure 1.2   Federal Court Hierarchy

Supreme Court

- Highest court in the federal system
- Nine justices, meeting in Washington, D.C.
- Appeals jurisdiction through certiorari process
- Limited original jurisdiction over some cases

Courts of Appeal

- Intermediate level in the federal system
- 12 regional "circuit" courts, including D.C. circuit
- No original jurisdiction; strictly appellate

District Courts

- Lowest level in the federal system
- 94 judicial districts in 50 states and territories
- No appellate jurisdiction
- Original jurisdiction over most cases

Sources: Administrative Office of the U.S. Courts; Supreme Court photo: © 2009 Jupiterimages Corporation; Courts of Appeal photo: © iStockphoto/David Lewis; District Courts photo: Public domain.

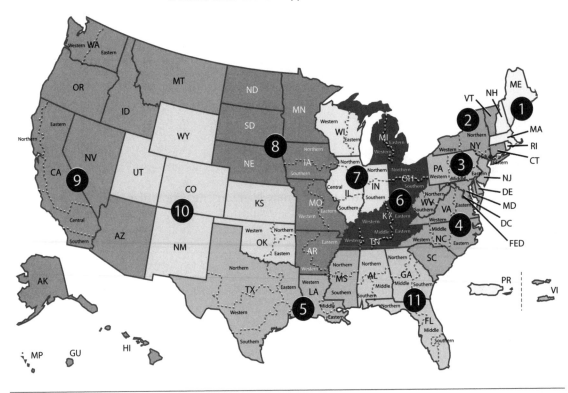

Figure 1.3 Map of Federal Court of Appeals

Geographic Boundaries
of United States Courts of Appeals and United States District Courts

Source: Curtis D. Edmonds, J.D. The Center for Assistive Technology and Environmental Access, Georgia Institute of Technology (GT) College of Architecture (COA), catea@coa.gatech.edu.

respect and influence within the legal community based on the reputation of the judges on the circuit. One measure of the importance of a circuit is the frequency with which the circuit court's decisions are affirmed by the U.S. Supreme Court.

The U.S. Supreme Court sits at the top of the hierarchy of federal and state courts. It is called the "court of last resort," because there is no appeal from a decision of the Supreme Court. The Supreme Court decision sets the **precedent** and is the binding authority on every state and every federal court in the United States on the meaning of the U.S. Constitution and on the meaning of a federal law. In other words, any court in the country that hears a case involving an issue on which the Supreme Court has ruled is required to follow the Supreme Court's judgment. Precedent is based on the judicial practice of following previous opinions or *stare decisis*, which literally translates as "to stand by precedent and to stand by settled points."

The U.S. Supreme Court consists of a chief justice and eight associate justices. The Court reviews a relatively limited number of cases. In an active year, the Supreme Court may rule on 150 of the 7,000 cases it is asked to consider. These cases generally tend to focus on issues in which different federal circuit courts of appeals have made different decisions or on significant issues that demand attention. There are two primary ways for a case to reach the Supreme Court.

• *Original jurisdiction.* The Court has **original jurisdiction** over disputes between the federal government and a state, between states, and in cases involving foreign ministers or ambassadors. Conflicts between states have arisen in cases of boundary disputes in which states

e

disagree over which state has a right to water or to natural resources. These types of cases are extremely rare.

• *Writ of certiorari.* The Court may hear an appeal from the decision of a court of appeals. The Supreme Court also will review state supreme court decisions that are decided on the basis of the U.S. Constitution. Four judges must vote to grant **certiorari** for a lower court decision to be reviewed by the Supreme Court. This is termed the **rule of four**.

The U.S. Supreme Court requires the lawyers for the opposing sides of a case to submit a **brief** or a written argument. The Court also conducts oral arguments, in which the lawyers present their points of view and are questioned by the justices. The party appealing a lower court judgment is termed the **appellant**, and the second name in the title of a case typically is the party against whom the appeal is filed, or the **appellee**.

Individuals who have been convicted and incarcerated and have exhausted their state appeals may file a constitutional challenge or **collateral attack** against their conviction. The first name in the title of the case on collateral attack is the name of the inmate bringing the case, or the **petitioner**, while the second name, or **respondent**, typically is that of the warden or individual in charge of the prison in which the petitioner is incarcerated. These habeas corpus actions typically originate in federal district courts and are appealed to the federal court of appeals and then to the U.S. Supreme Court. In a collateral attack, an inmate bringing the action files a petition for habeas corpus review, requesting a court to issue an order requiring the state to demonstrate that the petitioner is lawfully incarcerated. The ability of a petitioner to compel the state to demonstrate that he or she has been lawfully detained is one of the most important safeguards for individual liberty and is guaranteed in Article I, Section 9, Clause 2 of the U.S. Constitution.

Five of the nine Supreme Court justices are required to agree if they are to issue a **majority opinion**. This is a decision that will constitute a legal precedent. A justice may agree with the majority and want to write a **concurring opinion** that expresses his or her own view. A justice, for example, may agree with the majority decision but base his or her decision on a different reason. In some cases, four justices may agree and, along with various concurring opinions from other justices, constitute a majority. In this instance, there is a **plurality opinion**, and no single majority opinion. A justice who disagrees with the majority may draft a **dissenting opinion** that may be joined by other justices who also disagree with the majority decision. In some instances, a justice may disagree with some aspects of a majority decision while concurring with other parts of the decision. There are examples of dissenting opinions that many years later attract a majority of the justices and come to be recognized as the "law of the land." A fifth type of decision is termed a **per curiam** decision. This is an opinion of the entire court without any single justice being identified as the author.

In the event that a justice has a conflict of interest or is ill and does not participate in a case or there is an untimely death, the Court will sit with fewer than nine judges. An evenly divided court such as 4-to-4 is considered a "nondecision," and the lower court decision remains in effect.

Supreme Court justices and other federal judges are appointed by the U.S. president with the approval of the U.S. Senate, and they have lifetime appointments so long as they maintain "good behavior." The thinking is that this protects judges from political influence and pressure. There is a question whether Supreme Court justices should have limited tenure, rather than a lifetime appointment, to ensure that there is a turnover on the Court. The notion that an unelected judge should hold a powerful court appointment for many years strikes some commentators as inconsistent with democratic principles.

You should also be aware that there are a number of specialized federal courts with jurisdiction that is limited to narrow questions. Two special courts are the U.S. Court of Federal Claims, which considers suits against the government, and the Court of International Trade, which sits in New York and decides international trade disputes and tariff claims. There are also a number of other "non–Article III" courts. These are courts that the framers of the Constitution did not provide for in Article III of the U.S. Constitution and that have been created by Congress. These courts include the U.S. Tax Court, bankruptcy courts, the U.S. Court of Appeals for the Armed Forces and Court of Appeals for Veterans Claims, and the courts of administrative law judges who decide the cases of individuals who appeal an administrative agency's denial of benefits (e.g., a claim for social security benefits).

Figure 1.4   California State Court System

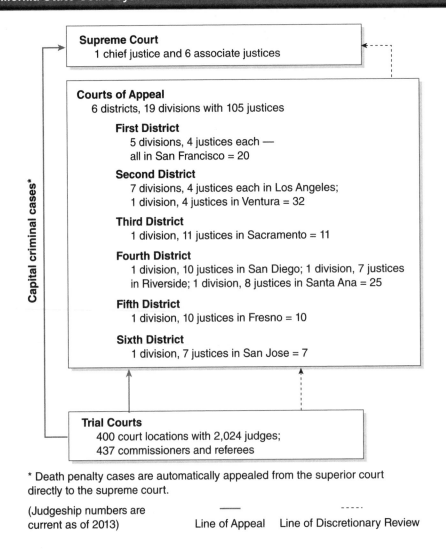

Supreme Court
1 chief justice and 6 associate justices

Courts of Appeal
6 districts, 19 divisions with 105 justices

First District
5 divisions, 4 justices each —
all in San Francisco = 20

Second District
7 divisions, 4 justices each in Los Angeles;
1 division, 4 justices in Ventura = 32

Third District
1 division, 11 justices in Sacramento = 11

Fourth District
1 division, 10 justices in San Diego; 1 division, 7 justices
in Riverside; 1 division, 8 justices in Santa Ana = 25

Fifth District
1 division, 10 justices in Fresno = 10

Sixth District
1 division, 7 justices in San Jose = 7

*Capital criminal cases**

Trial Courts
400 court locations with 2,024 judges;
437 commissioners and referees

* Death penalty cases are automatically appealed from the superior court
directly to the supreme court.

(Judgeship numbers are
current as of 2013)   ——   - - - - -
                    Line of Appeal   Line of Discretionary Review

Two types of courts
California has two types of courts: 58 trial courts, one in each county, and appellate courts. Trial courts are the superior courts; appellate courts are the six districts of the Courts of Appeal and the California Supreme Court. In the trial courts, a judge and sometimes a jury hear witnesses' testimony and other evidence and decide cases by applying the relevant law to the relevant facts. In the appellate courts, people who are not satisfied with a trial court decision appeal cases to judges. The California courts serve nearly 34 million people.

Trial courts. In June 1998, California voters approved Proposition 220, a constitutional amendment that permitted the judges in each county to merge their superior and municipal courts into a "unified," or single, superior court. As of February 2001, all of California's 58 counties have voted to unify their trial courts.

Superior courts now have trial jurisdiction over all criminal cases including felonies, misdemeanors, and traffic matters. They also have jurisdiction over all civil cases, including family law, probate, juvenile, and general civil matters. Nearly 8.8 million cases were filed in the trial courts at some 400 court locations throughout the state during 1998–1999. Appeals in limited civil cases (where $25,000 or less is at issue) and misdemeanors are heard by the appellate division of the superior court. When a small claims case is appealed, a superior court judge decides the case.

Appellate courts
Supreme Court: The state's highest court, the supreme court, may grant review of cases decided by the courts of appeal. Certain other cases, such as death penalty appeals and disciplinary cases involving judges and attorneys, are appealed directly to this court. At least four of the seven justices must agree on decisions of the court. The court's decisions are binding on all other state courts.

Courts of Appeals: Panels of three justices hear appeals from superior courts, except in death penalty cases, which are appealed automatically to the supreme court. The courts of appeal determine whether a trial court committed legal error in handling the cases that are presented on appeal.

Source: Superior Court of California, County of Glenn (2009). *Structure of California Court System,* http://www.glenncourt.ca.gov/general_info/teachers/structure.html. Updated by the author.

State Judicial Systems

There is significant variation among the states in the structure of their state court systems. Most follow the general structure outlined below. The organization of California courts in Figure 1.4 illustrates how one state arranges its judicial system. You may want to compare this with the structure of the judicial system in your state.

Prosecutions are first initiated or originate in **courts of original jurisdiction**. There are two types of courts in which a criminal prosecution may originate. First, there are trial **courts of limited jurisdiction**. These local courts are commonly called municipal courts, police courts, or magistrate's courts. The courts prosecute misdemeanors and in some instances specified felonies. Judges in municipal courts also hear traffic offenses, set bail, and conduct preliminary hearings in felony cases. In most instances, judges preside over criminal cases in these courts without a jury. A case in which a judge sits without a jury is termed a **bench trial**. Most jurisdictions also have specialized courts of limited jurisdiction to hear particular types of cases. These include juvenile courts, traffic courts, family or domestic courts, small claims courts, and courts that hear offenses against local ordinances.

Trial **courts of general jurisdiction** hear more serious criminal and civil cases. In some states, courts of general jurisdiction have jurisdiction over criminal appeals from courts of limited jurisdiction. This typically entails a **trial *de novo***, which means that a completely new trial is conducted that may involve the same witnesses, evidence, and legal arguments that formed the basis of the first trial. These courts of general jurisdiction commonly are referred to as circuit courts, district courts, or courts of common pleas; and they have jurisdiction over cases that arise in a specific county or region of the state. New York curiously names its court of general jurisdiction the supreme court.

Appeals from courts of general jurisdiction are taken in forty of the fifty states to **intermediate appellate courts**. An appeal as a matter of right may be filed to an intermediate court, which typically sits in panels of two or three judges. The court usually decides the case based on the transcript or written record of the trial from the lower court. The appeals court does not hear witnesses or consider new evidence.

The supreme court is the court of last resort in a state system and has the final word on the meaning of local ordinances, state statutes, and the state constitution. (Note that New York is different and refers to its court of last resort as the Court of Appeals.) A **discretionary appeal** may be available from an intermediate court. This means that the supreme court is not required to review the decision of a lower court and will do so at its discretion. In those states that do not have intermediate appellate courts, appeals may be directly taken from trial courts to the state supreme court. State supreme courts function in a similar fashion to the U.S. Supreme Court and hear every type of case. The U.S. Supreme Court has no authority to tell a state supreme court how to interpret the meaning of its state constitution.

State court judges are selected using a variety of procedures. Some states elect judges in a partisan election in which judges run under the label of a political party, while other states hold nonpartisan elections in which judges are not identified as belonging to a political party. In other states, judges are elected by the state legislature. A fourth approach is appointment by the governor with the consent of the legislature. The so-called Missouri Plan provides for appointment by the governor, and following a judge's initial period of judicial service, the electorate is asked whether to retain or to reject the judge's continuation in office. A minority of states provide for the lifetime appointment of judges. Most states limit the length of the judge's term in office. In many states, different procedures are used for different courts. There is a continuing debate over whether judges should be elected or appointed based on merit and qualifications.

PRECEDENT

We have seen that courts follow *stare decisis*, which means that once a court has established a legal principle, this rule constitutes a precedent that will be followed by courts in future cases that involve the same legal issue. The advantage of precedent is that courts do not have to reinvent the wheel each time that they confront an issue and, instead, are able to rely on the opinion of other judges. A judgment that is based on precedent and the existing law also takes on credibility and is likely to be respected and followed. Precedent is merely the method that all of us rely on when undertaking a new challenge: We ask how other people went about doing the same task.

Courts have different degrees of authority in terms of precedent. As noted, U.S. Supreme Court decisions constitute precedent for all other courts in interpreting the U.S. Constitution and federal laws. Circuit courts of appeals, U.S. district courts, and state courts are bound by Supreme Court precedent. Circuit courts of appeals and state supreme courts establish binding precedents within their territorial jurisdictions. In other words, a state supreme court decision constitutes precedent for all courts within the state.

What if there is no precedent? A case that presents an issue that a court has never previously decided is termed a case of **first impression**. In these instances, a court will look to see how other courts have decided the issue. These other court decisions do not constitute precedent, but they are viewed as **persuasive authority**, or cases to be considered in reaching a decision. For example, a federal court of appeals will look to see how other courts of appeals have decided an issue and will view these decisions as persuasive authority rather than as **binding authority**.

A decision of the Supreme Court of California has binding authority on all lower courts in California. The decision of a lower-level California court that fails to follow precedent likely will be appealed and reversed by the Supreme Court of California. The decisions of the Supreme Court of California do not have binding authority on courts outside of California, but they may be consulted as persuasive authority. Courts are viewed as carrying different degrees of status within the legal world in regard to their persuasive authority. For example, the U.S. Court of Appeals for the Second Circuit in New York is viewed as particularly knowledgeable on financial matters, because the judges are experienced in deciding cases involving Wall Street, banking, and finance. Courts are reluctant to overturn precedents, although this does occur on rare occasions. A court may avoid a precedent by distinguishing the facts of the case that the judges are deciding from the facts involved in the case that constitutes a precedent.

CHAPTER SUMMARY

Criminal law is the foundation of the criminal justice system. The law defines the acts that may lead to arrest, trial, and incarceration. We typically think about crime as involving violent conduct, but in fact a broad variety of acts are defined as crimes.

Criminal law is best defined as conduct that if shown to have taken place will result in the "formal and solemn pronouncement of the moral condemnation of the community." Civil law is distinguished from criminal law by the fact that it primarily protects the interests of the individual rather than the interests of society.

The purpose of criminal law is to prohibit conduct that causes harm or threatens harm to the individual and to the public interest, to warn people of the acts that are subject to criminal punishment, to define criminal acts and intent, to distinguish between serious and minor offenses, to punish offenders, and to ensure that the interests of victims and the public are represented at trial and in the punishment of offenders.

In analyzing individual crimes, we focus on several basic concerns that compose the general part of the criminal law. A crime is composed of a concurrence between a criminal act (*actus reus*) and criminal intent (*mens rea*) and the causation of a social harm. Individuals must be provided with notice of the acts that are criminally condemned in order to have the opportunity to obey or to violate the law. Individuals must also be given the opportunity at trial to present defenses (justifications and excuses) to a criminal charge.

The criminal law distinguishes between felonies and misdemeanors. A crime punishable by death or by imprisonment for more than one year is a felony. Other offenses are misdemeanors. Offenses are further divided into capital and other grades of felonies and into gross and petty misdemeanors. A third level of offenses are violations or infractions, acts that are punishable by fines.

Another approach is to classify crime in terms of "moral turpitude." *Mala in se* crimes are considered "inherently evil," and *mala prohibita* crimes are not inherently evil and are only considered wrong because they are prohibited by statute.

In this textbook, crimes are categorized in accordance with the subject matter of the offense, the scheme that is followed in most state criminal codes. This includes crimes against the state, crimes against the person, crimes against habitation, crimes against property, crimes against public order, and crimes against the administration of justice.

There are a number of sources of American criminal law. These include the common law, state and federal criminal codes, the U.S. and state constitutions, international treaties, and judicial decisions. The English common law was transported to the United States and formed the foundation for the American criminal statutes adopted in the nineteenth and twentieth centuries. Some states continue to apply the common law in those instances in which the state legislature has not adopted a criminal statute. In code jurisdiction states, however, crimes are punishable only if incorporated into law.

States possess broad police powers to legislate for the public health, safety, and welfare of the residents of the state. The drafting of state criminal statutes has been heavily influenced by the American Law Institute's Model Penal Code, which has helped ensure a significant uniformity in the content of criminal codes.

The United States has a system of dual sovereignty in which the state governments have provided the federal government with the authority to legislate various areas of criminal law. The Supremacy Clause provides that federal law takes precedence over state law in the areas that the U.S. Constitution explicitly reserves to the national government. There is a trend toward strictly limiting the criminal law power of the federal government. The U.S. Supreme Court, for example, has ruled that the federal government has unconstitutionally employed the Interstate Commerce Clause to extend the reach of federal criminal legislation to the possession of a firearm adjacent to schools.

The authority of the state and federal governments to adopt criminal statutes is limited by the provisions of federal and state constitutions. For instance, laws must be drafted in a clear and nondiscriminatory fashion and must not impose retroactive or cruel or unusual punishment. The federal and state governments possess the authority to enact criminal legislation only within their separate spheres of constitutional power.

A criminal felony in the federal criminal justice system progresses through a number of stages. A case may begin with a police investigation and may not conclude until the individual's claim for postconviction relief is exhausted. A striking feature of the criminal justice process is the number of procedures that exist to protect individuals against unjustified detention, arrest, prosecution, and conviction.

The United States has a federal system of government in which the U.S. Constitution divides powers between the federal government and the fifty state governments. As a result, there are parallel judicial systems. Federal courts address those issues that the U.S. Constitution reserves to the federal government, while state courts address issues that are reserved to the states. The federal judicial system is based on a pyramid of authority. At the lowest level are ninety-four district courts. District courts are the workhorses of the federal system and are the venue for prosecutions of federal crimes. The ninety-four district courts, in turn, are organized into eleven regional circuits. There is also a U.S. Court of Appeals for the District of Columbia. A thirteenth U.S. court of appeals is the Federal Circuit in Washington, D.C. Appeals may be taken from district courts to the court of appeals in each circuit. The U.S. Supreme Court sits at the top of the hierarchy of federal courts and may grant certiorari and hear discretionary appeals from circuit courts. The Supreme Court is called the "court of last resort," because there is no appeal from a decision of the Court. A Supreme Court decision sets precedent and has binding authority on every state and every federal court in the United States with respect to the meaning of the U.S. Constitution and on the meaning of federal laws.

There is significant variation in the structure of state court systems. Prosecutions are first initiated in courts of original jurisdiction. In courts of limited jurisdiction, misdemeanors and specified felonies are prosecuted. In trial courts of general jurisdiction, more serious criminal and civil cases are heard. In some states, courts of general jurisdiction have jurisdiction over criminal appeals from courts of limited jurisdiction. Appeals from courts of general jurisdiction are taken in most states to intermediate appellate courts. The state supreme courts are the courts of last resort in each state and have the final word on the meaning of local ordinances, state statutes, and the state constitution. A discretionary appeal is available from intermediate courts to the state supreme court.

Courts have different degrees of authority in terms of precedent. As noted, U.S. Supreme Court decisions constitute precedent for all other courts in interpreting the U.S. Constitution and federal laws. Circuit courts of appeals, district courts, and state courts are bound by U.S. Supreme Court precedent. Circuit courts of appeals and state supreme courts establish binding precedents within their territorial jurisdictions. In those instances in which there is no precedent, an appellate court may look to other coequal courts for persuasive authority.

CHAPTER REVIEW QUESTIONS

1. Define crime.

2. Distinguish between criminal and civil law. Distinguish between a criminal act and a tort.

3. What is the purpose of criminal law?

4. Is there a difference between criminal law and criminal procedure? Distinguish between the specific and general parts of the criminal law.

5. List the basic principles that compose the general part of the criminal law.

6. Distinguish between felonies, misdemeanors, capital felonies, gross and petty misdemeanors, and violations.

7. What is the difference between *mala in se* and *mala prohibita* crimes?

8. Discuss the development of the common law. What do we mean by common law states and code jurisdiction states?

9. Discuss the nature and importance of the state police power.

10. Why is the Model Penal Code significant?

11. What is the legal basis for federal criminal law? Define the preemption doctrine and dual sovereignty. What is the significance of the Interstate Commerce Clause?

12. What are the primary sources of criminal law? How does the U.S. Constitution limit the criminal law?

13. Outline the steps in the criminal justice system.

14. Describe the organization of the federal and state judicial systems.

15. What is the role of precedent in judicial decision making?

LEGAL TERMINOLOGY

appellant

appellee

bench trial

binding authority

brief

capital felony

certiorari

civil law

code jurisdiction

collateral attack

common law crimes

common law states

concurrent jurisdiction

concurring opinion

courts of general jurisdiction

courts of limited jurisdiction

courts of original jurisdiction

crime

criminal procedure

defendant

discretionary appeal

dissenting opinion

dual sovereignty

en banc

federal criminal code

felony

first impression

Gerstein hearing

gross misdemeanor

indictment

infamous crimes

information

infraction

intermediate appellate courts

Interstate Commerce Clause

magistrate

majority opinion

mala in se

mala prohibita

misdemeanor

Model Penal Code

original jurisdiction

per curiam

persuasive authority

petitioner

petty misdemeanor

plurality opinion

police power

precedent

preemption doctrine

reception statute

respondent

rule of four

stare decisis

substantive criminal law

Supremacy Clause

tort

trial *de novo*

violation

CRIMINAL LAW ON THE WEB

Visit **study.sagepub.com/lippmaness2e** to access additional study tools including suggested answers to the You Decide questions, reprints of cases and statutes, online appendices, and more!

2 CONSTITUTIONAL LIMITATIONS

Did Elonis's Facebook post constitute a criminal threat?

Anthony Douglas Elonis . . . began "listening to more violent music" and posting self-styled "rap" lyrics inspired by the music. Eventually, Elonis changed the user name on his Facebook page from his actual name to a rap-style nom de plume, "Tone Dougie," to distinguish himself from his "on-line persona." The lyrics Elonis posted as "Tone Dougie" included graphically violent language and imagery. This material was often interspersed with disclaimers that the lyrics were "fictitious," with no intentional "resemblance to real persons." Elonis posted an explanation to another Facebook user that "I'm doing this for me. My writing is therapeutic." . . . Elonis posted a photograph of himself and a co-worker at a "Halloween Haunt" event . . . In the photograph, Elonis was holding a toy knife against his co-worker's neck, and in the caption Elonis wrote, "I wish." . . . Elonis's posts frequently included crude, degrading, and violent material about his soon-to-be ex-wife. Shortly after he was fired, Elonis posted an adaptation of a satirical sketch that he and his wife had watched together. . . . [A] comedian explains that it is illegal for a person to say he wishes to kill the President, but not illegal to explain that it is illegal for him to say that. When Elonis posted the script of the sketch, however, he substituted his wife for the President. . . . (*Elonis v. United States*, 575 U.S. __ [2015])

In this chapter, learn about criminal threats and freedom of expression.

Learning Objectives

1. Know the rule of legality.

2. Appreciate the distinction between bills of attainder and *ex post facto* laws.

3. Understand the importance of statutory clarity and know the legal test for identifying laws that are void for vagueness.

4. Know the three levels of scrutiny under the Equal Protection Clause.

5. Appreciate the importance of freedom of expression and the categories of expression that are not protected by the First Amendment.

6. Understand the constitutional basis for the right to privacy and the type of acts that are protected within the "zone of privacy."

7. Know how the Supreme Court's interpretation of the Second Amendment right to bear arms has evolved in the past few years.

8. Appreciate the meaning of the Eighth Amendment prohibition on cruel and unusual punishment.

INTRODUCTION

In the American democratic system, various constitutional provisions limit the power of the federal and state governments to enact criminal statutes. For instance, a statute prohibiting students from criticizing the government during a classroom discussion would likely violate the First Amendment to the U.S. Constitution. A law punishing individuals engaging in "unprotected" sexual activity, however socially desirable, may unconstitutionally violate the right to privacy.

Why did the framers create a **constitutional democracy**, a system of government based on a constitution that limits the powers of the government? The Founding Fathers were profoundly influenced by the harshness of British colonial rule and drafted a constitution designed to protect the rights of the individual against the tyrannical tendencies of government. They wanted to ensure that the police could not freely break down doors and search homes. The framers were also sufficiently wise to realize that individuals required constitutional safeguards against the political passions and intolerance of democratic majorities.

The limitations on government power reflect the framers' belief that individuals possess natural and inalienable rights, and that these rights may only be restricted when absolutely necessary to ensure social order and stability. The stress on individual freedom was also practical. The framers believed that the fledgling new American democracy would prosper and develop by freeing individuals to passionately pursue their hopes and dreams.

At the same time, the framers were not wide-eyed idealists. They fully appreciated that individual rights and liberties must be balanced against the need for social order and stability. The striking of this delicate balance is not a scientific process. A review of the historical record indicates that, at times, the emphasis has been placed on the control of crime and, at other times, stress has been placed on individual rights.

Chapter 2 describes the core constitutional limits on the criminal law and examines the balance between order and individual rights. Do you believe that greater importance should be placed on guaranteeing order or on protecting rights? You should keep the constitutional limitations discussed in this chapter in mind as you read the cases in subsequent chapters. The topics covered in the chapter are as follows:

- The first principle of American jurisprudence is the rule of legality.
- Constitutional constraints include the following:
  - Bills of attainder and *ex post facto* laws
  - Statutory clarity
  - Equal protection
  - Freedom of speech
  - Freedom of religion
  - Privacy
  - The right to bear arms
  - Cruel and unusual punishment

RULE OF LEGALITY

The **rule of legality** has been characterized as "the first principle of American criminal law and jurisprudence."[1] This principle was developed by common law judges and is interpreted today to mean that an individual may not be criminally punished for an act that was not clearly condemned in a statute prior to the time that the individual committed the act. The doctrine of legality is nicely summarized in the Latin expression *nullum crimen sine lege, nulla poena sine lege*, meaning "no crime without law, no punishment without law." The doctrine of legality is reflected in two constitutional principles governing criminal statutes:

- the constitutional prohibition on bills of attainder and *ex post facto* laws, and
- the constitutional requirement of statutory clarity.

BILLS OF ATTAINDER AND *EX POST FACTO* LAWS

Article I, Sections 9 and 10 of the U.S. Constitution prohibit state and federal legislatures from passing bills of attainder and *ex post facto* laws. James Madison characterized these provisions as a "bulwark in favor of personal security and personal rights."

Bills of Attainder

A **bill of attainder** is a legislative act that punishes an individual or a group of persons without the benefit of a trial. The constitutional prohibition of bills of attainder was intended to safeguard Americans from the type of arbitrary punishments that the English Parliament directed against opponents of the Crown. The Parliament disregarded the legal process and directly ordered that dissidents should be imprisoned, executed, or banished and forfeit their property.

The prohibition of a bill of attainder was successfully invoked in 1946 by three members of the American Communist Party who were excluded by Congress from working for the federal government.[2] In 1965, in *United States v. Brown*, the U.S. Supreme Court held that a law prohibiting all members of the Communist Party from serving as officials of labor unions violated the prohibition on bills of attainder. The Court explained that Congress was free to ban all individuals who were likely to initiate strikes and disrupt the economy from holding office in unions, although Congress was prohibited from barring a specific group of "subversive" individuals from union office. Excluding all members of the Communist Party from union office made little sense because party members differ in their willingness to call strikes and to disrupt the economy.[3]

Ex Post Facto Laws

An *ex post facto* **law** is a law "passed after the fact." Alexander Hamilton explained that the constitutional prohibition on *ex post facto* laws was vital because "subjecting of men to punishment for things which, when they were done were breaches of no law, and the practice of arbitrary imprisonments, have been, in all ages, the favorite and most formidable instrument of tyranny."[4] In 1798, in *Calder v. Bull*, Supreme Court Justice Samuel Chase listed four categories of *ex post facto* laws[5]:

- Every law that makes an action, done before *the passing of the law,* and was *innocent* when done, criminal; and punishes such action.
- Every law that *aggravates* a crime, or makes it *greater* than it was, when committed.
- Every law that *changes the punishment,* and inflicts a *greater punishment,* than the law annexed to the crime, when committed.
- Every law that alters the *legal* rules of *evidence,* and receives less, or different, testimony, than the law required at the time of the commission of the offense, *in order to convict the offender.*

The constitutional rule against *ex post facto* laws is based on the familiar interests in providing individuals notice of criminal conduct and protecting individuals against retroactive "after the fact" statutes. Supreme Court Justice John Paul Stevens noted that all four of Justice Chase's categories are "mirror images of one another. In each instance, the government refuses, after the fact, to play by its own rules, altering them in a way that is advantageous only to the State, to facilitate an easier conviction."[6]

In summary, the prohibition on *ex post facto* laws prevents legislation being applied to *acts committed before the statute went into effect.* The legislature is free to declare that in the *future* a previously innocent act will be a crime. Keep in mind that the prohibition on *ex post facto* laws is directed against enactments that disadvantage defendants; legislatures are free to retroactively assist defendants by reducing the punishment for a criminal act. The distinction between bills of attainder and *ex post facto* laws is summarized as follows:

- A bill of attainder punishes a specific individual or specific individuals. An *ex post facto* law criminalizes an act that was legal at the time the act was committed.
- A bill of attainder is not limited to criminal punishment and may involve any disadvantage imposed on an individual; *ex post facto* laws are limited to criminal punishment.

- A bill of attainder imposes punishment on an individual without trial. An *ex post facto* law is enforced in a criminal trial.

The Supreme Court and *Ex Post Facto* Laws

Determining whether a retroactive application of the law violates the prohibition on *ex post facto* laws has proven more difficult than might be imagined given the seemingly straightforward nature of this constitutional ban.

In *Stogner v. California*, the Supreme Court ruled that a California law authorizing the prosecution of allegations of child abuse that previously were barred by a three-year statute of limitations constituted a prohibited *ex post facto* law. This law was challenged by Marion Stogner, who found himself indicted for child abuse after having lived the past nineteen years without fear of criminal prosecution for an act committed twenty-two years prior. Justice Stephen Breyer ruled that California acted in an "unfair" and "dishonest" fashion in subjecting Stogner to prosecution many years after the state had assured him that he would not stand trial. Justice Anthony Kennedy argued in dissent that California merely reinstated a prosecution that was previously barred by the three-year statute of limitations. The penalty attached to the crime of child abuse remained unchanged.[7] What is your view?

We now turn our attention to the requirement of statutory clarity.

STATUTORY CLARITY

The Fifth and Fourteenth Amendments to the U.S. Constitution prohibit federal and state governments from depriving individuals of "life, liberty or property without due process of law." Due process requires that criminal statutes should be drafted in a clear and understandable fashion. A statute that fails to meet this standard is unconstitutional on the grounds that it is **void for vagueness**.

Due process requires that individuals receive notice of criminal conduct. Statutes are required to define criminal offenses with sufficient *clarity* so that ordinary individuals are able to understand what conduct is prohibited.

Due process requires that the police, prosecutors, judges, and jurors are provided with a reasonably clear statement of prohibited behavior. The requirement of definite standards ensures the uniform and nondiscriminatory enforcement of the law.

In summary, due process ensures clarity in criminal statutes. It guards against individuals being deprived of life (the death penalty), liberty (imprisonment), or property (fines) without due process of law.

Clarity

Would a statute that punishes individuals for being members of a gang satisfy the test of statutory clarity? The U.S. Supreme Court, in *Grayned v. Rockford*, ruled that a law was void for vagueness that punished an individual "known to be a member of any gang consisting of two or more persons." The Court observed that "no one may be required at peril of life, liberty or property to speculate as to the meaning of [the term 'gang' in] penal statutes."[8]

In another example, the Supreme Court ruled in *Coates v. Cincinnati* that an ordinance was held unconstitutionally void for vagueness that declared that it was a criminal offense for "three or more persons to assemble . . . on any of the sidewalks . . . and there conduct themselves in a manner annoying to persons passing by." The Court held that the statute failed to provide individuals with reasonably clear guidance because "conduct that annoys some people does not annoy others," and that an individual's arrest may depend on whether he or she happens to "annoy" a "police officer or other person who should happen to pass by." This did not mean that Cincinnati was helpless to maintain the city sidewalks; the city was free to prohibit people from "blocking sidewalks, obstructing traffic, littering streets, committing assaults, or engaging in countless other forms of antisocial conduct."[9]

Definite Standards for Law Enforcement

The U.S. Supreme Court explained in *Kolender v. Lawson* that the void-for-vagueness doctrine was aimed at ensuring that statutes clearly inform citizens of prohibited acts and, simultaneously, at providing definite standards for the enforcement of the law.[10]

Broadly worded statutes are a threat to a democracy that is committed to protecting even the most extreme nonconformist from governmental harassment. The U.S. Supreme Court, in *Coates v. Cincinnati*, expressed concern that the lack of clear standards in the local ordinance might lead to the arrest of individuals who are exercising their constitutionally protected rights. Under the Cincinnati statute, association and assembly on the public streets would be "continually subject" to whether the demonstrators' "ideas, their lifestyle, or their physical appearance is resented by the majority of their fellow citizens."[11]

The Supreme Court has stressed that the lack of standards presents the danger that a law will be applied in a discriminatory fashion against minorities and the poor.[12] In *Papachristou v. Jacksonville*, the U.S. Supreme Court expressed the concern that a broadly worded vagrancy statute punishing "rogues and vagabonds"; "lewd, wanton and lascivious persons"; "common railers and brawlers"; and "habitual loafers" failed to provide standards for law enforcement and risked that the poor, minorities, and nonconformists would be targeted for arrest based on the belief that they posed a threat to public safety. The court humorously noted that middle-class individuals who frequented the local country club were unlikely to be arrested, although they might be guilty under the ordinance of "neglecting all lawful business and habitually spending their time by frequenting . . . places where alcoholic beverages are sold or served."[13]

A devil's advocate may persuasively contend that the void-for-vagueness doctrine provides undeserved protection to "wrongdoers." In *Nebraska v. Metzger*, a neighbor spotted Metzger standing naked with his arms at his sides in the large window of his garden apartment for roughly five seconds. The police were called and observed Metzger standing within a foot of the window eating a bowl of cereal and noted that "his nude body, from the mid-thigh on up, was visible." The ordinance under which Metzger was charged and convicted made it unlawful to commit an "indecent, immodest or filthy act within the presence of any person, or in such a situation that persons passing might ordinarily see the same." The Nebraska Supreme Court ruled that this language provided little advance notice as to what is lawful and what is unlawful and could be employed by the police to arrest individuals for entirely lawful acts that some might consider immodest, including holding hands, kissing in public, or wearing a revealing swimsuit. Could Metzger possibly believe that there was no legal prohibition on his standing nude in his window?[14]

You Decide

2.1 In *State v. Stanko*, Stanko was clocked at eighty-five miles per hour and was ticketed for speeding. The arresting officer testified that the portion of the road over which he clocked Stanko was narrow with curves and hills and obscured vision. The weather was dry, and visibility was good. Section 61-8-303(1), MCA (Montana Code Annotated), provides as follows:

A person operating or driving a vehicle of any character on a public highway of this state shall drive the vehicle in a careful and prudent manner and at a rate of speed no greater than is reasonable and proper under the conditions existing at the point of operation, taking into account the amount and character of traffic, condition of brakes, weight of vehicle, grade and width of highway, condition of surface, and freedom of obstruction to the view ahead. The person operating or driving the vehicle shall drive the vehicle so as not to unduly or unreasonably endanger the life, limb, property, or other rights of a person entitled to the use of the street or highway.

Is the Montana statute void for vagueness? See *State v. Stanko*, 974 P.2d 1132 (Mont. 1998).

You can find the answer at study.sagepub.com/lippmaness2e

EQUAL PROTECTION

Immediately following the Civil War, in 1865, Congress enacted and the states ratified the Thirteenth Amendment, which prohibits slavery and involuntary servitude. Discrimination against African Americans nevertheless continued, and Congress responded by approving the Fourteenth Amendment in 1866. Section 1 provides that "no state shall deprive any person of life, liberty or property without due process of law, or deny any person equal protection of the law." The Supreme Court declared in 1954 that the Fifth Amendment Due Process Clause imposes an identical obligation to ensure the **equal protection** of the law on the federal government.[15]

The Equal Protection Clause was rarely invoked for almost one hundred years. Justice Oliver Wendell Holmes Jr., writing in 1927, typified the lack of regard for the Equal Protection Clause when he referred to the amendment as "the last resort of constitutional argument."[16] The famous 1954 Supreme Court decision in *Brown v. Board of Education* ordering the desegregation of public schools with "all deliberate speed" ushered in a period of intense litigation over the requirements of the clause.[17]

Three Levels of Scrutiny

Criminal statutes typically make distinctions based on various factors, including the age of victims and the seriousness of the offense. For instance, a crime committed with a dangerous weapon may be punished more harshly than a crime committed without a weapon. Courts generally accept the judgment of state legislatures in making differentiations so long as a law is rationally related to a legitimate government purpose. Legitimate government purposes generally include public safety, health, morality, peace and quiet, and law and order. There is a strong presumption that a law is constitutional under this **rational basis test** or **minimum level of scrutiny test**.[18]

In *Westbrook v. Alaska*, nineteen-year-old Nicole M. Westbrook contested her conviction for consuming alcoholic beverages when under the age of twenty-one. Westbrook argued that there was no basis for distinguishing between a twenty-one-year-old and an individual who was slightly younger. The Alaska Court of Appeals recognized that there may be some individuals younger than twenty-one who possess the judgment and maturity to handle alcoholic beverages and that some individuals over twenty-one may fail to meet this standard. The court observed that states have established the drinking age at various points and that setting the age between nineteen and twenty-one years of age seemed to be rationally related to the objective of ensuring responsible drinking. As a result, the court concluded that "even if we assume that Westbrook is an exceptionally mature 19-year-old, it is still constitutional for the legislature to require her to wait until she turns 21 before she drinks alcoholic beverages."[19]

In contrast, the courts apply a **strict scrutiny test** in examining distinctions based on race and national origin. Racial discrimination is the very evil that the Fourteenth Amendment was intended to prevent, and the history of racism in the United States raises the strong probability that such classifications reflect a discriminatory purpose. In *Strauder v. West Virginia*, the U.S. Supreme Court struck down a West Virginia statute as unconstitutional that limited juries to "white male persons who are twenty-one years of age."[20]

Courts are particularly sensitive to racial classifications in criminal statutes and have ruled that such laws are unconstitutional in almost every instance. The Supreme Court observed that "in this context . . . the power of the State weighs most heavily upon the individual or the group."[21] In *Loving v. Virginia*, in 1967, Mildred Jeter, an African American, and Richard Loving, a Caucasian, pled guilty to violating Virginia's ban on interracial marriages and were sentenced to twenty-five years in prison, a sentence that was suspended on the condition that the Lovings leave Virginia. The Supreme Court stressed that laws containing racial classifications must be subjected to the "most rigid scrutiny" and determined that the statute violated the Equal Protection Clause. The Court failed to find any "legitimate overriding purpose independent of invidious racial discrimination" behind the law. The fact that Virginia "prohibits only interracial marriages involving white persons demonstrates that the racial classifications must stand on their justification, as measures designed to maintain White Supremacy. . . . There can be no doubt that restricting the freedom to marry solely because of racial classifications violates the central meaning of the Equal Protection Clause."[22] The strict scrutiny test also is used when a law limits the exercise of "fundamental rights" (such as freedom of speech).

The Supreme Court has adopted a third, **intermediate level of scrutiny** for classifications based on gender. The decision to apply this standard rather than strict scrutiny is based on the consideration that although women historically have confronted discrimination, the biological differences between men and women make it more likely that gender classifications are justified. Women, according to the Court, also possess a degree of political power and resources that are generally not found in "isolated and insular minority groups" and are able to combat discrimination through the political process. Intermediate scrutiny demands that the state provide some meaningful justification for the different treatment of men and women and not rely on stereotypes or classifications that have no basis in fact. Justice Ruth Ginsburg applied intermediate scrutiny in ordering that the Virginia Military Institute admit women and ruled that gender-based government action must be based on "an exceedingly persuasive justification . . . the burden of justification is demanding and it rests entirely on the State."[23]

In *Michael M. v. Superior Court*, the U.S. Supreme Court upheld the constitutionality of California's "statutory rape law" that punished "an act of sexual intercourse accomplished with a female not the wife of the perpetrator, where the female is under the age of 18 years." Is it constitutional to limit criminal liability to males? The Supreme Court noted that California possessed a "strong interest" in preventing illegitimate teenage pregnancies. The Court explained that imposing criminal sanctions solely on males roughly "equalized the deterrents on the sexes," because young men did not face the prospects of pregnancy and child rearing. The Court also deferred to the judgment of the California legislature that extending liability to females would likely make young women reluctant to report violations of the law.[24]

In summary, there are three different levels of analysis under the Equal Protection Clause:

- *Rational Basis Test.* A classification is presumed valid so long as it is rationally related to a constitutionally permissible state interest. An individual challenging the statute must demonstrate that there is no rational basis for the classification. This test is used in regard to the "nonsuspect" categories of the poor, the elderly, and the mentally challenged and to distinctions based on age.
- *Strict Scrutiny.* A law singling out a racial or ethnic minority must be strictly necessary, and there must be no alternative approach to advancing a compelling state interest. This test is also used when a law limits fundamental rights.
- *Intermediate Scrutiny.* Distinctions on the basis of gender must be substantially related to an important government objective. A law singling out women must be based on factual differences and must not rest on overbroad generalizations.

In 2013, in *United States v. Windsor*, the U.S. Supreme Court struck down part of the federal Defense of Marriage Act (DOMA), a law that defined marriage as "only a legal union between one man and one woman." The effect of DOMA was to deny roughly one thousand federal benefits to same-sex couples whose marriages were recognized under state law. The Court held that "no legitimate purpose overcomes the purpose and effect" of the law, which is to "injure" and to "demean" and to deny "equal status" to same-sex marriages.[25]

In 2015, in *Obergefell v. Hodges*, the U.S. Supreme Court held by a vote of 5-4 that the Fourteenth Amendment Due Process and Equal Protection Clauses guarantee same-sex couples the same fundamental right to marry as is afforded to opposite-sex couples and ruled that state prohibitions on same-sex marriage were unconstitutional. The Court also held that the Fourteenth Amendment requires states to recognize same-sex marriages performed in other states.[26]

You Decide  **2.2** Jeanine Biocic was walking on the beach on the Chincoteague National Wildlife Refuge in Virginia with a male friend. Biocic wanted to get some extra sun and removed the top of her two-piece bathing suit, exposing her breasts. She was observed by a U.S. Fish and Wildlife Service officer who issued a summons charging Biocic with an "act of indecency or disorderly conduct . . . prohibited on any national wildlife refuge." Biocic was convicted and fined $25; she appealed on the ground that her conviction violated equal protection under law. Her claim was based on the fact that the ordinance prohibited the exposure of female breasts and did not prohibit the exposure of male breasts. How would you rule? See *United States v. Biocic*, 928 F.2d 112 (4th Cir. 1991).

You can find the answer at study.sagepub.com/lippmaness2e

Read *Webster v. Virgin Islands* and *Wright v. South Carolina* on the study site: study .sagepub.com/ lippmaness2e.

We next look at the protections for freedom of speech and privacy, the right to bear arms, and the prohibition against cruel and unusual punishment.

THE BILL OF RIGHTS

Nationalization

The last half of the twentieth century witnessed the *nationalization* or what law professors refer to as the *constitutionalization* of the criminal justice process. This involved interpreting the Fourteenth Amendment **Due Process Clause** to extend most of the protections of the **Bill of Rights** (the first ten amendments to the Constitution) to the states. There now is a single standard of rights and liberties that all levels of government must satisfy. You may be prosecuted in Indiana, in Iowa, or in the federal system, and your rights are fundamentally the same. This *constitutionalization* or development of a single standard that applies to the federal government as well as to the states marked a true revolution in the law.

Professor Erwin Chemerinsky observed that if the Bill of Rights applies only to the federal government, the state and local governments "then are free to infringe even the most precious liberties" and to "violate basic constitutional rights."[27] A state, for example, might not provide an individual the right to a trial by jury or the right to a lawyer when charged with a serious criminal offense. On the other hand, there is a widespread belief that the federal government should not intrude into the affairs of state governments and that the citizens of each state should be left free to determine what rights and liberties they wish to preserve and to protect. Criminal justice, in particular, was viewed as a local matter.[28]

This system of states' rights did not fully survive the Civil War. Slavery in the states of the former Confederacy would no longer be tolerated, and former African American slaves were to enjoy the full rights of citizenship. The **Fourteenth Amendment** was added to the Constitution in 1868 in order to guarantee equal treatment and opportunity for African Americans. The amendment reads as follows:

> All persons born or naturalized in the United States, and subject to the jurisdiction thereof, are citizens of the United States and of the state wherein they reside. No state shall make or enforce any law which shall abridge the privileges and immunities of citizens of the United States nor shall any state deprive any person of life, liberty, or property without due process of law; nor deny to any person within its jurisdiction the equal protection of the laws.

The first sentence recognized that African Americans are citizens of the United States and of the state in which they reside. The purpose was to reverse the Supreme Court's 1857 decision in *Scott v. Sandford*, which held that African American slaves were not eligible to become U.S. citizens.[29]

The twentieth century witnessed continued efforts by defendants to extend the protection of the Bill of Rights to the states. There was an increasing call for fairer procedures in state courts. Lawyers argued that the Due Process Clause of the Fourteenth Amendment, which applied to the states, included various provisions of the Bill of Rights to the U.S. Constitution. Supreme Court justices have employed one of three approaches to incorporate aspects of the Bill of Rights into the Fourteenth Amendment and to extend these protections to the fifty states. The three theories of **incorporation** are as follows:

- *Fundamental Fairness.* The Supreme Court decides on a case-by-case basis whether rights are fundamental to the concept of ordered liberty and therefore apply to the states.
- *Total Incorporation and Total Incorporation Plus.* The entire Bill of Rights applies to the states. Total incorporation plus includes additional rights not in the Bill of Rights along with the entire Bill of Rights.
- *Selective Incorporation.* Particular rights in the Bill of Rights apply to the states. Selective incorporation plus includes additional rights not in the Bill of Rights along with the particular rights in the Bill of Rights.

The majority of judges favor selective incorporation. They argue that only those provisions of the Bill of Rights that are essential to liberty are incorporated into the Fourteenth Amendment.

The U.S. Supreme Court has incorporated a number of the fundamental rights included in the Bill of Rights into the Fourteenth Amendment Due Process Clause. The rights that are incorporated are listed in Table 2.1. The Court has not incorporated the following four provisions of the Bill of Rights into the Fourteenth Amendment, and therefore, a state is free although not required to adopt a law or include a provision in its constitution that extends these four protections to its citizens.

- *Third Amendment.* Prohibition against quartering soldiers without consent of the owner.
- *Fifth Amendment.* Right to indictment by a grand jury for capital or infamous crimes.
- *Seventh Amendment.* Right to trial in civil law cases.
- *Eighth Amendment.* Prohibition against excessive bail and fines.

FREEDOM OF SPEECH

The **First Amendment** to the U.S. Constitution provides that "Congress shall make no law . . . abridging the freedom of speech or of the press; or the right of the people peaceably to assemble, and to petition the Government for a redress of grievances." The U.S. Supreme Court extended this prohibition to the states in a 1925 Supreme Court decision in which the Court proclaimed that "freedom of speech and of the press . . . are among the fundamental personal rights and 'liberties' protected under the Due Process Clause of the Fourteenth Amendment from impairment by the States."[30]

The famous, and now deceased, First Amendment scholar Thomas I. Emerson identified four functions central to democracy performed by freedom of expression under the First Amendment[31]:

- Freedom of expression contributes to *individual self-fulfillment* by encouraging individuals to express their ideas and creativity.
- Freedom of expression ensures *a vigorous "marketplace of ideas"* in which a diversity of views are expressed and considered in reaching a decision.
- Freedom of expression *promotes social stability* by providing individuals the opportunity to be heard and to influence the political and policy-making process. This encourages the acceptance of decisions and discourages individuals from resorting to violence.
- Freedom of expression ensures that there is a steady stream of innovative ideas and enables the *government to identify and address newly arising issues.*

The First Amendment is vital to the United States' free, open, and democratic society. Justice William O. Douglas wrote in *Terminiello v. Chicago*[32] that speech

> may indeed best serve its high purpose when it induces a condition of unrest, creates dissatisfaction with the conditions as they are, or even stirs people to anger. Speech is often provocative and challenging. It may strike at prejudices and preconceptions and have profound unsettling effects as it presses for acceptance of an idea.

Justice Robert H. Jackson, reflecting on his experience as a prosecutor during the Nuremberg trials of Nazi war criminals following World War II, cautioned Justice Douglas that the choice is not between order and liberty. It is between liberty with order and anarchy without either. There is danger that if the Court does not temper its doctrinaire logic with a little practical wisdom, it will convert the constitutional Bill of Rights into a suicide pact. Justice Jackson is clearly correct that there must be some limit to freedom of speech. But where should the line be drawn? The Supreme Court articulated these limits in *Chaplinsky v. New Hampshire* and observed that there are "certain well-recognized categories of speech which may be permissibly limited under the First Amendment." The Supreme Court explained that these "utterances are no essential part of any exposition of ideas, and are of such slight social value as a step to truth that any benefit that may be derived from them is clearly outweighed by the social interest in order and morality."[33]

Table 2.1	Bill of Rights Provisions Related to Criminal Procedure Incorporated Into the Fourteenth Amendment

First Amendment

Fiske v. Kansas, 274 U.S. 380 (1927)
[freedom of speech]

Second Amendment

McDonald v. Chicago, 561 U.S. 742 (2010)
[right to bear arms]

Fourth Amendment

Wolf v. Colorado, 338 U.S. 25 (1949)
[unreasonable searches and seizures]
Mapp v. Ohio, 367 U.S. 643 (1961)
[exclusionary rule]

Fifth Amendment

Malloy v. Hogan, 378 U.S. 1 (1964)
[compelled self-incrimination]
Benton v. Maryland, 395 U.S. 784 (1969)
[double jeopardy]

Sixth Amendment

Gideon v. Wainwright, 372 U.S. 335 (1963)
[right to counsel]
Klopfer v. North Carolina, 386 U.S. 213 (1967)
[speedy trial]
In re Oliver, 333 U.S. 257 (1948)
[public trial]
Pointer v. Texas, 380 U.S. 400 (1965)
[right to confront witnesses]
Duncan v. Louisiana, 391 U.S. 145 (1968)
[impartial jury]
Washington v. Texas, 388 U.S. 14 (1967)
[right to compulsory process for obtaining favorable witnesses at trial]

Eighth Amendment

Robinson v. California, 370 U.S. 660 (1962)
[cruel and unusual punishment]

The main categories of speech for which *content is not protected by the First Amendment* and that may result in the imposition of criminal punishment are as follows:

• *Fighting Words.* Words directed to another individual or individuals that an ordinary and reasonable person should be aware are likely to cause a fight or breach of the peace are prohibited under the **fighting words** doctrine. In *Chaplinsky v. New Hampshire*, the Supreme Court upheld the conviction of a member of the Jehovah's Witnesses who, when distributing religious pamphlets, attacked a local marshal with the accusation that "you are a God damned racketeer" and "a damned Fascist and the whole government of Rochester are Fascists or agents of Fascists."

- *Incitement to Violent Action.* A speaker, when addressing an audience, is prohibited from **incitement to violent action**. In *Feiner v. New York*, Feiner addressed a racially mixed crowd of seventy-five or eighty people. He was described as "endeavoring to arouse" the African Americans in the crowd "against the whites, urging that they rise up in arms and fight for equal rights." The Supreme Court ruled that "when clear and present danger of riot, disorder, interference with traffic upon the public streets, or other immediate threat to public safety, peace, or order, appears, the power of the State to prevent or punish is obvious."[34] On the other hand, in *Terminiello v. Chicago*, the Supreme Court stressed that a speaker could not be punished for speech that merely "stirs to anger, invites dispute, brings about a condition of unrest, or creates a disturbance."[35] In *Brandenburg v. Ohio*, the Court clarified the standard for incitement when it overturned the conviction of an Ohio Ku Klux Klan leader for a speech that instructed the audience on the duty and necessity of violence against the government. The Court held that the government may outlaw speech when it is directed at inciting or producing "imminent lawless action" and is likely to incite or produce such action. The statute under which *Brandenburg* was convicted was unconstitutional because it did not distinguish between mere teaching and advocacy of violence from incitement to imminent lawless action.[36]

- *Threat.* A developing body of law prohibits threats of bodily harm directed at individuals. Judges must weigh and balance a range of factors in determining whether a statement constitutes a political exaggeration or a **true threat**. In *Watts v. United States*, the defendant proclaimed to a small gathering following a public rally on the grounds of the Washington Monument that if inducted into the army and forced to carry a rifle, "the first man I want to get in my sights is L.B.J. [President Lyndon Johnson]. . . . They are not going to make me kill my black brothers." The onlookers greeted this statement with laughter. Watts's conviction was overturned by the U.S. Supreme Court, which ruled that the government had failed to demonstrate that Watts had articulated a true threat and that these types of bold statements were to be expected in a dynamic and democratic society divided over the Vietnam War.[37]

  In *Elonis v. United States*, Anthony Douglas Elonis adopted the online name "Tone Dougie" and posted vicious and violent rap lyrics on Facebook against a former employer, his soon-to-be ex-wife, a kindergarten class, and an FBI agent. Elonis was convicted under a federal statute that prohibits the transmission in interstate commerce of any "threat . . . to injure another." The Supreme Court held that Elonis could not be convicted based solely on the reaction of a reasonable person to his posts and that the government was required to establish that Elonis possessed a criminal intent. Elonis claimed he was acting under his online persona and lacked a specific intent to threaten individuals. The Supreme Court asked the lower court to decide whether it was sufficient for a conviction under the federal law that Elonis may have been reckless in his Facebook posts.[38]

- *Obscenity.* Obscene materials are considered to lack "redeeming social importance" and are not accorded constitutional protection. Drawing the line between **obscenity** and protected speech has proven problematic. The Supreme Court conceded that obscenity cannot be defined with "God-like precision," and Justice Potter Stewart went so far as to pronounce in frustration that the only viable test seemed to be that he "knew obscenity when he saw it."[39] The U.S. Supreme Court was finally able to agree on a test for obscenity in *Miller v. California*. The Supreme Court declared that obscenity was limited to works that when taken as a whole, in light of contemporary community standards, appeal to the prurient interest in sex; are patently offensive; and lack serious literary, artistic, political, or scientific value. This qualification for scientific works means that a medical textbook portraying individuals engaged in "ultimate sexual acts" likely would not constitute obscenity.[40] Child pornography may be limited despite the fact that it does not satisfy the *Miller* standard.[41]

- *Libel.* You should remain aware that the other major limitation on speech, **libel**, is a civil law rather than a criminal action. This enables individuals to recover damages for injury to their reputations. In *New York Times v. Sullivan*, the U.S. Supreme Court severely limited the circumstances in which public officials could recover damages and held that a public official may not recover damages for a defamatory falsehood relating to his or her official conduct "unless . . . the statement was made with 'actual malice'—that is, with knowledge that it was false or with reckless disregard of whether it was false or not."[42] The Court later clarified that states were free to apply a more relaxed, simple negligence (lack of reasonable care in verifying the facts) standard in suits for libel brought by private individuals.[43]

Keep in mind that these are narrowly drawn exceptions to the First Amendment's commitment to a lively and vigorous societal debate. The general rule is that the government may neither require nor substantially interfere with individual expression. The Supreme Court held in *West Virginia v. Barnette* that a student may not be compelled to pledge allegiance to the American flag. The Supreme Court observed that "if there is any fixed star in our constitutional constellation, it is that no official, high or petty, can prescribe what shall be orthodox in politics, nationalism, religion or other matters of opinion or force citizens to confess by word or action their faith therein." This commitment to a free "marketplace of ideas" is based on the belief that delegating the decision as to what "views shall be voiced largely into the hands of each of us" will "ultimately produce a more capable citizenry and more perfect polity and . . . that no other approach would comport with the premise of individual dignity and choice upon which our political system rests."[44]

The Supreme Court has been reluctant to expand the categories of prohibited speech. In 2010, the Supreme Court held unconstitutional a federal law that punished depictions of animal cruelty. The Court noted that there was a long tradition of prohibiting animal cruelty in the United States. This, however, was "not a category of speech that historically had been prohibited and depictions of animal cruelty were protected under the First Amendment."[45]

Overbreadth

The doctrine of **overbreadth** is an important aspect of First Amendment protection. This provides that a statute is unconstitutional that is so broadly and imprecisely drafted that it encompasses and prohibits a substantial amount of protected speech relative to the coverage of the statute.[46] In *New York v. Ferber*, the U.S. Supreme Court upheld a New York child pornography statute that criminally punished an individual for promoting a "performance which includes sexual conduct by a child less than sixteen years of age." Sexual conduct was defined to include "lewd exhibition of the genitals." Justice Byron White was impatient with the concern that although the law was directed at hard-core child pornography, "[s]ome protected expression ranging from medical textbooks to pictorials in the National Geographic would fall prey to the statute." White doubted whether these applications of the statute to protected speech constituted more than a "tiny fraction of the materials" that would be affected by the law, and he expressed confidence that prosecutors would not bring actions against these types of publications. This, in short, is the "paradigmatic case of state statute whose legitimate reach dwarfs its arguably impermissible applications."[47]

Symbolic Speech

The Supreme Court has interpreted "expression" under the First Amendment to include **symbolic speech** or actions that have "communicative content." For example, the Court has held that the First Amendment protects high school students wearing black armbands to protest the Vietnam War[48] and a religious individual covering up the motto "Live Free or Die" on the New Hampshire license plate as a means of expressing the view that his ultimate loyalty was to God rather than to the state.[49]

In *Texas v. Johnson*, the U.S. Supreme Court addressed the constitutionality of Texas Penal Code Annotated Section 42.09, which punished the intentional or knowing desecration of a "state or national flag." Desecration under the statute was interpreted as to "efface, damage, or otherwise physically mistreat in a way that the actor knows will seriously offend one or more persons likely to observe or discover his action."[50]

Johnson participated in a political demonstration during the Republican National Convention in Dallas in 1984 to protest the policies of the Reagan administration and to dramatize the consequences of nuclear war. Johnson unfurled an American flag, doused the flag with kerosene, and set it on fire. The demonstrators chanted, "America, the red, white, and blue, we spit on you," as the flag burned.

Justice William Brennan observed that the Supreme Court had recognized that conduct may be protected under the First Amendment where there is an intent to convey a particularized message and there is a strong likelihood that this message will be understood by observers. Justice

Brennan observed that the circumstances surrounding Johnson's burning of the flag resulted in his message being "both intentional and overwhelmingly apparent." In those instances in which an act contains both communicative and noncommunicative elements, the standard in judging the constitutionality of governmental regulation of symbolic speech is whether the government has a substantial interest in limiting the nonspeech element (the burning). In the view of the majority of the judges, Johnson was being unconstitutionally punished based on the ideas he communicated when he burned the flag.

In 1989, the U.S. Congress adopted the Flag Protection Act, 18 U.S.C. § 700. The act provided that anyone who "knowingly mutilates, defaces, physically defiles, burns, maintains on the floor or ground, or tramples upon" a U.S. flag shall be subject to both a fine and imprisonment for not more than one year. This law exempted the disposal of a "worn or soiled" flag. In *United States v. Eichman*, Justice Brennan failed to find that this law was significantly different from the Texas statute in *Johnson* and ruled that the law "suppresses expression out of concern for its likely communicative impact."[51]

Hate Speech

Hate speech is one of the central challenges confronting the First Amendment. This is defined as speech that denigrates, humiliates, and attacks individuals on account of race, religion, ethnicity, nationality, gender, sexual preference, or other personal characteristics and preferences. Hate speech should be distinguished from hate crimes or penal offenses that are directed against an individual who is a member of one of these "protected groups."

The United States is an increasingly diverse society in which people inevitably collide, clash, and compete over jobs, housing, and education. Racial, religious, and other insults and denunciations are hurtful, increase social tensions and divisions, and possess limited social value. This type of expression also has little place in a diverse society based on respect and regard for individuals of every race, religion, ethnicity, and nationality. Regulating this expression, on the other hand, runs the risk that artistic and literary depictions of racial, religious, and ethnic themes may be deterred and denigrated. In addition, there is the consideration that debate on issues of diversity, affirmative action, and public policy may be discouraged. Society benefits when views are forced out of the shadows and compete in the sunlight of public debate.

The most important U.S. Supreme Court ruling on hate speech is *R.A.V. v. St. Paul*. In *R.A.V.*, several Caucasian juveniles burned a cross inside the fenced-in yard of an African American family.[52] The young people were charged under two statutes, including the St. Paul Bias-Motivated Crime Ordinance (St. Paul Minn. Legis. Code § 292.02), which provided that "whoever places on public or private property a symbol, object, including and not limited to, a burning cross or Nazi swastika, which one knows or has reasonable grounds to know arouses anger, alarm or resentment . . . on the basis of race, color, creed, religion or gender, commits disorderly conduct . . . [and] shall be guilty of a misdemeanor." The Supreme Court noted that St. Paul punishes certain fighting words, yet permits other equally harmful expressions. This discriminates against speech based on the content of ideas. For instance, what about symbolic attacks against greedy real estate developers or middle-class individuals who move into a gentrifying neighborhood that makes these economically privileged individuals fearful for their safety? A year later in 1993, in *Wisconsin v. Mitchell*, the Supreme Court ruled that a Wisconsin statute that enhanced the punishment of individuals convicted of hate crimes did not violate the defendant's First Amendment rights.[53] The Wisconsin court had increased Mitchell's prison sentence for aggravated assault from a maximum of two years to a term of four years based on his intentional selection of the person against "whom the crime is committed because of the race, religion, color, disability, sexual orientation, national origin or ancestry of that person."

Mitchell creatively claimed that he was being punished more severely for harboring and acting on racially discriminatory views in violation of the First Amendment. The Supreme Court, however, ruled that Mitchell was being punished for his harmful act rather than for the fact that his act was motivated by racist views. The enhancement of Mitchell's sentence was recognition that acts based on discriminatory motives are likely "to provoke retaliatory crimes, inflict distinct emotional harms on their victims, and incite community unrest." Mitchell also pointed out that the prosecution was free to introduce a defendant's prior racist comments at trial to prove a discriminatory motive or intent and that this would "chill" racist speech. The Supreme Court held that it was unlikely that a citizen would limit the expression of his or her racist views based on the fear that these statements would be introduced one day against him or her at a prosecution for a hate crime.

In 2003, in *Virginia v. Black*, the U.S. Supreme Court held unconstitutional a Virginia law prohibiting cross burning with "an intent to intimidate a person or group of persons."[54] This law, unlike the St. Paul statute, did not discriminate on the basis of the content of the speech. The Court, however, determined that the statute's provision that the jury is authorized to infer an intent to intimidate from the act of burning a cross without any additional evidence "permits a jury to convict in every cross burning case in which defendants exercise their constitutional right not to put on a defense." This provision also makes "it more likely that the jury will find an intent to intimidate regardless of the particular facts of the case." The Virginia law failed to distinguish between cross burning intended to intimidate individuals and cross burning intended to make a political statement by groups such as the Ku Klux Klan that view the flaming cross as a symbolic representation of their political point of view.

FREEDOM OF ASSEMBLY

The First Amendment right to freedom of nonviolent public assembly is integral to the ability of individuals to organize to influence public policy. In *DeJonge v. Oregon*, the Supreme Court stated that freedom of peaceful assembly is as fundamental as freedom of speech and the press to democracy.[55]

Demonstrations have been an important mechanism for groups of people to express their collective views on issues ranging from abortion to civil rights to immigration.

TIME, PLACE, AND MANNER RESTRICTIONS

The Supreme Court has upheld the reasonableness of laws that restrict the time, location, and manner of individuals' exercise of freedom of speech and assembly. A local government, for example, may limit the time or noise level or location of demonstrations. Time, place, and manner restrictions must be "content neutral," meaning that they are required to apply to all types of speech regardless of content. Individuals also must be provided or possess reasonable alternative means of expressing their message.

In *Grayned v. Rockford*, the U.S. Supreme Court upheld the restriction on demonstrations on the sidewalk adjacent to a school during school hours on the grounds that such protests may disrupt students' education. On the other hand, a demonstration nearby to the school during non–school hours likely would be constitutionally protected.[56]

The First Amendment protects freedom of religion as well as freedom of speech. The next section discusses the Free Exercise Clause of the First Amendment.

You Decide

2.3 Lori MacPhail, a peace officer in Chico, California, assigned to a high school, observed Ryan D. with some other students off campus during school hours. She conducted a pat-down, discovered that Ryan possessed marijuana, and issued him a citation.

Roughly a month later, Ryan turned in an art project for a painting class at the high school. The projects generally are displayed in the classroom for as long as two weeks. Ryan's painting pictured an individual who appeared to be a juvenile wearing a green hooded sweatshirt discharging a handgun at the back of the head of a female peace officer with badge No. 67 (Officer MacPhail's number) and the initials CPD (Chico Police Department). The officer had blood on her hair, and pieces of her flesh and face were blown away. An art teacher saw the painting and found it to be "disturbing" and "scary," and an administrator at the school informed Officer MacPhail.

An assistant principal confronted Ryan, who stated the picture depicted his "anger at police officers" and that he was angry with MacPhail and agreed that it was "reasonable to expect that Officer MacPhail would eventually see the picture." Ryan was charged with a violation of Section 422 and brought before juvenile court.

How would you rule? See *In re Ryan D.*, 123 Cal. Rptr. 2d 193 (Cal. App. 2002). Compare the decision in *Ryan D.* to the decision in *George T. v. California*, 93 P.3d 1007 (Cal. 2004).

You can find the answer at study.sagepub.com/lippmaness2e

FREEDOM OF RELIGION

The first part of the First Amendment provides that "Congress shall make no law respecting an establishment of religion, or prohibiting the free exercise thereof." The first portion of the clause is known as the "Establishment Clause," and the second part of the clause is referred to as the "Free Exercise Clause."

The Establishment Clause regulates the relationship between government and religion. One view is that the government may favor and support religion so long as the government does not promote any particular religion. Some legal thinkers take a broader interpretation and argue that there is a "wall of separation" between government and religion and that government should not have any connection whatsoever to religion. Under the first approach, the government could provide textbooks to all religious schools. In contrast, the second view would prohibit the government from providing textbooks to all religious schools.

In the area of criminal law, the central concern is the Free Exercise Clause. The rule is that individuals have complete freedom of religious belief, although religious practice may be limited. There are several ways in which government regulation may collide with an individual's religious belief.

The general rule is that the courts will uphold laws that may affect an individual's religious practice that are directed to all individuals whether or not they are members of a religion. In 1990, in *Employment Division v. Smith*, the U.S. Supreme Court held that a law prohibiting consumption of the hallucinogenic drug peyote did not violate the free exercise of religion of members of the Native American Church, whose adherents used peyote as a sacrament. The Court held that the law applied to all individuals and that members of the Native American Church were not singled out for prosecution.[57] In 1878, in *Reynolds v. United States*, the Supreme Court upheld the criminal prosecution of polygamist members of the Church of Jesus Christ of Latter-day Saints.[58]

On the other hand, courts are required to demonstrate a compelling interest to justify a law that targets members of a religious faith. In 1993, in *Church of the Lukumi Babalu Aye, Inc. v. Hialeah*, the Court struck down a city ordinance that prohibited the ritualistic sacrifice of animals, which was a sacred practice of the Santeria religion.[59] Justice Anthony Kennedy wrote that the "laws in question were enacted by officials who did not understand, failed to perceive, or chose to ignore the fact that their official actions violated the Nation's essential commitment to religious freedom."

Courts generally have held that while an adult may refuse medical treatment, a parent may not deny medical treatment to a child based on the parent's religious belief. The state's interest in protecting the life of the child takes precedence over the religious belief of the parent.[60]

In 1993, Congress adopted the Religious Freedom Restoration Act (RFRA), and various state legislatures have passed similar laws. The RFRA requires federal courts to apply a strict scrutiny test in determining whether a law that substantially burdens an individual's free exercise of religion is constitutional even if this burden results from a rule that applies to all religions. State RFRA laws typically provide that the laws do not provide legal protection to individuals who invoke religious reasons to justify discrimination against other individuals based on race, gender, national origin, or sexual preference.

In 2000, Congress passed the Religious Land Use and Institutionalized Persons Act (RLUIPA), 42 U.S.C. § 2000, which prohibits federal and state laws that burden the ability of prisoners to worship. In 2015, in *Holt v. Hobbs*, the U.S. Supreme Court held that an Arkansas prison regulation that prohibited inmates from growing beards other than for medical reasons violated the religious liberty of a Muslim inmate who sought to grow a "short," one-half-inch beard.[61]

The right to privacy is a relatively recent right that is increasingly at the center of political debate.

PRIVACY

The idea that there should be a legal right to **privacy** was first expressed in an 1890 article in the *Harvard Law Review* written by Samuel D. Warren and Louis D. Brandeis, who was later appointed to the U.S. Supreme Court. The two authors argued that the threats to privacy associated with the dawning of the twentieth century could be combated through recognition of a civil action (legal suit for damages) against those people who intrude into individuals' personal affairs.[62]

In 1905, the Supreme Court of Georgia became the first court to recognize an individual's right to privacy when it ruled that the New England Life Insurance Company unlawfully used the image of artist Paolo Pavesich in an advertisement that falsely claimed that Pavesich endorsed the company.[63] This decision served as a precedent for the recognition of privacy by courts in other states.

The Constitutional Right to Privacy

A constitutional right to privacy was first recognized in *Griswold v. Connecticut* in 1965.[64] The U.S. Supreme Court proclaimed that although privacy was not explicitly mentioned in the U.S. Constitution, it was implicitly incorporated into the text. The case arose when Griswold, along with Professor Buxton of Yale Medical School, provided advice to married couples on the prevention of procreation through contraceptives. Griswold was convicted of being an accessory to the violation of a Connecticut law that provided that any person who uses a contraceptive shall be fined not less than $50 or imprisoned not less than sixty days nor more than one year or be both fined and imprisoned.

Justice William O. Douglas noted that although the right to privacy was not explicitly set forth in the Constitution, this right was "created by several fundamental constitutional guarantees." According to Justice Douglas, these fundamental rights create a "zone of privacy" for individuals. In a famous phrase, Justice Douglas noted that the various provisions of the Bill of Rights possess "penumbras, formed by emanations from those guarantees . . . [that] create zones of privacy." Justice Douglas cited a number of constitutional provisions that together create the right to privacy.

The right of association contained in the penumbra of the First Amendment is one; the Third Amendment in its prohibition against the quartering of soldiers "in any house" in time of peace without the consent of the owner is another facet of that privacy. The Fourth Amendment explicitly affirms the "right of the people to be secure in their persons, houses, papers, and effects, against unreasonable searches and seizures." The Fifth Amendment's Self-Incrimination Clause "enables the citizen to create a zone of privacy that Government may not force him to surrender to his detriment." The Ninth Amendment provides that "[t]he enumeration in the Constitution of certain rights shall not be construed to deny or disparage others retained by the people."

In contrast, Justice Arthur Goldberg argued that privacy was found within the Ninth Amendment, which provides that the statement of certain rights does not mean that there are not other rights retained by the people, and Justice John Marshall Harlan contended that privacy is a fundamental aspect of individual "liberty" within the Fourteenth Amendment.

We nevertheless should take note of Justice Hugo Black's dissent in *Griswold* questioning whether the Constitution provides a right to privacy, a view that continues to attract significant support. Justice Black observed that "I like my privacy as well as the next one, but I am nevertheless compelled to admit that government has a right to invade [my privacy] unless prohibited by some specific constitutional provision."

The right to privacy recognized in *Griswold* guarantees that we are free to make the day-to-day decisions that define our unique personality: what we eat, read, and watch; where we live and how we spend our time, dress, and act; and with whom we associate and work. In a totalitarian society, these choices are made by the government, but in the U.S. democracy, these choices are made by the individual. The courts have held that the right to privacy protects several core concerns:

- *Sanctity of the Home.* Freedom of the home and other personal spaces from arbitrary governmental intrusion
- *Intimate Activities.* Freedom to make choices concerning personal lifestyle and an individual's body and reproduction
- *Information.* The right to prevent the collection and disclosure of intimate or incriminating information to private industry, the public, and governmental authorities
- *Public Portrayal.* The right to prevent your picture or endorsement from being used in an advertisement without permission or to prevent the details of your life from being falsely portrayed in the media[65]

In short, as noted by Supreme Court Justice Brandeis, "The makers of our Constitution undertook to secure conditions favorable to the pursuit of happiness. . . . They conferred as against the Government, the right to be let alone—the most comprehensive of rights and the right most valued by civilized men."[66] (See Table 2.2.)

Table 2.2 The Right to Privacy

Key U.S. Supreme Court Decisions on Privacy

Case Name and Citation	Case Summary
Eisenstadt v. Baird, 405 U.S. 438 (1972)	In 1971, the Supreme Court extended *Griswold* and ruled that a Massachusetts statute that punished individuals who provided contraceptives to unmarried individuals violated the right to privacy. Justice Brennan wrote that "if the right to privacy means anything, it is the right of the individual, married or single, to be free from unwarranted governmental intrusion into matters so fundamentally affecting a person as the decision whether to bear or beget a child."
Carey v. Population Services International, 431 U.S. 678 (1977)	The Supreme Court, in 1977, declared a New York law unconstitutional that made it a crime to provide contraceptives to minors and for anyone other than a licensed pharmacist to distribute contraceptives to persons over sixteen. Justice Brennan noted that this imposed a significant burden on access to contraceptives and impeded the "decision whether or not to beget or bear a child" that was at the "very heart" of the "right to privacy."
Roe v. Wade, 410 U.S. 113 (1973)	In 1973, in *Roe v. Wade,* the Supreme Court ruled a Texas statute unconstitutional that made it a crime to "procure an abortion." Justice Blackmun wrote that the "right to privacy . . . is broad enough to encompass a woman's decision whether or not to terminate her pregnancy." The Supreme Court later ruled in *Planned Parenthood v. Casey,* 505 U.S. 833 (1992), that Pennsylvania's requirement that a woman obtain her husband's consent unduly interfered with her access to an abortion.
Gonzales v. Carhart, 550 U.S. 124 (2007)	The Supreme Court upheld the authority of Congress to prohibit "partial-birth abortion." The Court reasoned that there is a substantial government interest in protecting the fetus and that it was uncertain whether this procedure ever is required to preserve the life of the mother.
Stanley v. Georgia, 394 U.S. 557 (1969)	A search of Stanley's home for bookmaking paraphernalia led to the seizure of three reels of film portraying obscene scenes. Justice Marshall, in his 1969 decision, concluded that "whatever the power of the state to control public dissemination of ideas inimical to the public morality, it cannot constitutionally premise legislation on the desirability of controlling a person's private thoughts."

The Constitutional Right to Privacy and Same-Sex Relations Between Consenting Adults in the Home

Precisely what activities are within the right of privacy in the home? In answering this question, we must balance the freedom to be left alone against the need for law and order. The issue of sodomy confronted judges with the question of whether laws upholding sexual morality must yield to the demands of sexual freedom within the home.

In 1986, in *Bowers v. Hardwick,* the Supreme Court affirmed Hardwick's sodomy conviction under a Georgia statute.[67] Justice White failed to find a fundamental right deeply rooted in the nation's history and tradition to engage in acts of consensual sodomy, even when committed in the privacy of the home. He pointed out that sodomy was prohibited by all thirteen colonies at the time the constitution was ratified, and twenty-five states and the District of Columbia continued to criminally condemn this conduct.

In 2003, in *Lawrence v. Texas*, the Supreme Court called in doubt the historical analysis in *Bowers*. The Court noted that only thirteen states currently prohibited sodomy and that in these states there is a "pattern of nonenforcement with respect to consenting adults in private."[68] The Court held that the right to privacy includes the fundamental right of two consenting males to engage in sodomy within the privacy of the home.

You Decide

2.4 The plaintiffs allege that the Florida law requiring motorcyclists to wear helmets violates their right to privacy under the U.S. Constitution. Are they correct? See *Picou v. Gillum*, 874 F.2d 1519 (11th Cir. 1989).

You can find the answer at study.sagepub.com/lippmaness2e

The Right to Privacy and the Fourth Amendment

The right to privacy is the philosophical basis of the **Fourth Amendment** protection of individuals' homes, papers, persons, and effects from "unreasonable searches and seizures" conducted without a search warrant founded on probable cause. In the famous case of *Katz v. United States*, Katz was suspected of using phones in two public phone booths to transmit unlawful interstate gambling information. The government without obtaining a search warrant placed a recording device on the phone booths and recorded Katz's conversations about gambling on college football. Katz's conviction for transmitting gambling information was overturned. The Supreme Court reasoned that when Katz shut the door of the phone booth and carried on his conversations he expressed a reasonable expectation of privacy and that what an individual "seeks to preserve as private, even in an area accessible to the public," merits constitutional protection. When the government undertakes a search and seizure that impedes on an individual's expectation of privacy, it is required to obtain a warrant from a judicial official that strictly limits the extent of the search. FBI agents in *Katz* improperly decided on their own whether and how long to listen to Katz's conversations. Note that the Supreme Court in *Katz* clarified that our words as well as physical objects and our persons are protected under the Fourth Amendment.[69]

The Fourth Amendment is at the core of the contemporary debates about technology. The U.S. Supreme Court in *United States v. Jones* held that law enforcement unconstitutionally attached a GPS to the automobile of a suspected drug trafficker without a valid search warrant and monitored his movements for twenty-eight days. Justice Samuel Alito noted that the government's surveillance of Jones violated his reasonable expectation of privacy because the twenty-eight-day warrantless surveillance could potentially reveal the most intimate aspects of Jones's life. A person who knows all of another person's travels "can deduce whether he is a weekly church goer, a heavy drinker, a regular at the gym, an unfaithful husband, an outpatient receiving medical treatment, an associate of particular individuals or political groups—and not just one such fact about a person, but all such facts."[70] The Court also has held that a search warrant is required to search the smartphone of an arrestee.[71] In *Kyllo v. United States*, government agents suspected that Danny Kyllo was growing marijuana using high-intensity lamps. The agents without a search warrant aimed a thermal-imaging device at Kyllo's home. Based on the results from the thermal imaging and other evidence, the agents obtained a search warrant to search Kyllo's home and seized one hundred marijuana plants. The government argued that a search warrant was not required because the thermal-imaging device measured heat emitted outside of the home that had no expectation of privacy. However, the late Justice Antonin Scalia concluded that the Fourth Amendment provides a high expectation of privacy to the home and that where the government uses a device that is not in general public use to explore details of the home that would have previously been unknown without a physical intrusion the government is required to obtain a search warrant before invading the privacy of a homeowner.[72]

The tension between privacy and the social interest in criminal investigation and detection arose when the FBI obtained a court order requiring Apple to help "unlock" the phone used by Syed Farook, one of the attackers who killed fourteen people in San Bernardino, California. The FBI argued that this information was essential to determine whether other individuals were involved in the terrorist attack, although Apple contended that the government was requiring the company to "bypass" or to "disable" a central security feature of the phone and compromise the privacy depended upon by users of the iPhone.

THE RIGHT TO BEAR ARMS

The **Second Amendment** to the U.S. Constitution provides that, "[a] well regulated Militia being necessary to the security of a free State, the right of the people to keep and bear Arms shall not be infringed."

The meaning of the Second Amendment has been the topic of considerable debate. Courts historically focused on the first clause of the amendment that recognizes the importance of a "well regulated Militia" and held that the amendment protects the right of individuals to possess arms in conjunction with service in an organized government militia. In 1939, in *United States v. Miller*, the Supreme Court upheld the constitutionality of a federal law prohibiting the interstate shipment of sawed-off shotguns, reasoning that the Second Amendment protections are limited to gun ownership that has "some reasonable relationship to the preservation or efficiency of a well regulated militia."[73]

Gun rights activists contended that the Second Amendment protection of the "right of the people to keep and bear Arms" was not limited to members of the militia. They argued that the Second Amendment also protects individuals' right to possess firearms "unconnected" with service in a militia. The Founding Fathers, according to gun activists, viewed gun ownership as essential to the preservation of individual liberty. A state or federal government could abolish the state national guard and leave citizens unarmed and vulnerable. The framers concluded that the best way to safeguard and to protect the people was to guarantee individuals' right to bear arms.

In *District of Columbia v. Heller*, the U.S. Supreme Court adopted the view of gun rights activists. The Court majority held that the Second Amendment protects the right of individuals to possess firearms.[74]

A District of Columbia (D.C.) ordinance prohibited the possession of handguns and declared that it was a crime to carry an unregistered firearm. A separate portion of the D.C. ordinance authorized the chief of police to issue licenses for one-year periods. Lawfully registered handguns were required to be kept "unloaded and dissembled or bound by a trigger lock or similar device" when not "located" in a place of business or used for lawful recreational activities.

Justice Scalia writing for a five-judge majority held that the D.C. ordinance was unconstitutional because the regulations interfered with the ability of law-abiding citizens to use a firearm for self-defense in the home, the "core lawful purpose" of the right to bear arms. "Undoubtedly some think that the Second Amendment is outmoded in a society where our standing army is the pride of our Nation, where well-trained police forces provide personal security, and where gun violence is a serious problem. That is perhaps debatable, but what is not debatable is that it is not the role of this Court to pronounce the Second Amendment extinct."

The Court decision noted that while D.C. could not constitutionally ban the possession of firearms in the home, the right to bear arms was subject to limitations. The judgment did not (1) limit the ability of states to prohibit possession of firearms by felons and the mentally challenged; (2) prohibit laws forbidding the carrying of firearms in "sensitive places," such as schools and government buildings; (3) prevent the regulation of the commercial sale of arms; or (4) prevent states and localities from banning the possession of dangerous and unusual weapons or from requiring the safe storage of weapons.

Heller, although important for defining the meaning of the Second Amendment, applied only to D.C. and to other federal jurisdictions. In 2010, in *McDonald v. Chicago*, residents of Chicago and the Chicago suburb of Oak Park, Illinois, challenged local ordinances that were almost identical to the law that the Court struck down as unconstitutional in the federal enclave of Washington, D.C.[75] The Supreme Court addressed whether the Second Amendment right of individuals to bear arms extended to the states as well as to the federal government.

The Second Amendment was one of the few amendments in the Bill of Rights that had not been incorporated into the Fourteenth Amendment and made applicable to the states. The result was that even after *Heller*, the right to possess firearms was not considered a fundamental right protected by the Fourteenth Amendment, and state governments were free to restrict or even to prohibit the possession of firearms.

The Fourteenth Amendment prohibits a state from denying an individual life, liberty, or property without due process of law. The question in *McDonald v. Chicago* was whether the right to keep and to bear arms was a liberty interest protected under the Due Process Clause of the Fourteenth Amendment that was applicable to the states. Justice Samuel Alito wrote that self-defense is a "basic right, recognized by many legal systems from ancient times to the present day." He concluded that the Second Amendment right to possess firearms in the home for the purpose of self-defense is incorporated into the Fourteenth Amendment and is applicable to the states. The right to keep and bear arms for purposes of self-defense is "among the fundamental rights necessary to our system of ordered liberty," which is "deeply rooted in this Nation's history and tradition." A number of state constitutions already protected the right to own and to carry arms. The incorporation of the Second Amendment into the Fourteenth Amendment clearly established that the right to bear arms for the purpose of self-defense is a fundamental right that may not be infringed by state governments.

In 2013, in *Moore v. Madigan*, the Seventh Circuit Court of Appeals in an important decision held unconstitutional an Illinois flat ban on carrying a loaded firearm within accessible reach outside the home. The only exceptions to this prohibition under Illinois law were police officers and other security personnel, hunters, and members of target shooting clubs. The Seventh Circuit Court of Appeals held that although both *Heller* and *McDonald* held that "'the need for defense of self, family, and property is most acute' in the home," this does not mean "it is not acute outside the home" and pointed out that *Heller* recognized a broader Second Amendment right than the right to have a gun in one's home when the decision noted that the Second Amendment "guarantee[s] the individual right to possess and carry weapons in case of confrontation." The Seventh Circuit noted that confrontations are not limited to the home, and that as a result the Illinois law therefore is in violation of individuals' Second Amendment rights.[76] In July 2013, the Illinois legislature subsequently passed a statute permitting individuals to obtain a license to carry a loaded or unloaded concealed weapon on their person or within a vehicle.

The precise meaning of the decisions in *Heller* and *McDonald* will not be clear until various state gun control laws are reviewed by the judiciary. This includes local and state laws restricting possession of firearms in schools, in religious institutions, and at other locations; laws limiting large-capacity magazines; laws prohibiting individuals convicted of domestic violence from possessing firearms; and laws restricting the possession of assault rifles. In 2015, in *Caetano v. Massachusetts*, the U.S. Supreme Court indicated that the Second Amendment protects Tasers and held that the protection of the Second Amendment is not limited to weapons in existence at the time the Second Amendment was drafted and is not limited to "weapons of war."[77]

In January 2016, President Barack Obama announced a number of measures intended to further regulate firearms in the United States. President Obama contended that most of these measures were within his executive authority, although some of the measures required congressional action. The president's most important measures involved the extension of background checks. The National Instant Criminal Background Check System (NICS) was created by Congress to prevent guns from being sold by licensed firearm dealers to prohibited individuals. Under President Obama's executive order, individuals considered to be in the business of selling guns whether in a store, at a gun show, or over the Internet must be federally licensed and conduct background checks on buyers. Federal law subjects individuals who fail to obtain a license or who fail to conduct a background check on a buyer to criminal penalties.

CRUEL AND UNUSUAL PUNISHMENT

The Eighth Amendment states that "[e]xcessive bail shall not be required, nor excessive fines imposed, nor cruel and unusual punishments inflicted." Professor Wayne LaFave lists three approaches to interpreting the clause: (1) it limits the *methods* employed to inflict punishment, (2) it restricts the *amount of punishment* that may be imposed, and (3) it *prohibits* the criminal punishment of certain acts.[78]

Methods of Punishment

There is agreement that the **Eighth Amendment** prohibits punishment that was considered cruel at the time of the amendment's ratification, including burning at the stake, crucifixion, breaking on the wheel, drawing and quartering, the rack, and the thumbscrew.

The vast majority of courts have not limited cruel and unusual punishment to acts condemned at the time of the passage of the Eighth Amendment and have viewed this as an evolving concept. The U.S. Supreme Court in *Trop v. Dulles* stressed that the Eighth Amendment "must draw its meaning from the evolving standards of decency that mark the progress of a maturing society."[79]

The death penalty historically has been viewed as a constitutionally acceptable form of punishment. The Supreme Court noted that punishments are "cruel when they involve torture or a lingering death; but the punishment of death is not cruel within the meaning of that word as used in the Constitution. [Cruelty] implies there is something inhuman and barbarous—something more than the mere extinguishment of life."[80]

The Supreme Court has rejected the contention that death by shooting and electrocution is cruel and barbarous, noting in 1890 that the newly developed technique of electricity was a "more humane method of reaching the result." In *Louisiana ex rel. Francis v. Resweber*, Francis was strapped in the electric chair and received a bolt of electricity before the machine malfunctioned.[81] The U.S. Supreme Court rejected the claim that subjecting the petitioner to the electric chair a second time constituted cruel and unusual punishment. The Court observed that there was no intent to inflict unnecessary pain, and the fact that "an unforeseeable accident prevented the prompt consummation of the sentence cannot . . . add an element of cruelty to a subsequent execution." In 2008, in *Baze v. Rees*, the U.S. Supreme Court affirmed the constitutionality of the execution of individuals through the use of lethal injection.[82] (See Criminal Law in the News below.)

In 2011, in *Brown v. Plata*, Justice Anthony Kennedy affirmed a lower court judgment requiring California prisons to release roughly forty-six thousand inmates to relieve prison overcrowding.[83] The California system housed twice as many prisoners as the institutions were designed to hold. Justice Kennedy concluded that the overcrowding of California prisons constituted unconstitutional cruel treatment because the prison system lacked the resources to provide adequate health and mental health care to the large prison population. Overcrowding also had led to rising tension and to violence.

The Amount of Punishment: The Death Penalty

The prohibition on cruel and unusual punishment has also been interpreted to require that punishment is proportionate to the crime. In other words, the "punishment must not be excessive"; it must "fit the crime." Judges have been particularly concerned with the proportionality of the

CRIMINAL LAW IN THE NEWS

European manufacturers of lethal injection drugs like sodium thiopental and pentobarbital in the past several years decided to stop selling these drugs to American states for use in executions. A shortage of these drugs led correctional authorities to experiment with new combinations of drug cocktails. The executions of Dennis McGuire in Ohio in January 2014, Clayton D. Lockett in Oklahoma in April 2014, and Joseph R. Wood III in Arizona in July 2014 led to a questioning of executions through lethal injection that included the sedative midazolam. Midazolam is used to induce a coma-like sleep. A second drug paralyzes the individual, and a third drug induces a heart attack. McGuire's execution in Ohio required roughly twenty-five minutes, although death normally should occur within ten minutes. Witnesses reported that McGuire appeared to be gasping for air and seemed to be conscious of the pain associated with the execution. Lockett's execution in Oklahoma took forty-three minutes. Lockett reportedly was moaning in pain because an improperly placed intravenous line prevented the drugs from flowing directly into his bloodstream. Wood also was executed using midazolam and according to observers gasped for air over six hundred times during the nearly two hours it took for him to die.

The three inmates all had been convicted of brutal crimes, and the families of the victims stressed that their loved ones had suffered to a much greater extent than their assailants. Lockett, for example, had been convicted of shooting a nineteen-year-old woman and burying her alive.

In reaction to the shortage of drugs used in lethal injection, Oklahoma and Utah have authorized the use of firing squads if the required chemicals are unavailable thirty days before an execution is

(Continued)

(Continued)

scheduled to take place. Oklahoma, in April 2015, also adopted legislation providing death by asphyxiation using nitrogen gas. Tennessee has authorized the use of the electric chair to execute individuals if lethal injection drugs are unavailable.

In June 2015 in *Glossip v. Gross* (576 U.S. __ [2015]), the Supreme Court in a 5-4 decision held that Oklahoma inmates challenging the state's use of midazolam as the first drug in a three-drug protocol "fail[ed] to establish a likelihood of success on the merits of their claim that the use of midazolam violates the Eighth Amendment." Justice Samuel A. Alito Jr. in his majority decision held that the inmates were unable to establish that the challenged drug created a substantial risk of severe pain and that the inmates had failed to identify a less painful alternative. Justice Alito also noted that the inmates should not benefit from the fact that anti–death penalty activists had pressured foreign pharmaceutical companies to "refuse to supply the drugs used to carry out death sentences."

Justice Sonia Sotomayor in her dissenting opinion pointed out that the three inmates had made the serious allegation that Oklahoma's three-drug protocol was the chemical equivalent to being "burned alive." Justice Sotomayor stressed that "under the court's rule [requiring a less painful alternative], it would not matter whether the state intended to use midazolam, or instead to have petitioners drawn and quartered, slowly tortured to death or actually burned alive."

States have become increasingly varied in the drugs they use to carry out executions. In January 2014, six executions were conducted in six different states using four different protocols. In October 2015, Oklahoma halted the execution of Glossip after prison officials found that the wrong drugs had been delivered by the state's supplier of execution drugs and discovered that in January 2014 the state had executed an inmate using the wrong drug. Glossip's attorneys have continued to insist on his innocence. Should states continue to rely on lethal injection to execute individuals?

death penalty. This reflects an understandable concern that a penalty that is so "unusual in its pain, in its finality and in its enormity" is imposed in an "evenhanded, nonselective, and nonarbitrary" manner against individuals who have committed crimes deserving of death.[84]

In *Gregg v. Georgia*, in 1976, the U.S. Supreme Court approved a Georgia statute designed to ensure the proportionate application of capital punishment.[85] The Georgia law limited the discretion of jurors to impose the death penalty by requiring jurors to find that a murder had been accompanied by one of several aggravating circumstances. This evidence was to be presented at a separate sentencing hearing and was to be weighed against any and all mitigating considerations. Death sentences were to be automatically reviewed by the state supreme court, which was charged with ensuring that the verdict was supported by the facts and that capital punishment was imposed in a consistent fashion. This system was intended to ensure that the death penalty was reserved for the "worst of the worst" homicides and offenders and was not "cruelly imposed on undeserving defendants." The Supreme Court has held that the question of aggravating circumstances and the determination of whether a defendant merits capital punishment is to be decided by the jury rather than by a judge.[86] In the recent case of *Hurst v. Florida*, the Supreme Court held that a Florida sentencing procedure was unconstitutional because the judge rather than the jury decided whether to impose capital punishment. The judge under the Florida law was to give the jury's recommendation whether to impose the death sentence "great weight" although the judge was authorized to independently find and weigh the aggravating and mitigating circumstances.[87]

Are there offenses other than aggravated and intentional murder that merit the death penalty? What of aggravated rape? In *Coker v. Georgia*, in 1977, the U.S. Supreme Court ruled that death was a grossly disproportionate and excessive punishment for the aggravated rape of an adult and constituted cruel and unusual punishment.[88] Thirty-one years later, in *Kennedy v. Louisiana*, the Supreme Court held that imposition of capital punishment for the rape of a child constituted cruel and unusual punishment.[89] The Court also has held that the Eighth Amendment prohibits execution of the mentally challenged[90] and individuals convicted of felony murder who neither killed nor attempted to kill nor intended to kill the victim.[91]

The Supreme Court held, in 1988 in *Thompson v. Oklahoma*, that it is unconstitutional to execute a person under the age of sixteen at the time of his or her offense.[92] In 2005, in *Roper v. Simmons*, the Supreme Court held that the execution of individuals who are sixteen or seventeen years of age constitutes cruel and unusual punishment.[93] Five years later, in *Graham v. Florida*, the Supreme Court ruled that sentencing a juvenile to life imprisonment without parole for a nonhomicide offense violated the Eighth Amendment prohibition on cruel and unusual punishment.[94] The Court held that a state is required to provide defendants like Graham "some meaningful opportunity to obtain release based on demonstrated maturity and rehabilitation." The Eighth Amendment, however, does not prohibit a state from concluding that a juvenile should remain in prison for life. In 2012, in *Miller v. Alabama*, the Supreme Court held that mandatory life imprisonment without parole for juveniles under eighteen convicted of homicide was unconstitutional. Judges are required to consider the offender's age, the nature of the offense, and other factors before sentencing a juvenile to life imprisonment without parole.[95] In 2016, in *Montgomery v. Louisiana*, the Supreme Court held that *Miller* should be applied to individuals sentenced to life imprisonment before the Court's decision in *Miller*. Justice Kennedy held that "[t]hose prisoners who have shown an inability to reform will continue to serve life sentences," although "the opportunity for release will be afforded to those who demonstrate the truth of *Miller*'s central intuition—that children who commit even heinous crimes are capable of change."[96]

In 2015, the twenty-eight executions carried out were the fewest since 1991 when there were fourteen executions. Only six states carried out executions. Texas accounted for thirteen executions, Missouri carried out six, and Georgia carried out five executions. Ten of the twenty-eight individuals executed were African American; six of the twenty-eight individuals executed were convicted of murdering an African American.

The forty-nine death sentences handed down to defendants by judges in 2015 marked a 33 percent decline from 2014 and the lowest number imposed since 1973. Riverside County, California, sentenced eight individuals to death, which was more than the number of death sentences handed down by any state other than Florida, which handed down nine death sentences. Six individuals on death row were exonerated in 2015.

As of January 2015, only thirty-one states authorized capital punishment.

The Amount of Punishment: Sentences for a Term of Years

The U.S. Supreme Court has remained sharply divided over whether the federal judicial branch is constitutionally entitled to extend its proportionality analysis beyond the death penalty to imprisonment for a "term of years." The Court appears to have accepted that the length of a criminal sentence is the province of elected state legislators and that judicial intervention should be "extremely rare" and limited to sentences that are "grossly disproportionate" to the seriousness of the offense.

In 2003, in *Lockyer v. Andrade*, the Supreme Court affirmed two consecutive twenty-five-years-to-life sentences for a defendant who on two occasions stole videotapes with an aggregate value of roughly $150 from two stores.[97] In *Ewing v. California*, decided on the same day as *Lockyer*, Justice Sandra Day O'Connor affirmed a twenty-five-year sentence for Daniel Ewing under California's "Three Strikes and You're Out" law.[98] Ewing, while on parole, was adjudged guilty of the grand theft of three golf clubs worth $399 apiece. He had previously been convicted of several serious or violent felonies. Justice O'Connor ruled that the Supreme Court was required to respect California's determination that it possessed a public safety interest in incapacitating and deterring recidivist felons like Ewing, whose previous offenses included robbery and three residential burglaries. In 2012, California voters passed a referendum requiring that the "third strike" involve a serious or violent crime.

Criminal Punishment and Status Offenses

In *Robinson v. California*, the U.S. Supreme Court overturned Robinson's conviction under a California law that declared it was a criminal offense "to be addicted to the use of narcotics."[99] The Supreme Court ruled that it was cruel and unusual punishment to impose criminal penalties on Robinson based on his conviction of the **status offense** of narcotics addiction, which a majority of the judges considered an addictive illness. Justice Potter Stewart noted that "even one day in prison would be cruel and unusual punishment for the 'crime' of having a common cold. It is unlikely that any state would make it a criminal offense for a person to be mentally ill, or a leper, or to be afflicted with venereal disease. [Such a] law would be universally thought to be an infliction of cruel and unusual punishment in violation of the Eighth and Fourteenth amendments."

CRIMINAL LAW AND PUBLIC POLICY

Barack Obama in 2015 became the first U.S. president to visit a federal prison and at the time asked whether "we really think it makes sense to lock so many people alone in tiny cells for 23 hours per day, often for months or years."

In 1993, Craig Haney, a social psychologist, interviewed inmates in solitary confinement at Pelican Bay State Prison in California, a super-maximum-security institution.[100] Twenty years later, he reinterviewed seven of the inmates who had spent two decades in windowless 6- by 11.6-foot isolation cells and other inmates who had spent at least ten years in solitary confinement at Pelican Bay. The inmates who were interviewed had been sentenced to prison for violent crimes although they primarily were confined in isolation because they were gang members or gang associates who posed a threat to correctional personnel or to other inmates. The only way out of isolation for these inmates was to become an informant and to risk retribution for being a snitch. Individuals in solitary confinement at Pelican Bay (Special Housing Unit or SHU) were denied personal phone calls and were prohibited from physically interacting with visitors. Haney found that there had been a complete mental and psychological deterioration of the inmates, who resembled zombies devoid of emotions and who possessed an inability to interact with other human beings.

Haney described the men as suffering from profound sadness. "They were grieving for their lost lives, for their loss of connectedness to the social world and their families outside, and also for their lost selves. . . . Most of them really did understand that they had lost who they were, and weren't sure of who they had become."

Sixty-three percent of inmates in solitary for more than ten years said they were on the verge of an "impending breakdown," but only 4 percent of the maximum-security inmates who were interviewed who were not in solitary confinement shared this feeling. Seventy-three percent of inmates in isolation reported chronic depression, and 78 percent felt emotionally empty, as compared to 48 percent and 36 percent among the maximum-security inmates who were not in solitary confinement. The inmates in long-term solitary also suffered from anxiety, paranoia, perceptual disturbances, and deep depression.

Even after being released, inmates who had spent extended time in solitary confinement were easily startled, were fearful of crowds, sought out confined spaces, were overwhelmed by sensory stimulation, and suffered from various psychological disorders. Studies also indicate that solitary confinement leads to higher rates of recidivism.

Juan E. Mendez, special rapporteur on torture for the United Nations, concluded that confinement of prisoners in solitary at Pelican Bay amounted "to torture or cruel, inhumane or degrading treatment or punishment" and was "contrary to the practices of civilized nations."

Roughly seventy-five thousand state and federal inmates as of 2015 were held in solitary confinement in the United States, most of whom are confined in their cells for twenty-three hours per day and only are allowed outside of their cells for showers, exercise, or medical visits.

The use of isolation cells escalated in the 1980s and 1990s when prison overcrowding and long-term sentences and the increased incarceration of gang members led to an escalation of violence that prison officials controlled through the isolation of inmates considered to pose a threat to the stability of institutions. Solitary confinement also was used to provide security for gay, bisexual, transgender, and physically challenged prisoners.

California, Colorado, Washington, Illinois, Oregon, and New York have introduced reforms to their system of solitary confinement. New York ended a system in which four thousand inmates were locked up for twenty-three hours a day, in 6- by 10-foot cells with little human contact or access to rehabilitative programs and a diet that at times was restricted to a slab of bread and potatoes known as "the loaf." In January 2016, President Obama issued an executive order prohibiting the use of solitary confinement in federal prisons against juveniles and prisoners who commit "low-level infractions." Obama recounted the story of sixteen-year-old Kalief Browder, who was sent to Rikers Island in New York City in 2010 to await trial after being accused of stealing a backpack. Kalief was released in 2013 after spending nearly two years in solitary confinement without ever standing trial or being convicted. Kalief subsequently committed suicide at age twenty-two. President Obama in explaining his executive order in an op-ed wrote, "How can we subject prisoners to unnecessary solitary confinement, knowing its effects, and then expect them to return to our communities as whole people? . . . It doesn't make us safer. It's an affront to our common humanity."

CASE ANALYSIS

At least eight states now have provisions allowing the carrying of concealed weapons on public postsecondary campuses. In Texas, the state legislature in 2015 approved carrying concealed weapons on campus starting in August 2016. In October 2015, California Governor Jerry Brown signed legislation prohibiting individuals from carrying concealed firearms on university campuses.

In *DiGiacinto v. Rector and Visitors of George Mason University*, the Virginia Supreme Court was asked to decide whether the prohibition on the "possession or carrying of any weapon" at George Mason University (GMU) was in violation of the right to bear arms protected under the Second Amendment and under the Virginia Constitution.

Is There a Second Amendment Right to Possess Firearms on a College Campus?

DiGiacinto v. Rector and Visitors of George Mason University, 704 S.E.2d 365 (Va. 2011)

In this appeal, we consider whether 8 VAC § 35-60-20, a George Mason University regulation governing the possession of weapons on its campus, violates the Constitution of Virginia or the United States Constitution. Possession or carrying of any weapon by any person, except a police officer, is prohibited on university property in academic buildings, administrative office buildings, student residence buildings, dining facilities, or while attending sporting, entertainment or educational events. Entry upon the aforementioned university property in violation of this prohibition is expressly forbidden. 8 VAC § 35-60-20.

DiGiacinto is not a student or employee of GMU, but he visits and utilizes the university's resources, including its libraries. He desires to exercise his right to carry a firearm not only onto the GMU campus but also into the buildings and at the events. DiGiacinto argued in his complaint that 8 VAC § 35-60-20 violates his constitutional right to carry a firearm, that GMU lacks statutory authority to regulate firearms, and that the regulation conflicts with state law. . . . Describing 8 VAC § 35-60-20 as "effectually a total ban" on the right to bear arms on GMU's campus . . . [DiGiacinto argues that it] violates the historic understanding of the right to bear arms.

Like the United States Constitution, the Constitution of Virginia also protects the right to bear arms. . . . The Virginia General Assembly incorporated the specific language of the Second Amendment—"the right of the people to keep and bear arms shall not be infringed"—into the existing framework of Article I, § 13 of the Constitution of Virginia. As a result, the language in Article I, § 13 concerning the right to bear arms is "substantially identical to the rights founded in the Second Amendment."

We hold that the protection of the right to bear arms expressed in Article I, § 13 of the Constitution of Virginia is co-extensive with the rights provided by the Second Amendment of the United States Constitution, concerning all issues in the instant case. Thus, for the purposes of this opinion, we analyze DiGiacinto's state constitutional rights and his federal constitutional rights concurrently.

The Supreme Court of the United States has held that the Second Amendment protects the right to carry and possess handguns in the home for self-defense. . . . In *McDonald*, the Court further held that the Second Amendment applies to the states by way of the Fourteenth Amendment.

The Supreme Court clearly stated in *Heller*, and a plurality of the Court reiterated in *McDonald*, that the right to carry a firearm is not unlimited. In *Heller*, the Supreme Court specifically recognized that:

> Nothing in our opinion should be taken to cast doubt on longstanding prohibitions on the possession of firearms by felons and the mentally ill, or laws forbidding the carrying of firearms in sensitive places such as schools and government buildings, or laws imposing conditions and qualifications on the commercial sale of arms.

The Supreme Court further explained its assertion by noting, "We identify these presumptively lawful regulatory measures only as examples; our list does not purport to be exhaustive."

Neither *Heller* nor *McDonald* casts doubt on laws or regulations restricting the carrying of firearms in sensitive places, such as schools and government buildings. Indeed, such restrictions are presumptively legal.

GMU has 30,000 students enrolled ranging from age 16 to senior citizens, and over 350 members of the incoming freshman class would be under the age of 18. Also approximately 50,000 elementary and high school students attend summer camps at GMU, and

(Continued)

(Continued)

approximately 130 children attend the child study center preschool there. All of these individuals use GMU's buildings and attend events on campus. The fact that GMU is a school and that its buildings are owned by the government indicates that GMU is a "sensitive place."

Unlike a public street or park, a university traditionally has not been open to the general public, "but instead is an institute of higher learning that is devoted to its mission of public education." Moreover, parents who send their children to a university have a reasonable expectation that the university will maintain a campus free of foreseeable harm. Recognizing the sensitivity of the university environment, the General Assembly established "a corporate body composed of the board of visitors of George Mason University" for the purpose of entrusting to that board the power to direct GMU's affairs. Although the real estate and personal property comprising GMU is property of the Commonwealth, the General Assembly has provided that this property "shall be transferred to and be known and taken as standing in the name and under the control of the rector and visitors of George Mason University."

GMU promulgated 8 VAC § 35-60-20 to restrict the possession or carrying of weapons in its facilities or at university events by individuals other than police officers. The regulation does not impose a total ban of weapons on campus. Rather, the regulation is tailored, restricting weapons only in those places where people congregate and are most vulnerable—inside campus buildings and at campus events. Individuals may still carry or possess weapons on the open grounds of GMU, and in other places on campus not enumerated in the regulation. We hold that GMU is a sensitive place and that 8 VAC § 35-60-20 is constitutional and does not violate Article I, § 13 of the Constitution of Virginia or the Second Amendment of the federal Constitution.

CHAPTER SUMMARY

The United States is a constitutional democracy. The government's power to enact laws is constrained by the Constitution. These limits are intended to safeguard the individual against the passions of the majority and the tyrannical tendencies of government. The restrictions on government also are designed to maximize individual freedom, which is the foundation of an energetic and creative society and dynamic economy. Individual freedom, of course, must be balanced against the need for social order and stability. We all have been reminded that "you cannot yell 'Fire!' in a crowded theater." This chapter challenges you to locate the proper balances among freedom, order, and stability. The rule of legality requires that individuals receive notice of prohibited acts. The ability to live your life without fear of unpredictable criminal punishment is fundamental to a free society. The rule of legality provides the philosophical basis for the constitutional prohibition on bills of attainder and *ex post facto* laws. Bills of attainder prohibit the legislative punishment of individuals without trial. *Ex post facto* laws prevent the government from criminally punishing acts that were innocent when committed. The constitutional provision for due process ensures that individuals are informed of acts that are criminally condemned and that definite standards are established that limit the discretion of the police. An additional restriction on criminal statutes is the Equal Protection Clause. This prevents the government from creating classifications that unjustifiably disadvantage or discriminate against individuals; a particularly heavy burden is imposed on the government to justify distinctions based on race or ethnicity. Classifications on gender are subject to intermediate scrutiny. Other differentiations are required only to meet a rational basis test.

Freedom of expression is of vital importance in American democracy, and the Constitution protects speech that some may view as offensive and disruptive. Courts may limit speech only in isolated situations that threaten social harm and instability. The right to privacy protects individuals from governmental intrusion into the intimate aspects of life and creates "space" for individuality and social diversity to flourish.

The First Amendment also protects the free exercise of religion. Laws that apply to all citizens constitutionally may interfere with religious practice. The government has a heavy burden to justify laws that single out a religion or religions.

The U.S. Supreme Court has held that the Second Amendment protects the right of individuals to possess handguns for the purpose of self-defense in the home. The full extent of the Second Amendment "right to bear arms" has yet to be determined.

The Supreme Court has narrowed the application of the death penalty in an effort to ensure that the punishment is proportionate to the character of the offender and the nature of his or her offense. The Court defers to the legislature in evaluating sentences for a term of years.

Keep these limitations on criminal punishment in mind as you read the remainder of the text.

CHAPTER REVIEW QUESTIONS

1. Explain the philosophy underlying the United States' constitutional democracy. What are the reasons for limiting the powers of state and federal government to enact criminal legislation? Are there costs as well as benefits in restricting governmental powers?

2. Define the rule of legality. What is the reason for this rule?

3. Define and compare bills of attainder and *ex post facto* laws. List the various types of *ex post facto* laws. What is the reason that the U.S. Constitution prohibits retroactive legislation?

4. Explain the standards for laws under the Due Process Clause.

5. Why does the U.S. Constitution protect freedom of expression? Is this freedom subject to any limitations?

6. What are the differences among the "rational basis," "intermediate scrutiny," and "strict scrutiny" tests under the Equal Protection Clause?

7. Discuss the constitutionality of laws that interfere with the free exercise of religion.

8. Where is the right to privacy found in the U.S. Constitution? What activities are protected within this right?

9. What is the relationship between the right to privacy and the Fourth Amendment prohibition against unreasonable searches and seizures?

10. Discuss the significance of recent cases interpreting the Second Amendment.

11. Summarize the requirements of the Eighth Amendment regarding methods of punishment, the amount of punishment, and punishment and status offenses.

12. Write a short essay on the constitutional restrictions on the drafting and enforcement of criminal statutes.

13. As a final exercise, consider life in a country that does not provide safeguards for civil liberties. How would your life be changed?

LEGAL TERMINOLOGY

bill of attainder

Bill of Rights

constitutional democracy

Due Process Clause

Eighth Amendment

equal protection

ex post facto law

fighting words

First Amendment

Fourteenth Amendment

Fourth Amendment

hate speech

incitement to violent action

incorporation

intermediate level of scrutiny

libel

minimum level of scrutiny test

nullum crimen sine lege, nulla poena sine lege

obscenity

overbreadth

privacy

rational basis test

rule of legality

Second Amendment

status offense

strict scrutiny test

symbolic speech

true threat

void for vagueness

CRIMINAL LAW ON THE WEB

Visit **study.sagepub.com/lippmaness2e** to access additional study tools including suggested answers to the You Decide questions, reprints of cases and statutes, online appendices, and more!

3 ELEMENTS OF CRIMES

Did the defendant negligently cause the death of the two-year-old victim?

The defendant did not allow the two-year-old victim to consume liquids after 8 p.m. in order to prevent him from wetting the bed. The defendant also prevented the victim from consuming liquids at other times in order to encourage him to consume solid food. . . . [T]he defendant gave the victim little or nothing to drink from the morning of February 22, 2009, to the morning of February 26, 2009.

Moreover, at some point during the victim's stay, the defendant attempted to discourage him from drinking out of cups belonging to other people. In order to accomplish this, the defendant placed a small amount of hot sauce in a cup and left it on the kitchen table. The victim consumed hot sauce from a cup on at least one occasion.

In the days immediately preceding his death, the victim began to exhibit numerous symptoms of dehydration. He had dry, cracked lips, a sunken face and a diminished appetite. He also had lost a significant amount of weight. On the morning of February 26, 2009, the defendant discovered that the victim was not breathing. Shortly thereafter, the defendant contacted emergency personnel by telephone. . . . The deputy chief medical examiner later confirmed that the child had died due to insufficient fluid intake. . . . The defendant possesses an IQ of 61. This score places her within the bottom one half of 1 percent of the population. (*State v. Patterson*, 27 A.3D 374 [Conn. App. 2011])

In this chapter, learn the difference between the criminal intents of purposely, knowingly, negligently, and recklessly.

Learning Objectives

1. Understand *actus reus* and *mens rea* and the requirement of concurrence.
2. Appreciate the difference between voluntary and involuntary acts.
3. Understand status offenses.
4. Know the circumstances in which an individual may be held liable for a failure to act.
5. Know the definition of possession and the different types of possession.
6. Appreciate the difference between specific intent, general intent, and constructive intent.
7. Know the difference between purposely, knowingly, recklessly, and negligently—the criminal intents established by the Model Penal Code.
8. Know the definition of a strict liability offense.
9. Understand transferred intent.
10. Know the significance of the concept of causality and the definition of cause in fact, proximate cause, intervening cause, coincidental intervening cause, and responsive intervening cause.

INTRODUCTION

A crime comprises an ***actus reus***, or a criminal act or omission (failure to act), and a ***mens rea***, or a criminal intent. Conviction of a criminal charge requires evidence establishing beyond a reasonable doubt that the accused possessed the required mental state and performed a voluntary act that caused the social harm condemned in the statute. Shortly, I will explain how an omission or failure to act may constitute a crime. At the moment, our focus is on criminal acts.

There must be a concurrence between the *actus reus* and *mens rea.* For instance, common law burglary is the breaking and entering of the dwelling house of another at night with the intent to commit a felony. A backpacker may force his or her way into a cabin to escape the sweltering summer heat and, once having entered, find it impossible to resist the temptation to steal hiking equipment. The requisite intent to steal developed following the breaking and entering, and our backpacker is not guilty of common law burglary. The requirement of concurrence is illustrated by the California Penal Code, which provides that "in every crime . . . there must exist a union or joint operation of act and intent."[1]

Actus reus generally involves three elements or components: (1) a voluntary act or failure to perform an act (2) that causes (3) a social harm condemned under a criminal statute. Homicide, for instance, may involve the voluntary shooting or stabbing (act) of another human being that results in (causation) death (social harm). The Indiana Criminal Code, in part, provides that a "person commits an offense only if he voluntarily engages in conduct in violation of the statute defining the offense."[2]

Keep in mind that certain offenses are strict liability offenses. An individual is held liable for a strict liability offense who is proven beyond a reasonable doubt to have committed a criminal act. There is no requirement of a criminal intent.

There are various other requirements to prove a criminal act in addition to an act and to an intent. First, keep in mind that an act may be innocent or criminal depending on the context or **attendant circumstances**. Entering an automobile, turning the key, and driving down the highway may be innocent or criminal depending on whether the driver is the owner or a thief. Second, crimes require differing attendant circumstances. An assault on a police officer requires an attack on a law enforcement official; an assault with a dangerous weapon involves the employment of an instrument capable of inflicting serious injury, such as a knife or firearm. A third point is that some offenses require that an act cause a specific harm. Homicide, for instance, involves an act that directly causes the death of the victim, while false pretenses require that an individual obtain title to property through the false representation of a fact or facts. In the case of these so-called **result crimes**, the defendant's act must be the "actual cause" of the resulting harm. An individual who dangerously assaults a victim who subsequently dies may not be guilty of homicide in the event that the victim would have lived and her death was caused by the gross negligence of an ambulance driver.

In this chapter, we discuss the concepts that constitute the foundation of a criminal offense:

Acts

Intent

Concurrence

Causality

CRIMINAL ACTS AND THOUGHTS

What is an act? It is sufficient to note that the popular view is that an act involves a bodily movement, whether voluntary or involuntary.

The significant point is that the criminal law punishes voluntary acts and does not penalize thoughts. Why?

- Punishing people for their thoughts would involve an unacceptable degree of governmental intrusion into individual privacy.
- It would be difficult to distinguish between criminal thoughts that reflect momentary anger, frustration, or fantasy, and thoughts involving the serious consideration of criminal conduct.
- Individuals should be punished only for conduct that creates a social harm or imminent threat of social harm and should not be penalized for thoughts that are not translated into action.
- The social harm created by an act can be measured and a proportionate punishment imposed. The harm resulting from thoughts is much more difficult to determine.

How should we balance the interest in freedom of thought and imagination against the social interest in the early detection and prevention of social harm in the case of an individual who records dreams of child molestation in his or her private diary?

A VOLUNTARY CRIMINAL ACT

A more problematic issue is the requirement that a crime consist of a voluntary act. The Indiana Criminal Law Study Commission, which assisted in writing the Indiana statute on criminal conduct, explains that *voluntary* simply means a conscious choice by an individual to commit or not to commit an act.[3] Professor Joshua Dressler compares an involuntary movement to the branch of a tree that is blown by the wind into a passerby. A voluntary act may involve pulling the trigger of a gun, hitting a victim, moving your mouth and inciting a riot, or offering another person money to commit a murder.[4]

The requirement of a voluntary act is based on the belief that it would be fundamentally unfair to punish individuals who do not consciously choose to engage in criminal activity and who therefore cannot be considered morally blameworthy. There also is the practical consideration that there is no need to deter, incapacitate, or rehabilitate individuals who involuntarily engage in criminal conduct.[5]

Once again, a voluntary act "requires an ability to choose which course to take—i.e., an ability to choose whether to commit the act that gives rise to criminal liability."[6] Consider several cases in Table 3.1 in which courts were required to determine whether to hold defendants criminally liable who claimed that they should be acquitted because they had committed an **involuntary act**.

An individual driving an automobile is not held liable for an unanticipated stroke or heart attack that involuntarily causes an accident and the death of another. Courts reason that the death resulted from an unanticipated, involuntary act. However, these types of situations can be complicated. Consider the frequently cited case of *People v. Decina*, in which the defendant was convicted of negligent homicide. The defendant's automobile jumped a curb and killed four children. The appellate court affirmed Decina's conviction despite the fact that the accident resulted from an

Table 3.1	Involuntary Acts

Sample of Court Decisions on Involuntary Acts

Involuntary Act	Court Decision
Sleepwalking	The Kentucky Supreme Court ruled that a defendant, who claimed that he was a "sleepwalker," should not be convicted in the event that he was "unconscious when he killed the deceased." See *Fain v. Commonwealth*, 78 Ky. 183 (1879).
Reflex Action	A California court of appeals concluded that the evidence supported the "inference" that a defendant who had been wounded in the abdomen had shot and killed a police officer as a reflex action and was in a "state of unconsciousness." See *People v. Newton*, 87 Cal. Rptr. 394 (Cal. App. 1970).
Drugs in Jail	Eaton was arrested for driving with his headlights turned off and failed a field sobriety test. He was arrested for DUI and taken to the county jail where he was searched, the officers seized methamphetamine, and he was charged with possession of a controlled substance. The prosecutor sought a sentence enhancement because Eaton introduced the narcotics into the county jail. The Washington Supreme Court held that Eaton was "forcibly taken" to the county jail and that a sentence enhancement could not be lawfully imposed. See *State v. Eaton*, 229 P.3d 704 (Wash. 2010). An Arizona appellate court based on similar facts held that the defendant's possession of a controlled substance was "voluntary in that, after being advised of the consequences of bringing drugs into the jail, [he] consciously chose to ignore the officers' warnings, choosing instead to enter the jail in possession of cocaine. Under these circumstances, the [defendant] was the author of his own fate." See *State v. Alvarado*, 200 P.3d 1037 (Ariz. App. 2008).

epileptic seizure. The judges reasoned that the statute "does not necessarily contemplate that the driver be conscious at the time of the accident" and that it is sufficient that the defendant "knew of his medical disability and knew that it would interfere with the operation of a motor vehicle." In other words, Decina committed a voluntary act when he voluntarily got behind the wheel of his auto, consciously turned the key, and drove the auto, although he was aware that he might experience a seizure.[7]

The notion that an act may be involuntary is not an easy concept to comprehend, and you may be justifiably skeptical about whether this is humanly possible. In a famous Canadian case in 1988, twenty-four-year-old Kenneth Parks was acquitted of murder after he was found to have driven fourteen miles to his mother-in-law's home and beat her to death with a tire iron. Parks successfully argued that he was sleepwalking, and friends testified that he had a history of sleepwalking. Expert medical witnesses testified that there were roughly thirty cases in which a "sleepwalker" committed murder.[8]

Model Penal Code (MPC) Section 2.01 provides a good summary of the requirement that a criminal act must include "a voluntary act or the omission to perform an act." The MPC avoids the difficulties involved in trying to unravel the differences between voluntary and involuntary acts by listing categories of involuntary acts.

MPC Section 2.01 defines the Requirement of Voluntary Act as follows (reprinted in partial):

Model Penal Code

Section 2.01. Requirement of Voluntary Act

(1) A person is not guilty of an offense unless his liability is based on conduct that includes a voluntary act or the omission to perform an act of which he is physically capable.

(2) The following are not voluntary acts within the meaning of this Section:

    (a) a reflex or convulsion;

    (b) a bodily movement during unconsciousness or sleep;

    (c) conduct during hypnosis or resulting from hypnotic suggestion;

    (d) a bodily movement that otherwise is not a product of the effort or determination of the actor, either conscious or habitual.

The Legal Equation

Actus reus	=	A voluntary act or failure to perform an act.
Voluntary act	=	A bodily movement that is the product of a conscious choice.

You Decide

3.1 Thomas F. Martino and his wife, Carmen Keenon, got into an argument. Martino shoved his wife down the front stairs of the home. He fell on Keenon and began choking her. The police arrived and observed Martino on top of Keenon on the stair landing outside of the couple's apartment. The officers ordered Martino to get off of Keenon who replied in a combative tone, "[Y]ou ain't going to ----ing do anything." After the police repeated these orders several more times, threatened to tase Martino, and began moving up the stairs, Martino stood up, moved to the front of the landing, and "'squared off' against the police in a way that indicated that he wanted to fight." Martino yelled at the police, "Come on." One of the officers tased Martino, who dropped to the ground, having lost control of his muscles because of being tased. He fell backward on top of Keenon, breaking her arm. The trial court found Martino guilty of aggravated domestic battery, aggravated battery, unlawful restraint, and two counts of resisting or obstructing a police officer. The defendant was sentenced to concurrent terms totaling 180 days in jail and four years of probation. Martino claims that his breaking of Keenon's arm was an involuntary act and that he may not be held criminally liable for a battery. Do you agree? See *People v. Martino*, 970 N.E.2d 1236 (Ill. App. 2012).

You can find the answer at study.sagepub.com/lippmaness2e

CRIMINAL LAW IN THE NEWS

Gilberto Valle, age thirty-one, the so-called "Cannibal Cop," was convicted of conspiracy to kidnap. A New York police officer, Valle was convicted in March 2013 based on his alleged secret plotting on "dark" Internet sites to abduct several women, including his own wife. He used online identities like Girlmeat Hunter and searched for methods of kidnapping, subduing, torturing, and killing women and used a law enforcement database to collect information about his victims. Valle also conducted Internet searches on topics such as "how to chloroform a girl."

Valle's wife discovered his postings about women on fetish chat rooms. In one e-mail, Valle described hanging a victim by her feet and "cutting her throat" and "[l]etting her bleed . . . [and] butcher[ing] her while she hangs." Other messages stated that "part of me wants to put her in the oven while she is still alive, but at a very low heat," and expressed a desire to "make some bacon strips off her belly."

Federal District Court Judge Paul G. Gardephe overturned Valle's conspiracy conviction, finding that he only engaged in "fantasy role-play." "No one was ever kidnapped, no attempted kidnapping [occurred] . . . and no real-world, non-Internet-based steps were ever taken to kidnap anyone." Judge Gardephe acknowledged that Valle's "depraved, misogynistic sexual fantasies about his wife, former college classmates and acquaintances undoubtedly reflected a mind diseased." However, Valle never met and did not know the men with whom he communicated and took no "non-Internet-based steps" to implement the plan. The dates for the kidnappings passed without comment or discussion or implementation.

Valle did receive a one-year sentence for using a law enforcement database to learn about the women about whom he fantasized and was required to continue mental health treatment. At the time of his sentencing, Valle had already been jailed for twenty months while awaiting trial.

In December 2015, the Second Circuit Court of Appeals affirmed Judge Gardephe's reversal of Valle's conviction. Judge Barrington D. Parker Jr. wrote that "fantasizing about committing a crime, even a crime of violence against a real person whom you know, is not a crime." Judge Parker cautioned that Valle's rhetoric was not harmless because it is both a "symptom of and a contributor to a culture of . . . massive social harm that demeans women." Valle in an interview following the reversal of his conviction recognized that the anonymity of the computer screen contributes to a culture in which "you try . . . [to] outdo the other person [as to] who can be the sicker one." Why did the appellate courts consider Valle to have engaged in fantasy? Do you agree with the decision to acquit Valle?

STATUS

An individual may not be held criminally liable for a **status**. A status is defined as a "characteristic" or a "condition" or "state of being." The rule is that you may not be criminally punished for "who you are"; you may be held liable only for "what you do." In other words, we cannot be held criminally responsible based on our race, religion, gender, or sexual preference or the fact that we have a disease or are a former offender. In 1969, in *Wheeler v. Goodman*, a federal district court judge held that the defendants had been improperly arrested and punished because they were unemployed "hippies."[9]

> A man is free to be a hippie, a Methodist, a Jew, a Black Panther, a Kiwanian, or even a Communist, so long as his conduct does not imperil others, or infringe upon their rights. In short, it is no crime to be a hippie. . . . Status—even that of a gambler or prostitute—may

not be made criminal. The acts of gambling, prostitution, and operating bawdy houses are criminally punishable, of course, but the state cannot create the special status of vagrant for persons who commit those illegal acts and then punish the status instead of the act.

What about the status of being a drug addict? In *Robinson v. California*, the U.S. Supreme Court was asked to determine whether Robinson could be held criminally liable for his status of being "addicted to narcotics." The Court found the California law unconstitutional because it did not "require possession or use of narcotics, or disorderly behavior resulting from narcotics, but rather imposed liability for the mere status of being addicted." The justices concluded that just as it would be cruel to make it a crime to be mentally ill or a leper or to be afflicted with venereal disease, it was cruel to convict an individual for the "disease of addiction" without requiring proof of narcotics possession or antisocial behavior.[10]

Six years later, the Court reached a different outcome in *Powell v. Texas*. Leroy Powell was an alcoholic with roughly one hundred arrests for public intoxication. He was arrested for "being found in a state of intoxication in a public place." Powell claimed that he could not control his urge to drink and that because of his status as an alcoholic, he should not be held guilty for being drunk in public. The Supreme Court rejected Powell's argument that he was being punished for being a chronic alcoholic and held that he was being punished for public behavior that posed "substantial health and safety hazards, both to himself and for members of the general public."[11]

Powell, according to the majority of the justices, was not suffering from a disease that made him unable to control his desire to drink. Each morning, Powell made a voluntary decision to start drinking and knew that by the end of the day, he would find himself drunk in public and subject to arrest.

In other words, although Robinson was improperly punished for being a "narcotics addict," Powell was properly punished for being "drunk and disorderly in public." Consider how the Court would have ruled if the scientific evidence indicated that alcoholics like Powell have a gene that makes them unable to resist drinking and getting drunk in public. Would Powell, on these facts, succeed in claiming that he was being punished for a status rather than for an act?

You might be thinking about the fact that sex offenders are prohibited from living nearby a school or church; suspected terrorists are prohibited from flying on commercial airliners; and, in many states, undocumented young people are denied state college tuition. Are these status offenses? The answer is that these disabilities are civil regulations designed to protect the public rather than "criminal punishments" imposed on individuals. A homeless individual who is convicted of sleeping in the park is being punished for his or her act rather than his or her status. On the other hand, some argue that a homeless individual is compelled by his or her homelessness and the lack of housing to sleep in the park.

You Decide **3.2** An FBI search of Bruce Black's home and home computer resulted in the seizure of photographs and computer diskettes containing unlawful child pornography. Black pled guilty to the receipt, possession, and distribution of child pornography that had been transmitted in interstate commerce. He was sentenced to eighteen months in prison and to three years of supervised release. The government stipulated in the plea agreement that Black was a "pedophile and/or ephebophile [sexually attracted to young men]" and that "the receipt, collection and distribution of child pornography was a pathological symptom of the defendant's pedophilia and/or ephebophilia." Psychiatric reports concluded that despite Black's illness, Black was able to appreciate the wrongfulness of his acts and was able to control his impulses and limit his involvement in child pornography to those periods in which his roommate was absent. Black appealed and claimed that he was unable to control his sexual urges and that he was being punished for his status as a pedophile and/or ephebophile. Do you agree with Black? Will his appeal be successful? See *United States v. Black*, 116 F.3d 198 (7th Cir. 1997).

You can find the answer at study.sagepub.com/lippmaness2e

OMISSIONS

Can you be held criminally liable for a failure to act? For casually stepping over the body of a dying person who is blocking the entrance to your favorite coffee shop? The MPC requires that criminal conduct be based on a "voluntary act or omission to perform an act of which [an individual] is physically capable." An **omission** is a failure to act or a "negative act."

Read *People v. Kellogg* on the study site: study .sagepub.com/ lippmaness2e.

The American and European Bystander Rules

The basic rule in the United States is that an individual is not legally required to assist a person who is in peril. This principle was clearly established in 1907 in *People v. Beardsley*. The Michigan Supreme Court ruled that the married Beardsley was not liable for failing to take steps to ensure the safety of Blanche Burns, a woman with whom he was spending the weekend. The court explained that the fact that Burns was in Beardsley's house at the time she overdosed on drugs and alcohol did not create a legal duty to assist her. The Michigan judges cited in support of this verdict the statement of U.S. Supreme Court Justice Stephen Johnson Field that it is "undoubtedly the moral duty of every person to extend to others assistance when in danger . . . and, if such efforts should be omitted . . . he would by his conduct draw upon himself the just censure and reproach of good men; but this is the only punishment to which he would be subjected by society."[12] Chief Justice Alonzo Philetus Carpenter of the New Hampshire Supreme Court earlier had recognized that an individual did not possess a duty to rescue a child standing in the path of an oncoming train. Justice Carpenter noted that "if he does not, he may . . . justly be styled a ruthless savage and a moral monster; but he is not liable in damages for the child's injury, or indictable under the statute for its death."[13]

This so-called **American bystander rule** contrasts with the **European bystander rule**, common in Europe, that obligates individuals to intervene. Five American states, Hawaii, Minnesota, Rhode Island, Vermont, and Wisconsin, have laws that require individuals to call for help or to intervene in certain circumstances to protect another person so long as they themselves are not placed in danger. **Good Samaritan laws**, in contrast, protect individuals who intervene to assist a person in peril from lawsuits for damages and should not be confused with criminal liability for a failure to intervene.[14]

Most Americans would likely agree that an Olympic swimmer is morally obligated to rescue a young child drowning in a swimming pool. Why, then, is this not recognized as a legal duty in the United States? There are several reasons for the American bystander rule:

- Individuals intervening may be placed in jeopardy.
- Bystanders may misperceive a situation, unnecessarily interfere, and create needless complications.
- Individuals may lack the physical capacity and expertise to subdue an assailant or to rescue a hostage and place themselves in danger. This is the role of criminal justice professionals.
- The circumstances under which individuals should intervene and the acts required to satisfy the obligation to assist another would be difficult to clearly define.
- Criminal prosecutions for a failure to intervene would burden the criminal justice system.
- Individuals in a capitalist society are responsible for their own welfare and should not expect assistance from others.
- Most people will assist others out of a sense of moral responsibility, and there is no need for the law to require intervention.

Critics of the American bystander rule contend that there is little difference between pushing a child onto the railroad tracks and failing to intervene to ensure the child's safety and that criminal liability should extend to both acts and omissions. This also would deter crime, because offenders may be reluctant to commit crimes in situations in which they anticipate that citizens will intervene. We can see how the readiness of passengers to confront terrorists on airplanes has prevented several attacks, most notably in the case of the "shoe bomber" Richard Reid. The European rule also assists in promoting a sense of community and regard for others.[15]

The conflict between law and morality was starkly presented in 1964 when thirty-eight residents of New York City were awakened by the desperate screams of Kitty Genovese, a twenty-eight-year-old woman returning home from work. Kitty parked her car in a lot roughly one hundred feet from her apartment and was confronted by Winston Moseley, a married father of two young children, who later would testify that he received emotional gratification from stalking women. The thirty-eight residents of the building turned on their lights and opened their windows and watched as Moseley returned on three separate occasions over a period of thirty-five minutes to stab Kitty seventeen times. The third time Moseley returned, he found that Kitty had crawled to safety inside a nearby apartment house, and he stabbed her in the throat to prevent her from screaming, attempted to rape her, and took $49 from her wallet. One person found the courage to persuade a neighbor to call the police, who arrived in two minutes to find Kitty's dead body. This event profoundly impacted the United States. Commentators asked whether we had become a society of passive bystanders who were concerned only with our own welfare.[16]

American criminal law does not impose a general duty on the individuals witnessing the murder of Kitty Genovese to intervene. There is a duty, however, to assist another under certain limited conditions. The primary requirement is that a duty must be imposed by either the common law or a statute.

- *Status.* The common law recognized that individuals possess an obligation to assist their child, spouse, or employee. In *State v. Mally*, the defendant was convicted of "hastening" the death of his wife who had fallen and broken both of her arms, precipitating severe shock and the degeneration of her kidneys. Michael Mally left his wife Kay alone in bed for two days, only bothering to provide her with a single glass of water. A Montana district court held that "the failure to obtain medical aid for one who is owed a duty is a sufficient degree of negligence to constitute involuntary manslaughter provided death results from the failure to act."[17]

- *Statute.* A **duty to intervene** may be created by a statute that imposes a duty of care. This may be a criminal statute requiring that a doctor report child abuse or a statute that sets forth the obligations of parents. In *Craig v. State*, the defendants followed the dictates of their religion and treated their child's fatal illness with prayer rather than medicine. They were subsequently convicted of failing to obtain medical care for their now-deceased six-year-old daughter. The court ruled that the parents had breached their duty under a statute that provided that a father and mother are jointly and individually responsible for the "support, care, nurture, welfare and education of their minor children." The statute failed to mention medical care, but the court had "no hesitancy in holding that it is embraced within the scope of the broad language used."[18]

- *Contract.* An obligation may be created by an agreement. An obvious example is a babysitter who agrees to care for children or a lifeguard employed to safeguard swimmers. In *Commonwealth v. Pestinikas*, Walter and Helen Pestinikas verbally agreed to provide shelter, food, and medicine to ninety-two-year-old Joseph Kly, who had been hospitalized with a severe weakness of the esophagus. Kly agreed to pay the Pestinikases $300 a month in return for food, shelter, care, and medicine. Kly was found dead of dehydration and starvation roughly nineteen months later. A Pennsylvania superior court ruled that although failure to provide food and medicine could not have been the basis for prosecuting a stranger who learned of Kly's condition, a "duty to act imposed by contract is legally enforceable and, therefore, creates a legal duty."[19]

- *Assumption of a Duty.* An individual who voluntarily intervenes to assist another is charged with a duty of care. In *People v. Oliver*, Oliver, knowing that Cornejo was extremely drunk, drove him from a bar to Oliver's home, where she assisted him to inject drugs. Cornejo collapsed on the floor, and Oliver instructed her daughter to drag Cornejo's body outside and hide him behind a shed. The next morning, Cornejo was discovered dead. A California superior court ruled that by taking Cornejo into her home, Oliver "took charge of a person unable to prevent harm to himself," and she "owed Cornejo a duty" that she breached by failing to summon medical assistance.[20]

In *People v. Burton*, the defendants, Sharon Burton and Leroy Locke, were convicted of first-degree murder. On January 22, 1996, Sharon Burton passively watched Leroy Locke chase her daughter Dominique with a belt, after learning that she had had a "toilet training accident" on the carpet, while shouting "the little bitch pissed again." Locke then filled the bathtub with water and forced Dominique's head under the water three times for fifteen seconds at a time. Dominique's body reportedly went limp in the water, and Locke and Burton left the three-year-old unattended in the bathtub for thirty minutes while they played cards. Burton, after discovering Dominique's lifeless body, called her mother rather than authorities and later falsely reported to investigators that the child had fallen off the toilet. An Illinois appellate court found that Burton possessed knowledge that Dominique was being subjected to an ongoing pattern of abuse and that there was a substantial likelihood that Dominique would suffer death or great bodily harm.[21]

Read *Jones v. United States* and *State v. Caldwell* on the study site: study .sagepub.com/ lippmaness2e.

The Legal Equation

Omission of a duty $=$ A failure to act

$+$ status, statute, contract, assume a duty, peril, control, landowner

$+$ knowledge that the victim is in peril

$+$ criminal intent

$+$ possession of the capacity to perform the act

$+$ would not be placed in danger.

You Decide

3.3 In May 1997, nineteen-year-old Jeremy Strohmeyer together with his friend David Cash played video games at a Las Vegas casino while Strohmeyer's father gambled. Seven-year-old Sherrice Iverson threw a wet paper towel at Strohmeyer, and a paper towel fight ensued. He followed her into the restroom to continue the game. The forty-six-pound Iverson threw a yellow floor sign at Strohmeyer and then began screaming. Strohmeyer covered her mouth and forced her into a bathroom stall. David Cash wandered into the restroom to look for Strohmeyer. He peered over the stall and viewed Strohmeyer gripping and threatening to kill Sherrice. Cash allegedly made an unsuccessful effort to get Strohmeyer's attention and left the bathroom. Strohmeyer then molested Sherrice and strangled her to suffocate the screams. As he was about to leave, Strohmeyer decided to relieve Sherrice's suffering and twisted her head and broke her neck. He placed the limp body in a sitting position on the toilet with Sherrice's feet in the bowl.

Strohmeyer confessed to Cash and, after being apprehended by the police three days later, explained that he wanted to experience death. His lawyer argued that Strohmeyer was in a "dream-like state" as a result of a combination of alcohol, drugs, and stress. In order to avoid the death penalty, Strohmeyer pled guilty to first-degree murder, first-degree kidnapping, and sexual assault of a minor, all of which carry a life sentence in Nevada.

Iverson's mother called for Cash to be criminally charged, but Nevada law required him neither to intervene nor to report the crime to the police. The administration at the University of California at Berkeley responded to a student demonstration calling for Cash's dismissal by explaining that there were no grounds to expel him from the institution because he had not committed a crime. Cash, who was studying nuclear engineering, refused to express remorse, explaining that he was concerned about himself and was not going to become upset over other people's problems, particularly a little girl whom he did not know.

Should David Cash be held criminally liable for a failure to rescue Sherrice Iverson? See Joshua Dressler, *Cases and Materials on Criminal Law*, 3rd ed. (St. Paul, MN: West, 2003), pp. 133–134.

You can find the answer at study.sagepub.com/lippmaness2e

POSSESSION

State criminal codes punish a number of crimes involving the possession of **contraband** (material that is unlawful to possess or to manufacture). Statutes typically punish the possession of narcotics, firearms, ammunition and explosives, burglar tools, stolen property, and child pornography and obscenity.

Possession is a preparatory offense. The thinking is that punishing possession deters and prevents the next step—a burglary, sale of narcotics, or the use of a weapon in a robbery. The possession of contraband such as drugs and guns may also provoke conflict and violence.[22] How does the possession of contraband meet the requirement that a crime involve a voluntary act or omission? This difficulty is overcome by requiring proof that the accused knowingly obtained or received the contraband (voluntary act) or failed to immediately dispose of the property.[23]

There are a number of central concepts to keep in mind in understanding possession.

- **Actual possession** refers to drugs and other contraband within an individual's physical possession or immediate reach.
- **Constructive possession** refers to contraband that is outside of an individual's actual physical control but over which he or she exercises control through access to the location where the contraband is stored or through ability to control an individual who has physical control over the contraband. A drug dealer has constructive possession over narcotics stored in his or her home or under the physical control of a member of his or her gang.
- **Joint possession** refers to a situation in which a number of individuals exercise control over contraband. Several members of a gang may all live in the home where drugs are stored. There must be specific proof connecting each individual to the drugs. The fact that a gang member lives in the house is not sufficient.
- **Fleeting possession** permits an innocent individual to take momentary possession and dispose of an illegal object. An example is when a teacher removes and disposes of narcotics seized in the classroom.

Possession typically requires a criminal intent. MPC Section 2.01 provides that the "possessor" must have "knowingly procured or received the thing possessed" or "was aware of his control thereof for a sufficient period to have been able to terminate his possession." In other words, the keys to possession are knowledge and either physical or constructive possession of the property.[24]

Perhaps the most difficult cases involve determining which of the residents of a house or occupants of an automobile are in constructive possession of contraband. In *State v. Cashen*, Ross Cashen was convicted of possession of marijuana, and he appealed. Cashen was one of six occupants of an automobile. Four individuals, including Cashen and his girlfriend, were in the backseat. Cashen was sitting next to a window with his girlfriend on his lap.[25]

An officer found a lighter and cigarette rolling papers on Cashen and cigarette rolling papers and a small baggie of marijuana seeds in his girlfriend's pants pocket. The officers found a baggie of marijuana wedged in the rear seat on the side where Cashen and his girlfriend had been seated. Both Cashen and his girlfriend stated that she owned the marijuana. The Iowa Supreme Court held that Cashen's physical closeness to the marijuana was not sufficient to prove possession beyond a reasonable doubt, and his conviction was overturned. His fingerprints were not on the bag of marijuana, the marijuana was not visible to the occupants of the car, and Cashen neither owned the car nor acted in a suspicious fashion when the police approached to search the automobile. Would you hold Cashen, his girlfriend, any of the passengers, or the driver liable for possession based on these facts? Would it make a difference to your answer if there was a large amount of marijuana in the backseat?

The doctrine of **willful blindness** holds an individual criminally liable who lacks actual knowledge of the existence of contraband although he or she is aware of a high probability of the existence of the contraband. Commentators note that individuals may not bury their head in the sand like an ostrich and thereby escape legal liability. Charles Jewell and a friend were approached in a Tijuana, Mexico, bar by a stranger who called himself "Ray." Ray asked them if they wanted to buy marijuana, and when they refused, he offered to pay them $100 for driving a car across the border. Jewell accepted the offer, although his friend refused. Customs agents stopped Jewell at the border and opened the trunk and seized 110 pounds of marijuana concealed in a secret compartment between the trunk and rear seat. Jewell testified at trial that he had seen the special compartment when he opened the trunk and that he did not investigate further. The jury convicted Jewell of drug possession and concluded that if Jewell was not actually aware of the marijuana, his "ignorance was solely and entirely a result of a conscious purpose to avoid learning the truth."[26]

The Legal Equation

Possession = Knowledge of presence of object

+ exercise of dominion and control

+ knowledge of character of object.

MENS REA CRIMINAL INTENT

In the last section, we noted that a criminal offense ordinarily requires the concurrence between a criminal act (*actus reus*) and a criminal intent (*mens rea*) that cause a social harm prohibited under the law. The prosecutor is required to establish beyond a reasonable doubt that the defendant possessed the required criminal intent.

It is said that one of the great contributions of the common law is to limit criminal punishment to "morally blameworthy" individuals who consciously choose to cause or to create a risk of harm or injury. Individuals are punished based on the harm caused by their decision to commit a criminal act rather than because they are "bad" or "evil people." Former Supreme Court justice Robert Jackson observed that a system of punishment based on a criminal intent is intended to direct punishment at individuals who consciously choose between "good and evil." Justice Jackson noted that this emphasis on individual choice and free will assumes that criminal law and punishment can deter people from choosing to commit crimes, and that those who do engage in crime can be encouraged through the application of punishment to develop a greater sense of moral responsibility in the future.[27]

We all pay attention to intent in evaluating individuals' behavior. You read in the newspaper that a rock star shot and killed one of her friends. There is no more serious crime than murder; yet, before condemning the killer, you want to know what was on her mind. The rock star may have intentionally aimed and fired the weapon. On the other hand, she may have aimed and fired the gun, believing that it was unloaded. We have the same act but a different reaction, based on whether the rock star intended to kill her friend or acted in a reckless fashion. As former Supreme Court justice Oliver Wendell Holmes Jr. famously observed, "even a dog distinguishes between being stumbled over and being kicked."[28]

It is a bedrock principle of criminal law that a crime requires an act or omission and a criminal intent. The importance of a criminal intent is captured by a frequently quoted phrase: "There can be no crime, large or small, without an evil mind" (*actus non facit reum nisi mens sit rea*).[29]

The common law originally punished criminal acts and paid no attention to the mental element of an individual's act. The killing of another was murder, whether committed intentionally or recklessly. Canon, or religious law, with its stress on sinfulness and moral guilt, helped to introduce the idea that punishment should depend on an individual's "moral blameworthiness." This came to be fully accepted in the American colonies. In 1978, the Supreme Court observed that *mens rea* is now the "rule of, rather than the exception to, the principles of American jurisprudence."[30] There are two primary reasons that explain why the criminal law requires "moral blameworthiness."

1. *Responsibility.* It is just and fair to hold a person accountable who intentionally chooses to commit a crime.

2. *Deterrence.* Individuals who act with a criminal intent pose a threat to society and should be punished in order to discourage them from violating the law in the future and in order to deter others from choosing to violate the law.

In many instances, it is difficult to establish a criminal intent beyond a reasonable doubt because we do not know what is going on inside an individual's mind. The easiest case is when an individual makes a statement of intent, such as "I will kill you," or makes a confession to the police. In most instances, we do not know what an individual is thinking and must rely on circumstantial evidence or the surrounding facts. In the Illinois case of *People v. Conley*, a district court found that the defendant possessed the intent to cause "permanent disability" based on the defendant's forcefully hitting the victim in the face with a full bottle of wine.[31]

Intent should not be confused with **motive**. Motive is the underlying reason that explains or inspires an individual to act. An individual who robs a bank may be motivated by greed or by a desire to feed his or her family. The individual's motive is not considered in determining whether the individual possessed a criminal intent and committed a criminal act. Motive may be considered by a judge at sentencing.

GENERAL AND SPECIFIC INTENT

The common law provided for two confusing categories of *mens rea*, a general intent and a specific intent. These continue to appear in various state statutes and decisions, although, as we shall see, a number of states have adopted the MPC framework.

A **general intent** is simply an intent to commit the *actus reus* or criminal act. There is no requirement that the prosecutors demonstrate that an offender possessed an intent to violate the law, an awareness that the act is a crime, or knowledge that the act will result in a particular type of harm. Proof of the defendant's general intent is typically inferred from the nature of the act and the surrounding circumstances. The crime of battery or a nonconsensual harmful touching provides a good illustration of a general intent crime. The prosecutor is required to establish only that the accused intended to commit an act that was likely to substantially harm another. In the case of a battery, this may be inferred from factors such as the force of the blow, the portion of the body that was targeted, and the defendant's statements and motive. Statutes that require a general intent typically use words such as *willfully* or *intentionally*.

A **specific intent** is a mental determination to accomplish a specific result. The prosecutor is required to demonstrate that the offender possessed the intent to commit the *actus reus* and then is required to present additional evidence that the defendant possessed the specific intent to accomplish a particular result. For example, a battery with an intent to kill requires proof of a battery along with additional evidence of a specific intent to murder the victim. Larceny requires the intent to and act of taking and carrying away property with the added intent permanently to deprive an individual of the property. The classic example is common law burglary. This requires the *actus reus* of breaking and entering and evidence of a specific intent to commit a felony inside the dwelling. Some commentators refer to these offenses as **crimes of cause and result** because the offender possesses the intent to "cause a particular result."

The difference between a specific intent and a general intent is nicely summarized by the Michigan Supreme Court: "The distinction between specific intent and general intent crimes is that the former involve a particular criminal intent beyond the act done, while the latter involve merely the intent to do the physical act."[32]

Courts at times struggle with whether statutes require a general or specific intent. The consequences can be seen from the Texas case of *Alvarado v. State*. The defendant was convicted of "intentionally and knowingly" causing serious bodily injury to her child by placing him in a tub of hot water. The trial judge instructed the jury that they were merely required to find that the accused deliberately placed the child in the water to find her criminally liable. The appellate court overturned the conviction and ruled that the statute required the jury to find that the defendant possessed the intent to place the child in hot water, as well as the specific intent to inflict serious bodily harm.[33]

Constructive intent is a third type of common law intent that was developed in situations in which a defendant lacked a specific intent, although a result was substantially likely to occur. This was applied in the early twentieth century to protect the public against reckless drivers; it provides that individuals who act with conscious disregard for the consequences of their actions are considered to intend the natural consequences of their actions. A reckless driver who caused an accident that resulted in death, under the doctrine of constructive intent, is guilty of a willful and intentional battery or homicide.

In 1980, in *United States v. Bailey*, the U.S. Supreme Court complained that the common law distinction between general and specific intent had caused a "good deal of confusion." A 1972 survey of federal statutes found seventy-six different terms used to describe the required mental element of criminal offenses. This laundry list included terms such as *intentionally, knowingly, fraudulently, designedly, recklessly, wantonly, unlawfully, feloniously, willfully, purposely, negligently, wickedly,* and *wrongfully*.[34]

Justice Robert Jackson noted "the variety . . . and confusion" of the judicial definition of the "elusive mental element" of crime. He observed that "[f]ew areas of criminal law pose more difficulty than the proper definition of *mens rea* required for a particular crime."

The MPC introduced a new approach to determining criminal intent, which is discussed in the next section. Professor Dressler writes that "[n]o aspect of the Model Penal Code has had greater influence on the direction of American criminal law than Section 2.02 [on criminal intent]."[35]

INTENT UNDER THE MODEL PENAL CODE

The MPC attempted to clearly define the mental intent required for crimes by providing four easily understood levels of responsibility. All crimes requiring a mental element (strict liability offenses do not) must include one of the four mental states provided in Section 2.02 of the MPC. These four types of intent, in descending order of culpability (responsibility), are as follows:

Purposely

Knowingly

Recklessly

Negligently

These criminal intents are illustrated in Table 3.2.

Purposely

The MPC established **purposely** as the most serious category of criminal intent. *Purposely* merely means that a defendant acted "on purpose" or "deliberately." In legal terms, the defendant must possess a specific intent or "conscious object" to cause a result. A person acts purposely when his or her conscious object is to achieve a result. A murderer pulls the trigger with the purpose of killing the victim, a burglar breaks and enters with the purpose of committing a felony inside the dwelling, and a thief possesses the purpose of permanently depriving an individual of the possession of his or her property.

Table 3.2	Criminal Intent Under the Model Penal Code
Mental State	*Illustration*
Purposely	"You borrowed my car and wrecked it on purpose."
Knowingly	"You may not have purposely wrecked my car, but you knew that you were almost certain to get in an accident because you had never driven such a powerful and fast automobile."
Recklessly	"You may not have purposely wrecked my car, but you were driving over the speed limit on a rain-soaked and slick road in heavy traffic and certainly realized that you were extremely likely to get into an accident."
Negligently	"You may not have purposely wrecked my car and apparently did not understand the power of the auto's engine, but I cannot overlook your lack of awareness of the risk of an accident. After all, any reasonable person would have been aware that such an expensive sports car would pack a punch and would be difficult for a new driver to control."

In *State v. Sanborn*, Sanborn attacked his wife, from whom he was separated, when she threatened to call his mother if he did not leave her apartment. Sanborn held his wife's head in an arm lock, hit her in the face four times, and beat her multiple times with a stainless steel toaster oven, a stainless steel coffee maker and carafe, and a microwave oven. Sanborn, while beating his wife, threatened to make her head explode and to kill her. The prosecution was required to establish that Sanborn acted with the "purpose" to cause serious bodily injury. The judge concluded that when Sanborn "slugs a five-foot-two-inch, 135-pound woman in the eye and side of the head and back of the head several times, and then attempts to smash down a microwave on her head, and then hits her with a toaster oven in the head, that is clearly . . . an attempt, a purposeful attempt . . . to cause serious bodily injury."[36]

Knowingly

When he or she acts **knowingly**, an individual is aware that circumstances exist or a result is practically certain to follow from his or her conduct. An example of knowledge that circumstances exist is knowingly to "possess a firearm" or knowingly to possess narcotics. An illustration of a result that is practically certain to occur is a terrorist who bombs a public building knowing the people inside are likely to be maimed or injured, or to die.

Another example of a result that is practically certain to occur is *State v. Fuelling*. Michelle Fuelling left her twenty-three-month-old son, Raven, at home with her son's father, Carlos Mendoza. Mendoza beat Raven and inflicted severe brain injury and bruises resulting in Raven's death. An autopsy indicated that Raven's death resulted from severe head trauma. Mendoza was convicted of child abuse and murder.[37]

The evidence indicated that Fuelling knew that Mendoza had abused Raven in the past and that her family had warned her about leaving Raven with Mendoza. Fuelling was convicted of having "knowingly acted in a manner that created a substantial risk to the life, body and health of Raven . . . by leaving [him] in the care of Carlos Mendoza, knowing that said Mendoza abused the child." The prosecution established that Fuelling knew that her conduct was "practically certain to endanger the child." Keep in mind that she likely did not have the purposeful intent of Mendoza injuring Raven, although she was held liable for being aware that he likely would endanger Raven.

Recklessly

A person acts **recklessly** when he or she is personally aware of a severe and serious risk and acts in such a fashion that demonstrates a clear lack of judgment and concern for the consequences. This is an objective test, and the defendant's behavior must be a clear departure from what would be expected of law-abiding individuals.

In *Durkovitz v. State*, Gary Durkovitz was convicted of the offense of recklessly causing serious bodily injury to a child. Durkovitz, an experienced animal trainer, took his 350-pound grown lion to a flea market in Houston on eight occasions and charged patrons to be photographed with the lion. The court found that the defendant was aware that there were a number of children at the flea market and that the lion posed a danger to the children because of the animal's predatory instincts. The animal had injured two children in the past. Durkovitz nonetheless took the lion into the flea market and secured him only with a short, heavy chain. Durkovitz lost control of the lion, which grabbed and attempted to crush a child's head in its mouth.[38]

In *State v. Williams*, the Texas Court of Criminal Appeals noted other cases in which the court found the defendant possessed a reckless intent.[39]

Read *Hranicky v. State* on the study site: study .sagepub.com/ lippmaness2e.

These include holding a child's feet under extremely hot water, ramming a parked car that had an 18-month-old child in it, twisting and pulling a baby's leg, . . . and speeding and running through stop signs with a child passenger. In other reckless injury cases, the defendant failed to perform an act that directly resulted in the injury. In one case the defendant was held to have recklessly caused bodily injury to her children by failing to report to the authorities that her boyfriend had violently kidnapped them. In still other cases the actors have left a disabled victim lying in bleach for at least an hour; failed to immediately seek medical help for a lethargic child; and left four-year-old twins unsupervised and wandering around an apartment complex.

Negligently

An individual who acts **negligently** is unaware of and disregards a substantial and unjustifiable risk that other individuals would be aware of and, like the reckless individual, grossly deviates from the standard of care that a reasonable person would exhibit under a similar set of circumstances.

Latrece Jones, age eighteen, was riding in the front passenger seat of a rented Chevrolet Cavalier in Chattanooga, Tennessee. Her two-year-old son, Carlon Bowens Jr., was asleep in her lap. Carlon's aunt, Letitia Abernathy, had rented the car and was driving the automobile; five children and one adult sat in the backseat. A car failed to yield the right of way, causing an accident, which led the passenger-side air bag to deploy.[40]

The air bag struck Carlon, breaking his neck and killing him. Jones was charged with criminally negligent homicide. At the time of the accident, Tennessee's child restraint law required children under four years old to be in a "child passenger restraint system meeting federal motor vehicle standards." There also was evidence that a widespread media campaign in the past year had been directed at educating parents of the need to use child restraints and on the danger posed by air bags. This campaign, in part, was a recognition that it was only in 1999 that all automobiles were required to have air bags and that parents generally lacked knowledge of the danger posed by air bags. A newspaper study twelve days prior to the accident indicated that only 60 percent of children observed in motor vehicles were restrained and that a number of children continued to be seated in the front seat.

The Tennessee court concluded that the fact that there was a need for a large-scale public information campaign aimed at educating parents about child car safety indicates "how many people in the community simply were not using child safety restraints at the time of the accident. . . . If 40% of the children being transported in Ms. Jones' community were being transported without being properly restrained at the time of the accident, it would be difficult for a rational trier of fact to conclude that it was a gross deviation from the standard of care at the time of the accident for Ms. Jones to transport her child improperly."

As you might have concluded, it often is challenging to determine whether a defendant possessed a reckless or a negligent intent. In *People v. Stanfield*, Stanfield was convicted of reckless homicide. An appellate court held that the jury should have been provided the opportunity to determine whether the defendant was negligent rather than reckless. Stanfield pointed a pistol at his wife, whom he accused of being involved with another man during his absence. She told him to stop "fooling and slapped his hand." The gun discharged, fatally shooting his wife. Stanfield claimed that he neither pulled the trigger nor intended that she should be fatally shot. The appellate court held that "[i]t is obvious that one who fails to perceive the possible danger inherent in holding a gun to another when he has no intention of pulling a trigger is at least negligent. If he perceives the possibility that an outside blow, i.e., a slap of the hand, might discharge the weapon, then he is reckless. . . . It is the perception of possible risk to others which governs. On the evidence, the jury could easily have found that defendant was no more than negligent in not foreseeing the possibility of the slap."[41]

Keep in mind that purpose generally corresponds to the common law standard of specific intent and knowledge is thought to correspond to a general intent. Recklessness and negligence are based on the concept of constructive intent. New Jersey is a state that has adopted the MPC approach to criminal intent in order to achieve a clearer definition of the intent required for various crimes.[42] New Jersey statute 2C:2-2 provides that "a person is not guilty of an offense unless he acted purposely, knowingly, recklessly or negligently, as the law may require, with respect to each material element of the offense."

In 1978, Arizona adopted the MPC mental states for all offenses in the criminal code.[43] In reading the text, keep in mind that you will encounter statutes that rely on both the common law and the MPC approaches to criminal intent.

The next section discusses transferred intent, a doctrine that imposes liability on an individual whose criminal act harms an individual who was not the intended victim of the crime.

TRANSFERRED INTENT

The doctrine of **transferred intent** first developed in England in 1575 in the case of *Regina v. Saunders & Archer*. Saunders gave his wife a poison apple. She took a bite out of the apple and handed it to her daughter, who died after finishing the apple. Saunders's intent to kill his wife was transferred to his daughter, and the judge convicted him of the intentional killing of his daughter, although his intent was to poison his wife.[44]

The doctrine of transferred intent subsequently was adopted by courts in the United States. Transferred intent primarily is applied to cases of homicide and battery, although it applies to other types of crimes as well.

The California case of *People v. Scott* is one of the most important American cases on transferred intent. Calvin Hughes and Elaine Scott went through a bitter breakup of their relationship. Scott's two sons Damien Scott and Derrick Brown retaliated by attempting to shoot and kill Hughes. The bullet hit Hughes in the heel of his shoe and inadvertently killed Jack Gibson, an innocent teenager who was sitting in a nearby car.[45]

The California Supreme Court relied on transferred intent to hold Scott and Brown liable for the death of Gibson. The court explained that a "defendant who shoots with an intent to kill but misses and hits a bystander instead should be punished for a crime of the same seriousness as the one he tried to commit against his intended victim." A shorthand way to understand transferred intent is to remember that the defendant's intent follows the bullet. Why does the law recognize transferred intent in "wrong aim" cases?

Individual accountability. Defendants should be held responsible for the result (murder) that they intended to achieve (murder) and did achieve (murder).

Justice. There is a social interest in punishing defendants whose acts create the social harm that they intended to commit despite the fact that the wrong individual is victimized.

STRICT LIABILITY OFFENSES

We all have had the experience of telling another person that "I don't care why you acted in that way; you hurt me, and that was wrong." This is similar to a strict liability offense.

A **strict liability offense** is a crime that does not require a *mens rea*, and an individual may be convicted based solely on the commission of a criminal act.

Strict liability offenses have their origin in the industrial development of the United States in the middle of the nineteenth century. The U.S. Congress and various state legislatures enacted a number of **public welfare offenses** that were intended to protect society against impure food, defective drugs, pollution, and unsafe working conditions, trucks, and railroads. These *mala prohibita* offenses (an act is wrong because it is prohibited) are distinguished from those crimes that are *mala in se* (inherently wrongful, such as rape, robbery, and murder).

The common law was based on the belief that criminal offenses required a criminal intent; this ensured that offenders were morally blameworthy. The U.S. Supreme Court has pronounced that the requirement of a criminal intent, although not required under the Constitution, is "universal and persistent in mature systems of law."[46] Courts, however, have disregarded the strong policy in favor of requiring a criminal intent in upholding the constitutionality of *mala prohibita* laws. Congress and state legislatures typically indicate that these are strict liability laws by omitting language such as "knowingly" or "purposely" from the text of the law. Courts look to several factors in addition to the textual language in determining whether a statute should be interpreted as providing for strict liability:

- The offense is not a common law crime.
- A single violation poses a danger to a large number of people.
- The risk of the conviction of an "innocent" individual is outweighed by the public interest in preventing harm to society.
- The penalty is relatively minor.
- A conviction does not harm a defendant's reputation.
- The law does not significantly impede the rights of individuals or impose a heavy burden. Examples are the prohibition of acts such as "selling alcohol to minors" or "driving without a license."
- These are acts that most people avoid, and individuals who engage in such acts generally possess a criminal intent.

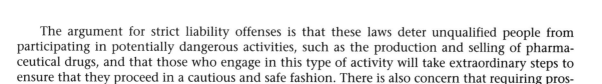

The argument for strict liability offenses is that these laws deter unqualified people from participating in potentially dangerous activities, such as the production and selling of pharmaceutical drugs, and that those who engage in this type of activity will take extraordinary steps to ensure that they proceed in a cautious and safe fashion. There is also concern that requiring prosecutors to establish a criminal intent in these relatively minor cases will consume time and energy and divert resources from other cases.

Courts traditionally have read an intent requirement into criminal statutes punishing common law *mala in se* offenses such as murder, robbery, kidnapping, and larceny. Judges reason that these serious offenses should be punished only when accompanied by an intent to violate the law. In *Morissette v. United States*, the defendant trespassed on an old government bombing range and was convicted of carting three truckloads of old bomb casings that appeared to have been abandoned.[47] The Supreme Court held that the lower court judge had improperly concluded that because the statute did not mention a criminal intent this was a strict liability offense. The Court reasoned that Congress had modeled the statute punishing "whoever steals government property" on the common law crime of larceny, and the fact that the statute did not mention intent did not mean that Congress had intended to omit an intent requirement. Larceny historically had required an "evil-meaning mind and an evil-doing hand."

There is a trend toward expanding strict liability into the non–public welfare crimes that carry relatively severe punishment. Many of these statutes are criticized for imposing prison terms without providing for the fundamental requirement of a criminal intent.

The U.S. Supreme Court indicated in *Staples v. United States* that it may not be willing to continue to accept the growing number of strict liability public welfare offenses.[48] The National Firearms Act was intended to restrict the possession of dangerous weapons and declared it a crime punishable by up to ten years in prison to possess a "machine gun" without legal registration. The defendant was convicted for possession of an AR-15 rifle, which is a semiautomatic weapon that can be modified to fire more than one shot with a single pull of the trigger. The Supreme Court interpreted the statute to require a *mens rea*, explaining that the imposition of a lengthy prison sentence has traditionally required that a defendant possess a criminal intent. The Court noted that gun ownership is widespread in the United States and that a strict liability requirement would result in the imprisonment of individuals who lacked the sophistication to determine whether they purchased or possessed a lawful or unlawful weapon.

A Michigan appellate court held that John Wesley Janes should not be held criminally liable for possession of a dangerous animal based on his pit bull's attack on an infant absent Janes's knowledge that the dog was dangerous. The court reasoned that dog ownership is widespread in the United States and the incidence of aggressive behavior by dogs is not so widespread to alert individuals that they should assume that absent a history of violent behavior a dog is a "dangerous animal." The court observed that "we find it unthinkable that the Legislature intended to subject law-abiding, well-intentioned citizens to a possible four-year prison term if, despite genuinely and reasonably believing their animal to be safe around other people and animals, the animal nevertheless harms someone. . . . [W]e are reluctant to impute to our Legislature the intent of dispensing with the criminal-intent requirement when it would mean easing the path to convicting persons whose conduct would not even alert them to the probability of strict regulation" under the statute.[49]

MPC Section 1.04(5) accepts the need for strict liability crimes, while limiting these crimes to what the code terms "violations." Violations are not subject to imprisonment and are punishable only by a fine, forfeiture, or other civil penalty; and they may not result in the type of legal disability (e.g., loss of the right to vote) that flows from a criminal conviction. You can find some examples of strict liability offenses in Table 3.3.

CONCURRENCE OF ACT AND INTENT

We now have discussed both *actus reus* and *mens rea*. The next step is to understand that there must be a **concurrence** between a criminal act and a criminal intent. *Chronological concurrence* means that a criminal intent must exist at the same time as a criminal act. An example of chronological concurrence is the requirement that a burglary involves breaking and entering into the dwelling house of another at night with the intent to commit a felony therein. A defendant who claimed

Table 3.3	Strict Liability Offenses
Offense	*Case Example*
Open Bottle	Steven Mark Loge was cited for a violation of a Minnesota statute that declares it a misdemeanor for the owner of a motor vehicle, or the driver when the owner is not present, "to keep or allow to be kept in a motor vehicle when such vehicle is upon the public highway any bottle or receptacle containing intoxicating liquors or 3.2 percent malt liquors which has been opened." Loge borrowed his father's pickup truck and was stopped by two police officers while on his way home from work. One of the officers observed and seized an open beer bottle underneath the passenger's side of the seat and also found one full unopened can of beer and one empty beer can in the truck. Loge was issued a citation for a violation of the open bottle statute. See *State v. Loge,* 608 N.W.2d 152 (Minn. 2000).
Students' Possession of Weapons in School	A juvenile court ordered C.R.M. to attend an Anoka County, Minnesota, juvenile day school. Students' coats are hung outside the classroom and inspected in the morning for contraband. A folding knife with a four-inch blade was discovered in C.R.M.'s coat. C.R.M. immediately reacted, "Oh man, I forgot to take it out, I was whittling this weekend." C.R.M. was convicted under a statute that makes possession of a dangerous weapon on school property a strict liability offense. The Minnesota statute provides that "[w]hoever possesses, stores, or keeps a dangerous weapon or uses or brandishes a replica firearm or a BB gun on school property is guilty of a felony and may be sentenced to imprisonment for not more than two years or to payment of a fine of not more than $5,000, or both." See *In re C.R.M.,* 611 N.W.2d 802 (Minn. 2000).
Teacher's Possession of Weapons in School	A Virginia law makes it a felony for an individual to possess a firearm "upon any public . . . elementary school, including building and grounds." Deena Esteban, a fourth-grade elementary school teacher, left a zippered yellow canvas bag in a classroom; the bag was found to contain a loaded .38 caliber revolver. Esteban explained that she placed the gun in the bag and took it to the store on the previous Saturday, and then she forgot that the pistol was in the bag and inadvertently carried it into the school. The Virginia Supreme Court affirmed Esteban's conviction on appeal. The court stressed that the fact that Esteban "innocently" brought a loaded revolver into the school "does not diminish the danger." A footnote in the decision indicated that Esteban possessed a concealed handgun permit that specifically did not authorize possession of a handgun on school property. See *Esteban v. Commonwealth,* 587 S.E.2d 523 (Va. 2003).

that he entered his mother's home with the intent to escape the cold and contended that he only later developed the intent to kill his mother would not be guilty of burglary, if he was believed by the jury.[50] The principle of concurrence is reflected in Section 20 of the California Penal Code, which provides that in "every crime . . . there must exist a union or joint operation of act and intent or criminal negligence."[51]

The Legal Equation

Concurrence = *Mens rea* (in unison with)

+ *actus reus.*

You Decide

3.4 Scott Jackson administered what he believed was a fatal dose of cocaine to Pearl Bryan in Cincinnati, Ohio. Bryan was pregnant, apparently as a result of her intercourse with Jackson. Jackson and a companion then transported Bryan to Kentucky and cut off her head to prevent identification of the body. Bryan, in fact, was still alive when she was brought to Kentucky, and she died as a result of the severing of her head. A state possesses jurisdiction over offenses committed within its territorial boundaries. Can Jackson be prosecuted for the intentional killing of Bryan in Ohio? In Kentucky? See *Jackson v. Commonwealth*, 38 S.W. 422 (Ky. App. 1896).

You can find the answer at study.sagepub.com/lippmaness2e

CRIMINAL LAW AND PUBLIC POLICY

We have seen throughout this chapter that a crime requires the concurrence of a criminal act and a criminal intent. In 2014, Vonte Skinner was convicted of attempted murder and aggravated assault for allegedly attempting to carry out a contract killing of a narcotics dealer who had withheld the proceeds from narcotics sales from a drug gang. A search of the defendant's car led to the seizure of three notebooks filled with rap lyrics authored by Skinner. A number of the lyrics are described as "violent" and were written under the moniker "Real Threat." Skinner has the word *Threat* tattooed on his arm.

The jury was unable to reach a verdict at Skinner's first trial. He was convicted at a second trial in which a detective testifying for the state of New Jersey read excerpts from the defendant's lyrics, testimony that ran for thirteen pages in the **trial transcript**. The prosecution successfully argued that although none of the lyrics mentioned the victim by name and that all of the lyrics had been composed prior to the shooting, the lyrics provided evidence of the defendant's criminal motive and intent and capacity for violence. Several of the lyrics are reprinted below.

On the block, I can box you down or straight razor ox you down, run in your crib with a four pound and pop your crown. Checkmate, put your face in the ground. I'll drop your queen and pawn, f–k–f–k wastin' around. They don't call me Threat for nothin'.

You pricks goin' to listen to Threat tonight. 'Cause feel when I pump this P-89 into your head like lice. Slugs will pass ya' D, like Montana and rice, that's five hammers, 16 shots to damage your life, leave you f—s all bloody.

After you die, I'll go to your Mom's house and f–k her until tomorrow and make ya' little brother watch with his face full of sorrow.

So get them answers right. Where's the case and stash of white. I got ya' wife tied to the bed and at her throat a knife.

An appellate court reversed Skinner's conviction and expressed doubt whether the jurors would have found the defendant guilty if they had not listened to an "extended reading" of these lyrics.

The New Jersey Supreme Court found that there was no connection between the various crimes with which Skinner was charged and the bad acts recounted in the lyrics. "We reject the proposition that probative evidence about a charged offense can be found in an individual's artistic endeavors absent a strong nexus between specific details of the artistic composition and the circumstances of the offense for which the evidence is being adduced." The Supreme Court also noted the risk that the introduction of the lyrics had prejudiced the jury against the defendant.

In other cases, courts have found a strong connection between rap lyrics and a defendant's mental determination to kill. In *Bryant v. State*, 802 N.E.2d 486 (Ind. Ct. App. 2004), the defendant was convicted of the murder of his stepmother. His lyrics were admitted to establish his motive to kill because the lyrics closely resembled the crime with which the defendant was charged. "'Cuz the 5-0 won't even know who you are when they pull yo ugly ass out of the trunk of my car." In the South Carolina trial of Gonzales Wardlaw (Snoop), the defendant's lyrics were introduced as an admission of guilt to a murder, and in a Pittsburgh case, two men were sentenced to prison after posting a rap video that threatened to harm two police officers who had arrested them.

(Continued)

(Continued)

Law enforcement officials now are trained to use rap lyrics to assist them in investigating crimes. The *New York Times* identified dozens of cases between 2012 and 2014 in which prosecutors attempted to introduce rap music at a defendant's trial. The American Civil Liberties Union of New Jersey found that courts admitted lyrics roughly 80 percent of the time. Studies find that juries are more likely to believe that defendants who have written violent rap lyrics are capable of committing a murder than defendants who have not written violent lyrics.

Commentators familiar with the culture of rap music point out that the lyrics are not necessarily autobiographical and that gangsta rap is characterized by exaggeration and violent and sexual language. Artists remain in "character" even when not performing to persuade their audience that they are "authentic" and "credible." Commentators also note that law enforcement officials are able to distinguish between the reality and fiction when it comes to other forms of music but do not seem willing to make this distinction when it comes to young African American artists. Under what circumstances should rap music be viewed as evidence of criminal intent and motive rather than artistic expression?

CAUSALITY

You now know that a crime entails a *mens rea* that *concurs* with an *actus reus*. The defendant must be shown to have *caused* the victim's death or injury, or to have damaged the property.

Causation is central to criminal law and must be proven beyond a reasonable doubt. The requirement of causality is based on two considerations:

1. *Individual Responsibility.* The criminal law is based on individual responsibility. Causality connects a person's acts to the resulting social harm and permits the imposition of the appropriate punishment.

2. *Fairness.* Causality limits liability to individuals whose conduct produces a prohibited social harm. A law that declares that all individuals in close proximity to a crime are liable regardless of their involvement would be unfair and would penalize people for being in the wrong place at the wrong time. If such a law were enacted, individuals might hesitate to gather in crowds or bars or to attend concerts and sporting events.

Establishing that a defendant's criminal act caused harm to the victim can be more complicated than you might imagine. Should an individual who commits a rape be held responsible for the victim's subsequent suicide? What if the victim attempted suicide a week before the rape and then killed herself following the rape? Would your answer be the same if the stress induced by the rape appeared to have contributed to the victim's contracting cancer and dying a year later? What if doctors determine that a murder victim who was hospitalized would have died an hour later of natural causes?

We can begin to provide an answer to these hypothetical situations by reviewing the two types of causes that a prosecutor must establish beyond a reasonable doubt at trial in order to convict a defendant: cause in fact and legal or proximate cause.

You will find that most causality cases involve defendants charged with murder who claim that they should not be held responsible for the victim's death.

Cause in Fact

The **cause in fact** or factual cause simply requires you to ask whether "but for" the defendant's act, the victim would have died. An individual aims a gun at the victim, pulls the trigger, and kills the victim. "But for" the shooter's act, the victim would be alive. In most cases, the defendant's act is the only factual cause of the victim's injury or death and is clearly the direct cause of the harm. This is a simple cause-and-effect question. The legal or proximate cause of the victim's injury or death may not be so easily determined.

A defendant's act must be the cause in fact or factual cause of a harm in order for the defendant to be criminally convicted. This connects the defendant to the result. The cause in fact or factual cause is typically a straightforward question. Note that the defendant's act must also be the legal or proximate cause of the resulting harm.

Legal or Proximate Cause

Just when things seem simple, we encounter the challenge of determining the legal or **proximate cause** of the victim's death. Proximate cause analysis requires the jury to determine whether it is fair or just to hold a defendant legally responsible for an injury or death. This is not a scientific question. We must consider questions of fairness and justice. There are few rules to assist us in this analysis.

In most cases, a defendant is clearly both the cause in fact and legal cause of the victim's injury or death. However, consider the following scenarios: You pull the trigger, and the victim dies. You point out that it was not your fault, since the victim died from the wound you inflicted in combination with a minor nonlethal gun wound that she suffered earlier in the day. Should you be held liable? In another scenario, an ambulance rescues the victim, the ambulance's brakes fail, and the vehicle crashes into a wall, killing the driver and victim. Are you or the driver responsible for the victim's death? You later learn that the victim died after the staff of the hospital emergency room waited five hours to treat the victim and that she would have lived had she received timely assistance. Who is responsible for the death? Would your answer be different in the event that the doctors protested that they could not operate on the victim because of a power outage caused by a hurricane? What if the victim was wounded from the gunshot and, although barely conscious, stumbled into the street and was hit by an automobile or by lightning? In each case, "but for" your act, the victim would not have been placed in the situation that led to his or her death. On the other hand, you might argue that in each of these examples you were not legally liable, because the death resulted from an **intervening cause** or outside factor rather than from the shooting. As you can see from the previous examples, an intervening cause may arise from any of the following:

- The act of the victim wandering into the street
- An act of nature, such as a hurricane
- The doctors who did not immediately operate
- A wound inflicted by an assailant in combination with a previous injury

Another area that complicates the determination of proximate cause is a victim's preexisting medical condition. This arises when you shoot an individual and the shock from the wound results in the failure of the victim's already seriously weakened heart.

Intervening Cause

Professor Dressler helps us address these causation problems by providing two useful categories of intervening acts: coincidental intervening acts and responsive intervening acts.

Coincidental Intervening Acts

A defendant is not considered legally responsible for a victim's injury or death that results from a **coincidental intervening act**. (Some texts refer to this as an *independent intervening cause*.) A coincidental intervening act is a cause that is unrelated to a criminal act of the accused. *Coincidental intervening acts arise when a defendant's act places a victim in a particular place where the victim is harmed by an unforeseeable event.*

The Ninth Circuit Court of Appeals offered an example of an unforeseeable event as hypothetical in the case of *United States v. Main*. The defendant in this example drives in a reckless fashion and crashes his car, pinning the passenger in the automobile. The defendant leaves the scene of the accident to seek assistance, and the semiconscious passenger is eaten by a bear. The Ninth Circuit Court of Appeals observed that reckless driving does not create a foreseeable risk of being eaten by a bear and that this intervening cause is so out of the ordinary that it would be unfair to hold the driver responsible for the victim's death.[52] Another example of an unforeseeable coincidental intervening event involves a victim who is wounded, taken to the hospital for medical treatment, and then killed in the hospital by a knife-wielding mass murderer. Professor Dressler notes that in this case, the unfortunate victim has found himself or herself in the "wrong place at the wrong time."[53]

Responsive Intervening Acts

The response of a victim to a defendant's criminal act is termed a **responsive intervening act** (some texts refer to this as a *dependent intervening act*). In most instances, the defendant is considered responsible because his or her behavior caused the victim to respond. A defendant is relieved of responsibility only in those instances in which the victim's reaction to the crime is both abnormal and unforeseeable. Consider the case of a victim who jumps into the water to evade an assailant and drowns. The assailant will be charged with the victim's death despite the fact that the victim could not swim and did not realize that the water was dangerously deep. The issue is the *foreseeability* of the victim's response rather than the *reasonableness* of the victim's response. Again, courts generally are not sympathetic to defendants who set a chain of events in motion, and they generally will hold such defendants criminally liable.

In *People v. Armitage*, David Armitage was convicted of "drunk boating causing [the] death" of Peter Maskovich. Armitage was operating his small aluminum speedboat at a high rate of speed while zigzagging across the river, when it flipped over. There were no flotation devices on board, and the intoxicated Armitage and Maskovich clung to the capsized vessel. Maskovich disregarded Armitage's warning, decided to try to swim to shore, and drowned. A California appellate court ruled that Maskovich's decision did not break the chain of causation. The "fact that the panic stricken victim recklessly abandoned the boat and tried to swim ashore was not a wholly abnormal reaction to the peril of drowning," and Armitage could not exonerate himself by claiming that the "victim should have reacted differently or more prudently."[54]

Defendants have also been held liable for the response of individuals other than the victim. For instance, in the California case of *People v. Schmies*, defendant Schmies fled on his motorcycle from a traffic stop at speeds of up to ninety miles an hour and disregarded all traffic regulations. During the chase, one of the pursuing patrol cars struck another vehicle, killing the driver and injuring the officer. Schmies was convicted of grossly negligent vehicular manslaughter and of reckless driving. A California court affirmed the defendant's conviction based on the fact that the officer's response and the resulting injury were reasonably foreseeable. The officer's reaction, in other words, was not so extraordinary that it was unforeseeable, unpredictable, and statistically extremely improbable.[55]

Medical negligence has also consistently been viewed as foreseeable and does not break the chain of causation. In *People v. Saavedra-Rodriguez*, the defendant claimed that the negligence of the doctors at the hospital rather than the knife wound he inflicted was the proximate cause of the death and that he should not be held liable for homicide. The Colorado Supreme Court ruled that medical negligence is "too frequent to be considered abnormal" and that the defendant's stabbing of the victim started a chain of events, the natural and probable result of which was the defendant's death. The court added that only the most gross and irresponsible medical negligence is so removed from normal expectations as to be considered unforeseeable.[56]

In sum, a defendant who commits a crime is responsible for the natural and probable consequences of his or her actions. A defendant is responsible for foreseeable responsive intervening acts.

The MPC eliminates legal or proximate causation and requires only "but-for causation." The code merely asks whether the result was consistent with the defendant's intent or knowledge or was within the scope of risk created by the defendant's reckless or negligent act. In other words, under the MPC, you merely look at the defendant's intent and act and ask whether the result could have been anticipated. In cases of a resulting harm or injury that is "remote" or "accidental" (e.g., a lightning bolt or a doctor who is a serial killer), the MPC requires that we look to see whether it would be unjust to hold the defendant responsible.

You can find more cases on causality in Table 3.4.

Table 3.4	Causality
Act and Intent	Case Examples
Apparent Safety Doctrine	In an 1856 North Carolina case, Preslar kicked and choked his wife and beat her over the head with a thirty-inch-thick piece of wood. He also threatened to kill her with his axe. The victim gathered her children and walked over two miles to her father's home. Reluctant to reveal her bruises and injuries to her family, she spread a quilt on the ground and covered herself with cotton fabric and slept outside. The combination of the exhausting walk, her injuries, and the biting cold led to a weakened condition that resulted in her death. The victim's husband was acquitted by the North Carolina Supreme Court, which ruled that the chain of causation was broken by the victim's failure to seek safety. The court distinguished this case from the situation of a victim who in fleeing is forced to wade through a swamp or jump into a river. Is it relevant that the victim likely feared that her family would force her to return to her marital home and that she would have to face additional physical abuse from her husband? See *State v. Preslar,* 48 N.C. 421 (1856).
Drag Racing	In *Velazquez v. State*, the defendant Velazquez and the deceased Alvarez agreed to drag race their automobiles over a quarter-mile course on a public highway. Upon completing the race, Alvarez suddenly turned his automobile around and proceeded east toward the starting line. Velazquez also reversed direction. Alvarez was in the lead and attained an estimated speed of 123 miles per hour. He was not wearing a seat belt and had a blood alcohol level of between .11 and .12. Velazquez had not been drinking and was traveling at roughly 90 miles per hour. As both approached the end of the road, they applied their brakes, but Alvarez was unable to stop. He crashed through the guardrail and was propelled over a canal and landed on the far bank. Alvarez was thrown from his car, pinned under the vehicle when it landed, and died. The defendant crashed through the guardrail, landed in the canal, and managed to escape. A Florida district court of appeal determined that the defendant's reckless operation of his vehicle in the drag race was technically the cause in fact of Alvarez's death under the "but for" test. There was no doubt that "but for" the defendant's participation, the deceased would not have recklessly raced his vehicle and would not have been killed. The court, however, ruled that the defendant's participation was not the proximate cause of the deceased's death because the "deceased, in effect, killed himself by his own volitional reckless driving," and that it "would be unjust to hold the defendant criminally responsible for this death." The race was completed when Alvarez turned his car around and engaged in a "near-suicide mission." See *Velazquez v. State,* 561 So.2d 347 (Fla. Dist. Ct. App. 1990).
Medical Negligence	In *United States v. Hamilton*, the defendant knocked the victim down and jumped on him and kicked his face. The victim was rushed to the hospital, where nasal tubes were inserted to enable him to breathe, and his arms were restrained. During the night, the nurses changed his bedclothes and negligently failed to reattach the restraints on the victim's arms. Early in the morning the victim went into convulsions, pulled out the nasal tubes, and suffocated to death. The federal court held that regardless of whether the victim accidentally or intentionally pulled out the tubes, the victim's death was the ordinary and foreseeable consequence of the attack and affirmed the defendant's conviction for manslaughter. See *United States v. Hamilton,* 182 F. Supp. 548 (D.D.C. 1960).
Removal From Life Support	The defendant was convicted of vehicular manslaughter when the Toyota Camry he was driving struck a Chrysler LeBaron driven by William Patrick from behind. The LeBaron "sailed over the curb and slid along the guardrail, crashing into a utility pole before it ultimately came to rest 152 feet from the site of impact." The defendant's blood alcohol level was estimated at .18 or .19. As a result of the accident, Patrick suffered broken bones, paralysis, infections, organ failure, an inability to breathe on his own, brain damage, and severe psychological problems. Five months following the accident, Patrick's family in accordance with his wishes removed him from a ventilator, and he died two hours later. The New Jersey Supreme Court held that removal of life-sustaining treatment is a victim's right, and it is foreseeable that a victim may exercise his or her right not to be placed on, or to be removed from, life support systems. See *State v. Pelham,* 824 A.2d 1082 (N.J. 2003).

The Legal Equation

Causality	=	Cause in fact
	+	legal or proximate cause.
Cause in fact	=	"But for" the defendant's criminal act, the victim would not be injured or dead.
Legal or proximate cause	=	Whether it is just or fair to hold the defendant criminally responsible.
Intervening acts	=	Coincidental intervening acts limit liability where unforeseeable; responsive intervening acts limit liability where unforeseeable and abnormal.

You Decide

3.5 Defendant Israel Cervantes and fellow gang members of the Highland Street gang went to a birthday party for a member of the Alley Boys gang. The two gangs were not enemies. Cervantes approached a woman named Grace who refused his invitation to go to another party. Cervantes called her a "ho," and the two exchanged insults. Juan Cisneros, a member of the Alley Boys, told Cervantes that he was disrespecting his "homegirl." Richard Linares, a member of the Alley Boys, tried to calm the situation. Cisneros, however, drew a gun and threatened to "cap" Cervantes.

Cervantes pulled out his own gun. Linares responded by "pushing or touching" Cervantes in an effort to separate him from Cisneros. The defendant Cervantes stated that "nobody touches me" and shot Linares through the arm and chest. A large-scale fight ensued between the gangs, and gang "challenges were exchanged."

A short time later, a group of Highland Street gang members saw Hector Cabrera, a member of the Alley Boys, entering his car. Five gang members fired shots and participated in killing Cabrera.

Would you hold Cervantes liable for the murder of Cabrera? See *People v. Cervantes*, 29 P.3d 225 (Cal. 2001).

You can find the answer at study.sagepub.com/lippmaness2e.

CASE ANALYSIS

In *State v. Gargus*, the defendant, a certified nurse assistant (CNA), voluntarily assumed care of her eighty-one-year-old mother who was suffering from diabetes and had lost the capacity to walk. A Missouri appellate court was asked to decide whether the defendant possessed a duty to care for her mother and knowingly violated her duty of care by failing to provide her mother with adequate medical care and as a result was guilty of elder abuse.

Did Gargus Possess a Duty of Care Toward Her Mother, and Did Gargus's Breach of Her Duty of Care Cause the Death of Her Mother?

State v. Gargus, No. ED 99233 (Mo. 2013)

Gargus was convicted of the felony of elder abuse in the first degree stemming from the death of her mother, Lorraine Gargus (the victim), while in Gargus's care.

"A person commits the crime of elder abuse in the first degree if he attempts to kill, knowingly causes or attempts to cause serious physical injury . . . to any person sixty years of age or older. . . ." Criminal liability is premised on conduct involving voluntary acts. Voluntary acts include "[a]n omission to perform an act of which the actor is physically capable." The defendant was sentenced to ten years in prison.

The victim was an eighty-one-year-old woman suffering from diabetes. After falling in 2005, the victim determined she was unable to walk anymore and became bedbound. Gargus started staying with the victim and Gargus's father in 2008 to help out, and by December 2009 she had moved in to care for them. In January 2010, Gargus quit her job at the Clark County Nursing Home, where she had worked since 1973, to care for her parents full-time.

Gargus testified she cooked for the victim, gave her daily sponge baths, and changed her clothes daily. The victim had been using a bedpan, but in January 2010, she became incontinent. Gargus tried to give the victim her medicine, but the victim resisted medication, frequently hiding it or throwing it away.

Gargus first noticed a bedsore the size of a tennis ball on the victim's upper buttocks on January 20, 2010. To care for the bedsore, Gargus continued using egg crate and fleece cushioning for the victim's bed, stopped using Depends diapers on the victim to allow the sore to get air, and attempted to turn the victim every hour—however, the victim was reluctant to change positions, and Gargus described it as a "constant battle." The victim's husband died on January 31, 2010. At the funeral, family members indicated they wanted to visit the victim, but Gargus discouraged visits. After her husband's death, the victim stopped eating and did not want to drink.

Cindy Hickman (Cindy), the victim's granddaughter, visited the victim on February 2, 2010, and described the mobile home as dirty and smelly. The victim's bed was located in the living room with animal cages stacked around it from floor to ceiling. Cindy testified there were "hundreds" of mice everywhere. The victim was completely covered in a blanket and her eyes were matted shut and she did not recognize Cindy, calling her by her sister Sylvia Winger's name.

On February 22, 2010, Gargus called an ambulance after noticing a wound on the victim's foot. She had bathed the victim that morning and put lotion on her feet, but did not see an injury. The victim generally kept her feet uncovered, so any injury would be obvious. Gargus's son alerted her to the injury later that day. . . . The emergency personnel testified that the victim appeared confused and complained of a burning sensation in her rectum. As they moved the victim from her bed to the stretcher, a large mouse or small rat ran out of the bedclothes.

Dr. Neville Crenshaw . . . who was the victim's attending doctor, testified that when the victim was admitted to the hospital she was "acutely and critically ill." The victim had several large bedsores in various stages of development. The main bedsore was on the victim's upper buttocks, and Dr. Crenshaw described it as a "huge, gaping, infected wound." The infection had eaten the skin and subcutaneous fat around the bedsore, and an investigator for the Missouri Department of Health and Senior Services (DHSS) testified she could see the victim's tailbone through the basketball-sized wound. The infection tested positive for staphylococcus (staph) and had turned septic— that is, had spread to her bloodstream. The surgical floor nurse testified the bedsore smelled like rotting flesh. As well, the emergency room nurse testified the victim had open sores over most of her body and large bedsores on her heels.

Dr. Crenshaw further testified that the victim's second main injury was the trauma to her left foot. Her skin and tissue were removed down to tendon and bone, consistent with having been eaten by a rodent, as witnessed by the emergency personnel. . . . The following day, an orthopedic surgeon amputated the victim's leg and foot below the knee. He noted the leg was no longer getting any blood supply and was cold and blue. Moreover, he could feel gas under the skin, consistent with gangrene. Last, Dr. Crenshaw testified the victim was malnourished and "profoundly dehydrated."

The victim died on March 11, 2010. Her autopsy revealed that the cause of death was multiple-organ failure due to septicemia, stemming from the multiple bedsores and gangrene of the left foot. The medical examiner testified that the victim's death was caused by the bedsore on her back, and that early care of the bedsore could have stopped the disease from progressing. He noted bedsores occur when patients lie on their backs for long periods of time without moving. He further testified the failure to provide a clean environment, movement treatment for the bedsore, and medical care also led to the victim's death.

The record shows that Gargus had worked in a nursing home since 1973 and had been a CNA since 1989. Her supervisor testified that all CNAs received continuing training in infection control, pressure areas, and skin care. More importantly, Gargus's own testimony revealed that she knew of the importance of preventing and treating bedsores. . . . Despite Gargus's admitted knowledge about the treatment of bedsores and her testimony that she bathed the victim every day and saw the victim's body daily, Gargus let the bedsore progress to Stage IV before calling for medical assistance. When the victim was admitted to the hospital, the bedsore was a "huge, gaping, infected wound" through which the victim's tailbone was visible.

Moreover, when the victim was admitted to the hospital, she was malnourished and dehydrated. Gargus testified that the victim stopped eating when her husband died on January 31, yet Gargus did not call

(Continued)

(Continued)

for medical assistance until February 22. . . . Further, despite Gargus's testimony that she bathed the victim daily and rubbed lotion on the victim's feet as late as February 22, she somehow failed to notice that the victim's left leg was not getting any blood supply, was cold and blue, and had gas under the skin consistent with gangrene. The jury was entitled to infer that as a trained CNA, Gargus knew that failing to seek treatment for a diabetic whose leg was in such a necrotic condition was practically certain to cause serious physical injury or harm to the victim. Last, as a CNA, Gargus was trained in the importance of hygiene, but isolated the victim in a mobile home infected with mice that had feces on the floor, molding food in the kitchen, and a nonworking bathroom. Moreover, Gargus stated to investigators that she washed the victim's clothing in flea-ridden, foul-smelling muddy gray water. Because she was a CNA trained in the importance of hygiene, the jury could infer Gargus knew the condition of the home was certain to cause serious physical injury or harm to the victim, a diabetic with multiple bedsores in various stages of development. Indeed, the victim later died of a massive infection.

The evidence shows that Gargus had a duty to act to prevent injury to the victim and that Gargus knew about but failed to provide the proper treatment of bedsores, failed to ensure the victim ate and drank, and failed—despite her twenty-plus years as a CNA—to notice the condition of the victim's leg. . . . Therefore, we find there was sufficient evidence from which a reasonable trier of fact could conclude Gargus knowingly caused serious physical injury to the victim.

CHAPTER SUMMARY

A crime requires the concurrence of a criminal intent (*mens rea*) and criminal act (*actus reus*). An act, for purposes of the criminal law, must be a voluntary act. An individual also may be held liable for a failure to act in those instances in which law imposes a duty to act. A duty arises when there is a status relationship, statute, or contract, or when an individual assumes a duty. The possession of contraband constitutes an act.

A significant contribution of the common law is limiting criminal punishment to individuals who possess a "guilty mind." The common law established three types of criminal intent: specific intent, general intent, and constructive criminal intent. These intent standards proved confusing, and the Model Penal Code attempted to simplify the intent standard by establishing a hierarchy of criminal intent standards. The most serious intent standard is purposely, followed by knowingly, recklessly, and the least serious form of intent, negligently. A fifth type of intent is strict liability.

As noted, there must be a concurrence between a criminal act and a criminal intent. The criminal act must be the cause or proximate cause of a prohibited harm. This analysis is complicated by intervening causes. Individuals are not held liable for coincidental intervening causes, although they are held liable for responsive intervening causes.

CHAPTER REVIEW QUESTIONS

1. What are the elements of a crime?

2. Why are criminal thoughts not penalized by the criminal law?

3. Give some examples of behavior that is considered to be an involuntary act. Why are involuntary acts not criminally punished?

4. What is a status offense? Why are status offenses not criminally punished?

5. Define the American bystander rule. When is an individual criminally liable for an omission?

6. List the various types of possession.

7. Distinguish between specific intent and general intent and constructive intent.

8. Define the criminal intents of purposely, knowingly, recklessly, and negligently.

9. What are the characteristics of a strict liability offense?

10. Discuss the significance of concurrence.

11. Why is the criminal law concerned with causality?

12. Define cause in fact, proximate cause, intervening cause, coincidental intervening cause, and responsive intervening cause.

LEGAL TERMINOLOGY

actual possession

actus reus

American bystander rule

attendant circumstances

causation

cause in fact

coincidental intervening act

concurrence

constructive intent

constructive possession

contraband

crimes of cause and result

duty to intervene

European bystander rule

fleeting possession

general intent

Good Samaritan laws

intervening cause

involuntary act

joint possession

knowingly

mens rea

motive

negligently

omission

proximate cause

public welfare offenses

purposely

recklessly

responsive intervening act

result crimes

specific intent

status

strict liability offenses

transferred intent

trial transcript

willful blindness

CRIMINAL LAW ON THE WEB

Visit **study.sagepub.com/lippmaness2e** to access additional study tools including suggested answers to the You Decide questions, reprints of cases and statutes, online appendices, and more!

4 PARTIES TO CRIME

Did Gometz aid and abet the stabbing of the prison guard?

Three guards would escort Fountain and Silverstein (separately), handcuffed, every time they left their cells to go to or from the recreation room, the law library, or the shower (prisoners in Marion's control unit are confined, one to a cell, for all but an hour or an hour and a half a day, and are fed in their cells). But the guards would not be armed; nowadays guards do not carry weapons in the presence of prisoners, who might seize the weapons. . . . [That] morning, Silverstein, while being escorted from the shower to his cell, stopped next to Randy Gometz's cell, and while two of the escorting officers were for some reason at a distance from him, reached his handcuffed hands into the cell. The third officer, who was closer to him, heard the click of the handcuffs being released and saw Gometz raise his shirt to reveal a home-made knife ("shank")—which had been fashioned from the iron leg of a bed—protruding from his waistband. Silverstein drew the knife and attacked one of the guards, Clutts, stabbing him 29 times and killing him. While pacing the corridor after the killing, Silverstein explained that "this is no cop thing. This is a personal thing between me and Clutts. The man disrespected me and I had to get him for it." Having gotten this off his chest, he returned to his cell (*United States v. Fountain*, 768 F.2d 790 [7th Cir. 1985]).

In this chapter, learn about criminal liability under the law of parties.

Learning Objectives

1. Know the four categories of parties to a crime under the common law and the two categories of parties to a crime used in contemporary statutes.

2. Describe the *actus reus* and *mens rea* of accomplice liability.

3. Understand the natural and probable consequences doctrine.

4. Know the elements of accessory after the fact.

5. Understand the reasons that the law imposes vicarious liability.

INTRODUCTION

Thus far, we have established a number of building blocks of criminal conduct. First, there are *constitutional limits* on the government's ability to declare acts criminal. Second, *actus reus* requires that an individual commit a voluntary act or omission. People are punished for what they do, not for what they think or for who they are. Third, the existence of a criminal intent or *mens rea* means that punishment is limited to morally blameworthy individuals. Last, there must be a *concurrence* between a criminal act and a criminal intent. The criminal act must be established as both the *factual cause* and the *legal* or *proximate cause* of a prohibited harm or injury. We now add another building block to this foundation by observing that more than one individual may be liable for a crime. In this chapter, we will discuss two situations in which multiple parties are held liable for a crime.

- *Parties to a Crime or Complicity.* Individuals who assist the perpetrator of a crime before, during, or following the crime are held criminally responsible. In other words, individuals who assist in the commission of a crime are held liable for the criminal conduct of the perpetrator of the offense.
- *Vicarious Liability.* Individuals may be held liable based on their *relationship* with the perpetrator of a crime. The most common instance involves extending guilt to an employer for the acts of an employee or imposing liability on a corporation for the acts of a manager or employee.

In considering cases concerning complicity, you should ask yourself whether the appellant intended to assist and assisted a crime. As a matter of social policy, consider why we punish people who assist another to commit a crime. Should the parties to a crime be subject to the same punishment as the perpetrator? As for vicarious liability, consider whether criminal responsibility should be extended to individuals who were neither present, involved, nor perhaps even aware of the crime.

PARTIES TO A CRIME

Common law judges appreciated that criminal conduct often involves a range of activities: planning the crime, carrying out the offense, evading arrest, and disposing of the fruits of the crime. The common law divided the participants in a crime into *principals* and *accessories*. Principals were actually present and carried out the crime, while accessories assisted the principals. Holding individuals accountable for intentionally assisting the criminal acts of another is termed *accomplice* or *accessory liability*.

The four categories of **parties to a crime** under the common law are as follows:

- **Principals in the first degree** are the perpetrators of a crime—for example, the person or persons actually robbing a bank.
- **Principals in the second degree** are any individuals assisting the robbers. This includes lookouts, getaway drivers, and those disabling burglar alarms. Principals in the second degree are required to be either physically present at the bank or constructively present, meaning that they directly assist the robbery at a distance by engaging in such activities as serving as a lookout.
- **Accessories before the fact** are those individuals who help prepare for the crime. In the case of a bank robbery, accessories before the fact may purchase firearms or masks, plan the crime, or encourage the robbers. Accessories, in contrast to principals, are neither physically nor constructively present.
- **Accessories after the fact** are those individuals who assist the perpetrators, knowing that a crime has been committed. This includes those who help the bank robbers escape or hide the stolen money.

Both principals and accessories were punishable as felons under the common law. All felonies were subject to the death penalty. Common law judges desired to limit the offenses for which capital punishment might be imposed, and they developed various rules to frustrate the application of the death penalty. Judges, for instance, held that principals and accessories could be prosecuted only following the conviction of the principal in the first degree. This posed a barrier to prosecution in those instances in which the principal in the first degree was acquitted, fled, or died, or in which the principal's conviction was reversed. There were additional requirements that complicated prosecutions, such as the fact that an accessory who assisted a crime while living in another state could be prosecuted only in the state in which the acts of accessoryship occurred. These jurisdictions typically had little interest in prosecuting an accessory for crimes committed outside the state.[1]

Today we are no longer required to overcome these complications. Virtually every jurisdiction has abandoned the common law categories. States typically provide for two parties to a crime:

- **Accomplices** are individuals involved before and during a crime.
- **Accessories** are individuals involved in assisting an offender following a crime.

Returning to our bank robbery example, the perpetrator of the bank robbery and the individuals planning and organizing the robbery as well as the lookout, the driver of the getaway car, and the individuals disabling the bank guard will all be charged with bank robbery. In the event that the accomplices are convicted, they may receive the same sentence as the perpetrator of the crime.

Individuals who assist the perpetrators following a crime will be charged as accessories after the fact. Accessoryship is no longer viewed as being connected to the central crime. It is considered a separate, minor offense involving the frustration of the criminal justice process, and it is punishable as a misdemeanor. Despite these changes to the law of parties, you will find that common law categories are frequently referred to in judicial decisions and in various state statutes.

Holding an individual liable for the conduct of another seems contrary to the American value of personal responsibility. Why should we punish an individual who drives a getaway car in a bank robbery to the same extent as the actual perpetrator of the crime? The law presumes that the individuals who assisted the robber implicitly consented to be bound by the conduct of the principal in the first degree and, in the words of Joshua Dressler, "forfeited their personal identity." Professor Dressler refers to this as **derivative liability**, in which the accessory's guilt flows from the acts of the primary perpetrator of the crime.[2]

ACTUS REUS OF ACCOMPLICE LIABILITY

Statutes and judicial decisions describe the *actus reus* of accomplice liability using a range of seemingly confusing terms such as *aid*, *abet*, *encourage*, and *command*. Whatever the terminology, keep in mind that the *actus reus* of accomplice liability is satisfied by even a relatively insignificant degree of material or psychological assistance. In a well-known English case, a journalist bought a ticket to attend and review a concert by American jazz musician Coleman Hawkins. The journalist was convicted of encouraging and supporting Hawkins, who had not received permission to perform from British immigration authorities.[3] Some other examples of cases in which individuals satisfied the *actus reus* of accomplice liability are listed below.

- Two men attacked and broke Clifton Robertson's leg. The men initially approached Robertson's brother-in-law, Carl Brown, who pointed to Robertson. Following the attack, one of the assailants remarked to Brown, "You can pay me now." Brown was found guilty of aggravated assault for inciting, encouraging, or assisting the perpetrators of the assault.[4]
- Guadalupe Steven Mendez was an incarcerated felon who, over the phone, directed Patricia Morgan to molest and to take nude photos of her fourteen-year-old granddaughter. Mendez was found to have aided and abetted aggravated rape.[5]
- Prentiss Phillips was a high-ranking member of the Gangster Disciples street gang. He was convicted of the murder and aggravated kidnapping of Vernon Green, whom he suspected of standing outside of a meeting of the street gang in order to identify members of the Gangster Disciples for the rival Vice Lords. Phillips allegedly ordered gang members to seize Green and watched as Green was dragged upstairs, where he was beaten. Phillips later ordered three gang members to take Green outside and kill him. Phillips was convicted of aiding and abetting the murder and aggravated kidnapping of Green.[6]
- Anderson handed Palfrey a handgun before fighting Carter. At some point during the fight, Anderson retrieved the firearm and shot and killed Carter. The Louisiana Supreme Court held that "[a]cting in concert each man . . . became responsible . . . not only for his own acts but for the acts of the other."[7]

In the cases discussed previously, the defendants' acts clearly assisted, encouraged, or incited criminal conduct. The **mere presence rule** provides that being present and watching the commission of a crime is not sufficient to satisfy the *actus reus* requirement of accomplice liability. Why is that? A mere presence is ambiguous. On the one hand, it is sometimes the case that an individual's presence encourages and facilitates a defendant's criminal conduct. On the other hand, silence may indicate disapproval.

An exception to the mere presence doctrine arises where defendants possess a duty to intervene. In *State v. Walden*, a mother was convicted of aiding and abetting an assault with a deadly weapon when she failed to intervene to prevent an acquaintance from brutally beating her young son. The North Carolina Supreme Court reasoned that a parent's failure to protect his or her child communicates an approval of the criminal conduct.[8]

Read *State v. Ulvinen* on the study site: study .sagepub.com/ lippmaness2e.

You Decide

4.1 A woman entered a bar in New Bedford, Massachusetts, in March 1983, in order to purchase cigarettes. As she started to leave, she was knocked to the ground by two men who tore off her clothing. For the next seventy-five minutes, she was forced to commit various sexual acts, which she resisted. The victim cried for help, but the sixteen men in the bar yelled, laughed, and cheered. No one came to her assistance. Were all fifteen male customers and the male bartender accomplices to the sexual attack? Various procedural issues are discussed in *Commonwealth v. Cordeiro*, 519 N.E.2d 1328 (Mass. 1988), and *Commonwealth v. Vieira*, 519 N.E.2d 1320 (Mass. 1988).

You can find the answer at study.sagepub.com/lippmaness2e

MENS REA OF ACCOMPLICE LIABILITY

A conviction for accomplice liability requires that a defendant both assist and intend to assist the commission of a crime.

In most cases, an accomplice is required to intend or possess the purpose that an individual commit a specific crime. This is described as *dual intents*:

- the intent to assist the primary party, and
- the intent that the primary party commit the offense charged.

In the words of Judge Learned Hand in *United States v. Peoni*, "mere knowledge" is not sufficient to hold a defendant liable for aiding and abetting. A defendant must possess a "purposive attitude" and "associate himself with the venture . . . as in something that he wishes to bring about, that he seek by his action to make it succeed."[9]

In other words, an individual will not be held liable as an accomplice for knowingly rather than purposely

- selling a gun to an individual who plans to rob a bank,
- renting a room to someone who plans to use the room for prostitution, or
- repairing the car of a stranded motorist who intends to use the auto to rob a bank.

The question of whether an individual possessed the purpose to assist an individual in committing a crime is not always easily determined. In *State v. Barker*, Barbara Barker appealed her conviction of aiding and abetting her husband's possession of thousands of images of child pornography on their home computer. There was evidence that in one instance prior to James Barker's arrest Barbara had seen child pornography on the computer and nonetheless on several occasions "restored" the computer when the machine had "frozen up." A Missouri appellate court overturned Barbara's conviction on the grounds that the evidence that Barbara had seen child pornography on the machine did not support a reasonable inference that Barbara restored James's computer with the purpose or intent of aiding or encouraging James's possession of child pornography. The court noted that affirming Barbara's conviction would mean that "[t]he continued payment of a bill for the provision of internet access with knowledge that another in the home has previously used the internet to access child pornography would support accomplice liability. Giving money to a known drug addict where the money is thereafter used to buy drugs could support accomplice liability."[10]

Some judges have ruled that the *mens rea* requirement for accomplice liability in the case of serious crimes is satisfied by knowledge of a principal's criminal plans and that an accomplice is not required to share the principal's criminal purpose. An example may be knowingly selling explosives to an individual who plans to commit an act of terrorism.[11]

Regardless of whether a "purposive" or "knowledge" standard is employed, an accomplice is subject to the **natural and probable consequences doctrine**. This provides that a person encouraging or facilitating the commission of a crime will be held liable as an accomplice for the crime he or she aided and abetted as well as for crimes that are the natural and probable outcome of the criminal conduct.

You Decide

4.2 Mark Manes, twenty-two, met Eric Harris, a seventeen-year-old student at Columbine High School in Littleton, Colorado, at a gun show. Manes purchased a semiautomatic handgun for Harris and accompanied Harris to a target range. After hitting a target, Harris excitedly proclaimed that this could have been someone's brain. Several months later, Manes sold Harris one hundred rounds of ammunition for $25. The next day, Harris and Dylan Klebold entered Columbine High School and killed twelve students and a teacher and then took their own lives. Harris and Klebold left a tape recording thanking Manes for his help and urged that he not be arrested, because they would have eventually found someone else willing to sell them guns and ammunition.

As a prosecutor, would you charge Manes as an accomplice to the murders? To the suicides? What if Harris and Klebold arrived at the school armed with weapons and ammunition provided by Manes but used other weapons to kill? What if they left the weapons and ammunition provided by Manes at home? See Joshua Dressler, *Cases and Materials on Criminal Law*, 3rd ed. (St. Paul, MN: West, 2003), p. 886.

You can find the answer at study.sagepub.com/lippmaness2e

Natural and Probable Consequences Doctrine

The leading case on the natural and probable consequences doctrine is the Maine case of *State v. Linscott*.[12] Joel Fuller enlisted William Linscott in a robbery scheme. The plan was for Linscott and Fuller to enter through the back door to prevent Norman Grenier from grabbing a shotgun that he kept in the bedroom. Linscott carried a hunting knife and a switchblade, and Fuller was armed with his shotgun. As they approached the house, they saw that the snow blocked the back door and revised their plan. Linscott was to break the living room picture window, whereupon Fuller would freeze Grenier with the shotgun while Linscott seized the cash.

Linscott broke the window with his body, and Fuller immediately fired a shot through the broken window, killing Grenier. Fuller entered the house through the broken window and took $1,300 from Grenier's pocket. Fuller gave Linscott $500.

Linscott later was arrested. He claimed that it was not unusual for Fuller to carry a shotgun, although he was unaware that Fuller had a reputation for violence. He also claimed that although he may have been negligent, he had no intention of killing Grenier during the course of the robbery. Linscott was convicted of intentionally or knowingly killing Grenier. The court found that he possessed the intent to commit the crime of robbery and that the murder was a reasonably foreseeable consequence of Linscott's participation in the robbery. The court recognized that Linscott did not intend to kill Grenier and that he probably would not have participated in the robbery had he believed that Grenier would be killed during the course of the robbery. A small number of courts have rejected the natural and foreseeable consequences doctrine as unfair to an accessory who lacked the intent to commit the more serious offense.[13]

You Decide

4.3 Leon McCoy conspired with Keith Lamar Bellamy to rob a McDonald's restaurant where McCoy worked. Andre Randall, McCoy's coworker, was aware of the plan.

C.B. was working the evening shift as the assistant manager of a McDonald's in Wilmington, Delaware. She was assisted by defendant Leon McCoy (McCoy) and Andre Randall (Randall). C.B. locked the doors at 10:00 that night. Randall took out the trash, and, contrary to restaurant policy, failed to notify C.B. who ordinarily opened and locked the door. Randall simply opened the door and, rather than closing the door, turned the deadbolt so as to keep the door ajar. Bellamy, who was armed, entered at around 11:30 as McCoy was mopping the hallway and C.B. was preparing the night deposit. Bellamy put the gun to the side of C.B.'s head and seized the deposit money; he also took C.B.'s personal cash. He demanded a bag for the cash. McCoy, went to the front near the service counter and got a bag. Although there were several silent alarms in this area, McCoy did not activate any of the alarms.

Once he bagged the money, Bellamy told C.B. to undress. As she was unbuttoning her shirt, he said she was taking too long and he told her to just drop her pants and underwear. He then demanded that she spread her labia apart. He stooped down to inspect her genitals, and used the barrel of his gun to pull her labia further apart. He noticed that she had a tampon inserted, and told her that she was "lucky." Following the robbery, Bellamy fled and McCoy went to the front of the store and hit a silent alarm. There were security cameras in the store recording the robbery. Is McCoy guilty of sexual assault? See *State v. Bellamy*, 617 S.E.2d 81 (N.C. App. 2005).

You can find the answer at study.sagepub.com/lippmaness2e

ACCESSORY AFTER THE FACT

The Common Law

Conviction as an accessory after the fact at common law required that a defendant conceal or assist an individual whom he or she knew had committed a felony in order to hinder the perpetrator's arrest, prosecution, or conviction. For example, an individual would be held liable for assisting a friend, whom he or she knew had killed a member of an opposing gang, to flee to a foreign country.

Accessories after the fact at common law were treated as accomplices and were subject to the same punishment as the principal who had committed the offense. A wife, however, could not be held liable as an accessory after the fact because it was expected that she had assisted her husband.

The Elements of Accessory After the Fact

The elements of accessory after the fact are as follows:

- *Commission of a Felony.* There must be a completed felony. The crime need not have been detected or formal charges filed.

- *Knowledge.* The defendant must possess knowledge that the individual whom he or she is assisting has committed a felony. A reasonable but mistaken belief does not create liability. In *Browne v. People*, Marcella Browne was charged and convicted as an accessory after the fact under the Virgin Islands Code for making a false statement to the police. Marcella allegedly lied to protect her husband Jeffrey Browne and her brother, Luis Melendez, who were suspected of a killing in a public housing project. Marcella falsely told the police that Jeffrey and Luis were at her house at the time of the killing and that she was driving around in the couple's auto at the time of the killing. The Supreme Court of the Virgin Islands overturned Marcella's conviction and explained that although she was informed of the killing, she did not know that Browne and Melendez had been involved in the shooting.[14]

- *Affirmative Act.* The accessory must take affirmative steps to hinder the felon's arrest; a refusal or failure to report the crime or to provide information to the authorities is not sufficient. Examples of conduct amounting to accessoryship after the fact are hiding or helping a felon escape, destroying evidence, or providing false information to the police in order to mislead law enforcement officials. In *State v. Thomas*, an Illinois appellate court overturned the defendant's conviction and held that the defendant's failure to disclose the identity of a killer to the police did not constitute an "affirmative misrepresentation" and a "misleading" of the police.[15]

• *Criminal Intent.* The defendant must provide assistance with the intent or purpose of hindering the detection, apprehension, prosecution, conviction, or punishment of the individual receiving assistance. In *State v. Jordan*, Kenneth Jordan shot Christopher Pendley after seeing Pendley talking to Teresa Jordan, Kenneth's wife. Teresa was convicted of being an accessory after the fact based on her falsely reporting to friends, nurses, and the police and testifying at trial that Pendley had been shot while attempting to rape her. Kenneth pled guilty to the voluntary manslaughter of Pendley prior to Teresa's conviction.[16]

The modern view is that because accessories after the fact are involved following the completion of a crime, they should not be treated as harshly as the perpetrator of the crime or accomplices. Accessories after the fact are now held liable for a separate, less serious felony or for a misdemeanor. Some states have abandoned the crime of accessory after the fact and have created the new offense of "hindering prosecution," which punishes individuals frustrating the arrest, prosecution, or conviction of individuals who have committed felonies as well as misdemeanors. An example is Model Penal Code Section 242.3, which is reprinted in the text below.

Most states have abandoned the common law requirements that impeded the conviction of individuals for accessoryship after the fact. A spouse remains immune from prosecution as an accessory after the fact in fourteen states. In 1999, Florida amended the law to exclude child abuse or related crimes from the law protecting family members from liability.[17] The common law rule that an individual may be prosecuted only for being an accessory after the fact following the conviction of the principal has also been modified. Most states require only proof of a completed felony.

On April 15, 2013, two homemade bombs were ignited at the finish line of the Boston Marathon by Dzhokhar Tsarnaev and his older brother Tamerlan Tsarnaev, who later was killed in a shoot-out with the police. The bomb killed three people and wounded more than 260 others, a number of whom were severely injured (discussed in Chapter 14). Three college friends of Dzhokhar were found guilty in 2014 of obstruction of justice when following the bombing they removed a backpack containing incriminating evidence from Dzhokhar's dorm room and disposed of the backpack in a Dumpster.

Model Penal Code

Section 242.3. Hindering Apprehension or Prosecution

A person commits an offense if, with purpose to hinder the apprehension, prosecution, conviction or punishment of another for crime, he:

(1) harbors or conceals the other; or

(2) provides or aids in providing a weapon, transportation, disguise or other means of avoiding apprehension or effecting escape; or

(3) conceals or destroys evidence of the crime, or tampers with a witness, informant, document or other source of information, regardless of its admissibility in evidence; or

(4) warns the others of impending discovery or apprehension . . . or

(5) volunteers false information to a law enforcement officer.

Analysis

The Model Penal Code views accessory after the fact as obstruction of justice and does not require that the person providing assistance be aware that the alleged offender actually committed a crime. The essence of the crime is interference with the functioning of the legal process. An individual charged with accessory after the fact is thus not treated as a principal. Liability extends to assisting an individual avoid apprehension for a misdemeanor as well as a felony. The Model Penal Code specifies the type of assistance that is prohibited to prevent courts from too narrowly or too broadly interpreting the behavior that is prohibited.

Accessory after the fact is punished as a felony carrying five years' imprisonment if the person aided is charged or is liable to be charged with a felony of the first or second degree. Assisting a felony of the third degree (one to two years in prison) or a misdemeanor is punished as a misdemeanor. The fact that the person who provides assistance is related to the individual confronting a criminal charge is to be considered as a mitigating factor at sentencing rather than as a complete defense.

The Legal Equation

Accessory after the fact	=	Conceals or assists an individual
	+	whom he or she knows to have committed a felony
	+	in order to hinder the perpetrator's arrest, prosecution, or conviction.

You Decide

4.4 In a Mississippi case, Xavier Sherron began having intercourse with his thirteen-year-old step-daughter, Jane, in December 2001 or January 2002. Charlotte Sherron, Xavier's wife and Jane's mother, learned that Xavier had been having intercourse with Jane on a regular basis, and Xavier assured her that he would not continue to molest Jane. Charlotte directed Jane to lock her door. Charlotte needed Xavier's monthly disability checks to make ends meet and did not ask him to leave her house. Charlotte also was fearful that in the event the rape was revealed, her three children would be taken from her by state authorities.

In February 2002, Jane told Charlotte that she was pregnant and stated that an abortion was preferable to bearing Xavier's child. Charlotte agreed with other family members that she would not contact the police, and Charlotte arranged for an abortion for Jane in Tuscaloosa, Alabama. Both Charlotte and Xavier drove Jane to Tuscaloosa. In May 2002, Jane's uncle approached the police, and Xavier subsequently was arrested and convicted of statutory rape. Charlotte was arrested as an accessory after the fact to the statutory rape based on her assisting Jane in obtaining an abortion. There was no charge brought against Charlotte for failing to fulfill her obligation as a Mississippi school employee to inform the police of Jane's abuse.

The court analyzed Jane's abortion under the requirements of Mississippi law and noted that Alabama law presumably contained the same provisions. A child who desires to obtain an abortion in Mississippi either must get parental consent or must petition the court for permission to obtain an abortion. The appellate court stated that the question is whether Charlotte's consent to Jane's abortion was based on a desire to support her daughter or based on an intent to conceal her husband's crimes. There was testimony at trial that Charlotte was afraid of Xavier, who in the past had choked Charlotte and had thrown objects at her.

Would you convict Charlotte of being an accessory after the fact to Xavier's statutory rape? See *Sherron v. State*, 959 So. 2d 30 (Miss. App. 2006).

You can find the answer at study.sagepub.com/lippmaness2e

CRIMINAL LAW IN THE NEWS

In December 1996, Robert Lee Thompson, age twenty-one, and Sammy Butler, age nineteen, robbed a convenience store in Houston, Texas. This was part of a two-month crime spree. Thompson approached clerk Mobarakali Meredia; when Meredia hesitated, Thompson shot him four times. Thompson then put the gun to Meredia's neck, pulled the trigger, and found that the chamber was empty. Thompson in frustration pistol-whipped Meredia and hit him in the head with the cash tray from the register. Thompson next fired two shots that missed the other clerk, Mansoor Rahim, who was in the rear of the store. Thompson and Butler fled and drove away with Thompson behind the wheel. Rahim ran from the store into the parking lot and was shot and killed by Butler. Butler and Thompson were prosecuted and convicted in March 1998. Butler was sentenced to life imprisonment, and Thompson was sentenced to death.

Texas is the only state that authorizes the execution of an individual who "solicits, encourages, directs, aids or attempts to aid" the "triggerman" in a homicide. Five individuals had been executed under the Texas "law of parties" in the past. At the punishment stage, prosecutors alleged that Thompson had been involved in at least eight other robberies that resulted in fatalities, two of which took place in the twenty-four hours before the robbery–murder of the convenience store clerks.

The Texas Board of Pardons and Paroles voted 5-2 to recommend to Governor Rick Perry that he commute Thompson's sentence. Perry, in fact, had only recently commuted the death sentence of Kenneth Foster, who had been sentenced to death under the "law of parties." Governor Perry rejected the board's recommendation, and announced that "after reviewing all of the facts in the case of Robert Lee Thompson, who had a murderous history and participated in the killing of Mansoor Bhai Rahim Mohammed, I have decided to uphold the jury's capital murder conviction and capital punishment for this heinous crime." Thompson was executed almost immediately following Governor Perry's decision. Just before his execution, Thompson claimed to have converted to Islam and sought forgiveness from the victims' families and from Allah.

The prevailing law under the Eighth Amendment on the constitutionality of executing individuals who do not actually kill is not entirely clear. In *Enmund v. Florida*, the U.S. Supreme Court held that it was unconstitutional to execute the driver of a getaway car who lacked a criminal intent and who did not participate in a robbery and murder (458 U.S. 782 [1982]). On the other hand, in *Tison v. Arizona*, the Court noted that "substantial participation in a violent felony under circumstances likely to result in the loss of innocent life may justify the death penalty even absent an intent to kill" (481 U.S. 137 [1987]).

VICARIOUS LIABILITY

We have seen that *strict liability* results in holding a defendant criminally responsible for the commission of a criminal act without a requirement of a criminal intent. An act, in other words, is all that is required. **Vicarious liability** imposes liability on an individual for a criminal act committed by another. The other person acts, and you are responsible. *Accomplice liability*, in contrast, holds individuals responsible who affirmatively aid and abet a criminal act with a purposeful intent.

Vicarious liability is employed to hold employers and business executives and corporations (which are considered "legal persons") liable for the criminal acts of employees. Vicarious liability has also been used to hold the owner of an automobile liable for parking violations committed by an individual driving the owner's car. Another example of vicarious liability is imposing liability on parents for crimes committed by their children.

Vicarious liability is contrary to the core principle that individuals should be held responsible and liable for their own conduct. The primary reason for this departure from individual responsibility in the case of corporate liability is to encourage employers to control and to monitor employees so as to ensure that the public is protected from potential dangers, such as poisoned food.[18]

We have distinguished strict and vicarious liability. Keep in mind that statutes that are intended to protect the public health, safety, and welfare typically combine both doctrines. In the California case of *People v. Travers*, Greg Mitchell, a service station employee, misrepresented the quality of motor oil he sold to the public. The defendant, Charles Travers, was the owner of the station and was prosecuted along with Mitchell under a statute that punished the sale of a misbranded product. Travers objected that he was completely unaware of Mitchell's actions. The court reasoned that the importance of smoothly running motor vehicles and the right of the public to receive what they paid for justified the imposition of vicarious liability on Travers without the necessity of demonstrating that he possessed a criminal intent. The court explained that it was reasonable to expect a service station owner to supervise the sale of motor oil, and requiring the prosecution to establish criminal intent would permit owners to escape punishment by pleading that they were unaware of the quality or contents of the motor oil sold in their service stations.[19]

Is it fair to impose strict liability on Travers for the acts of Mitchell? Would a significant number of guilty people be acquitted in the event that the court required the prosecution to establish a criminal intent? Professor Wayne LaFave poses a choice between punishing one hundred people for selling tainted food under a strict liability statute and using an intent standard that would result in the conviction of five of the one hundred. The first alternative would result in some innocent people being convicted; the second alternative would result in some guilty people avoiding a criminal conviction. What is the better approach?[20]

The Legal Equation

Vicarious liability	=	Voluntary act or omission or possession by another
	+	status of employer, parent, or owner of automobile.

You Decide

4.5 A seventeen-year-old rented sexually oriented videotapes on two occasions from VIP Video in Millville, Ohio. The first time, the seventeen-year-old used his father's driver's license for identification. The second time, he paid in cash, and the clerk did not ask him for an identification or proof of age. The owner of the store, Peter Tomaino, did not post a sign in the store indicating that sexually oriented rentals would not be made to juveniles. Tomaino was absent from the store at the time of the rentals. He was convicted under a statute that provides that "no person, with knowledge of its character or content, shall recklessly . . . sell . . . material . . . that is obscene or harmful to juveniles."

Should Tomaino's conviction be overturned? Could he constitutionally be sentenced to prison? See *State v. Tomaino,* 733 N.E.2d 1191 (Ohio App. 1999).

You can find the answer at study.sagepub.com/lippmaness2e

CRIMINAL LAW AND PUBLIC POLICY

Susan and Anthony Provenzino of St. Clair Shores, Michigan, were aware that their son Alex was experiencing difficulties. He was arrested in May 1995, and the Provenzinos obtained Alex's release from juvenile custody in the fall of 1995, fearing that he would be mistreated by violent juveniles housed in the facility. Over the course of the next year, Alex was involved in a burglary, excessive drinking, and using and selling marijuana. Alex verbally abused his parents at home and, on one occasion, attacked his father with a golf club. In May 1996, the Provenzinos were convicted of violating a two-year-old local ordinance that placed an affirmative responsibility on parents to "exercise reasonable control over their children." The jury required only fifteen minutes to find them guilty; each was fined $100 and ordered to pay $1,000 in court fees.

Roughly seventeen states and cities today have similar **parental responsibility laws**. States have a long history of passing laws against parents who abuse, neglect, or abandon their children or fail to ensure that their children attend school. In 1903, Colorado was the first state to punish "contributing to the delinquency of a minor." Similar provisions were subsequently adopted by roughly forty-two states and the District of Columbia. These statutes are not limited to parents; and they require some affirmative act on the part of an adult that aids, encourages, or causes the child's delinquent behavior.

The first wave of parental responsibility statutes was passed in the late 1980s and early 1990s, when various states and municipalities adopted laws holding parents strictly and vicariously liable for the criminal conduct of their children. It was presumed that parents possess a duty to supervise their offspring and that this type of statute would encourage parents to monitor and to control their kids. These strict and vicarious liability statutes were ruled unconstitutional in Connecticut, Louisiana, Oregon, and Wyoming.

Parental responsibility statutes generally hold parents responsible for the failure to take reasonable steps to prevent their children from engaging in serious or persistent criminal behavior. A New York law, for instance, punishes a parent who "fails or refuses to exercise reasonable diligence in the control of . . . a child to prevent him from becoming . . . a 'juvenile delinquent' or a 'person in need of supervision.' . . ." These statutes, as illustrated by the New York law, generally lack clear and definite standards.

There are a variety of laws that hold adults liable for teenage drinking. **Social host liability laws** hold adults liable for providing liquor in their home to minors in the event that an accident or injury occurs. Variants are so-called teen party ordinances, which declare that it is criminal for an adult to host a party for minors at which alcohol is served. Some states impose misdemeanor liability on parents whose children fail to attend school on a regular basis. See *In re Gloria H.*, 979 A.2d 710 (Md. 2009).

In 1993, in *Williams v. Garcetti*, 853 P.2d 507 (Cal. 1993), the California Supreme Court upheld the constitutionality of a California parental responsibility statute. The law stated that a "parent or legal guardian to any person under the age of 18 years shall have the duty to exercise reasonable care, supervision, protection, and control over their minor child." A parent or guardian whose "act or omission causes or tends to cause or encourage a child to violate a curfew, be habitually truant or commit a crime" is held liable under the statute. In other words, parents are held liable who know or should know "that their child is at risk of delinquency and . . . they are able to control the child." A violation of the statute is punished as a misdemeanor, although the charges may be dismissed prior to trial against a parent or guardian who completes an education, treatment, or rehabilitation program. The legislature passed the law as part of an effort to combat "violent street gangs whose members threaten, terrorize, and commit a multitude of crimes against the peaceful citizens of . . . neighborhoods."

The California Supreme Court stressed that the provision for parental diversion from criminal prosecution in "less serious cases" means that parents will face criminal penalties for a "failure to supervise only in those cases in which the parent's culpability is great and the causal connection correspondingly clear." On one hand, it seems unfair to hold parents vicariously liable for the criminal acts of their children. On the other hand, parents would certainly seem to have certain obligations and responsibilities to society based on their decision to have children. Holding parents liable may lead them to closely supervise their children and may serve to protect society. What is your view?

CASE ANALYSIS

In *State v. Robinson*, the Michigan Supreme Court decided whether to hold Robinson liable for murder based on the natural and probable consequences doctrine.

Should Robinson Be Held Liable for Murder?

State v. Robinson, 715 N.W.2d 44 (Mich. 2006)

According to the evidence adduced at trial, defendant and Pannell went to the house of the victim, Bernard Thomas, with the stated intent to "f--- him up." Under Pannell's direction, defendant drove himself and Pannell to the victim's house. Pannell knocked on the victim's door. When the victim opened the door, defendant struck him. As the victim fell to the ground, defendant struck the victim again. Pannell began to kick the victim. Defendant told Pannell that "that was enough," and walked back to the car. When defendant reached his car, he heard a single gunshot.

Following a bench trial, the trial court found defendant guilty of second-degree murder. Specifically, the court found that defendant drove Pannell to the victim's house with the intent to physically attack the victim. The court also found that once at the victim's

(Continued)

(Continued)

home, defendant initiated the attack on the victim, and that defendant's attack enabled Pannell to "get the upper-hand" on the victim. The court sentenced defendant to a term of 71 months to 15 years.

The evidence establishes that the victim threatened Pannell's children in Pannell's presence, enraging Pannell. When defendant woke up at 10:00 that evening, Pannell was still "ranting and raving" in the house. Despite knowing that Pannell was in an agitated state, defendant agreed to drive to the victim's house with the understanding that he and Pannell would "f--- him up." When the pair arrived at the victim's home, defendant initiated the assault by hitting the victim once in the face and once in the neck with the

back of his hand. After the victim fell to the ground, Pannell punched him twice and began kicking him. In our judgment, a natural and probable consequence of a plan to assault someone is that one of the actors may well escalate the assault into a murder. . . . Pannell's anger toward the victim escalated during the assault into a murderous rage.

A "natural and probable consequence" of leaving the enraged Pannell alone with the victim is that Pannell would ultimately murder the victim. That defendant . . . left the scene of the crime moments before Thomas's murder does not under these circumstances exonerate him from responsibility for the crime.

CHAPTER SUMMARY

We have seen that under the common law there were four parties to a crime. The procedural requirements surrounding the prosecution of parties developed by judges were intended to impede the application of the death penalty. Today there are two parties to a crime:

1. *Accomplices.* Individuals participating before and during a crime

2. *Accessories.* Individuals involved following a crime

The *actus reus* of accomplice liability is described as "aiding," "abetting," "encouraging," and "commanding" the commission of a crime. This is satisfied by even a small degree of material or psychological assistance. Mere presence is not sufficient. The *mens rea* of accomplice liability is typically described as the intent to assist the primary party to commit the offense with

which he or she is charged. Some judges have argued for a knowledge standard, but other courts have recognized liability based on recklessness. The criminality of an accessory after the fact is distinguished from that of accomplices by the fact that the legal guilt of an accessory after the fact is not derived from the primary crime. Instead, accessory after the fact is now considered a separate and minor offense involving an intent and an act undertaken with the purpose of hindering the detection, apprehension, prosecution, conviction, or punishment of the individual receiving assistance.

Strict liability holds an individual liable based on the commission of a criminal act while dispensing with the requirement of a criminal intent. Vicarious liability imposes liability on an individual for the criminal act of another. Parents, under some state statutes, are held vicariously liable for the criminal conduct of their children based on their status relationship.

CHAPTER REVIEW QUESTIONS

1. What were the four categories of common law parties? How does this differ from the modern categorization of parties?

2. Illustrate the definition of common law accomplices and accessories using the example of a bank robbery. Should accomplices be held liable for the same crime as the primary perpetrator of the crime?

3. What *actus reus* is required for an accomplice? Provide some illustrations of acts satisfying the *actus reus* requirement. What is the mere presence rule? Is there an exception to the mere presence rule?

4. Discuss the *mens rea* of accomplice liability. Distinguish this from the minority position that "knowledge" is sufficient. How would these two

approaches result in a different outcome in a case? Which approach do you favor?

5. What are the requirements for an individual to be considered an accessory after the fact? Is this considered as serious a criminal violation as being an accomplice?

6. Distinguish accomplice liability, strict liability, and vicarious liability.

7. What constitutional considerations are involved in holding the owner of an automobile vicariously liable for the traffic tickets issued to the car?

8. Is it constitutional to hold parents strictly and vicariously liable for the criminal acts of their children? In your view, are there any situations in which parents should or should not be held vicariously liable?

9. Write a brief essay summarizing the law of parties.

LEGAL TERMINOLOGY

accessories

accessories after the fact

accessories before the fact

accomplices

derivative liability

mere presence rule

natural and probable consequences doctrine

parental responsibility laws

parties to a crime

principals in the first degree

principals in the second degree

social host liability laws

vicarious liability

CRIMINAL LAW ON THE WEB

Visit **study.sagepub.com/lippmaness2e** to access additional study tools including suggested answers to the You Decide questions, reprints of cases and statutes, online appendices, and more!

5 ATTEMPT, SOLICITATION, AND CONSPIRACY

Was the defendant guilty of an attempt to illegally kill a deer?

At approximately nine o'clock on the night of November 18, 1988, two state game wardens placed a deer decoy in a field. . . . The wardens constructed the decoy using [S]tyrofoam and wood, a deer hide covering, and a mounted deer head. They designed the body of the decoy to closely resemble the physique and proportions of a deer, covering its glass eyes with reflective tape to simulate the appearance of a live deer's eyes. The decoy was placed eighty-three feet from the road.

Positioning themselves so that they could observe the area undetected, the wardens saw defendant's pickup truck proceeding slowly along the town road. . . . The wardens saw the silhouette of a rifle emerge from the driver's window and heard a gun shot almost immediately thereafter. The wardens converged on the truck, identifying defendant as the operator of the truck and seizing a .22 caliber rifle, ammunition and lighting devices, the strongest of which was attached to a miner's cap, worn by defendant. . . . Upon examination of the decoy, the wardens determined that one eye [of the deer] had been shattered by a gun shot. (*State v. Curtis*, No. 89-621 [Vt. 1991])

In this chapter, learn about criminal attempts and impossibility.

Learning Objectives

1. Understand the *mens rea* and *actus reus* of criminal attempts.

2. Know the *mens rea* and *actus reus* of solicitation.

3. Understand the *mens rea* and *actus reus* of conspiracy.

INTRODUCTION

We live in fear of a terrorist bombing or hijacking and certainly do not want to wait for an attack to occur before arresting terrorists. On the other hand, at what point can we be confident that individuals are intent on terrorism?

Inchoate or "beginning" crimes provide that individuals can be convicted and punished for an intent to commit a crime when this intent is accompanied by a significant step toward the commission of the offense. At this point, society is confident that the individual presents a threat and is justified in acting to protect itself. There are three **inchoate crimes**:

1. *Attempt* punishes an unsuccessful effort to commit a crime.

2. *Conspiracy* punishes an agreement to commit a crime and an overt act in furtherance of this agreement.

3. *Solicitation* punishes an effort to persuade another individual to commit a crime.

The conviction of an individual for an inchoate crime requires

- a specific intent or purpose to accomplish a criminal offense, and
- an act to carry out the purpose.

Individuals who commit inchoate offenses may be punished less severely than or as severely as they would have been punished if they had completed the crime that was the object of the attempt, conspiracy, or solicitation.

ATTEMPT

Professor George Fletcher notes that attempts are failures.[1] A sniper misses an intended victim, two robbers are apprehended as they enter a store, and a pickpocket finds that the victim's pocket is empty. In this section, we will ask at what point an **attempt** is subject to criminal punishment. Must we wait until a bullet misses its mark and whistles past the head of an intended victim to arrest the shooter? What defenses are available? May a pickpocket plead that the intended victim's pocket was empty?

There are two types of attempts: **complete attempt** (but "imperfect") and **incomplete attempt**. A complete, but imperfect, attempt occurs when an individual takes every act required to commit a crime and yet fails to succeed. An example is an individual firing a weapon and missing the intended victim. In the case of an incomplete attempt, an individual abandons or is prevented from completing a shooting due to the arrival of the police or as a result of some other event outside his or her control. A third category that we should mention is the *impossible attempt*. This arises where the perpetrator makes a mistake, such as aiming and firing the gun only to realize that it is not loaded. You should keep these categories in mind as you read the cases on attempt.[2]

Judges and lawyers, as we mentioned, disagree over how far an individual must progress toward the completion of a crime to be held legally liable for an attempt. It is only when an assailant pulls the trigger that we can be confident that he or she possesses an intent to kill or to seriously wound a potential victim. Yet, the longer we wait to arrest an individual, the greater the risk that he or she may carry out the crime and wound or kill a victim. At what point do you believe the police are entitled to arrest a potential assailant?

In *People v. Miller*, Charles Miller, while slightly inebriated, threatened to kill Albert Jeans. Miller appeared that afternoon on a farm owned by Sheriff Ginochio where Jeans worked. Miller was carrying a .22-caliber rifle and walked toward Ginochio, who was 250 or 300 yards in the distance. Jeans stood roughly 30 yards behind Ginochio. The defendant walked about 100 yards, stopped, appeared to load his rifle, and then continued to walk toward Ginochio, who seized the weapon from Miller without resistance. Jeans, as soon as he saw Miller, fled on a right angle to Miller's line of approach, but it is not clear whether this occurred before or after Miller crouched and appeared to place a bullet in the rifle. The firearm was loaded with a high-speed cartridge. At no time did Miller raise and aim his rifle. Was this sufficient for an attempt?

What was Miller's intent, to frighten Jeans or to kill him? Should we consider Jeans's reaction in determining Miller's guilt? Consider the presence of Ginochio in formulating your view. Would you hold Miller liable for an attempt to kill Jeans? Should an attempt be punished to the same extent as the actual offense? Do you believe that the resources of the legal system should be devoted to prosecuting Miller under the circumstances?[3]

History of Attempt

Scholars and philosophers dating back to the ancient Greeks have wrestled with the appropriate punishment for an attempted crime. After all, an attempt arguably does not result in any harm. In 360 B.C., the famous Greek philosopher Plato argued that an individual who possesses "the purpose and intention to slay another . . . should be regarded as a murderer and tried for murder." Plato, however, also recognized that an attempt does not result in the death of the victim and that banishment rather than the death penalty would be an appropriate penalty.[4]

The early common law did not punish attempts. Henry of Bracton explained this by asking, "What harm did the attempt cause, since the injury took no effect?"[5] England, rather than relying on the prosecution of attempts to prevent and punish the first steps toward crime, adopted laws against unlawful assemblies, walking at night, and unemployed persons wandering in the countryside, as well as other prohibitions on activities that may result in crime, such as keeping guns or crossbows in the house, lying in wait, or drawing a sword to harm a judge. Gaps in the law were filled by the Court of Star Chamber, which was authorized by the king to maintain order by modifying common law rules where necessary. These were volatile and violent times, and the Star Chamber began to introduce the concept of attempts into the law by punishing threats and verbal confrontations that were likely to escalate into armed confrontations, challenges, and attempts to enter into duels. In 1614, Sir Francis Bacon prosecuted a case before the Star Chamber for dueling in which he argued that acts of preparation for a sword fight should be punished in order to discourage armed confrontations.

The law of attempt was finally recognized by the common law in the important decision of *Rex v. Scofield* in 1784. The defendant was charged with placing a lighted candle and combustible material in a house with the intent of burning down the structure. Lord Mansfield, in convicting the defendant, stressed the importance of intent, writing that "the intent may make an act, innocent in itself, criminal. . . . Nor is the completion of an act, criminal in itself, necessary to constitute criminality."[6] In 1801, the law of attempt was fully accepted in the case of *Rex v. Higgins*, which involved the indictment of an individual for urging a servant to steal his master's goods. The court proclaimed that "all offenses of a public nature, that is, all such acts or attempts as tend to the prejudice of the community, are indictable."[7] This common law rule was subsequently accepted by courts in the United States, which ruled that it was a misdemeanor to attempt to commit any felony or misdemeanor. An attempt "merges into the completed crime," and a defendant may not be convicted of both an attempt and the target crime and typically is punished less severely for the attempt than for the substantive offense.[8]

Public Policy and Attempt

Why punish an act that does not result in the successful commission of a crime? There are at least three good reasons:

- *Retribution.* An individual who shoots and misses or makes efforts to commit a murder is as morally blameworthy as a successful assailant. Success or failure may depend on unpredictable factors, such as whether the victim moved to the left or to the right or whether the police happened to drive by the crime scene.
- *Utility.* The lesser punishment for attempt provides an incentive for individuals to halt before completing a criminal act in order to avoid being subjected to a harsher punishment.
- *Incapacitation.* The individual has demonstrated that he or she poses a threat to society.

The Elements of Criminal Attempt

Criminal attempt comprises three elements:

1. an intent or purpose to commit a crime,
2. act or acts toward the commission of the crime, and
3. a failure to complete the crime.

A general attempt statute punishes an attempt to commit any criminal offense. Other statutes may be directed at specific offenses, such as an attempt to commit murder, robbery, or rape.

The Legal Equation

Attempt = Step toward the completion of a crime

+ specific intent or purpose to commit the crime attempted

+ failure to complete the crime.

Mens Rea of Attempt

A criminal attempt involves a dual intent.

- An individual must intentionally perform acts that are proximate to the completion of a crime.
- An individual must possess the specific intent or purpose to achieve a criminal objective.

In the case of an individual accused of attempted murder, the prosecution must demonstrate that (1) the defendant intentionally aimed and engaged in an act toward the shooting of the arrow, and (2) this was undertaken with the intent to kill a hunter walking on the trail. A defendant who did not notice the hunter and lacked the intent to kill would not be held liable for attempted premeditated murder.[9] As noted by an Illinois appellate court, "a finding of specific intent to kill is a necessary element of intent to kill."[10]

The commentary to the Model Penal Code (MPC) offers the example of an individual who detonates a bomb with the purpose of demolishing a building knowing that people are inside. In the event that the bomb proves defective, the commentary notes that the defendant likely would not be held responsible for attempted murder, because his or her purpose was to destroy the building rather than to kill the individuals inside the structure. MPC Section 5.01(1)(b), in this instance, adopts a broad approach to intent and argues that when a defendant knows that death is likely to result from the destruction of the building, it is appropriate to hold him or her liable for attempted murder.[11]

Actus Reus of Attempt

There are two steps in considering the *actus reus* of attempt. First, determine the legal test to be applied. Second, apply the legal test to the facts. There are a number of often-confusing legal tests that courts have adopted to determine attempt.

The MPC **substantial step test** simplifies matters by providing an understandable and easily applied test for attempt. The MPC states that to constitute an attempt, an act must be a *clear step* toward the commission of a crime. This step is not required to come close to the completion of the crime itself. The MPC does state that the act must be "strongly corroborative of the actor's criminal purpose." The focus is on the acts already taken by the defendant toward the commission of the crime. The code offers a number of factual examples:

- Lying in wait, searching for, or following the contemplated victim of a crime
- Enticing the victim of the crime to go to the place contemplated for its commission
- Surveillance of the site of the contemplated crime
- Unlawful entry of a building or vehicle that is the site of the contemplated crime
- Possession of materials specifically designed for the commission of a crime
- Soliciting an individual to engage in conduct constituting a crime

The MPC substantial step analysis concentrates on asking whether an individual has taken affirmative acts toward the completion of a crime that, in combination with other evidence, indicates a defendant possesses a criminal intent. These steps are not required to be physically proximate or close to the offense, and there is no firm distinction between **preparation** and perpetration of a crime. The concern is with detaining dangerous persons rather than with delaying an arrest until an individual comes close to committing a dangerous act.

Some courts continue to require an act that comes dangerously close to success and continue to require a *physical proximity* to the completion of the crime. In the well-known case of *People v. Rizzo*, the three defendants were driving along the route regularly traveled by an individual who was responsible for depositing business receipts at the bank. A New York court held that the "line has been drawn between those acts which are remote and those which are proximate and near to the consummation. . . . The act or acts must come . . . very near to the accomplishment of the intended crime." The defendants possessed the intent to rob the employee, although they did not commit an act that was sufficiently proximate to a robbery. The question remains, how close to the completion of the robbery would be required to find the defendants guilty of an attempt?[12]

The Physical Proximity and Substantial Step Tests

You are likely understandably confused by the broad and uncertain nature of the law of attempt. Keep in mind that the fundamental question is whether the law of attempt should be concerned with a defendant's intent or with the proximity of his or her acts to the completion of a crime.

An illustration of the difference between the substantial step test and the **physical proximity test** is *Commonwealth v. Gilliam*. Gilliam was a prisoner at the Dallas State Correctional Institution, and correctional officers discovered that the bars on the window in his cell had been cut and were being held in place by sticks and paper. A search of the cell revealed vise grips concealed inside Gilliam's mattress, and two knotted extension cords attached to a hook were found in a box of clothing. The vise grips were sufficiently strong to cut through the barbed wire along the top of the fence surrounding the prison compound, and the extension cords presumably were to be used to scale the surrounding penitentiary wall. A Pennsylvania superior court ruled that Gilliam's sawing through the bars and gathering of tools indicated a clear intent to escape from prison and constituted a substantial step under the MPC. The court, however, noted that these same acts would not constitute an attempt under a test that required that an act come close to the completion of the crime, because a number of additional steps were required to escape from the prison.[13]

A number of states avoid the complexities of attempt by providing that preparation for specific offenses constitutes a crime. For instance, California Penal Code Section 466 provides the following:

> Every person having upon him or her in his or her possession a picklock, crowbar, keybit, . . . or other instrument or tool with intent feloniously to break or enter into any building . . . is guilty of misdemeanor.[14]

You Decide

5.1 Kerry Van Bell was convicted of attempted rape of a child. The defendant was contacted by a police undercover agent who stated that she had a foster child who was available for sexual relations for money. Bell met with the undercover officer and expressed unhappiness that the child was not with the undercover agent. They negotiated a price for intercourse with the four-year-old foster child. Bell nodded his head at the price of $200 and agreed to follow the undercover officer to Elm Street by Elm Park roughly one mile away where the agent represented that the child was located. As the undercover officer exited Van Bell's car, she signaled to nearby police officers who arrested Van Bell as his vehicle began to pull out of his parking spot and turn toward the exit of the parking lot, in the direction of Elm Park. The court stated that in determining whether a defendant is guilty of an attempt in Massachusetts "we look to the actions left to be taken, or the 'distance or gap between the defendant's actions and the (unachieved) goal of the consummated crime—the distance must be relatively short, the gap narrow, if the defendant is to be held guilty of a criminal attempt.'" Was Van Bell guilty of attempted rape of a child? See *Commonwealth v. Kerry Van Bell*, 917, N.E.2d 740 (Sup. Jud. Ct. Mass. 2009).

You can find the answer at study.sagepub.com/lippmaness2e.

IMPOSSIBILITY

Consider whether the following defendants should be held liable for an attempted offense.

- A pickpocket reaches into your pocket, only to find that there is no wallet.
- An individual hands $100 to a seller in an effort to purchase narcotics and is arrested by the police before the seller is able to hand over what is later revealed to be baking powder.
- A doctor begins to perform an illegal abortion on a woman who is, in fact, a government undercover agent who is not pregnant.
- In an attempt to kill a romantic rival, an individual enters the rival's bedroom and shoots into the bed, not realizing that it is empty.
- A male forces himself on a sleeping female with the belief that she did not consent and then discovers that the victim died of a heart attack an hour prior.

Read *Bolton v. State* and *Young v. State* on the study site: study.sagepub.com/lippmaness2e.

In each instance, the defendant possessed an intent to commit a crime that was factually impossible to complete. The perpetrators would have successfully completed the offenses had the facts been as the individuals "believed them to be" (i.e., there was a wallet in the pocket, the seller possessed drugs, the woman was pregnant, the romantic rival was in his or her bed, and the potential victim was alive).

A **factual impossibility** is not a defense to an attempt to commit a crime. This is based on the fact that an offender who possesses a criminal intent and who takes steps to commit an offense should not be free from legal guilt. The factual circumstance that prevents an individual from actually completing the offense is referred to in some state statutes as an **extraneous factor**, or an event outside of an individual's control.

Factual impossibility should be distinguished from **legal impossibility**, which is recognized as a defense. Legal impossibility arises when an individual mistakenly believes that he or she is acting illegally. An example is taking a tax deduction that an individual believes is illegal but that, in fact, is perfectly permissible. A group of eighteen-year-old college freshmen will not be guilty of an attempt in the event that they go to a bar and order beers while mistakenly believing that the drinking age is twenty-one. As Professor Jerome Hall notes, it is not a crime to throw a Kansas steak into the garbage, and an individual who makes an effort to toss the steak into the garbage is not guilty of an attempted offense. The individual attempting to discard the steak possesses a criminal intent to violate a nonexistent law. Our old friend *the principle of legality* prohibits punishing an individual for a crime that is the product of his or her imagination.[15]

The rule is that a mistake concerning the facts is not a defense; a mistake concerning the law is a defense. Ask yourself whether the individual charged with an attempt was mistaken concerning the facts or mistaken concerning the law.

We also should refer to the defense of **inherent impossibility**. This occurs in those rare situations in which a defendant could not possibly achieve the desired result. The example that is cited is an individual who sticks pins in a voodoo doll and is acquitted of attempted murder. The reason is that the individual's act of sticking pins in the voodoo doll is so unlikely to result in death that it would be unfair to hold him or her criminally liable.[16] Is there a social benefit in punishing an individual who possesses a criminal intent to kill and who commits an inherently impossible act?

The MPC does not recognize the defense of factual impossibility under any circumstances. The code provides a "safety valve" in Section 5.05(2) by providing that an act should be treated as a minor offense in those instances in which neither the offender nor his or her conduct presents a serious threat to the public. A Colorado statute provides that neither factual nor legal impossibility is a defense "if the offense would have [been] committed had the attendant circumstances been as the actor believed them to be."[17]

In *State v. Damms*, the defendant put a gun to the head of his wife, from whom he was separated, and pulled the trigger. He exclaimed, "It won't fire. It won't fire." Police officers immediately arrested Damms and found that the weapon was unloaded. Damms told the officers that he thought that the gun was loaded. The Wisconsin Supreme Court affirmed Damms's conviction for attempted murder.[18]

In *State v. Glass*, the Ada County, Idaho, Sheriff's Office conducted an "online crimes" investigation directed against Internet chat rooms. The Sheriff's office created a profile for a fictional fourteen-year-old female with the screen name BBG14. BBG14 received an instant message from Glass, who was using the screen name "s3x-slave_for_u." Glass described in "graphic detail" the sex acts that he would like to perform with BBG14, arranged to meet her, and was arrested when he appeared, with a box of condoms, at the place that they arranged to meet. An Idaho appellate court "held that impossibility is not a recognized defense to attempt crimes in the State of Idaho. In determining that Idaho's attempt statute . . . does not allow for an impossibility defense, we stated that the statute provides no exception for those who intend to commit a crime but fail because they were unaware of some fact that would have prevented them from completing the intended crime."[19]

People v. Dlugash, decided by the New York Court of Appeals in 1977, is a well-known example of factual impossibility. A fight developed, and Bush shot Geller three times, killing Geller. Dlugash then approached the body and shot Geller five times in the head. The New York court determined that Dlugash believed at the time he fired his pistol that Geller was alive. As a prosecutor, would you charge Dlugash with attempted murder? Should we judge the dangerousness of Dlugash's acts by his intent or by the actual facts? What if Dlugash arrived following Bush's shooting of Geller and believed that Geller was lying wounded in bed and proceeded to shoot into the bed, only to discover that he shot a large toy bear?[20] Would you charge Dlugash with attempted murder?

You Decide

5.2 Francisco Martin Duran was a twenty-six-year-old upholsterer from Colorado. On September 13, 1994, Duran bought an assault rifle and roughly one hundred rounds of ammunition. Two days later, he purchased a thirty-round clip and equipped the rifle with a folding stock. Thirteen days later, Duran bought a shotgun and, the following day, additional ammunition. On September 30, 1993, Duran left work and, without contacting his family or employer, began a journey to Washington, D.C. He purchased another thirty-round clip and a large coat in Virginia. On October 10, Duran arrived in Washington, D.C., and he stayed in various hotels over the next nineteen days.

On October 29, 1994, Duran positioned himself outside the White House fence and observed a group of men in dark suits, one of whom was Dennis Basso,

who strongly resembled then-president Bill Clinton. Two eighth-grade students remarked that Basso looked like Bill Clinton. Duran almost immediately began firing twenty rounds at Basso, who managed to take cover. Duran was tackled by a pedestrian when attempting to reload a second clip. The Secret Service searched Duran's automobile and found incriminating evidence, including a map with the phrase "kill the Pres!" and an "X" drawn across a photo of President Clinton. A subsequent search of Duran's home led to the seizure of other incriminating evidence, including a business card on the back of which Duran called for the killing of all government officers and department heads.

Was Duran guilty of an attempt to kill the president of the United States, despite the fact that this was impossible given that President Clinton was not on the lawn of the White House? See *United States v. Duran*, 96 F.3d 1495 (D.C. Cir. 1996).

You can find the answer at study.sagepub.com/lippmaness2e

ABANDONMENT

An individual who abandons an attempt to commit a crime based on the intervention of outside or extraneous factors remains criminally liable. On the other hand, what about an individual who voluntarily abandons his or her criminal scheme after completing an attempt?

In *People v. Staples*, Staples intentionally rented an office above a bank.[21] He learned that no one was in the building on Saturday and received permission from the owner to move items into his office over the weekend. Staples took advantage of the fact that no one was in the building and drilled several holes partway through the floor, which he then covered with a rug. He placed the drilling tools in the closet and left the key in the office. Later, the landlord discovered the holes and notified the police. Staples was arrested and confessed, explaining that he abandoned his criminal plan after realizing that he could not enjoy life while living off stolen money.

Is Staples guilty of an attempt? Assuming that Staples committed an attempted burglary (breaking and entering with an intent to steal), does the defendant's change of heart or abandonment constitute a defense? Would it make a difference if the defendant changed his mind only after hearing voices in the bank?

The MPC, in Section 5.01(4), recognizes the affirmative defense of **abandonment** in those instances in which an individual committed an attempt and "abandoned his effort . . . under circumstances manifesting a complete and voluntary manifestation of criminal purpose." The important point is that an individual can commit an attempt and then relieve himself or herself from liability by voluntarily abandoning the criminal enterprise. A renunciation is not voluntary when motivated by a desire to avoid apprehension, provoked by the realization that the crime is too difficult to accomplish, or where the offender decides to postpone the crime or to focus on another victim. For example, abandonment has not been recognized as a defense where the lock on a bank vault or the door on a cash register proved difficult to open, the police arrived during the commission of a crime, or a victim broke free and fled. Once having completed the commission of a crime, the fact that an offender is full of regret and rushes the victim to the hospital also does not free the assailant from criminal liability. Abandonment, in short, is a defense to attempt when an individual freely and voluntarily undergoes a change of heart and abandons the criminal activity.[22]

In some cases, courts have continued to hold that once an attempt is complete, an individual cannot avoid criminal liability. Why should an attempt be treated differently than any other crime? The vast majority of decisions recognize that there are good reasons for recognizing the defense of abandonment, even in cases where the individual's acts are "dangerously close" to the completion of a crime.[23]

- *Lack of Purpose.* An individual who abandons a criminal enterprise lacks a firm commitment to complete the crime and should be permitted to avoid punishment.
- *Incentive to Renounce Crime.* The defense of abandonment provides an incentive for individuals to renounce their criminal conduct before completing the crime.

You Decide

5.3 Dorothy Henley was alone in her trailer when a stranger, Sammy Joe Ross, knocked on the door to ask for directions. Henley suggested that Ross consult a neighbor. When she turned her back, Ross pointed a handgun at her, ordered her into the house, told her to undress, and pushed her onto the couch. Ross, at one point, threatened to kill her; and Henley described herself as frightened and crying. Henley told Ross that her daughter would be home from school at any time.

She testified that "I started crying and talking about my daughter, that I was all she had because her daddy was dead, and he said if I had a little girl he wouldn't do anything, for me just to go outside and turn my back." Ross told Henley to walk outside behind the trailer. Ross then told her to keep her back to the road until he left. Ross later was arrested, and he claimed that he should be acquitted because he had abandoned the attempted rape. Did Ross abandon the attempted rape of Henley? See *Ross v. State*, 601 So.2d 872 (Miss. 1992).

You can find the answer at study.sagepub.com/lippmaness2e

Read *Le Barron v. State* on the study site: study .sagepub.com/ lippmaness2e.

SOLICITATION

Solicitation is defined as commanding, hiring, or encouraging another person to commit a crime. The crime was largely unknown until the prosecution of the 1801 English case of *Rex v. Higgins*, in which Higgins was convicted of unsuccessfully soliciting a servant to steal his master's goods. A number of states do not have solicitation statutes and continue to apply the common law of solicitation. States with modern statutory schemes have adopted various approaches. Some punish solicitation of all crimes, and others limit solicitation to felonies, particular felonies, or certain classes of felonies. Solicitation generally results in a punishment slightly less severe or equivalent to the punishment that is usual for the crime solicited.[24]

We all read about the greedy spouse who approaches a contract killer to murder his or her partner in order to collect insurance money. The act of proposing the killing of a spouse with the intent that the murder be carried out constitutes solicitation. Solicitation is a form of accomplice liability; and in the event that the spouse is murdered, both the greedy spouse and contract killer are guilty of homicide. In the event the assassination proves unsuccessful, both the greedy spouse and inaccurate assassin are guilty of attempted murder. An agreement between the two that leads to an overt act that is not carried out results in liability for a conspiracy. The contract killer, of course, may refuse to become involved with the greedy spouse. Nevertheless, the spouse is guilty of solicitation; the crime of solicitation is complete when a spouse attempts to hire the killer. Keep in mind that in contrast to solicitation, an attempt requires a substantial act toward the commission of a crime, and solicitation involves a communication directed to another individual. "The solicitation of another, assuming neither the solicitor nor solicitee . . . acts towards the crime's commission, cannot be held for an attempt."[25]

Public Policy

Solicitation remains a controversial crime; this accounts for the fact that some states have not yet enacted solicitation statutes. The thinking is that there is no necessity for the crime of solicitation. Solicitation, it is argued, is not a threat to society until steps are taken to carry out the scheme. At this point, the agreement can be punished as a conspiracy. A solicitor depends on the efforts of others, and simply approaching another person to commit a crime does not present a social danger. There is also the risk that individuals will be convicted based on a false accusation or as a result of a casual remark. Lastly, punishing individuals for solicitation interferes with freedom of speech. As observed by a nineteenth-century court, holding every individual who "nods or winks" to a married person on the sidewalk "indictable for soliciting to adultery . . . would be a dangerous and difficult rule of criminal law to administer."[26]

On the other hand, there are convincing reasons for punishing solicitation:

- *Cooperation Among Criminals.* Individuals typically encourage and support one another, which creates a strong likelihood that the crime will be committed.
- *Social Danger.* An individual who is sufficiently motivated to enlist the efforts of a skilled professional criminal clearly poses a continuing social danger.
- *Intervention.* Solicitation permits the police to intervene before a crime is fully implemented. The police should not be placed in the position of having to wait for an offense to occur before arresting individuals intent on committing a crime.

States typically protect individuals against wrongful convictions by requiring corroboration or additional evidence to support a charge of solicitation. This might involve an e-mail, a voice recording, or witnesses who overheard the conversation. As for the First Amendment, society possesses a substantial interest in prohibiting acts such as the solicitation of adolescents by adults for sexual activity on computer chat rooms that more than justifies any possible interference with individual self-expression.[27]

The Crime of Solicitation

Solicitation involves a written or spoken statement in which an individual intentionally advises, requests, counsels, commands, hires, encourages, or incites another person to commit a crime with the purpose that the other person commit the crime. You are not liable for a comment that is intended as a joke or uttered out of momentary frustration.

The *mens rea* of solicitation requires a specific intent or purpose that another individual commit a crime. You would not be liable in the event that you humorously advise a friend to "blow up" the expensive car of a neighbor who regularly parks in your friend's parking space. On the other hand, you might harbor a long-standing grudge against the neighbor and genuinely intend to persuade your friend to destroy the automobile.

The *actus reus* of solicitation requires an effort to get another person to commit a crime. A variety of terms are used to describe the required act, including *command, encourage,* and *request.* The crime of solicitation occurs the moment an individual urges, asks, or encourages another to commit a crime with the requisite intent. The individual is guilty of solicitation even in those instances in which the other person rejects the offer or accepts the offer and does not commit the crime.

There are four important points on *actus reus:*

1. The crime is complete the moment the statement requesting another to commit a crime is made. This is the case despite the fact that an additional step, such as a phone call or the payment of money, is required to trigger the crime.

2. A statement justifying or hoping that the neighbor's automobile is damaged is not sufficient. There must be an effort to get another person to commit the crime. A solicitation may be direct or indirect. For instance, in cases involving the enticement of children into sexual activity, courts will consider a defendant's use of suggestive and seductive remarks and materials.

3. The MPC provides that an individual is guilty of solicitation even in instances in which a letter asking others to commit a crime is intercepted by prison authorities and does not reach gang members outside of prison. States that do not follow the MPC require that the solicitation actually is received by the intended recipient.

4. The MPC provides it is a defense to a charge of criminal solicitation that an individual freely and voluntarily renounced his or her criminal purpose and prevented the commission of the crime.

In *State v. Cotton*, Cotton was arrested and charged with criminal sexual penetration of a minor and criminal sexual contact with a minor. The defendant, while in jail awaiting trial, wrote his wife in Indiana and requested that she persuade his stepdaughter whom he was accused of molesting not to testify against him. He also asked his wife to convince his stepdaughter to leave New Mexico and to return to Indiana so that she would be unavailable to testify against Cotton in the New Mexico trial. Cotton sealed the letter in an envelope and asked his cellmate Dobbs to obtain a stamp. Dobbs, unknown to Cotton, removed the letter from the envelope and replaced it with a blank sheet of paper, returned the sealed stamped envelope to Cotton, and gave the original letter to law enforcement authorities. Several days later, Cotton wrote another letter to his wife, which ultimately was handed over to law enforcement authorities. The New Mexico Supreme Court overturned Cotton's conviction of two counts of criminal solicitation for the bribery and intimidation of a witness on the grounds that New Mexico did not follow the MPC and required that solicitation should be communicated to the intended party. Do you favor the approach of New Mexico or the approach of the MPC toward criminal solicitation?[28]

Model Penal Code

Section 5.02. Criminal Solicitation

(1) . . . A person is guilty of solicitation to commit a crime if with the purpose of promoting or facilitating its commission he commands, encourages or requests another person to engage in specific conduct that would constitute such crime or an attempt to commit such crime or would establish his complicity in its commission or attempted commission.

(2) . . . It is immaterial . . . that the actor fails to communicate with the person he solicits to commit a crime if his conduct was designed to effect such communication.

(3) . . . It is an affirmative defense that the actor, after soliciting another person to commit a crime, persuaded him not to do so or otherwise prevented the commission of the crime, under circumstances manifesting a complete and voluntary renunciation of his criminal purpose.

Analysis

1. Solicitation for a felony or misdemeanor is a crime. This also includes solicitation for an attempt and aiding and abetting.

2. An individual is guilty of solicitation even in those instances that the solicitation is not communicated.

3. The defense of renunciation is recognized in those instances that the other person is persuaded not to commit or prevented from committing the offense.

The Legal Equation

Solicitation = Intent or purpose for another person to commit a crime (felony)

+ words, written statements, or actions inviting, requesting, or urging another to commit a crime.

You Decide

5.4 Cassandra Y. informed Lou Tong Saephanh, a California inmate, that she was pregnant with his child. Saephanh was excited to be a father, and they talked about the baby every week. Roughly six months later, Saephanh wrote a letter to fellow gang member Cheng Saechao: "By the way loc, could you & the homies do me a big favor & take care that white bitch, Cassie for me. ha, ha, ha!! Cuzz, it's too late to have abortion so I think a miss carrage would do just fine. I aint fista pay child sport for this bull-shit loc. You think you can get the homies or home girls do that for me before she have the baby on Aug. '98." Vicki Lawrence, a correctional officer, opened and read the letter. The letter was embargoed by prison authorities and was not sent to the addressee. Saephanh later explained that if Cassandra did not let him be a part of the baby's life, he wanted to "get rid of the baby" and did not want to pay child support. Is Saephanh guilty of solicitation? The California solicitation statute reads: "Every person who, with the intent that the crime be committed, solicits another to commit or join in the commission of murder shall be punished by imprisonment." See *People v. Saephanh*, 80 Cal. App. 4th 451 (Cal. Ct. App. 2000).

You can find the answer at study.sagepub.com/lippmaness2e

CRIMINAL LAW AND PUBLIC POLICY

In 2014, FBI Director James Comey pronounced that the recruitment of potential homegrown terrorists in the United States by the Islamic State (ISIS) takes place "24 hours a day" in "all fifty states." He stated that the challenge was to "stop them [these recruits] from acting" against the United States. According to CIA estimates, roughly two thousand Westerners have traveled to Iraq and Syria (most via Turkey) to join ISIS. More than one hundred of these individuals are from the United States, five hundred from the United Kingdom, and more than seven hundred from France. An additional 150 Americans have attempted to travel to Syria, and each day more and more Westerners are drawn to ISIS.

This recruitment of young people to join ISIS constitutes a crime under U.S. law, and individuals who recruit fighters for ISIS as well as the combatants themselves are criminally liable for providing "material support" to a terrorist organization (discussed in Chapter 14). The recruiters, however, are difficult to apprehend because their communications invariably are encrypted and they typically are outside the United States and beyond the reach of American law enforcement.

In October 2014, three American teenage girls from Colorado of Somali and Sudanese descent, age sixteen, seventeen, and eighteen, stole their passports and $2,000 in cash from their parents and boarded a flight to Germany where they were arrested by the FBI. In April 2014, Shannon Conley, a nineteen-year-old convert, was arrested at Denver International Airport attempting to board a flight to Turkey with the intent of marrying an ISIS member. Earlier in the year, Mohammed Khan, a Chicago teenager, was arrested before boarding a plane to the Middle East. These recruits not only bolster ISIS ranks overseas; they pose a potential threat when they return to the United States and Europe and are able to blend into these countries without raising suspicion. Most of the terrorists responsible for attacking sites in Paris in 2015 and in Belgium in 2016 had been trained by ISIS in Syria.

Mufid Elfgeeh, a Yemen-born manager of a pizza restaurant in Rochester, New York, was charged with recruiting members to ISIS. In announcing Elfgeeh's arrest, U.S. Attorney General Eric Holder proclaimed that "[w]e are focused on breaking up these activities on the front end, before supporters of ISI[S] can make good on plans to travel to the region or recruit sympathizers to this cause."

Commentators speculate that ISIS offers a sense of family and emotional support to the teenagers looking for purpose, meaning, self-esteem, and heroic adventure. ISIS recruits young people on social media with sophisticated appeals and videos. The terrorist organization's violent tactics provide the organization with an aura of strength and defiance that attracts young people who may feel isolated, alienated, and alone. Many of these American young people are from families that emigrated from the Middle East or that converted to Islam, and ISIS appeals to their sense of obligation to protect the Muslim faith from what ISIS portrays as an onslaught by the United States and Europe. Most of the individuals who have volunteered for ISIS lack a detailed knowledge of Islam and are susceptible to ISIS's distorted view of their religious obligations. This support for ISIS often seems particularly baffling because young women are drawn to ISIS despite the group's repressive treatment of women.

In another case, Ali Shukri Amin, a seventeen-year-old from Manassas, Virginia, pled guilty and was sentenced to eleven years in prison, a $100,000 fine, and federal supervision for the rest of his life, including monitoring of his Internet activities, for providing material support to ISIS and its radical agenda.

Amin was an honors student who at one time was in a program for gifted students and had been accepted to college. He was transformed by a recruiter from a small, shy, and sickly young person into a jihadist "rock star" who is notorious for his online "prank" of superimposing the black flag of ISIS onto the flagpole atop the White House and heralding the group's "upcoming conquest of the Americas." His Twitter account attracted thousands of followers including jihadists across the Middle East, and he posted more than seven thousand positive tweets about ISIS including instructions on how to use Bitcoin to send money to ISIS.

Why did these individuals, most of whom were financially well-off young people with the promise of educational opportunity and a successful career, turn to ISIS? Should these young people be sentenced to federal prison?

CONSPIRACY

The crime of **conspiracy** comprises an agreement between two or more persons to commit a criminal act. There are several reasons for punishing an agreement:

- *Intervention.* Protecting society involves arresting individuals before they commit a dangerous crime.
- *Group Activity.* Crimes committed by groups have a greater potential to cause social harm.
- *Deterrence.* Group pressure makes it unlikely that the conspirators will be deterred from carrying out the agreement.

The common law crime of conspiracy was complete with the agreement to commit a crime. The Florida conspiracy statute, along with roughly half of the state statutes, provides that a "person who agrees, conspires, combines, or confederates with another person or persons to commit any offense commits the offense of criminal conspiracy."[29] Other state statutes, including California and New York along with the federal conspiracy statute, require an overt act, however slight, toward carrying out the conspiracy. The Illinois conspiracy statute states that "[a] person commits conspiracy when, with intent that an offense be committed, he agrees with another to the commission of that offense. No person may be convicted of conspiracy to commit an offense unless an act in furtherance of such agreement is alleged and proved to have been committed by him or by a coconspirator."[30]

An overt act may be committed by any party to the conspiracy and is not required to be a criminal act; and any act in furtherance of the conspiracy, no matter how insignificant, is sufficient to satisfy the overt act requirement. This may involve purchasing masks to be used in a bank robbery or visiting the bank to evaluate the risks involved in the robbery. The important point is that the law of conspiracy permits law enforcement to arrest individuals at an early stage of criminal planning. The overt act requirement provides assurance that the conspirators are serious about implementing their criminal agreement.

Keep in mind that in common law, the conspiracy did not merge into the criminal act. Today, this continues to be the rule; conspiracy does not merge into the attempted or completed offense that is the object of conspiracy. *As a result, an individual may be convicted both of the substantive offense that is the object of the conspiracy and of a conspiracy. A defendant may be held liable both for armed robbery and for a conspiracy to commit armed robbery.* The MPC adopts the position that an individual may not be sentenced both for conspiracy and for criminal acts completed or attempted that are the object of the conspiracy. The MPC explains that conspiracy is punished to deter individuals from joining together to commit a crime and that once the crime occurs, there is no reason to punish the conspiracy.

State statutes differ on the punishment of a conspiracy. Some provide that a conspiracy is a misdemeanor, others that the sentence for conspiracy is the same as the target offense, and a third group of statutes provides a different sentence for conspiracies to commit a misdemeanor and for conspiracies to commit a felony. *In general, a conspiracy to commit a felony is a felony; a conspiracy to commit a misdemeanor is a misdemeanor.*[31]

The law of conspiracy is one of the most difficult areas of the criminal law to understand. As former Supreme Court justice Robert Jackson observed, "The modern crime of conspiracy is so vague that it almost defies definition."[32]

Actus Reus

The *actus reus* of conspiracy consists of

- entering into an agreement to commit a crime, and,
- under some modern statutes, an overt act in furtherance of the agreement is required.

The core of a conspiracy charge is an agreement. Individuals do not normally enter into a formal and open contractual agreement to commit a crime. Prosecutors typically are forced to point to circumstances that strongly indicate that the defendants agreed to commit a crime. In *Commonwealth v. Azim*, Charles Azim pulled his automobile over to the curb, and one of the passengers, Thomas Robinson, called to a nearby Temple University student. The student refused to respond, and Robinson and Mylice James exited the auto, beat and choked him, and took his wallet. The three then drove away from the area. The Pennsylvania Superior Court, in affirming Azim's conviction for conspiracy, pointed to Azim's association with the two assailants, his presence at the crime scene, and Azim's waiting in the automobile with the engine running and lights on as the student was beaten. The case for conspiracy would have been even stronger had this been part of a pattern of criminal activity or if there was evidence that the three divided the money.[33]

United States v. Brown is often cited to illustrate the danger that courts will find a conspiracy based on even the slightest evidence suggesting that the defendants cooperated with one another. An undercover officer approached Valentine on the street seeking to purchase marijuana. Brown joined the conversation and advised Valentine three times that the officer "looks okay to me." Brown told Valentine that there was no reason to distrust the customer or to take precautions and persuaded Valentine to personally hand the drugs over to the undercover agent. The federal Court of Appeals concluded that the facts indicated that Brown had agreed with Valentine to direct or advise Valentine on drug sales. Judge Oakes observed in dissent that there was not a "shred of evidence" that Brown was involved with Valentine and that when "numerous other inferences could be drawn from the few words of conversation . . . I cannot believe that there is proof of conspiracy . . . beyond a reasonable doubt." Judge Oakes asked, "What conspiracies might we approve tomorrow? The majority opinion will come back to haunt us, I fear."[34]

Overt Act

Under the common law, an agreement was sufficient to satisfy the elements of a conspiracy. Roughly half of the states and the federal statute now require proof of an **overt act** in furtherance of the conspiracy. The overt act requirement is satisfied by even an insignificant act that is far removed from the commission of a crime. As observed by Justice Oliver Wendell Holmes Jr., "The essence of the conspiracy is being combined for an unlawful purpose—and if an overt act is required, it does not matter how remote the act may be from accomplishing the purpose, if done to effect it."[35] Attending a meeting of the Communist Party was considered to constitute an overt act in furtherance of a Communist conspiracy to overthrow the U.S. government,[36] and purchasing large quantities of dynamite satisfied the overt act requirement for a conspiracy to blow up a school building.[37] In other cases, the overt act has been satisfied by observing the movements of an intended kidnapping victim or by purchasing stamps to send poison through the mail.[38]

An overt act by any party to a conspiracy is attributed to every member and provides a sufficient basis for prosecuting all the participants. The requirement of an overt act is intended to limit conspiracy prosecutions to agreements that have progressed beyond the stage of discussion and that therefore present a social danger.[39]

Mens Rea

The *mens rea* of conspiracy is the intent to achieve the object of the agreement. Some judges continue to express uncertainty over whether this requires a purpose to cause the result or whether it is sufficient that an individual knows that a result will occur. Under the knowledge standard, all that is required is that the seller be aware of a buyer's "intended illegal use." A purpose standard requires that the seller possess an intent to further, promote, and cooperate in the buyer's specific illegal objective.

A knowledge standard may deter individuals from providing assistance to individuals who they are aware or suspect are engaged in illegal activity. On the other hand, limiting liability to individuals with a criminal purpose targets individuals who intend to further criminal conduct.[40]

The MPC reflects the predominant view that a specific intent to further the object of the conspiracy is required. In *United States v. Falcone*, the U.S. Supreme Court ruled that individuals who provided large quantities of sugar, yeast, and cans to individuals who they knew were engaged in illegally manufacturing alcohol were not liable for conspiracy. The court held that the government was required to demonstrate that the suppliers intended to promote the illegal enterprise.[41]

In *People v. Lauria*, a California appellate court was confronted with the challenge of determining whether the operator of a telephone message service was merely providing a service to his clients knowing that they were prostitutes or whether he conspired to further acts of prostitution. The court rejected the prosecution's claim that Lauria's knowledge that three of the customers were prostitutes satisfied the mental element required to hold Lauria liable for conspiring to commit prostitution. The court ruled that the prosecution must demonstrate that Lauria possessed an intent to further a criminal enterprise and that there was insufficient evidence that "Lauria took any direct action to further, encourage or direct . . . call-girl activities."[42]

The California court provided some direction to prosecutors in future cases by observing that Lauria's intent to further prostitution might be established by evidence that he promoted and encouraged the prostitutes' pursuit of customers or received substantial financial benefits from their activities. It was significant that only a small portion of Lauria's business was derived from the prostitutes and that he received the same fee regardless of the number of messages left for his prostitute customers.

The **Pinkerton doctrine** provides that an individual is guilty of all criminal acts committed by one of the conspirators in furtherance of the conspiracy, regardless of whether the individual aided or abetted or was even aware of the offense. The court cautioned that the conspirators may not be liable for acts that are not the reasonably foreseeable acts.[43] This *Pinkerton* doctrine has been viewed by the MPC[44] and by some courts as contrary to the notion that an individual is accountable for his or her own actions and should not be held liable for the acts of another.[45]

Parties

A conviction for conspiracy requires that two or more persons intentionally enter into an agreement with the intent to achieve the crime that is the objective of the conspiracy. This is referred to as the **plurality requirement**. As noted by former Supreme Court justice Benjamin Cardozo, "It is impossible . . . for a man to conspire with himself."[46]

This joint or **bilateral** conception of conspiracy means that a charge of conspiracy against one conspirator will fail in the event that the other party to the conspiracy lacked the required *mens rea*. A conspirator in a two-person conspiracy, for example, would be automatically acquitted in the event that the other party was an undercover police officer or was legally insane and was legally incapable of entering into an agreement. In a joint trial of two conspirators at common law, the acquittal of one alleged conspirator resulted in the dismissal of the charges against the other conspirator. Keep in mind that under the bilateral approach, "[t]here must be at least two guilty conspirators or none."[47]

The MPC adopts a **unilateral** approach that examines whether a single individual agreed to enter into a conspiracy rather than focusing on whether two or more persons entered into an agreement. This scheme has been incorporated into a number of modern state statutes. Under the unilateral approach, the fact that one party is an undercover police officer or lacks the capacity to enter into a conspiracy does not result in the acquittal of the other conspirator. The commentary to the MPC notes that under the unilateral approach, it is "immaterial to the guilt of a conspirator . . . that the person or all of the persons with whom he conspired have not been or cannot be convicted."[48]

The unilateral approach has been criticized for permitting the prosecution of individuals for a conspiracy who, in fact, have not actually entered into a criminal agreement. The fear is expressed by civil libertarians that the unilateral approach enables undercover agents to manufacture crime by enticing individuals into unilateral conspiratorial agreements.[49]

The Structure of Conspiracies

The structure of a conspiracy is important. Defendants may be found guilty only of the conspiracy charged at trial and may offer the defense that there were separate agreements to commit different crimes rather than a single conspiracy. A defendant might admit that he or she was involved in a conspiracy to kidnap and hold a corporate executive for ransom and also argue that the other kidnappers entered into a separate conspiracy to kill the executive. Remember, in the event of a single conspiracy, our kidnapper would be held liable for all offenses committed in furtherance of the agreement to kidnap the executive, including the murder.[50]

Most complex conspiracies can be categorized as either a *chain conspiracy* or *wheel conspiracy*.

A **chain conspiracy** typically arises in the distribution of narcotics and other contraband. This involves communication and cooperation by individuals linked together in a vertical chain to achieve a criminal objective.

The classic case is *United States v. Bruno*, in which eighty-eight defendants were indicted for a conspiracy to import, sell, and possess narcotics. This involved smugglers who brought narcotics into New York and sold them to middlemen who distributed the narcotics to retailers who, in turn, sold narcotics to operatives in Texas and Louisiana for distribution to addicts. The petitioners appealed on the grounds that there were three conspiracies rather than one large conspiracy. The court ruled that this was a single chain conspiracy in which the smugglers knew that the middlemen must sell to retailers for distribution to addicts, and the retailers knew that the middlemen must purchase drugs from smugglers. In the words of the court, the "conspirators at one end of the chain knew that the unlawful business would not, and could not, stop with their buyers; and those at the other end knew that it had not begun with their sellers." Each member of the conspiracy knew "that the success of that part with which he was immediately concerned, was dependent upon the success of the whole." Remember that this means that every member of the conspiracy was liable for every illegal transaction carried out by his co-conspirators in Texas and in Louisiana.[51]

A circle or **wheel conspiracy** involves a single person or group that serves as a *hub*, or common core, connecting various independent individuals or spokes. The *spokes* typically interact with the hub rather than with one another. In the event that the spokes share a common purpose to succeed, there is a single conspiracy. On the other hand, in those instances that each spoke is unconcerned with the success of the other spokes, there are multiple conspiracies.

The most frequently cited case illustrating a wheel conspiracy is *Kotteakos v. United States*. Simon Brown, the hub, assisted thirty-one independent individuals to obtain separate fraudulent loans from the government. The Supreme Court held that although all the defendants were engaged in the same type of illegal activity, there was no common purpose or overall plan, and the defendants were not liable for involvement in a single conspiracy. Each loan "was an end in itself, separate from all others, although all were alike in having similar illegal objects. Except for Brown, the common figure, no conspirator was interested in whether any loan except his own went through." As a result, the Supreme Court found that there were thirty-two separate conspiracies involving Brown rather than one common conspiracy. Defendants only were liable for the conspiracy in which they were involved.[52]

Criminal Objectives

The crime of conspiracy traditionally punished agreements to commit a broad range of objectives, many of which would not be criminal if committed by a single individual. The thinking was that these acts assume an added danger when engaged in by a group of individuals.

In 1832, English jurist Lord Denman pronounced that a conspiracy indictment must "charge a conspiracy either to do an unlawful act or a lawful act by unlawful means."[53] English and American courts interpret "unlawful" to include acts that are not punishable under the criminal law. It was "enough if they are corrupt, dishonest, fraudulent, immoral, and in that sense illegal, and it is in the combination to make use of such practices that the dangers of this offense consist."[54]

The U.S. Supreme Court has recognized the danger that broadly defined conspiracy statutes may fail to inform citizens of the acts that are prohibited and may provide the police, prosecutors, and judges with broad discretion in bringing charges. The doctrine of conspiracy, for instance, was used against workers who went on strike in protest against a fellow employee who agreed to work below union wages.[55] The English House of Lords upheld the conviction of an individual for "conspiracy to corrupt public morals" who agreed to publish a directory of prostitutes.[56] In ruling that a Utah conspiracy statute that punished conspiracies to commit acts injurious to the public morals was unconstitutional, the U.S. Supreme Court noted that the statute

> would seem to be a warrant for conviction for an agreement to do almost any act which a judge and jury might find . . . contrary to his or its notions of what was good for health, morals, trade, commerce, justice or order.[57]

Modern statutes generally limit the criminal objectives of conspiracy to agreements to commit crimes. Several jurisdictions, however, continue to enforce broadly drafted statutes. California Penal Code Sections 182–185(5) punish a conspiracy to commit "any act injurious to the public health, to public morals, or to pervert or obstruct justice, or the due administration of justice." The U.S. government's conspiracy statute broadly punishes persons conspiring either to "commit any offense against the United States, or to defraud the United States." A conspiracy to commit a felony under this statute is punishable by up to five years in prison in addition to a fine, while a conspiracy to commit a misdemeanor is subject to the maximum penalty for the target offense.[58]

Pinkerton v. United States established that all criminal acts undertaken in furtherance of a conspiracy or that are "reasonably foreseeable as the necessary or natural consequences of the conspiracy" are attributable to each member by virtue of his or her membership. In *Pinkerton*, Daniel Pinkerton was held liable for conspiring with his brother Walter to avoid federal taxes. Daniel was held criminally responsible for Walter's failure to pay taxes, despite the fact that Daniel was in prison at the time that Walter submitted his fraudulent tax return. The MPC rejects the *Pinkerton* rule, because each conspirator may be held liable for "thousands of crimes" of which he or she was "completely unaware" and did not "influence at all." Consider the often-cited example of a woman who refers individuals to a criminal abortionist who may find herself being held liable for unlawful abortions performed on women referred to the abortionist by a co-conspirator whom she has never met.[59]

You also should be aware of **Wharton's rule**. This provides that an agreement by two persons to commit a crime that requires the voluntary and cooperative action of two persons cannot constitute a conspiracy. The classic examples of consensual crimes that require the participation of two individuals and do not permit a charge of conspiracy under Wharton's rule are adultery, bigamy, the sale of contraband, bribery, and dueling. These offenses already punish a cooperative agreement between two individuals to commit a crime, and there is no reason to further punish individuals for entering into a conspiratorial agreement. Wharton's rule does not prevent a conspiracy involving more than the required number of individuals. Three individuals, for example, may conspire for two of them to engage in bribery. Two individuals may also conspire for other individuals to pay and receive bribes.[60]

Another principle is the *Gebardi* **rule**. This provides that an individual who is in a class of persons who are excluded from criminal liability under a statute may not be charged with a conspiracy to violate the same law. In *Gebardi v. United States*, the U.S. Supreme Court reversed the conspiracy conviction of a man and woman for violation of the Mann Act. This statute prohibited and punished the transportation of a woman from one state to another for immoral purposes. The Court reasoned that the statute was intended to protect women from sexual exploitation and was defined so as to punish solely the individual transporting the women. The Court therefore reasoned that the two defendants could not enter into a criminal conspiracy and reversed their conviction.[61]

Conspiracy Prosecutions

Judge Learned Hand called conspiracy the "darling of the modern prosecutor's nursery."[62] Judge Hand was referring to the fact that conspiracy constitutes a powerful and potential tool for prosecuting and punishing defendants.[63]

- Conspiracies are not typically based on explicit agreements and may be established by demonstrating a commitment to a common goal by individuals sharing a criminal objective.

- Defendants may be prosecuted for both conspiracy and the commission of the crime that was the object of the conspiracy.
- A prosecution may be brought in any jurisdiction in which the defendants entered into a conspiratorial agreement or committed an overt act.
- The defendants all may be joined in a single trial, creating the potential for "guilt by association."
- All conspirators are held responsible for the criminal acts and statements of any co-conspirator in furtherance of the conspiracy. An individual may be held liable who is not present or even aware of a co-conspirator's actions.
- Individuals may abandon the conspiracy and escape liability for future offenses only if this abandonment is communicated to the other conspirators. Some statutes require that individuals persuade the other conspirators to abandon the conspiracy.

The federal law of conspiracy was further expanded in 1970 when Congress passed the Racketeer Influenced and Corrupt Organizations Act (RICO). This law is intended to provide prosecutors with a powerful and potent weapon against organized crime. The RICO law essentially eliminates the need to prove that individuals are part of a single conspiracy and, instead, holds defendants responsible for all acts of racketeering undertaken as part of an "enterprise." Racketeering includes a range of state and federal offenses typically committed by organized crime including murder, kidnapping, gambling, arson, robbery, bribery, extortion, and dealing in narcotics or obscene material. Critics have voiced concern over the government's power to bring a counterfeiter to trial for murders committed by individuals involved in an unrelated component of a criminal enterprise.[64]

Read *United States v. Garcia* on the study site: study .sagepub.com/ lippmaness2e.

Model Penal Code

Section 5.03. Criminal Conspiracy

(1) . . . A person is guilty of conspiracy with another person or persons to commit a crime if with the purpose of promoting or facilitating its commission he:

(a) agrees with such other person or persons that they or one or more of them will engage in conduct that constitutes such crime or an attempt or solicitation to commit such crime; or

(b) agrees to aid such other person or persons in the planning or commission of such crime or of an attempt or solicitation to commit such crime. . . .

(2) . . . If a person guilty of conspiracy . . . knows that a person with whom he conspires to commit a crime has conspired with another person or persons to commit the same crime, he is guilty of conspiring with such other person or persons, whether or not he knows their identity, to commit such crime.

(3) . . . If a person conspires to commit a number of crimes, he is guilty of only one conspiracy so long as such multiple crimes are the object of the same agreement or continuous conspiratorial relationship.

(4) . . .

(a) . . . two or more persons charged with criminal conspiracy may be prosecuted jointly. . . .

(6) [Withdrawal is a defense where the individual] thwarted the success of the conspiracy, under circumstances manifesting a complete and voluntary renunciation of his criminal purpose.

(7) [A withdrawal occurs] only if and when he advises those with whom he conspired of his abandonment or he informs the law enforcement authorities of the existence of the conspiracy and of his participation therein.

Analysis

1. The MPC limits conspiracies to crimes and does not extend conspiracy to broad categories of immoral or corrupt behavior.

2. A defendant must possess the purpose of promoting or facilitating the commission of a crime. Knowledge does not satisfy the intent requirement of conspiracy (§5.04(1)).

3. The essence of a conspiracy is an agreement. This determination should be based on clear evidence (§5.04(1)(a)).

4. A unilateral approach to conspiratorial agreements is adopted (§5.04(1)(b)).

5. The MPC does not use the terminology of wheel or chain conspiracies. The code, instead, examines whether a specific individual has entered into a conspiratorial agreement and whether the individual is aware that the person with whom he or she has conspired has entered into agreements with other individuals. The end result would not differ from the wheel or chain analysis (§5.04(2)).

6. An overt act is required other than in the case of serious felonies.

7. The *Pinkerton* rule is rejected (§2.06); individuals are responsible only for crimes that they solicited, aided, agreed to aid, or attempted to aid.

8. Conspiracy is punished to the same extent as the most serious offense that is attempted or solicited or is an object of the conspiracy (§5.05(1)).

9. The code does not permit punishment of both a conspiracy and the substantive crime that is the object of the conspiracy (§1.07)(1)(b).

10. The *Gebardi* rule is incorporated into the MPC (§5.04(2)).

The Legal Equation

Conspiracy $=$ Agreement (or agreement and overt act in furtherance of agreement)

$+$ specific intent or purpose to commit a crime. (Some courts employ a knowledge standard.)

CRIMINAL LAW IN THE NEWS

In May 2015, a violent confrontation in Waco, Texas, between members of two competing outlaw motorcycle gangs (OMGs) left nine dead and eighteen injured and led to the arrest of 171 individuals charged with organized criminal activity. The arrests also led to the seizure of over one hundred firearms and highlighted the criminal activity of motorcycle gangs. Several hundred chains, brass knuckles, knives, and clubs also were seized by the police.

The U.S. Department of Justice (DOJ) describes OMGs as organizations whose membership "uses their motorcycle clubs as conduits for criminal enterprises." The clubs according to the federal government are involved in manufacturing, smuggling, and distributing unlawful narcotics and in kidnapping, extortion, insurance fraud, prostitution, gun smuggling, and arson. OMGs according to the DOJ collect $1 billion a year from their illicit activities.

The FBI's 2011 National Gang Threat Assessment estimated that there are forty-four thousand members of OMGs affiliated with roughly three thousand active gangs. These gang members amount to 2.5 percent of all gang members in the United States. The membership of the most influential gangs ranges from 250 to 900, and the gangs tend to be dominant in specific areas of the country.

The FBI and the Criminal Intelligence Service Canada have named four motorcycle clubs as "outlaw motorcycle gangs." The co-called "Big Four" gangs are the Hells Angels, the Pagans, the Outlaws, and the Bandidos. The California Attorney General also includes the Mongols and the Vagabonds as important

OMGs. Two other gangs, the Sons of Silence and the Cossacks, also are categorized by some law enforcement agencies as outlaw gangs. The OMGs are aligned in coalitions with one another and are in conflict with other gang coalitions over the control of criminal activity within various states and regions. One of the most infamous conflicts was the so-called "Quebec Biker War" in 2002 between Canadian biker gangs that resulted in over 150 murders, eighty-four bombings, and 130 instances of arson.

The federal government has engaged in several mass arrests of the members of OMGs. In 1985, Operation Roughrider resulted in the arrest of over 125 individuals, most of whom were members of the Hells Angels motorcycle club in eleven states. The raid resulted in the seizure of unlawful narcotics with a street value of roughly $2 million.

Biker gangs are decentralized and according to gang analysts are based on "amoral individualism" in which members are free to pursue their own criminal plans. As a result, law-abiding club members often claim that the motorcycle club with which they are affiliated does not sponsor illicit activity and may justifiably contend that their club is being unfairly labeled as a criminal organization. Motorcycle gang members who engage in criminal activity refer to themselves as "one percenters" based on a statement by the American Motorcycle Association that 99 percent of bikers follow the law.

In 2015, the Bureau of Alcohol, Tobacco, Firearms and Explosives in a report leaked to the press warned that "insatiable appetite for dominance [of OMGs] has led to shootings, assaults and malicious attacks across the globe. OMGs continue to maim and murder over territory." The report concluded that as "tensions [between OMGs] escalate, brazen shootings are occurring in broad daylight."

The shoot-out in Waco allegedly was precipitated by the Bandidos Motorcycle Club claim that they were entitled to determine whether the Cossacks and other Texas motorcycle clubs were free to wear jackets ("colors") decorated with patches on their back with a "bottom rocker" that read "Texas," indicating that Texas was the geographic home territory of the club. There had been several confrontations between members of the Bandidos and Cossacks dating back to November 2013.

The May 2015 confrontation between the Bandidos and Cossacks occurred at a regularly scheduled meeting of the Texas Confederation of Clubs and Independents, a statewide organization that advocates for the rights of motorcyclists. The Bandidos reportedly had decided to mount a display of dominant force that symbolically proclaimed that Waco was a Bandidos town in which the Cossacks were unwelcome. The Cossacks, although not a part of the Confederation, decided to attend the meeting to make it clear that the Cossacks were entitled to ride their motorcycles in Waco. A shoot-out erupted over a dispute about a parking spot and escalated into a large-scale confrontation. Individuals arrested initially were held at $1 million bail, which later was reduced to $25,000. Defense attorneys alleged that most of the gunfire and fatalities resulted from the police rather than bikers. As a prosecutor, would you charge members of OMGs with conspiracy or a violation of RICO?

CASE ANALYSIS

In *People v. Johnson,* an Illinois appellate court was asked to determine whether the defendant was guilty of attempted arson.

Was Johnson Guilty of Attempted Arson?

People v. Johnson, 429 N.E.2d 905 (Ill. App. 1981)

Lee W. Johnson was convicted of attempted aggravated arson and resisting a peace officer after a jury trial in Kankakee County. He was sentenced to 10 years on the "attempt" charge and one year on the "resisting an officer" charge. The defendant . . . contends on appeal that his attempt aggravated arson conviction should be reversed because the evidence did not establish that he took a substantial step toward the crime or that he had the necessary specific intent to commit aggravated arson.

The unusual events involved in this case began on November 29, 1980, in Kankakee. Sometime between 2:30 and 3:30 p.m. on that day, two Kankakee police officers were dispatched to a house. . . . The defendant

(Continued)

(Continued)

Lee Johnson had called the police for the purpose of having them help him recover a gun that was within the house. . . . When the officers . . . arrived, Johnson was standing in front of the house. He told them that he had lived in the house with his former girlfriend, Glenda Pankey, and that he had left a gun with her, which she was refusing to return. The officers, accompanied by Johnson, proceeded onto the front porch and Officer Born then knocked on the door. Pankey eventually answered, and let Born in the house. When inside, he noticed that there were another woman and several children present. While Born was inside, Johnson could be heard speaking loudly on the front porch to Officer Osenga. Johnson was upset, repeating that he wanted his gun and that it was in the house. Osenga at the time requested to see Johnson's owner "I.D." card, which he produced, along with a receipt for the gun. The officer then told Johnson that they could not search the house for the gun. The defendant responded, "If I don't get this gun back, I will burn this m-----f---ing house down."

Officer Born came out of the house several minutes later, telling Johnson that Pankey claimed not to have the gun, but also offered to bring it to the police station when she did. With this, Johnson became even more upset and again threatened to burn the house. Born went back into the house, only to return again with another of Pankey's denials. Johnson became further agitated and continued to spout his threats. . . . [A]fter the warning, Johnson left the house, and he walked . . . to his own residence, about a half a block away. The two police officers, meanwhile, pulled into a lot, a block away . . . Within minutes, they observed Johnson . . . carrying a gasoline can. He walked to the . . . service station . . . put some gas in the can, paid for it and then headed back down Rosewood [to] Pankey's house. Osenga saw Johnson take two or three steps on the south side of the house while pouring gasoline. Johnson was about a foot away from the house, which had a 1 1/2- to 2-foot concrete foundation, and Osenga could not tell if the gas was hitting the ground or the house. The ground was snow-covered grass and earth. It was a cold and damp day.

When Johnson noticed Officer Osenga, he stopped pouring the gasoline and started to walk away from the house, still carrying the can. . . . Osenga, after subduing Johnson with the help of another officer who arrived at the scene, then retrieved the gas can, which was half full. The other officer then went to Glenda Pankey's residence, where he was given the defendant's rifle by a woman there. Pankey informed the officer at that time that the gun had been there, as Johnson had indicated, since the previous night. At the police station, a search of Johnson revealed that he had no matches, no lighter, and nothing else which could serve as an ignition source.

In the instant case, we find that the evidence is sufficient to establish that the defendant had performed acts which brought him in dangerous proximity to success in committing aggravated arson. He had threatened to burn the house down. He had purchased gasoline, carried it to the house and began pouring it beside the foundation of the wood frame structure. He ceased his activities only when the police officer drove up in front of the house. The only remaining step to be taken to complete the arson was the igniting of the gasoline. It is not necessary to prove that the defendant took the last step immediately preceding that which would render the substantive crime complete. Under the circumstances, we find that the evidence was sufficient for the jury to conclude that the defendant had taken a substantial step toward committing aggravated arson. Each case must be decided on its own facts. That he was later found to be without an ignition source does not alter our conclusion. The record does not indicate, nor will we presume, that Johnson knew that he was without an ignition source. It is as consistent with the evidence to conclude that he mistakenly believed that he did have an ignition source. We would note that it is no defense to an attempt charge that because of a misapprehension of circumstances it would have been impossible for him to commit the substantive offense.

As for a criminal intent, there is no indication that he knew he was without matches or a lighter and the evidence is as consistent with a mistaken belief conclusion. However, despite the evidence indicating intent, there is other evidence supporting a conclusion that he did not have the intent. It was he who called the police to the dispute in the first place. While he made threats to burn the house, he did so in the presence of the officers and in a loud enough voice so that Pankey would hear him. Though it was mid-afternoon, he marched openly to his house, from there proceeding to the gas station, while the squad cars waited in the lot across the street from the service station. He then marched openly to Pankey's house and poured an amount of gasoline on the ground next to the house. The house, a wooden frame structure, had a concrete foundation. The ground was wet, covered with melting snow. Additionally, there was the fact that no ignition source was found on the defendant's person. Certainly, this evidence was consistent with the defense version of the incident, that the defendant's only intent was to frighten Pankey into returning his gun. It is consistent with the defense position that the defendant had no intent to start the fire that afternoon. Essentially, the record in this case presents a close factual question on the question of the defendant's intent. The evidence could support a jury's conclusion either way on that issue. While we may not have reached the same result, the jury's conclusion that the defendant possessed the requisite intent is supported in the evidence. The evidence, however close, was sufficient to uphold the jury's verdicts.

CHAPTER SUMMARY

Attempt, solicitation, and conspiracy are inchoate crimes or offenses that punish the beginning steps toward a crime. All require a *mens rea* involving a specific intent or purpose to achieve a crime as well as an *actus reus* that entails an affirmative act toward the commission of a crime. Each of these offenses is subject to the same or a lesser penalty than the crime that is the criminal objective.

An attempt involves three elements:

1. an intent or purpose to commit the crime,
2. an act toward the commission of the crime, and
3. a failure to commit the crime.

A complete (but imperfect) attempt occurs when a defendant takes every act required to complete the offense and fails to succeed in committing the crime. An incomplete attempt arises when an individual abandons or is prevented from completing an attempt.

An individual must possess the intent to achieve a criminal objective. The Model Penal Code adopts a substantial step test. This requires that an act must strongly support an individual's criminal purpose. The approach of the MPC extends attempt to acts that might be considered mere preparation under the objective approach. Among the acts that constitute an attempt under the substantial step test and that are considered "strongly corroborative of an actor's criminal purpose" are

- lying in wait,
- enticing of a victim to go to the place contemplated for the commission of a crime,
- surveying a site contemplated for the commission of a crime,
- unlawful entry of a structure or vehicle in which a crime is contemplated,
- possession of materials to be employed in the commission of a crime, and
- soliciting an individual to engage in conduct constituting an element of a crime.

A factual impossibility does not constitute a defense to an attempt to commit a crime. This is based on the reasoning that the offender has demonstrated a dangerous criminal intent and a determination to commit an offense. The factual circumstance that prevents an individual from actually completing the offense is referred to in some state statutes as an extraneous factor. This should be distinguished from a legal impossibility that is recognized as a defense.

Legal impossibility arises in those instances in which an individual wrongly believes that he or she is violating the law. Inherent impossibility arises where an individual undertakes an act that could not possibly result in a crime.

An individual may avoid criminal liability by abandoning a criminal attempt under circumstances manifesting a complete and voluntary renunciation of a criminal purpose. Individuals abandoning a criminal purpose based on the intervention of outside or extraneous factors remain criminally liable.

Solicitation involves a written or spoken statement in which an individual intentionally advises, requests, counsels, commands, hires, encourages, or incites another person to commit a crime with the purpose that the other individual commit the crime. A solicitation is complete the moment the statement requesting another to commit a crime is made. The solicitation need not be actually communicated.

Conspiracy comprises an agreement between two or more persons to commit a criminal act. Most modern state statutes require an affirmative act in furtherance of this criminal purpose. The common law crime of conspiracy did not merge into the completed criminal act. Today an individual also may be convicted both of the substantive offense that is the object of the conspiracy and of the conspiracy itself.

The centerpiece of a charge of conspiracy is an agreement. There is rarely proof of a formal agreement, and an agreement typically must be established by examining the relationship, conduct, and circumstances of the parties. The overt act requirement is satisfied by even an insignificant act in furtherance of a conspiracy. The *mens rea* of conspiracy is the intent or purpose that the object of the agreement is accomplished.

The conspirators are liable for all criminal actions taken in furtherance of a conspiracy. Most complex conspiracies can be categorized as either a wheel conspiracy or a chain conspiracy. A chain conspiracy entails communication and cooperation by individuals linked together in a vertical relationship to achieve a criminal objective. A wheel conspiracy involves a single person or group that serves as a hub that provides a common core connecting various independent individuals or spokes.

A conspiracy charge provides prosecutors with various advantages, such as joining the conspirators in a single trial and bringing the charges in any jurisdiction in which an agreement or act in furtherance of the conspiracy is committed.

CHAPTER REVIEW QUESTIONS

1. What are the *mens rea* and *actus reus* of inchoate crimes?

2. Distinguish the three categories of inchoate crimes.

3. Provide an example of each crime.

4. Compare the subjective and objective approaches to criminal attempts.

5. How does the Model Penal Code substantial step test differ from the test of physical proximity to attempts? What types of acts satisfy the substantial step test?

6. Discuss and distinguish between legal and factual impossibility.

7. Why is there a defense of abandonment for attempts? What are the legal elements of this defense?

8. What are the reasons for punishing conspiracy?

9. Discuss the *mens rea* and *actus reus* of conspiracy.

10. Why do some states require an overt act for a conspiracy?

11. Is there a difference between the bilateral and unilateral approaches to a conspiratorial agreement?

12. Distinguish between the wheel and chain approaches to conspiracy. Explain why defendants may argue that there are multiple conspiracies rather than a single conspiracy.

13. How does a charge of conspiracy assist a prosecutor in convicting a defendant?

14. Why did Congress adopt the RICO statute?

15. What are the *mens rea* and *actus reus* of solicitation?

16. At what point is the crime of solicitation complete? Is a solicitation required to reach the individual to whom it is directed?

17. How does society benefit by punishing inchoate crimes? Would society suffer in the event that these offenses did not exist?

LEGAL TERMINOLOGY

abandonment

attempt

bilateral

chain conspiracy

complete attempt

conspiracy

criminal attempt

extraneous factor

factual impossibility

Gebardi rule

inchoate crimes

incomplete attempt

inherent impossibility

legal impossibility

overt act

physical proximity test

Pinkerton doctrine

plurality requirement

preparation

solicitation

substantial step test

unilateral

Wharton's rule

wheel conspiracy

CRIMINAL LAW ON THE WEB

Visit **study.sagepub.com/lippmaness2e** to access additional study tools including suggested answers to the You Decide questions, reprints of cases and statutes, online appendices, and more!

CRIMINAL DEFENSES

Justifications and Excuses

Will Belton be successful in relying on the necessity defense?

Calloway soon turned his aggression toward Belton and began directing insults at her. When Belton indicated that she might leave Calloway if he did not calm down, Calloway threatened to "whoop [Belton's] a[–]." Calloway repeated his threat to assault Belton numerous times. Belton feared that Calloway would follow through on his threat to assault her because he had previously done so on at least two separate occasions. Belton feared "that it would be worse" on "that particular night" because Calloway "was on drugs." Based on Calloway's demeanor, Belton "knew" that Calloway would assault her that night if she stayed.

Calloway . . . exited the vehicle without explanation and went back inside the home. Fearing for her safety, Belton took advantage of the opportunity by sliding over and into the driver's seat and driving away. Belton, who was "in a neighborhood [she] didn't know nothing about[,]" decided to drive in the direction of 16th Street and Bellefontaine Street, where some of her family resided.

After Belton had been driving for approximately seven or eight blocks, or approximately one-half of a mile, Indianapolis Metropolitan Police Officer Jason Ross initiated a traffic stop of the vehicle driven by Belton because it appeared that the vehicle's registration was expired. During the traffic stop, Belton admitted that her driver's license was suspended and stated that she only drove because of her need to remove herself from the situation involving Calloway. (*Belton v. State*, 6 N.E.3d 1043 [Ind. App. 2014])

In this chapter, learn about the necessity defense.

Learning Objectives

1. Understand the presumption of innocence.

2. Appreciate the distinction between justifications and excuses.

3. Know the tests for the insanity defense and the significance of "guilty but mentally ill" and of "diminished capacity."

4. Know the relationship between age and the capacity to form a criminal intent and the factors that a court will consider in determining whether a juvenile is capable of forming a criminal intent.

5. List and explain the elements of self-defense.

6. State the two tests for the defense of others.

7. Know the law on defense of the home and the significance of the "Castle Doctrine."

8. Understand the legal test for police use of deadly force.

9. Appreciate the distinction between the American and European rules for resistance to an unlawful arrest.

10. Understand the elements of the necessity defense.

11. Know the three situations in which the law recognizes consent as a defense to criminal conduct.

12. Understand the "new defenses" and the arguments for recognizing "new defenses."

INTRODUCTION

The Prosecutor's Burden

The American legal system is based on the **presumption of innocence**. A defendant may not be compelled to testify against himself or herself, and the prosecution is required as a matter of the due process of law to establish every element of a crime beyond a reasonable doubt to prove a defendant's guilt. This heavy prosecutorial burden also reflects the fact that a criminal conviction carries severe consequences and individuals should not be lightly deprived of their liberty. Insisting on a high standard of guilt assures the public that innocents are not being falsely convicted and that individuals need not fear that they will suddenly be snatched off the streets and falsely convicted and incarcerated.[1]

The prosecutor presents his or her witnesses in the **case-in-chief**. These witnesses are then subject to cross-examination by the defense attorney. The defense also has the right to introduce evidence challenging the prosecution's case during the **rebuttal** stage at trial. A defendant, for instance, may raise doubts about whether the prosecution has established that the defendant committed the crime beyond a reasonable doubt by presenting alibi witnesses.

A defendant is to be acquitted if the prosecution fails to establish each element of the offense beyond a reasonable doubt. Judges have been reluctant to reduce the beyond a reasonable doubt standard to a mathematical formula and stress that a "high level of probability" is required and that jurors must reach a "state of near certitude" of guilt.[2]

The classic definition of reasonable doubt provides that the evidence "leaves the minds of jurors in that condition that they cannot say they feel an abiding conviction, to a moral certainty of the truth of the charge."[3]

A defendant may present an **alibi** and claim that he or she did not commit the crime because the defendant was somewhere else at the time the crime was committed. A defense attorney is required to notify the prosecutor that the defendant will rely on the defense and provide the names of the witnesses that will testify. The Supreme Court has held that fairness dictates that the prosecutor disclose the witnesses that he or she plans to present to rebut the defendant's alibi defense.[4]

A defendant is entitled to file a motion for judgment of acquittal at the close of the prosecution's case or prior to the submission of the case to the jury. This motion will be granted if the judge determines that the evidence does not support any verdict other than acquittal, viewing the evidence as favorably as possible for the prosecution. The judge, in the alternative, may adhere to the standard procedure of submitting the case to the jury following the close of the evidence and instructing the jurors to acquit if they have a reasonable doubt concerning one or more elements of the offense.[5]

Affirmative Defenses

In addition to attempting to demonstrate that the prosecution's case suffers from a failure of proof beyond a reasonable doubt, defendants may present **affirmative defenses**, or defenses in which the defendant typically possesses the **burden of production** as well as the **burden of persuasion**.

Justifications and **excuses** are both affirmative defenses. The defendant possesses the burden of producing "some evidence in support of his defense." In most cases, the defendant then also has the burden of persuasion by a preponderance of the evidence, which is a balance of probabilities, or slightly more than 50 percent. In some jurisdictions, the prosecution retains the burden of persuasion and is responsible for negating the defense by a reasonable doubt.[6]

Assigning the burden of production to the defendant is based on the fact that the prosecution cannot be expected to anticipate and rebut every possible defense that might be raised by a defendant. The burden of rebutting every conceivable defense ranging from insanity and intoxication to self-defense would be overwhelmingly time-consuming and inefficient. Thus, it makes sense to assign responsibility for raising a defense to the defendant. The U.S. Supreme Court has issued a series of rather technical judgments on the allocation of the burden of persuasion. In the last analysis, states are fairly free to place the burden of persuasion on either the defense or the prosecution. As noted, in most instances, the prosecution has the burden of persuading the jury beyond a reasonable doubt to reject the defense.

There are two types of affirmative defenses that may result in acquittal:

1. *Justifications.* These are defenses to otherwise criminal acts that society approves and encourages under the circumstances. An example is self-defense.

2. *Excuses.* These are defenses to acts that deserve condemnation, but for which the defendant is not held criminally liable because of a personal disability such as infancy or insanity.

Professors Singer and La Fond illustrate the difference between these concepts by noting that justification involves illegally parking in front of a hospital in an effort to rush a sick infant into the emergency room, and an excuse entails illegally parking in response to the delusional demand of "Martian invaders."[7] In the words of Professor George Fletcher, "Justification speaks to the rightness of the act; an excuse, to whether the actor is [mentally] accountable for a concededly wrongful act."[8]

In the common law, there were important consequences resulting from a successful plea of justification or excuse. A justification resulted in an acquittal, whereas an excuse provided a defendant with the opportunity to request that the king exempt him or her from the death penalty. Eventually there came to be little practical difference between being acquitted by reason of a justification or an excuse.[9]

Scholars continue to point to differences between categorizing an act as justified as opposed to excused, but these have little practical significance for most defendants.

JUSTIFICATIONS AND EXCUSES

Defenses categorized as justifications typically include necessity, consent, self-defense, defense of others, defense of habitation and property, execution of public duties, and resisting unlawful arrest. There are various theories for the defense of justification, none of which fully account for each and every justification defense.[10]

Moral Interest. An individual's act is justified based on the protection of an important moral interest. An example is self-defense and the preservation of an individual's right to life.

Superior Interest. The interests being preserved outweigh the interests of the person who is harmed. The necessity defense authorizes an individual to break the law to preserve a more compelling value. An example might be the captain of a ship in a storm who throws luggage overboard to lighten the load and preserve the lives of those on board.

Public Benefit. An individual's act is justified on the grounds that it is undertaken in service of the public good. This includes a law enforcement officer's use of physical force against a fleeing felon.

Moral Forfeiture. An individual perpetrating a crime has lost the right to claim legal protection. This explains why a dangerous aggressor may justifiably be killed in self-defense.

A defendant who establishes a perfect defense is able to satisfy each and every element of a justification defense and is acquitted. An imperfect defense arises in those instances in which the requirements of the defense are not fully satisfied. For instance, a defendant may use excessive force in self-defense or possess a genuine, but unreasonable, belief in the need to act in self-defense. A defendant's liability in these cases is typically reduced, for example, in the case of a homicide to manslaughter and to a lower level of guilt in the case of other offenses.[11]

Excuses, in contrast, provide a defense based on the fact that although a defendant committed a criminal act, he or she is not considered responsible. The defendant claims that although "I broke the law and my act was wrong, I am not responsible. I am not morally blameworthy." This is illustrated by legal insanity that excuses criminal liability based on a mental disease or defect. Individuals are also excused due to youth or intoxication or in those instances when they lack a criminal intent as a result of a mental disease or defect. Defendants are further excused in those instances when they commit a criminal act in response to a threat of imminent harm or a mistake of fact or are manipulated and entrapped into criminal conduct.

Excuses are very different from one another, and each requires separate study. The common denominator of excuses is that the defendants are not morally blameworthy and therefore are excused from criminal liability. The defenses categorized as excuses typically include the insanity, intoxication, age, duress, mistake of law, mistake of fact, and entrapment.

The difference between justifications and excuses no longer has a great deal of importance. In this chapter, defenses are divided into five categories.

1. *Lack of Capacity.* Individuals claim a lack of mental capacity to commit a crime (insanity, intoxication, age).

2. *Justification and Excuse Defenses.* Individuals contend that under the circumstances, their criminal act was justified or excused (necessity, duress, consent, mistake of law, mistake of fact).

3. *Defenses Justifying the Use of Force.* Individuals confronting a threat to their person or property who claim a right to resort to armed force (self-defense, defense of others, defense of habitation and of property, resisting an arrest).

4. *Governmental Misconduct.* Individuals claiming a defense based on governmental misconduct (entrapment, selective prosecution).

5. *New Defenses.* Defendants have attempted to persuade judges to accept previously unrecognized defenses based on biology, psychology, and culture.

DEFENSES BASED ON A LACK OF CAPACITY TO COMMIT A CRIME

A defendant invoking a defense based on a lack of capacity to commit a crime concedes that he or she committed the required *actus reus*. The defendant, however, claims an inability to form the *mens rea* for the crime. The three primary defenses based on a lack of capacity to commit a crime are insanity, inebriation, and infancy.

The Insanity Defense

English common law initially did not consider a mental disturbance or insanity as relevant to an individual's guilt. In the thirteenth century, it was recognized that a murderer of "unsound mind" was deserving of a royal pardon, and as the century drew to a close, "madness" was recognized as a complete defense.[12] This more humanistic approach reflected the regrettable "wild beast" theory that portrayed "madmen" as barely removed from "the brutes who are without reason."[13]

The **insanity defense** is one of the most thoroughly studied and hotly debated issues in criminal law. The debate is not easy to follow because the law's reliance on concepts drawn from mental health makes this a difficult area to understand. Texas residents must have scratched their heads in 2004 when Deanna Laney was acquitted by reason of insanity for crushing the skulls of her three sons with heavy stones. She then proceeded to call the police and informed them that "I just killed my boys." The youngest at the time was a fourteen-month-old who was left brain injured and nearly blind. Two years earlier, another Texas mother, Andrea Yates, received a life sentence for drowning her five children in the bathtub. Yates told the police that the devil had told her to kill her children; and despite Yates's history of mental problems and claim of insanity, the jury found that she was able to distinguish right from wrong. Yates's conviction was overturned on appeal, and in July 2006, a Texas jury ruled Yates not guilty by reason of insanity (NGRI). Laney reportedly believed that she and Yates had been selected by God to be witnesses to the end of the world.

In 2015, military veteran Eddie Ray Routh was convicted of the murder of famed Navy SEAL Chris Kyle and Kyle's friend Chad Littlefield. The jury rejected Routh's insanity defense because they determined that he knew the difference between right and wrong at the time of the murder.

The prosecution expert witnesses testified that Routh was an alcohol and drug abuser who feigned post-traumatic stress disorder (PTSD) whenever he got in trouble with the law. He was sufficiently coherent to stop at a fast-food restaurant following the killings.

Defendants who rely on the insanity defense are typically required to provide notice to the prosecution. They are then subject to examination by a state-appointed mental health expert, and they will usually hire one or more of their own "defense experts." These experts will interview the defendant and conduct various psychological tests. The prosecution and defense experts will then testify at trial, and additional testimony is typically offered on behalf of the defendant by people who are able to attest to his or her mental disturbance. The nature of a defendant's criminal conduct is also important. The prosecutor may argue that a well-planned crime is inconsistent with a claim of insanity. The jury is then asked to return a verdict of either guilty, not guilty, or NGRI. In some jurisdictions, the jury considers the issue of insanity in a separate hearing in the event that the defendant is found guilty.

A defendant found NGRI in some states is subject to immediate committal to a mental institution until he or she is determined to be sane and no longer poses a threat to society. In most states, a separate **civil commitment** hearing is conducted to determine whether the defendant poses a danger and should be interned in a mental institution. Keep in mind that this period of institutionalization may last longer than a criminal sentence for the crime for which the defendant was convicted.

Why do we have an insanity defense? Experts cite three reasons:

1. *Free Will.* The defendant did not make a deliberate decision to violate the law. His or her criminal act resulted from a disability.

2. *Theories of Punishment.* A defendant who is unable to distinguish right from wrong or to control his or her conduct cannot be deterred by criminal punishment, and it would be cruel to seek retribution for acts that result from a disability.

3. *Humanitarianism.* An individual found NGRI may pose a continuing danger to society. He or she is best incapacitated and treated by doctors in a noncriminal rather than criminal environment.

In the United States, courts and legislators have struggled with balancing the protection of society against the humane treatment of individuals determined to be NGRI. There have been several tests for insanity:

- *M'Naghten* (twenty-eight states and the federal government recognize all or a part of this test)
- Irresistible impulse (seventeen states recognize this test in conjunction with another test)
- *Durham* product test (New Hampshire)
- American Law Institute, Model Penal Code (MPC) standard (fourteen states)

The fundamental difference among these tests is whether the emphasis is placed on a defendant's ability to know right from wrong or whether the stress is placed on a defendant's ability to control his or her behavior. You might gain some sense of what is considered an inability to tell right from wrong by considering a young child who has not been taught right from wrong and takes an object from a store without realizing that this is improper. As an example of an inability to control behavior, think about a motorist who suddenly erupts in "road rage" and violently threatens you for driving too slowly.

Keep in mind that an individual who is "mentally challenged" may not necessarily meet the legal standard for insanity. A serial killer, for instance, may be mentally disturbed but still not considered to be so impaired by a mental illness or so retarded as to be considered legally insane. The question is whether the individual was legally insane at the time that he or she committed the crime. Juries generally find the determination of insanity to be highly complicated, and they experience difficulty in following the often technical testimony of experts. As a result, jurors often follow their own judgment in determining whether a defendant should be determined to be NGRI.

You also should be aware that insanity is distinct from **competence to stand trial**. Due process of law requires that defendants should not be subjected to a criminal trial unless they possess the ability to intelligently assist their attorney and to understand and follow the trial. The prosecution of an individual who is found incompetent is suspended until he or she is found competent.

The Right–Wrong Test

Daniel M'Naghten was an ordinary English citizen who was convinced that British Prime Minister Sir Robert Peel was conspiring to kill him. In 1843, M'Naghten retaliated by attempting to assassinate the British leader and, instead, mistakenly killed Sir Robert's private secretary. The jury acquitted M'Naghten after finding that he "had not the use of his understanding, so as to know he was doing a wrong or wicked act." This verdict sent shock waves of fright through the British royal family and political establishment, and the judges were summoned to defend the verdict before the Parliament. The judges articulated a test that continues to be followed by a majority of American states and by the federal government. The **M'Naghten test** requires that at the time of committing the act, the party accused must have been suffering from such a defect of reason or a disease of the mind that he or she "did not know what he [or she] was doing" (did not know the "nature and quality of his or her act"); or the defendant "did not know he [or she] was doing wrong."[14]

The requirement that the defendant did not know the *"nature and quality of his or her act"* is extremely difficult to satisfy. The common example is that an individual squeezing the victim's neck must be so detached from reality that he or she believes that he or she is squeezing a lemon. Individuals suffering this level of mental disturbance are extremely rare, and the *M'Naghten* test assumes that these individuals should be detained and receive treatment and that criminal incarceration serves no meaningful purpose and is inhumane.[15]

There also is an ongoing debate whether a defendant must know that an act is a "legal wrong" or whether the defendant must know that the act is a "moral wrong." *State v. Crenshaw* attempted to resolve this conflict.[16] The defendant Rodney Crenshaw was honeymooning with his wife in Canada and suspected that she was unfaithful. Crenshaw beat his wife senseless, stabbed her twenty-four times, and then decapitated the body with an axe. He then drove to a remote area and disposed of his wife's body and cleaned the hotel room. Crenshaw claimed to be a member of the Moscovite faith, a religion that required a man to kill a wife guilty of adultery. He claimed he believed that his act, although illegal, was morally justified. Was Crenshaw insane based on his belief that his act was morally justified? Did he possess the capacity to distinguish between right and wrong?

Crenshaw was convicted and appealed on the grounds that the judge improperly instructed the jury that insanity required a finding that as a result of a mental defect or disease, Crenshaw believed that his act was lawful rather than moral. The Washington Supreme Court, however, concluded that under either a legal or moral wrongfulness test, Crenshaw was legally sane. The court noted that Crenshaw's effort to conceal the crime indicated that he was aware that killing his wife was contrary to society's morals as well as the law. The Washington Supreme Court ruled that in the future, courts should not define "wrongfulness," and that jurors should be left free to apply either a societal morality or legal wrongfulness approach.

It's likely you are fairly confused at this point. The right–wrong test is clearly much too difficult to be easily applied by even the most educated and sophisticated juror. In the end, juries tend to follow their commonsense notion of whether the defendant was legally sane or insane.

The Legal Equation		
M'Naghten right–wrong test	=	Defect of reason from a disease of the mind
	+	at the time of the act did not know
	+	the nature and quality of the act or that the act was wrong.

The Irresistible Impulse Test

The *M'Naghten* test is criticized for focusing on the mind and failing to consider emotions. Critics point out that an individual may be capable of distinguishing between right and wrong and still may be driven by emotions to steal or to kill. Many of us are aware of the dangers of smoking, drinking, or eating too much and yet continue to indulge in this behavior. Various states responded to this criticism by broadening the *M'Naghten* standard and adopting the irresistible impulse test. This is often referred to as the "third branch of *M'Naghten*."[17]

The **irresistible impulse test** requires the jury to find a defendant NGRI in the event that the jurors find that the defendant possessed a mental disease that prevented him or her from curbing his or her criminal conduct. A defendant may be found legally insane under this test despite the fact that he or she is able to tell right from wrong. The central consideration is whether the disease overcame his or her capacity to resist the impulse to kill, rape, maim, or commit any other crime.[18]

John Hinckley's acquittal by reason of insanity for the attempted assassination of Ronald Reagan sparked a reconsideration and rejection of the irresistible impulse test. After all, why should Hinckley be ruled legally insane because he attempted to kill President Reagan to fulfill an uncontrollable impulse to attract the attention of Jodie Foster, a young female film star? There was also a recognition that psychiatrists simply were unable to determine whether an individual experienced an irresistible impulse.

As a result, several jurisdictions abolished the irresistible impulse defense.[19] The U.S. Congress adopted the so-called John Hinckley Amendment that eliminated the defense in federal trials and adopted a strict *M'Naghten* standard.

The Legal Equation

Irresistible impulse test $=$ Mental disease or mental defect (psychosis or physical defect)

$+$ inability to resist criminal activity (may have ability to distinguish right from wrong).

The Durham *Product Test*

The ***Durham* product test** was intended to simplify the determination of legal insanity by eliminating much of the confusing terminology. The "product" test was first formulated by the New Hampshire Supreme Court in *State v. Pike* in 1869.[20] This standard was not accepted or even considered by any other jurisdiction until it was adopted in 1954 by the U.S. Court of Appeals for the District of Columbia.[21]

Durham provided that an accused is "not criminally responsible if his unlawful act was the product of mental disease or mental defect." Jurors were asked to evaluate whether the accused was suffering from a disease or defective mental condition at the time he or she committed the criminal act and whether the criminal act was the product of such mental abnormality. However, the decision left the definition of a mental disease or defect undefined.

The Court of Appeals for the District of Columbia abandoned this experiment after eighteen years, in 1972, after realizing that the "product test" had resulted in expert witnesses playing an overly important role at trial in determining what qualified as a mental disease or defect.[22]

The Legal Equation

Durham product test $=$ Unlawful act

$+$ product of disease or defect.

The Substantial Capacity Test

Psychiatric experts urged the American Law Institute (ALI) to incorporate the *Durham* product test into the MPC. The ALI, instead, adopted a modified version of the *M'Naghten* and irresistible impulse tests, known as the **substantial capacity test**. Section 4.01(1)(2) provides:

A person is not responsible for criminal conduct if at the time of such conduct as a result of mental disease or defect he lacks substantial capacity either to appreciate the criminality [wrongfulness] of his conduct or to conform his conduct to the requirements of law. . . . The terms "mental disease or defect" do not include an abnormality manifested only by repeated criminal or otherwise antisocial conduct.

The ALI test modifies *M'Naghten* by providing that a defendant may lack a substantial capacity to appreciate rather than know the criminality of his or her conduct. This is intended to highlight that a defendant may be declared legally insane and still know that an act is wrong because he or she still may not appreciate the full harm and impact of his or her criminal conduct. In other words, a defendant may know that sexual molestation is wrong without appreciating the harm a sexual attack causes to the victim.

The ALI's more tolerant and broader view of legal insanity was adopted by a number of states and by the federal judiciary. The test later was abandoned by all but a handful of state and federal courts following Hinckley's successful reliance on the insanity defense in his attempted assassination of President Reagan in 1981. The trend is to follow the lead of the U.S. Congress and to adopt the standard articulated in the *Insanity Defense Reform Act of 1984*.

The Legal Equation		
Substantial capacity test	=	Mental disease or defect
	+	substantial incapacity
	+	to appreciate criminality (wrongfulness) of an act or to conform conduct to requirements of the law.

Federal Standard

The U.S. Congress in the **Insanity Defense Reform Act of 1984** returned to the *M'Naghten* standard and abandoned the volitional prong of the ALI test. The act states that in federal courts

[i]t is an affirmative defense to a prosecution under any federal statute that, at the time of the commission of the acts constituting the offense, the defendant, as a result of a severe mental disease or defect, was unable to appreciate the nature and quality or the wrongfulness of his acts. Mental disease or defect does not otherwise constitute a defense.[23]

In *United States v. Duran*, in 1996, the District of Columbia Court of Appeals applied this new standard in upholding a jury's rejection of the insanity defense of Francisco Martin Duran who had attempted to assassinate President Bill Clinton.[24]

Burden of Proof

The defendant possesses the initial burden of going forward in every state. The defendant is presumed sane until evidence is produced challenging this assumption. The defendant's burden varies and ranges from a "reasonable doubt" to "some evidence," "slight evidence," or a "scintilla of evidence."[25]

The prosecution at this point in a number of states is required to establish the defendant's sanity beyond a reasonable doubt. In roughly half of the states, however, the defendant possesses the burden of proving his or her insanity by the civil standard of a preponderance of the evidence. In the federal system and in a small number of states, the defendant has the burden of establishing insanity by "clear and convincing evidence." Clear and convincing evidence requires the defendant to establish that it is "substantially more likely than not that it is true." This is a higher standard than a preponderance of the evidence and a slightly less demanding standard than beyond a reasonable doubt, which is the test required for a criminal conviction. Although placing this burden of proof on the defendant is controversial, the federal courts have held that this is constitutional.[26]

The Future of the Insanity Defense

Defenders of the insanity defense point out that critics exaggerate the significance of the insanity defense for the criminal justice system and that only a small number of deserving defendants are evaluated as legally insane. Statistics indicate that the defense results in an acquittal by reason of insanity in less than 1 percent of all criminal trials per year. This translates into an average of thirty-three defendants. These individuals may also spend more time institutionalized in a mental institution than they would serve were they criminally convicted.

Idaho, Montana, Kansas, and Utah have abolished the insanity defense and, instead, permit defendants to introduce evidence of a mental disease or defect that resulted in a lack of criminal intent. Idaho, for example, provides that a "[m]ental condition shall not be a defense to any charge of criminal conduct." Evidence of state of mind is admissible in Idaho to negate criminal intent, and a judge who finds that a defendant convicted of a crime suffers from a mental condition requiring treatment shall incarcerate the defendant in a facility where he or she will receive treatment. State supreme courts have ruled that the insanity defense is not fundamental to the fairness of a trial and that the alternative of relying on evidence of a mental disease or defect to negate criminal intent is consistent with due process. Defendants under this alternative approach, however, continue to rely on experts and highly technical evidence.

Thirteen states have adopted a verdict of **guilty but mentally ill (GBMI)**. Eleven of these states continue to retain the insanity defense, and in these states jurors may select from among four verdicts: guilty, not guilty, NGRI, and GBMI. A verdict of GBMI applies where the jury determines beyond a reasonable doubt that a defendant was mentally ill, but not legally insane, at the time of his or her criminal act. The defendant receives the standard criminal sentence of confinement and is provided with psychiatric care while interned. The intent is to provide jurors with an alternative to the insanity defense that affords greater protection to the public.

The GBMI verdict has thus far not decreased findings of legal insanity. Nevertheless, advocates of the insanity defense remain fearful that jurors will find the GBMI verdict more attractive than verdicts of NGRI.

You Decide

6.1 Michael L. Moler was living with Neil Wright and Neil's mother Nina Wright. Both Neil and Nina knew that Moler suffered from schizophrenia, but both also observed that Moler functioned normally on medication. Nina's mother Ethel Cummins moved into the house six months before the tragic events described below. In the morning, Moler was dropped off at a mental health facility where he received an injection of antipsychotic medication. Moler, Neil, and Cummins spent the afternoon watching television. Neil and Nina left in the evening and upon returning home found the bloodied Cummins lying on the floor. Moler was standing at the sink and pro-claimed that "I did not mean to do it. She's a witch. She turned into a witch." Moler later told the police that Nina's hair had "stood straight up" and that Nina had turned into a witch and that he had "twisted her head around and killed her." Despite testimony from Neil and Nina that Moler appeared normal both before and after the injection and testimony by the police that Moler appeared normal following the killing, two mental health experts concluded that in their opinion at the time of the killing Moler was unable to appreciate the wrongfulness of his acts. Moler was found guilty but mentally ill and sentenced to fifty-five years in prison. Do you agree with the verdict? See *Moler v. State*, 782 N.E.2d 454 (Ind. Ct. App. 2003).

You can find the answer at study.sagepub.com/lippmaness2e

Diminished Capacity

Diminished capacity is recognized in roughly fifteen states. This permits the admission of psychiatric testimony to establish that a defendant suffers from a mental disturbance that *diminishes* the defendant's capacity to form the required criminal intent. The diminished capacity defense merely recognizes that an individual has the right to demonstrate that he or she was incapable of forming the intent required for the offense and should be held culpable for a lesser offense. This is a compromise between finding an individual either NGRI or criminally liable. Some states confine diminished capacity to intentional murder and provide that an accused may still be convicted of second-degree murder or in some cases manslaughter, which does not require premeditation. Keep in mind that this rarely is successfully invoked.[27]

The far-reaching implications of the diminished capacity defense became apparent when a San Francisco jury convicted city official Dan White of manslaughter for the killings of his colleague Harvey Milk and Mayor George Moscone. The defense argued that White's depressions were exaggerated by junk food, which caused biochemical reactions in his brain, diminishing his capacity to control his behavior and to form a specific intent to kill, and he was convicted of voluntary manslaughter rather than intentional murder. In reaction to this "Twinkie defense," California voters adopted a statute that provides that the "defense of diminished capacity is hereby abolished" and shall not be admissible "to show or negate capacity to form the . . . intent . . . required for the commission of the crime charged." Evidence of diminished capacity or a mental disorder may be considered in California at sentencing.[28]

CRIMINAL LAW IN THE NEWS

In July 2012, James Holmes, twenty-seven, entered an Aurora, Colorado, movie theater showing the film *The Dark Knight*. Holmes was equipped with protective gear and carried an AR-15, a shotgun, and two Glock pistols and opened fire on a crowd of midnight moviegoers, killing twelve and wounding seventy.

Holmes had recently dropped out of the neuroscience doctoral program at the University of Colorado because of a series of academic setbacks. He pled guilty by reason of insanity to 166 counts, including twelve charges of first-degree murder. Colorado places the burden of proof on the prosecution to prove the defendant does not "suffer from a mental disease or defect that rendered him incapable of distinguishing from right and wrong."

The prosecution alleged that Holmes had engaged in meticulous planning in carrying out the attack that was inconsistent with his claim of legal insanity. Holmes's planning included purchasing guns, ammunition, and military equipment; practicing at a firing range; and surveying the theater that was the scene of his attack.

The prosecution also pointed to Holmes's personal diary in which he outlined a detailed plan for a "mass murder spree" and reflected on the time of day in which the attack would achieve the "maximum casualties." At one point in the diary, Holmes rejected attacking an airport because there is too great a risk of being apprehended and his attack might be mistaken for terrorism. He instead settled on attacking the movie theater at midnight because fewer police would be in the area and decided to lock the exit doors to increase the number of casualties.

Holmes's consciousness of the difference between right and wrong according to the prosecution was illustrated by his question to the police after being apprehended whether "any children had been killed." Holmes also booby trapped his apartment in anticipation that the police would enter the unit following the attack and purchased the arms and material he used in the attack with a credit card that his parents were unable to access. On an AdultFriendFinder.com profile several days before the shooting, he wrote, "Will you visit me in prison?"

Holmes's consciousness of guilt also allegedly was illustrated by his belief that the FBI was following him and fear that he would be arrested before he was able to carry out his plan. He called a mental health hotline moments before the attack "to see if I should turn back or not" and hung up without talking to anyone because he did not hear someone on the other end of the line.

Defense attorneys, on the other hand, stressed that Holmes's notebook was full of a "whole lot of crazy" and that he analyzed himself as suffering from a "broken mind." They pointed to page after page in which the word *why* appears in bold letters across the page.

The jury watched a video of Dr. William Reid, a court-appointed psychiatrist, speaking to Holmes. Dr. Reid concluded that Holmes was fully capable of "forming the intent and knowing what he was doing and the consequences of what he was doing." Dr. Jeffrey Metzner, a second court-appointed therapist, interviewed Holmes for twenty-five hours and agreed that he was able to distinguish right from wrong.

In his videotaped interview with Dr. Reid, Holmes testified that during the attack on the theater he wore headphones and turned up the music to drown out the screams. He stated that he expected to be killed, but accepted this fate was the price of completion of what he termed "the mission." Holmes explained that the purpose of the killings was to increase his self-esteem and that the wounded and dead were "collateral damage." He stated that following the shootings he felt "calm and collected" and "successful in the mission."

Dr. Jonathan Woodcock interviewed Holmes four days following the attack and concluded that he was legally insane. Woodcock testified that Holmes had a family history of mental illness, that as a child he was frightened of "Nail Ghosts" that would hammer on the walls at night, and that he had attempted suicide at age eleven. Holmes according to Dr. Woodcock was in the grip of an uncontrollable psychotic compulsion to kill. According to Dr. Woodcock, Holmes transitioned from suicide to homicide following the end of his romantic relationship with a fellow graduate student.

The jury of nine women and three men found Holmes guilty on all 165 counts, although one juror refused to endorse capital punishment, and as a result, Holmes was sentenced to life imprisonment. Would you have voted to sentence Holmes to death?

Intoxication

Voluntary Intoxication

Voluntary intoxication was not recognized as a defense under the early common law in England. Lord Hale proclaimed that the intoxicated individual "shall have no privilege by this voluntary contracted madness, but shall have the same judgment as if he were in his right senses." William Blackstone went beyond this neutral stance and urged that intoxication should be viewed "as an aggravation of the offense, rather than as an excuse for any criminal behavior." The common law rule was incorporated into American law. An 1847 textbook recorded that this was a "long established maxim of judicial policy, from which perhaps a single dissenting voice cannot be found."[29]

The rule that intoxication was not a defense began to be transformed in the nineteenth century. Judges attempted to balance their disapproval toward alcoholism against the fact that inebriated individuals often lacked the mental capacity to formulate a criminal intent. Courts created a distinction between offenses involving a specific intent for which voluntary intoxication was an excuse and offenses involving a general intent for which voluntary intoxication was not recognized as an excuse. An individual charged with a crime requiring a specific intent was able to introduce evidence that the use of alcohol prevented him or her from forming a specific intent to assault an individual with the intent to kill. A defendant who proved successful would be held liable for the lesser offense of simple assault. As noted by the California Supreme Court, the difference between an intent to commit a battery and an intent to commit a battery for the purpose of raping or killing "may be slight, but it is sufficient to justify drawing a line between them and considering evidence of intoxication in the one case and disregarding it in the other."[30]

MPC Section 2.08(1)(2) accepts the common law's distinction between offenses based on intent and substitutes "knowledge" or "purpose" for a specific intent and "negligence or recklessness" for a general intent. The commentary to the code notes that it would be unfair to punish an individual who, due to inebriation, lacks "knowledge or purpose," even when this results from voluntary intoxication.[31]

Professor Jerome Hall observes that *in practice*, the hostility toward the inebriated defendant has resulted in the voluntary intoxication defense only being recognized in isolated instances, typically involving intentional killing.[32] Courts have placed a heavy burden on defendants seeking to negate a specific intent. Even the consumption of large amounts of alcohol is not sufficient. The New Jersey Supreme Court observed that there must be a showing of such a "great prostration of the faculties that the requisite mental state was totally lacking. . . . [A]n accused must show that he was so intoxicated that he did not have the intent to commit an offense. Such a state of affairs will likely exist in very few cases." This typically requires an evaluation of the quantity and period of time that an intoxicant was consumed, blood alcohol content, and the individual's conduct and ability to recall events.[33]

The contemporary trend is to return to the original common law rule and refuse to recognize a defense based on voluntary alcoholism. Twelve states do not recognize the alcoholism defense: Delaware, Florida, Georgia, Hawaii, Idaho, Indiana, Missouri, Montana, Ohio, Oklahoma, Pennsylvania, and Texas. The thinking is that the defendant voluntarily created a situation in which he or she was unable to form a specific criminal intent.

The Arizona Criminal Code, in Section 13-503 of the Arizona Revised Statutes Annotated, provides that "[t]emporary intoxication resulting from the voluntary ingestion . . . of alcohol . . . or other psychoactive substances or the abuse of prescribed medications . . . is not a defense for any criminal act or requisite state of mind." Texas Penal Code Annotated Section 8.04 provides that "[v]oluntary intoxication does not constitute a defense to the commission of crime." The right of states to deny defendants the intoxication defense was affirmed by the U.S. Supreme Court in 1996, in *Montana v. Egelhoff;* Justice Antonin Scalia noted that Montana was merely returning to the law at the time of the drafting of the U.S. Constitution and that this rule served to deter excessive drinking.[34]

Involuntary Intoxication

Involuntary intoxication is a defense to any and all criminal offenses in those instances that the defendant's state of mind satisfies the standard for the insanity defense in the state. MPC Section 2.08(4) requires that the individual "lacks substantial capacity" to distinguish right from wrong or to conform his or her behavior to the law. The code also recognizes "pathological intoxication." This arises in those instances when an individual voluntarily consumes a substance and experiences an extreme and unanticipated reaction. Involuntary intoxication from alcohol or narcotics can occur in any of four ways[35]:

1. *Duress.* An individual is coerced into consuming an intoxicant.
2. *Mistake.* An individual mistakenly consumes a narcotic rather than his or her prescribed medicine.
3. *Fraud.* An individual consumes a narcotic as a result of a fraudulent misrepresentation of the nature of the substance.
4. *Medication.* An individual has an extreme and unanticipated reaction to medication prescribed by a doctor.

A Wisconsin statute provides that an intoxicated or drugged condition is a defense only if it is "involuntarily produced and renders the actor incapable of distinguishing between right and wrong in regard to the alleged criminal act at the time the act is committed." Involuntary intoxication under Wisconsin law also may be used to negate a criminal intent other than recklessness.[36]

Age

In 2000, on the last day of the school year, thirteen-year-old Nathaniel Brazill shot and killed one of his favorite teachers at his middle school, Barry Grunow. Brazill was prosecuted as an adult and convicted of first-degree murder and sentenced to twenty-eight years in prison. "As Grunow attempted to close the classroom door, Brazill pulled the trigger and Grunow fell to the floor, with a gunshot wound between the eyes. A school surveillance videotape of the hallway revealed that Brazill had pointed the gun at Grunow for nine seconds before shooting. Brazill exclaimed: 'Oh s--t,' and fled."[37] In a second Florida case, Lionel Tate, age twelve, wrestled and killed his six-year-old friend. He was convicted of first-degree murder and was sentenced to life imprisonment without parole. His sentence was overturned on appeal; he pled guilty to second-degree murder and was released in 2004. One year later, Tate committed an armed robbery and was sentenced to a thirty-year prison term.[38] Should juveniles like Brazill and Tate be punished as adults?

The early common law did not recognize **infancy** as a defense to criminal prosecution. Youthful offenders, however, were typically pardoned. A tenth-century statute softened the failure to recognize infancy as a defense by providing that an individual younger than the age of fifteen was not subject to capital punishment unless he or she made an effort to elude authorities or refused to surrender. A further refinement occurred in the fourteenth century when children younger than seven were declared to be without criminal capacity.

The common law continued to develop and reached its final form by the seventeenth century. Juveniles were divided into three categories based on the capacity of adolescents at various ages to formulate a criminal intent. Individuals were categorized on the basis of their actual rather than their mental age at the time of the offense.[39]

- *Children younger than seven lack a criminal capacity.* There was an *irrebuttable presumption*, an assumption that cannot be overcome by facts, that children younger than seven lack the ability to formulate a criminal intent.

- *Children older than seven and younger than fourteen* were presumed to be without capacity to form a criminal intent. This was a *rebuttable presumption*; the prosecution could overcome the presumption by evidence that the juvenile knew what he or she was doing was wrong. The older the child and the more atrocious the crime, the easier to overcome the presumption. Factors to be considered include the age of the child, efforts to conceal the crime and to influence witnesses, and the seriousness of the crime.

- *Children fourteen and older* possessed the same criminal capacity as adults. Juveniles capable of forming a criminal intent may be prosecuted as adults rather than remain in the juvenile system. Today, the age when a juvenile may be criminally prosecuted as an adult rather than being brought before a juvenile court is determined by state statute. There is no standard approach. One group of states maintains a conclusive presumption of incapacity for juveniles younger than a particular age (usually fourteen); however, other states provide that juveniles regardless of age may be treated as adults. A third group of states provide that juveniles charged with serious offenses may be treated as adults.

The common law presumptions of incapacity are not applicable to proceedings in juvenile court because the purpose of the court is treatment and rehabilitation rather than the adjudication of moral responsibility and punishment.[40]

There is a growing trend for state statutes to permit the criminal prosecution of any juvenile as an adult who is charged with a serious offense. These "transfer statutes" adopt various schemes, vesting "waiver authority" in juvenile judges or prosecutors or providing for automatic transfer for specified crimes.[41] The standard to be applied by judges was articulated by the U.S. Supreme Court in *Kent v. United States.* The factors to be considered in the decision whether to prosecute a juvenile as an adult include the seriousness and violence of the offense, the background and maturity of the juvenile, and the ability of the juvenile justice system to protect the public and rehabilitate the offender.[42]

You Decide  **6.2** K.R.L., eight years, two months old, was playing with a friend behind a building. Catherine Alder heard the boys playing and directed them to leave because the area was dangerous. K.R.L. responded in an angry manner and replied that he would leave "in a minute." Alder, with obvious irritation, told the two boys, "No, not in a minute, now, get out of there now." The boys then ran off.

Three days later, K.R.L. entered Alder's home without her permission. He removed a goldfish from a fishbowl, chopped it into several pieces with a steak knife and "smeared it all over the counter." He then went into Alder's bathroom and "clamped a 'plugged in' hair curling iron onto a towel." K.R.L's mother testified that he admitted to her that entering Alder's home was wrong after she had beaten him "with a belt, black and blue."

He told her that the "Devil was making him do bad things."

K.R.L. subsequently was charged with residential burglary. Earlier, he had taken "Easter candy" from a neighbor's home without permission. K.R.L. admitted to the police that he "knew it was wrong and he wouldn't like it if somebody took his candy." The same officer testified that on an earlier occasion, K.R.L. had been caught riding the bicycles of two neighbor children without having their permission. K.R.L. told the police officer that he "knew it was wrong" to ride the bicycles.

The assistant principal of K.R.L.'s elementary school testified that K.R.L. was of "very normal" intelligence. K.R.L.'s first-grade teacher said that K.R.L. had "some difficulty" in school and that he would place K.R.L. in a "lower age academically."

In Washington State, children younger than eight are incapable of a criminal intent. Children between

(Continued)

(Continued)

eight and twelve years of age are presumed to be incapable of committing a crime. This presumption may be overcome by proof that they have "sufficient capacity to understand the act or neglect, and to know that it was wrong." The Washington Supreme Court was asked to decide whether the trial court was correct in concluding that there was clear and convincing evidence that K.R.L. had the capacity to commit residential burglary.

What is your opinion? See *State v. K.R.L.*, 840 P.2d 210 (Wash. Ct. App. 1992).

You can find the answer at study.sagepub.com/lippmaness2e

DEFENSES BASED ON JUSTIFICATION OR EXCUSE

As previously pointed out, justification defenses are based on the circumstances confronting an individual and may be invoked by any individual in similar circumstances. Excuse defenses generally are available to individuals who lack the capacity to form a criminal intent.

Necessity

The **necessity defense** recognizes that conduct that would otherwise be criminal is justified when undertaken to prevent a significant harm. This is commonly called the **"choice of evils"** because individuals are confronted with the unhappy choice between committing a crime and experiencing a harmful event. The harm to be prevented was traditionally required to result from the forces of nature. A classic example is the boat captain caught in a storm who disregards a "no trespassing" sign and docks his or her boat on an unoccupied pier. Necessity is based on the assumption that had the legislature been confronted with this choice, the legislators presumably would have safeguarded the human life of sailors over the property interest of the owner of the dock. As a result, elected officials could not have intended that the trespass statute would be applied against a boat captain in this situation.[43]

The limitation of necessity to actions undertaken in response to the forces of nature has been gradually modified, and most modern cases arise in response to pressures exerted by medical emergencies and other situations in which individuals must act immediately to avert harm. *State v. Salin* is representative of this trend. Salin, an emergency medical services technician, was arrested for speeding while responding to a call to assist a two-year-old child who was not breathing. The Delaware court agreed that Salin reasonably assumed that the child was in imminent danger and did not have time to use his cell phone to check on the child's progress. His criminal conviction was reversed on the grounds of necessity. Judge Charles Welch concluded that Salin was confronted by a choice of evils and that his "slightly harmful conduct" was justified in order to "prevent a greater harm."[44]

Roughly half of the states possess necessity statutes, and the other jurisdictions rely on the common law defense of necessity. There is agreement on the central elements of the defense.[45]

Model Penal Code

Section 3.02. Justification Generally: Choice of Evils

(1) Conduct that the actor believes to be necessary to avoid a harm or evil to himself or to another is justifiable, provided that:

(a) the harm or evil sought to be avoided by such conduct is greater than that sought to be prevented by the law defining the offense charged; and

(b) neither the Code nor other law defining the offense provides exceptions or defenses dealing with the specific situation involved; and

(c) a legislative purpose to exclude the justification claimed does not otherwise plainly appear.

(2) When the actor was reckless or negligent in bringing about the situation requiring a choice of harms or evil or in appraising the necessity for his conduct, the justification afforded by this Section is unavailable in a prosecution for any offense for which recklessness or negligence, as the case may be, suffices to establish culpability.

Analysis

The commentary to the MPC observes that the letter of the law must be limited in certain circumstances by considerations of justice. The commentary lists some specific examples:

1. Property may be destroyed to prevent the spread of a fire.

2. The speed limit may be exceeded in pursuing a suspected criminal.

3. Mountain climbers lost in a storm may take refuge in a house or seize provisions.

4. Cargo may be thrown overboard or a port entered to save a vessel.

5. An individual may violate curfew to reach an air-raid shelter.

6. A druggist may dispense a drug without a prescription in an emergency.

Several steps are involved under the MPC:

- *A Belief That Acts Are Necessary to Avoid a Harm.* The actor must "actually believe" the act is necessary or required to avoid a harm or evil to him- or herself or to others. A druggist who sells a drug without a prescription must be aware that this is an act of necessity rather than ordinary lawbreaking.
- *Comparative Harm or Evils.* The harm or evil to be avoided is greater than that sought to be prevented by the law defining the offense. Human life generally is valued above property. A naval captain may enter a port from which the vessel is prohibited to save the life of a crew member. The question of whether an individual has made the proper choice is determined by the judge or jury rather than by the defendant's subjective belief.
- *Legislative Judgment.* A statute may explicitly preclude necessity; for instance, prohibiting abortions to save the life of the mother.
- *Creation of Harm.* The individual did not intentionally, negligently, or recklessly create the harm or negligently or recklessly misperceive the necessity to act. The boat captain who knowingly sets sail in a severe storm cannot rely on the necessity defense to justify docking the boat on a stranger's pier.
- *Alternatives.* An absence of legal alternatives.

The Legal Equation

Necessity	=	Criminal action believed to be necessary to prevent a harm
	+	the harm prevented is greater than will result from the criminal act
	+	absence of legal alternatives
	+	legislature did not preclude necessity
	+	did not intentionally, negligently, or recklessly create the harm.

You Decide

6.3 Matthew Ducheneaux was charged with possession of marijuana. He was arrested on a bike path in Sioux Falls, South Dakota, during the city's annual "Jazz Fest" in July 2000. He falsely claimed that he lawfully possessed the two ounces of marijuana as a result of his participation in a federal medical research project. Ducheneaux is thirty-six and was rendered quadriplegic by an automobile accident in 1985. He is almost completely paralyzed other than some movement in his hands. Ducheneaux suffers from spastic paralysis that causes unpredictable spastic tremors and pain throughout his body. He testified that he had not been able to treat the symptoms with traditional drug therapies and these protocols resulted in painful and potentially fatal side effects. One of the prescription drugs for spastic paralysis is Marinol, a synthetic tetrahydrocannabinol (THC). THC is the essential active ingredient of marijuana. Ducheneaux has a prescription for Marinol, but testified it causes dangerous side effects that are absent from marijuana. The South Dakota legislature has provided that "no person may knowingly possess marijuana" and has declined on two occasions to create a medical necessity exception. Would you convict Ducheneaux of the criminal possession of marijuana? The statute provides that the justification defense is available when a person commits a crime "because of the use or threatened use of unlawful force upon him or upon another person." See *State v. Ducheneaux*, 671 N.W.2d 841 (S.D. 2003).

You can find the answer at study.sagepub.com/lippmaness2e

Read *Commonwealth v. Kendall* and *People v. Michael S.* on the study site: study .sagepub.com/ lippmaness2e.

Duress

The common law excused an individual from guilt who committed a crime to avoid a threat of imminent death or bodily harm. In several seventeenth- and eighteenth-century cases involving treason or rebellion against the king, defendants were excused who joined or assisted the rebels in response to a threat of injury or death. The common law courts stressed that individuals were obligated to desert the rebels as soon as the threat of harm was removed.[46]

Duress differs from necessity in that an individual commits a crime because of an immediate threat from another individual rather than because of the situation confronting the individual.

Realism may be the most persuasive justification for duress. An English court nicely captured this concern in the observation that in the "calm of the courtroom, measures of fortitude or of heroic behavior are surely not to be demanded when they could not in moments for decision reasonably have been expected even of the resolute and the well-disposed."[47]

The defense of duress raises the difficult question whether the law should excuse the criminal acts of an individual who is forced to commit a crime in order to avoid the infliction of death or serious bodily harm to him- or herself. The individual was compelled against his or her will to act. On the other hand, why should we allow an individual who harms another to escape punishment? This debate is at the core of the defense of duress.

The defense of duress involves several central elements:

- The defendant's actions are to be judged in accordance with a reasonable person standard.
- There must be a threat of death or serious bodily harm from another individual that causes an individual to commit a crime. Most states also recognize that a threat directed against a member of the defendant's family or a third party may constitute duress. Psychological pressure or blackmail does not amount to a threat for purposes of duress.
- Duress does not excuse the intentional taking of the life of another.
- The threat must be immediate and imminent.
- An individual must have exhausted all reasonable and available alternatives to violating the law.
- The defendant must not create or assist in creating the circumstances leading to the claim of duress.

The most controversial duress cases involve prison escapes, in which inmates threatened with physical assault have been held to be entitled to rely on the defense of duress to excuse their escape. In *People v. Unger*, the defendant Francis Unger, a twenty-two-year-old full-blooded

Crete Indian, pled guilty to a theft charge and was imprisoned in Stateville Penitentiary in Joliet, Illinois.[48] During the first two months of Unger's imprisonment, he was threatened by an inmate wielding a six-inch knife who demanded that the defendant engage in homosexual activity. Unger was transferred to a minimum-security honor farm and, one week later, was beaten and sexually assaulted by a gang of inmates.

Unger was warned against informing authorities and, several days later, received a phone call informing him that he would be killed in retribution for having allegedly contacted correctional officials. Unger responded by escaping from the dairy farm, and he was apprehended two days later while still wearing his prison clothes. He claimed that he had intended to return to the institution.

The court determined that Unger, under these circumstances, was entitled to a jury instruction on duress because he may have reasonably believed that he had no alternative other than to escape, to be killed, or to suffer severe bodily harm. The Illinois appellate court held that it was unrealistic to require that a prisoner wait to escape until the moment that he was being "immediately pursued by armed inmates" and it was sufficient that Unger was threatened that he would be dead before the end of the evening.

Inmates relying on duress must establish that they did not use force or violence toward prison personnel or other innocent individuals in the escape and that they immediately contacted authorities once having reached a position of safety. The requirement that individuals turn themselves into authorities at the first opportunity in several federal court cases has been extended to individuals who acted as drug couriers after being threatened by gang leaders. In *United States v. Moreno*, the Ninth Circuit Court of Appeals held that "[t]he encounter with Officer Krajewski presented a clear opportunity for Moreno to save himself and alert authorities about the threat to his family. Instead, he kicked Officer Krajewski in the head twice in his attempt to escape to complete his illegal delivery."[49]

The duress defense is not fully embraced by all commentators; some argue that the law should encourage people to resist rather than to conform to the demands of violent and forceful individuals.

Model Penal Code

Section 2.09. Duress

(1) It is an affirmative defense that the actor engaged in the conduct charged to constitute an offense because he was coerced to do so by the use of, or a threat to use, unlawful force against his person or the person of another, that a person of reasonable firmness in his situation would have been unable to resist.

(2) The defense is unavailable if the actor recklessly [or negligently] placed himself in such a situation.

(3) It is not a defense that a woman acted on the command of her husband.

Analysis

The MPC significantly amends the common law standard:

1. The threat need not be limited to death or serious bodily harm. The commentary provides for a threat of unlawful force against the individual or another that would coerce an individual of "reasonable firmness" in the defendant's situation. Only threats to property or reputation are excluded in the commentary.

2. The threat is not required to be imminent or immediate.

3. Duress may be used as an excuse for homicide.

4. The threat may be to harm another person and is not limited to friends or relatives.

The Legal Equation

Duress = Reasonable belief of

+ an imminent threat by another

+ of death or severe bodily harm

+ against the defendant or close friend or relative (not limited in the Model Penal Code)

+ that causes defendant (reasonable person standard) to commit a criminal act

+ defendant did not place himself or herself in the situation

+ defendant did not kill another (not in Model Penal Code).

You Decide

6.4 Georgia Carradine was held in contempt of court based on her refusal to testify after witnessing a gang-related homicide, explaining that she was in fear for her life and the lives of her children. Carradine was sentenced to six months in the Cook County jail. She persisted in this refusal despite the government's offers to relocate her and her family to other areas in Chicago, Illinois, or the continental United States. Carradine had been separated from her husband for roughly four years and supported her six children aged five to eighteen through payments from her husband and supplemental welfare funds. She explained that she distrusted the State's Attorney and doubted that law enforcement authorities could protect her from the Blackstone Rangers youth gang. Carradine's fear was so great that she was willing to go to jail rather than to testify. The Illinois Supreme Court, in affirming the sentence, stated that criminals could not be brought to the bar of justice "unless citizens stand up to be counted." Do you agree with the decision to deny Carradine the defense of duress? See *People v. Carradine*, 287 N.E.2d 670 (Ill. 1972).

You can find the answer at study.sagepub.com/lippmaness2e

Consent

Read *United States v. Moreno* on the study site: study .sagepub.com/ lippmanness2e

The fact that an individual consents to be the victim of a crime ordinarily does not constitute a defense. For example, the Massachusetts Supreme Judicial Court held that an individual's consensual participation in a sadomasochistic relationship was not a defense to a charge of assault with a small whip. The Massachusetts justices stressed that as a matter of public policy, an individual may not consent to become a victim of an assault and battery with a dangerous weapon.[50]

In *State v. Brown*, a New Jersey Superior Court ruled that a wife's instructions to her husband that he should beat her in the event that she consumed alcoholic beverages did not constitute a justification for the severe beating he administered. Judge Bachman ruled that to "allow an otherwise criminal act to go unpunished because of the victim's consent would not only threaten the security of our society but also might tend to detract from the force of the moral principles underlying the criminal law."[51]

There are three exceptions or situations in which the law recognizes consent as a defense to criminal conduct, which are recognized in MPC Section 2.11:

- *Incidental Contact.* Acts that do not cause serious injury or harm customarily are not subject to criminal prosecution and punishment. People, for example, often are bumped and pushed on a crowded bus or at a music club.

- *Sporting Events.* Ordinary physical contact or blows are incident to sports such as football, boxing, or wrestling.
- *Socially Beneficial Activity.* Individuals benefit from activities such as medical procedures and surgery.

Consent must be free and voluntary and may not be the result of duress or coercion or fraud. Consent also is invalid if offered by an individual who lacks the legal capacity to consent based on age, a mental defect, or intoxication. An individual may limit the scope of consent by, for instance, authorizing a doctor to operate on only three of the five fingers on his or her left hand. The forgiveness of a perpetrator by the victim following a crime does not constitute consent to a criminal act. A recent area of concern involves fraternity hazing. A New York judge found that the beating inflicted on pledges exceeded the terms of consent and that consent must be voluntary and intelligent and must be "free of force or fraud."[52]

The Legal Equation

Consent	=	A justification, generally.
Consent	=	A justification only for
		1. incidental contact;
		2. foreseeable injury in legal sporting event; and
		3. beneficial medical procedure; where
	+	consent is voluntarily given by an individual with legal capacity.

You Decide

6.5 Givens Miller, an eighteen-year-old, 210-pound football player, had a disagreement with his parents following a high school football game. Givens's father, George, responded by taking away Givens's cell phone and car keys. Givens repeatedly shouted at his parents, telling his father to "take your G.D. money and 'f---' yourself with it." He then baited George, uttering "What the 'f---,' man. I'm going to—you going to hit me, man? Are you going to hit me? What the 'f---,' man."

George responded, "No, I'm not going to hit you," and shoved Givens away from him. Givens kicked and punched George in his side; and as Givens charged toward him, George punched Givens in the face. George then threw two more punches. Givens testified that at the time of the incident, he "was all jazzed up" from the game and "in an aggressive mood" and "kind of wanted to hit [George]" and he "kind of wanted [George] to hit [him]." Givens "suffered dental fractures and loose teeth. He also received two blows to the head, and testified that he may have lost consciousness for a brief moment." At the close of evidence, George objected to the jury charge because the court did not include an instruction on the defense of consent.

Was the judge correct in not issuing an instruction on consent? See *Miller v. State*, 312 S.W.3d 209 (Tex. Ct. App. 2010).

You can find the answer at study.sagepub.com/lippmaness2e

Mistake of Law and Mistake of Fact

A core principle of the common law is that only "morally blameworthy" individuals should be subject to criminal conviction and punishment. What about the individual who commits an act that he or she does not realize is a crime? Consider a resident of a foreign country who is flying to the United States for a vacation and is asked by a new American acquaintance to bring a vial of expensive heart medicine to his or her parents in the United States. The visitor is searched by

Read *State v. Dejarlais* on the study site: study.sagepub.com/lippmaness2e.

American customs officials as he or she enters the United States, and the heart medicine is discovered to be an illegal narcotic. Should the victim be held criminally liable for the knowing possession of narcotics despite this "mistake of fact"? What if the visitor was asked by his American friend to transport cocaine and was assured that there was nothing to worry about because the importation and possession of this narcotic is legal in the United States? How should the law address this "mistake of law"?

In the previous two hypothetical examples, the question is whether an individual who mistakenly believes that his or her behavior is legal should be held liable for violating the law. Professor Wayne R. LaFave has observed that no area has created "more confusion" than mistakes of law and fact—a confusion that has caused "ulcers in law students."[53]

Mistake of Law

The conventional wisdom is that *ignorantia legis non excusat*: "Ignorance of the law is no excuse." The rule that a **mistake of law** does not constitute a defense is based on several considerations, including the expectation that individuals should know the law.[54]

The expectation that individuals know the law may have made sense in early England. Critics contend, however, that people cannot realistically be expected to comprehend the vast number of laws that characterize modern society. An individual who, through a lack of knowledge, violates highly technical statutes regulating taxation or banking can hardly be viewed as "morally blameworthy."[55] Some observers note that courts seem to have taken this criticism seriously and, in several instances, have relaxed the rule that individuals are presumed to "know the law."[56] Three U.S. Supreme Court decisions illustrate this trend:

1. *Notice.* In *Lambert v. California*, the defendant was convicted of failure to adhere to a law that required a "felon" resident in Los Angeles to register with the police within five days. The U.S. Supreme Court found that convicting Lambert would violate due process because the law was unlikely to have come to his attention.[57]

2. *Intent.* In *Cheek v. United States*, an airline pilot had been counseled by antitax activists and believed that his wages did not constitute income and, therefore, he did not owe federal tax. He was convicted of willfully attempting to evade or defeat his taxes. The U.S. Supreme Court ruled that Congress required a showing of a willful intent to violate tax laws because the vast number of tax statutes made it likely that the average citizen might innocently fail to remain informed of the provisions of the tax code.[58]

3. *Reliance.* In the civil rights–era case of *Cox v. Louisiana*, the defendants were convicted of picketing a courthouse with the intent of interfering, obstructing, or influencing the administration of justice. The U.S. Supreme Court reversed the students' convictions on the grounds that the chief of police had instructed them that they could legally picket at a location 101 feet from the courthouse steps.[59]

MPC Section 2.04(3) recognizes an "ignorance of the law defense" when the defendant does not know the law and the law has not been published or made reasonably available to the public (notice). This defense also applies where the defendant has relied on an official statement of the law (reliance).

Mistake of Fact

A **mistake of fact** constitutes a defense in those instances when the defendant's mistake results in a lack of criminal intent. MPC Section 2.04(1) states that "ignorance or mistake is a defense when it negatives the existence of a state of mind that is essential to the commission of an offense." As a first step, determine the intent required for the offense and then compare this to the defendant's state of mind. A defendant may take an umbrella from a restaurant during a rainstorm believing that this is the umbrella that he or she left at the restaurant two years ago. The accused will be acquitted of theft because he or she lacked the intent to take, carry away, and permanently deprive the owner of the umbrella. Some courts require that a defendant's mistake must be objectively reasonable, meaning that a reasonable person would have made the same mistake. A trial court, for instance, might conclude that it was unreasonable for the defendant to believe after two years that his umbrella was still at the restaurant.[60]

Another aspect of the mistake of fact defense is that an individual may be mistaken but nonetheless will be held criminally liable in the event that the facts as perceived by the defendant still comprise a crime. For example, a defendant may be charged with receiving stolen umbrellas and contend that he or she believed that the package contained stolen raincoats. This would not exonerate the defendant. The charge is based on the receipt of stolen property, not stolen umbrellas.[61]

MPC Section 2.04(1)(a)(b) accepts that a mistake of fact constitutes a defense so long as it "negatives" the intent required under the statute.

The Legal Equation

Mistake of law = No excuse (some indication may excuse criminal liability in cases involving notice, intent, or reliance).

Mistake of fact = Mistake is an excuse if it negates the required criminal intent (may require reasonable mistake).

You Decide 6.6 The defendant and his cousin, knowing that their marriage would be illegal in Nebraska, married in Iowa, where such unions are not prohibited. The county prosecutor informed the defendant that he would be prosecuted for sexual relations without marriage ("fornication") in the event that the couple continued to live in Nebraska because the marriage was not recognized in the state.

Three private attorneys confirmed that the Iowa marriage was not valid in Nebraska. The defendant subsequently "separated" from his pregnant cousin and remarried another woman. It later was determined that, in fact, the Iowa marriage was valid in Nebraska, and the defendant was charged with bigamy (simultaneous marriage to more than a single spouse). Is the defendant guilty of bigamy? See *Staley v. State*, 89 Neb. 701 (1911).

You can find the answer at study.sagepub.com/lippmaness2e

DEFENSES JUSTIFYING THE USE OF FORCE

An individual who reasonably believes that he or she is threatened with an imminent threat of bodily harm is entitled to use force to protect himself or herself.

Self-Defense

It is commonly observed that the United States is a "government of law rather than men and women." This means that guilt and punishment are to be determined in accordance with fair and objective legal procedures in the judicial suites rather than by brute force in the streets. Accordingly, the law generally discourages individuals from "taking the law into their own hands." This type of "vigilante justice" risks anarchy and mob violence. One sorry example is the lynching of thousands of African Americans by the Ku Klux Klan following the Civil War.

Self-defense is the most obvious exception to this rule and is recognized as a defense in all fifty states. Why does the law concede that an individual may use physical force in self-defense? One federal court judge noted the practical consideration that absent this defense, the innocent victim of a violent attack would be placed in the unacceptable position of choosing between "almost certain death" at the hands of his or her attacker or a "trial and conviction of murder later." More fundamentally, eighteenth-century English jurist William Blackstone wrote that it was "lawful" for an individual who is attacked to "repel force by force." According to Blackstone, this was a recognition of the natural impulse and right of individuals to defend themselves. A failure to recognize this right would inevitably lead to a disregard of the law.[62]

The Central Components of Self-Defense

The common law recognizes that an individual is justified in employing force in self-defense. This may involve deadly or nondeadly force, depending on the nature of the threat. There are a number of points to keep in mind:

- *Reasonable Belief.* An individual must possess a reasonable belief that force is required to defend himself or herself. In other words, the individual must believe and a reasonable person must believe that force is required in self-defense.
- *Necessity.* The defender must reasonably believe that force is required to prevent the imminent and unlawful infliction of death or serious bodily harm.
- *Proportionality.* The force employed must not be excessive or more than is required under the circumstances.
- *Retreat.* A defendant may not resort to deadly force if he or she can safely **retreat**. This generally is not required when the attack occurs in the home or workplace, or if the attacker uses deadly force.
- *Aggressor.* An **aggressor**, or individual who unlawfully initiates force, generally is not entitled to self-defense. An aggressor may claim self-defense only in those instances that an aggressor who is not employing deadly force is himself or herself confronted by deadly force. Some courts require that under these circumstances, the aggressor withdraw from the conflict if at all possible before enjoying the right of self-defense. There are courts willing to recognize that even an aggressor who employs deadly force may regain the right of self-defense by withdrawing following the initial attack. The other party then assumes the role of the aggressor.
- *Mistake.* An individual who is mistaken concerning the necessity for self-defense may rely on the defense as long as his or her belief is reasonable.
- *Imperfect Self-Defense.* An individual who honestly, but unreasonably, believes that he or she confronts a situation calling for self-defense and intentionally kills is held liable in many states for an intentional killing. Other states, however, follow the doctrine of **imperfect self-defense**. This provides that although the defendant may not be acquitted, fairness dictates that he or she should be held liable only for the less serious crime of manslaughter.

Model Penal Code

Section 3.04. Use of Force in Self-Protection

(1) [T]he use of force upon or toward another person is justifiable when the actor believes that such force is immediately necessary for the purpose of protecting himself against the use of unlawful force by such other person on the present occasion.

(2) Limitations on Justifying Necessity for Use of Force.

    (a) . . .

    (b) The use of deadly force is not justifiable under this Section unless the actor believes that such force is necessary to protect himself against death, serious bodily injury, kidnapping or sexual intercourse compelled by force or threat; nor is it justifiable if:

        (i) the actor, with the purpose of causing death or serious bodily injury, provoked the use of force against himself in the same encounter; or

        (ii) the actor knows that he can avoid the necessity of using such force with complete safety by retreating or by surrendering possession of a thing to a person asserting a claim of right thereto or by complying with a demand that he abstain from any action that he has no duty to take. . . .

Analysis

The MPC makes some significant modifications to the standard approach to self-defense that will be discussed later in the text. The basic formulation affirms that the use of force in self-protection is justified in those instances in which an individual "employs it in the belief that it is immediately necessary for the purpose of protecting himself against the other's use of unlawful force on the present occasion." The code provides that an aggressor who uses deadly force may "break off the struggle" and retreat and regain the privilege of self-defense against the other party.

The Legal Equation

Self-defense	=	Reasonable belief
	+	immediately necessary
	+	to employ proportionate force
	+	to protect oneself against unlawful force.

Reasonable Belief

The common law and most statutes and modern decisions require that an individual who relies on self-defense must act with a reasonable belief in the imminence of serious bodily harm or death. The Utah statute on self-defense specifies that a person is justified in threatening or using force against another in those instances in which he or she "reasonably believes that force is necessary . . . to prevent death or serious bodily injury." . . . The reasonableness test has two prongs:

1. *Subjective.* A defendant must demonstrate an honest belief that he or she confronted an imminent attack.
2. *Objective.* A defendant must demonstrate that a reasonable person under the same circumstances would have believed that he or she confronted an imminent attack.

An individual who acts with an honest and reasonable, but mistaken, belief that he or she is subject to an armed attack is entitled to the justification of self-defense. The classic example is the individual who kills an assailant who is about to stab him or her with a knife, a knife that later is revealed to be a realistic-looking rubber replica. As noted by Supreme Court Justice Oliver Wendell Holmes Jr., "[d]etached reflection cannot be demanded in the presence of an uplifted knife."[63] Absent a reasonableness requirement, it is feared that individuals might act on the basis of suspicion or prejudice or intentionally kill or maim and then later claim self-defense.

The MPC adopts a subjective approach and only requires that a defendant actually believe in the necessity of self-defense. The subjective approach has been adopted by very few courts. An interesting justification for this approach was articulated by the Colorado Supreme Court, which contended that the reasonable person standard was "misleading and confusing." The right to self-defense, according to the Colorado court, is a "natural right and is based on the natural law of self-preservation. Being so, it is resorted to instinctively in the animal kingdom by those creatures not endowed with intellect and reason, so it is not based on the 'reasonable man' concept."[64]

A number of courts are moving to a limited extent in the direction of the MPC by providing that a defendant acting in an honest, but unreasonable, belief is entitled to claim *imperfect self-defense* and should be convicted of manslaughter rather than intentional murder.[65] In *Harshaw v. State*, the defendant and deceased were arguing, and the deceased threatened to retrieve his gun. They both retreated to their automobiles, and the defendant grabbed his shotgun in time to shoot the deceased as he reached inside his automobile. The deceased was later found to have been unarmed. The Arkansas Supreme Court ruled that the judge should have instructed the jury on manslaughter because the jurors could reasonably have found that Harshaw acted "hastily and without due care" and that he merited a conviction for manslaughter rather than murder.[66]

The New York Court of Appeals wrestled with the meaning of "reasonableness" under the New York statute in the famous "subway murder trial" of Bernhard Goetz. Goetz reacted to four young juveniles who asked him for money on the subway by brandishing a pistol and firing five shots in "self-defense." The court noted that a subjective standard would exonerate an individual who claimed to have acted in self-defense no matter how delusional his or her beliefs. The legal test according to the New York court is whether the defendant's subjective belief that he or she confronted an imminent threat was "reasonable under the circumstances." In evaluating the reasonableness of the defendant's belief, a number of factors are to be considered—including the relative "size" of the individuals involved, knowledge of the assailant's past involvement in violence, and past experiences of the defendant that could provide the defendant with a reasonable belief that he or she was threatened. The jury acquitted Goetz, who alleged that he had been threatened on the subway in the past, of all charges other than unlawful possession of a firearm.[67]

Imminence

A defendant must reasonably believe that the threatened harm is imminent, meaning that the harm "is about to happen."

In *State v. Schroeder*, the nineteen-year-old defendant stabbed a violent cellmate who threatened to make Schroeder his "sex slave" or "punk." Schroeder testified that he felt vulnerable and afraid and woke up at 1:00 a.m. and stabbed his cellmate in the back with a table knife and hit him in the face with a metal ashtray. The Nebraska Supreme Court ruled that the threatened harm was not imminent and that there was a danger in legalizing "preventive assaults."[68]

The MPC adopts a broad approach and provides that force is justifiable when the actor believes that he or she will be attacked on "the present occasion" rather than imminently. The broad MPC test has found support in the statutes of a number of states, including Delaware, Hawaii, Nebraska, New Jersey, and Pennsylvania. A dissenting judge in *Schroeder* cited the MPC and argued that the young inmate should have been acquitted on the grounds of self-defense. After all, he could not be expected to remain continuously on guard against an assault by his older cellmate or the cellmate's friends.

Battered Persons

The clash between the common law imminence requirement and the MPC's notion that self-defense may be justified where necessary to prevent an anticipated future harm is starkly presented by the so-called battered spouse defense. In *State v. Norman*, the defendant had been the victim of continual battering by her husband over a number of years, and he literally treated her like a "dog" and forced her to eat out of bowl and to sleep on the floor. The victim shot and killed her abusive spouse while he was asleep.[69] The North Carolina Supreme Court affirmed the trial court's refusal to issue a self-defense instruction. The court held that the evidence did not "show that the defendant reasonably believed that she was confronted by a threat of imminent death or great bodily harm." The court further observed that "relaxed requirements" for self-defense would "legalize the opportune killing of abusive husbands by their wives solely on the basis of the wives' . . . subjective speculation as the probability of future felonious assaults by their husbands."[70]

Various state courts have held that a "battered spouse" is entitled to present expert witnesses explaining what is termed the "battered spouse syndrome." This syndrome is defined as a mental state that results from a cycle of physical and psychological abuse. The expert testimony helps the jury understand why it was reasonable for the defendant to have viewed himself or herself as confronting a threat of imminent harm and that there was no reasonable alternative other than to kill his or her abuser.[71]

A number of state legislatures have adopted statutes on intimate partner violence.[72] A Missouri statute provides that evidence that the defendant suffered from battered spouse syndrome is admissible "upon the issue of whether the actor lawfully acted in self-defense."[73]

Several courts have recognized the "battered child syndrome." The Washington Supreme Court, in an important decision, concluded that a seventeen-year-old who shot and killed his stepfather was entitled to rely on the "battered child syndrome" and to introduce evidence supporting the reasonableness of his belief that he confronted the prospect of imminent abuse. Children are more likely than adults to feel helpless and to lack the capacity to seek outside help or to leave the abusive relationship and to see no other avenue of escape other than to kill their abuser.[74]

Now that we have discussed the imminence requirement, we turn our attention to other requirements for self-defense.

Read *State v. Norman* on the study site: study .sagepub.com/ lippmaness2e.

You Decide

6.7 The defendant, seventeen-year-old Andrew Janes, was abandoned by his alcoholic father at age seven. Along with his mother Gale and brother Shawn, Andrew was abused by his mother's lover, Walter Jaloveckas, for roughly ten years. As Walter walked in the door following work on August 30, 1988, Andrew shot and killed him; one 9-millimeter pistol shot went through Walter's right eye and the other through his head. The previous night, Walter had yelled at Gale, and Walter later leaned his head into Andrew's room and spoke in low tones that usually were "reserved for threats." Andrew was unable to remember precisely what Walter said. In the morning, Gale mentioned to Andrew that Walter was still mad. After returning from school, Andrew loaded the pistol, drank some whiskey, and smoked marijuana.

Examples of the type of abuse directed against Andrew by Walter included beatings with a belt and wire hanger, hitting Andrew in the mouth with a mop, and punching Andrew in the face for failing to complete a homework assignment. In 1988, Walter hit Andrew with a piece of firewood, knocking him out. Andrew was subject to verbal as well as physical threats, including a threat to nail his hands to a tree, brand his forehead, place Andrew's hands on a hot stove, break Andrew's fingers, and hit him in the head with a hammer.

The "battered child syndrome" results from a pattern of abuse and anxiety. "Battered children" live in a state of constant alert ("hypervigilant") and caution ("hypermonitoring") and develop a lack of confidence and an inability to seek help ("learned helplessness"). Did Andrew believe and would a reasonable person in Andrew's situation believe that Andrew confronted an imminent threat of great bodily harm or death? The Washington Supreme Court clarified that *imminent* means "near at hand . . . hanging threateningly over one's head . . . menacingly near." The trial court refused to instruct the jury to consider whether Andrew was entitled to invoke self-defense.

Should the Washington Supreme Court uphold or reverse the decision of the trial court? See *State v. Janes*, 850 P.2d 495 (Wash. 1993).

You can find the answer at study.sagepub.com/lippmaness2e

Excessive Force

An individual acting in self-defense is entitled to use that degree of force reasonably believed to be necessary to defend himself or herself. **Deadly force** is force that a reasonable person under the circumstances would be aware will cause or create a substantial risk of death or substantial bodily harm. This may be employed to protect against death or serious bodily harm. The application of excessive rather than proportionate force may result in a defender's being transformed into an aggressor. This is the case where an individual entitled to **nondeadly force** resorts to deadly force. The MPC limits deadly force to the protection against death, serious bodily injury, kidnapping, or rape. The Wisconsin statute authorizes the application of deadly force against arson, robbery, burglary, and any felony offense that creates a danger of death or serious bodily harm.[75]

In *State v. DeJesus*, DeJesus was attacked by two machete-wielding assailants, and he knocked them to the ground with a metal pipe and beat them to death. The Connecticut Supreme Court held that "[t]he jury could have reasonably concluded that the defendant did not reasonably believe that the degree of deadly force he exercised, in continuing to beat the victims in the manner established by the evidence, was necessary under the circumstances to thwart any immediate attacks from either or both of the victims."[76]

Retreat

The law of self-defense is based on necessity. An individual may resort to self-protection when he or she reasonably believes it necessary to defend against an immediate attack. The amount of force is limited to that reasonably believed to be necessary. Courts have struggled with how to treat a situation in which an individual may avoid resorting to deadly force by safely retreating or fleeing. The principle of necessity dictates that every alternative should be exhausted before an individual resorts to deadly force and that an individual should be required to **retreat to the wall** (as far as possible). On the other hand, should an individual be required to retreat when confronted with a violent wrongdoer? Should the law promote cowardice and penalize courage?

Virtually every jurisdiction provides that there is no duty or requirement to retreat before resorting to *nondeadly force*. A majority of jurisdictions follow the same **stand your ground rule** in the case of *deadly force*, although a "significant minority" of states require retreat to the wall.[77]

Most jurisdictions limit the right to "stand your ground" when confronted with nondeadly force to an individual who is without fault, a **true man**. An aggressor employing nondeadly force must clearly abandon the struggle, and it must be a **withdrawal in good faith** to regain the right of self-defense. Some courts recognize that even an aggressor using deadly force may withdraw and regain the right of self-defense. In these instances, the right of self-defense will limit the initial aggressor's liability to manslaughter and will not provide a **perfect self-defense**. A withdrawal in good faith must be distinguished from a **tactical retreat** in which an individual retreats with the intent of continuing the hostilities.

The requirement of retreat is premised on the traditional rule that only necessary force may be employed in self-defense. The provision for retreat is balanced by the consideration that withdrawal is not required when the safety of the defender would be jeopardized. The **Castle Doctrine** is another generally recognized exception to the rule of retreat and provides that individuals inside the home are justified in "holding their ground." Aggressors are not entitled to rely on the Castle Doctrine inside the home.[78]

New Jersey along with a minority of states requires that a co-occupant of the home retreat before employing deadly force against another co-occupant.[79] In 2009, the West Virginia Supreme Court after considering the plight of the victims of domestic violence reversed the "no retreat rule" for lawful occupants of a home confronting abuse. The court explained that women who flee the home in many instances are "caught, dragged back inside, and severely beaten again. [Even i]f she manages to escape, . . . [w]here will she go if she has no money, no transportation, and if her children are left behind in the care of an enraged man?" The West Virginia Court also reasoned that it was unfair that a woman attacked in the home by a stranger may stand her ground while a woman who is attacked by her husband or partner must retreat.[80]

MPC Section 3.04(b)(ii) provides that deadly force is not justifiable in those instances in which an individual "knows that he can avoid the necessity of using such force with complete safety by retreating." There is no duty to retreat under the MPC within the home or place of work unless an individual is an aggressor.

Defense of Others

The common law generally limited the privilege of **intervention in defense of others** to the protection of spouses, family, employees, and employers. This was based on the assumption that an individual would be in a good position to evaluate whether these individuals were aggressors or victims in need of assistance. Some state statutes continue to limit the right to intervene, but this no longer is the prevailing legal rule. The Wisconsin statute provides that a person is justified in "threatening or using force against another when . . . he or she reasonably believes that force is necessary to defend himself or a third person against such other's imminent use of unlawful force."

The early approach in the United States was the **alter ego rule**. This provides that an individual intervening "stands in the shoes" of or possesses the "same rights" as the person whom he or she is assisting. The alter ego approach generally has been abandoned in favor of the reasonable person or **objective test for intervention in defense of others** of the MPC. Section 3.05 provides that an individual is justified in using force to protect another who he or she reasonably believes (1) is in immediate danger and (2) is entitled under the MPC to use protective force in self-defense, and (3) such force is necessary for the protection of the other person. An intervener is not criminally liable under this test for a reasonable mistake of fact.

What is the difference between the alter ego rule and the objective test? Individuals intervening under the alter ego rule act at their own peril. The person "in whose shoes they stand" may in fact be an aggressor or may not possess the right of self-defense. The objective test, on the other hand, protects individuals who act in a "reasonable," but mistaken, belief.

Remember, you may intervene to protect another, but you are not required to intervene. George Fletcher notes that the desire to provide protection to those who intervene on behalf of others reflects the belief that an attack against a single individual threatens to erode the rule of law that protects each and every individual.[81]

Defense of the Home

The home has historically been viewed as a place of safety, security, and shelter. The eighteenth-century English jurist Lord Coke wrote that "[a] man's house is his castle—for where shall a man be safe if it be not his own house." Coke's opinion was shaped by the ancient Roman legal scholars who wrote that "one's home is the safety refuge for everyone." The early colonial states adopted the English common law right of individuals to use deadly force in those instances in which they reasonably believe that force is required to prevent an imminent and unlawful entry. The common law rule is sufficiently broad to permit deadly force against a rapist, burglar, or drunk who mistakenly stumbles into the wrong house on his or her way to a surprise birthday party.[82]

States gradually abandoned this broad standard and adopted statutes that restricted the use of deadly force in defense of the home. There is no uniform approach today, and statutes typically limit deadly force to those situations in which deadly force is reasonably believed to be required to prevent the entry of an intruder who is reasonably believed to intend to commit "a felony" in the dwelling. Other state statutes strictly regulate armed force and authorize deadly force only in those instances in which it is reasonably believed to be required to prevent the entry of an intruder who is reasonably believed to intend to commit a "forcible felony" involving the threat or use of violence against an occupant.[83] The first alternative would permit the use of deadly force against an individual who is intent on stealing a valuable painting, whereas the second approach would require that the art thief threaten violence or display a weapon.

The MPC balances the right to protect a dwelling from intruders against respect for human life and provides that deadly force is justified in those instances that the intruder is attempting to commit arson, burglary, robbery, other serious theft, or the destruction of property and has demonstrated that he or she poses a threat by employing or threatening to employ deadly force. Deadly force is also permissible under Section 3.06(3)(d)(ii)(A)(B) where the employment of nondeadly force would expose the occupant to substantial danger of serious bodily harm.

The most controversial and dominant trend is toward so-called **make my day laws** that authorize the use of "any degree of force" against intruders who "might use any physical force, no matter how slight, against any occupant."[84]

In *State v. Anderson*, the Oklahoma Court of Criminal Appeals stressed that under the state's make my day law, the occupant possesses unlimited discretion to employ whatever degree of force he or she desires based "solely upon the occupant's belief that the intruder might use any force against the occupant." In practice, this is a return to the original common law rule because a jury would likely find reasonable justification to believe that almost any intruder poses at least a threat of "slight" physical force against an occupant.[85] The make my day law raises the issue of the proper legal standard for the use of force in defense of the dwelling. Should a homeowner be required to wait until the intruder poses a threat of serious harm?

What about the protection of property? An individual is entitled to employ reasonable and necessary *nondeadly force* to protect property against a thief. Deadly force in protection of property is never justifiable. A victim of a theft who acts "promptly" and engages in hot pursuit against an assailant may use nondeadly force to recapture stolen property. Physical force generally may not be used by a "rightful owner" to "recapture" property that has been stolen and carried away by the perpetrator.[86]

The Castle Doctrine in Florida

Florida statute Section 776.013 is enormously influential and contains several provisions that have been followed by other states. A number of important provisions are reprinted below and are discussed in the Criminal Law and Public Policy feature.

776.013. Home protection; use of deadly force; presumption of fear of death or great bodily harm.—

(1) A person is presumed to have held a reasonable fear of imminent peril of death or great bodily harm to himself or herself or another when using defensive force that is intended or likely to cause death or great bodily harm to another if:

   (a) The person against whom the defensive force was used was in the process of unlawfully and forcefully entering, or had unlawfully and forcibly entered, a dwelling, residence, or occupied vehicle, or if that person had removed or was attempting to remove another against that person's will from the dwelling, residence, or occupied vehicle; and

(b) The person who uses defensive force knew or had reason to believe that an unlawful and forcible entry or unlawful and forcible act was occurring or had occurred.

(2) The presumption set forth in subsection (1) does not apply if:

(a) The person against whom the defensive force is used has the right to be in or is a lawful resident of the dwelling, residence, or vehicle, such as an owner, lessee, or titleholder, and there is not an injunction for protection from domestic violence or a written pretrial supervision order of no contact against that person; or

(3) A person who is not engaged in an unlawful activity and who is attacked in any other place where he or she has a right to be has no duty to retreat and has the right to stand his or her ground and meet force with force, including deadly force if he or she reasonably believes it is necessary to do so to prevent death or great bodily harm to himself or herself or another or to prevent the commission of a forcible felony.

(4) A person who unlawfully and by force enters or attempts to enter a person's dwelling, residence, or occupied vehicle is presumed to be doing so with the intent to commit an unlawful act involving force or violence.

CRIMINAL LAW AND PUBLIC POLICY

In 2005, Florida passed a Castle Doctrine law, also popularly referred to as the stand your ground law, which expands the right of self-defense. In the last five years, roughly thirty-one states have adopted some or all provisions of the Florida law. These laws are inspired by the common law doctrine that authorizes individuals to employ deadly force without the obligation to retreat against individuals unlawfully entering their home who are reasonably believed to pose a threat to inflict serious bodily harm or death. Individuals under the Castle Doctrine laws possess the right to stand their ground whether they are inside the home or in the curtilage outside the home. The Florida stand your ground law extends the right to stand your ground to individuals outside the home.

The National Rifle Association (NRA) has been at the forefront of the movement to persuade state legislatures to adopt these Castle Doctrine laws. The NRA argues that it is time for the law to be concerned with the rights of innocent individuals rather than to focus on the rights of offenders. The obligation to retreat before resorting to deadly force according to the NRA restricts the ability of innocent individuals to defend themselves against wrongdoers. The law of self-defense places victims in the position of having to make a split-second decision about whether they are obligated to retreat and whether they are employing proportionate force. The preamble to the Florida law states that "no person . . . should be required to surrender his or her personal safety to a criminal . . . nor . . . be required to needlessly retreat in the face of intrusion

or attack." In the words of the spokesperson for the National Association of Criminal Defense Lawyers, "Most people would rather be judged by 12 (a jury) than carried by six (pallbearers)."

The Florida Castle Doctrine law modified the state's law of self-defense and has three central provisions.

Public place. An individual in any location where he or she "has a right to be" and who is not engaged in criminal activity is presumed to be justified in the use of deadly force or threatened use of deadly force and has no duty to retreat and has the right to stand his or her ground. The individual must reasonably believe that such force is required to prevent imminent death or great bodily harm or to prevent the imminent commission of a forcible felony to himself or herself or to another. Three questions are involved. Did the defendant have a right to be where he or she was located? Was the defendant engaged in lawful activity? Was the defendant in reasonable fear of death or great bodily harm?

Home. Individuals are presumed to be justified in using deadly force against intruders who forcefully and unlawfully enter their residence or automobile. In the past under the Florida law, a jury when confronted with a claim of self-defense by an individual in the home who employed deadly force was asked to decide whether the defendant reasonably believed that an intruder threatened death or serious bodily injury. Under the new Florida law, the issue is whether an intruder forcibly and unlawfully entered the defendant's home.

Immunity. Individuals who are authorized to use deadly force are immune from criminal prosecution and civil liability.

Prosecutors after reviewing a case may decide against bringing charges despite a police decision to arrest an individual because the prosecutor concludes that the individual has a valid claim of self-defense. Claims of self-defense are adjudicated in a preliminary hearing in which the assailant is required to establish self-defense by a preponderance of the evidence. The immunity provision prevents an individual who possesses a credible claim of self-defense from being brought to trial in criminal or civil court. The failure of a court to find that a defendant is immune from prosecution may be appealed. The individual whose claim is rejected in a preliminary hearing also may seek a plea bargain or rely on self-defense at trial. In some instances, the stand your ground law may influence the decision making of jurors despite the fact that the defense does not explicitly rely on the law.

The *St. Petersburg Times* studied ninety-three Florida cases between 2005 and 2010 involving claims of self-defense and found that in well over half of these cases, either individuals claiming self-defense were not charged with a crime, or the charges were dropped by prosecutors or dismissed by a judge before trial.

The central criticism of stand your ground laws is that the laws create a climate in which people will resort to deadly force in situations in which they previously may have avoided armed violence. This, according to critics, threatens to turn communities into "shooting galleries" reminiscent of the "old West" in which a significant percentage of people feel the need to carry firearms. Since the passage of the Florida law in 2005, the number of individuals with concealed-carry permits has increased three times to 1.1 million permits.

There is evidence that in stand your ground states roughly 8 percent or six hundred more homicides have been committed than otherwise would be expected. Researchers speculate that this results from the fact that ordinary interpersonal conflicts escalate into violent confrontations. This in turn has led to an increase in the number of cases in which individuals claim that the violence was justified on the grounds of self-defense.

The *Tampa Bay Times* has compiled a database of stand your ground cases and has published several informative studies. Because of the failure of localities to keep accurate records, there is no fully accurate compilation of cases. Among the most important findings are these:

Number of cases. The stand your ground law is being applied in a growing number of cases. The *Tampa Bay Times* database of nonfatal cases increased five times between 2008 and 2011. Several hundred defendants are invoking the law each year. As a result, the court system is overburdened with expensive and time-consuming cases. On the other hand, individuals who acted in justifiable self-defense are able to avoid prosecution.

Acquittal. As of July 2012, 67 percent of defendants who invoked the law went free.

Background. Individuals with "records of crime and violence . . . have benefited most from the . . . law": In the study of one hundred fatal stand your ground cases, more than thirty of the defendants had been accused of violent crimes, and 40 percent had three or more arrests.

Race. Individuals asserting self-defense against African Americans were more successful than individuals who relied on self-defense against assailants of other races. Of individuals who killed an African American, 73 percent were not punished as compared to 59 percent of individuals killing an individual of another race. The race of the defendant appears to play little role in the result of cases. Proponents of the law claim that African American offenders are more likely to be armed.

Age. In February 2014, the *Tampa Bay Times* reported that 19 percent of stand your ground cases resulted in the deaths of children or teens. Another 14 percent involved individuals who were either twenty or twenty-one.

The *Tampa Bay Times* notes that although stand your ground generally is applied in a responsible fashion by Florida prosecutors, there are a number of similar cases treated differently by local prosecutors. The newspaper also found cases that make a "mockery" of the law. "In nearly a third of the cases . . . defendants [who] initiated the fight, shot an unarmed person or pursued their victim . . . still went 'free.'"

In 2006, Jason Rosenbloom was shot by his neighbor Kenneth Allen in the doorway to Allen's home. Allen had complained about the amount of trash that Rosenbloom was putting out to be picked up by the trash collectors. Rosenbloom knocked on Allen's door, and the two engaged in a shouting match. Allen claimed that Rosenbloom prevented Allen from closing the door to his house with his foot and that Rosenbloom tried to push his way inside the house. Allen shot the unarmed Rosenbloom in the stomach and then in the chest.

(Continued)

(Continued)

Allen claimed that he was afraid and that "I have a right . . . to keep my house safe."

The case came down to a "swearing contest" between Rosenbloom and Allen. Allen claimed that the unarmed Rosenbloom "unlawfully" and "forcibly" attempted to enter his home. Rosenbloom's entry created a presumption that Allen acted under reasonable fear of serious injury or death, and the prosecutors did not pursue the case. Under the previous law, the prosecution may have attempted to establish that Allen unlawfully resorted to deadly force because he lacked a reasonable fear that the unarmed Rosenbloom threatened serious injury or death.

The Florida stand your ground law became the topic of intense national debate when George Zimmerman, a neighborhood watch coordinator, was acquitted of the second-degree murder of seventeen-year-old Trayvon Martin. The controversy over stand your ground was further fueled by the conviction of Michael Dunn for the killing of seventeen-year-old Jordan Davis stemming from Dunn's complaint that Davis and his friends were playing music too loudly. Judge Russell Healey in sentencing Dunn to life imprisonment stated that this "exemplifies that our society seems to have lost its way. . . . We should remember that there's nothing wrong with retreating and deescalating the situation."

Despite the controversy over the provisions of the Florida law, a Florida gubernatorial task force reported in 2012 that the Castle Doctrine law has been effective in protecting citizens and in inspiring confidence in the criminal justice system and should be retained as part of the Florida criminal code.

Stand your ground cases have been equally controversial in other states. In 2015, Wayne Burgarello, seventy-four, was acquitted by a Nevada jury for firing five shots and killing one intruder and seriously wounding another intruder, both of whom were breaking into a vacant rental unit. Burgarello was tired of the burglary and vandalism of the empty rental unit and had lain in wait for the intruders.

A Nevada jury rejected a stand your ground defense by Markus Kaarma who baited an intruder by placing a purse in an open garage. After being alerted by motion sensors that an intruder was entering the garage, Kaarma killed the seventeen-year-old burglar with four shots from a pump action shotgun. The jury rejected Kaarma's defense that he was protecting his home, and he was sentenced to seventy years of imprisonment.

In Montana, in September 2012, Dan Fredenberg was fatally shot by Brice Harper. Fredenberg suspected that Harper was having an affair with Fredenberg's wife. The unarmed Fredenberg decided to confront Harper and was shot dead by Harper as he entered Harper's garage. Dan Corrigan, the local prosecutor, concluded that Harper had been justified in killing Fredenberg under the Montana stand your ground law and decided against pressing charges. Corrigan explained, "You don't have to claim that you were afraid for your life. You just have to claim that he [the assailant] was in the house illegally. If you think someone's going to punch you in the nose or engage you in a fistfight, that's sufficient grounds to engage in lethal force." Do you believe it is time to reconsider stand your ground laws?

Execution of Public Duties

The enforcement of criminal law requires that the police detain, arrest, and incarcerate individuals and seize and secure property. This interference with life, liberty, and property would ordinarily constitute a criminal offense. The law, however, provides a defense to individuals executing public duties. This is based on a judgment that the public interest in the enforcement of the law justifies intruding on individual liberty.

In 1985, the U.S. Supreme Court reviewed the **fleeing felon rule** in *Tennessee v. Garner*. The case was brought under a civil rights statute by the family of the deceased who was seeking monetary damages for deprivation of the "rights . . . secured by the Constitution," 42 U.S.C. § 1983. The Supreme Court determined that the police officer violated Garner's Fourth Amendment right to be free from "unreasonable seizures." Although this was a civil rather than criminal decision, the judgment established the standard to be employed in criminal prosecutions against officers charged with the unreasonable utilization of deadly force.[87]

When the officer has probable cause to believe that the suspect poses a threat of serious physical harm, either to the officer or to others, it is not constitutionally unreasonable to prevent escape by using deadly force. Thus, if the suspect threatens the officer with a weapon or there is probable cause to believe that he or she has committed a crime involving the infliction or threatened infliction of serious physical harm, deadly force may be used if necessary to prevent escape, and if, where feasible, some warning has been given.

Justice Sandra Day O'Connor in dissent wrote that "I cannot accept the majority's creation of a constitutional right to flight for burglary suspects seeking to avoid capture at the scene of the crime."

The U.S. Supreme Court in three "high speed pursuit" decisions affirmed the reasonableness of police officers' use of deadly force and other methods that pose a high likelihood of serious injury or death to halt a "fleeing motorist" so as to protect innocent members of the public who are placed at risk by the "fleeing motorist."[88]

The use of deadly force by the police became an issue of heated debate in August 2015 when Officer Darren Wilson of the Ferguson, Missouri, Police Department (FPD) shot and killed unarmed African American teenager Michael Brown. A St. Louis County, Missouri, grand jury after hearing evidence from sixty witnesses over the course of three months voted against indicting Officer Wilson for murder. In the aftermath of the grand jury decision, the Criminal Section of the Department of Justice Civil Rights Division initiated an investigation into Brown's death and concluded that Wilson had not violated the federal criminal statute, 18 U.S.C. § 242, which prohibits an individual under color of law (e.g., Officer Wilson) from willfully subjecting any person (e.g., Brown) to the deprivation of his or her constitutional rights or rights under the laws of the United States.

Resisting Unlawful Arrests

English common law recognized the right to resist an unlawful arrest by reasonable force. The U.S. Supreme Court, in *John Bad Elk v. United States* in 1900, ruled that "[i]f the officer had no right to arrest, the other party might resist the illegal attempt to arrest him, using no more force than was absolutely necessary to repel the assault constituting the attempt to arrest."[89] In 1948, the U.S. Supreme Court affirmed that "[o]ne has an undoubted right to resist an unlawful arrest . . . and courts will uphold the right of resistance in proper cases."[90]

Read *Tennessee v. Garner* on the study site: study .sagepub.com/ lippmaness2e.

The English common law rule that authorizes the right to resist an unlawful arrest by reasonable force was recognized as the law in forty-five states as late as 1963. The Mississippi Supreme Court proclaimed in *State v. King* that "every person has a right to resist an unlawful arrest; and, in preventing such illegal restraint of his liberty, he may use such force."[91] Today, only twelve states continue to recognize the **English rule for resistance to an unlawful arrest**. Thirty-eight states have now abandoned the right to resist arrest—known as the **American rule for resistance to an unlawful arrest**.

The abandonment of the recognition of the right to resist by an overwhelming majority of states and by the MPC is because the rule no longer is thought to make much sense. Individuals and the police often are heavily armed, and a violent exchange imperils the public. The common law rule reflected the fact that imprisonment, even for brief periods, subjected individuals to a "death trap" characterized by disease, hunger, and violence. However, today individuals who are arrested have access to a lawyer, and to release on bail while awaiting trial. Incarcerated individuals are no longer subjected to harsh, inhuman, and disease-ridden prison conditions that result in illness and death.[92]

Keep in mind that individuals continue to retain the right of self-defense to resist a police officer's application of unnecessary and unlawful force in executing arrest. Judges reason that individuals are not adequately protected against the infliction of death or serious bodily harm by the ability to bring a civil or criminal case charging the officer with the application of excessive force.[93]

The Legal Equation

| A lawful or unlawful arrest | = | resistance by physical force. |
| Excessive force in an arrest | = | proportionate self-defense. |

DEFENSES BASED ON GOVERNMENTAL MISCONDUCT

Individuals who are pressured, tricked, or coerced into committing a crime can rely on the defense of entrapment.

Entrapment

American common law did not recognize the defense of **entrapment**. The fact that the government entrapped or induced a defendant to commit a crime was irrelevant in evaluating a defendant's guilt or innocence.

The development of the defense is traced to the U.S. Supreme Court's 1932 decision in *Sorrells v. United States*. In *Sorrells*, an undercover agent posing as a "thirsty tourist" struck up a friendship with Sorrells and was able to overcome Sorrells's resistance and persuaded him to locate some illicitly manufactured alcohol. Sorrells's conviction for illegally selling alcohol was reversed by the U.S. Supreme Court.[94]

The decision in *Sorrells* defined entrapment as the "conception and planning of an offense by an officer, and his procurement of its commission by one who would not have perpetrated it except for the trickery, persuasion, or fraud of the officer." The essence of entrapment is the government's inducement of an otherwise innocent individual to commit a crime. Decisions have clarified that the prohibition on entrapment extends to the activities of undercover government agents, confidential informants, and private citizens acting under the direction of law enforcement personnel. The defense has been raised in cases involving prostitution; the illegal sale of alcohol, cigarettes, firearms, and narcotics; and public corruption. There is some indication that the defense may not be invoked to excuse a crime of severe violence.

There are good reasons for the government to rely on undercover strategies:

- *Crime Detection.* Certain crimes are difficult to investigate and to prevent without informants. These include narcotics, prostitution, and public corruption.
- *Resources.* Undercover techniques, such as posing as a buyer of stolen goods, can result in a significant number of arrests without expending substantial resources.
- *Deterrence.* Individuals will be deterred from criminal activity by the threat of government involvement in the crime.

Entrapment is also subject to criticism:

- The government may "manufacture crime" by individuals who otherwise may not engage in such activity.
- The government may lose respect by engaging in lawbreaking.
- The informants who infiltrate criminal organizations may be criminals whose own criminal activity often is overlooked in exchange for their assistance.
- Innocent individuals are often approached in order to test their moral virtue by determining whether they will engage in criminal activity. They likely would not commit a crime were they not approached.

The Law of Entrapment

In developing a legal test to regulate entrapment, judges and legislators have attempted to balance the need of law enforcement to rely on undercover techniques against the interest in ensuring that innocent individuals are not pressured or tricked into illegal activity. As noted by Chief Justice Earl Warren in 1958, "a line must be drawn between the trap for the unwary innocent and the trap for the unwary criminal."[95]

There are two competing legal tests for entrapment that are nicely articulated in the 1958 U.S. Supreme Court case of *Sherman v. United States*. Sherman's conviction on three counts of selling illegal narcotics was overturned by the Supreme Court; and the facts, in many respects, illustrate the perils of government undercover tactics. Kalchinian, a government informant facing criminal charges, struck up a friendship with defendant Sherman. They regularly talked during their visits to a doctor who was assisting both of them to end their addiction to narcotics. Kalchinian eventually was able to overcome Sherman's resistance and persuaded him to obtain and to split the cost of illegal narcotics.[96]

The U.S. Supreme Court unanimously agreed that Sherman had been entrapped. Five judges supported a *subjective test* for entrapment, and four supported an *objective test*. The federal government and a majority of states follow a subjective test, whereas the MPC and a minority of states rely on an objective test. Keep in mind that the defense of entrapment was developed by judges, and the availability of this defense has not been recognized as part of a defendant's constitutional right to due process of law. Entrapment in many states is an affirmative defense that results in the burden being placed on the defendant to satisfy a preponderance of the evidence standard. Other states require the defendant to produce some evidence, and then they place the burden on the government to rebut the defense beyond a reasonable doubt.[97]

The Subjective Test

The subjective test focuses on the defendant and asks whether the accused possessed the criminal intent or "predisposition" to commit the crime or whether the government "created" the offense. In other words, "but for" the actions of the government, would the accused have broken the law? Was the crime the "product of the creative activity of the government" or the result of the defendant's own criminal design?

The first step is to determine whether the government induced the crime. This requires that the undercover agent or informant persuade or pressure the accused. A simple offer to sell or to purchase drugs is a "mere offer" and does not constitute an "inducement." In contrast, an inducement involves appeals to friendship, compassion, promises of extraordinary economic or material gain, sexual favors, or assistance in carrying out the crime.

The second step is the most important and involves evaluating whether the defendant possessed a "predisposition" or readiness to commit the crime with which he or she is charged. The law assumes that a defendant who is predisposed is ready and willing to engage in criminal conduct in the absence of governmental inducements and, for this reason, is not entitled to rely on the defense of entrapment. In other words, the government must direct its undercover strategy against the unwary criminal rather than the unwary innocent. How is predisposition established? A number of factors are considered[98]:

- the character or reputation of the defendant, including prior criminal arrests and convictions for the type of crime involved;
- whether the accused suggested the criminal activity;
- whether the defendant was already engaged in criminal activity for profit;
- whether the defendant was reluctant to commit the offense; and
- the attractiveness of the inducement.

In *Sherman*, the purchase of the drugs was initiated by the informant, Kalchinian, who overcame Sherman's initial resistance and persuaded him to obtain drugs. Kalchinian, in fact, had instigated two previous arrests and was facing sentencing for a drug offense himself. The two split the costs. There is no indication that Sherman was otherwise involved in the drug trade, and a search failed to find drugs in his home. Sherman's nine-year-old sales conviction and five-year-old possession conviction did not indicate that he was ready and willing to sell narcotics. In other words, before Kalchinian induced Sherman to purchase drugs, he seemed to be genuinely motivated to overcome his dependency on narcotics.

The underlying theory is that the jury, in evaluating whether the defendant was entrapped, is merely carrying out the intent of the legislature. The "fiction" is that the legislature did not intend for otherwise innocent individuals to be punished who were induced to commit crimes by government trickery and pressure. The issue of entrapment under the subjective test is to be decided by the jury.

The Objective Test

The objective test focuses on the conduct of the government rather than on the character of the defendant. Justice Felix Frankfurter, in his dissenting opinion in *Sherman*, explained that the crucial question is "whether police conduct revealed in the particular case falls below standards to which common feelings respond, for the proper use of governmental power." The police, of course, must rely on undercover work, and the test for entrapment is whether the government, by offering inducements, is likely to attract those "ready and willing" to commit crimes "should the occasion arise" or whether the government has relied on tactics and strategies that are likely to attract those who "normally avoid crime and through self-struggle resist ordinary temptations."

The subjective test focuses on the defendant; the objective test focuses on the government's conduct. Under the subjective test, if an informant makes persistent appeals to compassion and friendship and then asks a defendant to sell narcotics, the defendant has no defense if he is predisposed to selling narcotics. Under the objective test, there would be a defense because the conduct of the police, rather than the predisposition of the defendant, is the central consideration.[99]

Justice Frankfurter wrote that public confidence in the integrity and fairness of the government must be preserved and that government power is "abused and directed to an end for which it was not constituted when employed to promote rather than detect crime and to bring about the downfall of those who, left to themselves, might well have obeyed the law."[100] These unacceptable methods lead to a lack of respect for the law and encourage criminality. Frankfurter argued that judges must condemn corrupt and uncivilized methods of law enforcement even if this judgment may result in the acquittal of the accused. Frankfurter criticized the predisposition test for providing protection for "innocent defendants," while permitting the government to employ various unethical strategies and schemes against defendants who are predisposed.

In *Sherman*, Frankfurter condemned Kalchinian's repeated requests that the accused assist him to obtain drugs. He pointed out that Kalchinian took advantage of Sherman's susceptibility to narcotics and manipulated Sherman's sympathetic response to the pain Kalchinian was allegedly suffering in withdrawing from drugs. The *Sherman* and *Sorrells* cases suggest that practices prohibited under the objective test include

- taking advantage of weaknesses;
- repeated appeals to friendship and sympathy;
- promising substantial economic gain;
- pressure or threats;
- providing the equipment required for carrying out a crime; and
- false representations designed to induce a belief that the conduct is not prohibited.

Critics complain that the objective test has not resulted in clear and definite standards to guide law enforcement. Can you determine at what point Kalchinian crossed the line? Critics also charge that it makes little sense to acquit a defendant who is "predisposed" based on the fact that a "mythical innocent" individual may have been tricked into criminal activity by the government's tactics. However, the objective test was adopted by the MPC, which follows Justice Frankfurter in assigning the determination of entrapment to judges rather than juries based on the fact that judges are responsible for safeguarding the integrity of the criminal justice process.

The Entrapment Defense

In the past, a disadvantage of pleading entrapment was that a defendant was required to admit that he or she was entrapped by the government into committing a crime. A defendant who was unsuccessful in pleading entrapment would be found guilty. The Supreme Court has recognized that in the federal judicial system, a defendant may assert "inconsistent defenses," both relying on entrapment and denying guilt. State courts take different approaches to this issue.[101]

We might question whether courts should be involved in evaluating law enforcement tactics and in acquitting individuals who are otherwise clearly guilty of criminal conduct. Can innocent individuals really be pressured into criminal activity? Do we want to limit the ability of the police to use the techniques they believe are required to investigate and punish crime? There also appear to be no clear judicial standards for determining predisposition under the subjective test and for evaluating acceptable law enforcement tactics under the objective test. This leaves the police without a great deal of guidance or direction. On the other hand, we clearly are in need of a legal mechanism for preventing government abuse.

In recent years, the Bureau of Alcohol, Tobacco, Firearms and Explosives has relied on a controversial undercover "sting operation" to combat the drug trade. An informant involved in the drug trade approaches individuals and tells them that there is a loosely guarded stash house in which drugs are stored. As the individuals approach the stash house, they are arrested by federal agents and charged with various firearms and narcotics offenses. This tactic has resulted in the arrest of nearly one thousand individuals.

The Legal Equation

Subjective test	=	Government inducement
	+	defendant is not predisposed to commit the crime.
Objective test	=	Police conduct falls below standards to which common feelings respond
	+	induces crime by those who normally avoid criminal activity.

You Decide

6.8 Detective Jason Leavitt of the Las Vegas Police Department was disguised as an "intoxicated vagrant." Twenty one-dollar bills were placed in his pocket and were visible to anyone standing close to him. Leavitt's words and actions were monitored by other officers.

Appellant Richard Miller, who was walking southbound on Main Street, approached Detective Leavitt and asked him for money. Leavitt responded that he would not give Miller any money. "Miller then pulled Detective Leavitt closer to him, quickly reached his hand into Detective Leavitt's pocket, and took the twenty dollars. Miller then loosened his grip on Detective Leavitt and again asked for money. Detective Leavitt said that he could not give Miller any money because his money was gone." Miller was arrested and charged with larceny.

May Miller successfully rely on the entrapment defense? See *Miller v. State*, 110 P.3d 53 (Nev. 2005).

You can find the answer at study.sagepub.com/lippmaness2e

NEW DEFENSES

The criminal law is based on the notion that individuals are responsible and accountable for their decisions and subject to punishment for choosing to engage in morally blameworthy behavior. We have reviewed a number of circumstances in which the law has traditionally recognized that individuals should be excused and should not be held fully responsible. In the last decades, medicine and the social sciences have expanded our understanding of the various factors that influence human behavior. This has resulted in defendants' offering various new defenses that do not easily fit into existing categories. These defenses are not firmly established and have yet to be accepted by judges and juries. Most legal commentators dismiss the defenses as "quackery" or "science" and condemn these initiatives for undermining the principle that individuals are responsible for their actions.

Read *United States v. Jacobsen* on the study site: study .sagepub.com/ lippmaness2e

One of the foremost critics is Professor Alan Dershowitz of Harvard Law School, who has pointed to fifty "abuse excuses." Dershowitz defines an **abuse excuse** as a legal defense in which defendants claim that the crimes with which they are charged result from their own victimization and that they should not be held responsible. Examples are the "battered wife" and "battered child syndromes."[102] A related set of defenses are based on the claim that the defendant's biological or genetic heredity caused him or her to commit a crime. George Fletcher has warned that these types of defenses could potentially undermine the assumption that all individuals are equal and should be rewarded or punished based on what they do, not on who they are. On the other hand, proponents of these new defenses argue that the law should evolve to reflect new intellectual insights.[103]

Some New Defenses

Four examples of *biological defenses* are as follows:

- *XYY Chromosome.* This is based on research that indicates that a large percentage of male prison inmates possess an extra Y chromosome that results in enhanced "maleness." (Each fetus has two sex chromosomes, one of which is an X. A female has two X chromosomes; a male, a Y and an X chromosome.) A Maryland appeals court dismissed a defendant's claim that his robbery should be excused based on the presence of an extra Y masculine chromosome that allegedly made it impossible for him to control his antisocial and aggressive behavior.[104]

- *Premenstrual Syndrome (PMS).* Many women experience cramps, nausea, and discomfort prior to menstruation. PMS has been invoked by defendants who contend that they suffered from severe pain and distress that drove them to act in a violent fashion. Geraldine Richter was detained by an officer for driving while intoxicated, and she verbally attacked and threatened the officer and kicked the Breathalyzer. A Fairfax County, Virginia, judge acquitted Richter of driving while intoxicated, resisting arrest, and other charges after an expert testified that her premenstrual condition caused her to absorb alcohol at an abnormally rapid rate.[105]

- *Postpartum Psychosis.* This is caused by a drop in the hormonal level following the birth of a child. The result can be depression, suicide, and in its extreme manifestations delusions, hallucinations, and violence. Stephanie Molina reportedly was a happy and outgoing young woman who suffered severe depression and a paranoid fear of being killed. She subsequently killed her child, attempted suicide, and made an effort to burn her house down. A California appellate court ruled that the jury should have been permitted to consider evidence of Molina's condition in evaluating her guilt for the intentional killing of her child.[106]

- *Environmental Defense.* The Massachusetts Supreme Judicial Court rejected a defendant's effort to excuse a homicide based on the argument that the chemicals he used in lawn care work resulted in involuntary intoxication and led him to violently respond to a customer's complaint.[107]

- *Brainwashing.* Brainwashing is an example of a psychological defense in which an individual claims to have been placed under the mental control of others and to have lost the capacity to make independent decisions. A well-known example is newspaper heiress Patricia Hearst who, in 1974, was kidnapped by a small terrorist group, the Symbionese Liberation Army (SLA). Several months later, she entered a bank armed with a machine gun and assisted the group in a robbery. Hearst testified at trial that she had been abused and brainwashed by the SLA and had been programmed to assume the identity of "Tanya the terrorist." The jury dismissed this claim and convicted Hearst.

- *Post-Traumatic Stress Disorder (PTSD).* PTSD is another example of a psychological defense. A Tennessee Court of Appeals ruled that a veteran of the Desert Shield and Desert Storm military campaigns, who recently had returned to the United States, should be permitted to introduce evidence demonstrating that his wartime experiences led him to react in an emotional and violent fashion to his wife's romantic involvement with the victim.[108]

Defendants relying on *sociological defenses* claim that their life experiences and environment have caused them to commit crimes. These include the following:

- *Black Rage.* Colin Ferguson, a thirty-five-year-old native of Jamaica, in December 1993, boarded a commuter train in New York City and embarked on a shooting spree against Caucasian and Asian passengers that left six dead and nineteen wounded. The police found notes in which Ferguson expressed a hatred for these groups as well as for "Uncle Tom Negroes." His lawyer announced that Ferguson would offer the defense of extreme racial stress precipitated by the destructive racial treatment of African Americans. Ferguson ultimately represented himself at trial and did not raise this defense, which nonetheless has been the topic of substantial discussion and debate.[109]

- *Urban Survivor.* Daimion Osby, a seventeen-year-old student, shot and killed two unarmed cousins who had been demanding that Osby provide them with the opportunity to win back the money they had lost to him while gambling. At one point, a white pickup apparently belonging to one of the cousins pulled alongside Osby's automobile, and a rifle barrel was allegedly pointed out the window. Two weeks later, the same truck approached and Osby shot and killed the occupants, Marcus and Willie Brooks, neither of whom were armed. The defense offered the "urban survivor defense" during Osby's first trial. This resulted in a hung jury. He then was retried and convicted. The defense unsuccessfully appealed the fact that Osby was prohibited from introducing experts supporting his claim of the "urban survivor syndrome" at the second trial. The "urban survivor defense" consists of the contention that young people living in poor and violent urban areas do not receive adequate police protection and develop a heightened awareness and fear of threats.[110]

- *Media Intoxication.* Defendants have claimed that their criminal conduct is caused by "intoxication" from television and pornography. Ronald Ray Howard, nineteen, unsuccessfully argued in mitigation of a death sentence that he had killed a police officer while listening to "gangsta rap."[111]

- *Rotten Social Background.* In *United States v. Alexander*, the defendant shot and killed a white Marine who had uttered a racial epithet. The African American defendant claimed that he had shot as a result of an irresistible impulse that resulted from his socially deprived childhood. Alexander's early years were marked by abandonment, poverty, discrimination, and an absence of love. This "rotten social background" (RSB) allegedly created an irresistible impulse to kill in response to the Marine's remark. The U.S. Court of Appeals for the District of Columbia Circuit affirmed the trial judge's refusal to issue a jury instruction on RSB. Judge David Bazelon dissented and questioned whether society had a right to sit in judgment over a defendant who had been so thoroughly mistreated.[112]

- *Agent Orange/PTSD.* Defendant Bruce Franklin Jerrett was charged with first-degree murder, breaking and entering, kidnapping, and armed robbery. Jerrett and his mother testified to six or seven incidents following the Vietnam War in which he "blacked out," and on one occasion he attacked his sister. He attributed the incidents to the downward spiral of his health and to PTSD as a result of having been exposed to the chemical Agent Orange. Following his blackouts, Jerrett had no memory of what he had done. Jerrett appealed his conviction; and the North Carolina Supreme Court overturned his conviction on the grounds that the jurors should have received an instruction that if they found that the defendant suffered from PTSD and was unconscious at the time of his crime, he should be acquitted.[113]

The Cultural Defense

Defendants in several cases have invoked the "cultural defense." This involves arguing that a foreign-born defendant was following his or her culture and was understandably unaware of the requirements of American law. Those in favor of the "cultural defense" argue that it is unrealistic to expect that new immigrants will immediately know or accept American practices in areas as important as the raising and disciplining of children. The acceptance of diversity, however, may breed a lack of respect for the law among immigrant groups and lead Americans who are required to conform to legal standards to believe that they are being treated unfairly. Judges and juries may also lack the background to determine the authentic customs and traditions of various immigrant groups and may be forced to rely on expert witnesses to understand different cultures.[114]

Read *State v. Kargar* on the study site: study.sagepub.com/lippmaness2e.

In *State v. Kargar*, the Maine Supreme Judicial Court held that the defendant, who had emigrated to the United States three years earlier, should not be held liable for gross sexual conduct because his kissing of his eighteen-month-old son in sensitive areas of his anatomy was part of his cultural tradition.[115]

CASE ANALYSIS

In *State v. Plueard*, a Washington Appellate court decided whether Spenser James Plueard, when he was under twelve years of age, knew that it was wrong to sexually molest his sisters.

Did Spenser James Plueard When He Was Under Twelve Years Old Know That It Was Wrong to Sexually Molest His Sisters MKM and CLM?

State v. Plueard, No. 42167-4-II (Wash. Ct. App. Feb. 20, 2013)

Spenser James Plueard was born in November 1988. He lived with his grandparents and in foster care while his mother was in prison. In approximately 1998 or 1999, when Plueard was around 10 years old, his mother regained custody of him, and he moved in with her, his stepfather, and his two half sisters, MKM and CLM. Shortly after moving in with his half sisters, Plueard developed a "sexual attraction" for MKM, which he thought she also shared. When he was 10 years old and MKM was 5, he started going into her bedroom at night, touching her body, and telling her that it was "normal."

Plueard also touched his other half sister, CLM, beginning in 2000 or 2001 on multiple occasions, when he was around 11 1/2 or 12 1/2 years old and CLM was 8 or 9. Plueard also touched her vagina on two occasions when they were driving in a car. This sexual contact occurred two or three times a week for a year. CLM eventually told Plueard that she would tell on him, and he stopped touching her.

Later that year, in 2001, when Plueard was 13 years old, his mother called Child Protective Services (CPS) and reported that he had touched MKM's "privates." CPS dismissed the charges against Plueard as a "you show me yours, I'll show you mine" situation. Plueard attended counseling after this incident. Despite this counseling, Plueard continued to touch MKM in a sexual manner, which grew more intense over time.

On a weekly basis between 2001 and 2007, when Plueard was 13 to 19 years old, he touched MKM's bare vagina with his hand and with his penis, and he began having sexual intercourse with her when they were alone in her bedroom. Plueard repeatedly threatened MKM not to tell anyone about their sexual contact because "CPS would take her away" and "no one would believe her." He once became so angry at MKM for threatening to tell on him that he hit her in the face. Plueard last had sexual contact with MKM in 2007, when he was around 19 years old.

In 2010, when MKM went to the doctor for a yeast infection, she became very upset and did not want the doctor to examine her vagina. When her mother asked what was wrong, MKM disclosed that Plueard's sexual contact had continued after 2001 and the counseling. When MKM's mother confronted Plueard about the sexual contact, he denied it.

Law enforcement and CPS were again contacted, and MKM and CLM underwent child forensic interviews. After viewing a video recording of MKM's forensic interview, the police determined that they had

probable cause to arrest . . . Plueard admitted several incidents of "touching" or "fondling" MKM before he was 12 years old; but he denied having sexual intercourse with her, and he denied touching CLM at all. . . .

Plueard eventually admitted that there may have been "more than one" touching incident. He specifically recalled one incident during which he had gone into MKM's bedroom at night when he had believed no one else was present. According to Plueard, he and MKM had talked for a while; eventually, MKM had pulled down her pants and they had started fondling each other. Plueard had unzipped his zipper, pulled out his penis, and touched the outside of her vagina with his hand; but he denied having stuck his finger or his penis inside her vagina. When the police asked why he had stopped before penetration, Plueard replied that he remembered thinking at the time that their sexual contact was "wrong" but that it was like the song lyrics, "[T]his is so wrong, but it feels so right." Plueard also explained that he had shown MKM "sexual positions" when they were fully clothed and admitted that he might have rubbed his penis against her vagina "once or twice."

Plueard . . . estimated that he had fondled MKM "once a week" for "six months" when he was around 10 years old and she was 5. He was adamant, however, that none of their sexual contact continued after he was 11 years old because he was "very afraid of his stepfather" after the "first incident came to light." . . .

The State charged Plueard with two counts of first degree child molestation committed against CLM and MKM, respectively. Both counts included a charging period when Plueard was under 12 years old: Count I was based on Plueard's sexual contact with CLM between May 21, 2000, and May 20, 2002, when Plueard was between 11 1/2 and 13 1/2 years old. Count II was based on Plueard's sexual contact with MKM between December 6, 1999, and December 5, 2005, when Plueard was between 11 and 17 years old. The trial court found Plueard guilty of both counts.

When the superior court finds capacity under RCW 9A.04.0507 we review the record to determine whether there is substantial evidence establishing that the State met its burden of overcoming the statutory presumption that children under 12 years of age are incapable of committing a crime. In order to overcome the presumption of incapacity, the State must provide clear and convincing evidence that the child had sufficient capacity both to understand the act and to know that it was wrong.

Washington courts have held that the State carries a greater burden of proving capacity when a juvenile is charged with a sex crime and that it must present a higher level of proof that the child understood the illegality of his act.

Nevertheless, the State need not prove that the child understood the act's legal consequences—that the act would be punishable under the law. Instead, the focus is on "'whether the child appreciated the quality of his . . . acts at the time the act was committed.'"

Substantial evidence supports the trial court's determination that Plueard understood his acts were wrong before age 12. . . . His admissions during the police interview summary provided evidence of his knowledge that this sexual contact was wrong and support the following . . . factors: (1) Plueard fondled MKM when he was around 10 or 11 years old, close to the age of 12, when capacity is presumed; (2) he admitted fondling MKM late one evening when he believed no one else was around, suggesting his desire for secrecy; (3) he stated that although he could not remember whether he had threatened MKM not to tell their parents, it "wouldn't surprise him" if he had because he knew his parents would "get mad"; and (4) he spontaneously described having thought while fondling MKM several years earlier that his sexual contact with her was like the song lyrics, "[T]his is so wrong, but it feels so right."

Plueard's thinking "this is so wrong, but it feels so right" differs from the "after-the-fact" acknowledgement that the Washington Supreme Court held insufficient to show that a child knew his act was wrong in *J.P.S.* [In that case,] JPS, a child with cognitive disabilities, admitted, "'I know it was bad and I feel really guilty about it,'" only after he was interrogated by the police three times over a month-long period and was shunned by his neighbors and classmates. The Supreme Court held that this admission alone was insufficient to overcome the presumption of incapacity by clear and convincing evidence because it was not particularly probative of what JPS knew at the time of his conduct. In contrast, Plueard's statement provided insight into what he was thinking as he was engaging in sexual contact with MKM, namely that it was "wrong" but it felt "right" to him.

We hold, therefore, that substantial evidence supports (1) the trial court's finding that Plueard knew his sexual contact was wrong when he committed his sexual acts before age 12, and (2) its conclusion that Plueard had capacity to commit the charged child molestation crimes before he turned 12 years old.

CHAPTER SUMMARY

Excuses comprise a broad set of defenses in which defendants claim a lack of responsibility for their criminal acts. This lack of "moral blameworthiness" is based on a lack of criminal intent or on the involuntary nature of the defendant's criminal act.

Justification defenses provide that acts that ordinarily are criminal are justified and carry no criminal liability under certain circumstances. This is based on the reasoning that a violation of the law under these conditions promotes important social values, advances the social welfare, and is encouraged by society.

The *M'Naghten* "right–wrong" formula is the predominant test for *legal insanity*. The criminal justice system has experimented with broader approaches that resulted in a larger number of defendants being considered legally insane.

- *Irresistible Impulse.* Emotions cause loss of control to conform behavior to the law.
- Durham *Product Test.* The criminal act was the product of a mental disease or defect.
- *Substantial Capacity.* The defendant lacks substantial (not total) capacity to distinguish right from wrong or to conform his or her behavior to the law.

The diminished capacity defense permits defendants to introduce evidence of mental defect or disease to negate a required criminal intent. This typically is limited to murder. Other defenses based on a lack of a capacity to form a criminal intent include the following:

- *Age.* The common law and various state statutes divide age into three distinct periods. Infancy is an excuse (younger than seven at common law). There is a rebuttable presumption that adolescents in the middle period lack the capacity to form a criminal intent (between seven and fourteen at common law). Individuals older than fourteen are considered to have the same capacity as adults.
- *Intoxication.* Voluntary intoxication is recognized as a defense to a criminal charge requiring a specific intent. The trend is for abolition of the excuse of voluntary intoxication. Involuntary intoxication is a defense where, as a result of alcohol or drugs, the individual meets the standard for legal insanity in the jurisdiction.

A number of defenses were discussed under the category of justification and excuse defenses.

A defendant who commits a crime under a reasonable belief that he or she is threatened with imminent serious physical harm or death is excused from culpability based on the defense of duress. Necessity or "choice of evils" justifies illegal acts that alleviate an imminent and greater harm. The defense of consent is recognized in certain isolated instances in which the defendant's criminal conduct advances the social welfare. These include incidental contact, sports, and medical procedures. The defense of mistake falls into two categories.

A mistake of law is never a defense; a mistake of fact may be relied on to demonstrate a lack of a specific criminal intent. Some courts require that the mistake of fact be objectively reasonable.

Another group of defenses justify the use of physical force. Self-defense preserves the right to life and bodily integrity of an individual confronting an imminent threat of death or serious bodily harm. Individuals are also provided with the privilege of intervening to defend others in peril. Defense of the dwelling preserves the safety and security of the home. The execution of public duties justifies the acts of individuals in the criminal justice system that ordinarily would be considered criminal. A police officer, for instance, may use deadly force against a "fleeing felon" who poses an imminent threat to the police or to the public.

The right to resist an illegal arrest is still recognized in several states, but it has been sharply curtailed based on the fact that the state and federal governments provide effective criminal and civil remedies for the abuse of police powers.

Entrapment is a defense based on "governmental misconduct." Entrapment asks whether the government "implanted a criminal intent" in an otherwise innocent individual. The subjective approach to entrapment focuses on the defendant. This version of the defense requires proof that the government induced an individual who lacked a criminal predisposition to commit a crime. The objective test centers on the government. This test requires a judge to determine whether the government's conduct falls below accepted standards and would have induced an otherwise innocent individual to engage in criminal conduct. Courts have been reluctant to find that the Due Process Clause protects individuals against outrageous governmental misconduct.

The new defenses surveyed illustrate the effort to base excuses on new developments in biology, psychology, and sociology. Critics contend that many of these are "abuse excuses," in which defendants manipulate the law by claiming that they are victims. On the other hand, defendants ask why some traits and conditions are considered to excuse criminal activity while factors such as poverty, inequality, or abuse are not recognized as a defense. The general trend is for the law to limit rather than to expand criminal excuses.

CHAPTER REVIEW QUESTIONS

1. Distinguish the affirmative defenses of justification and excuse.

2. Define and distinguish between the four major approaches to legal insanity.

3. Discuss the purpose of the diminished capacity defense. What is the result of the application of the defense to a defendant charged with a crime requiring a specific intent?

4. Why did some states permit juries to return a verdict of GBMI?

5. Distinguish between the defenses of voluntary and involuntary intoxication.

6. Describe the common law defense of infancy. How has this been modified under contemporary statutes?

7. What are the elements of the duress defense?

8. What are the elements of the necessity defense? Provide some examples of the application of the defense.

9. Why do most state legal codes provide that an individual cannot consent to a crime? What are the exceptions to this rule?

10. List the elements of self-defense. Explain the significance of reasonable belief, imminence, retreat, withdrawal, the Castle Doctrine, and defense of others.

11. What are the two approaches to intervention in defense of another? Which test is preferable?

12. What is the law pertaining to the defense of the home? Discuss the policy behind this defense. Compare the laws pertaining to defense of habitation and self-defense.

13. Discuss the importance of the Florida Castle Doctrine law.

14. How does the rule regulating police use of deadly force illustrate the defense of execution of public duties? Does this legal standard "handcuff" the police?

15. Why have the overwhelming majority of states abandoned the defense of resistance to an illegal arrest? Distinguish this from the right to resist excessive force.

16. Discuss the difference between the mistake of law and mistake of fact defenses.

17. What are the two tests of entrapment? How do these two tests differ from one another? Explain the relationship between these two tests for entrapment and the due process approach.

18. Provide some examples of the "new defenses." How do these differ from established criminal law defenses? Do you agree that some of these defenses deserve to be criticized as "abuse excuses"?

19. Write a brief essay outlining justification defenses.

LEGAL TERMINOLOGY

abuse excuse

affirmative defenses

aggressor

alibi

alter ego rule

American rule for resistance to an unlawful arrest

burden of persuasion

burden of production

case-in-chief

Castle Doctrine

choice of evils

civil commitment

competence to stand trial

deadly force

diminished capacity

duress

Durham product test

English rule for resistance to an unlawful arrest

entrapment

excuses

fleeing felon rule

guilty but mentally ill (GBMI)

ignorantia legis non excusat

imperfect self-defense

infancy

insanity defense

Insanity Defense Reform Act of 1984

intervention in defense of others

involuntary intoxication

irresistible impulse test

justification

make my day laws

mistake of fact

mistake of law

M'Naghten test

necessity defense

nondeadly force

objective test for intervention in defense of others

perfect self-defense

presumption of innocence

rebuttal

retreat

retreat to the wall

self-defense

stand your ground rule

substantial capacity test

tactical retreat

true man

voluntary intoxication

withdrawal in good faith

CRIMINAL LAW ON THE WEB

Visit **study.sagepub.com/lippmaness2e** to access additional study tools including suggested answers to the You Decide questions, reprints of cases and statutes, online appendices, and more!

7 HOMICIDE

Was Schnopps guilty of first-degree murder or voluntary manslaughter, murder in the heat of passion?

On the day of the killing, Schnopps had asked his wife to come to their home and talk over their marital difficulties. Schnopps told his wife that he wanted his children at home, and that he wanted the family to remain intact. Schnopps cried during the conversation, and begged his wife to let the children live with him and to keep their family together. His wife replied, "No, I am going to court, you are going to give me all the furniture, you are going to have to get the Hell out of here, you won't have nothing." Then, pointing to her crotch, she said, "You will never touch this again, because I have got something bigger and better for it."

On hearing those words, Schnopps claims that his mind went blank, and that he went "berserk." He went to a cabinet and got out a pistol he had bought and loaded the day before, and he shot his wife and himself. . . . Schnopps claims, however, that his wife's admission of adultery was made for the first time on the day of the killing, and hence the evidence of provocation was sufficient to trigger jury consideration of voluntary manslaughter as a possible verdict. (*Commonwealth v. Schnopps*, 417 N.E.2d 1213 [Mass. 1981])

In this chapter, learn about first- and second-degree murder and voluntary manslaughter.

Learning Objectives

1. Understand the development of the common law of homicide and the historical distinction between murder and manslaughter.
2. Describe the *actus reus* of homicide.
3. Know the elements of first-degree premeditated murder.
4. Understand the characteristics of capital and aggravated first-degree murder.
5. Know the difference between first- and second-degree murder.
6. List the elements of depraved heart murder.
7. State the law of felony murder and compare and contrast the agency theory of felony murder with the proximate cause theory of criminal responsibility for felony murder.
8. State the elements of voluntary and involuntary manslaughter.
9. Explain misdemeanor manslaughter.
10. Know the differing views on when life begins for purposes of homicide and the legal tests for determining death.

INTRODUCTION

Why is homicide considered the most serious criminal offense? What is the reason that it is the only crime subject to the death penalty?

Supreme Court Justice William Brennan noted that in a society that "so strongly affirms the sanctity of life," it is not surprising that death is viewed as the "ultimate" harm. Justice Brennan went on to observe that death is "truly awesome" and is "unusual in its pain, in its finality, and in its enormity. . . . Death, in these respects, is in a class by itself. . . . [It is] degrading to human dignity. It is this regard for life that reminds us to respect one another and to treat each individual with dignity and regard."[1] In *Coker v. Georgia*, Supreme Court Justice Byron White, in explaining why the death penalty is imposed for murder while it is not imposed for rape, noted that the "murderer kills; the rapist, if no more than that, does not. Life is over for the victim of the murderer; for the rape victim, life may not be nearly so happy as it was, but it is not over and normally is not beyond repair."[2]

There are also religious grounds for treating murder as the most serious of crimes. The influential eighteenth-century English jurist William Blackstone observed that murder is a denial of human life and that human life is a gift from God. He stressed that a mere mortal has no right to take a life and to disrupt the divine order of the universe. Professor George Fletcher expands on this notion and explains that in the view of the Bible, a killer was thought to acquire control over the blood of the victim. The execution of the killer was the only way that the blood could be returned to God.[3]

At common law, murder was defined as the unlawful killing of another human being with **malice aforethought**. (We will discuss the meaning of malice aforethought in the next section.) Initially, the common law did not distinguish between types of **criminal homicide**. The taking of a life was treated equally as serious whether committed intentionally, in the heat of passion, recklessly, or negligently.

The development of the modern law of homicide can be traced to fifteenth-century England. Members of the clergy were prosecuted for homicide before ecclesiastical or religious courts that, unlike royal courts, were not authorized to impose the death penalty. Offenders, instead, were subject to imprisonment for a year, the branding of the thumb, and the forfeiture of goods. Judges in the religious courts gradually expanded the *benefit of clergy* to any individual who could read, in order to avoid the harshness of the death penalty. Defendants who could not read typically claimed the benefit of clergy by memorizing passages from the Bible in order to prove that they were literate.

The English monarchy resisted expanding the power of religious courts and enacted a series of statutes that established the jurisdiction of royal courts over the most atrocious homicides. These statutes denied the benefit of clergy and provided for the death penalty. The royal courts began to distinguish between murder, which was committed with malice aforethought and was not eligible for the benefit of clergy, and manslaughter, which was committed without malice aforethought and was eligible for the benefit of clergy. This distinction persisted even after royal courts asserted jurisdiction over all homicides. Murder under the royal courts was subject to the death penalty unless a royal pardon was issued, whereas manslaughter was viewed as a less serious offense that did not result in capital punishment. Most state statutes continue to recognize the distinction between murder and manslaughter. Over time, judges created several other categories of homicide, a process that culminated in modern homicide statutes.

In this chapter, we will review the distinctions between these various grades of criminal homicide. Your challenge is to understand these distinctions.

TYPES OF CRIMINAL HOMICIDE

By the eighteenth century, the law recognized four types of homicide:

1. **Justifiable homicide** includes self-defense, defense of others, defense of the home, and police use of deadly force.

2. **Excusable homicide** is murder committed by individuals who are considered to be legally insane, by individuals with a diminished capacity, or by infants.

3. **Murder** includes all homicides that are neither excused nor justified.

4. **Manslaughter** includes all homicides without malice aforethought that are committed without justification or excuse.

As we have seen, by the end of the fifteenth century, criminal homicide had been divided into murder, or the taking of the life of another with malice aforethought, and manslaughter, or the taking of the life of another without malice aforethought. Malice aforethought is commonly defined as the intent to kill with an ill will or hatred. Aforethought requires that the intent to kill be undertaken with a design to kill. The classic example of a plan to kill is murder committed while "lying in wait" for the victim.

The commentary to the Model Penal Code (MPC) notes that judges gradually expanded malice aforethought to include various types of murder that have little relationship to the original definition. As observed by the Royal Commission on Capital Punishment in England, malice aforethought has come to be a general name for "a number of different mental attitudes which have been variously defined at different stages in the development of the law, the presence of any one of which has been held by the courts to render a homicide particularly heinous and therefore to make it murder."

The MPC notes that as the common law developed, malice aforethought came to be divided into several different mental states, each of which was subject to the penalty of death. The first is intent to kill or murder. A second category of murder entails knowingly causing grievous or serious bodily harm. A third category of murder is termed **depraved heart murder** or killing committed with extreme recklessness or negligence. This involves a "depraved mind" or an "abandoned and malignant heart" and entails a wanton and willful disregard of an unreasonable human risk. A fourth category involves the intent to resist a lawful arrest. There is one additional category of murder committed with malice aforethought. This is murder committed during a felony, which today is termed **felony murder**.

Remember that murder requires a demonstration of malice. The Nevada criminal code states that murder is the "unlawful killing of a human being, with malice aforethought, either express or implied. . . . The unlawful killing may be effected by any of the various means by which death may be occasioned." Individuals who have a deliberate intent to kill possess *express malice*. *Implied malice* exists in those cases that an individual possesses the intent to cause great bodily harm or the intent to commit an act that may be expected to lead to death or great bodily harm. Nevada defines express malice as a "deliberate intention unlawfully to take away the life of a fellow creature which is manifested by external circumstances." The Nevada law goes on to provide that malice may be implied "when all the circumstances of the killing show an abandoned and malignant heart."[4]

What about manslaughter? The common law of manslaughter developed into two separate categories. The first entails an intentional killing committed without malice in the heat of passion upon adequate provocation. Murder was also considered manslaughter when it was committed without malice as a result of conduct that was insufficiently reckless or negligent to be categorized as depraved heart murder. Courts typically describe the first category as **voluntary manslaughter** and the second as **involuntary manslaughter**.

In 1794, Pennsylvania adopted a statute (ch. 257, §§ 1, 2) creating separate grades of murder and manslaughter that continue to serve as the foundation for a majority of state statutes today. The Pennsylvania statute divided homicide into two separate categories and limited the death penalty to first-degree murder, the most serious form of homicide. Second-degree murder was punishable by life imprisonment.

> All murder, which shall be perpetrated by means of poison, by lying in wait, or by any other kind of willful, deliberate, or premeditated killing or which shall be committed in perpetration or attempt to perpetrate any arson, rape, robbery, or burglary shall be deemed murder in the first degree; and all other kinds of murder shall be deemed murder in the second degree.

Modern state statutes typically divide murder into first- and second-degree murder, both of which require the prosecutor to establish intent and malice. **First-degree murder** is the most serious form of murder, and the prosecutor has the burden of establishing **premeditation and deliberation**. This involves demonstrating that the defendant reflected for at least a brief period of time before intentionally killing another individual. **Second-degree murder** usually includes all murders not involving premeditation and deliberation. Manslaughter typically comprises an additional grade or grades of homicide. These general categories are described in Table 7.1, starting with the most serious degree of homicide. Keep in mind that state statutes differ widely in their approach to defining homicide.

Some states also single out vehicular manslaughter as a special form of involuntary manslaughter. This typically is defined as the "reckless killing of another by the operation of an automobile, airplane, motorboat or other motor vehicle involving conduct creating a substantial risk of death or serious bodily injury to a person; or as the proximate result of the driver's intoxication."[5]

Homicide primarily is prosecuted under state law. The federal government has jurisdiction over the killing of officers and employees of the U.S. government as well as the killing of various foreign officials. Federal statutes provide for the same division of offenses as state law.[6]

Table 7.1 Contemporary Approaches to Homicide	
Type of Criminal Homicide	*Definition*
First-Degree Murder	Premeditation and deliberation and murder committed in the perpetration of various dangerous felonies. Some statutes explicitly include the killing of a police officer and murder committed while lying in wait or as a result of torture or poison. Capital or aggravated first-degree murder may result in the death penalty in the states that provide for capital punishment.
Second-Degree Murder	Killing with malice and without premeditation. This may include a death resulting from the intent to cause serious bodily harm and killing resulting from the distribution of certain unlawful narcotics.
Depraved Heart Murder	Reckless conduct that results in the death of another.
Voluntary Manslaughter	Murder in the heat of passion.
Involuntary Manslaughter	Gross negligence that results in the death of another.

ACTUS REUS AND CRIMINAL HOMICIDE

State statutes define the *actus reus* of criminal homicide as the "unlawful killing of a human being" or "causing the death of a person." This may involve an infinite variety of acts, including shooting, stabbing, choking, poisoning, beating with a bat or axe, and "a thousand other forms of death."[7] Homicides can also be carried out without landing a single blow. A husband was held criminally liable for the murder of his young wife when he threatened to beat her unless she jumped into a stream that subsequently carried her away in the current.[8]

The Legal Equation

Criminal homicide $=$ Unlawful killing of human being

$+$ purposely or knowingly or recklessly or negligently.

MENS REA AND CRIMINAL HOMICIDE

The *mens rea* of criminal homicide encompasses all of the mental states that we discussed in Chapter 3. The Utah criminal code provides that an individual commits criminal homicide "if he intentionally, knowingly, recklessly, with criminal negligence" or acting with the "mental state . . . specified in the statute defining the offense, causes the death of another human being, including an unborn child at any stage of development."[9]

Two forms of criminal homicide that we will review later in the chapter, felony murder and misdemeanor manslaughter, involve strict liability. The **grading**, or assignment of degrees to homicide, is based on a defendant's criminal intent. As we shall see, an individual who kills as a result of premeditation and deliberation is considered more dangerous and morally blameworthy than an individual who kills as a result of a reckless disregard or negligence.

MURDER

We have seen that murder is the unlawful killing of an individual with malice aforethought. Several types of murder are discussed in this chapter, and your challenge is to learn the difference between each of these categories of homicide:

- First-degree murder
- Capital and aggravated first-degree murder
- Second-degree murder
- Depraved heart murder
- Felony murder

Table 7.2 lists the states with the highest rates of homicide in 2014.

First-Degree Murder

First-degree murder is the most serious form of homicide and can result in the death penalty in thirty-one states.

The *mens rea* of first-degree murder requires deliberation and premeditation as well as malice. Premeditation means the act was thought out prior to committing the crime. Deliberation entails an intent to kill that is carried out in a cool state of mind in furtherance of the design to kill.

An intent to kill without deliberation and premeditation generally is considered second-degree murder.

Why is first-degree murder treated more seriously than other forms of homicide? First, an individual who is capable of consciously devising a plan to take the life of another obviously poses a threat to society. A harsh punishment both is deserved and may deter others from cold and calculated killings. Some commentators dispute whether a deliberate and premeditated murderer poses a greater threat than an impulsive individual who lacks self-control and may explode at any moment in reaction to the slightest insult. Assuming that you were asked to formulate a sentencing scheme, which of these two killers would you punish most severely?

Table 7.2 Ten* Highest Murder Rates in 2014 per 100,000 Population	
State	Rate
Louisiana	10.3
Mississippi	8.6
Missouri	6.6
South Carolina	6.4
Maryland	6.1
Nevada	6.0
Delaware	5.8
Florida	5.8
Tennessee	5.7
Arkansas	5.7
Georgia	5.7
National Rate = 4.5	

Source: Kathleen O'Leary Morgan and Scott Morgan, eds. *State Rankings 2016: A Statistical View of America.* Thousand Oaks, CA: CQ Press, 2016, p. 36.

*Eleven are included due to the three-way tie of Tennessee, Arkansas, and Georgia.

The general rule is that premeditation may be formed in the few seconds it takes to pull a trigger or deliver a fatal blow. A West Virginia court observed that the "mental process necessary to constitute 'willful, deliberate and premeditated' murder can be accomplished very quickly or even in the proverbial 'twinkling of an eye.'"[10] The California Penal Code in Section 189 provides that to prove a killing was "deliberate and premeditated, it shall not be necessary to prove the defendant maturely and meaningfully reflected upon the gravity of his or her act."

What evidence might have established premeditation? In order to establish premeditation and deliberation, judges generally require either evidence of planning or evidence that the defendant possessed a motive to kill and that the killing was undertaken in a fashion that indicates that it was planned, such as "lying in wait" or the use of a bomb or poison or the carrying out of the killing in a brutal fashion.

A number of judges continue to resist the trend toward recognizing that a premeditated intent to kill need only exist for an instant. These jurists point out that unless the prosecution is required to produce proof of premeditation and deliberation, it is difficult to tell the difference between first- and second-degree murder.[11] California Penal Code Section 189 adopts a modern approach to defining first-degree murder by listing specific criminal acts that are categorized as first-degree murder. The acts listed in the statute generally require some planning and reflection.

All murder which is perpetrated by means of a destructive device or explosive, a weapon of mass destruction, knowing use of ammunition designed primarily to penetrate metal or armor, poison, lying in wait, torture, or by any other kind of willful, deliberate, and premeditated killing, . . . or any murder which is perpetrated by means of discharging a firearm from a motor vehicle, intentionally at another person outside of the vehicle with the intent to inflict death, is murder of the first degree. All other kinds of murders are of the second degree.

Felony murder, which is covered later in the chapter, also is considered first-degree murder under California law.

A particularly difficult issue is so-called mercy killing. In *State v. Forrest*, Forrest shot and killed his dying father and was convicted of first-degree murder and sentenced to life imprisonment. A judge noted in dissent that

Read *State v. Forrest* on the study site: study .sagepub.com/ lippmaness2e.

[a]lmost all would agree that someone who kills because of a desire to end a loved one's physical suffering caused by an illness which is both terminal and incurable should not be deemed in law as culpable and deserving of the same punishment as one who kills because of unmitigated spite, hatred, or ill will. Yet the Court's decision in this case essentially says there is no legal distinction between the two kinds of killing.[12]

CRIMINAL LAW AND PUBLIC POLICY

Suicide at common law was considered the felony of "self murder" because it deprived the King of one of his subjects and therefore was a crime against the Crown and against God. The punishment for suicide entailed forfeiture of the deceased person's estate and loss of the right to a formal burial. In 1961, England abolished the offense of suicide, although assisting suicide remains a crime.

In the United States, suicide in most states also no longer is considered a criminal offense. Assisting suicide, however, remains a crime. New York provides that an individual who "intentionally causes or aids another person to commit suicide" is guilty of manslaughter in the second degree (N.Y. Penal Law § 125.15).

In November 1997, the Oregon "death with dignity" law went into effect. The law provides for physician-assisted suicide (Ore. Rev. Stat. §§ 127.800, et seq). In 2006, the U.S. Supreme Court held that the federal government had no legal authority under the Controlled Substances Act (CSA) to prevent Oregon doctors from prescribing legal drugs to be used in suicide. Roughly six hundred individuals have made use of the Oregon law. See *Gonzales v. Oregon*, 546 U.S. 243 (2006).

Washington passed a similar law in 2008. Wash. Rev. Code § 70.122.070(1) provides that the withholding or withdrawal of life-sustaining treatment at a patient's request "shall not . . . constitute a suicide or

a homicide." In May 2009, a sixty-six-year-old woman suffering from pancreatic cancer became the first person in Washington to make use of the law to end her life. Approximately 150 persons have made use of the law in Washington.

In both Oregon and Washington, two doctors are required to certify that a patient has six months or less to live. After receiving these separate, independent certifications, the patient is eligible to terminate his or her life. Then, the patient must request lethal drugs on two occasions, fifteen days apart. The fatal dose must be self-administered.

The Oregon and Washington laws are opposed by various religious organizations and by the American Medical Association, which believes that doctors should not be involved in assisting in the taking of human life.

In Oregon, an equal number of men and women have made use of the law, and the median age of these individuals is seventy-one years of age. Of these individuals, 81 percent were suffering from cancer. Studies determined that most of these individuals were motivated by a desire to control their fate rather than to eliminate pain. There was apprehension when the Oregon law was passed that poor individuals would be pressured into suicide because of the cost of their care. Studies, however, indicate that most people employing the law were solidly middle class.

In 2014 in Oregon, prescriptions for lethal medications were written for 155 people as compared to 122 people in 2013 and 116 in 2012. There were seventy-one "assisted deaths" during 2013, nearly all of which involved individuals who were over sixty-five years of age and died at home. These people expressed concern for a loss of autonomy, for decreasing capacity to participate in activities that made life enjoyable, and for a loss of dignity.

In 2009, in *Baxter v. State*, 224 P.3d 1211 (Mont. 2009), the Montana Supreme Court held that a doctor is not criminally liable for assisting a mature, aware, and terminally ill patient to take his or her life. The court reasoned that state public policy respected the end-of-life autonomy of patients and that doctors had an ethical obligation to respect a patient's wishes. The Alaska Supreme Court earlier had held that terminally ill patients have no right to a physician's assistance in committing suicide. See *Sampson v. State*, 31 P.3d 88 (Alaska 2001). In May 2014, the Vermont legislature recognized that terminally ill patients have a right to assistance in dying.

In other states in the United States, the law continues to treat aiding and abetting a suicide as a crime. In 1999, the late Dr. Jack Kevorkian was convicted of the second-degree murder of Thomas Youk and was sentenced to serve from ten to twenty-five years in prison. Youk was in the final stages of Lou Gehrig's disease and had signed a consent form authorizing Kevorkian

to take his life. See *People v. Kevorkian,* 639 N.W.2d 291 (Mich. 2001). Kevorkian had videotaped the process leading to Youk's death. The tape was played on CBS's *60 Minutes* and was used by the prosecution at trial. Kevorkian was unrepentant and claimed that he was providing a "medical service for an agonized human being."

The U.S. Supreme Court in two decisions has upheld the constitutionality of a state's criminally punishing assisted suicide. See *Vacco v. Quill*, 521 U.S 793 (1997); and *Washington v. Glucksberg*, 521 U.S. 702 (1997). The Court noted in *Washington v. Glucksberg* that an examination of "our Nation's history, legal traditions, and practice demonstrates that Anglo-American common law has punished . . . assisting suicide for over seven hundred years."

In 2014, twenty-nine-year-old Brittany Maynard, diagnosed with terminal brain cancer, moved from California to Oregon to take her life under Oregon law. She wrote, "My question is: Who has the right to tell me that I don't deserve this choice?" Brittany's death led to the California legislature's adoption in 2015 of the End of Life Option Act, which legalized physician-assisted suicide. The California law requires two doctors to certify that a patient has six months or less to live before lethal drugs may be prescribed. Patients are required to be physically able to swallow the medication themselves and must have the mental capacity to make medical decisions.

The Legal Equation

First-degree murder $=$ Premeditated and deliberate intent to kill another person (or intent to commit felony in felony murder)

$+$ act that is the factual and legal cause of death

$+$ death of another person.

Capital and Aggravated First-Degree Murder

Thirty-one states and the federal government authorize the death penalty. In some states, this is called **capital murder**. The statutes in these jurisdictions typically provide for the death penalty or a life sentence in the case of a first-degree murder committed under conditions that make the killing deserving of the punishment of death or life imprisonment. Other states create a category termed *aggravated murder* that is subject to the death penalty or to life imprisonment. Those states that do not possess the death penalty punish aggravated murder by life imprisonment rather than death.

State capital murder or aggravated murder statutes typically reserve this harsh punishment for premeditated killings committed with the presence of various **aggravating factors** or special circumstances. The Virginia capital murder statute, for instance, includes willful, deliberate, and premeditated killing of a police officer, killing by an inmate, and killing in the commission of or following a rape or sexual penetration, along with other factors.[13] These statutes differ from one another but typically include the following aggravating circumstances:

- *Victim.* A killing of a police officer, a juvenile thirteen years of age or younger, or more than one victim.
- *Offender.* An escaped prison inmate or an individual previously convicted of an aggravated murder.
- *Criminal Act.* Terrorism, murder for hire, killing during a prison escape, or killing to prevent a witness from testifying.
- *Felony Murder.* Killing committed during a dangerous felony.

The jury, in order to sentence a defendant to death, must find one or more aggravating circumstances and is required to determine whether these outweigh any **mitigating circumstances** that may be presented by the defense attorney. Some statutes list mitigating circumstances that the jury should consider. The Florida death penalty statute specifies a number of mitigating circumstances, including the fact that the defendant does not possess a significant history of criminal activity or that he or she suffered from a substantially impaired mental capacity, or that the defendant was under the influence of extreme mental or emotional disturbance or acted under duress, or the victim participated in the defendant's conduct or consented to the act, or the defendant's participation was relatively minor.[14]

An example of a crime involving extreme and outrageous depravity is the Florida case of *Owen v. State.* The Florida Supreme Court recounted that the victim was stabbed or cut eighteen times and was alive when all the wounds were inflicted and "undoubtedly had a belief of her impending doom." The puncturing of Karen Slattery's lung "caused her to literally drown in her own blood. She experienced air deprivation. Each of the eighteen cuts, slashes, and/or stab wounds caused pain by penetrating nerve endings in Miss Slattery's body."[15]

Second-Degree Murder

State second-degree murder statutes typically punish intentional killings that are committed with malice aforethought that are not premeditated, justified, or excused. Most statutes go beyond this simple statement and provide that killings committed with malice aforethought that are not specifically listed as first-degree murder are considered second-degree murder. For instance, several states include felony murder as second- rather than first-degree murder.

Washington State provides that a person is guilty of murder in the second degree when, with "the intent to cause the death of another person but without premeditation, he causes the death of such person." That statute also includes as second-degree murder a killing committed in furtherance of or in flight from a felony.[16] Idaho provides that all killings that are not explicitly included in the first-degree murder statute "are of the second degree."[17] This means that an Idaho prosecutor is authorized to charge second-degree murder in all instances in which a murder does not fall within the state's first-degree murder statute.

The Louisiana statute states that second-degree murder is the killing of a human being when the "offender has a specific intent to kill or to inflict great bodily harm." The law also provides that second-degree murder includes[18]

- a killing that occurs during the perpetration or attempted perpetration of aggravated rape, arson, burglary, kidnapping, escape, a drive-by shooting, armed robbery, or robbery, despite the fact that the individual possesses no intent to kill or to inflict great bodily harm;
- a killing that occurs in the perpetration of cruelty to juveniles, despite the fact that an individual has no intent to kill or to inflict great bodily harm; and
- a killing that directly results from the unlawful distribution of an illegal narcotic.

Some states include **intent-to-do-serious-bodily-harm murder** under second-degree murder. In *Midgett v. State*, Ronnie Midgett Sr. was convicted of second-degree murder under an Arkansas statute that punished a killing committed with the "purpose of causing serious physical injury."[19] The three-hundred-pound Midgett starved and abused eight-year-old Ronnie Jr. for a number of months. The Arkansas Supreme Court held that Midgett's intent had been "not to kill his son but to further abuse him" and there was no "substantial evidence" that Midgett "premeditated and deliberated the killing."[20]

The Legal Equation

Second-degree murder	=	Intentional act dangerous to the life of another
	+	intent to kill without premeditation and deliberation or intent to commit underlying felony for felony murder
	+	causing the death of another person.

Depraved Heart Murder

An individual may be held criminally responsible for depraved heart murder in those instances that he or she kills another as a result of the "deliberate perpetration of a knowingly dangerous act with reckless and wanton unconcern and indifference as to whether anyone is harmed or not."[21] A defendant who acts in this fashion is viewed as manifesting an "abandoned and malignant heart" or "depraved indifference to human life." Reckless homicide is based on the belief that acts undertaken without an intent to kill that severely and seriously endanger human life are "just as antisocial and . . . just as truly murderous as the specific intent to kill and to harm."[22] Malice is implied in the case of depraved heart murder, and this is typically punished as second-degree murder. The California Penal Code states that malice is "implied . . . when the circumstances attending the killing show an abandoned and malignant heart."[23]

Depraved heart murder requires the following:

- *Conduct.* The defendant's act must create a very high degree of risk of serious bodily injury. Keep in mind that the act must be highly dangerous.
- *Intent.* The defendant must be aware of the danger created by his or her conduct. Some courts merely require that a reasonable person would have been aware of the risk.
- *Danger.* The common law appeared to require that a number of individuals were placed in danger; the modern view is that it is sufficient that a single individual is at risk.

Kansas Statutes Annotated Section 21-3402 (2003 Supp.) defines depraved heart murder as the killing of a human being committed "unintentionally but recklessly under circumstances manifesting extreme indifference to the value of human life." John Doub drank six beers following a party, struck two parked vehicles, and immediately drove off because he was concerned that the police would detect that he had been drinking. He subsequently drank additional liquor and smoked crack cocaine. Roughly two hours later, he collided into the rear of an automobile, killing nine-year-old Jamika Smith. The accident investigator determined that Doub was traveling at a rapid rate and drove "up on top of [the car]," driving it down into the pavement and propelling the automobile off the street and into a tree. Would you convict Doub?[24]

There is no mathematical formula for determining whether an act satisfies the highly dangerous standard of depraved heart murder. This is decided based on the facts of each case. Examples of depraved heart murder include the following:

- A defendant plays a game of "Russian Roulette" in which he loads a revolver with one bullet and six "dummy bullets" and spins the chamber. He places the gun to the victim's head and pulls the trigger three times; the third pull kills the victim.[25]
- A defendant shoots into a passing train, unintentionally killing a passenger.[26]
- Two street gangs engage in a lengthy shoot-out on a street in downtown Baltimore, killing an innocent fifteen-year-old.[27]

In *State v. Davidson*, the Kansas Supreme Court found that Sabine Davidson had killed Christopher Wilson "unintentionally but recklessly under circumstances manifesting extreme indifference to the value of human life." Davidson had a number of "powerful" and "aggressive" dogs and, despite warnings, failed to train or restrain the dogs, which terrorized the neighborhood. The dogs mauled an eleven-year-old child to death, and the court affirmed her conviction for depraved heart murder finding that she "created a profound risk and ignored foreseeable consequences that her dogs could attack or injure someone."[28]

The Legal Equation

Depraved heart murder = Dangerous act creating a high risk of death

+ knowledge of danger created by act.

You Decide

7.1 Michael Berry was charged with depraved heart murder. The defendant purchased a pit bull, Willy, from a breeder of fighting dogs. Berry trained Willy and entered the dog in "professional fights" as far away as South Carolina. Willy was described as possessing stamina, courage, and a particularly "hard bite." He was tied to the inside of a six-foot unenclosed fence so as to discourage access to the 243 marijuana plants that Berry was illegally growing in an area in the back of his house. Berry's next-door neighbor momentarily left her two-year-old child, James Soto, playing on the patio of her home. James apparently wandered across Berry's yard to the other side of Berry's home, where he encountered Willy and was mauled to death. An animal control officer testified that pit bulls are considered "dangerous unless proved otherwise." Is Berry guilty of killing with an abandoned and malignant heart? See *Berry v. Superior Court*, 256 Cal. Rptr. 344 (Cal. Ct. App. 1989).

You can find the answer at study.sagepub.com/lippmaness2e

Felony Murder

A murder that occurs during the course of a felony is punished as murder. In *People v. Stamp*, Michael John Koory and Jonathan Earl Stamp robbed a store while armed with a gun and a blackjack. The defendants ordered the employees along with the owner, Carl Honeyman, to lie down on the floor so that no one "would get hurt" while they removed money from the cash register. Fifteen or twenty minutes following the robbery, Honeyman collapsed on the floor and was pronounced dead on arrival at the hospital. He was found to suffer from advanced and dangerous hardening of the arteries, but doctors concluded that the fright from the robbery had caused the fatal seizure. A California appellate court affirmed the defendants' conviction for felony murder and sentence of life imprisonment.[29]

This use of the felony murder conviction to hold defendants liable for murder was criticized by another California appellate court, which observed that such a "harsh result destroys the symmetry of the law by equating an accidental killing . . . with premeditated murder."[30] Despite this criticism, the fact remains that "but for" the robbery, Honeyman would not have died. Severely punishing Koory and Stamp deters other individuals contemplating thievery and protects society. As you read this section of the textbook, consider whether the felony murder rule is a fair and just doctrine.

The felony murder doctrine, as previously noted, provides that any homicide that occurs during the commission of a felony or attempt to commit a felony is murder. This is true regardless of whether the killing is committed with deliberation and premeditation, intentionally, recklessly, or negligently. The intent to commit the felony is considered to provide the malice for the conviction of murder. The doctrine can be traced back to Lord Coke in the early 1600s and is illustrated by Judge Stephen's example that "if a man shot at a fowl with intent to steal it, and accidentally killed a man, he was to be accounted guilty of murder, because the act was done in the commission of a felony."[31]

This common law rule was not viewed as unduly harsh because all felonies in England were subject to the death penalty, and it made little difference whether an individual was convicted of murder or of the underlying felony. Felony murder, however, came under increasing criticism in England as the number of felonies subject to the death penalty was gradually reduced. English lawmakers came to view felony murder as making little sense and abandoned the doctrine in 1957.

The 1794 Pennsylvania murder statute included, within first-degree murder, killings committed in the perpetration or attempt to perpetrate "any arson, rape, robbery, or burglary." Killings committed in furtherance of other felonies under the Pennsylvania law were considered second-degree murder. The federal government along with virtually every state has continued to apply the felony murder rule; only Ohio, Hawaii, Michigan, and Kentucky resist the rule. Four reasons are offered for the felony murder rule:

1. *Deterrence.* Individuals are deterred from committing felonies knowing that a killing will result in a murder conviction.

2. *Protection of Life.* Individuals are deterred from committing felonies in a violent fashion knowing that a killing will result in a murder conviction.

3. *Punishment.* Individuals who commit violent felonies that result in death deserve to be harshly punished.

4. *Prosecution.* Prosecutors are relieved of the burden of establishing a criminal intent. The fact that a killing occurred during a felony is sufficient to establish first-degree murder. The imposition of liability on all the felons carrying out the crime provides an efficient method for incarcerating dangerous felons.

There is some question whether the felony murder rule is an important tool in the fight against crime. The U.S. Supreme Court, for example, cites statistics indicating that only half of 1 percent of all robberies result in homicide.[32]

State felony murder statutes generally classify killings committed in the perpetration or attempt to commit dangerous felonies, such as arson, rape, robbery, or burglary, as first-degree murder deserving life imprisonment or in states with the death penalty as a capital felony punishable with either life imprisonment or the death penalty. Killings committed in furtherance of other less dangerous felonies typically are not explicitly mentioned and are prosecuted under second-degree murder statutes that punish "all other kinds of murder that are not listed as first-degree murder."[33] Several states have statutes that punish as second-degree murder a killing that results from the commission or attempt to commit "any felony."[34]

Statutes that do not list specific felonies present courts with the challenge of determining which felonies are sufficiently serious to provide the foundation for felony murder. What felonies should serve as the foundation or predicate for felony murder? Judges have generally limited felony murder to "inherently dangerous felonies." One approach is to ask whether a particular felony can be committed "in the abstract" without creating a substantial risk that an individual will be killed. The other method is to examine whether the manner in which a particular felony was committed in the specific case before the court created a high risk of death.

The approach of the California Supreme Court is to ask whether the "underlying felony" can be committed without endangering human life. In *People v. Burroughs*, the California Supreme Court ruled that the defendant's felonious unlicensed practice of medicine did not constitute an "inherently dangerous felony" because an unlicensed practitioner may be treating a common cold, a sprained finger, or an individual who suffers from the delusion that he or she is president of the United States. The California Supreme Court accordingly reversed the defendant's conviction for felony murder.[35]

The felony also must have "caused" the victim's death to support a felony murder conviction, and the state must establish "that the homicide was committed in the perpetration of the felony." A Florida court held that there was "a break in the chain of circumstances when someone stole a car in the early morning hours and, later that evening, Allen [the defendant] was involved in an accident while driving the stolen car."[36] In *Lester v. State*, although the defendant "believed the police were following him," he was not fleeing the scene of the crime, and "his reckless driving was too [distant] from the grand theft of the car the previous evening to support a felony murder conviction."[37] These cases are distinguished from a situation in which a fatal accident occurred while the defendant was fleeing the scene of the robbery with the police in high-speed pursuit.[38]

Keep in mind that under the theory of accomplice liability, all the co-felons will be liable for a killing committed in furtherance of the felony that is the natural and probable result of the crime.

Felony murder can become complicated where a nonfelon, such as a police officer or victim, kills one of the felons or a bystander. In *Campbell v. State*, a police officer killed an armed fleeing felon who had robbed a taxicab driver. An unarmed co-felon was later apprehended by another officer and was charged with the first-degree murder of his co-felon. The Maryland Court of Appeals adopted the **agency theory of felony murder** that limits criminal liability to the acts of felons and co-felons and acquitted the defendant.[39] This theory was first stated by the Massachusetts Supreme Judicial Court in *Commonwealth v. Campbell*, which held that a felon was criminally responsible only for acts "committed by his own hand or by some one acting in concert with him in furtherance of a common object or purpose" and that a felon is not liable for the acts of a "person who is his direct and immediate adversary . . . [who is] actually engaged in opposing and resisting him and his confederates."[40]

Other courts have adopted a **proximate cause theory of felony murder** that holds felons responsible for foreseeable deaths that are caused by the commission of a dangerous felony. In *Kinchion v. State*, the defendant acted as a lookout while his armed accomplice entered a store. The clerk shot and killed Kinchion's co-conspirator in self-defense, and Kinchion was convicted of first-degree felony murder. The Oklahoma court affirmed the defendant's conviction, explaining that his planning and carrying out of the armed robbery "set in motion 'a chain of events so perilous to the sanctity of human life' that the likelihood of death was foreseeable."[41]

Consider whether this doctrine makes sense. Oliver Wendell Holmes Jr., in his famous book *The Common Law*, argues that if a felon stealing chickens accidentally kills a farmer, the defendant should be punished for reckless homicide rather than felony murder. Why should the prosecutor rely on felony murder rather than establishing the elements of implied malice second-degree murder? Note that Holmes argues that prosecuting the defendant for felony murder serves little purpose because few chicken thieves will be deterred from stealing chickens by a conviction of the thief for felony murder, and it would not occur to most chicken thieves to carry a weapon in any event.[42]

Read *People v. Lowery* on the study site: study .sagepub.com/ lippmaness2e.

The MPC shares Holmes's point of view and restricts felony murder to killings that are committed under certain circumstances. Section 210.2 punishes, as a felony of the first degree, killings committed purposely or knowingly as well as killings that result from "circumstances manifesting extreme indifference to the value of human life." Reckless indifference is presumed when a killing is committed during the commission, attempted commission, or flight from a robbery, sexual attack, arson, burglary, kidnapping, or felonious escape. The jury must find beyond a reasonable doubt that the defendant possessed a reckless indifference to human life. Would you recognize felony murder if you were drafting a new criminal code for your state?

The Legal Equation		
Felony murder	=	Killing of another
	+	intent to commit a dangerous felony
	+	killing during perpetration of a dangerous felony
	+	caused by felon or co-felon as a consequence of the felony.

You Decide 7.2 Sanexay Sophophone and three other individuals broke into a house in Emporia, Kansas. Police officers responded to a call from residents and spotted four individuals leaving the back of the house. They shined a light on the suspects and ordered them to stop. An officer ran down Sophophone, handcuffed him, and placed him in a police car.

Another officer chased fellow suspect Somphone Sysoumphone. Sysoumphone crossed railroad tracks, jumped a fence, and then stopped. The officer approached with his weapon drawn and ordered Sysoumphone to the ground and not to move. Sysoumphone complied with the officer's command but, while lying face down, rose up and fired at the officer, who returned fire and killed him. Sophophone was charged with conspiracy to commit aggravated burglary, obstruction of official duty, and felony murder. The question of law before the Kansas Supreme Court was whether Sophophone could be convicted of felony murder for the "killing of a co-felon not caused by his acts but by the lawful acts of a police officer acting in self-defense in the course and scope of his duties in apprehending the co-felon fleeing from an aggravated burglary."

The Kansas Supreme Court held that the "overriding fact . . . is that neither Sophophone nor any of his accomplices 'killed' anyone. . . . We believe that making one criminally responsible for the lawful acts of a law enforcement officer is not the intent of the felony-murder statute." The dissent pointed out that the rationale for felony murder is that it serves as a general deterrent. Potential felons will be hesitant to engage in criminal activity if they realize that they risk being convicted of first-degree murder in the event that a death occurs during the commission of a felony. "Sophophone set in motion acts which would have resulted in the death or serious injury of a law enforcement officer had it not been for the highly alert law enforcement officer." This "could have very easily resulted in the death of a law enforcement officer . . . [and] is exactly the type of case the legislature had in mind when it adopted the felony-murder rule. . . . It does not take much imagination to see a number of situations where a death is going to result from an inherently dangerous felony and the majority's opinion is going to prevent the accused from being charged with felony murder."

What is your view? Should the Kansas court use the agency or proximate cause theory? See *State v. Sophophone*, 19 P.3d 70 (Kan. 2001).

You can find the answer at study.sagepub.com/lippmaness2e

MANSLAUGHTER

Manslaughter comprises a second category of homicide and is defined as an unlawful killing of another human being without malice aforethought.

The common law distinction between voluntary manslaughter and the less severe offense of involuntary manslaughter continues to appear in many state statutes. Other statutes distinguish between degrees of manslaughter, and a third approach combines both voluntary and involuntary manslaughter within a single statute that punishes the crime of manslaughter. Voluntary manslaughter is the killing of another human being committed in a sudden heat of passion in response to adequate provocation. Adequate provocation is considered a provocation that would cause a reasonable person to lose self-control. Involuntary manslaughter is the killing of another human being as a result of criminal negligence. Criminal negligence involves a gross deviation from the standard of care that a reasonable person would practice under similar circumstances.

Voluntary Manslaughter

One function of criminal law is to remind us that we will be prosecuted and punished in the event that we allow our anger or frustration to boil over and assault individuals or destroy their property. Voluntary manslaughter seemingly is an exception to the expectation that we control our emotions. This offense recognizes that a reasonable person, under certain circumstances, will be provoked to lose control and kill. In such situations, it is only fair that an individual should receive a less serious punishment than an individual who kills in a cool and intentional fashion.

Voluntary manslaughter requires that an individual kill in a sudden and intense **heat of passion** in response to adequate provocation. Heat of passion is commonly described as anger but is sufficiently broad to include fear, jealousy, and panic.

The law of provocation is based on the reaction of the **reasonable person**, a fictional balanced, sober, and fair-minded human being with no physical or mental imperfections. *Adequate provocation* is defined as conduct that is sufficient to excite an intense passion that causes a reasonable person to lose control. The common law restricted adequate provocation to a limited number of situations: aggravated assault or battery, mutual combat defined as a fight voluntarily entered into by the participants, a serious crime committed against a close relative of a defendant, and one spouse observing the adultery of the other spouse. Keep in mind that the provocation must cause a reasonable person to lose control (objective component) and the defendant, in fact, must have lost control and killed in the heat of passion (subjective component).

The defense of sudden heat of passion is unavailable if a reasonable person's passion would have experienced a **cooling of blood** between the time of the provocation and the time of the killing. Some common law courts followed an ironclad rule that limited the impact of provocation to twenty-four hours. The modern approach is to view the facts and circumstances of a case and to determine whether a reasonable person's "blood would have cooled" and whether the defendant's "blood had cooled." In a frequently cited case, the victim was sodomized while unconscious. The perpetrator spread news of the defendant's victimization throughout the community and subjected the victim to what the victim viewed as humiliating comments and embarrassment. The defendant boiled over in rage after two weeks of this harassment and killed the perpetrator. The court ruled that the cumulative impact of the harassment would not be taken into consideration and that too much time had passed to recognize involuntary manslaughter.[43]

Voluntary Manslaughter Reconsidered

Voluntary manslaughter involves several "hurdles":

- *Provocation.* An individual must be reasonably and actually provoked and must kill in the heat of passion.
- *Cooling of Blood.* An individual must have *reasonably* and *actually* not "cooled off."

The question remains whether the law should recognize voluntary manslaughter. An individual who loses control and impulsively kills clearly poses a threat to society and might be viewed to be as dangerous as an individual who intentionally and calmly kills. Should we accept that a "reasonable person" can be driven to kill in the heat of passion and therefore should be subject to less severe punishment than other categories of killers?

Another question is whether the states should follow MPC Section 210.3(1) and allow the jury to decide for itself whether there is adequate provocation to reduce a defendant's guilt from murder to manslaughter. California, in reaction to a series of cases in which defendants unsuccessfully claimed they had acted in a heat of passion when the victim had attempted to sexually molest them, adopted a law in 2014 prohibiting defendants from raising the "gay panic defense."

The Legal Equation

Voluntary manslaughter	=	Killing another person
	+	intent to kill
	+	sudden heat of passion based on adequate provocation.

You Decide

7.3 Steven S. and Joyce M. Girouard had been married for about two months on October 28, 1987, after having known each other for roughly three months. They met while working together in the military.

Their relationship was rocky, and there is some indication that Joyce resumed a relationship with a former boyfriend.

Steven overheard Joyce tell her friend on the telephone that she had asked for a discharge because her husband did not love her anymore. Joyce refused to answer Steven's question; and, upset by her lack of response, Steven kicked away Joyce's plate of food.

Joyce followed Steven into the bedroom and climbed onto Steven's back, pulled his hair, and said, "What are you going to do, hit me?" Joyce added, "I never did want to marry you and you are a lousy f— and you remind me of my dad [who had impregnated her when she was 14]. . . . What are you going to do?" She added that she had filed charges against him in the Judge Advocate General (JAG) and that he would probably be court-martialed.

Steven left the bedroom with his pillow and entered the kitchen. He took a long-handled kitchen knife, which he hid behind the pillow. Joyce continued taunting Steven, claiming that the marriage had been a mistake. Steven lunged at Joyce and stabbed her nineteen times. Steven was convicted of first-degree murder and, on appeal, claimed that he should have been convicted of voluntary manslaughter.

Do you agree with Steven? See *Girouard v. State*, 583 A.2d 718 (Md. 1991).

You can find the answer at study.sagepub.com/lippmaness2e

Involuntary Manslaughter

Involuntary manslaughter involves the unintentional killing of another without malice and typically includes **negligent manslaughter**, the negligent creation of a risk of serious injury or death of another, as well as **misdemeanor manslaughter** (also referred to as unlawful-act manslaughter), the killing of another during the commission of a criminal act that does not amount to a felony. Some states, such as California, also provide for **vehicular manslaughter**, or the killing of another that results from the grossly negligent operation of an automobile or from driving under the influence of intoxicants.

Negligent Manslaughter

Negligent manslaughter arises when an individual commits an act that he or she is unaware creates a high degree of risk of human injury or death under circumstances in which a reasonable person would have been aware of the threat. Some courts require **recklessness**, meaning that a defendant must have been personally aware that his or her conduct creates a substantial risk of death or serious bodily harm. Other courts do not clearly state whether they require negligence or recklessness.

Alabama Criminal Code Section 13A-6-4(a) provides that a person "commits the crime of criminally negligent homicide if he causes the death of another person by criminal negligence." Missouri Criminal Code Section 565.024 provides that the crime of involuntary manslaughter involves "recklessly" causing the death of another person. The MPC uses a negligence standard and holds individuals criminally responsible where they are "grossly insensitive to the interests and claims of other persons in society" and their conduct constitutes a "gross deviation from ordinary standards of conduct."

You Decide  **7.4** Robert Strong, age fifty-seven, emigrated from "Arabia" to China and then to Rochester, New York, three years later. The defendant articulated the three central beliefs of his religion as "cosmetic consciousness, mind over matter and psysiomatic psychomatic consciousness." He contended that "mind over matter" empowered a "master" or leader to lie on a bed of nails without bleeding, walk through fire, and perform surgical operations without anesthesia. He also claimed that on count-less occasions he had stopped a follower's heartbeat and breathing and had plunged knives into the individual's chest without injuring the person. The defendant performed this ceremony on Kenneth Goings, a recent recruit to the religion, and the wounds from the hatchet and three knives that Strong inserted proved fatal. One of Strong's followers testified that the defendant had previously performed this ritual without causing injury. Was Strong "guilty only of the crime of criminally negligent homicide?" See *People v. Strong*, 37 N.Y.2d 568 (1975).

You can find the answer at study.sagepub.com/lippmaness2e

CRIMINAL LAW IN THE NEWS

On June 17, 2015, Dylann Storm Roof, age twenty-one, a slight young Caucasian man with a bowl haircut, entered Emanuel African Methodist Episcopal (AME) Church in Charleston, South Carolina, during Bible Study and asked for and took a seat next to Pastor Clementa C. Pinckney. An hour after arriving, Roof suddenly stood and pulled out a pistol and in response to an effort to calm him down announced that "[y]ou [African Americans] are raping our women and taking over the country. And you have to go." When Tywanza Sanders, twenty-six, told Roof to shoot him rather than Susie Jackson, his eighty-seven-year-old aunt, Roof replied, "[i]t doesn't matter [because] I'm going to shoot all of you." Roof told one woman that he would allow her to live "so she can tell the story of what happened." All of the African American victims were shot multiple times by Roof, whose image was captured by a number of security cameras.

Nine people—three men and six women age twenty-nine to eighty-seven—were killed by Roof, including pastor, state senator, and civil rights leader Pinckney, age forty-one. Pinckney was a highly respected voice for justice and a conciliatory figure in South Carolina. The other deceased individuals included a library manager, a former county administrator, a speech therapist who also worked for the church, and two ministers.

Emanuel AME Church, known as "Mother Emanuel," is the oldest African American congregation south of Baltimore, Maryland. The members of the congregation convened in secret in the years prior to the Civil War when African American churches were prohibited, and the church contains a shrine to one of its founders, Denmark Vesey, who helped to organize a slave revolt in 1822. Vesey, along with thirty-five other African American slaves, was executed when the plans for a slave revolt were uncovered and 313 suspected conspirators were arrested. The church was burned down by a white mob in retribution and subsequently was rebuilt in 1891. In the 1960s, "Mother Emanuel" was a center of civil rights activity, and the Reverend Dr. Martin Luther King Jr. spoke at the church in 1962. Observers were struck by the fact that at Roof's arraignment family members of the victims, while wanting to see Roof punished, expressed forgiveness and prayed for Roof's soul.

Roof, who had not finished high school, purchased a 45-caliber handgun with money given to him by his parents. According to friends, in the days leading to the killings, he seemed obsessed with defending the white race against what he viewed as the rising power of African Americans and advocated segregation between African Americans and whites. Roof's friends reportedly did not take him seriously when he talked about starting a race war by undertaking the mass killing of African Americans. He had been arrested five months earlier for unlawful possession of a prescription drug and was arrested two weeks later for misdemeanor trespass at a shopping mall from which he earlier had been banned. At the time of Roof's arrest, the police seized assault rifle parts and six 40-round magazines in his trunk.

South Carolina indicted Roof for nine counts of murder. The federal government later announced that it would charge Roof with a hate crime. South Carolina is one of five states that does not enhance penalties for bias-motivated offenses. U.S. Department of Justice officials pointed out that Roof had knowingly entered a renowned African American church and had selected African American victims. Nationally, roughly half of hate crimes are based on race, 20 percent are motivated by religion, 18 percent are directed against individuals because of their sexual orientation, and the remainder are based on ethnicity or because of an individual's disability. Some commentators called for Roof to be charged with terrorism and pointed out that similar acts when carried out by Muslims are labeled as terrorism although are considered ordinary crimes when directed against African Americans and Muslim Americans.

In the aftermath of the attack, South Carolina governor Nikki R. Haley called on the state legislature to remove the Confederate flag from the grounds of the state capitol. The flag originally was flown over the state house in 1962 as a symbol of resistance to the civil rights movement. Supporters of the flag objected to the legislature's removal of the flag and insisted that it is a symbolic acknowledgment of the heritage of their ancestors who fought in the Civil War. Would you prosecute Roof for a hate crime? Can crimes like those committed by Roof be deterred?

THE BEGINNING OF HUMAN LIFE

We have seen that murder entails the killing of a human being. Shooting a corpse under the false belief that the individual is alive is not murder. At what point does life begin? The common law rule adopted in 1348 provided that a defendant was not criminally responsible for the murder of a child in a mother's womb unless the child was born alive with the capacity for an independent existence. Following the child's birth, the question was whether the defendant's acts were the proximate cause of death. This rule reflected the fact that doctors were unable to determine whether an unborn child was alive in the mother's womb at the time of an attack.

In *Keeler v. Superior Court*, the California Supreme court held that the "born alive" rule barred the defendant's conviction for the death of a fetus.[44] The California legislature responded by amending the definition of murder to include the unlawful killing of "a human being, or a fetus, with malice aforethought."[45]

Roughly twenty states continue to follow some form of the born alive rule. In *State v. Lamy*, the New Hampshire Supreme Court reversed a defendant's manslaughter and negligent homicide conviction. The inebriated defendant drove at one hundred miles per hour down the wrong side of the street, hit a taxi, and killed a passenger who was seven months pregnant. The state was unable to show that the fetus was born alive because the prosecutor failed to demonstrate that the child was able to live on its own without a life support machine. D.E. "was never able to breathe without the aid of a respirator, required medication to maintain his blood pressure and never acquired . . . any brain function. . . . D.E. never exhibited any spontaneous sign of life such as beating of the heart, pulsation of the umbilical cord, or definite movement of voluntary muscles."[46]

A number of states have abandoned the common law born alive rule in the last few decades. Roughly fifteen states impose criminal liability when the prosecution is able to establish beyond a reasonable doubt that the fetus at the time of injury was viable, meaning that the fetus was capable of living separate and apart from the mother. In *Commonwealth v. Cass* in 1984, the Massachusetts Supreme Judicial Court ruled that the "infliction of prenatal injuries resulting in the death of a viable fetus, before or after it is born, is homicide. . . . We believe that our criminal law should extend its protection to viable fetuses."[47]

Keep in mind that the U.S. Supreme Court recognized in *Roe v. Wade* in 1973 that women have a right to an abortion as part of their constitutional right to privacy. A state may limit this right during the last phase of pregnancy, other than in those instances when an abortion is necessary to protect the health or life of the mother. The decision to hold an attacker criminally responsible for the death of a viable fetus does not limit the right of a woman to voluntarily consent to an abortion by a licensed physician. The MPC maintains the common law born alive rule in order to avoid a possible conflict between the law of abortion and the criminal law rule concerning the fetus.[48]

The trend is to extend homicide laws to the "earliest stages of pregnancy." In *People v. Davis*, the California Supreme Court held that California Penal Code Section 187(a), which defined murder as the "unlawful killing of a human being, or a fetus," extended protections to the postembryonic stage that occurs in humans "seven or eight weeks after fertilization."[49] Other state statutes are broader than the decision of the California Supreme Court. These state laws use the terms *gestation*, *conception*, *fertilization*, and *postfertilization*. Alabama Code Section 13A-6-1 defines human beings as "unborn children in utero at any stage of development, regardless of viability." South Carolina Code Section 16-3-1083 has a similar law that states that the murder of a pregnant woman results in liability for a "double homicide."

The U.S. Congress adopted the Unborn Victims of Violence Act of 2004, which declares that it is a crime to cause the death of a fetus in utero when the offender has knowledge of the victim's pregnancy or when the offender intended to injure or cause the death of the fetus.[50]

A significant number of state courts have ruled that child abuse statutes as well as homicide statutes apply to a fetus.[51] The South Carolina Supreme Court, however, held that a woman was properly convicted of child neglect who caused her baby to be born with cocaine metabolites in its system by reason of her ingestion of crack cocaine during the third trimester of her pregnancy.[52]

THE END OF HUMAN LIFE

The question of when life ends seems like a technical debate that should be the concern of doctors and philosophers rather than lawyers and criminal justice professionals.

The traditional definition of death required the total stoppage of the circulation of the blood and the cessation of vital functions, such as breathing. This definition was complicated by technology that, over the last decades, developed to the point that a "brain dead" individual's breathing and blood flow could be maintained through artificial machines despite the fact that the brain had ceased to function.

In 1970, Kansas became the first state to legislate that death occurs when an individual experiences an irreversible cessation of breathing and heartbeat or there is an absence of brain activity. A majority of state legislatures and courts now have adopted a **brain death test** for death. The circulatory and respiratory and brain death tests are incorporated as alternative approaches in the Uniform Determination of Death Act, a model law developed by the American Bar Association and American Medical Association.

The brain death test has also been adopted by courts in states without a statute defining death. In the Arizona case of *State v. Fierro*, the deceased, Victor Corella, was shot in the chest and head by a rival gang member. Corella was rushed to the hospital where he was operated on and, although his brain had ceased to function, he was placed on a life support system. The doctors, convinced that nothing could be done to save Corella's life, removed him from the life support machine after four days. The defendant argued that the removal of Corella from the life support machine was the proximate cause of death. The Arizona Supreme Court ruled that under Arizona law, death could be shown by either a lack of bodily function or brain death and concluded that the victim was legally dead before being placed on life support.[53]

Terri Schiavo

In 1976, the New Jersey Supreme Court held that Karen Ann Quinlan was entitled to the removal of her feeding tube. The Court noted that "[w]e have no doubt . . . that if Karen were herself miraculously lucid for an interval . . . and perceptive of her irreversible condition, she could effectively decide upon discontinuance of the life-support apparatus, even if it meant the prospect of natural death." See *In re Quinlan*, 355 A.2d 647 (N.J. 1976).

In *Cruzan v. Director, Missouri Department of Health*, 497 U.S. 261 (1990), the U.S. Supreme Court held that an individual in a persistent vegetative state has a liberty interest in refusing medical treatment, which must be balanced against the state interest in the preservation of life and ensuring that decisions reflect a patient's wishes. A state, according to the Court, may require that the individual's preferences be demonstrated by "clear and convincing evidence" and is not required to accept the "substituted" judgment of family members.

In 1990, Terri Schiavo, age twenty-six, collapsed in her Florida home and suffered massive brain damage as a result of a lack of oxygen. She remained in a coma for ten weeks. Terri was diagnosed as being in a persistent vegetative state in which she experienced normal sleep–wake cycles, although she did not respond to external stimuli.

A total of nine state court decisions between 2000 and 2003 culminated in a judicial order ordering removal of Terri's feeding tube. In October 2003, one week after the final judicial order removing the feeding tube, the Florida state legislature passed a law giving Governor Jeb Bush the authority to intervene in the case. Governor Bush ordered reinstatement of the feeding tube. The law subsequently was overturned as unconstitutional by the Florida Supreme Court. Terri's parents insisted that Terri responded to familiar voices and music, and they filed a series of unsuccessful judicial appeals before turning to the federal government. The Congress, with strong support from Republicans, passed and President George W. Bush signed an order transferring jurisdiction to the federal courts. The federal courts refused to intervene.

Terri passed away on March 31, 2005, at age forty-one. She managed to live for thirteen days following the removal of the feeding tube. Terri's death had been the subject of nineteen state and federal court decisions, legislation at both the state and federal levels, and four Supreme Court denials of review.

The Schiavo case raised the issue of whether the courts and the medical profession should make life and death decisions based on their view of the "value and quality of human life." Michael Schiavo and two other witnesses testified that Terri had remarked that she would not want her life perpetuated on a machine. On the other hand, we have no idea what Terri would have decided under the circumstances, and the notion that individuals have a "right to die" is open to debate. Critics warn that there is a temptation, as the population grows increasingly older, to make the denial of food and fluids ("passive euthanasia") an accepted part of the practice of medicine.

THE YEAR-AND-A-DAY RULE

The common law **year-and-a-day rule** was established in 1278 and provides that an individual is criminally responsible only for a death that occurs within one year of his or her criminal act. The basis for the rule was that medicine was not as advanced as it is today and that if an individual remained alive for a year and a day before dying, the victim's death may have resulted from a cause other than the criminal attack. Under such circumstances, a defendant would not be held liable for murder.

The trend is for state courts and legislatures to abolish the year-and-a-day rule. In 2001, the U.S. Supreme Court affirmed Tennessee's rejection of the year-and-a-day [rule] and explained that "practically every court recently to have considered the rule has noted advances in medical and related science have so undermined the usefulness of the rule as to render it without question obsolete."[54] Another argument against the year-and-a-day rule is that a family should not be forced to remove a crime victim from life support in order to prevent a defendant from escaping prosecution for murder.[55] California has adopted a presumption that a death that occurs three years and a day following a criminal attack is based on factors not related to the criminal attack.[56]

CORPUS DELICTI

Corpus delicti or "body of crime" or "substance of the crime" is a confusing common law doctrine that arises most frequently in homicide cases. Think about corpus delicti as proof that a crime has been committed. Professor LaFave explains that corpus delicti is satisfied by evidence that a crime has been committed without establishing the additional fact that the defendant was responsible for the crime. Keep in mind that corpus delicti also is used at times to refer to the fact that the prosecution must establish all elements of a crime beyond a reasonable doubt.[57]

Corpus delicti provides that a criminal prosecution requires proof of the prohibited harm (death) and proof that the harm resulted from a criminal act rather than as a consequence of natural causes or accident. In an arson case at common law, corpus delicti required proof of the intentional burning and damage of the dwelling house of another. The prosecution at trial, after establishing the corpus delicti, has the burden of establishing beyond a reasonable doubt that the defendant was responsible for the unlawful burning.

The elements of corpus delicti may not be based solely on an individual's extrajudicial confession or statements, and this evidence is required to be supplemented by evidence that corroborates the details of the defendant's confession or statements. There is fear that an extrajudicial confession may result from coercion or confusion, and the corroborating evidence requirement protects a defendant from being convicted of a crime that he or she did not commit. The corpus delicti rule was embraced in the United States following an early nineteenth-century Vermont case in which two brothers confessed to the murder of an individual who later was found to be alive and living in New Jersey.

The corpus delicti rule ordinarily is easily established in a homicide case based on the testimony of the police, medical personnel and records, scientific evidence, and eyewitnesses. In homicide cases involving a "missing body," corpus delicti is more difficult to establish. The prosecution in these cases must rely on a defendant's extrajudicial statements or confession along with circumstantial evidence. Allowing the prosecution to rely on circumstantial evidence to establish the death of the victim and to establish the cause of death prevents a guilty individual from escaping punishment by disposing of the victim's body.

In a recent Maryland case, a state court of appeals relied on the defendant's statements to the police along with circumstantial evidence to "sufficiently establish" that the defendant's wife, who had disappeared, was the victim of foul play. The victim, who was described as responsible and organized, had no contact with her family or friends for a number of years. During that time, she had not used her credit cards, and she had abandoned her car and dogs. Her calendar indicated that she had made plans for the next several months, and she had not been located despite a nationwide media blitz.

In a Virginia "missing body" case, the corpus delicti of the victim's murder was established by the defendant's incriminating statements, along with the discovery of the victim's blood-soaked clothes and indications of a violent struggle at the house where the victim was last seen.

CASE ANALYSIS

In *People v. Mehserle*, Officer Johannes Mehserle was convicted of the negligent manslaughter of Oscar Grant. Why did the California appellate court find that Mehserle was negligent? This verdict led to demonstrations protesting the verdict of negligent homicide. Would you have held Mehserle liable of a more serious offense?

Did Officer Mehserle Negligently Kill Oscar Grant?

People v. Mehserle, 206 Cal. App. 4th 1125 (2012), Marchiano, P. J.

Defendant Johannes Mehserle served as a police officer for the Bay Area Rapid Transit District (BART). Shortly after 2:00 a.m. on January 1, 2009, while responding to a report of a fight on a BART train, he shot and killed BART passenger Oscar Grant during a tense confrontation. The defendant was attempting to arrest and handcuff Grant for the misdemeanor of obstructing a police officer. While Grant was lying facedown on the BART platform, the defendant shot Grant, who was unarmed, in the back. The defendant contended he meant to pull his Taser and shock Grant to subdue him, but drew his handgun by mistake and fired the fatal shot.

Defendant carried two weapons: a black model 226 40-caliber Sig Sauer handgun and a bright yellow Taser International X26 Taser. The handgun weighed more than three times as much as the Taser. The handgun had no manual safety switch, while the Taser had a safety switch that also functioned as an on/off switch. The Taser had a red laser sight; the handgun did not.

In the small hours of the early morning of New Year's Day 2009, Grant boarded a BART train in San Francisco with his fiancée, Sophina Mesa, and several other friends. The group was bound for the Fruitvale BART station. The train was very crowded with New Year's Eve celebrants, and people were standing in the aisles.

As the train approached the Fruitvale BART station in Oakland, Grant began to argue with a fellow passenger and the two men started "tussling around." They attempted to strike each other, but the train was so crowded they were reduced to pushing and shoving. The aggression spread into a large fistfight, involving at least 10 men.

Passengers used the train intercom to report the fight to the operator, who in turn contacted BART central control. Central control apparently contacted BART police, whose dispatcher contacted officers in the field with a report of a fight at the Fruitvale BART station in the train's "lead car, no weapons, all black clothing, large group of B[lack] M[ales]."

Officer Anthony Pirone ordered Grant off the train. . . . Grant did not comply. Pirone said, "I've asked you politely. I'm going to have to remove you in front of all these people now." Pirone grabbed Grant by his hair and the scruff of his neck and forced him off the train. . . . Pirone forced Grant to his knees. A passenger's video shows Pirone drawing his Taser and pointing it. . . . Grant pleaded with Pirone not to "Tase" him because "I have a daughter."

Pirone and defendant placed Grant on his stomach. Pirone used his knees to pin Grant's neck to the ground. Grant protested, "I can't breathe. Just get off of me. I can't breathe. I quit. I surrender. I quit." Defendant ordered Grant to give up his arms, presumably so he could handcuff him. Grant responded that he could not move. Defendant repeatedly pulled at Grant's right arm, which apparently was under Grant's body.

Defendant testified as follows.

He did not intend to shoot Grant, but only to "Tase" him. He mistakenly drew and fired his handgun. . . . Defendant did not hear Grant complain that he could not breathe. Defendant did not notice that Officer Pirone had restrained Grant by placing his knee on Grant's neck.

Defendant saw Grant's right hand go into his pocket as if he were grabbing for something. Although he did not see a weapon, he thought Grant might be reaching for one. He decided to "Tase" Grant. He stood up to get sufficient distance to properly deploy the Taser, and announced, "I'm going to tase him. I'm going to tase him."

Defendant was not aware he had mistakenly drawn his handgun until he heard the shot. He looked down and saw he was holding his handgun, . . . and did not notice the lack of a red laser sight which would have emanated from his Taser.

We find sufficient evidence that [the defendant's] conduct of mistakenly drawing and firing his handgun instead of his Taser constitutes criminal negligence. . . . [H]e believed he was "Tasing" an arrestee, but mistakenly, and criminally negligently, drew and fired his handgun with lethal results.

CALCRIM No. 580 defines criminal negligence as follows. "A person acts with criminal negligence when:

1. He or she acts in a . . . way that creates a high risk of death or great bodily injury; AND

2. A reasonable person would have known that acting in that way would create such a risk.

[T]he jury could have reasonably found that when defendant did decide to use his Taser, he was criminally negligent in mistaking his handgun for his Taser. . . . Defendant had drawn his Taser earlier. The handgun weighed more than three times as much as the Taser. The Taser was bright yellow. The handgun was black. The Taser had an on/off safety switch. The handgun did not. The Taser had a red laser sight.

The handgun did not. The handgun was holstered on defendant's right, or dominant side, with a two-step release mechanism requiring defendant to push down and forward and then back on a separate safety switch. The Taser, in contrast, was holstered on defendant's left, or nondominant side, for a cross-draw by defendant's right hand and had only a safety strap and safety hood. After . . . incidents of handgun/Taser confusion, . . . several police agencies changed their Taser policies to require nondominant-side holstering and the Taser's bright yellow color as measures to prevent handgun/Taser confusion. A reasonable jury could conclude that a reasonably prudent person could distinguish between the two weapons, and drawing the deadly weapon—heavier, of a different color, and on the dominant side of the body with a complicated release mechanism—under the circumstances, amounted to criminal negligence. Thus, the jury could have reasonably found defendant's conduct . . . was not a mere mistake.

CHAPTER SUMMARY

The killing of another human being violates the fundamental right to life and is considered the most serious criminal offense. The common law gradually distinguished between murder (killings committed with malice aforethought) and the less serious crime of manslaughter (killings committed without malice aforethought).

We generally measure the beginning of human life from viability, the point at which a fetus is able to live independently from the mother. Death is measured by the brain death test, or the failure of the brain function.

Malice is the intent to kill with ill will or hatred. Aforethought means a design to kill. Malice aforethought is expressed when there is a deliberate intent to kill or implied where an individual possesses the intent to cause great bodily harm or the intent to commit an act that may lead to death or great bodily harm. Judges gradually expanded the concept of malice aforethought to include various forms of criminal intent.

There is no single approach to defining the law of murder or manslaughter in state statutes. The division of homicide into degrees is intended to divide killings by the "moral blameworthiness of the individual." This division is typically based on factors such as the perpetrator's intent, the nature of the killing, and the surrounding circumstances of the killing.

First-degree murder is the deliberate and premeditated killing of another with malice aforethought. An individual who is capable of devising a plan to take the life of another is considered a serious threat to society. Premeditation may be formed instantaneously and does not require a lengthy period of reflection.

Thirty-one states recognize the death penalty. Killings viewed as deserving of capital punishment are categorized as capital first-degree murder or aggravated first-degree murder. Conviction results in the death penalty or life imprisonment. In non-death-penalty states, aggravated murder carries life imprisonment. A homicide qualifies as aggravated or capital murder when it is found to have been committed in a heinous or atrocious fashion.

Second-degree murder involves the intentional killing of a human being with malice aforethought that is not committed in a premeditated and deliberate fashion. Depraved heart murder includes killings resulting from a knowingly dangerous act committed with reckless and wanton disregard as to whether others are harmed. Felony murder entails the death of an individual during the commission of or attempt to commit a felony. This category of murder tends to be limited to dangerous felonies; and in various states, felony murders are categorized as first-degree murder rather than second-degree murder.

Manslaughter comprises voluntary and involuntary manslaughter. Voluntary manslaughter is the killing of another in a sudden and intense heat of passion in response to an adequate provocation. Adequate provocation is defined as conduct that is sufficient to excite an intense passion that would cause a reasonable person to lose control. Only a limited number of acts are considered to constitute adequate provocation, but some judges have vested the discretion to determine provocation in jurors. The heat of passion is considered to have "cooled" after a reasonable period of time.

Involuntary manslaughter includes negligent manslaughter and misdemeanor manslaughter, also termed unlawful-act manslaughter. Negligent manslaughter involves the creation of a risk of the serious injury or death of another. Courts, in practice, do not clearly distinguish between a negligence and recklessness standard. Misdemeanor manslaughter involves a killing committed during the commission of a misdemeanor. Some states expand misdemeanor manslaughter to include nonviolent felonies and, for this reason, term this offense unlawful-act manslaughter.

CHAPTER REVIEW QUESTIONS

1. Discuss the historical origins and development of criminal homicide into murder and manslaughter. Can you distinguish between murder and manslaughter?

2. Differentiate first-degree murder from first-degree capital or aggravated homicide.

3. What is the difference between first- and second-degree murder?

4. Define depraved heart murder.

5. Why does the law provide for the offense of felony murder? What are the arguments for and against the felony murder rule?

6. Define voluntary manslaughter.

7. What acts constitute adequate provocation? What must the defendant prove to establish heat of passion? At what point does a defendant's blood "cool"?

8. Should the law recognize the offense of voluntary manslaughter? Why not?

9. Discuss the difference between negligent homicide and misdemeanor manslaughter. Why is misdemeanor manslaughter termed unlawful-act manslaughter in some states?

10. Discuss the purpose of the various grades of murder and dividing homicide into murder and manslaughter. Why do we make all these technical distinctions between types of homicide?

LEGAL TERMINOLOGY

agency theory of felony murder

aggravating factors

brain death test

capital murder

cooling of blood

corpus delicti

criminal homicide

depraved heart murder

excusable homicide

felony murder

first-degree murder

grading

heat of passion

intent-to-do-serious-bodily-harm murder

involuntary manslaughter

justifiable homicide

malice aforethought

manslaughter

misdemeanor manslaughter

mitigating circumstances

murder

negligent manslaughter

premeditation and deliberation

proximate cause theory of felony murder

reasonable person

recklessness

second-degree murder

vehicular manslaughter

voluntary manslaughter

year-and-a-day rule

 # CRIMINAL LAW ON THE WEB

8 OTHER CRIMES AGAINST THE PERSON

Was Dominguez guilty of kidnapping based on dragging the victim twenty-five feet from the side of the road into an embankment?

Forensic evidence determined Perez had been beaten and choked to death and that she had been forcibly raped, causing substantial bruising to her posterior vaginal wall and cervix. . . . [Dominguez] followed the victim after she got out of the taxi and, with the intent to rape her, forced her from the side of Southside Road, down an embankment and into an orchard. Once there, he (possibly with Martinez's assistance) raped and killed her, burying her jeans and discarding her shoes at the scene before dragging her lifeless body further into the walnut orchard and burying her. An investigating officer testified the drop from the surface of Southside Road to where the victim's bloody jeans were buried was approximately 10 to 12 feet, down a "fairly steep" hill. This place, which is where the prosecutor argued the rape occurred, was about 25 feet from the road. (*People v. Dominguez*, 39 Cal.4th 1141 [2006])

In this chapter, learn about sexual assault and kidnapping.

Learning Objectives

1. Describe the difference between simple and aggravated battery and between attempted battery assault and the placing of another in fear of a battery assault.

2. Know the elements of the crime of stalking.

3. Know the definition of rape under the common law and the strict requirements for rape under the common law.

4. List some of the changes in the law of rape resulting from rape reform in the 1970s and 1980s.

5. Compare and contrast the extrinsic and intrinsic tests for the *actus reus* of rape/sexual assault.

6. Know the difference between fraud in the *factum* and fraud in inducement.

7. Understand the standard for the *mens rea* of rape/sexual battery.

8. Summarize the law of statutory rape.

9. State the law on rape/sexual battery and the withdrawal of consent.

10. Understand rape shield statutes.

11. Know the role of testimony on rape trauma testimony at trial.

12. Describe the intent and act requirement for kidnapping.

13. Distinguish between kidnapping and false imprisonment.

INTRODUCTION

This chapter discusses three categories of crimes against the person. The first is protection against the threat and infliction of bodily harm (assault and battery), and the second is freedom from sexual violations (rape and sexual assault and battery). A third category is freedom of movement (kidnapping and false imprisonment).

Next to homicide, sexual offenses are considered the most serious offenses against the person and are punished as felonies, even when the victim is not physically injured. This harsh punishment reflects the fact that nonconsensual acts of sexual intimacy can cause severe physical injury as well as psychological trauma. Assaults and batteries and false imprisonment are typically misdemeanors (other than when committed in an aggravated fashion that risks or results in physical injury). Kidnapping is considered a serious offense that places people in danger and was subject to the death penalty under the common law.

There clearly is no more fundamental or important interest than protecting the life and bodily integrity of the individual. This is the basic and essential expectation of all members of a community. Imagine a society in which each of us was constantly fearful of an attack to our bodily integrity. Are there geographic areas of American society and the world that come close to this type of "lawlessness"?

ASSAULT AND BATTERY

Assault and battery, although often referred to as a single crime, in fact are separate offenses. A battery is the application of force to another person. An assault may be committed either by attempting to commit a battery or by intentionally placing another in fear of a battery. Notice that an assault does not involve physical contact. An assault is the first step toward a battery, and the law takes the position that it would be unfair to hold an individual liable for both an assault and a battery. As a result, the assault "merges" into the battery, and an individual is held responsible only for the battery. A Georgia statute provides that an individual "may not be convicted of both the assault and completed crime."[1]

State statutes typically include assault and battery under a single "assault statute." Both offenses are considered misdemeanors. Serious assaults and batteries are punished as aggravated misdemeanors, and aggravated batteries are categorized as felonies.

The Elements of Battery

Modern battery statutes require physical contact that results in bodily injury or offensive touching, contact that is likely to be regarded as offensive by a reasonable person. Assault and battery are satisfied under the Model Penal Code (MPC) by an intentional, purposeful, reckless, or negligent intent. The Texas Penal Code follows the MPC and declares that it is a battery to "intentionally, knowingly, or recklessly [cause] bodily injury to another."[2]

Most state statutes narrowly limit the required intent. Illinois punishes the intentional or knowing causing of bodily harm to an individual or physical contact with an individual of an insulting or provoking nature.[3] Georgia limits battery to the intentional causing of "substantial physical harm or visible bodily harm to another." This includes, but is not limited to, substantially blackened eyes, substantially swollen lips, and substantial other bruises to body parts.[4] California defines a battery as "any willful and unlawful use of force or violence upon the person of another."[5]

In thinking about battery, you should be aware that a battery is not confined to the direct application of force by an individual. It can include causing substantial bodily harm by poisoning, bombing, a motor vehicle, illegal narcotics, or an animal. Minnesota, for instance, punishes causing "great or substantial harm" by intentionally or negligently failing to keep a dog properly confined.[6] In *State v. Sherer*, the defendant placed random phone calls to over thirty women in Bozeman, Montana, in which he impersonated a doctor treating urinary tract infections.[7] He directed the women to engage in a self-exam over the phone involving a knife, a razor blade, or fingernail polish remover. The Montana Supreme Court ruled that aggravated assault does not require that the defendant personally direct force toward a victim, and that the resulting injury was precisely what Sherer intended to accomplish. Sherer's communications were held to be the cause of the victims' personal physical abuse. In states with statutes punishing offensive physical contact, an uninvited kiss or sexual fondling may be considered a battery. A Washington court held that assault and battery includes spitting.[8]

You should also keep in mind that not every physical contact is a battery. We imply consent to physical contact in sports, in medical operations, while walking in a crowd, or when a friend greets us with a hug or kiss. The law accepts that police officers and parents are justified in employing reasonable force. Reasonable force may also be used in self-defense or in defense of others.

The last point is that, as illustrated in the next section, states differ significantly in their approach to defining aggravated batteries or batteries that deserve a longer sentence.

Simple and Aggravated Battery

We earlier mentioned that a battery is a misdemeanor. Aggravated batteries are felonies. An **aggravated battery** typically requires

- serious bodily injury,
- the use of a dangerous or deadly weapon, or
- the intent to kill, rape, or seriously harm.

The Georgia battery statute punishes a second conviction for a simple battery with imprisonment of between ten days and twelve months with the possibility of a fine of not more than $1,000.[9] An aggravated battery in Georgia requires an attack that renders a "member" of the victim's body "useless" or "seriously disfigured" and is punishable by between one and twenty years in prison. The penalty is enhanced to between ten and twenty years when the offense was knowingly directed at a police or correctional officer, and to between five and twenty years when directed at an individual over sixty-five, committed in a public transit vehicle or station, or directed at a student or teacher. An aggravated battery is punished by between three and twenty years in prison when directed at a family member.[10]

Some idea of the range of acts that are punished as aggravated battery is illustrated by examining various provisions of state criminal codes. For example, Illinois lists as an aggravated battery a battery committed by an individual who is "hooded, robed or masked, in such manner as to conceal his identity."[11] South Dakota considers the serious physical injury on an unborn child to be an aggravated assault.[12] Florida punishes as aggravated a battery that intentionally or knowingly is committed against a woman who is pregnant and who the offender knows is pregnant.[13] A Minnesota statute punishes as an aggravated battery the selling or provision of illegal narcotics that "causes great bodily harm" by imprisonment for not more than ten years and by payment of a fine of not more than $20,000.[14]

California considers a battery aggravated when committed with a deadly weapon, a caustic or flammable chemical, a Taser or stun gun, or when the battery results in grievous bodily harm. A battery also is aggravated in California when committed against any person on school or park property, on the grounds of a public or private hospital, or against police officers, firefighters, correctional officers, public transportation operators, the elderly, and other specified individuals.[15]

States also have adopted statutes punishing caregivers who intentionally or recklessly cause injury to a "vulnerable elderly person," endanger the health of a "vulnerable elderly individual," or subject the elderly individual to sexual abuse.[16]

In 2012, Samuel Mullet Sr., along with fifteen members of a breakaway Amish sect, were convicted in federal district court of assault and other crimes for attacking and cutting the beards of men and the hair of women who opposed Mullet's dissident sect.[17]

Dangerous Weapon Battery

Dangerous weapon battery is considered an aggravated battery under state statutes. In Massachusetts, a battery through the use of a dangerous weapon may result in imprisonment for ten years.[18]

A dangerous weapon is an instrumentality that may be used to inflict serious bodily harm. This may be an object like a gun, knife, or hatchet designed to inflict substantial bodily harm or an object that may be used to inflict substantial harm. Ordinary objects may be transformed into dangerous weapons based on how they are used. This includes beer bottles, wooden boards, pool cues, and boots. In *State v. Basting*, the Minnesota Supreme Court held that a trained boxer's landing of two blows that broke the victim's nose did not constitute a battery with the use of a dangerous weapon.[19] The court examined the totality of the circumstances and concluded that the use of fists or feet may constitute a dangerous weapon based on the size and strength of the parties, the vulnerability of the victim, the duration and severity of the attack, the presence or absence of victim provocation, and the nature and extent of the injuries.

A defendant's hands or feet have been determined to constitute a dangerous weapon when a "brutal and prolonged attack" is directed against a "vulnerable" and "defenseless" victim. In *State v. Davis*, the victim was seven months pregnant at the time the defendant attacked her. When she tried to run from the defendant, he grabbed her, and she fell to the ground on her hands and knees. The defendant slapped her and repeatedly kicked her as if he was "jump-starting a Harley and the defendant punched the victim five to ten times in her face, torso and chest."[20] Kicking a victim who is on the ground in the head with cowboy boots also was found to constitute a dangerous weapon battery.[21] In *State v. Coauette*, a Minnesota appellate court held that the firing of a paint ball gun at a young girl, which resulted in swelling and scratching, did not constitute a battery with the use of a dangerous weapon.[22] The court noted that paint ball guns "are designed and manufactured to launch paintballs. And paintballs are intended and designed to break on contact and simply—as part of the game—splash a dose of nontoxic liquid paint on the human target. A paintball gun is not—by design or intent—'calculated or likely to produce death or great bodily harm.'"

Mayhem

The common law crime of **mayhem** is included in the criminal codes of several states, including California. California defines mayhem as depriving a human being of a "member of his or her body, or disabl[ing], disfigur[ing], or render[ing] it useless, or cut[ting] or disabl[ing] the tongue, or put[ting] out an eye, or slit[ting] the nose, ear, or lip." Mayhem includes intentionally depriving a "human being of a limb, organ, or member of his or her body" and is punishable by life imprisonment with the possibility of parole.[23] A well-known case of "malicious wounding" involved Lorena Bobbitt who, while her husband John was asleep, dismembered his sexual organ and left the house and tossed it out the car window onto the highway. Lorena claimed that John had raped her. She was subsequently found not guilty by reason of insanity and was committed to a mental institution for observation.

California Penal Code Section 206 punishes **torture** with life imprisonment. "Every person who, with the intent to cause cruel or extreme pain and suffering for the purpose of revenge, extortion, persuasion, or for any sadistic purpose, inflicts great bodily injury as defined . . . upon the person of another, is guilty of torture."[24] In 2006, attorney Richard Hamlin was convicted of torture for a course of abuse against his wife over a four-year period. Hamlin was found to have beat her, stabbed her, pistol-whipped her, threatened her with a sword, and punched her.

In summary, a battery involves the following:

- *Act.* The application of force that results in bodily injury or offensive contact. Aggravated battery statutes require a serious bodily injury, the intent to cause great bodily harm, or the use of a dangerous weapon. The contact must be regarded as offensive by a reasonable person.
- *Intent.* The intentional or knowing application of force. Some states include a reckless or negligent intent.
- *Consent.* An implied or explicit consent may constitute a defense under certain circumstances.

Assault

An assault may be committed by an attempt to commit a battery or by placing an individual in fear of a battery. Georgia defines an assault as an attempt to "commit a violent injury to the person of another; or . . . an act which places another in reasonable apprehension of immediately receiving a violent injury."[25]

California limits assault to an "an unlawful attempt, coupled with a present ability, to commit a violent injury on the person of another."[26] Illinois, on the other hand, provides that a person commits an assault when, "without lawful authority, he engages in conduct that places another in reasonable apprehension of receiving a battery."[27] An assault is a misdemeanor, punishable in California by imprisonment by up to six months in the county jail and by a possible fine of $2,000.[28] Ohio is among the states whose criminal code uses the term *menacing* rather than *assault.*[29]

A small number of states, including New York, recognize the offense of an attempted assault. The overwhelming majority of jurisdictions reject that an individual may be prosecuted for an "attempt to attempt a battery" on the grounds that this risks the conviction of individuals who have yet to take clear steps toward an assault.[30] A Georgia court in the nineteenth century also pointed out that prosecuting an individual for an attempt to commit a battery "is simply absurd. As soon as any act is done towards committing a violent injury on the person of another, the party doing the act is guilty of an assault, and he is not guilty until he has done the act. . . . An attempt to act is too [confused] for practical use."[31] Do you agree that an attempt to commit an assault is "absurd"?

Aggravated Assault

Aggravated assault is a felony and is generally based on factors similar to those constituting an aggravated battery.

Georgia provides three forms of aggravated assault that are punishable by between five and twenty years in prison: assault with intent to murder, rape, or rob; assault with a deadly weapon; and discharge of a firearm from within an automobile. The statute also punishes as an aggravated assault an assault on a police or correctional officer, a teacher, or an individual sixty-five years of age or older, or an assault committed during the theft of a vehicle engaged in public or commercial transport.[32]

Illinois lists as an aggravated assault an assault committed while "hooded, robed or masked," and an assault committed with "a deadly weapon or any device manufactured and designed to be substantially similar in appearance to a firearm." An individual also commits an aggravated assault in Illinois when he or she knowingly and without lawful justification "shines or flashes a laser gunsight or other laser device that is attached or affixed to a firearm . . . so that the laser beam strikes near or in the immediate vicinity of any person."[33] Illinois also punishes under a separate statute "vehicular endangerment," the dropping of an item off a bridge with the intent to strike a motor vehicle.[34]

The Elements of Assault

In considering an *attempted battery assault*, keep in mind:

- *Intent.* An attempt in most states to commit a battery requires an intent (purpose) to commit a battery.
- *Act.* An individual is required to take significant steps toward the commission of the battery.
- *Present Ability.* Some states require the present ability to commit the battery. In these jurisdictions, an individual would not be held liable for an assault where the assailant is unaware that a gun is unloaded. South Dakota, on the other hand, provides for a battery "with or without the actual ability to seriously harm the other person."[35]
- *Victim.* The victim need not be aware of the attempted battery.

The *assault of placing another in fear of a battery* requires the following:

- *Intent.* The intent (or purpose) to cause a fear of immediate bodily harm.
- *Act.* An act that would cause a reasonable person to fear *immediate* bodily harm. Words ordinarily are not sufficient and typically must be accompanied by a physical gesture that, in combination with the words, creates a reasonable fear of imminent bodily harm.
- *Victim.* The victim must be aware of the assailant's act and possess a reasonable fear of imminent bodily harm. A threat may be conditioned on the victim's meeting the demands of the assailant.

Model Penal Code

Section 211.1. Assault

(1) Simple Assault. A person is guilty of assault if he

(a) attempts to cause or purposely, knowingly, or recklessly causes bodily injury to another; or

(b) negligently causes bodily injury to another with a deadly weapon; or

(c) attempts by physical menace to put another in fear of imminent serious bodily injury.

Simple assault is a misdemeanor unless committed in a fight or scuffle entered into by mutual consent, in which case it is a petty misdemeanor.

(2) Aggravated Assault. A person is guilty of aggravated assault if he

(a) attempts to cause serious bodily injury to another, or causes such injury purposely, knowingly, or recklessly under circumstances manifesting extreme indifference to the value of human life; or

(b) attempts to cause or purposely or knowingly causes bodily injury to another with a deadly weapon.

Aggravated assault under paragraph (a) is a felony of the second degree; aggravated assault under paragraph (b) is a felony of the third degree.

Analysis

1. The MPC eliminates the common law categories and integrates assaults and batteries into a single assault statute.

2. Assaults are graded into categories based on the gravity of the harm intended or actually caused.

3. Grading is not based on the identity of the victim.

4. Actual or threatened bodily injury or serious bodily injury is required. Offensive contact is excluded.

5. Deadly weapons include poisons, explosives, caustic chemicals, handguns, knives, and automobiles.

The Legal Equation		
Battery	=	Unlawful bodily injury or offensive contact with another
	+	purposeful, knowing, reckless, negligent bodily injury, or offensive contact with another.
Attempted battery assault	=	Intent to injure
	+	an act undertaken to commit a battery.
Threatened battery assault	=	Intent to place in immediate fear of a battery
	+	act undertaken that places a reasonable person in fear of battery.

You Decide **8.1** Officer O'Donnell pulled over an automobile for speeding in a "high crime area" of Charlottesville, Virginia, at 11 p.m. O'Donnell asked the driver for his license and registration, and the driver responded in a "hostile" fashion. Officer O'Donnell examined the interior of the car with his flashlight. Carter was seated in the front passenger seat with his right hand extended down toward his leg. "Extending the index finger on his right hand straight out and the thumb straight up, [Carter] pointed his index finger at the officer and said, 'Pow.'" O'Donnell, "'[t]hinking Carter had a weapon and was going to shoot,'" reached for his weapon. A "split second" later, O'Donnell realized "it was only [Carter's] finger." O'Donnell testified: "The first thing I thought was that I was going to get shot—it's a terrifying experience, and if I could have gotten my weapon, I would have shot him." O'Donnell, who was "visibly shaken," asked Carter "if he thought it was funny," and Carter stated, "Yes, I think it is funny." Is Carter guilty of assaulting Officer O'Donnell? See *Carter v. Commonwealth*, 594 S.E.2d 284 (Va. Ct. App. 2004).

You can find the answer at study.sagepub.com/lippmaness2e

STALKING

The crime of **stalking** is recognized in every state. Some of you may recall the stalking and killing of young television actress Rebecca Schaeffer and rock star and former member of the Beatles John Lennon, as well as the attack on tennis star Monica Seles. Margaret Mary Ray stalked late-night talk show host David Letterman for a number of years. A recent study estimates that one out of every six women and one out of every nineteen men in the United States will be the victim of stalking during her or his lifetime.[36] In the late 1980s, California and Florida became the first states to adopt legislation punishing the crime of stalking. Every state and the District of Columbia over the course of the next ten years adopted similar legislation. The offense of stalking was developed because the type of acts that constitute stalking in many instances did not fall within the definition of a criminal assault or other types of crime. Stalking often involves a series of legal acts such as telephone calls, e-mails, and driving past an individual's home, which create anxiety, fear, and terror.

Stalking statutes, although differing from one another, share several general elements.

Acts. The acts that constitute stalking include following another person, placing another under surveillance, repeated unwanted contact, lying in wait, threatening, vandalizing, or a combination of these acts.

Cyberstalking. Stalking is punished when carried out through electronic communication or a combination of electronic communication, verbal expressions, and acts.

Multiple Acts. A series of acts of harassment are needed. A single act is sufficient where an individual violates an order of protection prohibiting contact with the victim.

Intent. A purposeful or knowing intent to harass and to place another person in fear of harm.

Victim. The victim or the victim's family must have a reasonable apprehension of immediate or future injury, and a reasonable person would possess such apprehension.

Gender Neutral. The victim may be a man or a woman.

Order of Protection. A judicial order of protection shields a victim by prohibiting an individual from continuing to engage in stalking.

Punishment. Stalking is a felony, and the penalty is aggravated when the stalking takes place in violation of a court order specifically prohibiting these types of acts.

There have been more than fifty constitutional challenges to stalking statutes in over twenty states based on the claim that the laws are vague and fail to inform individuals of the conduct that is prohibited. These challenges for the most part have been rejected by the judges.

The Illinois statute provides that a person commits stalking when he or she "on at least 2 separate occasions" follows another person or places the person under surveillance or any combination of these two acts. This must be combined with the transmittal of a threat of immediate or future bodily harm, or the placing of a person in reasonable apprehension of immediate or future bodily harm, or the creation of a reasonable apprehension that a family member will be placed in immediate or future bodily harm. These acts, when combined with the causing of bodily harm, the restraining of the victim, or the violation of a judicial order prohibiting such conduct, constitute aggravated stalking.[37]

The California stalking statute, Penal Code Section 649, provides that "[a]ny person who willfully, maliciously, and repeatedly follows or willfully and maliciously harasses another person, and who makes a credible threat with the intent to place that person in reasonable fear for his or her safety, or the safety of his or her immediate family, is guilty of the crime of stalking." Stalking is punished by imprisonment in a county jail for not more than one year, or by a fine of not more than $1,000, or by both a fine and imprisonment, or by imprisonment in the state prison. The punishment is enhanced where the stalker is in violation of a court order prohibiting the behavior.

A federal law, 18 U.S.C. § 2261(A)(1), makes it a crime to cross state lines with the intent to kill, injure, harass, or intimidate an individual and punishes one who commits an act of violence against a spouse, intimate partner, or dating partner.

Illinois, along with other states and the federal government, has passed laws to combat the new crime of **cyberstalking**. This involves transmitting a threat through an electronic device of immediate or future bodily harm, sexual assault, confinement, or restraint against an individual or family member of that person. The threat must create a "reasonable apprehension of immediate or future bodily harm, sexual assault, confinement, or restraint."[38]

The California Penal Code, in Section 646.9(h), provides that a credible threat may be made through an electronic communication device, "including telephones, cellular phones, computers, video recorders, fax machines or pagers."

Florida, in Section 784.048, defines cyberstalking as "to engage in a course of conduct to communicate, or to cause to be communicated, words, images, or language by or through the use of electronic mail or electronic communication, directed at a specific person, causing substantial emotional distress to that person and serving no legitimate purpose."

The courts confront the challenge of distinguishing between free speech and freedom of movement and stalking.

You Decide

8.2 Defendant Kevin Ellis and Sarah S. attended the same high school and met while they both were sophomores. They shared a table at lunchtime, and Sarah allegedly felt sorry for Kevin because he did not have a lot of friends. During the spring of their junior year, Kevin sent Sarah an e-mail revealing that he had a crush on her. Sarah responded that she had a boyfriend and that there was "no chance" they could ever be anything other than friends. Kevin waited outside her classes to talk to her and bought her a number of small gifts and continued to send her e-mails. Sarah occasionally included the defendant on e-mails she sent to a large group.

Kevin during the summer break called Sarah twice at her home. The second time, she quickly ended the conversation, and the defendant sent Sarah several e-mails. Sarah responded that she wanted to be friends, but "you need to back off a little bit." Kevin replied with an expletive-filled angry e-mail that asked why she was

punishing him and asking how she could want to be friends and yet not want to talk to him. Defendant sent her an additional e-mail in which he asked Sarah to give him a chance to be her friend again. Kevin approached her several weeks later and apologized and asked if they could do something together. Sarah responded "perhaps." He then e-mailed Sarah, who stated she was unavailable. Kevin explained that he was only trying to be her friend. At some point over the summer, Sarah requested that Kevin never call her at home again. Kevin, following an after-school sporting event, approached Sarah and her brother and asked for a ride to his car in an adjacent lot, which they refused. In October, Kevin spotted the victim along with her brother and mother at a shopping mall and approached the victim's brother in the checkout line and attempted to engage him in a conversation.

Sarah's father was the chief of police and approached Kevin and told him not to contact or harass Sarah. Kevin approached Sarah the next day at school, and Sarah told him that she had been trying to tell him to leave her alone for months. Defendant sent her an e-mail that day in which he said that he "just need[ed] a friend" and that he was "only asking for some closure now." Kevin later approached Sarah between classes at school, and her boyfriend stepped between them. The prosecution argued that the defendant engaged in a course of conduct that "would cause a reasonable person to fear for his or her physical safety or would cause a reasonable person substantial emotional distress."

Would you convict Kevin of stalking Sarah? *State v. Ellis*, 979 A.2d 1023 (Vt. 2009).

You can find the answer at study.sagepub.com/lippmaness2e

THE COMMON LAW OF RAPE

The common law treated rape as a capital crime punishable by death.[39] In the United States, only homicide has been historically considered more serious than rape. In 1925, nineteen states and the District of Columbia, as well as the federal government, punished rape with capital punishment. This was particularly controversial because the penalty of death for rape was almost exclusively employed against African Americans, particularly when accused of raping Caucasian women. By 1977, only Georgia provided capital punishment for rape. In that same year, the U.S. Supreme Court declared the death penalty for rape unconstitutional on the grounds that it was disproportionate to the harm caused by the rape.[40] This holding was affirmed in *Kennedy v. Louisiana*, in which the Court held that the death penalty was excessive punishment for the rape of a child.[41]

Today, most states divide rape into degrees of seriousness that reflect the circumstances of the offense. Aggravated rape may result in incarceration for a significant period of time and, in some jurisdictions, for life in prison. As discussed below, the term *rape* has been replaced in a number of state statutes by the term *sexual assault*.

The law of rape was rooted in the notion that a man's daughters and wife were his property, and that rape involved a trespass on a male's property rights. In fact, for a brief period of time, the common law categorized rape as a trespass subject to imprisonment and fine. William Blackstone recounts that under ancient Hebraic law, the rape of an unmarried woman was punishable by a fine of fifty shekels paid to the woman's father and by forced marriage without the privilege of divorce. The commentary to the MPC observes that the notion of "the wife as chattel" is illustrated by the fact that as late as 1984, forty states recognized a "marital exemption" that provided that a husband could not be held liable for the rape of his wife. Seventeenth-century English jurist Sir Matthew Hale explained that this exemption was based on the fact that a wife by "matrimonial consent and contract" had forfeited the privilege of refusing sexual favors to her husband.[42]

The law of rape is no longer an expression of property rights and today is designed to punish individuals who violate a victim's bodily integrity, psychological health and welfare, and sexual independence. The stigma and trauma that result from rape contribute to the reluctance of rape victims to report the crime to law enforcement authorities. Another factor contributing to the hesitancy of victims to report a rape is a lack of confidence that the criminal justice system will seriously pursue the prosecution and conviction of offenders.[43]

The criminal justice system is fairly effective in prosecuting what Professor Susan Estrich calls "real rape," or cases in which the victim is attacked by an unknown male. In such instances, the prosecution has little difficulty in demonstrating that the victim was forcibly subjected to sexual molestation. A greater challenge is presented in the area of so-called **acquaintance rape**, or date rape. In these cases, although no less serious, the perpetrator typically admits that sexual intercourse occurred and claims that it was consensual, while the victim characterizes the interaction as rape.[44] The reluctance to report rape may be most prevalent in the largely undocumented area of same-sex rape, which is a particularly serious problem in correctional institutions.[45]

In reading about rape, keep in mind that jurors and judges are likely to bring a host of prejudices and preconceptions regarding the proper behavior of men and women to their consideration of the facts. Although rape is categorized as a sexual offense, commentators stress that rape is a crime that involves the assertion of control and power over victims, most of whom are women. What types of issues do you anticipate may arise in rape prosecutions?[46]

The Elements of the Common Law of Rape

The common law defined rape as the forcible carnal knowledge of a woman against her will. Carnal knowledge for purposes of rape is defined as vaginal intercourse by a man with a woman who is not his wife. The vaginal intercourse is required to be carried out by force or threat of severe bodily harm ("by force or fear") without the victim's consent.[47]

The common law of rape reflects a distrust of women, and various requirements were imposed to ensure that the **prosecutrix** (victim) was not engaged in blackmail or in an attempt to conceal a consensual affair or was not suffering from a psychological illness. The fear of an unjust conviction was reflected in Sir Hale's comment that rape "is an accusation easy to be made, hard to be proved, but harder to be defended by the party accused though innocent." Sir Hale stressed that there was a danger that a judge and jury would be emotionally carried away by the seriousness of the charge and convict a defendant based on false testimony.[48]

The prosecution, as noted, was required to overcome a number of hurdles under the common law in order to convict the defendant.[49]

- *Immediate Complaint.* The absence of a **prompt complaint** by the victim to authorities was evidence that the complaint was not genuine.
- *Corroboration Rule.* The victim's allegation of rape required **corroboration**, evidence such as physical injury or witnesses.
- *Sexual Activity.* The victim's past sexual conduct or reputation for chastity was admissible as evidence of consent or on cross-examination to attack her credibility.
- *Judicial Instruction.* The judge was required to issue a cautionary instruction to the jury that the victim's testimony should be subject to strict scrutiny because rape is a crime easily charged and difficult to prove.

The crucial evidence in a prosecution for rape under the common law was a demonstration that the female "victim" did not consent to the sexual intercourse. Blackstone writes that a "necessary ingredient" in the crime of rape is that it is against the woman's will. He notes that it is a felony to forcibly ravish "even a concubine or harlot because the woman may have forsaken that unlawful course of life."[50]

The victim's lack of consent was demonstrated through outward resistance. In reference to sexual advances, a victim was required to **resist to the utmost** in order to establish a lack of consent. This expectation of combat against an attacker was viewed as reflecting "the natural instinct of every proud female to resist."[51] In *Brown v. State*, a sixteen-year-old woman recovering from the measles was attacked on a path near her family farm. The young woman was a virgin and testified that she tried as "hard as I could to get away" and "screamed as hard as I could . . . until I was almost strangled." The Wisconsin Supreme Court ruled that the prosecutrix failed to demonstrate that "she did her utmost" to resist. This not only requires "escape or withdrawal," but involves resistance "by means of hands and limbs and pelvic muscles." The alleged victim also failed to corroborate her complaint by "bruises, scratches and ripped clothing."[52] Courts did rule that resistance to the "utmost" was not required when the woman reasonably believed that she confronted a threat of "great and immediate bodily harm that would impair a reasonable person's will to resist."[53]

In the mid-twentieth century, judges began to relax this harsh resistance requirement. A few courts continued to require a fairly heavy burden of **earnest resistance**. Most, however, adopted the position that a victim was required to engage in **reasonable resistance** under the circumstances.[54]

Resistance is not required under the common law standard when a victim is incapable of understanding the nature of intercourse as a result of intoxication, sleep, or a lack of consciousness.[55] Another exception is so-called **fraud in the *factum*** or "fraud in the nature of the act." In *People v. Minkowski*, a woman consented to treatment for menstrual cramps by a doctor who proceeded to insert a metal instrument. During the procedure, he withdrew the metal object and without the consent of the patient inserted his sexual organ. The California court ruled that this was rape because the victim consented to a medical procedure and did not consent to intercourse.[56]

This is distinguished from **fraud in inducement** or consent to intercourse that results from a misrepresentation as to the purpose or benefits of the sexual act. In one well-known case, a female consented to intercourse with a donor after being tricked into believing that the donor had been injected with a serum that would cure her alleged disease. The California appellate court ruled that this was not rape because the victim consented to the "thing done" and the fraud related to the underlying purpose rather than to the fact of the sexual interaction.[57]

Rape Reform

During the 1970s and 1980s, a number of states abolished the special procedures surrounding the common law of rape. This included the corroboration and prompt reporting provisions and the judge's cautionary instructions to the jury. Another important development that we will discuss later in the chapter is the adoption of **rape shield laws** prohibiting the introduction of evidence concerning a victim's past sexual activity.

The commentary to the MPC justifies these reforms on the grounds that rape trials had become focused on the sexual background and resistance of victims rather than on the conduct of defendants. The extraordinary resistance standard placed women in a "no win" situation. Resistance might lead to violent retaliation; a failure to resist might result in the defendant's acquittal.[58]

A number of states adopted new sexual assault statutes that fundamentally changed the law of rape. The statutes treat rape as an assault against the person rather than as an offense against sexual morality. These statutes refer to "criminal sexual conduct" or "sexual assault" rather than rape. The modified statutes widely differ from one another and typically incorporate one or more of the following provisions[59]:

- *Gender Neutral.* A male or a female may be the perpetrator or the victim of rape.
- *Degrees of Rape.* Several degrees of rape are defined that are distinguished from one another based on the seriousness of the offense. These statutes provide that involuntary sexual penetration is more serious than involuntary contact and that the use of force results in a more serious offense than an involuntary contact or penetration that is accomplished without the use of force.
- *Sexual Intercourse.* "Sexual intercourse" is expanded to include a range of forced sexual activity or forced *intrusions* into a person's body, including oral and anal intercourse and the insertion of an object into the genital or anal opening of another. Some statutes also prohibit "*sexual contact*" or the intentional and nonconsensual touching of an intimate portion of another individual's body for purposes of sexual gratification.
- *Consent.* Some statutes provide that consent requires free, affirmative, and voluntary cooperation or that resistance may be established by either words or actions.
- *Coercion.* There is explicit recognition that coercion may be achieved through fraud or psychological pressure as well as through physical force.
- *Marital Exemption.* A husband or wife may be charged with the rape of a spouse.
- *Rape Shield Statutes.* Evidence of a victim's prior sexual activity with individuals other than the defendant is inadmissible in evidence.[60]

The important point to keep in mind is that these statutes have removed the barriers that have made rape convictions so difficult to obtain. States such as Michigan have adopted far-reaching reforms, whereas states such as Georgia have introduced only modest changes. A number of states as noted above now use the term *sexual assault* rather than *rape* in their criminal statutes to avoid the adjudication of criminal charges being influenced by the preconceptions and prejudices associated with rape.

An additional modern innovation in the law of rape is that some courts permit victims to present expert witnesses on the issue of **rape trauma syndrome** (discussed in this chapter). This expert evidence is intended to support the victim's contention that she was raped by pointing out that the victim's psychological and medical condition is characteristic of rape victims. In other instances, experts are employed to educate the jurors that rape victims often have a delayed reaction and that the jurors should not conclude that an individual was not raped because the complainant did not immediately bring charges of rape or was seemingly calm and collected following the alleged attack.[61]

Punishment and Sexual Assault

Sexual assault in Vermont involves compelling another person to participate in a sexual act without consent by threatening or coercing the other person, by placing the other person in fear of imminent bodily injury, by substantially impairing the ability of the other person through drugs or intoxicants without his or her knowledge or against his or her will, or when the victim is under fifteen years of age and the perpetrator is at least nineteen years of age. Sexual assault is punishable by a minimum of three years and a maximum of life imprisonment and by a fine of up to $25,000. **Aggravated sexual assault** in Vermont entails any one of a long list of factors including causing serious physical injury to the victim or to another; the perpetrator being joined by others in restraining, assaulting, or sexually assaulting the victim; the sexual act being committed under circumstances that constitute kidnapping; the perpetrator previously having been committed of sexual assault; the perpetrator being armed and threatening the victim with a deadly weapon or threatening to cause imminent serious bodily injury or applying deadly force; or the victim being under the age of thirteen and the perpetrator being at least eighteen. Aggravated sexual assault is punishable by between ten years in prison and life in prison and by a fine of up to $25,000. The statute of limitations for bringing a charge of sexual assault is six years, although there is no statute of limitations for aggravated sexual assault.[62]

In Indiana, an individual commits the crime of rape by engaging in sexual penetration with a person by force or threat of force, when the victim is unaware that sexual intercourse is occurring, or when the victim is unable to consent because of a mental disability. Rape is punishable by six to twenty years in prison and by a fine of up to $10,000. **Aggravated rape** involves sexual intercourse when the perpetrator uses or threatens to use deadly force, severely injures an individual other than the victim, is armed with a deadly weapon, gives the victim drugs, or knew that the victim had been given drugs without the victim's knowledge. Aggravated rape is punishable by twenty to fifty years in prison and by a fine of up to $10,000. Indiana extends the five-year statute of limitations an additional five years if DNA evidence is discovered or in the event of a confession by the perpetrator or other new evidence.[63] Roughly thirty-four states have a statute of limitations of between three and thirty years for rape or sexual assault, although some states extend the statute of limitations if DNA evidence is discovered.

Individuals convicted of sexual offenses in virtually every state are required to register as sexual offenders. The U.S. Supreme Court in *Stogner v. California*[64] and in *Smith v. Doe*[65] held that registration does not constitute criminal punishment and does not result in an offender being subjected to "double jeopardy." Offenders are required to register with government authorities, and their name, criminal conviction, photo, residence, and other information is posted on the Internet. The Court held that this does not constitute "double jeopardy" because it is a civil regulation intended to inform and to protect the public rather than to punish sexual offenders. Offenders are free to live their life without physical restraint. A number of communities restrict sexual offenders' ability to live near schools, playgrounds, and other areas in which children are found. In 2014, the Pennsylvania Supreme Court held that the sex offender law, which required juvenile sex offenders to register for life, violated due process because it was not "universally true" that these offenders continue to pose a threat to the community for their entire lives.[66]

The *Actus Reus* of Modern Rape

The *actus reus* of rape or what in most states is termed sexual assault requires the sexual penetration of the body of a rape victim by force. There are three approaches to defining the *actus reus*. One group of states adheres to the common law and punishes genital copulation. A second group of states that has followed the MPC expands this to include anal and oral copulation. A third group of states includes digital penetration and penetration with an instrument as well as genital, anal, and oral sex. The MPC and states such as Utah punish this last form of penetration as a less serious form of sexual assault.[67]

The FBI, until recently, followed the common law definition of rape in the Uniform Crime Reports. The definition of rape was modified and is defined as "[t]he penetration, no matter how slight, of the vagina or anus with any body part or object, or oral penetration by a sex organ of another person, without the consent of the victim."

Virtually all jurisdictions have adopted gender-neutral statutes that provide that women as well as men may be the perpetrators or victims of rape. A woman, for instance, may be an accomplice to the rape of a male by restraining a male victim while he is being subjected to homosexual rape. As for sexual penetration, California's statute reflects the majority rule by providing that "sexual penetration, however slight, is sufficient to complete the crime." An emission is not required.[68] An Arizona appellate court noted that it was following the majority rule in affirming the rape conviction of an impotent defendant who was unable to attain an erection and only achieved a penetration of roughly one inch.[69]

The essence of the *actus reus* of the common law crime of rape remains the employment of force to cause another individual to submit to sexual penetration without consent. How much force is required? Professor Wayne LaFave observes that courts have followed two distinct approaches.[70]

The first is the **extrinsic force** approach that requires an act of force beyond the physical effort required to accomplish penetration. This ensures that the penetration is without the victim's consent. A young college student entered Berkowitz's dorm room to visit Berkowitz's roommate. Berkowitz approached the young woman who had taken a seat on the floor, straddled her, and began fondling her. The victim objected, and Berkowitz attempted to place his penis in her mouth. She continued to say "no." Berkowitz pushed the victim down on the bed and had intercourse with her. She did not physically resist or vocally protest although she continued to say "no." The Pennsylvania Supreme Court reversed Berkowitz's rape conviction and held that "[w]here there is a lack of consent, but no showing of either physical force, a threat of physical force, or psychological coercion, [the] 'forcible compulsion' requirement . . . is not met." The degree of "forcible compulsion must be sufficient to prevent resistance by a person of reasonable resolution." In other words, in *Berkowitz*, the Pennsylvania Supreme Court held that the defendant did not use sufficient force or sufficient threat of force to prevent a reasonable female from physically resisting the assault. Absent resistance, the Supreme Court concluded that the prosecution had failed to establish a lack of consent on the part of the victim.[71]

Keep in mind that the force requirement may be satisfied by a threat of force as well as by the application of force. Statutes make this clear by stating that penetration may be accomplished by "force or threat of force," by "force or coercion," or by "force or fear." In other words, actual force is not required. There are two requirements that must be satisfied. First, there must be a threat of death or serious personal injury. Second, the victim's fear that the assailant will carry out the threat must be reasonable. The California statute provides that sexual intercourse constitutes rape where accomplished by "threatening to retaliate in the future . . . and there is a reasonable possibility that the perpetrator will execute the threat. . . . Threatening to retaliate means a threat to kidnap or falsely imprison or to inflict extreme pain, serious bodily injury, or death." The California statute also states that the threat requirement is satisfied where a public official threatens to "incarcerate, arrest, or deport the victim or another."[72] Michigan provides that a person is guilty of criminal sexual conduct where an individual engages in sexual penetration with another under circumstances in which the "actor is armed with a weapon or any article . . . fashioned . . . to lead the victim to reasonably believe it to be a weapon."[73]

The **intrinsic force** standard requires only the amount of force required to achieve penetration. The intrinsic force standard is based on the insight that there may be a lack of consent despite the fact that the perpetrator employs little or no force to achieve penetration. The thinking is that the stress on force and resistance under the extrinsic standard has "worked to the unfair disadvantage of the woman who, when threatened with violence, chose . . . quite rationally to submit to her assailant's advances rather than risk death or serious bodily harm."[74]

In *M.T.S.*, the seventeen-year-old defendant and fifteen-year-old victim were kissing one another when the defendant unexpectedly "penetrated" the young woman on three instances in rapid succession. The New Jersey Supreme Court held that M.T.S. had committed a rape based on the young woman's lack of consent. The Court stressed that the New Jersey statute had categorized rape as a sexual battery and did not employ the term *rape*. This suggests that the focus of the law is on whether the female consented to the sexual interaction and that "in order to convict under the sexual assault statute . . . the State must prove beyond a reasonable doubt that there was sexual penetration and that it was accomplished without the affirmative and freely given permission of the alleged victim."[75] Professor Joshua Dressler notes that the central question under the intrinsic test is whether the female expressed a "'yes' in words or action—before proceeding."[76]

We have already mentioned that force is not required where penetration is achieved through fraud or when the victim is unconscious, asleep, or insane and is unaware of the nature of the sexual penetration. The California statute provides for rape when the victim is "prevented from

Read
*Commonwealth
v. Berkowitz* and
*In the Interest of
M.T.S.* on the
study site: study
.sagepub.com/
lippmaness2e.

resisting by any intoxicating or anesthetic substance, or any controlled substance" or where an individual is "unconscious of the nature of the act."[77]

Several states have extended the *actus reus* for rape and declare that it is criminal to use a position of trust to cause another person to submit to sexual penetration. Texas, for instance, has provisions covering public servants, therapists, and nurses. Clergy are held liable for causing another person to submit or participate in a sexual act by "exploiting the other person's emotional dependency."[78] Pennsylvania defines "forcible compulsion" to mean "physical, intellectual, moral, emotional or psychological force either express or implied."[79]

Mens Rea

Rape at common law required that the male defendant intended to engage in vaginal intercourse with a woman who he knew was not his wife, through force or the threat of force. There was no clear guidance as to whether a defendant was required to be aware that the intercourse was without the female's consent. This issue remained unsettled for a number of years and only has been resolved in the last several decades with the view that rape is a general intent crime.

The majority of states accept an "objective test" that recognizes it is a defense to rape that a defendant honestly and reasonably believed that the rape victim consented. This doctrine was first recognized by the California Supreme Court in *People v. Mayberry.* The prosecutrix claimed that she had been kidnapped while shopping and had involuntarily accompanied the kidnapper to an apartment where she was raped by the defendant and another male. The defendant denied the accusations and characterized the victim's story as "inherently improbable."

The California Supreme Court ruled that the defendant was entitled to have the jury receive a mistake of fact instruction, reasoning that the state legislature must have intended that such a defense be available, given the seriousness of the charge. The court accordingly held that a defendant who "entertains a reasonable and bona fide belief that a prosecutrix voluntarily consented to accompany him and to engage in sexual intercourse . . . does not possess the wrongful intent that is a prerequisite . . . to a conviction of rape by means of force or threat."[80]

The objective test typically requires *equivocal conduct,* meaning that the victim's nonconsensual reactions were capable of being reasonably, but mistakenly, interpreted by the assailant as indicating consent. In the prosecution of heavyweight boxing champion Mike Tyson for the rape of a contestant in a beauty pageant that he was judging, the Indiana Court of Appeals held that Tyson was not entitled to a reasonable mistake of fact defense. Tyson's testimony indicated that the victim freely and fully participated in their sexual relationship. The victim, on the other hand, testified that Tyson forcibly imposed himself on her. The appellate court ruled that "there is no recitation of equivocal conduct by D.W. [the victim] that reasonably could have led Tyson to believe that D.W. . . . appeared to consent . . . [N]o gray area existed from which Tyson can logically argue that he misunderstood D.W.'s actions."[81]

CRIMINAL LAW AND PUBLIC POLICY

A 2007 Department of Justice study determined that one in five college women has been a victim of sexual assault. In 2014, California followed the recommendation of a White House task force on sexual assault on campus and adopted a "Yes Means Yes" law designed to combat sexual assaults on campus. Colleges and universities receiving state financial aid funds under the California statute are required to adopt an affirmative consent standard in determining whether a sexual assault occurred. New York later became the second state to adopt a statewide, campus affirmative consent law, and it is estimated that as many as eight

hundred public and private institutions have adopted the "Yes Means Yes" standard. Affirmative consent under the California law is defined as follows:

"Affirmative consent" means affirmative, conscious, and voluntary agreement to engage in sexual activity. It is the responsibility of each person involved in the sexual activity to ensure that he or she has the affirmative consent of the other or others to engage in the sexual activity. Lack of protest or resistance does not mean consent, nor does silence mean consent. . . . The existence of a dating relationship between the persons involved, or the fact of past sexual relations between them, should never by itself be assumed to be an indicator of consent. An individual who is inebriated or under the influence of narcotics is considered to be incapable of consent and the fact that the individual accused of sexual assault is intoxicated is not a defense.

This legal standard does not modify the legal standard followed in prosecutions in the criminal or civil justice systems.

Affirmative consent is ongoing, meaning that the fact that two individuals were in a relationship or have engaged in sexual activity in the past is not a defense. Consent may be revoked at any time. In adjudicating guilt, disciplinary committees are required by the U.S. Department of Education to apply a "preponderance of the evidence" standard (51 percent) rather than the "beyond a reasonable doubt" standard that is followed in the criminal justice process.

The rationale for the affirmative consent standard is that the traditional requirement that the assailant must use a degree of force inconsistent with consent in most instances requires women to say "no" and to resist in order to successfully establish a sexual assault. The California and New York laws by requiring that that an individual provide affirmative consent are thought to provide a needed degree of restraint on overly aggressive sexual partners, particularly when one or both of the partners are inebriated.

Proponents of the affirmative consent law argue that there is a need for a clear standard that will prevent misunderstandings between the individuals involved in a sexual interaction and that is easily applied by university panels. The affirmative consent standard also will provide greater confidence in the fairness of the process of adjudicating sexual assaults on campus.

Critics assert that the law is unworkable because there is a lack of certainty regarding what is required to establish affirmative consent and as a result individuals will be subject to liability without definite standards. Legally regulating sexual relationships between young people is bound to fail. Sexual interactions are not based on contract negotiations and often are spontaneous without either party asking for the consent of the other. A university panel will find it almost impossible to reconstruct the sexual interaction between the individuals and to disentangle conflicting versions of what transpired.

Critics also point out that the consequences of a student being held liable for sexual assault are too serious for guilt to be based on a "more likely than not" rather than "beyond a reasonable doubt" standard. Application of the "more likely than not" standard in the past has led to a number of legal actions against universities by individuals who have been determined to be responsible for sexual assault and expelled or suspended by college disciplinary committees.

In the last analysis, critics contend that the affirmative consent law is part of a trend toward the introduction of an unhealthy degree of political correctness on college campuses. Do you support the California affirmative consent law?

You Decide

8.3 The victim was an eighteen-year-old high school senior who at the time was working as a sales clerk. She was at work when the defendant, Randy Jay Goldberg, entered the store and claimed that he was a freelance talent agent and that the victim was an excellent candidate for a successful modeling career. The defendant actually was a community college student driving his mother's Cadillac Eldorado. Goldberg drove the victim to a condominium, which he said was his studio. They entered the bedroom, and the defendant persuaded the victim to remove one item of clothing after another. The victim said that she removed her clothes because she "was really scared of him" and that "[t]here was nothing I could do." When asked what caused her to be frightened, she said, "Because he

was—he was so much bigger than I was, and, you know, I was in a room alone with him, and there was nothing, no buildings around us, or anything, and I mean [it] wouldn't [have] helped if I wouldn't—help me if I didn't. It was like being trapped or something." On cross-examination, she said she was "afraid" she was "going to be killed."

Goldberg "pushed" her down on the bed and tried "to move [her legs] in different ways, and [she] kept pulling them together, and telling him that [she] didn't want to do it, and just wanted to go home." He kept telling her "just to relax." But she was "just really scared," and she was "shaking and my voice was really shaking" and she "kept on telling him [she] wanted to go home" and that "[she] didn't want to do this"; that she "didn't want to be a model, and [she] didn't want to do it any more. Just to let [her] alone." When asked "And what

(Continued)

(Continued)

was his reaction?" she testified that Goldberg was "really cool."

> And then he put his arms up on my stomach and his torso was in between my legs. He said just take your time; take a deep breath. And then he moved up on me and placed his penis in my vagina.
>
> . . . I squeezed my legs together and got really tense, and I just started crying real hard. And I told him not to do that to me. . . . [After ejaculating h]e got up and he said that if I can't enjoy it, then he can't enjoy it.

The relevant Maryland statute for first-degree rape at the time read as follows:

A person is guilty of rape in the first degree if the person engages in vaginal intercourse with another person by force against the will and without the consent of the other person *and*:

. . .

(3) threatens or places the victim in fear that the victim . . . will be imminently subjected to death, suffocation, strangulation, disfigurement, serious physical injury, or kidnapping.

Would you convict Goldberg of rape? See *Goldberg v. State*, 41 Md. App. 58 (1979).

You can find the answer at study.sagepub.com/lippmaness2e

Statutory Rape

Having sexual relations with a juvenile was not a crime under early English law as long as there was consent. This was modified by a statute that declared that it was a felony to engage in vaginal intercourse with a child younger than the age of ten, regardless of whether there was consent. This so-called **statutory rape** was incorporated into the common law of the United States. American legislatures gradually raised the age at which a child was protected against sexual intercourse to between eleven and fourteen. Statutory rape is based on several considerations[82]:

- *Understanding.* A minor is considered incapable of understanding the nature and consequences of his or her act.
- *Harmful.* Sexual relations are psychologically damaging to a minor and may lead to pregnancy.
- *Social Values.* This type of conduct is immoral and is contrary to social values.
- *Vulnerability.* The protection of females is based on the fact that males are typically the aggressors and take advantage of the vulnerability of immature females.

The general rule is that statutory rape is a strict liability offense in which a male is guilty of rape by engaging in intercourse with an "underage" female. This rule is intended to ensure that males will take extraordinary steps to ensure that females are of the age of consent.

Commentators have viewed strict liability for statutory rape as unjust in the case of a young woman who is physically mature and misrepresents her age. Defendants also have unsuccessfully claimed that males are singled out for prosecution while females rarely are charged with statutory rape. One reform is to provide that defendants can offer a "promiscuity defense" and document that the victim has had multiple sex partners and can be presumed to have possessed the capacity to appreciate the nature of her act and to have knowingly consented to a sexual relationship. A second approach is to divide the offense into various categories and to provide for more severe penalties for sexual relationships involving younger women. A third approach involves so-called **Romeo and Juliet laws**, which recognize that young people will engage in sexual experimentation and that statutory rape should not be a crime where the parties are roughly the same age, or it should be punished less severely. Forty-five states now recognize statutory rape as a gender-neutral offense; only five states still restrict guilt to males.[83]

You Decide

8.4 The Maryland statutory rape law in 1993 provided that it was a felony punishable by not more than twenty years in prison for a person to engage in vaginal intercourse with an individual "who is under 14 years of age and the person performing the act is at least four years older than the victim."

Raymond Leonard Garnett is described as a twenty-year-old, mentally challenged young man with an IQ of fifty-two. He read on the third-grade level, performed arithmetic on a fifth-grade level, and interacted with others socially at the level of someone eleven or twelve years of age. Raymond was unable to pass any of Maryland's functional tests required for graduation and received only a certificate of attendance rather than a high school diploma. He was introduced by a friend to Erica Frazier, thirteen, and was told that she was sixteen. The two of them talked on various occasions, and one evening they engaged in sexual intercourse after she invited him to climb through her bedroom window. Erica subsequently gave birth to a baby. Raymond was convicted of statutory rape and was sentenced to a suspended sentence of five years in prison and five years' probation, and was ordered to pay restitution to Erica and to Erica's family.

Do you agree with the verdict and the sentence? See *Garnett v. State*, 632 A.2d 797 (Md. 1993).

You can find the answer at study.sagepub.com/lippmaness2e

Withdrawal of Consent

In 2003, Illinois became the first state to pass a law on the **withdrawal of consent**. This legislation provides that a person "who initially consents to sexual penetration or sexual conduct is not deemed to have consented to any sexual penetration or sexual conduct that occurs after he or she withdraws consent during the course of that sexual penetration or conduct."[84]

Read *People v. John Z.* on the study site: study .sagepub.com/ lippmaness2e.

The Illinois law was passed in reaction to disagreement among courts in California as to whether an individual who continues sexual intercourse following the other party's withdrawal of consent is guilty of rape. The California Supreme Court resolved this conflict in *People v. John Z.*, holding that "forcible rape occurs when the act of sexual intercourse is accomplished against the will of the victim by force or threat of bodily injury and it is immaterial at what point the victim withdraws her consent, so long as that withdrawal is communicated to the male and he thereafter ignores it."[85] The decision in *John Z.* has been followed by courts in a majority of states. Do you believe that a male who continues sexual relations under such circumstances is guilty of rape?

Rape Shield Statute

The common law permitted the defense to introduce evidence concerning a victim's prior sexual relations with the accused, prior sexual relations with individuals other than the accused, and evidence concerning the alleged victim's reputation for chastity. Would you find this type of evidence valuable in determining the defendant's guilt or innocence?

The law continues to permit the introduction of evidence relating to sexual activity between the accused and victim. The assumption is that an individual who voluntarily entered into a relationship with a defendant in the past is more than likely to have again consented to enter into a relationship with the accused. The thinking is that the defendant is entitled to have the jury consider and determine the weight (importance) to attach to this evidence in determining guilt.

Rape shield laws prohibit the defense from asking the victim about or introducing evidence concerning sexual relations with individuals other than the accused or introducing evidence concerning the victim's reputation for chastity. The common law assumed that such evidence was relevant in that an individual who has "already started on the road of [sexual unchastity] would be less reluctant to pursue her way, than another who yet remains at her home of innocence and looks upon such a [pursuit] with horror."

The other reason for this evidence was the belief that the jury should be fully informed concerning the background of the alleged victim in order to determine whether her testimony was truthful or was the product of perjury or of a desire for revenge.[86]

Rape shield laws prohibiting evidence relating to a victim's general sexual activity are based on several reasons:

- *Harassment.* To prevent the defense attorney from harassing the victim.
- *Relevance.* The evidence has no relationship to whether the victim consented to sexual relations with the defendant and diverts the attention of the jury from the facts of the case.
- *Prejudice.* The evidence biases the jury against the accused.
- *Complaints.* Victims are not likely to report rapes if they are confronted at trial with evidence of their prior sexual activity.

Rape shield laws do not prohibit the introduction of an accused's past sexual activity in every instance. The Sixth Amendment to the U.S. Constitution guarantees individuals a fair trial and provides that individuals have the right to confront the witnesses against them. Courts have permitted the introduction of a victim's past activity with others in those instances when it is relevant to the source of injury or semen or reveals a pattern of activity or a motive to fabricate. For instance, the fact that a victim had a sexual relationship with a man other than the accused before going to the hospital may be relevant for the source of injury or semen.

Consider the issue that confronted the trial court in *State v. Colbath.* The defendant and victim were in a bar. The victim made sexually provocative remarks to the defendant and permitted him to feel her breast and buttocks and rubbed his sexual organ. The two went to the defendant's trailer where they had sexual intercourse. The defendant's significant other arrived and assaulted the woman, who defended her behavior by contending that she had been raped by the defendant. The trial judge rejected the defendant's effort to introduce evidence of the alleged victim's public sexual displays with other men in the bar and evidence that the victim had left the bar with other men prior to her approaching the defendant. The New Hampshire Supreme Court, however, held that despite the rape shield law, the defendant's Sixth Amendment right to confront witnesses against him required admission of evidence of the victim's conduct in the bar because it might indicate that at the time the victim met the defendant, she possessed a "receptiveness to sexual advances."[87]

On the other hand, in *People v. Wilhelm,* a Michigan appellate court upheld a ruling excluding evidence that the victim had exposed her breasts to two men who were sitting at her table in a bar and that she permitted one of them to fondle her breasts. The court ruled that the victim's conduct in the bar did not indicate that she would voluntarily engage in sexual intercourse with the defendant.[88]

You Decide

8.5 Stephen F. (Child) appeals his convictions for two counts of criminal sexual penetration and argues that the trial court improperly excluded evidence of the alleged victim's past sexual activities. Child claimed that this evidence would have demonstrated her motive to fabricate. Under Sections 30-9-11 through 30-9-15 of New Mexico Statutes, evidence of the victim's past sexual conduct and opinion evidence of the victim's past sexual conduct or of reputation for past sexual conduct shall not be admitted unless, and only to the extent, the court finds that the evidence is material to the case and that its inflammatory or prejudicial nature does not outweigh its probative value.

Child (age fifteen) and the alleged victim (B.G., age sixteen) engaged in sexual intercourse. Child, B.G., and B.G.'s brother had been watching movies in B.G.'s

bedroom. Child had been a friend of B.G.'s brother and family for nine years, and he usually slept on the couch in the living room when he spent the night. B.G. testified that after Child had headed for bed in the living room, he returned to her room and forced her to engage in sexual conduct, including oral, vaginal, and anal intercourse. The morning after the incident, B.G. told her mother that Child had raped her. Child was convicted of two counts of criminal sexual penetration. Child contended that the intercourse was consensual and claimed that B.G. lied because she feared that she would be punished by her religious parents. B.G. previously had been punished by her parents after having had consensual sexual relations with her then boyfriend. B.G. reportedly had told Child that her mother "was really upset . . . [about my having engaged in sex with my boyfriend;] she said that it was going to take her a long time to trust me again, . . . about three or four months[,] . . . and I wasn't allowed to go out on dates with guys." Child's theory was that B.G. was motivated to fabricate the claim of rape because she feared the punishment and disapproval of her parents, devout Christians who "don't believe in sex before marriage." The State of New Mexico opposed Child's motion to permit the cross-examination of the complaining witness in regard to her prior sexual conduct with her boyfriend on the grounds that this was intended to portray the complaining witness as an individual who is likely to engage in sexual activity outside of marriage. According to the appellate court, there are five areas to consider in making a decision on this issue: (1) whether there is a clear showing that complainant committed the prior acts; (2) whether the circumstances of the prior acts closely resemble those of the present case; (3) whether the prior acts are clearly relevant to a material issue, such as identity, intent, or bias; (4) whether the evidence is necessary to the defendant's case; [and] (5) whether the probative value of the evidence outweighs its prejudicial effect.

As a judge, would you permit Child to cross-examine the complaining witness in regard to her sexual conduct with her boyfriend? See *State v. Stephen F.,* 152 P.3d 842 (N.M. Ct. App. 2007).

You can find the answer at study.sagepub.com/lippmaness2e

Rape Trauma Syndrome

Rape trauma syndrome refers to attitudes and behaviors that scientists have identified after exhaustive study as being associated with being a rape victim (see discussion of rape trauma syndrome earlier in the chapter). The Kansas Supreme Court was the first court to admit expert witness testimony on rape trauma syndrome.[89] Every state court system has recognized the discretion of the trial court judge to permit the prosecution to introduce expert witness testimony on rape trauma syndrome.[90]

The expert witness testifies as to the behavior characteristic of an individual suffering from rape trauma syndrome evidence. Expert witnesses are witnesses whose academic or practical background and experience make them specially qualified to testify on a technical area that is outside the experience and knowledge of the average juror. The expert, in most instances, may not testify as to whether the victim is suffering from rape trauma syndrome. This is a determination for the jury.

Courts have allowed experts to testify on rape trauma syndrome where the behavior of the alleged victim following the rape does not conform to the type of behavior that the average juror may believe is uncharacteristic of a rape victim. The Colorado Supreme Court explained that expert testimony is required because "[t]he lay notion of what behavior logically followed the experience of being raped may not be consistent with the actual behavior which social scientists have observed from studying rape victims."[91]

Expert witnesses testifying on the rape trauma syndrome also may be used by the prosecution to help the jury understand the possible explanation for the victim's delayed report of rape and submissive behavior and to help resolve the dispute over whether the victim consented.[92]

The jury has responsibility for determining whether the victim's reaction following the rape is consistent with the rape trauma syndrome. Expert witness testimony on rape trauma syndrome provides the jurors with prosecution evidence to help them understand the victim's behavior following the alleged rape. The jurors may determine that even if the victim's behavior matches the

Table 8.1	Top Ten States' Rates of Rape in 2014 (per 100,000 Population)
State	**Rate**
Alaska	75.3
New Mexico	51.4
South Dakota	48.4
Montana	42.0
Michigan	40.9
Arkansas	39.8
Colorado	39.6
North Dakota	37.3
Kansas	37.0
Arizona	36.6
National rate, 26.4	

Source: Kathleen O'Leary Morgan and Scott Morgan, eds. *State Rankings 2016: A Statistical View of America.* Thousand Oaks, CA: CQ Press, 2016, p. 39.

rape trauma syndrome, they doubt her credibility (believability) or find the defense witnesses more credible. The Indiana Supreme Court allowed a defendant to introduce expert witness testimony on rape trauma syndrome to impeach the credibility of a victim who returned the evening following the alleged rape to the bar from which she claimed she had been abducted for a night of drinking and dancing.[93]

SEXUAL BATTERY

Battery, as noted, also may involve an uninvited, offensive physical contact. California defines **sexual battery** as the "touching against the will of the person touched" for the "specific purpose of sexual arousal, sexual gratification or sexual abuse." Sexual battery is punished by incarceration in jail for up to six months and a fine of as much as $2,000. The fine is enhanced when the defendant is the employer of the victim. In those instances when the defendant has a prior felony and the victim is a minor, the defendant is subject to a prison sentence of between two and four years and a fine of up to $10,000.[94]

A **domestic battery** in California against a spouse, a former spouse, or the mother or father of the assailant's child that results in a "traumatic condition" is punished as an aggravated felony. This includes a "wound or external or internal injury including an injury resulting from strangulation or suffocation."[95]

Domestic battery typically is incorporated into statutes punishing **domestic violence** or violent crimes committed against any member of a household. Indiana defines the crime of domestic violence as an "offense or the attempt to commit an offense" that "has as an element" of the "use of physical force" or "the threatened use of a deadly weapon." A court may impose a civil order of protection against an individual who is demonstrated by a preponderance of the evidence to pose a credible threat to an individual protected under the domestic violence statute. The order of protection may require that the assailant vacate the home, pay child support, remain at a distance from the victim, and turn over all firearms to the police. Individuals convicted of domestic violence also may be required to attend counseling sessions.[96]

The U.S. Congress established the offense of "interstate domestic violence" in 18 U.S.C. § 2261. This statute establishes criminal penalties for any "person who travels in interstate or foreign commerce . . . with the intent to kill, injure, harass, or intimidate a spouse, intimate partner, or dating partner, and . . . in the course or as a result of such travel, commits or attempts to commit a crime of violence against that spouse or intimate partner." A violation of this statute is punishable by a minimum penalty of five years in prison.

The federal government and sixteen states provide criminal penalties for female *genital mutilation*, a practice in which the sexual organs of young women are bound, to prevent premarital sexual relations. The federal statute punishes "whoever knowingly circumcises, excises, or infibulates the whole or any part of the labia majora or labia minora or clitoris of another person." Those who violate this statute are subject to a fine and imprisonment of not more than five years when the victim is a person younger than eighteen.[97]

CRIMINAL LAW IN THE NEWS

In late November 2004, Eagle County, Colorado, prosecutor Mark Hurlbert charged Los Angeles Lakers superstar basketball player Kobe Bryant with sexually assaulting a nineteen-year-old woman. Fifteen months later, the same prosecutor stood before the trial court and was granted a motion by the judge to dismiss the case. The prosecutor explained that the victim no longer desired to testify against Bryant.

The Eagle County prosecutor's office had spent $230,000 on this unsuccessful prosecution, 10 percent of its entire budget. Basketball fans of the Lakers expressed relief that the twenty-four-year-old Bryant, who if convicted faced a possible prison sentence of up to life, would be available to play for the Lakers.

Bryant entered the National Basketball Association right out of high school at age eighteen and had been selected to play in the NBA All-Star Game five times and already had played on three championship teams. Experts predicted that he would rank among the best players in league history by the time he retired.

Bryant insisted that the intercourse had been consensual. Observers, nevertheless, predicted that Bryant would never recover from the public humiliation. His squeaky clean public image had been tarnished by the public admission that he had committed adultery against his wife of two years, who had given birth to the couple's first child in January. In fact, he admitted during a police interview following his arrest that he earlier had been involved with yet another woman. The transcript of Bryant's conversation with the police indicates that he was primarily concerned with whether his public image would be damaged and with the reaction of his wife. He initially denied intercourse with the complainant and changed his mind after the investigators informed him that the physical evidence indicated that the two had engaged in intercourse.

Several days following Bryant's arrest, he purchased a $4 million diamond ring for his wife, who supported her husband throughout his legal ordeal. It later was revealed that Bryant had contemplated divorce several months earlier and that, as a result, his wife had been hospitalized and placed on life support. The mere bringing of the sexual assault charge against Bryant resulted in his losing multimillion-dollar endorsements with leading American corporations.

The alleged victim worked at the front desk at a spa located in a small mountain town one hundred miles west of Denver where Bryant was staying while preparing for knee surgery at a nearby clinic. Bryant invited her to his room. She initially alleged that he immediately assaulted her and then later indicated that Bryant unexpectedly escalated a consensual encounter and that she had cried and at least twice said "no" as he pushed her over a chair and entered her from the rear.

The media quickly shifted the focus from Bryant to the unnamed victim, whose name later was mistakenly posted on an Eagle County court Web site. Press reports indicated that she was a former high school cheerleader who reportedly had auditioned for the show *American Idol* and was described by some acquaintances as desperate for attention and notoriety. Other sources told of two suicide attempts during the past year and her hospitalization by the University of Northern Colorado campus police, who feared that she posed a "danger to herself." The media interviewed every resident of the victim's hometown who

was willing to speak, leading to a blizzard of supportive as well as skeptical comments. Two Lakers fans were sufficiently upset to issue death threats against the complainant, resulting in their imprisonment.

Documents and testimony from closed court hearings were leaked to the press. This information indicated that the complainant had sexual intercourse with at least one other individual after she left Bryant and before she contacted the police. The judge would later rule that the defense was entitled to introduce evidence of the complainant's sexual activity during the three days prior to her hospital examination on July 1, 2003, on the grounds that this was relevant to the cause of her injuries, the source of DNA, and her credibility as a witness. Information was also leaked documenting that she received a substantial amount of money from a state victim compensation fund to address mental health concerns stemming from her alleged sexual assault by Bryant.

The news stories on Bryant marveled over the fact that he was able to attend court hearings and then fly hundreds of miles to Lakers games and still perform at a high level. Speculation focused on whether Bryant would continue to play with the Lakers when his contract expired. This question was answered several months prior to the dismissal of the charges, when Bryant signed a seven-year contract for more than $136.4 million.

Following the dismissal of the charges against Bryant, fans expressed relief, and the Lakers issued a statement of support. Bryant circulated a press release in which he recognized that although he viewed the affair as consensual, "she did not," and he issued an apology to the complainant and her family for his behavior. Advocates for victims of sexual assault were quoted as bemoaning that the Bryant case would have the impact of discouraging women from bringing complaints of rape to prosecutors who, in turn, would be reluctant to file charges.

In 2016, Bryant retired from the NBA having played on five championship teams and having earned an Olympic gold medal. Even his harshest critics rank him as an all-time great player.

As a prosecutor, would you have brought the Bryant case to trial? Do athletes receive preferential treatment when accused of sexual abuse? On the other hand, are they more often than not the target of false allegations?

KIDNAPPING

Kidnapping at common law was the forcible abduction or stealing away of a person from his or her own country and sending him or her into another country. This misdemeanor was intended to punish the taking of an individual to an isolated location where the victim was outside of the protection of the law. Imagine the fear you would experience in the event that you were locked in a basement under the complete control of an abusive individual.

Kidnapping became of concern in 1932 with the kidnapping of the twenty-month-old son of Charles Lindbergh, the aviation hero who piloted the "Spirit of St. Louis" in the first flight across the Atlantic. Lindbergh paid the $50,000 ransom demanded for the return of Charles Jr., who later was found dead in the woods five miles from the Lindbergh home. A German immigrant, Bruno Hauptmann, was prosecuted for felony murder, convicted, and executed. The question whether Hauptmann was the perpetrator continues to be a topic of intense debate.

The Lindbergh kidnapping resulted in the adoption of the Federal Kidnapping Act, known as the "Lindbergh Law." This law prohibits the kidnapping and carrying of an individual across state lines for the purpose of obtaining a ransom or reward. Six states shortly thereafter adopted new statutes significantly increasing the penalty for kidnapping. This trend continued, and by 1952, all but four states punished kidnapping with death or life imprisonment.

The Lindbergh Law excluded parents from coverage. In 1981, Congress addressed the 150,000 abductions of children by a parent involved in a custody dispute in the Parental Kidnapping Prevention Act. The statute provides for FBI jurisdiction when a kidnapped child is transported across state lines. The abduction of children by a parent or relative involved in a custody dispute is also the subject of specific state statutes punishing a "relative of a child" who "takes or entices" a child younger than eighteen from his or her "lawful custodian."

The last decades have been marked by a string of high-profile kidnappings of wealthy corporate executives and members of their families. In 1974, Patricia Hearst, heiress to the Hearst newspaper fortune, was kidnapped from her campus apartment at the University of California at Berkeley. The abduction was carried out by the Symbionese Liberation Army (SLA), a self-proclaimed revolutionary group. The case took on a bizarre character when Hearst participated in bank robberies intended to finance the activities of the group. Hearst was later apprehended and convicted at trial despite her claim of "brainwashing." The major figures in the SLA were subsequently killed in a shoot-out with the Los Angeles police.

More recently, we have seen the 1993 abduction and killing of twelve-year-old Polly Klaas and the kidnapping, in 2002, of twelve-year-old Elizabeth Smart. Elizabeth was later found to have been forced into a "marriage" with her abductor, a handyman in the Smart home. In 2009, Jaycee Lee Dugard was rescued eighteen years after having been abducted at age eleven. The latest tragic incident involves the kidnapping and decade-long confinement of three young women by a Cleveland bus driver.

Following American intervention into Iraq, foreigners were regularly kidnapped by criminal gangs who "sold" the victims to political groups opposed to the presence of the United States. The terrorists typically threatened to kill the hostage unless the company for which the prisoner worked or his or her country of nationality agreed to withdraw from Iraq. In a related incident, *Wall Street Journal* reporter Daniel Pearl was kidnapped and beheaded by an extremist group in Pakistan. The terrorist group's Britain-born leader, Ahmed Omar Saeed Sheikh, was later prosecuted and sentenced to death in Pakistan. The taking of hostages is recognized as a crime under the International Convention Against the Taking of Hostages, which requires countries signing the treaty either to prosecute offenders or to send them to a nation claiming the right to prosecute the offender.

The U.S. Congress has also enacted the Victims of Trafficking and Violence Protection Act of 2000 and the PROTECT Act of 2003 that together combat the international sexual trafficking industry. Roughly one million children, most of whom are girls, have been persuaded to leave or are forcibly abducted from their mostly rural villages in poor countries and forced into sexual slavery or low-wage industrial labor.

Kidnapping Statutes

Kidnapping statutes vary widely in their requirements. California Penal Code Section 202 provides that

> [e]very person who forcibly, or by any other means of instilling fear, steals or takes, or holds, detains, or arrests any person in this state, and carries the person into another country, state, or county, or into another part of the same county, is guilty of kidnapping.

The *mens rea* of kidnapping, although subject to dispute, is commonly thought to be an intent to move or to confine the victim without his or her consent. Wisconsin Statute Section 940.31 provides that kidnapping is the carrying of another from one place to another without his or her consent and with the "intent to cause him or her to be secretly confined or imprisoned or to be carried out of this state or to be held to service against his or her will." Some statutes require holding an individual for a specific purpose such as detaining a person for ransom or as a hostage. Florida requires a specific intent, whether to hold an individual for ransom or reward, to serve as a shield or hostage, to inflict bodily harm, to terrorize the victim, or to interfere with the performance of any governmental or political function. Texas considers the intentional or knowing abduction of another person with the intent to commit these acts as "aggravated kidnapping."

Criminal Act

The essence of kidnapping is the *actus reus* of the forcible movement of a person as provided under the North Carolina statute "from one place to another." The central issue is the extent of the movement required. The traditional rule in American law is that any movement, no matter how limited, is sufficient. In the well-known California case of *People v. Chessman*, Caryl Chessman was convicted of kidnapping when he forced a rape victim to move twenty-two feet into his car. The California Supreme Court noted that it is "the fact, not the distance of forcible removal, which constitutes kidnapping in this State."[98]

Most courts abandoned this approach after realizing that almost any rape, battery, or robbery involves some movement of a victim. This led to prosecutors charging defendants with the primary crime as well as kidnapping and resulted in life imprisonment for crimes that otherwise did not merit this harsh penalty. In 1969, the California Supreme Court rejected the *Chessman* standard in *People v. Daniels*. The defendants entered the victims' apartments and forced them at knifepoint to move a few feet into another room where they were robbed and raped. The court reversed the kidnapping convictions on the grounds that the victims' movements were a central step in the rape or robbery and should not be considered as constituting the independent offense of kidnapping.[99]

Courts now generally limit the application of kidnapping statutes to "true kidnapping situations and [do] not . . . apply it to crimes which are essentially robbery, rape or assault . . . in which some confinement or asportation occurs as a subsidiary incident." The MPC requires that the individual is moved a "substantial distance" from where he or she is "found."

Kidnapping statutes are no longer thought to include unlawful confinements or movements incidental to the commission of other felonies. Under this standard, courts require that for a movement to be considered kidnapping, it "must be more than slight, inconsequential, or an incident inherent in the crime." Judges have ruled that for the movement to constitute kidnapping, it must meaningfully contribute to the commission of the primary crime by preventing the victim from calling for help, reducing the defendant's risk of detection, facilitating escape, or increasing the danger to the victim.

In *Faison v. State*, the defendant moved a woman from her office to a bathroom in the rear of the office to commit a rape. A Florida District Court affirmed the defendant's conviction and established a three-part test for kidnapping.[100]

> [I]f a taking or confinement is alleged to have been done to facilitate the commission of another crime, to be kidnapping the resulting movement or confinement:
>
> (a) Must not be slight, inconsequential and merely incidental to the other crime;
>
> (b) Must not be of the kind inherent in the nature of the other crime; and
>
> (c) Must have some significance independent of the other crime in that it makes the other crime substantially easier of commission or substantially lessens the risk of detection.

In *People v. Aguilar*, the defendant followed Nancy C., age sixteen, as she walked down a residential street. He grabbed her and inserted his fingers in her vagina. She screamed, and he dragged her 133 feet down the street to an area that was not illuminated by a street light and pushed her onto the hood of a car and reinserted his fingers in her vagina. The California appellate court held that Nancy's movement was not merely incidental to the rape. Her movement facilitated the rape and increased the danger to Nancy. Once having moved Nancy, the defendant threw her to the ground, grabbed her neck, choked her, bit her, slammed her onto a car hood, and held her down on the hood with a knife at her neck.[101]

The movement or detention of the victim must be unlawful, meaning without the victim's consent by force or threat of force. The Wisconsin statute requires that the movement of an individual must be undertaken "without his or her consent" and by "force or threat of imminent force." This excludes movements undertaken as a result of a lawful arrest, court order, or consent. An Arkansas court held that where the victim voluntarily accepted the defendant's offer of a ride to a friend's house, the victim revoked her consent when the perpetrator prevented her from leaving the automobile by displaying and threatening her with a firearm, ordering her to place her hands under her thighs, and taking her to his home where she was raped.

Courts are divided over whether an individual is "forcibly" moved where the defendant fraudulently misrepresents his or her intended destination. The California Supreme Court held that a victim's movement was "accomplished by force or any other means of instilling fear" where a rapist falsely represented that he was a police officer and informed the eighteen-year-old victim that she faced arrest unless she accompanied him to a store from which she was suspected of having stolen merchandise. The court concluded that this "kind of compulsion is qualitatively different than if defendant had offered to give Alesandria [the victim] a ride, or sought her assistance in locating a lost puppy, or any other circumstance suggesting voluntariness on the part of the victim."[102]

Some states follow the MPC in reducing the seriousness of the kidnapping where the victim was "voluntarily released . . . in a safe place." This provides an incentive for a defendant to limit the harm inflicted on victims.

Read *People v. Aguilar* on the study site: study .sagepub.com/ lippmaness2e.

A related crime is **child abduction**, an offense that requires the state to prove that the defendant "intentionally lure[d] or attempt[ed] to lure a child under the age of 16 into a motor vehicle . . . without the consent of the parent . . . of the child for other than a lawful purpose."[103] In *People v. Hampton*, the defendant was convicted for attempting to persuade a young woman, who told him that she was in eighth grade, into his car with the promise that "I will buy you anything you want."[104]

Model Penal Code

Section 212.1. Kidnapping

A person is guilty of kidnapping if he unlawfully removes another from his place of residence or business, or a substantial distance from the vicinity where he is found, or if he unlawfully confines another for a substantial period in a place of isolation, with any of the following purposes:

(a) to hold for ransom or reward, or as a shield or hostage; or

(b) to facilitate commission of any felony or flight thereafter; or

(c) to inflict bodily injury on or to terrorize the victim or another; or

(d) to interfere with the performance of any governmental or political function.

Kidnapping is a felony of the first degree unless the actor voluntarily releases the victim alive and in a safe place prior to the trial, in which case it is a felony of the second degree (ten years). A removal or confinement is unlawful . . . if it is accomplished by force, threat, or deception, or, in the case of a person who is under the age of 14 or incompetent, if it is accomplished without the consent of a parent, guardian, or other person responsible for general supervision of his welfare.

Analysis

1. Kidnapping is defined to include any of three acts. First, removing victims from the protection of the home or business is intended to punish the taking of individuals from the safety and security of a home or business and placing them in danger. Second, removing individuals

"a substantial distance from the vicinity" where they are located is intended to ensure that punishment is not imposed for "trivial changes of location." Third, confining an individual for a substantial period of time in an isolated location with a specified intent is intended to punish the "frightening and dangerous" removal of a victim from a safe environment to an "isolated" location where he or she is outside the protection of the law. No movement or asportation is required in regard to confining an individual. The requirement that the detention is for a "substantial period of time" in a "place of isolation" is intended to avoid punishing a defendant for a detention that is merely incidental to a rape or other crime of violence.

2. Kidnapping is defined to require one of four specified purposes that commonly appear in kidnapping statutes.

3. An unlawful removal must be accomplished through force, threat, or deception, or in the case of an "incompetent" juvenile under the age of fourteen, without the consent of a parent or guardian.

4. The reduction in punishment for kidnapping to a second-degree felony when the perpetrator releases the victim "alive and in a safe place" provides an incentive for the kidnapper to abandon the criminal enterprise. The defendant would remain liable for any battery or sexual assault.

The Legal Equation

Kidnapping $=$ Intent to detain and move or to detain and hide without consent

$+$ act of detention and moving or detention and hiding

$+$ through the unlawful use of force or threat of force.

FALSE IMPRISONMENT

Within the common law and in state statutes, **false imprisonment** is defined as the intentional and unlawful confinement or restraint of another person. The Idaho statute simply states that false imprisonment is the "unlawful violation of the personal liberty of another." False imprisonment is generally considered a misdemeanor, punishable in Idaho by a fine not exceeding $5,000, or by imprisonment in the county jail for no more than one year, or both.[105]

As with kidnapping, false imprisonment is a crime that punishes interference with the freedom and liberty of the individual. False imprisonment requires an intent to restrain the victim. Arkansas and other states follow the MPC and provide that false imprisonment may be committed by an individual who "without consent and without lawful authority . . . knowingly restrains another person so as to interfere with his liberty."[106] The detention must be unlawful and without the victim's consent. A restraint by an officer acting in accordance with the law or by a parent disciplining his or her child does not constitute false imprisonment. The consent of the victim constitutes a defense to false imprisonment. A farmer who secured his wife with a chain while he went to town was not held liable for false imprisonment where the evidence indicated that she requested him to manacle her to the bed.[107]

The *actus reus* is typically described as compelling the victim to "remain where he did not want to remain or go where he did not want to go."[108] The confinement may be accomplished by physical restraint or by a threat of force of which the victim is aware. Confinement may also be achieved without force or the threat of force when, for instance, the perpetrator locks a door. Professors Perkins and Boyce point out that an individual is not confined because he is prevented from moving in one or in several directions so long as he may proceed in another direction. An individual may also be confined in a moving bus or in a hijacked airplane.[109]

False imprisonment may overlap with kidnapping or with assault and battery or robbery, and several states have eliminated the crime. In these states, people who are unlawfully detained are able to seek damages in civil court. The major difference between the crimes of kidnapping and false imprisonment is that false imprisonment does not require an asportation (movement). In addition, kidnapping statutes that punish the confinement as well as the movement of a victim often provide that the victim must be "secretly confined" or "held in isolation" for a specific purpose (e.g., to obtain a ransom). The MPC provides that the confinement for kidnapping must be for a "substantial period."[110] False imprisonment, in contrast, requires a detention that may take place in public or in the privacy of a home and may be for a brief or lengthy period. States such as Alabama provide for the punishment of aggravated false imprisonment where an individual "restrains another person under circumstances which expose the latter to a risk of serious physical injury."[111]

The challenge often is to distinguish false imprisonment from kidnapping. In *Cole v. State*, a Florida appellate court held that the robber ordering store employees to move into a closet to prevent them from phoning the police was the type of act that normally accompanied the robbery of a store and that this constituted false imprisonment rather than kidnapping.[112]

Model Penal Code

Section 212.3. False Imprisonment

A person commits a misdemeanor if he knowingly restrains another unlawfully so as to interfere substantially with his liberty.

Section 212.2. Felonious Restraint

A person commits a felony of the third degree if he knowingly:

(1) restrains another unlawfully in circumstances exposing him to risk of serious bodily injury; or

(2) holds another in a condition of involuntary servitude.

Analysis

1. The MPC requires a substantial interference with an individual's liberty. This eliminates prosecutions for relatively modest interference with an individual's liberty.

2. An individual must knowingly restrain another person. As a result, it is sufficient that a defendant is aware that his or her conduct will result in the detention of another individual.

3. Felonious restraint is intended to punish as felonies restraints that create a risk of serious bodily injury or involuntary servitude.

The Legal Equation

False imprisonment	=	Restraint by
	+	force, threat of force, or constructive force.

You Decide

8.6 Joy Salem and Sarah Gibeson were employed by the Jewelry Mart. Victor Maurice Hoard entered the store shortly after it opened one Sunday afternoon. He displayed a gun and ordered the women to give him the key to the jewelry cases. Hoard demanded the keys to Gibeson's car and directed the women into the office at the back, fifty feet from where they were standing, tied their ankles and wrists with duct tape, and taped their mouths. He then began taking jewelry from the cases. When customers entered the store, Hoard told them it was closed for maintenance or performing inventory.

Gibeson tried to call 911 on her cell phone, but she dropped the phone. Hoard returned to the office,

threatened the women, pulled the office phone out of the wall, and left the store. After some other customers helped release the women, Gibeson saw that her car had been stolen by Hoard.

Was Hoard guilty of kidnapping? *People v. Hoard*, 103 Cal. App. 4th 599 (2002).

You can find the answer at study.sagepub.com/lippmaness2e

CASE ANALYSIS

In *State v. Jones*, the Idaho Supreme Court decided whether Jones was guilty of raping A.S.

Was There Sufficient Evidence of A.S.'s Resistance to Hold Jones Guilty of Forcible Rape?

State v. Jones, 299 P.3d 219 (Idaho 2013)

On May 27, Jones went to A.S.'s apartment to watch movies. He spent the night and remained there in the morning after Carpenter left for work and A.S.'s children went to school. At the time, A.S. was taking an antihistamine for a bee sting and a prescription anti-anxiety medication, both of which caused her to feel drowsy. As a result of her drowsiness she laid down on the living room couch and started to "drift off." Jones went into the living room, sat next to her, and started stroking her hair. A.S. testified that after he "grabbed a handful of hair and pulled" hard enough to hurt her, she was nonresponsive in hopes that "if [she] just laid there and didn't move he would leave [her] alone." She further stated that:

> After he was done pulling my hair, he left me alone for a little bit. And then he grabbed my chest and squeezed my breast really hard. . . . He apparently didn't get the reaction he wanted, and he moved down to my vaginal area. . . . He started touching me outside, and then he started putting his fingers inside me really hard. Jones then proceeded to pull down A.S.'s pants and underwear, and "pushed [her] legs apart and started having sex with [her]." In response, A.S. "just froze," and testified that she was "paralyzed" with fear.

Afterwards, Jones and A.S. went to the bedroom and shared a cigarette. Jones helped A.S. into bed and once again started to have sexual intercourse with her. She testified that:

> [H]e got off me and pulled his clothes back on and put mine back on. And then he sat me back up and asked me if he could have sex with me. And I just kept saying over and over again, no, my kids are going to be home soon. Eventually, Jones left the apartment.

A.S. drove to Carpenter's brother's house and told the brother's girlfriend that she had been raped. They took A.S. to the hospital where she told the staff that she had been sexually assaulted, but that she did not want to press charges. But law enforcement was contacted, and A.S. provided a statement to police while at the hospital.

On May 29, A.S. met with a detective, who arranged for A.S. to make a recorded call to Jones. A.S. confronted Jones regarding the incidents, and Jones is heard on tape apologizing. . . . Additionally, A.S. is clearly heard saying, "You think this is okay to do to people who are unconscious?" . . . Toward the end of the tape, A.S. asks Jones to describe what he did to her—he states that: "I think that I pushed things too

(Continued)

(Continued)

far and I guess it's rape. I did it. You obviously didn't want any part of it."

The Idaho Code defines forcible rape as follows:

Rape is defined as the penetration, however slight, of the oral, anal or vaginal opening with the perpetrator's penis accomplished with a female under any one (1) of the following circumstances:

. . .

(3) Where she resists but her resistance is overcome by force or violence. I.C. § 18-6101(3).

The statute only requires "resistance." It does not differentiate between physical or verbal resistance. . . . Whether the evidence establishes the element of resistance is a fact-sensitive determination based on the totality of the circumstances, including the victim's words and conduct. Based on the plain language of I.C. § 18–6101(3), we hold that the extrinsic force standard applies in Idaho. Section 18–6101(3) defines forcible rape as "penetration, however slight," "[w]here [a woman] resists but her resistance is overcome by force or violence." Were we to construe "force" as encompassing the act of penetration itself, it would effectively render the force element moot. . . . [W]e conclude that some force beyond that which is inherent in the sexual act is required for a charge of forcible rape.

We hold that there is insufficient evidence to support a charge of forcible rape. . . . By her own admission, A.S. "didn't respond" physically, or even verbally, to Jones' advances—she "just froze." Idaho's forcible rape statute expressly requires resistance. Satisfying this element with inactivity strains the definition of resistance, essentially nullifying the resistance requirement. Though studies have shown that "freezing up" is indeed a legitimate, understandable reaction of victims of sexual assault, this Court has no authority to jettison the resistance requirement—modifying this State's statutes is the Legislature's province alone. As the statute is plainly written, some quantum of resistance is required, and A.S. did not resist Jones' advances on May 28. There was insufficient evidence on the element of resistance to support the conviction of forcible rape I so we need not consider the issue of force. The conviction . . . is accordingly reversed.

[We recognize] that many women demonstrate "psychological infantilism"—a frozen fright response—in the face of sexual assault. . . . The "frozen fright" response resembles cooperative behavior. . . . Indeed, . . . the "victim may smile, even initiate acts, and may appear relaxed and calm." . . . Subjectively, however, she may be in a state of terror. [Also] the victim may make submissive signs to her assailant and engage in propitiating behavior in an effort to inhibit further aggression. . . . These findings belie the traditional notion that a woman who does not resist has consented. They suggest that lack of physical resistance may reflect a "profound primal terror" rather than consent.

CHAPTER SUMMARY

There are four categories of offenses discussed in this chapter: assault and battery, stalking, sexual assault, and kidnapping and false imprisonment.

Assault and battery, although often referred to as a single crime, are separate offenses. A battery is the application of force to another person. An assault may be committed by attempting to commit a battery or by intentionally placing another in imminent fear of a battery. Aggravated assaults and batteries are felonies.

Stalking entails a series of acts that intentionally or knowingly are undertaken to intimidate, frighten, or terrorize another individual. This may involve surveillance, repeated unwanted contact, lying in wait, threatening, vandalizing, or a combination of these acts. States also have adopted cyberstalking laws that prohibit stalking when carried out through electronic communication or a combination of electronic communication and verbal expression and acts.

Rape at common law was punishable by death, and only homicide was historically considered a more severe crime. Common law rape required the intentional vaginal intercourse by a man of a woman who was not his wife by force or threat of serious bodily injury against her will. The fear of false conviction led to the imposition of various barriers that the victim was required to overcome. These included immediate complaint, corroboration, the admissibility of evidence pertaining to a victim's past sexual activity, and a cautionary judicial instruction. The focus was on the victim, who was expected to demonstrate her lack of consent by the utmost resistance.

The law of rape was substantially modified by the legal reforms of the 1970s and 1980s that treated rape as an assault against the person rather than as an offense against sexual morality. Sexual intercourse was expanded to include the forced intrusion into any part of another person's body, including the insertion of an object into the genital or anal opening. Rape was defined in gender-neutral terms; the marital exemption was abolished; and rape was divided into simple and aggravated rape based on the type of the penetration, use of force, or resulting physical injury. Various statutes no longer employ the term *rape* and punish vaginal intercourse as one of several forms of sexual assault.

The intent of rape reform is to shift attention from resistance by the victim to the force exerted by the perpetrator. There are two approaches to analyzing force. The extrinsic force standard requires an act of force beyond the physical effort required to achieve sexual penetration. The intrinsic force standard requires only that amount of force required to achieve penetration. Sexual assault may also be accomplished by threat of force, through penetration obtained by fraud, or when the victim is incapable of consent stemming from unconsciousness, sleep, or insanity.

The *mens rea* of rape at common law was the intent to engage in vaginal intercourse with a woman who the defendant knew was not his wife through force or the threat of force against her will. There was no clear guidance as to whether a defendant was required to know that the intercourse was without the female's consent. A majority of states now accept an objective test that recognizes the defense that a defendant honestly and reasonably believed that the victim consented. This requires equivocal conduct by the victim that is capable of being reasonably, but mistakenly, interpreted by the assailant as indicating consent. The English House of Lords rule, in contrast, adopts a subjective approach and examines whether a defendant "knows" whether the victim consented. The third approach is the imposition of strict liability that holds defendants guilty whatever their personal belief or the objective reasonableness of their belief.

Recent legal and statutory developments recognize that individuals may withdraw their consent. The continuation of sexual relations under such circumstances constitutes rape.

Statutory rape is a strict liability offense that holds a defendant guilty of rape based on his intercourse with an "underage" female. Several states permit the defense of a reasonable mistake of age. Rape shield laws prohibit the prosecution from asking the victim about or introducing evidence concerning sexual relations with individuals other than the accused or introducing evidence relevant to the victim's reputation for chastity.

Kidnapping is the unlawful and forcible seizure and asportation (carrying away) of another without his or her consent. This requires the specific intent to move the victim without his or her consent. The *actus reus* is the moving or detention of the victim. Courts differ on the extent of this movement, variously requiring slight or, under the Model Penal Code standard, substantial movement. The majority rule is that the movement must not be incidental to the commission of another felony and must contribute to the primary crime by preventing the victim from calling for help, reducing the defendant's risk of detection, facilitating escape, or increasing the danger to the accused.

False imprisonment is the intentional and unlawful confinement or restraint of another person. The restraint may be achieved by force, by threat of force, or by other means and does not require the victim's asportation or secret confinement. False imprisonment is a misdemeanor other than when committed in an aggravated fashion.

CHAPTER REVIEW QUESTIONS

1. Distinguish an assault from a battery.

2. What are the requirements of a battery? Describe the difference between a simple battery and an aggravated battery.

3. Discuss the two ways to commit an assault.

4. What is the relationship between the crime of stalking and a criminal assault?

5. What was the original justification for the crime of rape?

6. Why does "date rape" present a challenge to prosecutors?

7. How did the common law define rape? List some of the barriers to establishing rape under the common law.

8. Describe the changes in the law of rape introduced by the reform statutes of the 1970s and 1980s.

9. What elements distinguish a simple or second-degree rape from aggravated or first-degree rape?

10. Distinguish the standard of extrinsic force from the intrinsic force standard in the law of rape.

11. In addition to force, what other means might a perpetrator employ to satisfy the *actus reus* requirement in the law of rape?

12. What are the three approaches to the defense of mistake of fact in the *mens rea* of rape?

13. Is a defendant's belief that another individual is above the age of lawful consent a defense to statutory rape? What of the female's past sexual experience?

14. May an individual who withdraws consent claim to be the victim of rape?

15. What is the purpose of rape shield laws? Are there exceptions to rape shield laws?

16. What is the definition of kidnapping? What are the various approaches to the asportation requirement?

17. Distinguish between false imprisonment and kidnapping.

LEGAL TERMINOLOGY

acquaintance rape

aggravated assault

aggravated battery

aggravated rape

aggravated sexual assault

assault and battery

child abduction

corroboration

cyberstalking

dangerous weapon battery

domestic battery

domestic violence

earnest resistance

extrinsic force

false imprisonment

fraud in inducement

fraud in the *factum*

intrinsic force

kidnapping

mayhem

prompt complaint

prosecutrix

rape shield laws

rape trauma syndrome

reasonable resistance

resist to the utmost

Romeo and Juliet laws

sexual assault

sexual battery

stalking

statutory rape

torture

withdrawal of consent

CRIMINAL LAW ON THE WEB

Visit **study.sagepub.com/lippmaness2e** to access additional study tools including suggested answers to the You Decide questions, reprints of cases and statutes, online appendices, and more!

9 CRIMES AGAINST PROPERTY

Is Alvarez guilty of false pretenses as a result of his false claim of having received the Congressional Medal of Honor?

Xavier Alvarez won a seat on the Three Valley Water District Board of Directors in 2007. On July 23, 2007, at a joint meeting with a neighboring water district board, newly seated Director Alvarez arose and introduced himself, stating "I'm a retired marine of 25 years. I retired in the year 2001. Back in 1987, I was awarded the Congressional Medal of Honor. I got wounded many times by the same guy. I'm still around." Alvarez has never been awarded the Congressional Medal of Honor, nor has he spent a single day as a marine or in the service of any other branch of the United States armed forces. . . . The summer before his election to the water district board, a woman informed the FBI about Alvarez's propensity for making false claims about his military past. Alvarez told her that he won the Medal of Honor for rescuing the American ambassador during the Iranian hostage crisis, and that he had been shot in the back as he returned to the embassy to save the American flag. Alvarez reportedly told another woman that he was a Vietnam veteran helicopter pilot who had been shot down but then, with the help of his buddies, was able to get the chopper back into the sky. . . . After the FBI obtained a recording of the water district board meeting, Alvarez was indicted in the Central District of California on two counts of violating 18 U.S.C. § 704(b), (c)(1). Specifically, he was charged with "falsely represent[ing] verbally that he had been awarded the Congressional Medal of Honor when, in truth and as [he] knew, he had not received the Congressional Medal of Honor." (*United States v. Alvarez*, 567 U.S. ___ [2012])

In this chapter, learn about false pretenses.

Learning Objectives

1. Know the elements of larceny.
2. Understand embezzlement and the difference between larceny and embezzlement.
3. State the elements of false pretenses and the distinction between false pretenses and larceny by trick.
4. Explain the purpose of theft statutes.
5. List the elements of receiving stolen property and the purpose of making it a crime to receive stolen property.
6. Define forgery and uttering.
7. Know the elements of robbery and the difference between robbery and larceny.
8. State the elements of carjacking and the difference between carjacking and robbery.
9. Understand the difference between robbery and extortion.
10. Know the common law of burglary and the changes to the law of burglary introduced by burglary statutes.
11. Understand the law of trespass and the difference between burglary and trespass.
12. Know the *mens rea* and *actus reus* of arson.
13. State the law of criminal mischief and the three categories of acts that constitute criminal mischief under the Model Penal Code.

INTRODUCTION

Seventeenth-century English philosopher John Locke asserted in his influential *Second Treatise of Government* that the protection of private property is the primary obligation of government. Locke argued that people originally existed in a "state of nature" in which they were subject to the survival of the fittest. These isolated individuals, according to Locke, came together and agreed to create and to maintain loyalty to a government that, in return, pledged to protect individuals and to safeguard their private property. Locke, as noted, viewed the protection of private property as the most important duty of government and as the bedrock of democracy.

Locke's views are reflected in the Fifth Amendment to the U.S. Constitution, which prohibits the taking of property without due process of law. Even today, those individuals who may not completely agree with Locke recognize that the ownership of private property is a right that provides us with a source of personal enjoyment, pride, profit, and motivation and serves as a measure of self-worth.

A complex of crimes was developed by common law judges and legislators to protect and punish the wrongful taking of private property. As we shall see, each of these crimes was created at a different point in time to fill a gap in the existing law. The development of these various offenses was necessary because prosecutors ran the risk that a defendant would be acquitted in the event that the proof at trial did not meet the technical requirements of a criminal charge. Today, roughly thirty states have simplified the law by consolidating these various property crimes into a single theft statute.

In this chapter, we will review the main property crimes. These include the following:

- *Larceny.* A pickpocket takes the wallet from your purse and walks away.
- *Embezzlement.* A bank official steals money from your account.
- *False Pretenses.* You sell a car to a friend who lies and falsely promises that he or she will pay you in the morning.
- *Receiving Stolen Property.* You buy a car knowing that it is stolen.
- *Forgery and Uttering.* A friend takes one of your checks, makes it payable to himself or herself, signs your name, and cashes the check at your bank.
- *Robbery.* You are told to hand over your wallet by an assailant who points a loaded gun at you.
- *Extortion.* You are told to pay protection to a gang leader who states that otherwise you will suffer retaliatory attacks in the coming months.

We also will look at the newly developing area of *carjacking*. In thinking about the property crimes discussed in this chapter, consider that they all involve the seizure of the property of another individual through a wrongful taking, fraud, or force.

The last part of the chapter discusses four crimes that threaten the security of an individual's home. The notion that the home is an individual's castle is deeply ingrained in the American character. The home is a safe and secure shelter where we are free to express our personalities and interests without fear of uninvited intrusions.

- *Burglary.* An individual breaks into your home with the intent to commit a felony.
- *Trespass.* Members of a street gang gather in your front yard to sell narcotics.
- *Arson.* An angry neighbor sets your house on fire.
- *Malicious Mischief.* A neighbor angry over your parking in his or her space defaces your home.

LARCENY

Early English law punished the taking of property by force, a crime that evolved into the offense of robbery. It became apparent that additional protections for property were required to meet the needs of the expanding British economy. Goods now were being produced, transported, bought, and sold. Robbery did not cover acts such as the taking of property under the cover of darkness from a loading dock. Robbery also did not punish employees who stole cash from their employers or a commercial shipper who removed goods from a container that was being transported to the market. Accordingly, the law of larceny was gradually developed to prohibit and punish the nonviolent taking of the property of another without his or her consent. The goods that are stolen were not required to be in the immediate presence of the individual.

Common law **larceny** is the trespassory taking and carrying away of the personal property of another with the intent to permanently deprive that individual of possession of the property. You should be certain that you understand each element of larceny:

- Trespassory
- taking and
- carrying away of the
- personal property of another with the
- intent to permanently deprive that individual of
- possession of the property.

Actus Reus: Trespassory Taking

The "trespassory taking" in larceny is different from the trespass against land. The term *trespassory taking* in larceny is derived from an ancient Latin legal term and refers to a wrongdoer who removes goods (chattel) or money from the possession of another without consent. **Possession** means physical control over property with the ability to freely use and enjoy the property. Consent obtained from a person in possession of property by force, fraud, or threat is not valid. An individual with title or ownership of property typically also has possession of property. The common law, as we shall soon see, established various rules to distinguish possession from **custody**, or the temporary and limited right to control property.[1]

As we observed earlier, the law of larceny developed in response to evolving economic conditions in Great Britain. In the fifteenth century, England changed from an agricultural country into a manufacturing center. Industry depended on carriers to transport goods to markets and stores. These carriers commonly would open and remove goods from shipping containers and sell them for personal profit. An English tribunal ruled in the *Carrier's Case*, in 1473, that the carrier was a bailee (an individual trusted with property and charged with a duty of care) who had possession of the container and custody over the contents. The carrier was ruled to be liable for larceny by "break[ing] bulk" and committing a trespassory taking of the contents. How did the judge reach this conclusion? The judge in the *Carrier's Case* reasoned that possession of the goods inside the crate continued to belong to the owner and that the shipper was liable for a trespassory taking when he broke open the container and removed the contents. Of course, the carrier might avoid a charge of larceny by stealing an unopened container.[2]

The law of larceny was also extended to employees. An employee is considered to have custody rather than possession over materials provided by an employer, such as construction tools or a delivery truck. The employer is said to enjoy *constructive possession* over this property or the authority and intent to control the property. An employee who walks away with the tools or truck with the intent to deprive the owner of possession of the tools or truck is guilty of larceny. A college student who drives a pizza delivery truck for a local business has custody over the truck. In the event that the student steals the truck, he or she has violated the owner's possessory right and has engaged in a "trespassory taking."[3]

Larceny is not limited to business and commerce. Professors Rollin Perkins and Ronald Boyce note that when eating in a restaurant, you have custody over the silverware, and removing it from the possession of the restaurant by walking out the door with a knife in your pocket constitutes larceny. Another illustration is a pickpocket who, by removing a wallet from your pocket, has taken the wallet from your possession.[4] Professor Joshua Dressler offers the example of an individual who test drives an automobile at a dealership, returns to the lot, and drives off with the car when the auto dealer climbs out of the vehicle. The test driver would be guilty of larceny for dispossessing the car dealer of the auto.[5]

Asportation

There must be a taking (caption) and movement (asportation) of the property. The movement of the object provides proof that an individual has asserted control and intends to steal the object. You might notice that an individual waiting in line in front of you has dropped his or her wallet.

Your intent to steal the wallet is apparent when you place the wallet in your pocket or seize the wallet and walk away at a brisk pace in the opposite direction.

A taking requires asserting "dominion and control" over the property, however briefly. The property then must be moved, and even "a hair's breath" is sufficient.[6] A pickpocket who manages to move a wallet only a few inches inside the victim's pocket may be convicted of larceny.[7]

Larceny may be accomplished through an innocent party. A defendant was convicted of larceny by falsely reporting to a neighbor that the defendant owned the cattle that wandered onto the neighbor's property. The neighbor followed the defendant's instructions to sell the cattle and then turned the proceeds over to the defendant. The defendant was held responsible for the neighbor's caption (taking) and asportation (carrying away), and the defendant was convicted of larceny.[8] A defendant was also found guilty of larceny for unlawfully selling a neighbor's bicycle to an innocent purchaser who rode off with the bike.[9]

Various modern state statutes have followed the Model Penal Code (MPC) in abandoning the requirement of asportation and provide that a person is guilty of theft if he or she "unlawfully takes, or exercises unlawful control," over property. The Texas statute provides that an individual is guilty of larceny where there is an "appropriation of property" without the owner's consent. Under these types of statutes, a pickpocket who reaches into an individual's purse and seizes a wallet would be guilty of larceny; there is no requirement that the pickpocket move or carry away the wallet.[10]

Property of Another

At common law, only tangible personal property was the subject of larceny. Tangible property includes items over which an individual is able to exercise physical control, such as jewelry, paintings, tools, crops and trees removed from the land, and certain domesticated animals. Property not subject to larceny at common law included *services* (e.g., painting a house), *real property* (e.g., real estate, crops attached to the land), and *intangible property* (e.g., property that represents something of value such as checks, money orders, credit card numbers, car titles, and deeds demonstrating ownership of property). Crops were subject to larceny only when severed from the land. For instance, an apple hanging on a tree that was removed by a trespasser was part of the land and was not subject to larceny. An apple that fell from the tree and hit the ground, however, was considered to have entered into the possession of the landowner and was subject to larceny. In another example, wild animals that were killed or tamed were transformed into property subject to larceny. Domestic animals, such as horses and cattle, were subject to larceny, but dogs were considered to possess a "base nature" and were not subject to larceny. These categories are generally no longer significant, and all varieties of property are subject to larceny under modern statutes.

The property must be "of another." Larceny is a crime against possession and is concerned with the taking of property from an individual who has a superior right to possess the object. A landlord who removes the furniture from a furnished apartment that he or she rents to a tenant is guilty of larceny.

Modern statutes, as noted, have expanded larceny to cover every conceivable variety of property. For example, the California statute protects personal property, animals, real estate, cars, money, checks, money orders, traveler's checks, phone service, tickets, and computer data.[11] A number of states follow Section 223.7 of the MPC and have specific statutes punishing the "Theft of Services." These statutes punish the theft of services in restaurants, hotels, transportation, and professional services as well as the theft of telephone, electric, and cable services.

Mens Rea

The *mens rea* of larceny is the intent to permanently deprive another of the property. There must be a concurrence between the intent and the act. The intent to borrow your neighbor's car is not larceny. It is also not larceny if, after borrowing your neighbor's car, you find that it is so much fun to drive that you decide to steal the auto. In this example, the criminal intent and the criminal act do not coincide with one another. Several states have so-called joyriding statutes that make it a crime to take an automobile with an intent to use it and then return it to the owner.

Professor Wayne LaFave points out that in addition to a specific intent to steal, there are cases holding that larceny is committed when an individual has an intent to deprive an individual of possession for an unreasonable length of time or has an intent to act in a fashion that will probably dispossess a person of the property. For instance, you may drive your neighbor's car from New York to Alaska with the intent of going on a vacation. The trip takes two months and deprives your neighbor of possession for an unreasonable period, which constitutes larceny. After arriving in Alaska, you park and leave the car in a remote area. You did not intend to steal the car, but it is unlikely that the car will be returned to the owner, and you could also be held liable for larceny based on your having acted in a fashion that will likely dispossess the owner of the car.[12]

Lost property or property that is misplaced by the owner is subject to larceny when a defendant harbors the intent to steal at the moment that he or she seizes the property. The defendant is held guilty of larceny, however, only when he or she knows who the owner is or knows that the owner can be located through reasonable efforts. Property is lost when its owner is involuntarily deprived of an object and has no idea where to find or recover it; property is misplaced when the owner forgets where he or she intentionally placed an object. Property that is abandoned has no owner and is not subject to larceny, because it is not the "property of another individual." Property is abandoned when its owner no longer claims ownership. Property delivered to the wrong address is subject to larceny when the recipient realizes the mistake at the moment of delivery and forms an intent to steal the property.

An individual may also claim property "as a matter of right" without committing larceny. This occurs when an individual seizes property that he or she reasonably believes has been taken from his or her possession or seizes money of equal value to the money owed to him or her. In these cases, the defendant believes that he or she has a legal right to the property and does not possess the intent to "take the property of another."

You can see that intent is central to larceny. What if you go to the store to buy some groceries and discover that you left your wallet in the car? You decide to walk out of the store with the groceries and intend to get your wallet and return to the store and pay for the groceries. Is this larceny?

Grades of Larceny

The common law distinguished between **grand larceny** and **petit larceny**. Grand larceny was the stealing of goods worth more than twelvepence, the price of a single sheep. The death penalty applied only to grand larceny.

State statutes continue to differentiate between grand larceny and petit larceny. The theft of property worth more than a specific dollar amount is the felony of grand larceny and is punishable by a year or more in prison. Property worth less than this designated amount is a misdemeanor and is punished by less than a year in prison. States differ on the dollar amount separating petit and grand larceny. South Carolina punishes the theft of an article valued at less than $2,000 as a misdemeanor. Stealing an object worth more than $2,000 but less than $10,000 is subject to five years in prison.[13] Theft of an article valued at $10,000 or more is punishable by ten years in prison. Texas uses the figure of $1,500 to distinguish a theft punishable as a misdemeanor from a theft punishable as a felony. Harsher punishment is imposed as the value of the stolen property increases.[14]

How is property valued? In the case of the theft of money or of a check made out for a specific amount, this is easily calculated. What about the theft of an automobile? Should this be measured by what the thief believes is the value of the property? The Pennsylvania statute is typical and provides that "value means the market value of the property at the time and place of the crime." Courts often describe this as the price at which the minds of a willing buyer and a willing seller would meet.

The application of this test means that judges will hear evidence concerning how much it would cost to purchase a replacement for a stolen car. What about a basketball jersey worn and autographed by megastar Michael Jordan? You cannot go to the store and purchase this item. The Pennsylvania statute states that if the market value "cannot be satisfactorily ascertained, [the value of the property is] the cost of replacement of the property within a reasonable time after the crime." In other words, the court will hear evidence concerning the value of a Michael Jordan autographed jersey in the same condition as the jersey that was stolen. One difficulty is that courts consider the absolute dollar value of items and do not evaluate the long-term investment or sentimental value of the property. The Pennsylvania statute also provides that when multiple items are stolen as part of a single plan or through repeated acts of theft, the value of the items may be aggregated or combined. This means that the money taken in a series of street robberies will be combined and that the perpetrator will be prosecuted for a felony rather than a series of misdemeanors.[15]

The value of property is not the only basis for distinguishing between grand and petit larceny. California uses the figure of $950 to distinguish between grand and petit larceny but also categorizes as grand larceny the theft of "domestic fowls, avocados, olives, citrus or deciduous fruits . . . vegetables, nuts, artichokes, or other farm crops" of a value of more than $250. California also considers grand larceny to include the theft of "fish, shellfish, mollusks, crustaceans, kelp, algae . . . taken from a commercial or research operation."[16]

Theft of a firearm, theft of an item from the "person of another," and theft from a home all pose a danger to other individuals and are typically treated as grand larceny. The penalty for stealing property may be increased where the stolen items belong to an "elderly individual" or to the government.

An interesting application of the law of larceny is shoplifting from self-service stores in which customers examine merchandise and try on clothes in dressing rooms, and carry merchandise around the store. In *People v. Gasparik*, the New York Court of Appeals held that stores consent to customers' possession of goods for a "limited purpose." The court held that a customer is not required to leave the store to be held liable for shoplifting and that there is probable cause to arrest an individual who acts in a fashion that is "inconsistent with the store's continued rights" in the merchandise.[17]

Read *People v. Gasparik* on the study site: study .sagepub.com/ lippmaness2e.

In many cases, it will be particularly relevant that the defendant concealed the goods under clothing or in a container. Such conduct is not generally expected in a self-service store and may, in a proper case, be deemed an exercise of dominion and control inconsistent with the store's continued rights. Other furtive or unusual behavior on the part of the defendant should also be weighed. Thus, if the defendant surveys the area while secreting the merchandise or abandons his or her own property in exchange for the concealed goods, this may evince larcenous rather than innocent behavior. Relevant too is the customer's proximity to or movement toward one of the store's exits. Certainly, it is highly probative of guilt that the customer was in possession of secreted goods just a few short steps from the door or moving in that direction. Finally, possession of a known shoplifting device actually used to conceal merchandise, such as a specially designed outer garment or a false-bottomed carrying case, would be all but decisive.

The Legal Equation

Larceny $=$ Unlawful taking and carrying away

$+$ intent to permanently deprive another of property.

You Decide

9.1 Carter entered a paint store and placed four 5-gallon buckets of paint, valued at $398.92, in a shopping cart. Browning waited for Carter by the "return desk" where customers take items they previously purchased and wish to return for a refund. As planned, Browning falsely stated that the paint had been purchased from the store and requested a refund for the paint. A store manager recognized Browning as someone she had been told to look for and contacted an employee of the store who summoned the police. Was Carter guilty of larceny? See *Carter v. Commonwealth*, 694 S.E.2d 590 (Va. 2010).

You can find the answer at study.sagepub.com/lippmaness2e

EMBEZZLEMENT

We have seen that larceny requires a taking of property from the possession of another person with the intent to permanently deprive the person of the property. In the English case of *Rex v. Bazeley*, in 1799, a bank teller dutifully recorded a customer's deposit and then placed the money in his pocket. The court ruled that the teller had taken possession of the note and that he therefore could not be held convicted of larceny and ordered his release from custody. The English Parliament responded by almost immediately passing a law that held servants, clerks, and employees criminally liable for the fraudulent misdemeanor of embezzlement of property. Today, embezzlement is a misdemeanor or felony depending on the value of the property.[18]

The law of **embezzlement** has slowly evolved, and although there is no uniform definition of embezzlement, the core of the crime is the fraudulent conversion of the property of another by an individual in lawful possession of the property. The following elements are central to the definition of the crime:

> *Fraudulent* (deceitful) *conversion* (serious interference with the owner's rights) *of the property* (statutes generally follow the law of larceny in specifying the property subject to embezzlement) *of another* (you cannot embezzle your own property) *by an individual in lawful possession of the property* (the essence of embezzlement is wrongful conversion by an individual in possession).

The distinction between larceny and embezzlement rests on the fact that in embezzlement, the perpetrator lawfully takes possession and then fraudulently converts the property. In contrast, larceny involves the unlawful trespassory taking of property from the possession of another. Larceny requires an intent to deprive an individual of possession at the time that the perpetrator "takes" the property. The intent to fraudulently convert property for purposes of embezzlement, however, may arise at any time after the perpetrator takes possession of the property.

Typically, embezzlement is committed by an individual to whom you entrust your property. Examples would be a bank clerk who steals money from the cash drawer, a computer repair technician who sells the machine that you left to be repaired, or a construction contractor who takes a deposit and then fails to pave your driveway or repair your roof. Embezzlement statutes are often expressed in terms of "property which may be the subject of larceny." In some states, embezzlement is defined to explicitly cover personal as well as real property (e.g., land).

Keep in mind that if an individual who is not entrusted with property steals the property, then it is not embezzlement. In *Batin v. State*, Marlon Javar Batin's conviction for embezzlement of money from the "bill validator" of a slot machine was overturned by the Nevada Supreme Court. Batin worked as a slot mechanic at a casino, and his responsibilities included refilling the "hopper," the part of the machine that "pays coin back," which is separate from the "bill validator" of the slot machine where the paper currency is kept. Batin had no duties or authorized access in regard to the paper currency in the "bill validator," and he was prohibited from handling the money in the "bill validator." The Nevada Supreme Court concluded that Batin was not entrusted with actual or constructive "lawful possession" of the money he stole, and as a result, his conviction for embezzlement was overturned. What would have been the result had Batin been charged with larceny?[19]

Read *Thomas v. State* on the study site: study .sagepub.com/ lippmaness2e.

Model Penal Code

Section 223.2. Theft by Unlawful Taking or Disposition

Movable Property. A person is guilty of theft if he unlawfully takes or exercises unlawful control over movable property of another with purpose to deprive him thereof.

Immovable Property. A person is guilty of theft if he unlawfully transfers immovable property of another or any interest therein with purpose to benefit himself or another not entitled thereto.

Analysis

- The MPC consolidates larceny and embezzlement.
- The phrase "unlawfully takes" is directed at larceny, while the exercise of "unlawful control" over the property of another is directed at embezzlement. In both instances, the defendant must be shown to possess an intent to "deprive" another of the property. This includes an intent to permanently deprive the other individual of the property as well as treating property in a manner that deprives another of its use and enjoyment.

- Property is broadly defined to include "anything of value," including personal property, land, services, and real estate.
- Asportation is not required for larceny.
- Combining larceny and embezzlement means that the prosecution is able to avoid the confusing issues of custody and possession. The "critical inquiry" is "whether the actor had control of the property, no matter how he got it, and whether the actor's acquisition or use of the property was authorized."

The Legal Equation

Embezzlement $=$ Conversion of property of another

$+$ intent to permanently deprive another of property.

FALSE PRETENSES

Larceny punishes individuals who "take and carry away" property from the possession of another with the intent to permanently deprive the individual of the property. Obtaining possession through misrepresentation or deceit is termed **larceny by trick**. In both larceny and larceny by trick, the wrongdoer unlawfully seizes and takes your property.

Embezzlement punishes individuals who fraudulently "convert" to their own use the property of another that the embezzler has in his or her lawful possession. In other words, you trusted the wrong person with the possession of your property.

Common law judges confronted a crisis when they realized that there was no criminal remedy against individuals who tricked another into transferring title or ownership of personal property or land. Consider the case of an individual who trades a fake diamond ring that he or she falsely represents to be extremely valuable in return for a title to farmland.

The English Parliament responded, in 1757, by adopting a statute punishing an individual who "knowingly and designedly" by false pretense shall "obtain from any person or persons money, goods, wares or merchandise with intent to cheat or defraud any person or persons of the same." American states followed the English example and adopted similar statutes.

State statutes slightly differ from one another in their definitions of false pretenses. The essence of the offense is that a defendant is guilty of **false pretenses** who

- obtains title and possession of property of another by
- a knowingly false representation of
- a present or past material fact with
- an intent to defraud that
- causes an individual to pass title to his or her property.

Actus Reus

The *actus reus* of false pretenses is a false representation of a fact. The expression of an opinion or an exaggeration ("puffing"), such as the statement that "this is a fantastic buy," does not constitute false pretenses. The most important point to remember is that the false representation must be of a past (this was George Washington's house) or present (this is a diamond ring) fact. A future promise does not constitute false pretenses ("I will pay you the remaining money in a year"). Why? The explanation is that it is difficult to determine whether an individual has made a false promise, whether an individual later decided not to fulfill a promise, or whether outside events prevented the performance of the promise. Prosecuting individuals for failing to fulfill a future promise would open the door to individuals being prosecuted for failing to pay back money they borrowed or might result in business executives being held criminally liable for failing to fulfill the terms of a contract to deliver consumer goods to a store. The misrepresentation must be material (central to the transaction; the brand of the tires on a car is not essential to a sale of a car) and must

cause an individual to transfer title. It would not be false pretenses where a buyer knows that the seller's claim that a home has a new roof is untrue or where the condition of the roof is irrelevant to the buyer.

Silence does not constitute false pretenses. A failure to disclose that a watch that appears to be a rare antique is in reality a piece of costume jewelry is not false pretenses. The seller, however, must disclose this fact in response to a buyer's inquiry as to whether the jewelry is an authentic antique.

Mens Rea

The *mens rea* of false pretenses requires that the false representation of an existing or past fact be made "knowingly and designedly" with the "intent to defraud." This means that an individual knows that a statement is false and makes the statement with the intent to steal. A defendant who sells for an exorbitant price a painting that he or she mistakenly or reasonably believes was painted by Elvis Presley is not guilty of false pretenses.

"Recklessness" or representations made without information, however, are typically sufficient for false pretenses. Representing that a painting was made by Elvis Presley when you are uncertain or are aware that you have no firm basis for such a representation would likely be sufficient for false pretenses.

In other words, the intent requirement is satisfied by *knowledge* that a representation is untrue, an *uncertainty* whether a representation is true or untrue, or an *awareness* that one lacks sufficient knowledge to determine whether a representation is true or false.

Defendants are not considered to possess an intent to defraud a victim of property when they reasonably believe that they actually own or are entitled to own the property. You cannot steal what you believe you are entitled to own.

Keep in mind that when possession passes to an individual and the owner retains the title, the defendant is guilty of larceny by trick rather than false pretenses. An individual who obtains the permission of an auto dealer to take a car for a drive and intends to and, in fact, does steal the car is guilty of larceny by trick. Obtaining the title to the car with a check that the buyer knows will "bounce" constitutes false pretenses. Another important difference is that larceny requires a taking and carrying away of the property. False pretenses require only a transfer of title and possession.

In *United States v. Alvarez*, the U.S. Supreme Court considered the constitutionality of the federal Stolen Valor Act of 2005, 18 U.S.C. § 704(b). The law provides:

> Whoever falsely represents himself or herself, verbally or in writing, to have been awarded any decoration or medal authorized by Congress for the Armed Forces of the United States, any of the service medals or badges awarded to the members of such forces, the ribbon, button, or rosette of any such badge, decoration, or medal, or any colorable imitation of such item shall be fined under this title, imprisoned not more than six months, or both.

The prescribed prison term is enhanced to one year if the decoration involved is the Congressional Medal of Honor, Distinguished Service Cross, Navy Cross, Air Force Cross, Silver Star, or Purple Heart.

Xavier Alvarez won a seat on the Three Valley Water District Board of Directors in 2007 (see opening vignette). At a joint meeting with a neighboring water district board, Alvarez introduced himself and noted that "I'm a retired marine of 25 years. I retired in the year 2001. Back in 1987, I was awarded the Congressional Medal of Honor. I got wounded many times by the same guy. I'm still around." Alvarez had neither served in the military nor been awarded the Congressional Medal of Honor. In the past, Alvarez had falsely claimed to have rescued the American ambassador during the Iran hostage crisis and to have been a helicopter pilot during the Vietnam War. Other misrepresentations included playing hockey for the Detroit Red Wings, working as a police officer, and having been secretly married to a Mexican movie star.

The U.S. Supreme Court upheld a Court of Appeals decision overturning Alvarez's conviction. Justice Anthony Kennedy stated that the government may validly limit false speech that is used to fraudulently obtain a material benefit such as money or employment. However, "[w]ere the Court to hold that the interest in truthful discourse [on military medals] alone is sufficient to maintain a ban on speech, absent any evidence that the speech was used to gain material advantage it would give government a broad censorial power unprecedented in the Court's case or in our constitutional tradition."[20]

Model Penal Code

Section 223.3. Theft by Deception

A person is guilty of theft if he purposely obtains property of another by deception. A person deceives if he purposely:

(1) creates or reinforces a false impression, including false impressions as to law, value, intention or other state of mind; but deception as to a person's intention to perform a promise shall not be inferred from the fact alone that he did not subsequently perform the promise;

(2) prevents another from acquiring information which would affect his judgment of a transaction;

(3) fails to correct a false impression which the deceiver previously created or reinforced, or which the deceiver knows to be influencing another to whom he stands in a fiduciary or confidential relationship;

(4) fails to disclose a lien, adverse claim or other legal impediment to the enjoyment of property which he transfers or encumbers in consideration for the property obtained, whether such impediment is or is not valid, or is or is not a matter of official record.

The term "deceive" does not, however, include falsity as to matters having no pecuniary significance or puffing by statements unlikely to deceive ordinary persons in the group addressed.

Analysis

- The term *deception* is substituted for "false pretense or misrepresentation."
- The defendant must possess the intent to defraud. This entails a purpose to obtain the property of another and a purpose to deceive the other person.
- The act requirement is satisfied by a misrepresentation as well as by reinforcing faulty information. False future promises are considered to constitute false pretenses.
- There is no duty of disclosure other than when the defendant contributes to the creation of a false impression or where the defendant has a duty of care toward the victim (fiduciary or confidential relationship) or there is a legal claim on the property. A seller also may not interfere with (destroy or hide) information.
- False pretenses do not include a misrepresentation that has no significance in terms of the value of the property (e.g., the political or religious affiliation of a salesperson) or puffing or nondisclosure.

The Legal Equation

False pretenses = Misrepresentation or deceit

+ intent to steal property

+ victim relies on misrepresentation and conveys title and possession.

THEFT

A number of states have consolidated larceny, embezzlement, and false pretenses into a single **theft statute**. The MPC and several state provisions also include within their theft statutes the property offenses of receiving stolen property, blackmail or extortion, the taking of lost or mistakenly delivered property, theft of services, and the unauthorized use of a vehicle.

Larceny, embezzlement, and false pretenses are all directed against wrongdoers who unlawfully interfere with the property interests of others, whether through "taking and asportation," "converting," or "stealing." The commentary to MPC Section 223.1 explains that each of these property offenses involves the "involuntary" transfer of property, and in each instance, the perpetrator "appropriates property of the victim without his consent or with a consent that is obtained by fraud or coercion." An example is the Texas law on consolidation of theft offenses, which combines theft, false pretenses, embezzlement, and other offenses against property.[21]

How do these consolidated theft statutes make it easier for prosecutors to charge and convict defendants of a property offense? A prosecutor under these consolidated theft statutes may charge a defendant with "theft" and, in most jurisdictions, is not required to indicate the specific form of theft with which the defendant is charged. The defendant will be convicted in the event that the evidence establishes beyond a reasonable doubt either larceny, embezzlement, or false pretenses. A prosecutor under the traditional approach would be required to charge a defendant with the separate offense of larceny, embezzlement, or false pretenses. The defendant would be acquitted in the event that he or she was charged with deceitfully obtaining possession and title (false pretenses) but the evidence established that the defendant had only obtained possession.[22]

The Pennsylvania consolidated theft statute, Section 3902, provides that conduct considered theft "constitutes a single offense. An accusation of theft may be supported by evidence that it was committed in any manner that would be theft under this chapter, notwithstanding the specification of a different manner in the complaint or indictment."

Consolidated statutes typically grade the severity of larceny, embezzlement, and false pretenses in a uniform fashion based on the value of the property, whether the stolen property is a firearm or motor vehicle, and factors such as whether the offense took place during the looting of a disaster area.

Model Penal Code

Section 223.1. Consolidation of Theft Offenses

(1) Conduct denominated theft in this Article constitutes a single offense. An accusation of theft may be supported by evidence that it was committed in any manner that would be theft under the Article, notwithstanding the specification of a different manner in the indictment or information, subject only to the power of the Court to ensure a fair trial by granting a continuance or other appropriate relief where the conduct of the defense would be prejudiced by lack of fair notice or by surprise.

(2) Grading of Theft Offenses:

(a) Theft constitutes a felony of the third degree if the amount involved exceeds $5,000, or if the property stolen is a firearm, automobile, airplane, motorcycle, motorboat, or other motor-propelled vehicle, or in the case of theft by receiving stolen property, if the receiver is in the business of buying or selling stolen property.

(b) Theft not within the preceding paragraph constitutes a misdemeanor, except that if the property was not taken from the person or by threat, or in breach of a fiduciary obligation, and the author proves by a preponderance of the evidence that the amount involved was less than $50, the offense constitutes a petty misdemeanor.

(c) The amount involved in a theft shall be deemed to be the highest value, by any reasonable standard, of the property or services which the actor stole or attempted to steal. Amounts involved in thefts committed pursuant to one scheme or course of conduct . . . may be aggregated in determining the grade of the offense.

(3) It is an affirmative defense to prosecution for theft that the actor:

(a) was unaware that the property or service was that of another;

(b) acted under an honest claim of right to the property or service involved or that he had a right to acquire or dispose of it as he did; or

(c) took property exposed for sale, intending to purchase and pay for it promptly, or reasonably believing that the owner, if present, would have consented.

(4) It is no defense that theft was from the actor's spouse except that misappropriation of household and personal effects, or other property normally accessible to both spouses, is theft only if it occurs after the parties have ceased living together.

CRIMINAL LAW AND PUBLIC POLICY

In May 2012, a teaching fellow in a government class at Harvard discovered that 125 students or almost half of the class had been cheating. In some instances, students submitted identical answers on the take-home test including typographical errors. Roughly half of the students implicated in the scandal received disciplinary probation and were suspended from Harvard for a year. Harvard has an average of seventeen cases a year in which students are suspended for academic dishonesty.

This is only one of various large-scale incidents of cheating on college exams. In 2007, thirty-four students or nearly 10 percent of the entering MBA class at Duke were expelled, were suspended, or flunked for collaborating on a take-home test. In the same year, it was revealed that eighty-four present and past students at Diablo Valley College in California paid employees in the registrar's office to change their grades and went so far as to trade sexual favors for grade changes. Many of these community college students had their grades raised from F to A and, on the strength of these grades, were admitted to highly competitive four-year colleges.

In 2014, the Air Force Academy launched an investigation into whether forty first-year students cheated on a chemistry lab report. This was the fourth investigation into cheating at the Air Force Academy since 2004. In a demonstration of how a culture of cheating can be perpetuated following college, it earlier was disclosed that dozens of nuclear missile officers at Malmstrom Air Force Base in Montana cheated on their launch proficiency exams.

Dental schools are not immune from cheating. In 2007, dental students at the University of Indiana hacked into a computer system containing X-rays that the students would be asked to analyze on an exam. Nine students were expelled, sixteen were suspended, and twenty-one received letters of reprimand. More recently, there has been an investigation of cheating at Stanford.

In 2015, thousands of foreign students were expelled from U.S. universities for academic nonperformance or cheating. The Department of Justice has indicted fifteen Chinese nationals in an elaborate scheme in which they were paid thousands of dollars to take the SAT and various graduate entrance examinations on behalf of individuals applying to U.S. universities.

Two well-known economists, Steven Levitt of the University of Chicago and Ming-Jen Lin at National Taiwan University, studied a classroom in which the instructor suspected that cheating was taking place. The two economists examined test results and found that 10 percent of the students likely cheated on the midterm because they had a number of the same incorrect answers as the person sitting next to them.

On the final exam, Levitt and Lin randomly assigned seats to students and increased the number of teaching assistants proctoring the test, and the evidence of cheating disappeared. The professor forwarded the names of students suspected of cheating to the dean, four of whom admitted to cheating. Pressure from parents resulted in the investigation into cheating being dropped by the university.

Are these incidents the exception or part of a general trend? As many as 75 percent of undergraduates admit that they have cheated, and over 40 percent of graduate students admit to cheating to improve their grade. Some researchers dispute whether cheating among college students has increased over the years, although they agree that in recent years it is the best as well as the worst students who now engage in cheating. A survey by the Center for Academic Integrity conducted between 2010 and 2011 of 1,800 students at nine separate state universities found that

70 percent admitted to cheating on exams,

84 percent admitted to cheating on written assignments, and

52 percent had copied one or more sentences from a Web site without citation.

Males and females cheat in equal numbers. Cheating is not confined to four-year colleges; the survey found that 45.6 percent of community college students have cheated during their two years at the institution.

The pressure to cheat begins early in students' academic careers. Most students who cheat in college also cheat in high school. Roughly 15 percent of students who engage in academic dishonesty state that they have no regrets over cheating. Researchers contend that this pattern of "cutting corners" continues throughout an individual's life and may result in unethical behavior, corporate criminality, and marital infidelity.

A number of elite high schools have been rocked by cheating scandals in recent years. Eric Anderman, a professor of educational psychology at The Ohio State University, concludes that 85 percent of all high school students cheat at least once prior to their graduation. At elite Stuyvesant High School in New York City, a student photographed pages of a state standardized examination and sent the photos to other students who had yet to take the test. In Great Neck, New York, students were caught paying another person to take their SAT, and some of the leading high schools in Texas also experienced widespread cheating.

A number of factors are viewed as motivating students to cheat: a misunderstanding of the definition of academic dishonesty, competition for good grades, a lack of respect for instructors who seem uninterested in the class, heavy academic workloads, the small probability of being detected, and the ease of cheating using the Internet. Some educators, rather than blaming students, blame a significant amount of cheating on the structure of college curricula in which students are required to take large classes in which they have little interest and in which grades are based on limited number of "high-

stakes" machine-graded assignments. In these types of learning environments, learning becomes secondary to the pursuit of grades, and there is little sense that education is a rewarding and creative experience. What is your view of the causes of college cheating? Do you believe this is a "problem" in need of a remedy? Is cheating on a class assignment a criminal offense?

RECEIVING STOLEN PROPERTY

There was no offense of **receiving stolen property** under the common law. An English court, in 1602, condemned a defendant who knowingly purchased a stolen pig and cow as an "arrant knave" and complained that there was "no separate crime of receiving stolen property." In the late seventeenth century, the English Parliament passed a law providing that an individual who knowingly bought or received stolen property was liable as an accessory after the fact to theft. In 1827, Parliament passed an additional statute declaring that receiving stolen property was a criminal offense. This law was later incorporated into the criminal codes of the American states and, today, is punished as a misdemeanor or felony, depending on the value of the property.

The offense of receiving stolen property requires that an individual

- receive property,
- knowing the property to be stolen,
- with the intent to permanently deprive the owner of the property.

Why do we punish receiving stolen property as a separate offense? Thieves typically sell stolen property to "fences," individuals who earn a living by buying and then selling stolen property. The offense of receiving stolen property is intended to deter "fencing." Generally, an individual may not be charged with both stealing and receiving stolen property.

Actus Reus

The *actus reus* of receiving stolen property requires that an individual control the stolen property, however briefly. An individual receiving the stolen items may take either actual possession of the property or constructive possession of the property by arranging for the property to be delivered to a specific location or to another individual.

Receiving stolen property traditionally was limited to goods that were taken and carried away in an act of larceny. The trend is to follow the approach of the MPC and to punish the receipt of stolen property, whether taken through larceny, embezzlement, false pretenses, or another illegal method.

Most state statutes on receiving stolen property cover both personal and real property. The MPC limits the statute to personal property on the grounds that this property is disposed of through fences and that this is not the case with real estate.

Mens Rea

State statutes typically require the *mens rea* of actual knowledge that the goods are stolen. Other statutes broaden this standard by providing that it is sufficient for an individual to believe that the goods are stolen. A court would likely conclude that a jeweler believed that a valuable watch was stolen that he or she inexpensively purchased from a known dealer in stolen merchandise. A third group of statutes applies a recklessness or negligence standard to the owners of junkyards, pawnshops, and other businesses where they neglect to investigate the circumstances under which the seller obtained the property. Consider the case of the owner of an art gallery specializing in global art who regularly buys rare and valuable Asian and African artwork that is thousands of years old and who, in one instance, buys a piece for next to nothing from individuals who wander into the shop. These statutes would hold the buyer guilty of receiving stolen property for failing to investigate how the seller obtained the property.

How can we determine whether an individual knows or honestly believes that property is stolen? Courts generally hold that it is sufficient if a reasonable person would have possessed this awareness. In most cases, this is inferred from the price, the seller, whether the type of property is frequently the subject of theft, the circumstances of the sale, and whether the recipient purchased stolen merchandise from the same individual in the past.

The recipient of stolen property must also have the *mens rea* to permanently deprive the owner of possession. A defendant does not possess the required intent who believes that he or she is the actual owner of the property, because there is no intent to deprive another of possession. The required intent is also lacking where the recipient intends to return the property to the rightful owner.

The required intent to permanently deprive an individual of possession must concur with the receipt of the property. The MPC, however, provides that the required intent may arise when an individual receives and only later decides to deprive the owner of possession.

Read *Hurston v. State* on the study site: study .sagepub.com/ lippmaness2e.

Model Penal Code

Section 223.6. Receiving Stolen Property

(1) A person is guilty of theft if he purposely receives, retains, or disposes of movable property of another knowing that it has been stolen, or believing that it has probably been stolen, unless the property is received, retained, or disposed with purpose to restore it to the owner. "Receiving" means acquiring possession, control or title, or lending on the security of the property.

(2) The requisite knowledge or belief is presumed in the case of a dealer who:

(a) is found in possession or control of property stolen from two or more persons on separate occasions;

(b) has received stolen property in another transaction within the year preceding the transaction charged; or

(c) being a dealer in property of the sort received, acquires it for a consideration which he knows is far below its reasonable value.

"Dealer" means a person in the business of buying or selling goods, including a pawnbroker.

Analysis

- Receiving stolen property is limited to property that can be moved and does not include real estate.
- There is no requirement that the purchaser know that the property is in fact stolen; it is sufficient that an individual believe that the property probably has been stolen.
- A defendant must know or believe that the property probably has been stolen. The intent to restore the property to the owner is a defense.
- The required intent may arise after the property is in the possession of the defendant.
- Knowledge is assumed under certain circumstances, including the fact that an individual is a "dealer."
- The receiver is liable regardless of the method employed by the thief, whether larceny, embezzlement, false pretenses, or other form of theft.

The Legal Equation

Receiving stolen property = Control over stolen property

+ purposely knowing (recklessly, negligently) that property is stolen

+ intent to permanently deprive individual of property.

You Decide

9.2 John L. Clough discovered various items missing from his music club. These items included four amplifier speakers, which were used by bands that played at the club. An employee, Gaylord Burton, worked at the club for several months and disappeared at the same time that the speakers were discovered to be missing. An employee reportedly had seen Burton taking the speakers on the morning of November 2, 1989. The equipment later was discovered at a pawnshop. An employee of the pawnshop, Anthony Smith, testified that two men had tried to pawn the speakers. Smith refused to accept the speakers without identification. The two men returned later with Olga Lee Sonnier, who presented a driver's license and pawned the speakers for $225. The four speakers were worth at least $350. Sonnier appealed her conviction for "theft by receiving." There are three elements of this offense: first, a theft by another person. Second, the defendant received the stolen property. Third, the defendant received the stolen property knowing that it was stolen. Was Sonnier in possession of the speakers? Sonnier also claimed that she lacked actual knowledge that the speakers were stolen. The speakers were pawned for a reasonable amount of money, and a reasonable person would have no notion of the monetary value of the speakers. Should the Texas appellate court affirm Sonnier's conviction? See *Sonnier v. State*, 849 S.W.2d 828 (Tex. App. 1992).

You can find the answer at study.sagepub.com/lippmaness2e

FORGERY AND UTTERING

The law of forgery originated in the punishment of individuals who used or copied the king's seal without authorization. The seal was customarily affixed to documents that bestowed various rights and privileges on individuals, and employing this stamp without authorization was viewed as an attack on royal power and prerogative. The law of forgery was gradually expanded to include private as well as public documents. **Forgery** is defined as creating a false legal document or the material modification of an existing legal document with the intent to deceive or to defraud others. The crime of forgery is complete upon the drafting of the document regardless of whether it is actually used to defraud others. **Uttering** is a separate and distinct offense that involves the *actus reus* of circulating or using a forged document.

Forgery and uttering are typically limited to documents that possess "legal significance." This means that the document, if genuine, would carry some legal importance, such as conveying property or authorizing an individual to drive. A falsified document is not a forgery when it merely impacts an individual's reputation or professional advancement, such as a fabricated newspaper account of a political candidate's evasion of military service.

The MPC extends forgery and uttering to all varieties of documents. This would include the attempt several years ago to sell a manuscript that was alleged to be Adolf Hitler's diary but, in truth, was a skillfully produced fraud. Fraudulent documents that may be punished as a forgery under state statutes include checks, currency, passports, driver's licenses, deeds, diplomas, tickets, credit cards, immigration visas, and residency and work permits.

There are several elements to establish forgery. Each must be proven beyond a reasonable doubt:

- a false document or material modification of an existing document that is
- written with intent to defraud and,
- if genuine, would have legal significance.

The elements of uttering are

- offering a
- forged instrument that is
- known to be false and is
- presented as authentic
- with the intent to defraud or deceive.

Forgery is similar to other property crimes in that the forger is unlawfully obtaining a benefit from another individual. The larger public policy behind criminalizing forgery is to ensure that people are able to rely on the authenticity or truth of documents. You want to be confident that when you buy a car, the title you receive is genuine and that the automobile has not been stolen.

Combating the forgery of passports and visas has taken on particular importance in securing the borders of the United States against the entry of terrorists.

Actus Reus

The important point to remember is that forgery is falsely making or materially altering an existing document. This may entail creating a false document or materially (fundamentally) changing an existing document without authorization. A material modification is a change or addition that has legal significance.

A forgery may involve manufacturing a "false identification" for a friend who is too young to drink, creating false passports for individuals seeking to illegally enter the United States, or fabricating tickets to a sold-out rock concert. Forgery may also involve materially or fundamentally altering or modifying an existing document. Stealing a check, signing the name of the owner of the account without authorization, and making the check payable to yourself for $100 is forgery. In this example, although the check itself is genuine, the details do not reflect the intent of the owner of the check. On the other hand, merely filling in the date on an undated check would ordinarily not constitute a material alteration because this change typically has no legal significance.

In other words, the question in forgery is whether a document is a "false writing." The document itself may be false, or the material statements in the document may be materially false.

Mens Rea

Forgery requires an intent to defraud; this need not be directed against a specific individual.

Uttering

Uttering is offering a document as genuine that is known to be false with the intent to deceive. This is a different offense from forgery, although the two are often included in a single statute. Merely presenting a forged check to a bank teller for payment knowing that it is inauthentic completes the crime of uttering. The teller need not accept the forged check as genuine.

Simulation

Several states follow the MPC in providing for the crime of **simulation**. This punishes the creation of false objects with the purpose to defraud, such as antique furniture, paintings, and jewelry. Simulation requires proof of a purpose to defraud or proof that an individual knows that he or she is "facilitating a fraud."

Model Penal Code

Section 224.1. Forgery

(1) A person is guilty of forgery if, with purpose to defraud or injure anyone, or with knowledge that he is facilitating a fraud or injury to be perpetrated by anyone, the actor:

(a) alters any writing of another without his authority; or

(b) makes, completes, executes, authenticates, issues or transfers any writing so that it purports to be the act of another who did not authorize that act, or to have been executed at a time or place or in a numbered sequence other than was in fact the case, or to be a copy of an original when no such original existed; or

(c) utters any writing which he knows to be forged in a manner specified in paragraphs (a) or (b).

"Writing" includes printing or any other method of recording information, money, coins, tokens, stamps, seals, credit cards, badges, trademarks, and other symbols of value, right, privilege, or identification.

(2) Forgery is a felony of the second degree if the writing is or purports to be part of an issue of money, securities, postage or revenue stamps, or other instruments issued by the government, or part of an issue of stock, bonds or other instruments representing interests in or claims against any property or enterprise. Forgery is a felony of the third degree if the writing is or purports to be a will, deed, contract, release, commercial instrument, or other document evidencing, creating, transferring, altering, terminating, or otherwise affecting legal relations. Otherwise forgery is a misdemeanor.

Analysis

- This section applies to "any writing" and to "any other method of recording information, money, coins, credit cards and trademarks and other symbols." Forgery is not limited to documents having legal significance. As a result, documents such as medical prescriptions, diplomas, and trademarks are encompassed within this provision. The section is not limited to economic harm and may include circulating a false document that injures an individual's reputation.
- Serious forgeries that have the most widespread and serious impact are second-degree felonies, carrying a maximum penalty of ten years. Other forgeries are punishable as felonies of a third degree, carrying a maximum of five years. Forgeries of documents that do not have legal significance, such as diplomas, are misdemeanors.
- Counterfeiting of currency is included in this section rather than being made a separate offense.
- Section 1(c) punishes uttering.

The Legal Equation

Forgery = Creation of a false document (of legal significance) or material alteration of an existing document

+ fraudulent intent.

Uttering = Passing of a false document (of legal significance)

+ purposely or knowingly deceitful.

You Decide

9.3 McGovern owed $1,800 to Scull. McGovern purchased $2,400 in traveler's checks from Citibank for purposes of repaying Scull. The checks may be redeemed for money at most banks or stores when signed by the individual to whom the check is issued. Scull and McGovern entered into a corrupt arrangement designed to reimburse Scull. Scull practiced McGovern's signature and took McGovern's driver's license and the traveler's checks and proceeded to cash the checks at two banks and collected $2,400. McGovern then reported to the police that the checks had been stolen from his car, and in accordance with the highly advertised policy concerning traveler's checks, McGovern was provided with replacement checks in the amount of $2,400 by Citibank. Did Scull's impersonation of McGovern constitute forgery? See *United States v. McGovern*, 661 F.2d 27 (3rd Cir. 1981).

You can find the answer at study.sagepub.com/lippmaness2e

ROBBERY

Robbery is typically described as aggravated larceny. You should think of robbery as larceny from an individual with the use of violence or intimidation. Professors Perkins and Boyce observe that in ancient law, the thief who stole quietly and secretly was viewed as deserving harsher punishment than the robber who openly employed violence. The common law reversed this point of view and categorized robbery as among the most serious of felonies, which should be treated as a separate offense deserving of harsher punishment than larceny.[23]

Robbery is the trespassory taking and carrying away of the personal property of another with intent to steal. Robbery is distinguished from larceny by additional requirements:

- The personal property must be taken from the victim's person or presence.
- The taking of the personal property must be achieved by violence or intimidation.

The California criminal code defines robbery as the "felonious taking of personal property in the possession of another, from his person or immediate presence, and against his will, accomplished by means of force or fear." In this chapter, robbery is treated as a property crime, although the FBI categorizes robbery as a violent crime against the person.[24]

Actus Reus

The *property must be taken from the person or presence of the victim.* Property is considered to be on the person of the victim if it is in his or her hands or pockets or is attached to his or her body (an earring) or clothing (a key chain).

The requirement that an object must be taken from the "presence of the victim" is much more difficult to apply. The rule is that the property must be within the proximity and control of the victim. What does this mean? The prosecution is required to demonstrate that had the victim not been subjected to violence or intimidation, he or she could have prevented the taking of the property.

In one frequently cited case, the defendants forced the manager of a drugstore to open a safe at gunpoint. The defendants then locked the manager in an adjoining room and removed the money from the safe. An Illinois court found that the money was under the victim's personal control and protection and that he could have prevented the theft had he not been subjected to an armed threat.[25] Professor LaFave illustrates the requirement that property be taken from the presence of the victim by noting that it would not be robbery to immobilize a property owner at one location while a confederate takes the owner's property from a location several miles away, because the owner could not have prevented the theft.[26]

The *property must be taken by violence or intimidation.* The Florida statute provides that robbery involves a taking through "the use of force, violence, assault, or putting in fear."[27] Keep in mind that it is the use of violence or intimidation that distinguishes robbery from larceny. The line between robbery and larceny, however, is not always clear. In general, any degree of force is sufficient for robbery. You are walking down the street loosely carrying your backpack when a thief snatches the backpack out of your grasp. You are so surprised that you fail to resist. Is this robbery? The consensus is that the incident is not a robbery. This would qualify as robbery in the event that you are pushed, are shoved, or struggle to hold on to the backpack. It is also robbery where force is applied to remove an item attached to your clothing or body, such as an earring or necklace. Does it make sense to distinguish between robbery and larceny based on whether the perpetrator employed a small amount of force?

The MPC attempts to avoid this type of technical analysis and provides that robbery requires "serious bodily injury." This approach has been rejected by most states on the grounds that it excludes street crimes in which victims are pushed to the ground or receive minor injuries. Before we leave this topic, we should note that it is a robbery when an assailant steals your personal items by rendering you helpless through liquor or drugs.

Property may also be seized as a result of intimidation or the fear of immediate infliction of violence. The threat of immediate harm must place the victim in fear, meaning in apprehension or in anticipation of injury.

The threat may be directed against members of the victim's family or relatives, and some courts have extended this to anyone present as well as to the destruction of the home. The threat must also be shown to have caused the victim to hand over the property.

Again, a threat may be "implied." This might involve a large and imposing panhandler who follows an elderly pedestrian down a dark and isolated street and angrily and repeatedly demands that the pedestrian "give up the money in his or her pocket." The threat must place the victim in apprehension of harm and cause him or her to hand over the property. The jury is required to find that the victim was actually frightened into handing over his or her property. Some courts require that a reasonable person would have acted in a similar fashion.

Mens Rea

The assailant must possess the intent to permanently deprive an individual of his or her property. The defendant may rely on the familiar defense that he or she intended only to borrow the property or was playing a practical joke. Courts are divided over whether it is a defense that the thief acted under a "claim of right," that the thief acted under an honest belief that the victim owed him money, or that the defendant reasonably believed that he or she owned the property. Some courts hold that even a claim of right does not justify the resort to force or intimidation to reclaim property.

Concurrence

The traditional view is that the intent to steal and the application of force or intimidation must coincide. The violence or intimidation must be employed for the purpose of the taking. This means that the threat or application of force must occur at the time of the taking. An individual does not commit a robbery who seizes property and then employs force or intimidation. A pickpocket who removes a victim's wallet and resorts to force only in response to the victim's accusation of theft is not guilty of robbery.

A number of states have followed the MPC in adopting language that provides that force or intimidation may occur "in the course of committing a theft." This is interpreted to mean that force or threat occurs "in an attempt to commit theft or in flight after the attempt or commission." The commentary explains that a thief's use of force against individuals in an effort to escape indicates that the thief would have employed force "to effect the theft had the need arisen." Even under this more liberal approach, an assailant who knocks the victim unconscious and then forms an intent to steal would not be guilty of robbery.[28] The Florida robbery statute defines robbery to include force or intimidation "in the course of the taking" of money or other property. This includes force or threats "prior to, contemporaneous with, or subsequent to the taking of the property . . . if it and the act of taking constitute a continuous series of acts or events."[29]

Grading Robbery

At common law, the theft of property that terrorized the victim resulted in the death penalty. Today, robbery statutes generally distinguish between simple and aggravated robbery. This is based on the degree of dangerousness caused by the defendant's act and the fear and apprehension experienced by the victim, rather than the value of the property. The factors that aggravate robbery include

- the robber was armed with a dangerous or deadly weapon or warned the victim that the robber possessed a firearm;
- the robber used a dangerous instrumentality, such as a knife, hammer, axe, or aggressive animal;
- the robber inflicted serious bodily injury; and
- the robber carried out the theft with an accomplice.

You might question whether we need the crime of robbery. Is there any justification for the crime of robbery other than historical tradition? Why not simplify matters and merely charge a defendant with larceny along with assault and battery?

Model Penal Code

Section 222.1. Robbery

(1) A person is guilty of robbery if, in the course of committing a theft, he:

   (a) inflicts serious bodily injury upon another; or

   (b) threatens another with or purposely puts him in fear of immediate serious bodily injury; or

   (c) commits or threatens immediately to commit any felony of the first or second degree.

   An act shall be deemed "in the course of committing a theft" if it occurs in an attempt to commit theft or in flight after the attempt or commission.

(2) Robbery is a felony of the second degree, except that it is a felony of the first degree if in the course of committing the theft the actor attempts to kill anyone, or purposely inflicts or attempts to inflict serious bodily harm.

Analysis

- The infliction or threat of harm is limited to "serious bodily injury." The inclusion of the commission or threat to commit a felony of the first or second degree as an element of robbery is intended to encompass the threat or commission of serious injury to an individual other than the victim as well as the threat to destroy or the destruction of property.
- The harm may be inflicted or threatened "in the course of committing the theft." This includes violence or the threat of violence to obtain or retain property and to prevent pursuit or to escape.
- The commentary explains that the same punishment is imposed for both robbery and attempted robbery. It is immaterial whether the assailant actually succeeds in the taking of property. This reflects the view that the essence of robbery is the placing of individuals in danger rather than the deprivation of property.
- The infliction or threat of harm must be immediate.
- The taking is not required to be from the person or in the presence of the victim. An offender might threaten the victim in order to extract ransom from an individual who is not present.
- Robbery is generally punished as a felony of the second degree, subject to ten years' imprisonment. Life imprisonment is viewed as an extreme penalty that is reserved for violent offenders.

The Legal Equation

Robbery $=$ Taking of the property of another from the person or presence of the person

$+$ by violence or threat of immediate violence placing another in fear

$+$ intent to permanently deprive another individual of property.

You Decide

9.4 Elaine Barker was moving items from a shopping cart into the trunk of her car. Karl Messina grabbed Barker's purse from the shopping cart and fled. Barker gave chase. Messina managed to get into his car and closed the door. Barker sat on the hood of Messina's car in an effort to prevent him from driving away. Messina started and stopped the car "several times while Barker held on to a windshield wiper to keep from falling off." Messina "turned the car sharply causing Barker to fall to the ground" causing her to suffer a broken foot and lacerations that required stitches. Was Messina guilty of a robbery? Consider that Florida law requires that force be used "in the course of the taking." See *Messina v. State*, 728 So. 2d 818 (Fla. Dist. Ct. App. 1999).

You can find the answer at study.sagepub.com/lippmaness2e

CARJACKING

Carjacking is a newly recognized form of property crime that is punished under both federal and state statutes. California is typical in defining carjacking as a form of robbery and punishes the taking of a motor vehicle "in the possession of another, from his or her person or immediate presence . . . against his or her will." This must be accomplished by "force or fear." The perpetrator is not required to intend to permanently steal the automobile. The California statute is satisfied by an intent to either "permanently or temporarily deprive the victim of possession of the car."[30]

Several state statutes provide that force must be directed against an occupant of the car. The New Jersey statute requires that while committing the unlawful taking of the automobile, there must be the infliction or use of force against an occupant or person in possession or control of the motor vehicle.[31] Virginia stipulates that the taking be carried out by violence to the person, by assault, or by otherwise putting a person in fear of serious bodily injury.[32]

The trend is to find a defendant guilty of carjacking when an automobile is seized and not to require that the perpetrator move the automobile. A carjacking may be directed against an occupant of the car or against an individual outside the car who is in possession of the keys and is sufficiently close to control the vehicle.

The punishment of carjacking is based on the degree of harm and apprehension caused by the offense. New Jersey punishes carjacking by between ten and twenty years in prison and a fine of up to $200,000. The Florida statute punishes carjacking with life imprisonment when committed with a firearm or other deadly weapon.[33]

EXTORTION

The common law misdemeanor of **extortion** punished the unlawful collection of money by a government official. William Blackstone defined extortion as "an abuse of public justice, which consists in any officer's unlawful taking, by color of his office, from any man, any money or thing of value that is not due to him, or more than is due, or before it is due."[34] The law of extortion was gradually expanded to punish threats by private individuals as well as public officials. The elements of the statutory crime of extortion are as follows:

- the taking of property from another by
- a present threat of future violence or threat to circulate secret, embarrassing, or harmful information; threat of criminal charges; threat to take or withhold official government action; or threat to inflict economic harm and other harms listed in the state statute, with
- a specific intent to deprive a lawful possessor of money or property.

Note that while robbery involves a threat of immediate violence, extortion entails a threat of future violence or other harms. The threat to disclose secret or embarrassing information is commonly referred to as the crime of **blackmail**. Robbery must be committed in the presence of the victim, while extortionate threats may be communicated over the phone or in a letter.

The majority of state statutes provide that the crime of extortion is complete when the threat is made. The prosecution must demonstrate that the victim believed that there was a definite threat and believed that this threat would be carried out. A Michigan statute punishes "any person who shall . . . maliciously threaten to accuse another of any crime . . . or . . . maliciously threaten any injury to . . . [a] person or property . . . with intent to thereby . . . extort money or any pecuniary advantage . . . or . . . to compel the person to do . . . any act against his will."[35] Other statutes require the handing over of money, property, or valuable items in response to the threat. The prosecution must establish a causal relationship between the threat and the conveying of the money or property. The "handing over" requirement is illustrated by the language of the New York statute, which provides that an individual is guilty of extortion when he or she "compels . . . another person to deliver . . . property to himself or to a third person by means of instill[ing] . . . fear."[36]

The object of extortion may be money, property, or "anything of value," including labor or services. The Iowa Supreme Court ruled that a college student who attempted to extort a date from a female acquaintance had attempted to extort "something of value for himself" and that value should be broadly interpreted to include "relative worth, utility, or importance" rather than "monetary worth."[37]

Harrington, a divorce lawyer, represented in a divorce action a female who had been the victim of severe physical abuse by her husband. Harrington arranged for another female to seduce the husband, and while the two were in a romantic embrace in bed, Harrington entered and took photographs. Harrington subsequently threatened to disclose the husband's adultery unless he paid his wife a divorce settlement of $175,000. The Vermont Supreme Court ruled that Harrington "acted maliciously and without just cause . . . with the intent to extort a substantial fee . . . to [Harrington's] personal advantage."[38]

Several commentators contrast extortion with *bribery*. Extortion involves taking money, property, or anything of value from another through threat of violence or harm. In bribery, money or a valuable benefit is offered or provided to a public official in return for an official's action or inaction. This act may involve a legislator voting in favor of or against a law, a judge acquitting or convicting a defendant, or a clerk giving priority to an applicant for a driver's license or passport. The inaction entails a failure to act, such as a building inspector overlooking safety violations in a music club. There must be an intent to corruptly influence an official in the conduct of his or her office. Individuals are held guilty of bribery for offering as well as accepting a bribe.

We next look at the common law offenses developed to protect an individual's dwelling and at the incorporation of these common law crimes in state statutes that cover a broad range of structures and vehicles.

The Legal Equation

Extortion $=$ Specific intent to deprive person of possession of property

$+$ threat of future violence, circulation of harmful information, economic harm, or government action.

BURGLARY

Burglary at common law was defined as the breaking and entering of the dwelling house of another at night with the intention to commit a felony. Burglary was punished by the death penalty, reflecting the fact that a nighttime invasion of a dwelling poses a threat to the home, which is "each man's castle . . . and the place of security for his family, as well as his most cherished possessions."[39] Blackstone observed that burglary is a "heinous offense" that causes "abundant terror," which constitutes a violation of the "right of habitation" and which provides the inhabitant of a dwelling with the "natural right of killing the aggressor."[40] The crime of burglary protects several interests:

- *Home.* The right to peaceful enjoyment of the home.
- *Safety.* The protection of individuals against violent attack and fright within the home.
- *Escalation.* The prevention of a dangerous confrontation that may escalate into a fatal conflict.

In 1990, the U.S. Supreme Court noted that state statutes no longer closely followed common law burglary and that these statutes, in turn, did not agree on a common definition of burglary. This means that in thinking about burglary, you should pay particular attention to the definition of burglary in the relevant state statute. As you read this section, analyze how burglary has been modified by state statutes. In addition, consider whether we continue to need the crime of burglary. What does burglary contribute that is not provided by other offenses?[41]

Table 9.1 lists the top ten states for property crimes per hundred thousand.

Breaking

Common law burglary requires a "breaking" to enter the home by a trespasser, an individual who enters without the consent of the owner. A breaking requires an act that penetrates the structure,

Table 9.1 Top Ten States for Property Crimes* in 2014 per 100,000 Population	
State	*Rate*
Washington	3,706.1
New Mexico	3,542.3
South Carolina	3,460.3
Louisiana	3,458.8
Florida	3,415.5
Arkansas	3,338.0
Georgia	3,281.2
Arizona	3,197.5
Alabama	3,177.6
Tennessee	3,060.6
National Rate = 2,596.1	

Source: Kathleen O'Leary Morgan and Scott Morgan, eds. *State Rankings 2016: A Statistical View of America.* Thousand Oaks, CA: CQ Press, 2016, p. 47.

*Property crimes are offenses of larceny theft, burglary, and motor vehicle theft.

such as breaking a window or pushing open an unlocked door. Permanent damage is not required; the slightest amount of force is sufficient. Why did the common law require a breaking? Most commentators conclude that this requirement was intended to encourage homeowners to take precautions against intruders by closing doors and windows. In addition, an individual who resorts to breaking also typically lacks permission to enter, and the breaking is evidence of an "unlawful" or "uninvited" entry. A breaking may also occur through constructive force. This entails entry by fraud, misrepresentation, or threat of force; entry by an accomplice; or entry through a chimney.

Most statutes no longer require a breaking. Burglary is typically defined as an unlawful or uninvited entry (e.g., lacking permission to enter). Note that it is not burglary under this definition for an individual to enter a store that is open to the general public. Some courts have interpreted statutes to cover the entry into a store by arguing that an individual who enters a store while concealing that he or she plans to commit a crime has committed a fraud and therefore has entered unlawfully. Courts have ruled that breaking into an ATM or other structure "too small for a human being to live in or do business in is not a 'building' or 'structure' for the purpose of burglary."[42]

Entry

The next step after the breaking is "entry." This requires only that a portion of an individual's body enters the dwelling; a hand, foot, or finger is sufficient. Courts also find burglary when there is entry by an instrument that is used to carry out the burglary. This might involve reaching into a window with a straightened coat hanger to pull out a wallet or reaching an arm through a window to pour flammable liquid into a home. In a recent case, an individual launched an aggressive verbal attack on his lover's husband while reaching his arm threateningly through the open door of the husband's motor home. A Washington appellate court determined that this was sufficient to constitute an intent to assault and a conviction for burglary.[43] Note the general rule is that it is not a burglary when an instrument is used solely to break the structure, such as tossing a brick through a window.[44]

Another point to keep in mind is that the breaking must be the means of entering the dwelling. You might break a window and then realize that the front door is open and walk in and steal a television. There is no burglary because the breaking is not connected to the entry. A burglary may also be accomplished constructively by helping a small, thin co-conspirator enter a home through a narrow basement window.

Some statutes provide that a burglary may be committed by "knowingly . . . remaining unlawfully in a building" with the required intent or "surreptitiously (secretly) remaining on the premises with the intent to commit a crime." In *Dixon v. State*, for example, the defendant entered a church during Sunday services, wandered into the church sanctuary, and stole money from the collection plate in the pastor's office. A Florida appellate court ruled that the defendant illegally entered the sanctuary and surreptitiously remained in the structure when he closed the door to the pastor's office during the robbery.[45]

The important point to keep in mind is that the entry for a burglary must be trespassory, meaning without consent. Note that stealing a computer from your own dorm room would not be a burglary. The essence of burglary is the unlawful interference with the right to habitation of another. In *Stowell v. People*, the Colorado Supreme Court observed that there is no burglary "if the person entering has a right to do so, although he may intend to commit and may actually commit a felony." Otherwise, a schoolteacher "using the key furnished to her . . . to re-open the schoolhouse door immediately after locking it in the evening, for the purpose of taking (but not finding) a pencil belonging to one of her pupils, could be sent to the penitentiary."[46]

Dwelling House

The common law limited burglary to a "dwelling house," a structure regularly used as a place to sleep. A structure may be used for other purposes and still constitute a dwelling so long as the building is used for sleep. The fact that the residents are temporarily absent from a summer cottage does not result in the building's losing its status as a dwelling. However, a structure that is under construction and not yet occupied or a dwelling that has been permanently abandoned is not considered a dwelling. The Illinois burglary statute provides that a dwelling is a "house, apartment, mobile home, trailer, or other living quarters in which at the time of the alleged offense the owners or occupants actually reside or in their absence intend within a reasonable period of time to reside."[47]

A dwelling at common law included the curtilage, or the land and buildings surrounding the dwelling, including the garage, tool shed, and barn. A recently decided Washington case held a defendant liable for a burglary when, with the intent to assault his former wife, he jumped over a six-foot wooden fence in the backyard of the house she shared with her current lover.[48]

Most statutes no longer limit burglaries to dwelling houses and typically categorize the burglary of a dwelling as an aggravated burglary. The California statute extends protection to "any house, room, apartment, . . . shop, warehouse, store, mill, barn, stable, outhouse, . . . tent, vessel, . . . floating home, railroad car, . . . inhabited camper, . . . aircraft, . . . or mine."[49] Other statutes are less precise and provide that a burglary involves a "building or occupied structure, or separately secure or occupied portion thereof."[50]

Dwelling of Another

The essence of burglary under the common law is interference with an individual's sense of safety and security within the home. In determining whether the home is "of another," you need to examine who resides in the dwelling rather than who owns the dwelling. For example, a husband who separates from his wife and moves out of the home that he owns with his spouse may be liable for the burglary of his former home. In *Ellyson v. State*, the defendant was convicted of burglary for breaking into the house that he and his estranged wife owned together with the intent of raping his former wife. The couple was undergoing a divorce, and the court found that his "wife alone controlled access to the home."[51] Also, an individual generally cannot burglarize a dwelling that he or she shares with another. A burglary of this dwelling is possible only when the individual enters into portions of the home under the exclusive control of his or her roommate with the requisite criminal intent.

The requirement that an entry be of the dwelling of another is not explicitly stated in most statutes. Despite the failure to include this language, you still cannot burglarize your own home because an entry must be unlawful, meaning without a legal right, and you clearly are entitled to enter your own home.

Nighttime

A central requirement of burglary at common law was that the crime be committed at night. The nighttime hours are the time when a dwelling is likely to be occupied and when individuals are most apt to be resting or asleep and vulnerable to fright and to attack. Perpetrators are also less likely to be easily identified during the nighttime hours. The common law determined whether it was nighttime by asking whether the identity of an individual could be identified in "natural light."

State statutes no longer require that a burglary be committed at night. However, a breaking and entering during the evening is considered an aggravated form of burglary and is punished more severely. States typically follow the rule that night extends between sunset and sunrise or from thirty minutes past sunset to thirty minutes before sunrise. English law defines nighttime as extending from six at night until nine in the morning.[52]

Intent

The common law required that individuals possess an intent to commit a felony within the dwelling at the time that they enter the building. An individual is guilty of a burglary when he or she enters the dwelling, regardless of whether he or she actually commits the crime or abandons his or her criminal purpose. The intent must be concurrent with the entry; it is not a burglary when the felonious intent is formed following entry.

Some judges recognize that individuals who enter a building are guilty of a burglary in the event that they develop a felonious intent after entering into a building and unlawfully break into a secured space, such as an office or dorm room.

Barry L. Jewell broke into his estranged wife's house through a window and beat her lover Chris Jones in the head with a board until he was unconscious, amputated Jones's sexual organ with a knife, and fed the severed organ to the dog. An Indiana appellate court affirmed Jewell's conviction for burglary with a deadly weapon along with other offenses. The court found that Jewell had expressed his intention to "get" Jones. The court noted that "although the fact of breaking and entering is not itself sufficient to prove that the entry was made with the intent to commit the felony, such intent may be inferred from the subsequent conduct of the defendant inside the premises."[53]

Statutes have adopted various approaches to modifying the common law intent standard. Pennsylvania requires an intent to commit a crime.[54] California broadens the intent to include any felony or any misdemeanor theft.[55] The expansion of the intent standard is justified on the grounds that an intrusion into the home is threatening to the occupants regardless of whether the intruder's intent is to commit a felony or misdemeanor.

Aggravated Burglary

Burglary is typically divided into degrees. Aggravated first-degree burglary statutes generally list various circumstances as deserving enhanced punishment, including the nighttime burglary of a dwelling, the possession of a dangerous weapon, or the infliction of injury to others. Second-degree burglary may include the burglary of a dwelling, store, automobile, truck, or railroad car. The least serious grade of burglary typically involves entry with the intent to commit a misdemeanor or nonviolent felony.

Arizona punishes as first-degree burglary the entering of or remaining in a residential or nonresidential structure with the intent to commit a felony or theft while knowingly possessing explosives or a deadly weapon or dangerous instrument. The burglary of a residential structure is a second-degree burglary, and the least serious form of burglary involves a nonresidential structure or fenced-in commercial or residential yard.[56]

Most states also prohibit possession of burglar tools. Idaho punishes as a misdemeanor the possession of a "picklock, crow, key, bit, or other instrument or tool with intent feloniously to break or enter into any building." One is guilty of a misdemeanor "who shall . . . knowingly make or alter any key . . . [to] fit or open the lock of a building, without being requested to do so by some person having the right to open the same."[57]

Burglary is a distinct offense and does not merge into the underlying offense. An individual, as a result, may be sentenced for both burglary and assault and battery or for both burglary and larceny. Pennsylvania, however, provides that a burglary merges into the offense "which it was his intent to commit after the burglarious entry" unless the additional offense was a serious felony.[58]

Do We Need the Crime of Burglary?

Do we really need burglary statutes? Why not just severely punish a crime committed inside a dwelling or other building?

The commentary to the MPC points out that punishment for burglary can lead to illogical results. An individual entering a store with the intent to steal an inexpensive item under some statutes would be liable for both burglary and shoplifting. On the other hand, an individual who developed an intent to steal only after having entered the store would only be liable for shoplifting. Does this make sense?

In *State v. Stinton*, Matthew Allen Stinton violated an order of protection issued by a judge that prohibited Stinton from harassing his former lover, Tyna McNeill. Stinton nevertheless entered and attempted to remove his personal property from the home the two formerly shared. He was held liable for the misdemeanor of violating the order of protection in addition to the felony of burglary for entering a dwelling with the intent to commit a crime. Stinton unsuccessfully argued that this unfairly transformed his violation of an order of protection into a burglary. Had he confronted McNeill on the street, Stinton would be held liable only for a misdemeanor. Do you agree with Stinton's contention?[59]

On the other hand, burglary statutes recognize that there clearly is a difference in the degree of fear, terror, and potential for violence resulting from an assault or theft in the home as opposed to an assault and theft on the street. Do burglary statutes require reform? Should we return to the common law definition of burglary? The MPC provides a reformed version of the law of burglary.

Read *Bruce v. Commonwealth*, 469 S.E.2d 64 (Va. Ct. App. 1996), on the study site: study .sagepub.com/ lippmaness2e.

Model Penal Code

Section 221.1. Burglary

(1) A person is guilty of burglary if he enters a building or occupied structure, or separately secured or occupied portions thereof, with purpose to commit a crime therein, unless the premises are at the time open to the public or the actor is licensed or privileged to enter. It is an affirmative defense to prosecution for burglary that the building or structure was abandoned.

(2) Burglary is a felony of the second degree (maximum sentence of ten years) if it is perpetrated in the dwelling of another at night, or if, in the course of committing the offense, the actor:

  (a) purposely, knowingly or recklessly inflicts or attempts to inflict bodily injury on anyone; or

  (b) is armed with explosives or a deadly weapon.

  Otherwise, burglary is a felony of the third degree (a maximum sentence of five years). An act shall be deemed "in the course of committing" an offense if it occurs in an attempt to commit the offense or in flight after the attempt or commission.

(3) A person may not be convicted both for burglary and for the offense which it was his purpose to commit after the burglarious entry or for an attempt to commit that offense, unless the additional offense constitutes a felony of the first or second degree.

Analysis

- A burglary is limited to an occupied building or structure. The building or structure need not be occupied at the precise moment of the burglary; the important point is that the structure is "normally occupied." There is no breaking and entering requirement. The MPC does not punish remaining unlawfully on the premises as burglary.
- The MPC does not include stores open to the public or motor vehicles or railcars.
- A burglary may be committed in a separate portion or unit of a building.
- A burglary involves an intent to commit a "crime" and is not limited to a felony. The burglary is aggravated when perpetrated at night or when it involves the infliction or attempted

infliction of bodily harm or in those instances that the perpetrator is armed with explosives or a deadly weapon.

- Most burglaries are punished as felonies in the third degree. The burglary merges into the completed crime unless the underlying offense is a felony in the second degree (maximum sentence of ten years) or a serious felony such as rape, violent robbery, or murder (maximum imprisonment for life).

The Legal Equation

Burglary = Breaking and entering or unlawfully remaining or unlawful entry

+ specific intent to commit a felony or crime

+ inside a dwelling or other structure at night and other aggravating factors.

You Decide **9.5** Anthony Holt attempted to remove a window screen from Carolyn Stamper's home. The window was open roughly four inches, and the curtains over the window were drawn other than for a gap of about four inches. Stamper saw Holt at the window as he attempted to remove the aluminum window screen. Holt removed the screen halfway from the window and attempted to get the screen free of the track at the bottom of the window frame. Stamper testified that "while holding the screen, the man's 'fingers were . . . in that area between the window and the screen.'" Holt, after noticing Stamper, stated, "Oh, I'm sorry," and turned and left the premises without opening the window and was convicted of one count of breaking and entering.

Stamper reported that the screen was "'pretty well destroyed'" and had to be replaced.

The defendant claimed that this was not burglary because he did not penetrate the structure of the home. The New Mexico Statute, UJI 14-1410 NMRA, requires the jury to find that (1) "[t]he defendant entered [the structure] without permission" and (2) "[t]he entry was obtained by breaking or dismantling a part of the structure." Holt "contends that only penetration of an interior protected space, not the outermost plane of a structure, constitutes an 'entry' for purposes of the breaking-and-entering statute" and that his conviction should be overturned.

Would you convict Holt of breaking and entering into Stamper's home? See *State v. Holt*, 352 P.3d 702 (NMCA 2015).

You can find the answer at study.sagepub.com/lippmaness2e

TRESPASS

Criminal trespass is the unauthorized entry or remaining on the land or premises of another. The *actus reus* is entering or remaining on another person's property without his or her permission. An example is disregarding a "no trespassing" sign and climbing over a fence in order to swim at a private beach. You also may commit a trespass when you swim with the owner's permission and then disregard his or her request to leave.

A **defiant trespass** occurs when an individual knowingly enters or remains on a premises after receiving a clear notice that he or she is trespassing. Keep in mind that the police, firefighters, and emergency personnel are privileged to enter any land or premises.

Criminal trespass entails an unauthorized entry, and unlike burglary, there is no requirement that the intruder intend to commit a felony. Another important point is that statutes punish a trespass on a broad range of private property. The Texas statute provides that an individual commits a trespass who "knowingly and unlawfully" enters or remains in the dwelling "of another" as well as in a motor vehicle, hotel, motel, condominium, or apartment building or on agricultural land. The federal and many state governments also have special statutes that punish trespass in schools, military facilities, and medical facilities.

A recent development in the law of trespass is the felony of *computer trespassing.* New York's law punishes an individual who "intentionally and without authorization" accesses a computer, computer system, or network with the intent to delete, damage, destroy, or disrupt a computer, computer system, or computer network.

Model Penal Code

Section 221.2. Criminal Trespass

(1) A person commits an offense if, knowing that he is not licensed or privileged to do so, he enters or surreptitiously remains in any building or occupied structure, or separately secured or occupied portion thereof. An offense under this Subsection is a misdemeanor if it is committed in a dwelling at night. Otherwise it is a petty misdemeanor.

(2) A person commits an offense if, knowing that he is not licensed or privileged to do so, he enters or remains in any place as to which notice against trespasser is given by:

  (a) actual communication to the actor; or

  (b) posting in a manner prescribed by law or reasonably likely to come to the attention of intruders; or

  (c) fencing or other enclosure manifestly designed to exclude intruders.

An offense under this Subsection constitutes a petty misdemeanor if the offender defies an order to leave personally communicated to him by the owner of the premises or other authorized person. Otherwise it is a violation (punishable by fine).

(3) It is an affirmative defense to prosecution under this Section that:

  (a) a building or occupied structure involved in an offense under Subsection (1) was abandoned; or

  (b) the premises were at the time open to members of the public and the actor complied with all lawful conditions imposed on access to or remaining in the premises; or

  (c) the actor reasonably believed that the owner of the premises or other persons empowered to license access thereto, would have licensed him to enter or remain.

Analysis

- An accused is guilty of trespass and a petty misdemeanor in the event that the accused knows that he or she lacks permission to enter and nevertheless enters or surreptitiously (hiding) remains in any building or occupied structure. This is a misdemeanor if committed in a dwelling at night and is a petty misdemeanor if committed during the daytime.
- It is a violation (fine) to enter any other "place" without authorization in which a notice against trespass is posted or in which a prohibition against trespass is clear from the enclosure surrounding the area. This is a petty misdemeanor where the trespasser defies an order personally communicated to him.
- The code requires knowledge of trespass. An individual who accidentally enters on property or mistakenly believes that he or she possesses authorization to enter or remain upon property is not guilty of a trespass.
- There are three affirmative defenses to trespass.

The Legal Equation

Criminal trespass = Entry or remaining on the property of another without authorization

+ purposely, knowingly, or strict liability.

ARSON

Common law **arson** is defined as the willful and malicious burning of the dwelling house of another. The purpose is to protect the home along with the occupants and their possessions. Common law arson has been substantially modified by state statutes.

Burning

The common law requires a burning. This is commonly defined as the "consuming of the material" of the house or the "burning of any part of the house." The burning is not required to destroy the structure or seriously damage the home. The burning is required to affect only a small portion of the dwelling, no matter how insignificant or difficult to detect. Even a small "spot" on the floor is sufficient.

The burning need not involve an actual flame and need merely result in a "charring" of the structure. This does not include "soot," "smudging," "blackening or discoloration or shriveling from heat," or "smoke damage." The common law did not consider an explosion as arson unless the combustion resulted in a fire.

The trend is for state statutes and courts to broadly interpret arson statutes and to find that smoke damage and soot are sufficient for arson.[60] Some statutes punish the setting of a fire without regard to damage to property. A New Jersey statute defines third-degree arson without requiring damage and provides that an individual commits arson when he or she "purposely starts a fire and recklessly places a person in danger of death or bodily injury or recklessly places a building or structure in danger of damage or destruction."[61] The Florida statute and other state laws include explosions that damage dwellings and other protected property under arson.[62]

Dwelling

Arson at common law must be committed against a dwelling. This is defined by the familiar formula as a place regularly used for sleeping. The definition reflects the fact that criminal laws against arson are designed to protect individuals and their right to the peace and security in the home. The occupants may be absent at the time of the arson, so long as the structure is regularly used for sleep. The definition of dwelling extends to all structures within the curtilage, the area immediately surrounding the home. This includes a barn, garage, or tool shed.

Statutes no longer limit arson to a dwelling. Illinois, in addition to prohibiting residential arson, punishes damage to real property (buildings and land) and to personal property (e.g., personal belongings). Aggravated arson is directed against injury to individuals resulting from the arson of "any building or structure, including any adjacent building . . . including . . . a house trailer, watercraft, motor vehicle or railroad car." Statutes that include personal property extend arson to the burning of furniture in a house regardless of whether the fire damages the dwelling.[63]

Dwelling of Another

The common law required that the burned dwelling was occupied by another individual. As with burglary, the central issue is occupancy rather than ownership. A tenant would not be guilty of arson for burning his or her rented apartment that is owned by the landlord; the landlord would be guilty of arson for burning the house that he or she owns and rents to the tenant. A husband would not be guilty of arson for burning the home he shares with his wife.

Modern statutes have eliminated the requirement that the arson must be directed at the dwelling "of another." Florida holds an individual liable for arson in the first degree "whether the property [is] of himself or herself or another."[64] Courts have reasoned that a fire poses a threat to firefighters, as well as to the neighbors, and have held that it is not an unreasonable limitation on property rights to hold a defendant liable for burning his or her own property. Do you agree?

Willful and Malicious

The *mens rea* of common law arson is malice. This does not require dislike or hatred. Malice in arson entails either a purpose to burn or a knowledge that the structure would burn or the creation of an obvious fire hazard that, without justification or excuse, damages a dwelling. An "obvious fire hazard" is created when an individual recklessly burns a large pile of dry leaves on a windy day and in the process creates an unreasonable hazard that burns a neighbor's house. A negligent or involuntary burning does not satisfy the requirement for common law arson.

State statutes typically retain the common law intent standard and include language such as "willfully and maliciously." Separate statutes often punish a reckless burning. A number of states also punish a burning committed by an individual with the specific intent to defraud an insurance company.

Grading

State statutes are typically divided into arson and aggravated arson. Some states provide for additional categories. Washington provides for knowing and malicious arson and aggravated arson, as well as for reckless burning. The Washington statute categorizes arson as aggravated based on various factors, including causing a fire or explosion that damages a dwelling or that is dangerous to human life. Aggravated arson also includes causing a fire or explosion on property valued at $10,000 or more with the intent to collect insurance.[65] Washington state punishes aggravated arson by life imprisonment, along with a possible fine of up to $50,000, while arson is punishable by ten years, by a fine of up to $20,000, or by both confinement and a fine.[66] California enhances the punishment of "willful and malicious" burning and of "reckless" burning when the perpetrator has been previously convicted of either offense, a police officer or firefighter is injured, more than one victim suffers great bodily injury, multiple structures are burned, or the defendant employed a device designed to accelerate the fire.[67]

Model Penal Code

Section 220.1. Arson and Related Offenses

(1) Arson. A person is guilty of arson, a felony of the second degree, if he starts a fire or causes an explosion with the purpose of:

(a) destroying a building or occupied structure of another; or

(b) destroying or damaging any property, whether his own or another's, to collect insurance for such loss. It shall be an affirmative defense . . . that the actor's conduct did not recklessly endanger any building or occupied structure of another or place any other person in danger of death or bodily injury.

(2) Reckless Burning or Exploding. A person commits a felony of the third degree if he purposely starts a fire or causes an explosion whether on his own property or another's, and thereby recklessly:

(a) places another person in danger of death or bodily injury; or

(b) places a building or occupied structure of another in danger of damage or destruction.

(3) Failure to Control or Report Dangerous Fire. A person who knows that a fire is endangering a life or a substantial amount of property of another and fails to take reasonable measures to put out or control the fire, when he can do so without substantial risk to himself, or to give a prompt fire alarm, commits a misdemeanor if:

(a) he knows that he is under an official, contractual, or other legal duty to prevent or combat the fire;

(b) the fire was started . . . lawfully, by him or with his assent, or on property in his custody or control.

(4) Definitions. "Occupied structure" means any structure, vehicle or place adapted for overnight accommodation of persons, or for carrying on business therein, whether or not a person is actually present. Property is that of another, for the purposes of this section, if anyone other than the actor has a possessory or proprietary interest therein. If a building or structure is divided into separately occupied units, any unit not occupied by the actor is an occupied structure of another.

Analysis

- MPC Section 220.1(1)(a) defines arson in terms of starting a fire or causing an explosion with the purpose of destroying a building or occupied structure of another.
- Directing punishment at individuals who start or cause a fire or explosion results in their being held liable for arson despite the fact that the fire is extinguished before damage results.
- Arson is punishable by a maximum of ten years in prison under the MPC. This would be in addition to punishment for any resulting injury to individuals.
- The requirement of a purpose to destroy a building or occupied structure or to destroy or damage property means that a specific intent is required for arson.
- The commentary states that the terms *building* and *occupied structure* are intended to refer to structures that are capable of occupancy. This restricts arson to fires or explosions dangerous to the life of inhabitants and firefighters. An individual need not be actually present in the dwelling.
- Arson to defraud in Section 220.1(1)(b) includes property owned by the defendant as well as another. There must be an intent to defraud an insurance company, and this provision includes all types of property.
- An individual is not liable for arson where the property of another or other persons is not endangered. This is designed to avoid the harsh penalties for arson when another person or his or her property is not recklessly endangered.
- Reckless burning or exploding is punishable by five years in prison. There is no requirement of a purpose to destroy a structure.
- The duty to undertake affirmative action to prevent and control fires is imposed.

The Legal Equation

Arson = Setting fire to a dwelling (other structures under state statutes) or structures in cartilage

+ intent to burn, knowing will burn, or reckless creation of risk of burning

+ burning of dwelling (smoke damage is sufficient under state statutes).

Read *People v. Fox* on the study site: study .sagepub.com/ lippmanness2e.

CRIMINAL MISCHIEF

The common law misdemeanor of malicious mischief is defined as the destruction of, or damage to, the personal property (physical belongings) of another. The MPC refers to this offense as **criminal mischief**, and under modern statutes, criminal mischief includes damage to both personal and real (land and structures) **tangible property** (physical property as opposed to ownership of **intangible property**, such as ownership of a song or the movie rights to a book). The offense is directed against interference with the property of another and punishes injury and destruction to an individual home or personal possessions.

Malicious mischief under most statutes is a minor felony, and the punishment is reduced or increased based on the dollar amount of the damage. A sentence may also be increased when the damage is directed against a residence or interferes with the delivery of essential services, such as phone, water, or utilities.

Actus Reus

The MPC specifies that criminal mischief is composed of three types of acts:

1. *Destruction or Damage to Tangible Property.* Injury to property, including damage by a fire, explosion, flood, or other harmful force.

2. *Tampering With Tangible Property So as to Endanger a Person or Property.* Interference with property that creates a danger—for example, the removal of a stop sign or one-way road sign.

3. *Deception or Threat Causing Financial Loss.* A trick that dupes an individual into spending money. An example is sending a telegram falsely informing an individual that his or her mother is dying in a distant city, causing the individual to spend several hundred dollars on an unnecessary plane flight.

Mens Rea

The MPC requires that these acts be committed purposely or recklessly. Damage to property by "catastrophic means," such as an explosion or flood, may be committed negligently. The punishment of criminal mischief under the MPC is based on the monetary damage of the harm. Keep in mind that property damage resulting from a fire or explosion that purposely endangers the person or property of another may be punished as arson.

The Legal Equation

Criminal mischief $=$ Destruction or damage or tampering with tangible property or deception or threat causing financial loss

 $+$ purposely, knowingly, recklessly, or negligently.

You Decide

9.6 Nicholas Y. wrote on a glass window of a projection booth at an AMC theater with a Sharpie marker. After his arrest, appellant admitted to police that he had written "RTK" on the window. Police saw "approximately 30 incidents" in red magic marker throughout the theater, including the one on the glass. Appellant said the initials stood for "The Right to Crime."

At the close of the prosecution's case, appellant's counsel argued that no defacing of or damage to property had been proved, stating: "It's a piece of glass with a marker on it. You take a rag and wipe it off. End of case. It's ridiculous." The prosecutor countered that appellant trespassed and left fresh marks on the window, thus defacing the window with graffiti. The court found that appellant violated Penal Code Section 594, subdivision (a), a misdemeanor.

Penal Code Section 594 provides, in relevant part:

(a) Every person who maliciously commits any of the following acts with respect to any real or personal property not his or her own . . . is guilty of vandalism:

(1) Defaces with graffiti or other inscribed material.

(2) Damages.

(3) Destroys. . . .

(4) (A) If the amount of defacement, damage, or destruction is less than four hundred dollars ($400), vandalism is punishable by imprisonment in a county jail for not more than six months, or by a fine of not more than one thousand dollars ($1,000) or by both that fine and imprisonment. . . .

(e) As used in this section the term "graffiti or other inscribed material" includes any unauthorized inscription, word, figure, mark, or design that is written, marked, etched, scratched, drawn, or painted on real or personal property.

Should Nicholas Y. be held guilty of vandalizing property belonging to the AMC theater? See *People v. Nicholas Y.*, 102 Cal. Rptr.2d 511 (Cal. Ct. App. 2000).

You can find the answer at study.sagepub.com/lippmaness2e

CRIMINAL LAW IN THE NEWS

On January 10, 2011, thousands of Auburn University football fans gathered at historic Toomer's Corner to celebrate the team's national college championship. Toomer's Corner has been called the Times Square or center of Auburn University, the site where students, alumni, and fans traditionally have gathered to mark major football victories. The corner is dotted with historic 130-year-old oak trees, which students roll in toilet paper as a traditional part of their celebrations.

On January 28, Auburn officials discovered that an herbicide had been applied in "lethal amounts" to the area surrounding two trees. The poisoning was discovered following a call to a Birmingham radio station from "Al from Dadeville" who claimed that he used "Spike 80DF" to poison the trees and that the trees "definitely will die." "Al" proclaimed that he was a dyed-in-the-wool University of Alabama Crimson Tide fan and that he had poisoned the trees following the annual Iron Bowl, in which Auburn scored 28 straight points and overcame what seemed like an insurmountable 24-point Alabama lead. Al signed off by exclaiming "Roll Damn Tide."

Jay Gogue, the president of Auburn, responded to the poisoning by vowing: "We will take every step we can to save the Toomer's oaks, which have been the home of countless celebrations and a symbol of the Auburn spirit for generations of students, fans, alumni, and the community."

A police investigation led to the arrest of Harvey Almorn Updyke, 62, a resident of Dadeville, Alabama, who is a retired Texas State Trooper. Updyke explained that he believed that Auburn was paying outstanding athletes "under the table" to play football and that he was enraged by the gloating of Auburn fans on the radio. He also alleged that he had seen photos of Auburn fans celebrating following the death of beloved Alabama coach Paul "Bear" Bryant.

Updyke initially characterized the tree poisoning as the type of prank that is a traditional part of college football rivalries. A grand jury charged Updyke with six criminal counts, including two counts of the felony of criminal mischief. Updyke's initial defiance and defense of his actions gradually gave way to a sense of remorse and regret. He stated that he had "done a lot of good things" and he did not want to go to his grave with "Harvey the tree poisoner" as his legacy. He stated that as a Texas trooper, he had arrested a record number of drunk drivers and that he also had been responsible for a significant number of drug busts.

Updyke explained that his entire life people had told him that he cared too much about Alabama football and that he "just had too much 'Bama in me." He admitted that he was a "very unhealthy Alabama fan. . . . I live it, I breathe it. I think about Alabama football 18 hours a day." Updyke explained that his father had died when he was a youngster and that he had been drawn to Alabama's legendary coach Paul "Bear" Bryant as a father substitute. He named his daughter Crimson Tyde and his son Bear and called his dogs Bama and Nicky (after Coach Nick Saban). Updyke owned 46 Alabama hats and had bought out the complete supply of Alabama football championship shirts at a local store. He planned to be buried in a crimson casket.

Updyke pled guilty to criminal damage to an agricultural facility and was sentenced to six months in jail, a $1,000 fine, and five years' probation. During his probation, he must adhere to a 7 p.m. curfew and is banned from college sporting events and may not enter the confines of Auburn University. He was credited with time served and was released after 76 days in jail. Updyke also was ordered to pay $800,000 in restitution in quarterly payments and to perform community service work for the police to help pay off the restitution. Auburn has replaced the soil at Toomer's Corner and expects to see the new oak trees begin to show significant signs of growth in 2016.

CASE ANALYSIS

In *Lee v. State,* the court decided whether the defendant committed a larceny of two bottles of cognac in a self-service liquor store.

Was Lee Guilty of Larceny?

Lee v. State, 474 A.2d 537 (Ct. App. Md. 1984)

Appellant, Joe William Lee, Jr. (Lee)[,] was convicted by the Circuit Court for Baltimore County of two separate charges of theft under $300.00 and sentenced to the Division of Correction for two consecutive one year sentences.

In the second conviction, however, Lee urges this Court to decide that his concealment of a bottle of liquor in his trousers while shopping in a self-service liquor store does not constitute evidence sufficient to convict him of theft. Since Lee was accosted with the merchandise in the store, abandoned it and then departed from the premises, this case poses a substantial question regarding the law of theft which has never specifically been resolved in this state: May a person be convicted of theft for shoplifting in a self-service store if he does not remove the goods from the premises of that store?

An employee of a pharmacy-liquor store observed Lee displacing two $16.47 bottles of cognac. Lee concealed one of the bottles in his pants and held the other in his hand. When approached by the employee, Lee returned both bottles to the shelf and fled the store. He was chased by the employee who flagged down a passing police cruiser. Subsequently, Lee was arrested and convicted. For the reasons set forth in our discussion, we uphold the theft conviction despite the fact Lee was accused and "returned" the merchandise before he left the store.

Larceny at common law was defined as the trespassory taking and carrying away of personal property of another with intent to steal the same. The requirement of a trespassory taking made larceny an offense against possession. . . . [T]he courts gradually broadened the offense by manipulating the concept of possession to embrace misappropriation by a person who with the consent of the owner already had physical control over the property. . . . [T]he courts began to distinguish "possession" from "custody," thereby enabling an employer to temporarily entrust his merchandise to an employee or a customer while still retaining "possession" over the goods until a sale was consummated. These distinctions and delineations, which ultimately laid the foundation for the statutory offense of theft as it exists today, provided the courts with the judicial machinery with which to sustain a larceny conviction when the customer who had rightful "custody" or "physical possession" converted the property to his own use and thereby performed . . . the requisite "trespassory taking."

The evolution of theft law is particularly relevant to thefts occurring in modern self-service stores where customers are impliedly invited to examine, try on, and carry about the merchandise on display.

In a self-service store, the owner has[,] in a sense, consented to the customer's custody of the goods for a limited purpose. . . . [T]he fact that the owner temporarily consents to custody does not preclude a conviction for larceny if the customer exercises dominion and control over the property by using or concealing it in an unauthorized manner. Such conduct would satisfy the element of trespassory taking as it could provide the basis for the inference of the intent to deprive the owner of the property.

From this perusal of cases, we conclude that several factors should be assessed to determine whether the accused intended to deprive the owner of property. First, concealment of goods inconsistent with the store owner's rights should be considered. "Concealment" is conduct which is not generally expected in a self-service store and may in many cases be deemed "obtaining unauthorized control over the property in a manner likely to deprive the owner of the property." Other furtive or unusual behavior on the part of the defendant should also be weighed. For instance, if a customer suspiciously surveys an area while secreting the merchandise this may evince larcenous behavior. Likewise, if the accused flees the scene upon being questioned or accosted about the merchandise, as in the instant case, an intent to steal may be inferred. The customer's proximity to the store's exits is also relevant. Additionally, possession by the customer of a shoplifting device with which to conceal merchandise would suggest a larcenous intent. One of these factors or any act on the part of the customer which would be inconsistent with the owner's property rights may be taken into account as relevant in determining whether there was a larcenous intent.

In the instant case, Lee knowingly removed the bottle of liquor from the shelf and secreted it under his clothing. This act in itself meets the requirement of concealment.

The fact that this concealment was brief or that Lee was detected before the goods were removed from the owner's premises is immaterial. The intent to deprive the owner of his property can be inferred from his furtive handling of the property. Lee not only placed the bottle in the waistband of his pants, but did so in a particularly suspicious manner by concealing the bottle such that it was hidden from the shop owner's view. It cannot be so as a matter of law that these circumstances failed to establish the elements of theft. Once a customer goes beyond the mere removal of goods from a shelf and crosses the threshold into the realm of behavior inconsistent with the owner's expectations, the circumstances may be such that a larcenous intent can be inferred.

CHAPTER SUMMARY

The common law initially punished only the violent taking of property. This soon proved insufficient. Individuals accumulated farm animals, crops, and consumer goods that were easily stolen by stealth and under the cover of darkness. Larceny developed to protect individuals against the wrongful taking and carrying away of their personal property by individuals harboring the intent to deprive the owner of possession. The economic development of society resulted in clear shortcomings in the coverage of the law that led to the development of embezzlement, false pretenses, and receiving stolen property.

A number of states have consolidated larceny, embezzlement, and false pretenses into a single theft statute. These statutes provide a uniform grading of offenses and, in some states, serve to prevent a defendant from being acquitted based on the prosecutor's failure to satisfy the technical factual requirements of the property crime with which the defendant is charged. The grading of larceny, embezzlement, and false pretenses is generally based on the monetary value of the property. Modern theft statutes also provide protection to all varieties of personal property and do not distinguish between tangible (physical objects) and intangible (legal documents) personal property. As noted, various states also extend protection to real property (real estate).

Forgery involves the creation of a false legal document or the material modification of an existing legal document with the intent to deceive or to defraud others. The crime of forgery is complete upon the drafting and modification of the document with the intent to defraud others, regardless of whether the document is actually used to commit a fraud. Uttering is the separate offense of circulating or using a forged document.

Robbery is a crime that threatens both the property and the safety and security of the individual. It involves the taking of personal property from the victim's person or presence through violence or intimidation. The grading of robbery depends on the harm inflicted or threatened. Carjacking is an increasingly prevalent offense that involves the use of force to unlawfully gain control and possession over a motor vehicle.

Robbery involves a threat of immediate violence, and extortion is distinguished from robbery by the fact it entails a threat of future violence or other harms. Robbery must be committed in the presence of the victim, while extortionate threats may be communicated over the phone or in a letter.

Crimes against habitation protect individuals' interest in safe and secure homes free from uninvited intrusions. Burglary and arson are the cornerstones of the criminal law's protection of dwellings. Modern statutes have significantly expanded the structures protected by burglary and arson.

Burglary at common law was defined as the breaking and entering of the dwelling house of another at night with the intention to commit a felony. State statutes have significantly modified the common law and differ in their approach to defining the felony of burglary. In general, a breaking no longer is required, and burglary has been expanded to include a range of structures and vehicles. Statutes provide that a burglary may involve entering as well as remaining in a variety of structures with the requisite purposeful intent. The intent standard has been broadened under various statutes to include "any offense" or a "felony or misdemeanor theft." Also, burglary is no longer required to be committed at night.

Criminal trespass is the unauthorized entry or remaining on the land or premises of another. Trespass is distinguished from burglary in that it does not require an intent to commit a felony or other offense and extends to property beyond the curtilage, including agricultural land. Statutes provide that a trespass may be committed knowingly or purposefully, and Missouri defines trespass as a strict liability offense.

Arson at common law is defined as the willful and malicious burning of the dwelling house of another. This is treated as a felony based on the danger posed to inhabitants and neighbors. Statutes no longer require a burning; even smoke damage or soot is sufficient. Arson also extends to a broad range of structures and is no longer limited to the dwelling of another. Arson requires either a purpose to burn or knowledge that a structure will burn. It may also be committed recklessly by creating an unreasonable hazard on an individual's own property that burns a neighbor's dwelling.

Criminal mischief under modern statutes punishes the damage, destruction, or tampering with personal and real tangible property or may involve a deception causing financial loss. Criminal mischief is generally punished as a misdemeanor and may be committed purposefully or recklessly.

CHAPTER REVIEW QUESTIONS

1. Provide an example of how the common law of larceny developed in response to the growth of business and commerce.

2. Distinguish between the requirements of larceny, embezzlement, and false pretenses.

3. Why did various states adopt consolidated theft statutes?

4. What is a prosecutor required to prove beyond a reasonable doubt in order to establish the crime of receiving stolen property? How does the punishment of this offense deter theft?

5. What is the difference between forgery and uttering?

6. How does robbery differ from larceny?

7. Discuss the use or threat of harm requirement in regard to robbery.

8. Distinguish robbery from the elements of carjacking.

9. Distinguish extortion from robbery.

10. What is the definition of burglary? How have the elements of the common law crime of burglary been modified by modern statutes?

11. What is the difference between burglary and trespass?

12. Define arson. How have modern statutes modified the common law crime of arson?

13. What are the three types of acts that satisfy the *actus reus* of criminal mischief?

14. Compare and contrast arson and criminal mischief.

15. What are some factors that aggravate burglary, arson, trespass, and criminal mischief?

16. Discuss the justifications for crimes against habitation. Is it accurate to continue to categorize burglary and arson as crimes against habitation?

LEGAL TERMINOLOGY

arson	embezzlement	petit larceny
blackmail	extortion	possession
burglary	false pretenses	receiving stolen property
carjacking	forgery	robbery
criminal mischief	grand larceny	simulation
criminal trespass	intangible property	tangible property
custody	larceny	theft statutes
defiant trespass	larceny by trick	uttering

CRIMINAL LAW ON THE WEB

Visit **study.sagepub.com/lippmaness2e** to access additional study tools including suggested answers to the You Decide questions, reprints of cases and statutes, online appendices, and more!

10 WHITE-COLLAR AND ORGANIZED CRIME

Did Reverend Davis engage in money laundering?

Reverend Davis became the preacher at the 15th Street Baptist Church in the mid-1980s. Shortly thereafter he began to sell drugs, and by mid-1987 was actively selling crack from two houses. . . . Davis deposited some of the cash he collected from the houses in bank accounts maintained in the names of the 15th Street Baptist Church Development Corporation . . . and the 15th Street Baptist Church . . . at Illini Federal, a local savings and loan. . . . Davis could write checks on these accounts. Some of these checks were made out to cash, which Davis diverted to his personal use. Others were made out to local vendors who provided services such as beepers and mobile telephones. Still others were made out to the landlord who owned the Swansea, Illinois, residence where Davis lived. Davis also purchased numerous cars, spending over $79,000 on a variety of vehicles for personal and church use. (*United States v. Jackson,* 935 F.2d 832 [7th Cir. 1991])

In this chapter, learn about money laundering.

Learning Objectives

1. Know the different approaches to defining white-collar crime.

2. Recite the argument for and against holding corporations criminally liable.

3. List the types of acts prohibited by environmental statutes.

4. Know the purpose of the Occupational Safety and Health Act.

5. Understand securities fraud and insider trading.

6. Know the elements of mail fraud and wire fraud.

7. Explain the Travel Act.

8. Outline the type of acts involved in health care fraud.

9. Understand the purpose of the Sherman Antitrust Act.

10. Explain money laundering.

11. Understand access device fraud.

12. Explain the elements of identity theft.

13. Know the basic elements of currency violations and tax crimes.

14. List the various types of computer crime.

15. Explain the purpose of the criminal law in protecting intellectual property, trademarks, and trade secrets.

16. Know the purpose of RICO and the types of acts prohibited under RICO.

INTRODUCTION

In 1949, sociologist Edwin H. Sutherland published his pioneering study, *White Collar Crime*. This volume called attention to the largely overlooked criminal behavior of business managers, executives, and professional groups, which Sutherland labeled **white-collar crime**. Sutherland defined white-collar crime as an offense committed by a "person of respectability and high social status in the course of his [or her] occupation." This definition stresses the social background of offenders and focuses on nonviolent offenses committed in the course of employment. Sutherland's central thesis is that theories that explain crime based on poverty, low social class, and lack of education fail to account for "crimes in the suites." The focus on the poor and disenfranchised diverts our attention from the fact that the financial cost of white-collar crime is several times greater than the economic consequences of common crimes. A second point raised by Sutherland is that despite the social harm caused by the crimes of the powerful, these offenses are typically punished by fines and less severe penalties than the offenses committed by average individuals.[1]

The U.S. Justice Department's definition of white-collar crime focuses on the nature of the criminal activity as well as on the job of the offender. This definition also does not limit white-collar crime to employment-related offenses. White-collar crime is defined as follows:

- Illegal acts that employ deceit and concealment rather than the application of force
- to obtain money, property, or service;
- to avoid the payment or loss of money; or
- to secure a business or professional advantage.
- White-collar criminals occupy positions of responsibility and trust in government, industry, the professions, and civil organizations.

A third approach defines white-collar crime in terms of the type of criminal activity involved. This has the advantage of drawing attention to the fact that tax and consumer fraud and other offenses characteristic of white-collar crime are committed by individuals of various socioeconomic backgrounds.

You might want to review our previous discussions of property offenses, a number of which may be committed by corporate criminals in the course of carrying out fraudulent schemes. These include larceny, false pretenses, and embezzlement.

The focus of the present chapter differs from our previous discussions in that most white-collar crime prosecutions are brought by the U.S. government rather than by state and local officials. You may recall that we discussed the division between federal and state powers in Chapter 1. In this chapter, we primarily examine the federal statutes that most frequently are used to combat white-collar crime, which include the following:

- *Environmental Crimes.* Offenses harming and polluting the environment.
- *Occupational Safety and Health.* Injury and harm to workers.
- *Securities Fraud.* Manipulation of stocks and bonds.
- *Mail and Wire Fraud.* The use of the mail and telephone to commit a fraud.
- *The Travel Act.* Committing certain offenses through the use of interstate travel or the mail.
- *Health Fraud.* Obtaining reimbursement or payment for unwarranted and undelivered medical treatments.
- *Antitrust Violations.* Interference with the competitive marketplace.
- *Identity Theft.* The fraudulent use of another individual's credit card or other financial information to purchase items or to obtain employment or other economic goods. A related crime is access device fraud involving the theft of a personal identification number (PIN) or other identifying information used to access money.
- *Money Laundering.* Transactions involving money derived from illegal activities.
- *Currency Violations.* The transfer of money in the banking system without completing the required paperwork.
- *Computer Crimes.* The use of a computer to engage in a variety of criminal activity.

- *Tax Crimes.* The intentional failure to report income to the Internal Revenue Service (IRS) or the knowing claim of a higher deduction than an individual is entitled to under the law.
- *Theft of Intellectual Property, Trademarks, and Trade Secrets.* The unauthorized use of the intellectual product developed by other individuals or businesses.

White-collar crime offenses are often committed in the regular course of business in an effort to make or save money. These offenses generally involve a betrayal of the trust that we place in business and government. Let me caution that this chapter cannot cover the entire field of white-collar crime.

Despite the fact that white-collar crime is one of the most active areas of federal prosecution, textbooks generally do not devote significant attention to the subject. This is partially based on the belief that white-collar crime is not a distinct category of crime. It is argued that there is little difference between the theft of money by a corporate executive and the theft of money by a waitress or the theft of tools by a construction worker. As you read this chapter, consider whether the concept of white-collar crime is useful. Should we pay special attention to "crimes in the suites"? Do you believe that the government should devote additional resources to the prosecution and punishment of corporate misconduct? Another question concerns the appropriate form of punishment for white-collar offenders. Should respectable business executives be punished like any other criminals?

CORPORATE CRIMINAL LIABILITY

The early common law adopted the logical position that corporations are not living and breathing human beings and therefore cannot be held criminally liable. There was no doctrine of **corporate liability**, prosecution, and punishment. Prosecution and punishment were limited to corporate officers and employees. Over time, corporations were subject to fines for failing to maintain the repair of public works such as roads and bridges. The increasing power and prominence of large-scale business enterprises resulted in the gradual growth of the idea of corporate criminal liability and the punishment of corporations through the imposition of financial penalties. The U.S. Supreme Court noted in 1909 that acts of an employee "may be controlled in the interests of public policy, by imputing his act to his employer and imposing penalties upon the corporation for which he is acting."[2]

The U.S. Supreme Court, in *United States v. Dotterweich*, affirmed in 1943 that corporations, along with corporate executives and employees, could be held criminally liable under the Federal Food and Drugs Act. The Court stressed that holding the president of the corporation and the corporation vicariously liable for the strict liability crimes of employees was intended to ensure that company executives and managers closely monitor the distribution of potentially dangerous drugs to the public.[3] In *United States v. Park*, the Supreme Court upheld the conviction of a large national food store chain, along with the president of the company, for shipping adulterated food in interstate commerce.[4]

Keep in mind that a corporate crime may result in the criminal conviction of the employee committing the offense as well as the extension of vicarious liability to the owner and the corporation. There is nothing mysterious about a corporation. It is a method of organizing a business that provides certain financial benefits in return for complying with various state regulations. Most small corporations typically are run by an owner or by several partners, although moderately sized and larger corporations may be organized with boards of directors and outside investors or shareholders. The corporation possesses a life of its own separate and apart from all the executives, managers, and employees and is considered a "person" under the law.

The first step in determining whether a corporation may be criminally liable is to examine whether the legislature intends the criminal statute to apply to corporations. In *United States v. Dotterweich*, the U.S. Supreme Court affirmed the conviction of the defendant and corporation under the Federal Food, Drug, and Cosmetic (FD&C) Act for introducing an "adulterated or misbranded" drug into interstate commerce. The Court stressed that "a person" under the act was defined to include corporations. Courts have ruled in other instances that the term *person* was limited to "natural persons" and did not include "corporate persons."[5]

Once it is determined that a statute encompasses corporations, there are two primary tests for determining whether a corporation should be criminally liable under the statute:

1. Respondeat Superior *or the Responsibility of a Superior.* A corporation may be held liable for the conduct of an employee who commits a crime within the scope of his or her employment who possesses the intent to benefit the corporation.

2. *Model Penal Code (MPC) Section 2.07.* Criminal liability is imposed in those instances that the criminal conduct is authorized, requested, commanded, performed, or recklessly tolerated by the board of directors or by a high managerial official acting on behalf of the corporation within the scope of his or her office or employment.

Respondeat superior extends vicarious criminal liability to a corporation for the acts of employees, even when such acts are contrary to corporate policy. It may seem unfair to impose liability on a corporation for the independent criminal acts of an employee that may be unknown to company officials, such as Mitchell, a service station employee who misbranded low-quality motor oil and sold it to motorists while representing that it was high-quality motor oil. On the other hand, Mitchell's sale of misbranded motor oil increased the company's profits and should have been prevented by his employer.[6] The MPC test limits vicarious liability to acts approved or tolerated by high-level corporate officials. Managers, corporate boards, and corporate entities under this approach are liable only for acts that they direct or tolerate. Under this test, decision makers may not possess an incentive to closely monitor employees to ensure that they are not engaging in acts that have not been approved by management. A corporation, for instance, would not be convicted for Mitchell's independent decision to misrepresent the quality of motor oil sold to consumers. Which test do you favor?

In the past several years there has been an increasing trend toward holding corporations criminally liable. The aim is to encourage corporate executives to vigorously prevent and punish illegal activity. Executives know that a criminal conviction may lead to a decline in consumer sales and investment in the firm as well as to criminal fines, and they have a powerful incentive to ensure that the corporation acts in a legal fashion. The prevention of corporate misconduct is important, because we depend on large firms to provide safe and secure health care, transportation, food, and products in the home. Holding a corporation vicariously liable also makes good sense because business decisions often involve a large number of individuals, and it often is difficult to single out a specific individual or individuals as responsible for designing, manufacturing, marketing, and delivering a defective drug or automobile.[7]

On the other hand, it seems unfair to hold a corporation strictly liable and to impose a heavy fine for crimes that may have been committed by low-level employees or managers or secretly approved by a high-level corporate executive. A criminal fine against a corporation is merely paid out of the corporate treasury, and the threat of a financial penalty may not encourage corporate officials to monitor the activities of employees. A fine may also be passed on to consumers, who will be charged a higher price. In the final analysis, the profits to be gained from misrepresenting the effectiveness of a drug may far outweigh any fine that may be imposed. Critics of corporate liability argue that it makes more sense to limit criminal liability to the individuals who committed the offense.[8]

Are there penalties other than fines that might be used against corporations? One federal district court imposed a three-year prison sentence on a corporation that was later suspended. The court observed that this could be carried out by ordering the U.S. marshal to seize corporate assets such as computers, machinery, and trucks. This type of punishment has the advantage of completely shutting down a business. On the other hand, it would likely result in innocent individuals losing their jobs.[9]

In *Commonwealth v. Penn Valley Resorts, Inc.*, the resort and owner were convicted of involuntary manslaughter. The resort was fined $10,000. A Pennsylvania statute, Section 307(a)(2), provides that a corporation may be convicted of an offense "authorized, requested, commanded, performed or recklessly tolerated by the board of directors or by a high managerial agent acting in behalf of the corporation within the scope of employment." The court held that the resort owner qualified as a "high managerial agent" under the statute and that the law did not limit the vicarious responsibility of corporations to strict liability health, safety, and welfare offenses.[10]

In *Penn Valley*, Edwin Clancy, the president of the resort, permitted a group of underage students to engage in a drinking binge at the resort. William Frazer, a twenty-year-old, drank excessively for five or six hours. Clancy personally served alcohol to Frazer. He seized and later handed Frazer back the keys to Frazer's automobile and encouraged the drunk and hostile student to leave the resort. Frazer was subsequently killed when his car drove off the road and hit a bridge. He was found to possess a blood alcohol content of .23. The Supreme Court of Pennsylvania concluded that the resort, "through its managerial agent, committed involuntary manslaughter and reckless endangerment." How can a corporation act with gross disregard for the safety of customers? On the other hand, Clancy was president, and his acts legally obligated and financially benefited the corporation.

In 2012, the British bank HSBC agreed to pay the government more than $1.9 million in fines because of the bank's involvement in assisting drug cartels and terrorist groups in transferring money into the United States.

The U.S. Department of Justice (DOJ) in the past few years came under increasing criticism for reaching "deferred prosecution" agreements with corporations. In the agreement, the corporation agrees to institute reforms to prevent additional criminal conduct and to pay a fine, and in return, the DOJ agrees not to pursue a criminal prosecution against the corporation so long as the corporation satisfies the terms of the agreement. In 2015, Attorney General Loretta Lynch announced that the DOJ would focus on prosecuting and punishing individual corporate criminals rather than prosecuting large corporations. This change was based on the fact that crimes are committed by "flesh and blood" human beings.

CRIMINAL LAW AND PUBLIC POLICY

Should a corporation be held liable for murder? In 1980, the Ford Motor Company was prosecuted for reckless homicide stemming from the 1978 death of three Indiana teenagers. The three were burned to death when their 1972 Ford Pinto was hit from behind by a van. Prosecutors charged that Ford was aware that the Pinto's gasoline tanks were in danger of catching fire when impacted by a rear-end collision. Ford was alleged to have decided that fixing the problem or recalling the Pinto would deeply cut into profits and that it would be less expensive to pay any damage awards that might result from civil suits filed by consumers. By 1977, the Pinto no longer was able to meet tough federal safety standards, and in late 1978, Ford recalled 1.5 million 1971–1976 Pinto sedans. Unfortunately, this recall was not issued in time to save the lives of the three teenagers.

In 1999, a Florida jury found airline maintenance company SabreTech guilty of contributing to the 1996 crash of ValuJet Flight 593, an accident that resulted in the death of 110 passengers. The company allegedly had been responsible for placing prohibited hazardous materials on the ValuJet aircraft that exploded during flight. SabreTech was convicted on eight counts of mishandling hazardous materials and one count of failing to properly train employees.

In 2003, Motiva Enterprises pled "no contest," or **nolo contendere** (a guilty plea for purposes of a particular prosecution), to one felony count of criminally negligent homicide and six misdemeanor counts of assault in the third degree. This plea arose out of a July 2001 explosion and fire at a company factory that resulted in the death of one employee and injury to six others. Prosecutors alleged that Motiva, a joint venture between Saudi Aramco and Royal Dutch Shell, ignored warnings and continued to operate the plant in order to maximize profits. The company's conviction resulted in a fine of $11,500 on the homicide charge and $5,750 for each of the assault charges for a total of $46,000, the maximum then permitted under Delaware law.

In 2005, Far West Water & Sewer Inc. was convicted of the murder of two workers who died from exposure to toxic chemicals while working on an underground sewer tank. The company was fined $1.7 million and required to pay restitution to the families of the dead workers.

In 2015, General Motors reached a deferred prosecution agreement with the Department of Justice and agreed to pay a $900 million penalty. General Motors admitted to knowing about a defective ignition switch, which reportedly was responsible for the death of 124 individuals. General Motors stated that it knew as early as 2004 that many of its vehicles contained defective ignition switches and that it was aware by 2012 that the defective switches could cause airbags to fail.

(Continued)

(Continued)

Despite this awareness, General Motors did not recall 2.6 million affected vehicles for nearly two years.

These cases illustrate that a corporation may be held liable for **corporate murder** in those cases in which conduct is performed or approved by corporate managers or officials. Of course, individual managers and executives may also be held criminally responsible. The extension of criminal responsibility to corporations is based on an interpretation of the term *person* in homicide statutes to encompass both natural persons and corporate entities. Other states have homicide statutes that extend liability for murder to corporations. In Illinois, a corporation is criminally responsible for offenses "authorized, requested, commanded, or performed by the board of directors or by a high managerial agent acting within the scope of his employment." A corporation "is responsible whenever any of its high managerial agents possess the requisite mental state and is responsible for a criminal offense while acting within the scope of its employment."

A corporation clearly cannot be incarcerated and, instead, is punished by the imposition of a fine. It is reasoned that the threat of a fine will motivate corporate officials and individuals owning stock in the firm to ensure that the corporation follows the law. On the other hand, some would argue that criminal responsibility is properly limited to the individuals who commit the crimes. A fine on a business hurts only the workers and stockholders who depend on strong corporate profits and creates a poor business climate that leads corporations to move their factories to other countries.

Ask yourself whether it serves any purpose to hold the corporation liable or whether responsibility should be limited to corporate officials.

ENVIRONMENTAL CRIMES

At times, the drive for corporate profit may lead business executives to disregard their legal obligation to protect the natural environment. There are considerable costs involved in environmental safety and clean-up that can absorb a significant percentage of corporate revenues. The FBI notes that **environmental crimes** threaten the health and natural resources of the United States and that such crimes range from air and water pollution to the illegal transportation and disposal of hazardous waste.

Americans were exposed to the potential danger that illegal business practices pose to the environment when a public health emergency was declared at Love Canal in Niagara Falls, New York. In 1978, a local paper reported that in 1953, Hooker Electrochemical Company had buried more than twenty-one thousand tons of toxic waste on land that the company and city government knew was now the site of a housing development and school. Studies revealed that women living nearby experienced an excessive rate of miscarriages and that children suffered high rates of birth defects and disorders of the nervous system. The state and federal government ultimately evacuated the area at a cost of over $42 million, and the area would not be reclaimed for housing until 1990. A second well-known case in Woburn, Massachusetts, in 1979, involved the pollution of the water supply by industrial waste. The industrial firms responsible for the pollution ultimately agreed to a clean-up that cost more than $70 million.

In 1980, Pennsylvania authorities discovered that Hudson Oil Refining Corporation of New Jersey had been dumping waste down an old mine shaft. The waste accumulated and, in July 1979, began pouring out of the mine tunnel into the Susquehanna River. Millions of gallons of toxic waste linked to cancer and birth defects formed an oil slick that threatened the water supply of Danville, Pennsylvania. The company was fined $750,000, and the president of Hudson Oil, the first corporate official imprisoned for illegal environmental dumping in U.S. history, was sentenced to one year in prison. In the mid-1980s, Pennsylvania convicted a corporate executive of illegally dumping ten thousand drums of waste in a Scranton, Pennsylvania, landfill.

In 1989, Rockwell International, a company that had managed the Rocky Flats nuclear weapons plant since 1975, pled guilty to ten federal counts and paid $18.5 million in fines stemming from its mismanagement of the 6,500-acre site fifteen miles northwest of Denver, Colorado. The plant was described as being littered with over 12.9 metric tons of dangerous plutonium, asbestos, lead, and other toxic chemicals.

On March 24, 1989, the oil tanker *Exxon Valdez* ran aground in Alaska, spilling eleven million gallons of oil into Prince William Sound and polluting roughly 1,300 miles of Alaskan shoreline.

Exxon agreed to pay a $150 million criminal fine. In 2008, the U.S. Supreme Court reduced the civil monetary judgment imposed on Exxon by a jury. The Court did affirm the jury's judgment that Exxon was responsible for the actions of the ship's captain, finding that the jury could have reasonably concluded that Exxon "knowingly allowed a relapsed alcoholic repeatedly to pilot a vessel filled with millions of gallons of oil" and that "it was only a matter of time before a crash or spill . . . occurred."

Today, the increased concern with environmental crimes has led the federal and various state governments to establish special prosecution units. The federal government now highlights the seriousness of these offenses through an annual National Environmental Crime Prevention and Education Week. The national dedication to combating environmental crime is illustrated by a recent federal case in which DOJ prosecutors obtained the conviction of two individuals for violating the Clean Air Act and the Toxic Substances Control Act. This resulted in the longest federal jail sentences for environmental crimes in history. Alexander Salvagno received twenty-five years in prison and was ordered to forfeit more than $2 million in illegal proceeds and to provide more than $23 million in restitution to the victims. His father, Raul Salvagno, was sentenced to nineteen years in prison and was required to forfeit close to $2 million in illegal proceeds and to pay more than $22 million in restitution. The two falsely represented to clients that they had completely removed dangerous toxic asbestos from homes and schools and directed their young workers to enter into asbestos "hot zones" without adequate protection, exposing more than five hundred of their employees to the risk of cancer.

In 2012, BP agreed to plead guilty to fourteen criminal counts and to pay $4.5 billion in fines stemming from the explosion of the Deepwater Horizon oil rig, which resulted in the death of eleven workers and created a giant oil spill in the Gulf of Mexico. Two BP supervisors were indicted for manslaughter, and a BP official was indicted for obstructing a congressional investigation.

In 2016, criminal charges were filed against two state officials and a city employee involved in the contamination of the drinking water supply in Flint, Michigan, with lead.

The FBI reports that at any given time, there are roughly 450 environmental criminal cases pending, roughly half of which involve violations of the Clean Water Act. Roughly 25 percent of white-collar crime prosecutions between 2001 and 2012 involved environmental crimes. The FBI's investigative priorities are protecting workers against hazardous wastes and pollutants, preventing large-scale environmental damage that threatens entire communities, pursuing organized crime interests that illegally dump solid waste, and monitoring businesses with a history of damaging the environment. The FBI notes that a single instance of dumping can poison a river and cost the public millions of dollars in cleanup costs. In Tampa, Florida, Durex Industries repeatedly disregarded warnings to safely dispose of hazardous materials used in the manufacture of aluminum cans. In 1993, two nine-year-old boys playing in a Dumpster died when they were overcome by fumes from materials that Durex had illegally discarded. The company was ordered to pay a $1.5 million fine, and several Durex officials were criminally convicted.

Most prosecutions for environmental crimes are undertaken by the federal government. Criminal provisions and penalties are typically incorporated into civil statutes regulating the environment. Investigations in this area, for the most part, are carried out by the Environmental Protection Agency (EPA), which refers matters to the DOJ for criminal prosecution. The central environmental laws include the following:

- *Refuse Act—Section 13 of the Rivers and Harbors Appropriation Act (1899).* Imposes criminal penalties for improper discharge of refuse (foreign substances and pollutants) into navigable or tributary waters of the United States.
- *Clean Water Act (1972).* Imposes criminal penalties for the discharge of certain pollutants beyond an authorized limit into navigable waterways and a prohibition on unauthorized dredging, the filling of wetlands, and the failure to clean up oil and other hazardous substances.
- *Resource Conservation and Recovery Act (RCRA, 1976).* Punishes knowingly storing, making use of, or disposing of hazardous wastes without a permit. Severe penalties are imposed for placing individuals in danger.
- *Comprehensive Environmental Response, Compensation, and Liability Act (CERCLA, 1980, revised 1986).* Regulates and finances the clean-up of hazardous waste sites. Criminal penalties are imposed for failing to report the "release" of hazardous wastes to the government.

- *Clean Air Act (1973, amended in 1990).* Establishes air-quality standards and regulates sources of air pollution. Criminal penalties are imposed for the knowing emission of hazardous pollutants and for violation of emission standards. Enforcement is delegated to state environmental agencies.
- *Safe Drinking Water Act (1974).* Prohibits contamination of the public water system.
- *Toxic Substances Control Act (1976).* Imposes criminal penalties for the failure to follow standards for use of toxic chemicals in manufacturing and industry.
- *Federal Insecticide, Fungicide, and Rodenticide Act (FIFRA, 1996).* Imposes criminal penalties for the failure to follow standards for the manufacture, registration, transportation, and sale of toxic pesticides.

The *mens rea* for most of these statutes is knowingly committing the prohibited act. A defendant is not required to have knowledge that the act is contrary to a federal statute or that the act poses a health hazard.[11]

OCCUPATIONAL SAFETY AND HEALTH

In 1970, Congress responded to the increasingly high number of job-related deaths and injuries by passing the **Occupational Safety and Health Act (OSHA)** and establishing an agency within the Department of Labor, the Occupational Safety and Health Administration, also known as OSHA, to enforce the act. The act declared that workplace injuries and deaths were resulting in lost production and wages and in preventable medical expenses and disability compensation payments. The act also stated that every working person should be guaranteed safe and healthful working conditions.[12]

OSHA primarily relies on the civil process and financial penalties to ensure compliance. A criminal misdemeanor carrying a fine of not more than $10,000 or a prison sentence of up to six months, or both, is provided in the case of a willful violation of the law that results in the death of an employee. A second conviction carries a fine of not more than $20,000 or a prison sentence of up to a year, or both. False statements in any document submitted or required to be maintained under the act may also result in a fine of not more than $10,000 or imprisonment for not more than six months, or both.[13]

OSHA refers cases of intentional, knowing, or reckless violations that result in death for prosecution by state authorities and, in recent years, by the Justice Department. Data compiled by OSHA found that 4,405 workers died on the job in 2013. The most dangerous industry sectors in 2013 were farming, fishing, forestry, and transportation. The overall fatality rate for all industries in 2014 was 3.2 workers per 100,000. Between 2007 and 2010, OSHA referred forty-nine cases for criminal prosecution and has increased criminal referrals in recent years.

One comprehensive study examined data between 1982 and 2002 and found that corporate executives generally have not been criminally prosecuted either by the federal government or by the five states with their own forms of OSHA. The study found that OSHA and state agencies initiated 1,798 workplace death investigations and sent a total of 196 cases to federal or state authorities for prosecution. This, in turn, led to 104 prosecutions, eighty-one convictions, and sixteen jail sentences totaling thirty years.[14]

In 1992, the owner of a poultry plant in North Carolina pled guilty to twenty-five counts of involuntary manslaughter and was sentenced to twenty years in prison. The plant was not equipped with either a fire alarm or a sprinkler system, which resulted in the death of twenty-five employees and injury to thirty-six workers. One of the most important worker safety cases involved Film Recovery Systems, an Illinois firm that extracted silver from used X-ray plates. Stefan Golab died after ingesting poisonous cyanide fumes while working at a plant operated by Film Recovery and its sister corporation, Metallic Marketing. Golab reportedly trembled and foamed at the mouth before losing consciousness. The air inside the plant was found to be foul, breathing was difficult and painful, and the ventilation was inadequate. Workers experienced dizziness, nausea, headaches, and vomiting. The plant workers were never informed that they were working with cyanide or of the danger of breathing cyanide gas. OSHA subsequently cited the firm for seventeen separate safety violations. Workers were provided with neither safety instructions nor protective clothing. Homicide convictions against executives and the firm were reversed on appeal based on a technicality. The case nonetheless established the principle that individuals as well as corporations would be held criminally liable for disregarding worker safety.[15] In another important case, *People v. Pymm*, OSHA fined Pymm Thermometer plant in New York for failing to protect workers against mercury poisoning.[16]

Several senior executives of Massey Energy Company pled guilty to various charges resulting from the 2010 explosion at the Upper Big Branch Mine in West Virginia that killed twenty-nine miners. Massey Energy paid $209 million in restitution and in civil and criminal fines as a result of the company's misconduct in causing the worst U.S. mine disaster in the past forty years. In another recent case, the former owner of Peanut Corporation of America, Stewart Parnell, was sentenced to twenty-eight years in prison for knowingly shipping salmonella-tainted peanut butter, which was linked to nine deaths and 714 illnesses in 2009.

SECURITIES FRAUD

Stock market fraud emerged as a subject of intense public interest when it was announced, in June 2002, that domestic diva Martha Stewart was the subject of a criminal investigation for lying to investigators about the sale of stock.

On December 27, 2001, Stewart sold 3,928 shares of stock in the biotech company ImClone, one day before the Food and Drug Administration (FDA) announced that it would not approve the company's new cancer drug, Erbitux. Stewart made roughly $228,000 by selling the stock. Following the FDA announcement, ImClone's stock rapidly fell in value, and had Stewart waited to sell, she would have lost an estimated $45,000. It later was revealed that Stewart lied to federal authorities when she denied having been informed by her stockbroker, Peter Bacanovic, and his assistant, Douglas Faneuil, that the head of ImClone, Sam Waksal, was selling his family's shares at a profit of $7.3 million after learning of the test results.

Stewart and Bacanovic were each sentenced to five months in prison and five months of home detention as a result of their convictions for lying to investigators. Waksal was sentenced to seven years and three months in prison and was ordered to pay more than $4 million in fines and taxes stemming from a variety of criminal offenses, including insider trading. Faneuil, in return for cooperating with authorities, was fined $2,000. Following Stewart's release from prison, she was confined to home detention on her $16 million estate while being permitted to receive her $900,000 salary and leave her home for up to forty-eight hours a week to work or run errands. Stewart reportedly devoted herself to running her company, Martha Stewart Living Omnimedia Inc.; writing a magazine column; and preparing for two television shows.

Critics contended that Stewart had been targeted because she was a woman and that the government had wasted valuable resources prosecuting her for the minor offense of lying to authorities about the fact that she had relied on inside information concerning the test results on ImClone's cancer drug. Why does the law punish individuals for buying or selling stocks based on information that is not available to the public at large?

Insider Trading

The stock market, rather than banks, is increasingly where Americans deposit and look to grow their savings. The average individual has twice as much money in the stock market as in banks. As a result, the federal government has become increasingly concerned with ensuring that the stock market functions in a fair fashion and has aggressively brought criminal charges against individuals for stock market fraud.

A corporation that wants to raise money to build new plants, hire workers, or manufacture innovative products typically sells stocks to the public. Individuals purchase stock in hopes that as corporate profits rise, the stock will increase in value, and they eventually will be able to sell it at a substantial profit. This investment in stocks not only is an important source of money for businesses but also provides individuals with the opportunity to invest their money and to save for a house or retirement. Corporate executives and corporate boards of directors possess a **fiduciary relationship** (a high duty of care) to safeguard and to protect the investments of stockholders.

The federal Securities and Exchange Commission (SEC) is charged with ensuring that corporate officials comply with the requirements of the Securities Exchange Act of 1934 in the offering and selling of stocks. The act, for instance, requires corporations to provide accurate information on their economic performance in order to enable the public to make informed investment decisions. The SEC typically seeks civil law financial penalties against corporations that violate the law and refers allegations of fraud to the DOJ for prosecution. In 2002, Congress passed the **Sarbanes-Oxley Act**. This is a corporate criminal fraud statute that requires the heads of corporations to certify that their firms' financial reports are accurate. A violation of this act is punishable by up to twenty years in prison and a maximum fine of $5 million.[17]

In the past decade, the DOJ has focused its white-collar crime investigations on **insider trading** in violation of Section 10(b) and Rule 10b-5 of the 1934 act. The enforcement of these provisions is intended to ensure that the stock market functions in a fair and open fashion. Insider trading entails the purchase or sale of securities based on information that is not available to the public at large. The Insider Trading and Securities Fraud Enforcement Act establishes a maximum sentence of ten years and a fine as high as $1 million for individuals convicted of insider trading. A corporation found to engage in insider trading may be liable for a fine as high as $2.5 million.

Let us return to the ImClone example. Imagine that you are an executive at ImClone and are informed that the company has invented a cure for cancer that has been approved by the federal government. You know that once the information is made public, everyone will be looking to buy ImClone stock and that this will mean that the price of the stock will increase. You tell your relatives the good news and ask them to buy the stock in their names before the announcement and then to sell the stock and to divide the profits with you. When the information is announced, you and your grateful family find that you have made a substantial profit. You believe that this is a just reward for your dedication to the company. The government unfortunately indicts you (the tipper) and your relatives (the tippees) for insider trading. Why is this illegal? Because most people would not put their money in the stock market if a small number of people exploited information that was not available to the public at large to make a profit. This would reduce the money available to businesses and would harm the economy.

Several business law textbooks illustrate insider trading by *Diamond v. Oreamuno*. In this case, several executives of Management Assistance Inc., a computer firm, sold 56,500 shares of company stock for $28 a share at a time when they were aware that the firm's profits were rapidly falling. Then, they publicly announced the company's poor economic performance, and the stock declined to $11 a share. The defendants, by selling the stock prior to their announcement, made $800,000 more than they would have earned had they waited to sell the stock. The New York court ruled that "there can be no justification for permitting officers and directors . . . to retain . . . profits which . . . they derived solely from exploiting information gained by virtue of their inside position as corporate officials."[18]

There are two theories of insider trading, both of which prohibit the use of information that is not available to the public to buy or sell a stock. Both theories impose criminal liability on **tippers** (individuals who transmit information) and **tippees** (individuals who receive the information). The **disclose or abstain doctrine** states that corporate officials must publicly reveal information to the public relating to the economic condition of a corporation before they buy or sell the company's stock. The **misappropriation doctrine** expands the law beyond individuals who work for a corporation and criminally punishes all individuals who take and use inside corporate information that is in the possession of their employer. An example is the U.S. Supreme Court case of *United States v. O'Hagan*, in which a lawyer was convicted of using information that his law firm obtained from a corporate client to make a profit of $4.3 million.[19]

A conviction for insider trading requires that an individual who is a corporate official or stockholder or who has access to material, nonpublic information use this information intentionally and deliberately to buy or sell securities for his or her own benefit. Material information is information that is likely to affect the price of a stock, such as government approval for a drug company to produce a new anticancer drug.

Between 2009 and 2012, the SEC filed 168 insider trading cases, more than in any three-year period in the agency's history. These cases involved roughly four hundred individuals and organizations whose unlawful activities involved roughly $600 million. In 2014, the SEC filed 807 enforcement actions involving a wide variety of violations of the law, and in 2015, the SEC filed 755 enforcement actions. Roughly 8–10 percent of these cases involve insider trading. Insider trading is difficult to establish. Investigators must look at who purchases or sells stock and determine whether these individuals relied on inside information in purchasing the securities. The prosecution also must prove a fraudulent intent. In other words, the government must establish that a defendant intentionally purchased or sold the stock knowing that the transaction was in violation of the law. What type of facts would you use to establish a case of insider trading by a corporate executive?

Insider trading is one example of securities fraud. **Pump and dump** involves spreading false information about a company to drive up the stock price. The individuals behind the scheme then sell the shares that they inexpensively purchased for a significant profit. In 2002, seventeen-year-old Cole Bartiromo was sentenced to thirty-three months in prison for using the Internet to spread false information about various companies in which he had invested. As a result of his scheme, Bartiromo made a $91,000 profit when he sold the securities.

Securities violations also may be prosecuted under financial fraud statutes rather than statutes regulating the sale and purchase of securities.

Keep in mind that federal courts recently have disagreed over whether the person receiving the tip in an insider trading case must be aware that the tipper has received a substantial benefit (e.g., a monetary bribe) for transmitting the tip. Courts have reasoned that otherwise an individual would be criminally liable for information provided to a family member or friend. On the other hand, this type of inside information gives tippees knowledge that is not available to the general public.

Read *United States v. Carpenter* on the study site: study.sagepub.com/lippmanness2e.

CRIMINAL LAW IN THE NEWS

In December 2008, prominent New York investment broker Bernard L. Madoff called his sons into his office and announced that his business was a "big lie" and "basically a giant Ponzi scheme." Madoff sadly noted that there was "nothing left" and that he expected to "go to jail." He was arrested on December 11 and confessed to the FBI that he had looted investors of as much as $50 billion, making this the largest fraud in U.S. history. Madoff's Ponzi scheme was relatively unsophisticated. He would use the money provided by new investors to pay returns to old investors. This enabled Madoff to pay investors a consistent return of 10–15 percent a year. He was so successful that he could afford to turn investors away who lacked the "right background" and required most people who wanted to invest their money to provide at least $1 million. Other Wall Street brokers made millions of dollars by turning all their clients' funds over to Madoff for investment. This "house of cards" collapsed when the U.S. economy took a downturn and a large number of Madoff's investors asked for the return of their money and found that their money had disappeared.

A portion of the money undoubtedly was used to support Madoff's quiet but luxurious lifestyle. This included memberships in most of the leading golf clubs in New York and Florida; partial ownership of two corporate jets and of two boats; and ownership of multiple homes, including one in France. Despite his affluent lifestyle, Madoff was respected for his public service and his charitable foundation. He gave generously to worthy organizations in New York City including Carnegie Hall, the Public Theater, the Special Olympics, and the Gift of Life Bone Marrow Foundation.

Madoff defrauded his friends, his own sister, and the institutions that trusted him. He demonstrated that even the most educated and sophisticated members of U.S. society can be tricked by a skilled con man. Madoff's clients included the family that owned the New York Mets baseball team and the former owner of the Philadelphia Eagles football team. His victims included Yeshiva University, the institution that had embraced and honored him. New York Law School and Tufts University also suffered a loss of portions of their endowments. A number of charitable organizations lost most of their resources, including the foundation of Elie Wiesel, the famed Holocaust survivor and commentator. The collapse of charitable foundations meant that many nonprofit foundations that had received donations now found that they had a shortage of money and confronted the prospect of closing their doors.

There is no obvious explanation for Madoff's corrupt conduct. He was from an extremely modest background, had lifted himself out of poverty through sheer intelligence, and had saved the money he earned as a young man from menial jobs and proceeded to build one of the most successful firms on Wall Street. Madoff pioneered the use of computers for investing, was a past president of a national organization of financial analysts, and served on the group's board of governors. It was Madoff's prominence and his powerful clientele that may have intimidated the Securities and

(Continued)

(Continued)

Exchange Commission and deterred the organization from investigating the performance of his investments, which most experts agreed was "too good to be true." Some observers have commented that investors were willing to tolerate Madoff's suspected illegalities as long as they were benefiting financially.

Judge Denny Chin later explained that he had considered a sentence that would have allowed Madoff to be released when he reached ninety years of age, but that he had wanted to send the "strongest possible message" to other individuals contemplating white-collar crimes that they would be harshly punished. He also wanted the victims to know that the justice system had taken their financial loss and suffering seriously and noted that he was particularly affected by the story of a widow whose life savings had been stolen by Madoff. Judge Chin noted that an offender should be punished in proportion to his blameworthiness and that Madoff's crimes were "extraordinarily evil" and his sentence should fit his "moral culpability."

Madoff currently is serving a 150-year sentence and is in minimum security in Butner, North Carolina. In an interview, Madoff accused Judge Chin of making him into the "human piñata of Wall Street" and caustically observed that he was surprised that the judge did not "suggest stoning in the public square." He said that "serial killers get a death sentence, but that's virtually what he gave me." Was Madoff's 150-year sentence disproportionate?

MAIL AND WIRE FRAUD

The U.S. government has relied on the mail and wire fraud statutes to prosecute a variety of corrupt schemes that are not specifically prohibited under federal laws. **Fraud** may be broadly defined as an intentional and knowing misrepresentation of a material (important) fact intended to induce another person to hand over money or property. Mail and wire fraud prosecutions range from fraudulent misrepresentations of the value of land and the quality of jewelry to offering and selling nonexistent merchandise. The common element in these schemes that permits the assertion of federal jurisdiction is the use of the U.S. mail or wires across state lines (phone, radio, television). The federal **mail fraud** statute, 18 U.S.C. § 1341, reads as follows:

> Whoever, having devised or intending to devise any scheme or artifice to defraud, or for obtaining money or property by means of false or fraudulent pretenses . . . for the purpose of executing such scheme . . . places in any . . . authorized depository for mail . . . any matter or thing whatever to be sent or delivered by the Postal Service, . . . or takes or receives therefrom, any such matter or thing, . . . shall be fined under this title or imprisoned not more than 20 years, or both. . . .

A conviction for mail fraud requires the prosecution to demonstrate each of the following:

- *Scheme.* Knowing participation in a scheme or artifice to defraud.
- *Falsehood.* Intentional false statement or promise.
- *Money or Property.* Intent to obtain money or property.
- *Reliance.* Statement or promise of a kind that would reasonably influence a person to part with money or property.
- *Mail.* Using the mail for the purpose of executing the scheme. This includes private mail delivery services. The mail is required to be only incidental to an essential part of the criminal design. The mail also may be used to "lull" a victim who has been defrauded into a "false sense of security."

The requirements of mail and **wire fraud** are similar, with the exception that the wire communication must cross interstate or foreign boundaries.[20] A conspiracy to commit mail or wire fraud is also prohibited under federal statutes. Under the conspiracy statute, a prosecutor is required to demonstrate that the use of the mail or wires would naturally occur in the course of the scheme or that the use of the mail or wires was reasonably foreseeable, although not actually intended.[21]

In *United States v. Duff*, Duff and other co-conspirators were convicted of mail fraud based on falsely representing that various firms were minority- or women-owned businesses. Chicago reserved certain contracts for firms that were at least 51 percent minority or female owned. A federal district court held that the City of Chicago had been defrauded of $100 million in contracts that had been set aside for "minority firms." The court held that the mail was "incidental to an essential part of the scheme" because the fraud depended on the City of Chicago mailing payments to the conspirators.[22]

In 2010, Congress established the Consumer Financial Protection Bureau (CFPB) to protect consumers. The CFPB states that it is charged with the following functions:

Read *United States v. Duff* on the study site: study .sagepub.com/ lippmaness2e.

* Write rules, supervise companies, and enforce federal consumer financial protection laws
* Restrict unfair, deceptive, or abusive acts or practices
* Take consumer complaints
* Promote financial education
* Research consumer behavior
* Monitor financial markets for new risks to consumers
* Enforce laws that outlaw discrimination and other unfair treatment in consumer finance

---

You Decide

10.1 Norby Walters is a sports agent who signed contracts with fifty-eight college football players, naming him as their representative in negotiating contracts with pro football teams. He offered cars and money to players who would sign with him. Walters was to receive a percentage of the players' income if they were drafted and signed with a team. The National Collegiate Athletic Association (NCAA) rules stipulate that a student who signs a contract with an agent is a professional, ineligible to play on collegiate teams. Walters, to avoid jeopardizing his clients' careers, dated the player contracts following the end of the player's eligibility and locked the contracts in a safe. He promised to lie to the universities about the date that the contracts had been signed in response to any inquiries. Walters consulted with lawyers who concluded that his plan would violate the NCAA rules, although it was not in violation of any laws.

Only two of the fifty-eight players signed by Walters fulfilled their understanding with Walters and allowed him to negotiate with the teams that drafted them; the other players kept the cars and the money and signed with other agents. Walters threatened several players with physical retaliation unless they repaid Walters's firm for the money and cars that they had been provided during their years in college. A seventy-five-page indictment against Walters included a mail fraud count. The fraud involved causing the universities to fund the scholarship of athletes who, unknown to the schools, had become ineligible as a result of having signed contracts with Walters to represent them. The fraud made use of the mail because each university required athletes to verify their eligibility to play and then sent copies of the eligibility forms by mail to the intercollegiate athletic conference with which the school was affiliated (e.g., the Big Ten).

Would you convict Walters of mail fraud? See *United States v. Walters*, 997 F.2d 1219 (7th Cir. 1993).

You can find the answer at study.sagepub.com/lippmaness2e

THE TRAVEL ACT

The **Travel Act** of 1961 was intended to assist state and local governments to combat organized crime. The Travel Act, 18 U.S.C. § 1952, authorizes the federal government to prosecute what are ordinarily considered the state criminal offenses of gambling, the illegal shipment and sale of alcohol and controlled substances, extortion, bribery, arson, prostitution, and money laundering. Federal jurisdiction is based on the fact that the crimes have been committed following travel in interstate or foreign commerce or through the use of the U.S. mail or any other facility in interstate or foreign commerce.

In *United States v. Jenkins*, the Second Circuit Court of Appeals stated that a conviction under the Travel Act requires (1) travel or the use of the mail or some other facility (e.g., wires) in interstate or foreign commerce (2) with the intent to commit a criminal offense listed in the Travel Act or a crime of violence or to distribute the proceeds of an illegal activity and (3) the commission of a crime or attempt to commit a crime. Performing or attempting to perform an act of violence is punishable by not more than twenty years in prison or a fine or both. Other offenses are punishable by not more than five years in prison or a fine or both.[23]

In *United States v. Goodman*, Goodman promoted records by contacting and persuading radio stations to place records from the companies he represented on their "playlists." Goodman, however, went beyond mere persuasion and was found to have illegally paid as much as $182,615 a year in cash through the mail to program directors and disc jockeys in return for placing records on their playlists. Goodman was convicted under the Travel Act of the use of interstate mail to commit bribery. The federal appellate court rejected the argument that the payments occurred after the records were added to the playlists and that the payments therefore did not constitute a bribe to induce station managers and disc jockeys to play specific records. The court noted that the receipt of the mailed money was intended both to "reward a past transgression and to influence or promote a future one."[24]

Goodman was also convicted under 47 U.S.C. § 508, the Payola Act, which prohibits the payment of money to radio station employees for the inclusion of material as part of a program unless the payment is disclosed to the recipient's employer. The federal appellate court ruled that the offense is complete upon the payment of money and that the records need not actually be played.

HEALTH CARE FRAUD

Roughly one-fifth of the federal budget is devoted to health care, most of which involves reimbursing doctors and health care workers for services provided under various federal and state programs to the elderly, children, the physically and mentally challenged, and economically disadvantaged individuals. The difficulty of administering programs of this size and complexity creates an opportunity for doctors and other health care providers to submit fraudulent claims for the reimbursement of services that, in fact, were never provided or to seek payment for unnecessary procedures. In 1996, Congress acted to prevent this type of fraud when it adopted a statute on **health care fraud** that punishes health care providers or consumers who knowingly and willfully execute or attempt to execute a scheme involving false statements intended to obtain, keep, or qualify for benefits or to increase benefits under a federal health care program. Health care fraud is punishable by a fine and imprisonment of up to ten years or both. Fraudulent acts that cause serious injury are punishable by a term of imprisonment of up to twenty years, while fraudulent acts that result in death are punishable by up to life in prison.[25]

It is estimated that health care fraud costs the taxpayers $68 billion annually. In *United States v. Baldwin*, the defendants were convicted of submitting a false claim of $275,000 for four dental chairs.[26] The health care fraud statute was interpreted to cover individuals outside the medical profession in *United States v. Lucien*. The defendants paid individuals to cause collisions with other vehicles and to claim that they suffered serious injuries. The defendants referred these alleged "victims" to various medical clinics in return for a fee. The clinics sought reimbursement from New York for medical procedures that, in fact, had not been provided. The "victims" then sued the drivers of the other vehicles in hopes of obtaining a settlement from the drivers' insurance companies.[27]

The type of extreme and grossly fraudulent abuse of the health care system that can take place is illustrated by *United States v. Miles*. Affiliated Professional Home Health (APRO) was formed in 1993 in Houston, Texas, by Carrie Hamilton, Alice Miles, and Richard Miles. Richard Miles, a vice principal of a Houston-area high school, was married to Alice Miles, a registered nurse, and is the brother of both Hamilton, also a registered nurse, and Harold Miles, an APRO employee. When APRO obtained certification from the Texas Department of Health and a Medicare provider number, the company began to treat Medicare-covered patients and to obtain reimbursement for in-home visits to such patients.[28]

The government presented evidence that the defendants, through APRO, submitted cost reports that grossly inflated expenses for items ranging from mileage to employee salaries. For example, Hamilton was reimbursed for a whopping 282,000 travel miles from 1994 to 1996, a period when she frequently visited Louisiana casinos. Alice Miles, another avid gambler, was reimbursed for 150,000 travel miles over three years, while her husband, whose primary job kept him occupied for most of the workday, was reimbursed for 180,000 miles over four years.

APRO also obtained reimbursement for costs that included personal expenses, such as renovations to the Hamiltons' home, renovations to the Mileses' parents' residence, and the purchase of various home appliances. The defendants billed expenses to Medicare for two or three times the actual cost incurred. At times, they engaged in more intricate schemes involving the splitting of large reimbursement checks into smaller cashier's checks that were then deposited into the APRO principals' bank accounts or used for personal expenses. On one occasion, Hamilton split an APRO check into cash and three cashier's checks at one bank. She deposited two of the cashier's checks into her own account at another bank and used a portion of the funds to obtain a fourth cashier's check to purchase a new Ford Mustang convertible. The third cashier's check from the original bank was cashed at the Star Casino.

Medicaid provides federal assistance for medical care for the elderly and for the poor, and Medicaid fraud is covered by the Medicaid False Claims Statute, 42 U.S.C. § 1320a-7b(a). In *United States v. Franklin-El*, the defendants headed a clinic for individuals addicted to alcohol and narcotics. They were convicted of health care fraud based on their filing of roughly 1,331 false claims for federal Medicaid reimbursements and submitting false claims for treating individuals who were not enrolled at the clinic, some of whom were young children. The scheme netted the defendants over $1.2 million. In May 2012, more than one hundred individuals were arrested in seven cities for a conspiracy involving more than $450 million in fraudulent medical billings.[29]

Another relevant statute is the Medicaid Anti-Kickback Statute, 42 U.S.C. § 1320a-7b(b), which prohibits an individual from promising or receiving payments for directing a patient to a health care provider.

ANTITRUST VIOLATIONS

The **Sherman Antitrust Act of 1890** is intended to ensure a free and competitive business marketplace. The Sherman Act, according to former Supreme Court justice Hugo Black, is designed to be a "comprehensive charter of economic liberty aimed at preserving free unfettered competition as the rule of trade."[30] Imagine if every bar and restaurant in a college town engaged in *price fixing* and agreed to sell beer at an inflated price rather than compete with one another for the business of students. The theory behind the Sherman Act, as explained by Justice Black, is that economic competition results in low prices and high quality and promotes self-reliance and democratic values. Can you explain why free competition leads to these benefits?

The criminal provisions of the Sherman Act state that any person "who shall make any contract or engage in any combination or conspiracy" to interfere with interstate commerce is guilty of a felony. A corporation shall be punished with a fine not exceeding $10 million and an individual by a fine of $1 million or by imprisonment not exceeding ten years, or both.[31]

A conviction requires proof that two or more persons or organizations

- knowingly entered into a contract or formed a combination or conspiracy, and that
- the combination or conspiracy produced or potentially produced an unreasonable restraint of interstate trade.

In *United States v. Azzarelli Construction Co. and John F. Azzarelli*, the defendant was the owner of a construction company who agreed with the owners of other construction businesses to engage in *bid-rigging* and fix the process of bidding on state contracts to ensure that each firm would receive state contracts. One firm would be designated to receive a contract and would submit an unreasonably high bid on the job. The competing firms would submit grossly inflated bids, ensuring that the first firm would receive the contract. The firms that intentionally lost the job then would be compensated by receiving a kickback from the successful contractor. The court noted that this fraudulent practice interfered with interstate commerce by raising the cost of highway construction and resulted in less money being available to upgrade the highway system.[32]

Antitrust violations directly affect consumers. A price-fixing conspiracy by two major soft-drink bottling companies in the Baltimore–Washington and Richmond, Virginia, areas was estimated by a federal district court judge to have resulted in consumers paying between $10 and $12 million more to purchase soft drinks than they would have paid had the companies competed against one another rather than artificially fixing the price.[33]

IDENTITY THEFT

William Shakespeare wrote that stealing "my good name" enriches the thief, while making the victim "poor indeed." Today **identity theft**, the theft of your name and identifying information, can lead to economic damage and has been called the crime of the twenty-first century. The stealing of your Social Security number, bank account information, credit card number, and other identifying data enables thieves to borrow money and make expensive purchases in your name. The end result is the ruining of your credit and the creation of financial hardship, forcing you to spend months restoring your "good name."

In the past, thieves threatened to "take and carry away" tangible property. Today, the theft of intangible property, such as a credit card or Social Security number, may lead to even greater harm because the thief can employ the number to make repeated purchases, to borrow money, or to establish phone service or cable access. You might not even be aware that the information was taken until you apply for credit and are rejected.

Thieves collect data by examining receipts you abandon in the trash, observing the numbers you enter at an ATM, intercepting mail from credit card companies, or enticing you to surrender information to what appears to be a reputable e-mail inquiry. A lost or stolen wallet or burglary of a home or automobile can result in valuable numbers and documents falling into the hands of organized identity theft gangs. Information can also be obtained by breaking into a company database. Individuals falsely portraying themselves as legitimate business executives, for instance, gained access to ChoicePoint in 2005 and stole roughly 145,000 credit files. Shortly thereafter, computer hackers copied the files of thirty thousand individuals contained on the database of LexisNexis. Bank of America reported the disappearance of a computer tape containing the files of more than a million customers.

Even strict protections over your personal information may not be effective. A study by the Federal Trade Commission (FTC), a federal agency concerned with consumer protection, determined that roughly 15 percent of identity thefts are committed by a victim's family members, friends, neighbors, or coworkers. The perpetrators of identity theft often transfer the information to sophisticated gangs of identity thieves in return for drugs, cell phones, guns, and money.

The Congressional Research Service estimates that over one million Americans are victimized by identity theft each year and find themselves with unwarranted financial obligations or may even be charged with crimes as a result of another person assuming their identity.

In 1998, the U.S. Congress passed the Identity Theft and Assumption Deterrence Act. This legislation created the new offense of identity theft and prohibits the knowing transfer or use without lawful authority of the "means of identification of another person with the intent to commit, or to aid or abet, any unlawful activity" that constitutes a violation of federal law or a felony under state or local law. A "means of identification" includes an individual's name, date of birth, Social Security number, driver's license number, passport number, bank account or credit card number, fingerprints, voiceprint, or eye image. Note that merely obtaining another individual's personal documents can result in a year or more in prison. Sentences for violation of the Identity Theft Act can be as severe as fifteen years in prison and a significant fine in those instances in which the perpetrator obtains items valued at $1,000 or more over a one-year period. The perpetrators of identity theft typically are also in violation of statutes punishing credit card fraud, mail fraud, or wire fraud.

Table 10.1 lists the top ten states for identity theft complaints in 2014.

The Utah statute on identity theft punishes an individual who knowingly or intentionally obtains "personal identifying information of another person" and uses or attempts to use this information "with fraudulent intent, including to obtain, or attempt to obtain credit, goods, services . . . or medical information in the name of another person." Obtaining items valued at more than $1,000 is a felony under the Utah law.[34]

In *Flores-Figueroa v. United States*, Ignacio Flores-Figueroa, a Mexican citizen, in 2006 presented his employer with counterfeit Social Security and alien registration cards. These cards used his real name but used arbitrarily selected numbers that unknown to Flores-Figueroa belonged to another individual. The U.S. Supreme Court held that the federal identity theft statute requires that a defendant know that the "means of identification" he or she transfers, possesses, or uses belongs to "another person." Flores-Figueroa, as a result, could not be held liable for identity theft under federal law.[35]

State courts have overturned convictions on the grounds that the identification numbers did not belong to another person. The Kansas statute K.S.A. 2000 Supp. 21-4018 requires that a defendant "obtain, possess, transfer, use, or attempt to obtain the identification documents or personal identification numbers of 'another person.'" This would occur, for example, when a defendant "'took' another person's social security number and used that number when applying for a credit card or bank account." In *City of Liberal, Kansas, v. Vargas*, Juan Vargas purchased a Missouri identification and a Social Security card belonging to Guillermo Hernandez. He was acquitted because there was no evidence that Hernandez was a real person whose identity had been stolen.[36]

Table 10.1	Top Ten* States for Identity Theft Complaints in 2014 per 100,000 Population
State	Rate
Florida	186.3
Washington	154.8
Oregon	124.6
Missouri	118.7
Georgia	112.7
Michigan	104.3
California	100.5
Nevada	100.2
Arizona	96.0
Maryland	95.9
Texas	95.9
National Rate = 104.3	

Source: Kathleen O'Leary Morgan and Scott Morgan, eds. *State Rankings 2016: A Statistical View of America*. Thousand Oaks, CA: CQ Press, 2016, p. 56.

* Eleven are included due to the two-way tie of Maryland and Texas.

ACCESS DEVICE FRAUD

The spread of credit cards, debit cards, ATM cards, PINs, and other means of gaining access to money, goods, and services has led states to adopt statutes on **access device fraud**. The Pennsylvania statute, § 4106, prohibits the use of an access device to obtain or to attempt to obtain property or services, knowing that the device is "counterfeit, altered or incomplete," that the device was issued to another person who has not authorized the use, or that the device has been revoked or canceled. The statute also makes criminal the sale, transfer, or possession of "altered" or "counterfeit" access devices. An unlawful transaction valued at more than $500 is a felony.

MONEY LAUNDERING

Individuals involved in criminal fraud or drug or vice transactions confront the problem of accounting for their income. These individuals may want to live a high-profile lifestyle and buy a house or automobile that they cannot afford based on the income reported on their tax forms. An obvious gap between lifestyle and income may attract the attention of the IRS or law enforcement. How can individuals explain their ability to purchase a million-dollar house when they report an income of only $30,000 a year? Where did the cash come from that they used to buy the house? Bank regulations require that deposits of more than $10,000 be reported by the bank to the federal government. How can individuals explain to government authorities the source of the $50,000 that they deposit in a bank?

The solution is **money laundering**. This involves creating some false source of income that accounts for the money used to buy a house, purchase a car, or open a bank account. This typically involves schemes such as paying the owner of a business in cash to list a drug dealer as an employee of the individual's construction business. In other instances, individuals involved in criminal activity may claim that their income is derived from a lawful business such as a restaurant. The federal laundering statute, 18 U.S.C. §§ 1956 and 1957, is intended to combat the "washing" of money by declaring that it is criminal to use or transfer illegally obtained money or property.

This is punishable by a fine of up to $500,000 or a fine of up to twice the value of the property and imprisonment for up to twenty years.

Money laundering includes the following elements:

- the defendant knowingly engaged or attempted to engage in a monetary transaction;
- the defendant knew the transaction involved the "profits" (funds or property) from one or more of a long list of criminal activities listed in the statute;
- the transaction was intended to conceal or disguise the source of the money or property; or
- the transaction was intended to promote the carrying on of a specified unlawful activity.

In *United States v. Johnson*, the defendant generated millions of dollars from a fraudulent scheme involving Mexican currency. The Tenth Circuit Court of Appeals ruled that the use of these funds to purchase an expensive home and a Mercedes violated the money laundering statute in that these purchases furthered the defendant's continued illegal activities by providing him with a legitimacy that he used to impress, attract, and ultimately victimize additional investors.[37]

In *United States v. Jackson*, Reverend Joseph Davis was convicted of engaging in transactions intended "to conceal or disguise the . . . proceeds" of profits from an unlawful cocaine drug scheme (see opening vignette). He directed the manufacture and distribution of cocaine at two crack houses. He then deposited the profits in cash into various accounts, listed under the name of the 15th Street Baptist Church, in which the proceeds of legitimate activities also were deposited. Funds were used for church expenses as well as for Reverend Davis's rent; credit card charges; and purchases of automobiles, cellular phones, and beepers used to direct the sale of cocaine. Davis was sentenced to thirty years in prison.[38]

In 2012, HSBC agreed to pay federal and state governments $1.92 billion in fines for assisting Mexican drug cartels to launder money through the U.S. banking system. The individual banking officials responsible for money laundering were not held criminally liable.

CURRENCY VIOLATIONS

In the 1970s, the federal government enacted a series of laws to monitor individuals who conducted banking transactions involving large amounts of cash that potentially might be the proceeds of unlawful activity. These laws work in combination with money laundering statutes to detect criminal activity. Banks and "trades or businesses" are required to report to the IRS transactions involving cash of more than $10,000. It is a crime to "structure" transactions to evade the reporting requirements of these *currency transaction reports*.[39] For example, in *Ratzlaf v. United States*, the defendant attempted to pay a $100,000 gambling debt to a Las Vegas casino by a check. The casino informed Ratzlaf that it was required to report the payments of over $10,000 to the IRS. Ratzlaf responded by obtaining a series of $10,000 checks. Ratzlaf was found guilty of evading the $10,000 reporting requirement, although his conviction later was overturned because the judge failed to instruct the jury that they were required to find that Ratzlaf "knew that the structuring in which he engaged was unlawful."[40]

Congress later amended the law to provide that an individual may be held liable for a "structuring offense" who like Ratzlaf knowingly violates the reporting requirement regardless of whether he or she knows that this constitutes a crime. Financial institutions also are required to report "any suspicious transactions." These reports typically are filed when there is a transaction of $5,000 that a bank suspects involves money laundering or an effort to evade a reporting requirement or that is an unusually large amount of money for the customer involved in the transaction.

In 2016, former Speaker of the House of Representatives Dennis Hastert was sentenced to fifteen months in prison and a $250,000 fine along with two years of supervised release after pleading guilty to "illegal structuring." Hastert on a number of occasions withdrew less than $10,000 from the bank in order to evade the withdrawals being reported to the federal government. He admitted that his intent was to conceal payments to a young man whom he had molested while a wrestling coach.

TAX CRIME

We all are required to file a yearly tax form reporting our income to the IRS. The five primary types of tax crimes are listed below.

1. *Tax Evasion.* The willful underpayment of taxes may result in a fine of up to $100,000 for an individual and $500,000 for a corporation and/or imprisonment for five years. The failure to pay taxes owed may result from a failure to disclose income or overstating the amount of a tax deduction (e.g., for a charitable deduction) to which an individual is entitled.[41]

2. *Failure to Collect Taxes.* The willful failure of an employer to collect taxes or to pay taxes owed to the IRS is a criminal offense.[42]

3. *False Returns.* The willful misrepresentation of a material fact on a tax form constitutes "tax perjury." This typically involves a failing to report income or claiming a larger deduction than the individual is entitled to claim.[43]

4. *Failure to File a Return.* A willful failure to file a return or the filing of blank or incomplete return is a misdemeanor subject to a fine of $25,000 for an individual or $100,000 for a corporation and/or imprisonment for not more than one year.[44]

5. *Tax Preparer.* A tax preparer may be criminally liable for willfully aiding and assisting in the preparation of a false tax reform.[45]

Criminal liability under these statutes requires that an individual act "willfully." This requires that an individual knows of the law and intends to violate the law. In other words, the defendant must possess a "full knowledge" of the provision of the tax code and must voluntarily and intentionally violate the law. An individual who breaks the law who is unaware of the requirements of the law does not possess a willful criminal intent. An individual who knows the requirements of the law and who intentionally and deliberately violates the law because he or she disagrees with the requirements of the law possesses a willful criminal intent.[46]

COMPUTER CRIME

Computer crime or **cybercrime** is a crime committed through the use of a computer. Computer crime poses a challenge for criminal law. Larceny historically has protected tangible (material) property. Courts have experienced difficulty applying the traditional law of larceny to individuals who gain access to intangible property without authorization (nonmaterial property that you cannot hold in your hands). The primary property offenses committed in cyberspace include unauthorized computer access to programs and databases and unlawfully obtaining personal information through deceit and trickery. Can you take and carry away access to a computer program?

In *Lund v. Commonwealth*, the defendant, a graduate student in statistics at Virginia Polytechnic Institute, was charged with larceny and the fraudulent use of "computer operation and services" valued at $100 or more. The customary procedure at the university was for departments to receive computer dollar credits. These dollar credits were deducted from the departmental account as faculty and students made use of the university's central computer. This was a bookkeeping procedure, and no funds actually changed hands. Lund's adviser failed to arrange for his use of the university computer, and Lund proceeded to gain access to the university computer without authorization and spent as much as $26,384.16 in unauthorized computer time. The Virginia Supreme Court ruled that computer time and services could not be the subject of either false pretenses or larceny "because neither time nor services may be taken and carried away. . . . It [the Virginia statute] refers to a taking and carrying away of a certain concrete article of personal property."[47]

State legislatures and the federal government responded to *Lund* by passing statutes addressing computer theft and crime. These statutes punish various types of activity including unauthorized access to a computer or to a computer network or program; the modification, removal, or disabling of computer data, programs, or software; causing a computer to malfunction; copying computer data, programs, or software without authorization; and falsifying e-mail transmissions in connection with the sending of unsolicited bulk e-mail. The question remains whether law enforcement possesses the expertise and resources to track sophisticated cybercriminals.

State statutes on computer crimes, as noted above, address a number of areas:

- *Computer Fraud and Theft.* The use of a computer to obtain property or services by false pretenses, embezzlement, larceny, or extortion.
- *Computer Hacking.* The entry into a computer system without authorization with the intent temporarily or permanently to halt or to disable a computer, computer programs, or software; to erase or to remove computer data or a computer program; or to make an unauthorized copy of computer data or a computer program.
- *Computer Trespass.* The intentional entrance into a computer system without permission and with the intent to cause injury to an individual.
- *Spam.* Knowingly transmitting a commercial, unsolicited e-mail that contains false or misleading information on a subject line or uses another individual or organization's Internet address or domain name without permission.
- *Computer Tampering.* The insertion of a program into a computer knowing that the program contains information or commands that may cause damage to the computer or to any other computer accessed by the computer or that accesses the computer. This is directed against computer viruses, worms, and "rogue programs."
- *Computer Stalking.* The use of the Internet or other electronic communication devices to stalk an individual.

In 2013 in *People v. Puesan*, the defendant, a suspended Time Warner employee, installed a keystroke logger on three of Time Warner's computers and used the information he wrongfully obtained with the keystroke logger to gain access to a Time Warner program that stores confidential customer information. He subsequently was convicted of almost every offense defined in the New York State computer crime statute (Article 156) including computer trespass, computer tampering, unlawful duplication of computer-related material, and criminal possession of computer-related material.[48]

In 1984, Congress passed the Computer Fraud and Abuse Act, 18 U.S.C. § 1030, which has been amended on several occasions. The act is intended to provide a comprehensive statute on computer crime, which previously was prosecuted under more than forty different federal laws, most of which originally were drafted to combat conventional crime. The federal government's jurisdiction is based on the interest in protecting government computers and the computers of financial institutions regulated by the U.S. government, and on the interest in protecting against the use of computers to transmit information across state lines or to attack government computers. Several important provisions are listed below.

Passwords. The act prohibits "knowingly and with intent to defraud, trafficking in passwords to permit unauthorized access to a government computer, or to affect interstate or foreign commerce."[49]

Extortion. The act proclaims that it is unlawful to transmit in interstate commerce any threat to cause damage to a protected computer with the intent to extort something of value.[50]

Damage to Computer. It is a crime to "knowingly cause the transmission of a program, information code, or command" in interstate commerce intended to cause damage to a computer used by the U.S. government or by a financial institution.[51]

Theft of Information. The act prohibits intentionally accessing a computer without authorization and obtaining information from a financial institution, credit card company, or department of the U.S. government.[52]

The CAN-SPAM Act of 2003 is a federal antispam act that directs the FTC to formulate rules regulating commercial e-mails. Spam is defined as unsolicited e-mail messages sent to a large number of recipients. The act provides the following[53]:

Header. The header of the commercial e-mail may not contain materially false or materially misleading information.

Subject Line. The subject line may not contain deceptive information.

Identification. The e-mail is required to carry a "clear and conspicuous" identification that it is an advertisement or solicitation.

Opt Out. The e-mail must contain "clear and conspicuous" notice of the opportunity to opt out of receiving future e-mails from the sender.

Notice. An e-mail may not be sent after the sender received notice that the recipient no longer wishes to receive e-mail from the sender (i.e., has "opted out").

Postal Address. The e-mail contains the sender's physical postal address.

In 2006, the United States joined over forty other countries in ratifying the International Convention on Cybercrime. The treaty requires states to adopt a number of computer crimes already punished under U.S. laws and attempts to increase cooperation among countries in combating computer crime. This type of collaboration in attacking crime is necessary because of the ability of computer criminals in one country to commit crimes in other countries.

In 2011, Aaron Swartz, twenty-six, a leading advocate for open access to information, broke into the computer network at Massachusetts Institute of Technology and downloaded millions of documents from JSTOR, a nonprofit online organization that sells access to scholarly articles to libraries. Swartz believed that information should be available to everyone and that it was wrong that only faculty and students whose library could afford access to JSTOR had access to scholarly research. Swartz hoped to bring attention to JSTOR's monopoly over research, some of which had been funded by federal dollars. Swartz was charged with multiple counts of computer fraud, carrying a potential sentence of up to thirty-five years in prison and $1 million in fines. He reportedly was extremely depressed over his impending criminal prosecution and committed suicide before the case was brought to trial.[54]

You Decide  **10.2** Lori Drew, forty-nine, created a Myspace account in 2007 under the name of Josh Evans, a fictitious sixteen-year-old male. "Josh" started corresponding with thirteen-year-old Megan Meier. "Josh" told Megan that he recently had moved to a nearby town, and they corresponded for several weeks. Josh's tone changed at some point during the correspondence, and he wrote in an instant message that "the world would be a much better place without you." Megan responded to Josh that he was the kind of boy that "a girl would kill herself over," and shortly thereafter, on October 16, 2008, Megan committed suicide. Lori was angry over Megan's alleged gossip about her daughter Sarah and knew that Megan suffered from depression and harbored thoughts of suicide. Lori was prosecuted by federal authorities under the Computer Fraud and Abuse Act (CFAA). The jury found that Lori intentionally had violated the terms of service of Myspace and that as a result she was guilty of "accessing a computer involved in interstate or foreign communication without authorization or in excess of authorization to obtain information." Is the intentional breach of a Web site's terms of service sufficient to constitute a criminal violation of the CFAA? See *United States v. Lori Drew*, 259 F.R.D. 449 (C.D. Cal. 2009).

You can find the answer at study.sagepub.com/lippmaness2e

THEFT OF INTELLECTUAL PROPERTY

Intellectual property refers to the content of books, films, artistic works, musical scores, and other "products of the mind." The protection of intellectual property is intended to safeguard the creative product of individuals and to allow the "creators" to profit economically from their work. This provides an incentive for individuals to go through the demanding process of writing books, carving a sculpture, producing a film, or developing a computer program.

The framers of the U.S. Constitution appreciated the importance of intellectual property; and in Article 1, Section 8, Clause 8, Congress was given the power to secure for authors and inventors the exclusive rights to their writings and discoveries for a limited period of time. The federal government possesses exclusive jurisdiction over civil and criminal actions for the violation of intellectual property rights.

Federal law provides that the "creator" of an intellectual work is free to sell or license the rights to his or her intellectual product to other individuals, and under federal law a **copyright** is protected for the life of the author plus seventy years.[55]

The "piracy" of intellectual property both within and outside the United States has increased in recent years because of the ability of individuals to scan books and films onto the Web and to send this material across the globe. It is estimated that theft of intellectual property costs the U.S. economy over $250 billion a year. For example, a pirated film that is sold by traffickers in stolen intellectual property deprives the movie studio and all of the individuals who worked on the film of compensation for the pirated copies of the film. Other businesses also suffer because consumers can view the bootlegged copies of the film without going to a movie theater or renting a copy of the film.

Copyright

The Copyright Act safeguards books, films, and songs that have been published. An *infringement* of a copyrighted work involves reprinting or distributing the work without authorization.[56] The "fair use doctrine" permits limited copying of a work for educational, and other listed purposes.[57] You likely have been in a class in which the instructor relies on the fair use doctrine and makes a small number of copies of a book available for the class.

Most prosecutions for *copyright infringement* involve civil actions for damages, although the piracy of intellectual property is in violation of the criminal law. Title 17 U.S.C. § 506(a) provides for the criminal punishment of individuals who willfully infringe a copyright for purposes of "commercial advantage or private financial gain." The severity of the punishment depends on the value of the property that is pirated and the number of copies. The reproduction or distribution during any 180-day period of ten copies of one or more copyrighted works that have a total retail value of more than $2,500 can result in imprisonment for up to five years as well as a fine. Congress subsequently provided for the criminal punishment of the recording of the live performance of a performer or performers without permission and also prohibits the distribution or commercial exploitation of such recordings.[58]

A particularly important criminal provision punishes by up to five years individuals who "traffic" in counterfeit goods by designing a counterfeit label or affixing a counterfeit label to a recording, computer program, motion picture, or other audiovisual work or book or artistic creation. Criminal penalties also are provided for the fraudulent placement of a copyright notice on an article, for removal of a copyright notice, and for a false representation of fact in an application for a copyright.[59]

In 1997, Congress amended the law to combat file sharing in the No Electronic Theft (NET) Act. The NET Act provides criminal punishment for the reproduction or distribution of a work carrying a copyright, even in those instances in which the individual lacks a commercial or financial motive. The reproduction or distribution of one or more copies of a copyrighted work with a value of more than $1,000 is a misdemeanor that may be punished by up to one year in prison and a fine of up to $100,000. An offense involving ten or more copyrighted works that have a total value of more than $2,500 is subject to punishment of up to five years in prison and a fine of up to $250,000.[60]

Trademark Fraud

A **trademark** is a specific word, phrase, symbol, or logo used to label a commercial product and to distinguish the product from competitors. Think about the logo or slogan associated with your favorite restaurant, line of clothing or shoes, or computer, or with a memorable phrase identified with a city or state. The "branding of products" is important because we are inclined to embrace products that are identified with a particular lifestyle or point of view. Trademarks that are registered with the U.S. Patent and Trademark Office enjoy nationwide protection. Trademark infringement legal actions generally are civil matters, although federal law provides criminal penalties for *trademark counterfeiting*. An individual who "intentionally traffics or attempts to traffic in goods or services, and knowingly uses a counterfeit mark on or in connection with such goods or services" shall be imprisoned not more than ten years and fined not more than $2 million. It also is a crime to affix a genuine trademark to counterfeit goods.[61]

THEFT OF TRADE SECRETS

A **trade secret** is confidential information that a business relies on for a competitive advantage. The trade secret may involve a drug formula, a computer program, the ingredients of a restaurant's signature dish, or the inner workings of machinery or other specialized information. In 2007, a former Coca-Cola employee was convicted of attempting to sell information from the company files to a competing company. Foreign countries allegedly have engaged in industrial espionage and have undertaken a concerted effort to hack into the computers of U.S. businesses in an effort to obtain valuable trade secrets. In 1996, Congress enacted the Economic Espionage Act (EEA) that punishes the domestic theft of trade secrets and prohibits the theft of trade secrets by foreign governments. An individual is criminally liable who "acts with the intent to convert a trade secret to the economic benefit of anyone other than owner . . . intending or knowing that the offense will injure any owner of that trade secret." A related section requires that the individual intend to benefit a foreign power.[62]

RACKETEER INFLUENCED AND CORRUPT ORGANIZATIONS

In 1970, Congress passed the Organized Crime Control Act of 1970. Title IX of the act, **RICO** (Racketeer Influenced and Corrupt Organizations), was enacted to counter the infiltration of legitimate businesses engaged in interstate commerce by organized crime. Various states have their own RICO statutes to cover businesses that are not engaged in interstate commerce and that, as a consequence, do not fall within federal jurisdiction. An individual convicted under the federal RICO statute is punishable by up to twenty years in prison. This is in addition to the sentence imposed for any other crimes for which the defendant may be convicted. RICO also provides for the forfeiture of any money or property acquired as part of the defendant's racketeering activities.[63]

The federal RICO statute is complicated, and the requirements of the law are far from clear. The first step is to define a *pattern of racketeering* as used in the statute. This requires at least two specified criminal acts or the collection of an unlawful debt committed within a period of ten years. These so-called *predicate criminal acts* may be any of thirty-seven federal offenses or nine serious state felonies. These two crimes are required to be "related" and to have the "same or similar purposes, results, participants, victims, or methods of commission, or otherwise are interrelated by distinguishing characteristics and are not isolated events."

The second concept that is important in the RICO statute is an *enterprise*. An enterprise is an organization, partnership, corporation, association or gang, or unlawful conspiratorial group of individuals working together with an unlawful purpose.

The next step is to demonstrate a relationship between the pattern of racketeering and an enterprise engaged in interstate commerce. There are three types of scenarios punished under RICO, listed below.

1. It is a crime for any person to take income from a pattern of racketeering and use or invest that income in an enterprise engaged in interstate or foreign commerce. In *United States v. Robertson*, the defendant was convicted of a RICO violation for investing proceeds from illegal narcotics sales in an Alaskan gold mine.[64]

2. It is a crime for any person to acquire or to maintain control of an enterprise engaged in interstate or international commerce through racketeering activity. In *United States v. Local 560 of the International Brotherhood of Teamsters*, the defendants were found to have taken control of a union organization through extortion and murder.[65]

3. It is a crime for any person "employed by or associated" with any enterprise engaged in interstate or international commerce "to conduct or to participate in an enterprise's affairs through a pattern of racketeering activity." This provision is aimed at lower-level employees or participants in the enterprise. Three defendants in the Tennessee governor's office were convicted of conspiring to solicit and to accept bribes for influencing the granting of pardons and paroles and for delaying the extradition to other states of individuals who had been convicted or charged with crimes. The "Office of the Governor of Tennessee" was held to be a RICO enterprise.[66]

You Decide

10.3 Rajat K. Gupta was convicted of securities fraud for providing inside information to the head of the Galleon investment firm. Gupta, who formerly was managing director of the prestigious global consulting firm McKinsey, obtained this information as a board member of the investment bank Goldman Sachs, enabling Galleon both to profit and to avoid losses totaling more than $5 million. Gupta was sentenced to two years in prison and fined $5 million. The sentencing judge observed that the evidence before the Court established beyond dispute that Gupta had "selflessly devoted a huge amount of time and effort" to a wide variety of socially beneficial causes, such as the Global Fund to Fight AIDS, Tuberculosis and Malaria; the Public Health Foundation of India; the Indian School of Business; the Pratham Foundation (which provides quality education to underprivileged children in India); the Cornell medical school; the Rockefeller Foundation; and many, many other worthy causes. His lawyer wrote in the sentencing memorandum submitted to the judge that these activities illustrate Gupta's "big heart and helping hand," which he "extended without fanfare or self-promotion, to all with whom he came in contact." Was Gupta's punishment too lenient or too harsh? See *United States v. Gupta* (Sentencing memorandum, 2012).

You can find the answer at study.sagepub.com/lippmaness2e

CASE ANALYSIS

In *State v. Far West*, an Arizona appellate court considered whether to affirm a negligent homicide against Far West Water & Sewer Inc.

Should Far West Water & Sewer Inc. Be Held Liable for Negligent Homicide?

State v. Far West Water & Sewer Inc., 228 P.3d 909 (Ariz. App. 2010)

Far West Water & Sewer, Inc. ("Far West") appeals its convictions and sentences for negligent homicide, aggravated assault, two counts of endangerment and violating a safety standard or regulation which caused the death of an employee.

The charges arose from an incident that occurred on October 24, 2001 at a sewage collection and treatment facility owned and operated by Far West, an Arizona corporation. At that time, Santec Corporation ("Santec") was a subcontractor of Far West. A Far West employee, James Gamble, and a Santec employee, Gary Lanser, died in an underground tank after they were overcome by hydrogen sulfide gas. Another Far West employee, Nathan Garrett, suffered severe injuries when he attempted to rescue Gamble from the tank. Other Far West and Santec employees were involved in rescue attempts, but none was injured to a significant degree.

Far West was indicted for [various charges]. . . . Far West's president, Brent Weidman, one of its forepersons, Connie Charles, and Santec were also indicted for the same or similar charges. Santec pled guilty to one count of violating a safety standard or regulation that caused the death of its employee, Lanser. It was placed on probation for two years and fined $30,000. Foreperson Connie Charles pled guilty to two counts of endangerment as to Gamble and Garrett and was placed on concurrent one-year terms of probation.

The jury acquitted Far West of both counts of manslaughter as to James Gamble and Gary Lanser, but found it guilty of one count of the lesser-included offense of negligent homicide for the death of Gamble, one count of aggravated assault as to Nathan Garrett, two counts of endangerment as to Gamble and Garrett, and one count of violating a safety standard or regulation that caused the death of Gamble.

The court ordered the sentences suspended and placed Far West on four years' probation for negligent homicide, five years' probation for aggravated assault and three years' probation for each count of endangerment and for violating a safety standard or regulation that caused the death of an employee. It ordered some terms of probation to run concurrently and others to run consecutively. The court imposed fines and penalties totaling $1,770,000.

In 1977, the Arizona legislature enacted A.R.S. § 13-305, which permits an enterprise to be held criminally liable. An enterprise includes a corporation. A.R.S. § 13-105(15)(2001). Section 13-305 provides in relevant part:

A. [A]n enterprise commits an offense if:

   1. The conduct constituting the offense consists of a failure to discharge a specific duty imposed by law; or

   2. The conduct undertaken in behalf of the enterprise and constituting the offense is engaged in, authorized, solicited, commanded or recklessly tolerated by the directors of the enterprise in any manner or by a high managerial agent acting within the scope of employment.

Arizona's criminal code defines "person" as "a human being and, as the context requires, an enterprise, a public or private corporation, an unincorporated association, a partnership, a firm, a society, a government, a governmental authority or an individual or entity capable of holding a legal or beneficial interest in property." A.R.S. § 13-105(26) (2001). . . . Further, not only did the legislature include corporations in the definition of person, the legislature described how corporations, as enterprises, can commit criminal offenses through the acts or omissions of their directors, high managerial agents and/or agents. A.R.S. § 13-305(A).

On appeal, Far West argues there was insufficient evidence to support its convictions for the charged offenses. "Far West owned and operated several wastewater treatment plants in Yuma. Weidman, who has a master's degree in industrial engineering and a Ph.D. in construction engineering, had been Far West's president and chief operating officer for nine years. Rex Noll, who had extensive training and experience in sewage and wastewater treatment plants, was the supervisor for the sewage division of Far West and reported directly to Weidman. Charles was in charge of the sewer crews and was under Noll's supervision.

Prior to the incident, Far West acquired the Mesa Del Oro Plant and hired Santec to renovate equipment in an underground sewage tank called the Mesa Del Oro Tank ("the Tank"). The 3,000 gallon tank was approximately nine feet underground. The interior of the Tank could only be accessed by descending down a ladder into a manhole approximately four feet wide. Two sewer lines fed into the Tank. The gravity line carried sewage downhill by gravitational force. The force main line carried sewage pumped by force main pumps from another tank or lift station, approximately one mile away.

On October 24, 2001, Far West and Santec began work on the Tank. . . . After the force main pumps at the lift station were shut off, Gamble and Garrett pumped out the sewage from the surface and cleaned out the remaining sewage from inside the Tank. As part of this process, Gamble inserted a plug into the gravity line to stop the flow of sewage. After the Santec crew finished upgrading the Tank, it was ready to have sewage pumped into it.

Normally, the crew would pull the gravity line plug and exit the Tank before turning on the force main pump. On this occasion, however, Charles wanted to turn the force main pumps on first because she was concerned that the lift station was overflowing. . . . Charles told Gamble to enter the Tank to pull out the gravity line plug once the Tank was about half-full of sewage. Charles then drove to the lift station, turned on the pumps and sewage began flowing into the Tank. In a radio communication, Charles asked Gamble if the Tank was half-full and inquired, "[i]s the plug out yet? Is the plug out yet?" As sewage was flowing into the Tank, Gamble climbed inside the Tank to unplug the gravity line. When the lower part of his body was in the Tank, he passed out and fell into the sewage.

Garrett saw Gamble floating facedown in the Tank. In an effort to rescue him, Garrett tied a rope around his waist, told Andre to hold it and climbed down a ladder into almost waist-deep sewage. Not able to get Gamble out of the Tank, Garrett tried to climb up the ladder but passed out before he reached the top. Lanser then climbed down the manhole in

(Continued)

(Continued)

an attempt to rescue both Gamble and Garrett, passed out and fell into the Tank. At some point, Hackbarth radioed to Charles to turn off the pumps and call 911. Charles rushed back to the Tank and entered it in an effort to rescue Gamble, Garrett and Lanser. She, too, passed out, but eventually regained consciousness.

Dr. Daniel Teitelbaum, a physician specializing in occupational medicine and toxicology, and an OSHA expert and consultant, concluded that Gamble and Lanser died from acute hydrogen sulfide poisoning which occurred in a confined space. . . . Although Garrett survived, he suffered life-threatening respiratory distress syndrome and aspiration pneumonia and sustained injuries to his lungs and eyes.

The State presented substantial evidence that Weidman and Noll were high managerial agents of Far West acting within the scope of their authority. Weidman was President and Chief Operating Officer of Far West and a member of the board of directors. Noll was the supervisor for the sewage division of Far West, answered to Weidman and had considerable authority over Far West's employees. He was in charge of Far West's safety program. He and Weidman together formulated and developed policies and practices of Far West regarding entry into underground sewage tanks. . . . A jury could reasonably conclude that Weidman and Noll were high managerial agents of Far West and were acting within the scope of their authority.

The State presented substantial evidence that Weidman and Noll were aware of the extreme risks to employees working at Far West. Both were industry professionals with extensive training and experience in sewage treatment plants. They knew the dangers associated with confined spaces and sewer environments. They knew about potentially lethal dangers posed by toxic gases found in underground tanks.

Weidman posited that the death and injuries occurred due to the toxic gases. Noll admitted that working in underground tanks was unsafe. The State presented substantial evidence that Weidman and Noll knew and understood the OSHA permit-required confined space regulations. . . .

A jury could reasonably conclude that Noll and Weidman consciously disregarded a substantial and unjustifiable risk of death or physical injury by knowingly violating OSHA regulations and permitting Far West employees to enter dangerous, life-threatening underground tanks without training, equipment, safety measures or rescue capability. A reasonable jury could find from this evidence that Weidman and Noll did more than "fail to perceive a substantial and unjustifiable" risk of death or serious physical injury for purposes of criminal negligence; they acted recklessly by being "aware of" and "consciously disregard[ing] a substantial and unjustifiable risk" of death or serious physical injury for purposes of aggravated assault and endangerment; and knowingly violated A.R.S. § 23-403 and OSHA regulations for purposes of A.R.S. § 23-418(E).

The State presented substantial evidence that the conduct of Weidman and Noll constituted a gross deviation from the required standard of care and/or conduct. Moreover, there was substantial evidence to show that Weidman and Noll engaged in conduct necessary to satisfy not only the elements of the criminal statutes defining the offenses but also the elements necessary to impose enterprise liability on Far West. See A.R.S. § 13-305(A) ("failure to discharge a specific duty imposed by law" and/or conduct undertaken which constitutes offense and "is engaged in, authorized, solicited, commanded or recklessly tolerated" by directors or high managerial agents).

CHAPTER SUMMARY

Sociologist Edwin H. Sutherland pioneered the concept of white-collar crime, defining this as crime committed by an individual of respectability and high social status in the course of his or her occupation. The Justice Department, in contrast, focuses on the types of offenses that constitute white-collar crime as well as on the economic status of the offender. The Justice Department defines white-collar crime as offenses that employ deceit and concealment rather than the application of force to obtain money, property, or service; to avoid the payment or loss of money; or to secure

a business or professional advantage. The definition notes that white-collar criminals occupy positions of responsibility and trust in government, industry, the professions, and civil organizations. In this chapter, we discussed some of the common white-collar criminal offenses.

Most white-collar crime prosecutions are undertaken by the federal government. These laws are based on the federal authority over interstate and foreign commerce and other constitutional powers. Environmental crimes threaten the health and natural resources of the United States and range from air and water pollution to the illegal transport and disposal of hazardous waste and pesticides. OSHA protects the health and safety of workers. Willful violations of the act that result in death are punished as a misdemeanor and may result in both a fine and imprisonment. A modest number of these violations have been pursued, and cases are increasingly being referred for prosecution.

The stock market is an important source of investment and retirement income for Americans. Securities law is designed to ensure a free and fair market in order to maintain investor trust and confidence. The most active area of prosecution is insider trading, the use of information that is not publicly available, to buy and sell stocks. Prosecutions for trading on the basis of inside information are brought against corporate insiders under a theory of "disclose or abate" and against corporate outsiders under a theory of "misappropriation."

A significant number of white-collar crime prosecutions are undertaken under the federal mail and wire fraud statutes. The mail fraud statute prohibits the knowing and intentional participation in a scheme or artifice to defraud money or property, the execution of which is undertaken through the use of the mail. The wire fraud statute requires the execution of an artifice or fraud through the use of wires that cross interstate or foreign boundaries. The mail or wires need only be used incident to an essential aspect of the scheme. A conspiracy to commit either of these offenses requires that the use of mail or wires will naturally occur in the course of the scheme or was reasonably foreseeable, although not actually intended.

The Travel Act is intended to assist state and local governments in combating organized crime and is directed at what ordinarily are considered the status offenses of illegal gambling, the shipment and sale of alcohol and controlled substances, extortion, bribery, arson, prostitution, and money laundering. This law punishes interstate or foreign travel or the use of the mail or any facility in interstate or foreign commerce with the intent to distribute the proceeds of one of the unlawful activities listed in the statute, to commit a crime of violence, or to commit a crime listed in the Travel Act. The law requires that a defendant thereafter attempts to commit or does commit a criminal offense.

Health fraud is an increasingly frequent and serious area of criminal activity. The federal health fraud statute addresses frauds against health insurance programs or the fraudulent obtaining of money or property from a health care benefit program. This typically involves claims by doctors to be reimbursed for unnecessary medical care or for medical care that was never provided.

The Sherman Antitrust Act is intended to ensure free and competitive markets and declares that it is a crime knowingly to enter into a contract or to form a combination or conspiracy to interfere with interstate commerce. An example is price-fixing.

Identity theft and access device fraud are two prevalent and costly forms of theft. Identity theft statutes typically require that an individual knowingly use the identification of another individual.

A challenge confronting criminal offenders is to convert money or property obtained from illegal activity into what individuals can claim to be lawful income. The federal money laundering statute combats the "washing of money" by declaring that it is a crime to knowingly conduct a financial transaction involving the proceeds of a crime or to engage in a transaction involving property derived from criminal activity with the intent to conceal the source of the money or property or to promote an illegal enterprise.

Currency regulations are a law enforcement tool that is used to limit the ability of individuals to deposit money obtained from illicit activities in banks and to transfer money into various accounts. The tax laws provide another set of laws that can be used against individuals who conceal the source of their income. These laws cover individuals who fail to report income, take undeserved deductions, or report false information on their returns.

Computer crime has posed a challenge for the criminal law because historically statutes were concerned with tangible property rather than with intangible property, like information or data. The federal government and states have adopted cybercrime statutes that address a broad range of computer-related offenses such as computer fraud, computer hacking, computer trespassing, and spam.

The Copyright Act safeguards the rights of authors in books, films, and songs that have been published. An *infringement* of the copyright of a work involves reprinting or distributing the work without authorization. Trademarks that are registered with the U.S. Patent and Trademark Office enjoy nationwide protection. Trademark infringement generally is a civil matter, although federal law provides criminal penalties for *trademark counterfeiting*. In 1996, Congress enacted the Economic Espionage Act, which punishes the domestic theft of trade secrets and prohibits the theft of trade secrets by foreign governments.

RICO has provided a strategy for countering the infiltration of private industry and public institutions by criminal gangs.

In thinking about this chapter, consider whether sufficient attention is paid to the investigation and prosecution of white-collar crime. Would you punish white-collar criminals more or less severely than other offenders?

CHAPTER REVIEW QUESTIONS

1. What are the various approaches to defining white-collar crime?

2. Should corporations be held criminally liable for white-collar crime?

3. List some of the acts that are considered environmental crimes.

4. What is the purpose of criminal prosecutions under OSHA?

5. Define insider trading. Why is insider trading considered a crime?

6. What are the elements of mail and wire fraud? How do they differ from one another?

7. Discuss the purpose of the Travel Act.

8. What areas are covered under the 1996 federal health care fraud act?

9. Discuss the purpose of the Sherman Antitrust Act. Give an example of an antitrust violation.

10. What are the elements of identity theft?

11. Describe access device fraud.

12. Discuss the purpose of laws against money laundering and explain what is involved in money laundering.

13. Outline currency violations.

14. What acts constitute tax crimes?

15. Describe the purpose of criminal laws against the theft of intellectual property, trademarks, and trade secrets.

16. Should the government place a greater emphasis on prosecuting white-collar crime? Do you believe that white-collar criminals should receive harsh prison sentences?

LEGAL TERMINOLOGY

access device fraud

computer crime

copyright

corporate liability

corporate murder

cybercrime

disclose or abstain doctrine

environmental crimes

fiduciary relationship

fraud

health care fraud

identity theft

insider trading

intellectual property

mail fraud

misappropriation doctrine

money laundering

nolo contendere

Occupational Safety and Health Act (OSHA)

pump and dump

RICO

Sarbanes-Oxley Act

Sherman (Antitrust) Act of 1890

tippees

tippers

trade secret

trademark

Travel Act

white-collar crime

wire fraud

CRIMINAL LAW ON THE WEB

Visit **study.sagepub.com/lippmaness2e** to access additional study tools including suggested answers to the You Decide questions, reprints of cases and statutes, online appendices, and more!

11 CRIMES AGAINST PUBLIC ORDER AND MORALITY

Was Whatley guilty of appearing in a state of nudity in public?

Whatley is an independent operator who owns a semi-trailer truck equipped with a sleeping berth. Whatley was driving his semi northbound on Interstate 65 when he pulled into a weigh station. . . . A state police motor carrier inspector approached the semi to check whether the driver was wearing a seat belt or in possession of firearms, or drugs. . . . Whatley was completely nude . . . [and stated] he was in too big a hurry to get dressed. Ind. Code § 35-45-4-1(a) provides in pertinent: "[a] person who knowingly or intentionally, in a public place: (1) engages in sexual intercourse; (2) engages in deviate sexual conduct; (3) appears in a state of nudity; or (4) fondles the person's genitals or the genitals of another person; commits public indecency. . . . Characterizing his truck as a "home on wheels" Whatley argues that he was not in a public place. (*Whatley v. State*, 36A05-9806-CR-307 [Ind. Ct. App. 1999])

In this chapter, learn about crimes against public order and morality.

Learning Objectives

1. Know the definition of crimes against public order and morality.

2. Understand the elements of disorderly conduct and the types of acts punished by the crime of disorderly conduct.

3. Distinguish the crime of riot from the crime of disorderly conduct.

4. Understand crimes against the quality of life and the broken windows theory.

5. Know the types of laws that regulate the driving of motor vehicles.

6. Discuss vagrancy and loitering and the use of the law to regulate homelessness.

7. Understand the debate on the overreach of criminal law.

8. Know the definition of the crime of prostitution and various crimes related to prostitution.

9. Understand the definition of obscenity and the difference between obscenity and child pornography.

10. Discuss the reason for the crime of cruelty to animals.

INTRODUCTION

You undoubtedly have been walking down the street and have been approached by a "panhandler" asking for money in an annoying or aggressive manner. He or she might even have followed you down the street or blocked the sidewalk. You may have felt that your "personal space" was invaded or that you were being

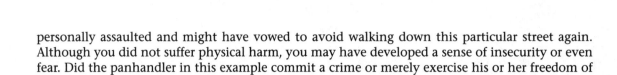

personally assaulted and might have vowed to avoid walking down this particular street again. Although you did not suffer physical harm, you may have developed a sense of insecurity or even fear. Did the panhandler in this example commit a crime or merely exercise his or her freedom of speech and assembly?

Crimes against public order and morality are intended to ensure that individuals walking on sidewalks, traveling on the streets, or enjoying the public parks and facilities are free from harassment, fear, threat, and alarm. This category of crime includes a large number of seemingly unrelated offenses that threaten the public peace, quiet, and tranquility. The challenge presented by these offenses is to balance public order and morality with the right of individuals to exercise their civil liberties.

A prime example of a crime against public order is individual disorderly conduct. This broadly defined offense involves acts that create public inconvenience and annoyance by directly threatening *individuals'* sense of physical safety. Disorderly conduct entails offenses ranging from intentionally blocking the sidewalk and acting in an abusive and threatening manner to discharging a firearm in public. Group disorderly conduct (riot) entails tumultuous or violent conduct by three or more persons. Another set of laws is designed to ensure road safety and security by regulating motor vehicles.

A second category of crimes against public order and morality covered in this chapter includes offenses against the public order that threaten the order and stability of a *neighborhood*. We focus on two so-called quality-of-life crimes. At common law, vagrancy was defined as moving through the community with no visible means of support. Loitering at common law was defined as idly standing on the corner or sidewalk in a manner that causes people to feel a sense of threat or alarm for their safety. These broad vagrancy and loitering statutes historically have been employed to detain and keep "undesirables" off the streets. The U.S. Supreme Court in recent years has consistently found these laws void for vagueness and unconstitutional. The same constitutional arguments are being used today to challenge ordinances directed against the homeless and gangs.

The second section of the chapter on crimes against public order and morality examines the overreach of the criminal law or so-called victimless crimes. These are offenses against *morality*. The individuals who voluntarily engage in victimless crimes typically do not view their involvement as harmful to themselves or to others. We initially center our discussion of victimless crimes on prostitution and soliciting for prostitution. The next section on victimless crimes examines whether the prohibition on obscenity should be extended to violent video games that are thought to harm children or whether these games are protected under the First Amendment to the U.S. Constitution. We conclude our discussion of crimes against public order and morality by examining the use of the criminal law to protect domestic animals.

In this chapter, several issues arise. Ask yourself whether the statutes punishing crimes against public order and morality are, at times, employed to target certain undesirable individuals in order to keep them off the streets rather than to protect society. Are some of these laws so broadly drafted that the police are provided with an unreasonable degree of discretion in determining whether to arrest individuals? Last, consider whether the criminal law reaches too far in punishing so-called victimless crimes. The overriding question is whether the enforcement of offenses against public order and morality is required in order to maintain social order and stability.

DISORDERLY CONDUCT

The common law punished a **breach of the peace**. This was defined as an act that disturbs or tends to disturb the tranquility of the citizenry. The great common law eighteenth-century commentator William Blackstone notes that breaches of the peace included both acts that actually disrupted the social order, such as fighting in public, and what he terms constructive breaches of the peace or conduct that is reasonably likely to provoke or to excite others to disrupt social order. Blackstone cites as examples of constructive breaches of the peace both the circulation of material causing a person to be subjected to public ridicule or contempt and the issuing of a challenge to another person to fight.[1]

The common law crime of breach of the peace constitutes the foundation for U.S. state statutes punishing **disorderly conduct**. An example of a statutory definition of the misdemeanor of disorderly conduct is the Wisconsin law that punishes anyone who, "in a public or private place, engages in violent, abusive, indecent, profane, boisterous, unreasonably loud or otherwise disorderly conduct under circumstances in which the conduct tends to cause or provoke a disturbance."[2] Other statutes specify the conduct constituting disorderly conduct. The Illinois statute defines disorderly conduct as any act knowingly committed in an unreasonable manner so as to "alarm or disturb another and to provoke a breach of the peace." The Illinois law then elaborates on this definition and lists specific acts that constitute a breach of the public peace, including a false fire alarm or false report of criminal activity to the police, a false report of an explosive device, a false report of child or elder abuse, and an annoying or intimidating telephone call made to collect a debt.[3] The Arizona statute requires an act committed with a specific intent to disturb the peace or quiet of a neighborhood, family, or person or committed with the knowledge that it is disturbing the peace, including fighting, unreasonable noise, use of abusive or offensive language to any person likely to cause retaliation, commotion intended to prevent a meeting or procession, refusal to obey a lawful order to disperse, and recklessly handling, displaying, or discharging a deadly weapon or dangerous instrument.[4]

We can see that the *mens rea* of the Illinois statute is knowingly, while the *mens rea* of the Arizona statute is an intentional or knowing intent. Other state statutes extend disorderly conduct to include the reckless disturbance of the peace. The Illinois and Arizona statutes differ in one other respect. The Arizona law covers acts intended to disturb or that knowingly disturb the peace or quiet of a neighborhood, family, or person, while the Illinois statute is generally directed at threats or acts that alarm the community. The commentary to the Model Penal Code (MPC) notes that defining disturbing the peace to include disturbing individuals authorizes the police to intervene and arrest individuals whose playing of their radio or television is considered unreasonably loud by their next-door neighbor. Disorderly conduct is a misdemeanor, although some states punish as felonies acts that create or threaten to create a significant disturbance.

As you can see, a broad range of conduct is punished under disorderly conduct statutes. For instance, a parent was convicted of disorderly conduct who loudly and aggressively disputed a referee's decision at his son's football game, refused the referee's request to leave the stadium, swore at spectators, placed his hands on the referee, and caused a halt in the game. A Minnesota court of appeals ruled that the parent's profanity combined with his aggressive acts caused anxiety and concern to the spectators and referees and constituted disorderly conduct.[5] How does the court know that the defendant's behavior "disturbed the peace"? Do people assume the risk that they will be subjected to emotional outbursts by spectators attending a football game? In an Illinois case, a defendant who declared to ticketing agents at the airport that he had a bomb in his shoe was sentenced to more than six months in prison. An appellate court affirmed the defendant's conviction for transmitting a false alarm relating to a bomb or other explosive device. The court noted that disorderly conduct under Illinois law requires only the uttering of a threat regardless of the response of other individuals. The court explained this strict standard by observing that the defendant must have known that there was a strong probability that the threat of a bomb in an airport would "cause alarm and mass disruption."[6]

Another challenge that is frequently presented by prosecutions for disorderly conduct is drawing the line between disorderly conduct and constitutionally protected speech. The Wisconsin Supreme Court affirmed that the statement by a thirteen-year-old that he was going to kill everyone at his school and make people suffer constituted disorderly conduct. The court explained that speech alone could constitute disorderly conduct where "a reasonable speaker . . . would foresee that reasonable listeners would interpret his statements as serious expressions of an intent to intimidate or inflict bodily harm."[7]

Disorderly conduct addresses relatively minor acts of criminality. Nevertheless, the commentary to the MPC stresses that this is an important area because disorderly conduct statutes affect a large number of defendants. Arrests for disorderly conduct in a given year are generally equal to the number arrested for all violent crimes combined. Thus, the enforcement of disorderly conduct statutes is critical in shaping public perceptions as to the fairness of the criminal justice system. A final point is that the concern of Americans with balancing crime control with civil liberties dictates that we take the time to consider whether disorderly conduct statutes intrude upon the rights of individuals and are in need of reform.

Model Penal Code

Section 250.2. Disorderly Conduct

(1) A person is guilty of disorderly conduct if, with purpose to cause public inconvenience, annoyance or alarm, or recklessly creating a risk thereof, he

(a) engages in fighting or threatening, or in violent or tumultuous behavior; or

(b) makes unreasonable noise or offensively coarse utterances, gesture or display, or addresses abusive language to any person present; or

(c) creates a hazardous or physically offensive condition by any act which serves no legitimate purpose of the actor.

"Public" means affecting or likely to affect persons in a place to which the public or substantial group has access; among the places included are highways, transport facilities, schools, prisons, apartment houses, places of business or amusement, or any neighborhood.

(2) An offense under this section is a petty misdemeanor if the actor's purpose is to cause substantial harm or serious inconvenience, or if he persists in disorderly conduct after reasonable warning or request to desist. Otherwise disorderly conduct is a violation [subject to a fine].

Analysis

- The MPC limits disorderly conduct to specific acts likely to create what the code terms a public nuisance. The commentary notes that the proposed statute does not include conduct tending to corrupt or to annoy other individuals.
- The act must be committed with the purpose to cause public inconvenience, annoyance, or alarm or recklessly creating a risk thereof. Guilt cannot be based on the argument that an individual should have foreseen the risk of public annoyance or alarm; "nothing less than conscious disregard of a substantial and justifiable risk of public nuisance will suffice for liability. Conviction cannot be had merely on proof that the actor should have foreseen the risk of public annoyance or alarm."
- Disorderly conduct is directed at disturbing the peace and quiet of the community. The code excludes family disputes within the home.
- The section limits imprisonment to circumstances in which an individual's purpose is to cause significant harm or serious inconvenience or in which an individual continues the crime despite warnings or requests to halt.
- The MPC also includes specific sections on the abuse of a corpse; cruelty to animals; desecration of graves, monuments, and places of worship; disruption of meetings and processions; false public alarms; harassment; loitering or prowling; obstructing highways or other public passages and processions; public drunkenness; unlawful eavesdropping; surveillance; and breaching the privacy of messages.

You Decide

11.1 Sergeant Loran Baker testified that on November 19, 2009, at 12:30 p.m., he was driving slowly on Laurel Street near downtown Santa Cruz, California. He was in plain clothes and driving an unmarked car. Baker spotted sixteen-year-old Cesar and seventeen-year-old Antonio walking along the sidewalk. Their attention was "directed towards the traffic and [they were] making some hand signs." Baker was particularly concerned about this activity because a sixteen-year-old had been stabbed to death "where the same kind of exchange was occurring" just a month earlier in the same vicinity.

Baker "couldn't tell if" the hand signs being made by Cesar and Antonio were directed at "a car or somebody on the [other side of the] street," but he saw that "their gestures . . . seemed to be getting more aggressive and [they were] moving towards them like they were challenging them to fight. I realized then, hey, this is for real, and they are challenging somebody." Since their behavior was "aggressive," Baker could tell that they were not "fooling around." Cesar and Antonio "changed directions" and "were moving towards the street." Cesar and Antonio put their hands up in the air while taking "a few steps towards the cars like, hey, let's go," a gesture that Baker "took as a challenge." They "held their arms up in an inviting manner," which was "like, hey, it's on, you're open to somebody approaching you."

Baker was concerned that violence would develop, so he "did a U-turn in traffic," drove up behind Cesar and Antonio, activated his lights, called for backup, and told Cesar and Antonio to "wait right there." Antonio told Baker that he had "been using hand signals to display a gang slogan . . . towards a car." He told Baker that "one of the occupants in the rear seat [of the Cadillac] had actually thrown him a four, meaning Norteño sign," which would identify that person as a Norteño gang member. Antonio told Baker that he had made signs for *P*, *S*, and *C* to signify the Poor Side Chicos, a Watsonville Sureño gang. The Poor Side Chicos gang consists of the "younger members" of the Poor Side Gang. Poor Side Chicos, like other Sureño gangs, associate with the color blue and the number thirteen. Poor Side Chicos members "hate" Norteños.

Antonio asserted that he "took it [the occupant's alleged sign] as being a challenge, a form of disrespect." He said he was "not really afraid because . . . there was a girl in the car." Antonio told Baker that he thought a fight was unlikely to occur because "typically there won't be a gang fight when the girl was present."

Antonio acknowledged that he was aware that his conduct had occurred in an area "where Norteños and Sureños would actually cross paths and it would be not good." Antonio also admitted that the blue "swoosh" on the Nike shoes he was wearing was intended to "signify" his Sureño affiliation.

Cesar maintained that he "was just holding his ground and not trying to challenge the occupants" of the Cadillac.

The prosecution's gang expert testified that a gesture of putting one's hands up in the air would be seen as "challenging the other person." He also opined that the "common response" to someone making a gang sign is violence. The expert testified that there was "no other reason" for a person to make a gang sign besides "challenging them to fight." The presence of a girl would not eliminate the risk of violence in such a situation. The gang expert testified that the Poor Side Chicos gang would benefit from a challenge such as that made by Cesar and Antonio because "[i]t would further the violent reputation" of the gang "within the community."

California Penal Code Section 415, Subdivision (1) provides that "[a]ny person who unlawfully fights in a public place or challenges another person in a public place to fight" commits a misdemeanor. Antonio and Cesar assert that their conduct was not a "challenge . . . to fight" because they were merely responding to a gang sign displayed by an occupant of a white Cadillac. Are they guilty of a challenge to fight? See *In re Cesar*, 192 Cal. App. 4th 989 (2011).

You can find the answer at study.sagepub.com/lippmaness2e

RIOT

The common law punished group disorderly conduct as a misdemeanor. An **unlawful assembly** was defined as the assembling of three or more persons with the purpose to engage in an unlawful act. Taking steps toward the accomplishment of this common illegal purpose was punished as a **rout**. The law recognized a **riot** where three or more individuals engaged in an unlawful act of violence. The participants must have agreed to the illegal purpose prior to engaging in violence. However, the individuals were not required to enter into a common agreement to commit an illegal act prior to the assembly; the illegal purpose could develop during the course of the meeting. The English Riot Act of 1549 punished as a felony an assembly of twelve or more persons gathered together with an unlawful design that failed to obey an order to disperse within one hour of the issuance of the order to disband. The Riot Act was reintroduced in 1714. You may be interested to know that it is the reading of the act to an assembly that constitutes the basis of the popular phrase "reading the riot act."[8]

The American colonists were understandably reluctant to adopt a British statute that had been employed by the English Crown to punish people who gathered for purposes of political protest. However, all the states eventually adopted riot laws loosely based on the English statute. These laws continue to remain in force and, in effect, punish group disorderly conduct.

Why is there a separate offense of riot? After all, we could merely punish riot as aggravated disorderly conduct. A group has a mind of its own and both poses a greater threat to society and is less easily deterred than a single individual. Collective action also presents a problem for the police, who may have to resort to aggressive force to control the crowd. Courts have recognized that a clear distinction must be made between riots and the right of individuals to freely assemble to petition the government for the redress of grievances. In 1949, the U.S. Supreme Court upheld the constitutionality of an Arkansas riot statute, holding that it did not abridge free speech or assembly for the "state to fasten themselves upon one who has actively and consciously assisted" in the "promoting, encouraging and aiding of an assembly the purpose of which is to wreak violence."[9]

Under a New York statute, an individual is guilty of misdemeanor riot when, with four other persons, he or she engages in "tumultuous and violent conduct" and thereby "intentionally or recklessly causes or creates a grave risk of causing public alarm." The New York statutory scheme punishes riot as a felony when a group of ten or more persons engages in "tumultuous and violent conduct and thereby intentionally or recklessly causes or creates a grave risk of causing public alarm" and a person other than one of the participants suffers "physical injury or substantial property damage." What is the difference between misdemeanor and felony riot under the New York statute?[10]

New York also punishes the misdemeanor of unlawful assembly. An unlawful assembly is defined as the assembly of an individual with four or more others for the purpose of engaging or preparing to engage with them in "tumultuous and violent conduct likely to cause public alarm, or when, being present at an assembly which either has or develops such a purpose, he remains there with intent to advance that purpose." How does this differ from a riot? New York punishes incitement to riot when an individual "urges ten or more persons to engage in tumultuous and violent conduct of a kind likely to create public alarm."[11] Other states provide criminal penalties for the English statutory crime of a knowing failure to obey an order to disperse. An Ohio statute punishes five or more persons engaged in a course of disorderly conduct "who knowingly fail to obey an order to disperse where there are other persons in the vicinity whose presence creates the likelihood of physical harm to persons or property or of serious public inconvenience, annoyance, or alarm."[12]

Riot statutes are typically used when a conspiracy or accessoryship cannot be easily applied. The Utah riot statute provides that an individual is guilty of riot if "he assembles with two or more other persons with the purpose of engaging, soon thereafter, in tumultuous or violent conduct, knowing that two or more other persons in the assembly have the same purpose." In *J.B.A. v. State*, a Utah appellate court convicted a juvenile of riot and held him to be a delinquent. J.B.A. was determined to have been aware that his friends were collecting weapons and preparing to return to school to "settle some differences." The defendant voluntarily stood as part of a show of force in support of his friends as they fought with members of a rival group. The Utah court noted that J.B.A. was not an uninterested bystander and that he would have been expected to intervene in the event that his friends were in jeopardy of losing the fight.[13] Does this situation fit your conception of participation in a riot? Why not merely punish this as conspiracy or as aiding and abetting disorderly conduct?

Model Penal Code

Section 250.1. Riot; Failure to Disperse

(1) A person is guilty of riot, a felony of the third degree, if he participates with two or more others in a course of disorderly conduct:

(a) with purpose to commit or facilitate the commission of a felony or misdemeanor;

(b) with purpose to prevent or coerce official action; or

(c) when the actor or any other participant to the knowledge of the actor uses or plans to use a firearm or other deadly weapon.

(2) Where three or more persons are participating in a course of disorderly conduct likely to cause substantial harm or serious inconvenience, annoyance or alarm, a peace officer or other public servant engaged in executing or enforcing the law may order the participants and others in the immediate vicinity to disperse. A person who refuses or knowingly fails to obey such an order commits a misdemeanor.

Analysis

- The MPC requires that an individual participate together with two or more other persons in a course of disorderly conduct with the required purpose or knowledge. It is not sufficient that an individual was present at the assembly or disturbance.
- The MPC also punishes a failure to disperse.

MOTOR VEHICLE VIOLATIONS

States and many local jurisdictions have a wide range of statutes regulating motor vehicles. These laws regulate activities such as parking; speeding; drag racing; failure to obey traffic signals, yield the right of way, signal a change of lanes, or signal a turn; driving with a revoked license or with malfunctioning equipment; and drunk driving. Most of these are strict liability laws, and there is no requirement to prove a criminal intent. The traffic laws in the United States are fairly uniform. Most states have adopted the provisions of the *Uniform Vehicle Code*, which was formulated by a group of experts whose goal was to create a single standard for regulating motor vehicles.

A violation of the traffic laws, until relatively recently, was treated as a criminal offense. The driver was arrested, incarcerated, and required to post bond to obtain his or her release from jail. In the past several decades, minor traffic violations have been decriminalized. They are considered *civil infractions* rather than criminal misdemeanors and are tried before a judge rather than before a jury. Violations are punished by fines and by suspension of a driver's license. A traffic violation also results in the accumulation of points on a driver's record, and the accumulation of a designated number of points results in suspension of a driver's license.

Serious traffic violations such as driving while under the influence of alcohol, reckless driving, and fleeing an officer generally are punished as misdemeanors, which result in the arrest of the driver. Individuals who are arrested will be taken into custody, incarcerated until released on bail, and subjected to a search of their person and perhaps their automobile. A search may lead to the seizure of unlawful narcotics and firearms and to additional criminal charges.

Keep in mind that the U.S. Supreme Court in *Atwater v. Lago Vista* held that states possess the right to provide a police officer with the discretion either to issue a citation or to conduct a custodial arrest for a violation of a minor traffic violation. The Court, as a result, affirmed the arrest of Gail Atwater for a failure to wear a seat belt, an offense punishable by a fine, which did not carry a jail sentence.[14]

A new area of legislation is **distracted driving**, which involves acts that divert a driver's attention. This includes eating, drinking, adjusting the radio, and glancing at the newspaper.

The two most dangerous examples of distracted driving are talking on a cell phone while driving and texting while driving. The National Highway Traffic Safety Administration (NHTSA) concludes that 80 percent of accidents and 16 percent of highway deaths result from distracted drivers. It is estimated that 1.6 million crashes (25 percent) are due to cell phone use and another 1 million (18 percent) are due to texting. The U.S. Department of Transportation concludes that reaching for a phone distracts a driver for 4.6 seconds, during which time the automobile will travel a distance equivalent to the length of a football field if the driver is traveling fifty-five miles per hour. Texting while driving increases the risk of an auto accident by twenty-three times.

Keep this material in mind when you read about driving while impaired by alcohol in Chapter 12.

PUBLIC INDECENCIES: QUALITY-OF-LIFE CRIMES

Criminal law texts traditionally devote very little attention to **public indecencies**. These offenses include public drunkenness, vagrancy, loitering, panhandling, graffiti, and urinating and sleeping in public. A significant number of arrests and prosecutions are devoted to these **crimes against the quality of life**; but for the most part, they receive limited attention because they are misdemeanors, are swiftly disposed of in summary trials before local judges, and disproportionately target young people, minorities, and individuals from lower socioeconomic backgrounds.

In the 1980s, scholars began to argue that seemingly unimportant offenses against the public order and morals were key to understanding why some neighborhoods bred crime and hopelessness while other areas prospered. This so-called **broken windows theory** is identified with criminologists James Q. Wilson and George Kelling. Why the name *broken windows*? Wilson and Kelling argue that if one window in a building is broken and left unrepaired, this sends a signal that no one cares about the house and that soon every window will be broken. The same process of decay is at work in a neighborhood. A home is abandoned, weeds sprout, the windows are smashed, and graffiti is sprayed on the building. Rowdy teenagers, drunks, and drug addicts are drawn to the abandoned structure and surrounding street. Residents find themselves confronting panhandlers, drunks, and addicts and develop apprehension about walking down the street. They flee the area as property values drop and businesses desert the community. The neighborhood now has reached a tipping point and is at risk of spiraling into a downward cycle of crime, prostitution, drugs, and gangs. The solution, according to Wilson and Kelling, is to address small concerns before they develop into large-scale crimes.[15]

We can question, along with some researchers, whether small incidents of disorder inevitably lead to petty crime, then to serious offenses, and finally to neighborhood decay. Nevertheless, surveys indicate that most people are more concerned with the immediate threat to their quality of life posed by rowdy juveniles, drug dealers, prostitutes, and public drunkenness than they are with the more distant threats of rape, robbery, and murder.

A central focus of the broken windows theory in cities where it has been adopted is combating vagrancy and loitering.

VAGRANCY AND LOITERING

Vagrancy is defined under the common law as wandering the streets with no apparent means of earning a living (without visible means of support). **Loitering** is a related offense defined as standing in public with no apparent purpose.

Vagrancy can be traced to laws passed in England as early as the thirteenth century. The early vagrancy statutes were passed in reaction to the end of the feudal system and required the vast army of individuals wandering the countryside to seek employment. These same laws were relied on during the labor shortage resulting from the Black Death in the fourteenth century to force individuals into the labor market. There was also the fear that these bands of men might loiter or gather together to engage in crime or rebellion.

The Ordinance of Labourers of 1349 authorized the imprisonment of males under sixty without means of financial support who refused to work. The Vagabonds Act of 1530 stipulated that an impotent beggar who wandered from home and was engaged in begging was to be whipped or placed in stocks for three days and nights on bread and water. Able-bodied but unemployed wanderers were later subjected to harsh penalties, including branding and slicing off portions of the ear. Another provision stated that any person found begging or wandering shall be "stripped naked from the middle upwards, and be openly whipped until his or her body be bloody." An English law in force in the second half of the nineteenth century divided vagrants into three criminal classes: idle and disorderly persons (people who refuse to work), rogues and vagabonds (wanderers), and incorrigible rogues (repeat offenders).[16] This descriptive language eventually found its way into the texts of U.S. statutes.

Statutes punishing vagrancy were adopted in virtually every U.S. state. These laws typically punished a broad range of behavior, including wandering or loitering, living without employment and having no visible means of support, begging, failing to support a wife and child, and sleeping outdoors. Individuals were also punished for their status or lifestyle. Laws, for instance, condemned and categorized as criminal prostitutes, drunkards, gamblers, gypsies engaged in telling fortunes, nightwalkers, corrupt persons, and individuals associating with thieves.[17]

The fear and distrust of the poor and unemployed led the U.S. Supreme Court to observe, in reference to an 1837 effort by New York City to prevent the inflow of the poor, that it is as necessary for a "state to provide precautionary measures against the moral pestilence of paupers, vagabonds, and possibly convicts; as it is to guard against the physical pestilence, which may arise from unsound and infectious articles imported or from a ship, the crew of which may be laboring under an infectious disease."[18]

By 1941, the U.S. Supreme Court had adopted a more sympathetic attitude toward the poor. California passed a statute in the early twentieth century preventing the influx of indigents. This was an unapologetic effort to limit budgetary expenditures for the poor and to prevent the introduction into the state of disease, rape, incest, and labor unrest. The Supreme Court criticized California and observed that it now was recognized in an industrial society that "the relief of the needy has become the common responsibility and concern of the whole nation" and that "we do not think it will now be seriously contended that because a person is without employment and without funds he constitutes a 'moral pestilence.' Poverty and immorality are not synonymous." Justice Robert Jackson added that it is contrary to the history and tradition of the United States to make an individual's rights dependent on his or her economic status, race, creed, or color. As Justice William O. Douglas noted, to hold a law constitutional that prevented those labeled as "indigents, paupers, or vagabonds" from seeking "new horizons" in California would be to reduce these individuals to an "inferior class of citizenship."[19]

In 1972, in the case of *Papachristou v. City of Jacksonville*, the U.S. Supreme Court held a Jacksonville, Florida, ordinance unconstitutional that authorized the arrest of vagrants. This was a typical statute that classified a wide range of individuals as vagrants, including rogues; vagabonds; dissolute persons who go about begging; common gamblers; persons who use juggling or unlawful games; common drunkards; nightwalkers; pilferers or pickpockets; keepers of gambling places; common brawlers; habitual loafers; persons frequenting houses of ill fame, gambling houses, and places where alcoholic beverages are sold; and individuals living on the earnings of their wives or minor children.[20]

The U.S. Supreme Court ruled that the statute was void for vagueness in that it failed to give a person of ordinary intelligence fair notice of the conduct prohibited by the statute and encouraged the police to engage in arbitrary and erratic arrests and convictions. The Court explained that the true evil in the law was its employment by the police to target the young, the poor, and minorities. The "rule of law, evenly applied to minorities as well as majorities, to the poor as well as the rich, is the great mucilage that holds society together."

Eleven years later, in *Kolender v. Lawson*, the U.S. Supreme Court ruled a California loitering statute unconstitutional that authorized the arrest of persons who loiter or wander on the streets and who fail to provide "credible and reliable" identification and to "account for their presence." The lack of a clear statement of what constitutes credible and reliable identification, according to the Court majority, left citizens uncertain how to satisfy the letter of the law and empowered the police to enforce the law in accordance with their individual biases and discretion.[21]

States now have amended their vagrancy and loitering statutes and have followed the MPC in punishing loitering or prowling under specific circumstances that "warrant alarm for the safety of persons or property."

Model Penal Code

Section 250.6. Loitering or Prowling

A person commits a violation if he loiters or prowls in a place, at a time, or in a manner not usual for law-abiding individuals under circumstances that warrant alarm for the safety of persons or property in the vicinity. Among the circumstances which may be considered in determining whether such alarm is warranted is the fact that the actor takes flight upon appearance of a peace officer, refuses to identify himself, or manifestly endeavors to conceal himself or any object. Unless flight by the actor or other circumstance makes it impracticable, a peace officer shall prior to any arrest for an offense under this section afford the actor an opportunity to dispel any alarm which would otherwise be warranted, by requesting him to identify himself and explain his presence and conduct. No person shall be convicted of an offense under this Section if the peace officer did not comply with the preceding sentence, if it appears at trial that the explanation given by the actor was true and, if believed by the peace officer at the time, would have dispelled the alarm.

HOMELESSNESS

City and local governments have increasingly relied on municipal ordinances to stem the tide of a growing homeless population. The National Law Center on Homelessness and Poverty and the National Coalition for the Homeless issued a report in 2009 titled *Homes Not Handcuffs: The Criminalization of Homelessness in U.S. Cities* that documents the increase and enforcement of laws prohibiting urban camping, sleeping in the parks and subways, aggressive panhandling, trespassing in areas under bridges and adjacent to parks, and blocking sidewalks. The report also finds laws against loitering, jaywalking, and open alcoholic containers. Several cities also prohibit charities, churches, and other organizations from serving food to the needy outside designated areas. The report concludes that these local ordinances have the effect of making it a crime to be homeless. The National Coalition for the Homeless singles out the ten "meanest cities" toward the homeless. These cities are Los Angeles, California; St. Petersburg, Florida; Orlando, Florida; Atlanta, Georgia; Gainesville, Florida; Kalamazoo, Michigan; San Francisco, California; Honolulu, Hawaii; Bradenton, Florida; and Berkeley, California. A survey of 187 cities published in 2014 found a continued increase in laws criminalizing homelessness.

In 1992, in *Pottinger v. City of Miami*, a federal district court ruled that the Miami police had employed the criminal law for the purpose of "eliminating or eradicating the presence of the homeless" or for "getting the homeless to move out of certain locations." One component of this strategy was to starve the homeless by preventing them from congregating in areas where pantries made free food available. The federal court found that the evidence supported the complainants' assertion that "there is no public place where they can perform basic, essential acts such as sleeping without the possibility of being arrested" and issued a judicial order directing the Miami police to halt this abuse of the criminal law. Another troubling trend is random violence by groups of young people against the homeless.[22]

A more typical decision is *Joyce v. City and County of San Francisco*, in which a federal district court refused to issue an injunction to halt San Francisco's enforcement of the Matrix Program on the grounds that the homeless plaintiffs were unlikely to be successful in constitutionally challenging the program. The Matrix Program was intended to combat the growing homeless population in San Francisco by stringently enforcing a number of criminal laws including "public drinking and inebriation; obstruction of sidewalks; lodging, camping, or sleeping in public parks; littering; public urination and defecation; aggressive panhandling; dumping of refuse; graffiti; vandalism; street prostitution; and street sales of narcotics."[23]

A number of jurisdictions have adopted ordinances prohibiting street begging or panhandling. The Second Circuit Court of Appeals, in *Loper v. New York City Police Department*, held that a statute that prohibited all panhandling on city sidewalks and streets violated the First Amendment.[24]

The City of Indianapolis, in July 1999, responded by prohibiting "aggressive panhandling." This illegal activity was defined as touching the solicited person, approaching an individual standing in line to be admitted to a commercial establishment, blocking an individual's entrance to any building or vehicle, following a person who walks away from the panhandler, using profane or abusive language or statements or gestures that would "cause a reasonable person to be fearful or feel compelled," and panhandling in a group of two or more persons. The ordinance also prohibited soliciting at various locations, including bus stops, sidewalk cafes, vehicles parked or stopped on a public street, and within twenty feet of an ATM. Panhandling is prohibited under the ordinance after sunset or before sunrise. Each act in violation of the ordinance is punishable by a fine of not more than $2,500. A court was authorized to issue an injunction or order prohibiting an individual convicted of violating the ordinance from repeating this behavior. Violation of the injunction was punishable with imprisonment.[25]

Panhandling is defined as a solicitation made in person upon any street, public place, or park in which a person requests an immediate donation of money or other gratuity. Individuals are free to directly ask for money during the day so long as they do not violate the ordinance. In addition, individuals have the right during the daytime or evening hours to engage in "passive panhandling" in which they display signs or engage in street performances during the evening.

The Seventh Circuit Court of Appeals ruled that Indianapolis possessed a legitimate interest in promoting the safety and convenience of its citizens on the public streets, places, and parks and that the ordinance was a reasonable time, place, and manner restriction of speech. The court noted that the ordinance does not ban all panhandling; it merely restricts solicitations to situations that are considered "especially unwanted or bothersome" in which people would "feel a heightened sense of fear or alarm, or might wish especially to be left alone."

You Decide **11.2** The Ninth Circuit Court of Appeals held that arresting homeless individuals for "sitting, lying, or sleeping on a public street and sidewalks at all times and in all places within Los Angeles" is cruel and unusual punishment. The so-called Skid Row area of Los Angeles has the largest concentration of homeless in the United States, and there generally is a shortage of more than a thousand beds each evening. The area is dominated by single-residence hotels, which charge $379 per month. The monthly welfare stipend for single adults in Los Angeles County is $221. Waiting lists for public housing and for housing assistance vouchers in Los Angeles are from three to ten years. Does the Eighth Amendment prohibit Los Angeles "from punishing involuntary sitting, lying, or sleeping on public sidewalks that is an unavoidable consequence of being homeless without shelter in the City of Los Angeles"? See *Jones v. City of Los Angeles*, 444 F.3d 1118 (9th Cir. 2006). (The decision was withdrawn following a settlement between the plaintiffs and Los Angeles.)

You can find the answer at study.sagepub.com/lippmaness2e

GANGS

It is estimated that that there are roughly twenty-one thousand gangs active in the United States with an estimated seven hundred thousand gang members. Gangs are no longer limited to large urban areas and today are active in nearly every city, suburb, and rural area. These gangs are involved in criminal activity ranging from drugs and prostitution to extortion and theft; and some have members throughout the United States as well as in Mexico and Central America. The Illinois legislature made several legislative "findings" concerning the peril posed by gangs:

- Urban, suburban, and rural communities are being "terrorized and plundered by street gangs."
- Street gangs are often "controlled by criminally sophisticated adults" who manipulate or threaten young people into serving as drug couriers and into carrying out brutal crimes on behalf of the gang.
- Street gangs present a "clear and present danger to public order and safety."[26]

An example is the Varrio Sureño Town gang that was described by the California Supreme Court, in the 1997 case of *Gallo v. Acuna*, as having converted the four-square-block neighborhood of Rockspring in San Jose, California, into an "urban war zone." The gang members were described as congregating on sidewalks and lawns and in front of apartment complexes at all hours. They openly drank, smoked dope, sniffed glue, snorted cocaine, and transformed the neighborhood into a drug bazaar. The court's opinion described drive-by shootings, vandalism, arson, and theft as commonplace. Garages were used as urinals; homes were "commandeered as escape routes" and served as storage sites for drugs and guns; and buildings, sidewalks, and automobiles were "turned into a . . . canvas of gang graffiti." The California Supreme Court concluded that community residents had become "prisoners in their own homes." Individuals wearing the color of clothing identified with rival gangs were at risk, and relatives and friends were reluctant to visit. Verbal and physical retaliation was directed against anyone who complained to the police or who served as an informant.[27]

In *Gallo*, the California Supreme Court affirmed an injunction (a court order halting certain acts) issued by a California trial court. The order declared the Varrio Sureño Town gang a "public nuisance," meaning that the gang's continued presence in the community prevented residents from the enjoyment of life and property, disrupted the quiet and security of the neighborhood, and interfered with the use of the streets and parks. Thirty-eight members of the gang were ordered to "abate" (end) the nuisance by halting conduct ranging from spray painting to the possession and sale of drugs and the playing of loud music, public consumption of alcohol, littering, urinating in a public place, communicating through the use of gang signals, and wearing gang insignia. An individual or group violating the injunction would be in contempt of court and subject to punishment by a fine or short-term incarceration. At last count, there were nearly fifty gang injunctions against fifty-seven gangs in Los Angeles with a total membership of eleven thousand.

States have adopted various legal approaches to controlling gangs. Special gang statutes make it a crime to solicit, to cause any person to join, or to deter any person from leaving a gang or to commit a crime intended to promote or further the interests of a gang. Enhanced punishment is provided for crimes committed to further the interests of gangs. Gang members have been prosecuted under organized crime statutes, and laws also provide for the vicarious civil liability of parents for the conduct of their children. Various school districts prohibit the display of gang paraphernalia and colors, and some correctional systems provide rewards for gang members who leave the gang and cooperate with authorities. In 2009, the City of Los Angeles successfully sued and collected a multimillion-dollar judgment for damages against individual gang members.

Critics of these antigang efforts question whether we are sacrificing the civil liberties of both gang members and innocent young people in order to combat the violence perpetrated by a relatively small number of individuals. They point to the fact that young minority males who, in fact, may not be gang members are often targeted for harassment, detention, interrogation, and arrest by the police. One of the most significant efforts to curb gang activity was the gang ordinance adopted by the Chicago City Council in 1992. This local law authorized the police to order suspected gang members who, along with at least two other individuals, were "loitering" in public to vacate the area. Between 1992 and 1995, the police issued eighty-nine thousand orders to disperse and arrested more than forty-two thousand people for disobeying an order to move on. In *City of Chicago v. Morales*, the U.S. Supreme Court considered the constitutionality of the ordinance and held that the ordinance unconstitutionally failed to provide clear standards to guide the police and the public and potentially applied to a large amount of innocent conduct. The city "enacted an ordinance that affords too much discretion to the police and too little notice to citizens who wish to use the public streets."[28]

Read *City of Chicago v. Morales* on the study site: study .sagepub.com/ lippmaness2e.

On February 16, 2000, the Chicago City Council revised the 1992 Gang Congregation Ordinance. The amended ordinance defined "gang loitering" as remaining in any one place under circumstances "that would warrant a reasonable person" to believe that the purpose or effect of that behavior is to enable a criminal street gang "to establish control over identifiable areas, to intimidate others from entering these areas, or [to] conceal illegal activities." The new ordinance authorizes the Superintendent of Police to designate areas of Chicago in which enforcement is required because "gang loitering has enabled street gangs to establish control over identifiable areas, to intimidate others from entering the areas or to conceal illegal activities."[29]

THE OVERREACH OF CRIMINAL LAW

Criminologists Norval Morris and Gordon Hawkins, writing in 1969, argue that the function of criminal law is to protect property and persons, particularly juveniles and those in need of special protection. They point out that roughly 50 percent of all arrests are for acts threatening public morality. These, for the most part, are acts that individuals engage in voluntarily and do not view as harmful to themselves or to others. In other words, people are arrested who do not believe that they should be treated as criminals or victims and who are not deterred by the threat of either arrest or punishment. This list of victimless crimes includes drunkenness, narcotics offenses, gambling, prostitution, the possession of obscene materials, and various sexual offenses. Some may include under the heading of victimless offenses seat belt and motorcycle helmet laws, **adultery** and **fornication**, and the prohibition on assisted suicide. Morris and Hawkins criticize what they view as the moralist orientation of U.S. criminal law and the long tradition of employing the law as an instrument for coercing men and women into acting in a virtuous fashion. In their view, people possess a complete right to choose a path that may lead to purgatory so long as they do not directly injure the person or property of another. Morris and Hawkins also point to the fact that criminalizing consensual, private behavior actually increases rather than decreases crime.[30]

- *Crime Tariff.* Making an activity illegal means that those engaged in the activity do not confront competition from legal businesses and will be free to charge a high price. This profit, in turn, is used to fund other organized crime activities. Also, addicts must resort to crime to support their expensive gambling, drug, and alcohol addictions.
- *Inconsistency.* The condemnation of activities such as gambling is undermined by the fact that there are legal lotteries and gambling casinos in Atlantic City, in Las Vegas, and on Native American reservations. This creates an inconsistency in legal rules and contributes to a lack of respect for the law.
- *Romanticism.* Declaring an activity illegal tends to make it appear romantic and appealing to younger people.
- *Law Enforcement.* Scarce law enforcement resources are devoted to enforcing these laws rather than to preventing more harmful offenses. Often, there are no complaining victims, and the police must resort to controversial undercover and sting operations. The amount of money involved in activities such as drug trafficking and the absence of complaining victims creates a situation with the potential for bribery, extortion, and corruption.
- *Criminal Subculture.* Making activities like gambling and prostitution illegal means that people involved in these activities are driven into a criminal environment and may be victimized or become involved in other crimes. Prostitutes often are exploited by pimps who offer protection and threaten customers.

This view is challenged by English Lord Patrick Devlin, who argues that society must be equally vigilant in protecting itself against threats from abroad and at home. Lord Devlin contends that the loosening of moral bonds is typically the first step toward the disintegration of the social order and that the maintenance of values is the proper concern of government. Lord Devlin argues that the notion that allegedly private behavior does not affect society is misguided. He concedes that while great social harm may not result from a single individual engaging in an alcoholic or gambling binge, society would crumble if the same activity were embraced by a quarter or more of the population. These so-called victimless crimes, according to Lord Devlin, impose hardships on the families of addicts, require society to spend money in treating addictions, corrupt the young, and ruin the lives of addicts. In short, a compassionate society does not permit individuals to "do their own thing." Lord Devlin concludes that we cannot, on the one hand, encourage people to live in a moral fashion and, on the other hand, tolerate immoral behavior. Where do you stand on the debate over so-called victimless crimes?[31]

The next section considers prostitution, an activity that the famous British *Wolfenden Report* argued, in 1957, should not be subject to criminal punishment when carried on between consenting adults.

PROSTITUTION

Prostitution is defined as engaging in sexual intercourse or other sexual acts in exchange for money or other items of value. You undoubtedly have heard someone refer to prostitution as "the world's oldest profession." Why is an activity that has been characteristic of both ancient and modern societies considered a crime? There are several reasons:

Disease. Encourages transmission of infections such as AIDS.

Family. Weakens marriage and the family.

Exploitation. Exploits and degrades women.

Immorality. Promotes social immorality and a culture tolerant of alcoholism, drug abuse, gambling, and acts of immorality.

Critics of laws punishing prostitution point out that the legitimacy of law enforcement is undermined by the fact that the police typically must resort to posing as "prostitutes" or "customers" in order to enforce prostitution laws and that this lowers respect for law enforcement. There is also an inconsistency in the fact that the police target street prostitutes while "call girls" who service the relatively wealthy are rarely arrested. Critics further note that despite the resources devoted to eliminating prostitution, the police have not been able to deter individuals from engaging in this activity. The argument is also made that categorizing prostitution as a crime ensures that it will be controlled by organized crime and pimps (individuals who live off the proceeds of prostitution). This results in prostitutes being labeled as criminals, places them in danger, and deprives the government of tax revenues. Others argue that prostitution laws deprive women of the opportunity to utilize their bodies to advance their economic well-being. The most radical commentators point to the fact that prostitutes are no different than the large number of people who engage in sex with the intent of obtaining employment or material gain. Some favor decriminalization of prostitution and subjecting the practice to state regulation, the policy followed in the Netherlands. State regulation has the advantage of ensuring that precautions are taken against the spread of HIV and other sexually transmitted diseases. A small number of commentators favor complete legalization. Judge Stanley Gartenstein of the Criminal Court of New York City noted that "morality cannot be legislated" and that it might be more productive to punish the individuals who exploit prostitutes rather than the prostitute herself.[32]

Nevada is the only state in which prostitution is legal. Each county in the state with a population of fewer than four hundred thousand is free to determine whether to permit prostitution, and the practice is heavily regulated. Brothels must pay a licensing fee, and prostitutes are required to submit to monthly HIV tests. Condoms are required, and prostitutes must be at least twenty-one years old. Prostitution is not permitted anywhere other than in the brothels, and the brothels may not advertise in counties in which the practice is illegal. Nevada possesses roughly thirty legal brothels that employ roughly three hundred prostitutes.

The Crime of Prostitution

Prostitution punishes both men and women who

- solicit or engage in
- any sexual activity
- in exchange for money or other consideration.

As you can see, prostitution is committed by exchanging sexual activity for money or other consideration or by **solicitation for prostitution**, asking or requesting another person to engage in prostitution. Note that it is the solicitation or actual exchange of money or value for sex that distinguishes prostitution from the legal act of approaching another person for consensual sexual activity. The crime of prostitution is not limited to sexual intercourse and encompasses all varieties of sexual interaction. Georgia's prostitution law provides that a person "commits the offense of prostitution when he or she performs or offers or consents to perform a sexual act, including but not limited to sexual intercourse or sodomy, for money or other items of value."[33]

Pennsylvania follows the MPC by providing that a person is guilty of prostitution who "is an inmate of a house of prostitution or otherwise engages in sexual activity as a business." An inmate is a person who engages in prostitution as a business in conjunction with a house of prostitution or as a "call girl" who makes use of an agency to obtain clients. An individual is guilty under this provision who engages in prostitution in affiliation with a house of prostitution. It is unnecessary to establish that the accused engaged in a specific act of prostitution.[34]

State statutes also commonly punish loitering for prostitution. California declares that it is "unlawful for any person to loiter in any public place with the intent to commit prostitution." An individual's *mens rea* is demonstrated by acts that indicate an intent to induce, entice, or solicit prostitution. The California statute notes that this intent may be established by the stopping and soliciting of pedestrians or of the occupants of passing automobiles. This type of provision recognizes that public loitering for solicitation is an essential step in engaging in the business of prostitution and that solicitation negatively impacts a neighborhood's sense of safety and stability.[35]

Prostitution statutes are gender neutral; prostitution may be committed by a male or female prostitute, and both prostitutes and customers may be guilty of soliciting or loitering for the purpose of prostitution. Several states explicitly punish a person who "hires a prostitute or any other person to engage in sexual activity . . . or if that person enters or remains in a house of prostitution for the purpose of engaging in sexual activity." Indiana punishes patronizing a prostitute with the same penalties that apply to sex workers. In *Banks v. State*, Banks was convicted when in response to a female undercover officer's question "so are you good for head for $20?" he nodded and said "yeah we're good."[36] Pennsylvania also provides that convictions and sentences for a second and all subsequent acts of prostitution shall be published in the newspaper.[37]

The federal Mann Act[38] prohibits the interstate transportation of an individual for prostitution or for any other prohibited sexual activity. The act applies when an individual is transported for an immoral purpose even when there is no financial motive involved.[39]

The federal criminal code also punishes **human trafficking**. The Victims of Trafficking and Violence Protection Act, first adopted in 2000 and renewed numerous times, punishes by twenty years in prison individuals who provide or obtain the labor of another through threat of serious harm or restraint or who traffic in persons who are to be subjected to slavery or forced labor. Aggravated forced labor and sex trafficking and the sex trafficking of minors is subject to punishment of up to life in prison.

Another prostitution-related offense is **pimping**, which involves procuring a prostitute for another individual, arranging a meeting for the purpose of prostitution, transporting an individual to a location for the purpose of prostitution, receiving money or another thing of value from a prostitute knowing that it was earned from prostitution, or owning, managing, or leasing a house of prostitution or prostitution business. **Pandering** is the encouraging and inducing of another to become or remain a prostitute; this is punished more harshly when duress or coercion is employed. **Living off prostitution** is committed by a person, other than a prostitute and the prostitute's minor child or other dependent, who is "knowingly supported in whole or substantial part by the proceeds of prostitution." **Keeping a place of prostitution** occurs "when [an individual] knowingly grants or permits the use of such place for the purpose of prostitution." Pimping, pandering, and keeping a place of prostitution are also generally encompassed under the crime of **promoting prostitution**, which involves aiding or abetting prostitution by "any means whatsoever." States also have extended their laws to criminally punish a "masseur or masseuse" who commits the offense of **masturbation for hire** when he or she "stimulates the genital organs of another, whether resulting in orgasm or not, by manual or other bodily contact exclusive of sexual intercourse or by instrumental manipulation for money or the substantial equivalent thereof."

Prostitution is a misdemeanor. It is typically punished somewhat more severely for the third and subsequent offenses and is a felony in the event that an individual knew that he or she was infected with HIV. Georgia provides a sentence of between five and twenty years and a fine of up to $10,000 for keeping a place of prostitution, pimping, pandering, or solicitation involving an individual under eighteen years old.[40]

We should note in passing that there are several other misdemeanor sexual offenses that appear in various state statutes:

- *Adultery.* Consensual sexual intercourse between a male and a female, at least one of whom is married.
- *Bigamy.* Marrying another while already having a living spouse.
- *Fornication.* An unmarried person engaging in voluntary sexual intercourse with another individual.
- *Lewdness.* Public acts offending community standards, including the display of genitals, sexual intercourse, lewd sexual contact, and deviant sexual intercourse.
- *Incest.* Sexual intercourse between individuals who are related to one another within certain prohibited degrees.
- *Seduction.* A female engaging in sexual intercourse with a male based on a false promise of marriage.
- *Polygamy.* Marriage at the same time to more than one person.

Legal Regulation of Prostitution

The difficulty of controlling prostitution through individual criminal prosecutions led the City of Milwaukee, Wisconsin, to obtain a court order declaring that prostitutes in designated areas of the city constituted a nuisance. A Wisconsin appellate court found that the police had received a high volume of complaints concerning prostitutes on the streets and private property in this neighborhood. The court further ruled that the enforcement of the laws against prostitution posed a danger

Read *Harwell v. State* on the study site: study .sagepub.com/ lippmaness2e.

to the police, who were forced to act undercover to apprehend prostitutes, and that these officers were endangered by the fact that the prostitutes frequently carried sharpened objects, knives with long blades, and razors. The injunction issued by the court prohibited prostitutes from soliciting customers by stopping pedestrians and automobiles and from waiting at bus stops and pay phones and loitering in the doorways of businesses.[41]

Model Penal Code

Section 251.2. Prostitution and Related Offenses

(1) A person is guilty of prostitution, a petty misdemeanor, if he or she:

(a) is an inmate of a house of prostitution or otherwise engages in sexual activity as a business; or

(b) loiters in or within view of any public place for the purpose of being hired to engage in sexual activity.

"Sexual activity" includes homosexual and other deviate sexual relations. A "house of prostitution" is any place where prostitution or promotion of prostitution is regularly carried on by one person under the control, management or supervision of another. An "inmate" is a person who engages in prostitution in or through the agency of a house of prostitution. "Public place" means any place to which the public or any substantial group thereof has access.

(2) Promoting Prostitution. . . . The following acts shall . . . constitute promoting prostitution:

(a) owning, controlling, managing, supervising or otherwise keeping . . . a house of prostitution or prostitution business; or

(b) procuring an inmate for a house of prostitution or a place in a house of prostitution for one who would be an inmate; or

(c) encouraging, inducing, or otherwise purposely causing another to become or remain a prostitute; or

(d) soliciting a person to patronize a prostitute; or

(e) procuring a prostitute for a patron; or

(f) transporting a person into or within this state with the purpose to promote that person engaging in prostitution, or procuring or paying for transportation with that purpose; or

(g) leasing or otherwise permitting a place controlled by the actor . . . to be regularly used for prostitution or the promotion of prostitution, or failure to make reasonable efforts to abate such use by ejecting the tenant, notifying law enforcement authorities, or other legally available means; or

(h) soliciting, receiving, or agreeing to receive any benefit for doing or agreeing to do anything forbidden by this Subsection.

(3) Grading of Offenses. An offense under Subsection (2) constitutes a felony of the third degree if:

(a) the offense falls within paragraph (a), (b) or (c) of Subsection (2); or

(b) the actor compels another to engage in or promote prostitution; or

(c) the actor promotes prostitution of a child under 16. . . .

(d) the actor promotes prostitution of his wife, child, ward or any person for whose care, protection or support he is responsible.

Otherwise the offense is a misdemeanor.

(4) Presumption From Living off Prostitutes. A person, other than the prostitute or the prostitute's minor child or other legal dependent incapable of self-support, who is supported in whole or substantial part by the proceeds of prostitution, is presumed to be knowingly promoting prostitution. . . .

(5) Patronizing Prostitutes. A person commits a violation if he hires a prostitute to engage in sexual activity with him, or if he enters or remains in a house of prostitution for the purpose of engaging in sexual activity.

(6) Evidence. On the issue whether a place is a house of prostitution the following shall be admissible evidence: its general repute; the repute of the persons who reside in or frequent the place; the frequency, timing and duration of visits by non-residents. Testimony of a person against his spouse shall be admissible to prove offenses under this Section.

CRIMINAL LAW AND PUBLIC POLICY

In 2015, the nongovernmental human rights organization Amnesty International (AI) took the controversial step of condemning the criminalization or punishment of activities relating to the buying or selling of consensual sex between adults. AI's position is based on the human rights principle that consensual sex between adults is entitled to protection so long as it does not involve trickery, threats, or violence. The organization continues to support the criminalization of individuals who exploit and abuse "sex workers" and who engage in sex trafficking.

AI advocates the decriminalization of sex work rather than criminal punishment. Customers (johns) who engage in consensual sexual activity with a "sex worker" and individuals involved in the "operational aspects" of the industry such as running a brothel under the AI proposal also would no longer be subject to arrest and to criminal punishment. An exception to decriminalization under AI's proposal are individuals who force others into sexual bondage or individuals who engage in sexual relations with children, who are considered to be incapable of a criminal intent.

AI argues that the present policy of criminalization of "sex work" across the globe leaves sex workers with little protection against harassment, violence, and sexual molestation by pimps, johns, and the police. As long as sex work is considered unlawful, sex workers also will be without access to the protections and benefits afforded to workers engaged in lawful activity, including unionization, health insurance, contributions to social security, or a retirement fund. Criminalization, according to AI, stigmatizes sex workers, results in their rejection by friends and family, and pushes them into a criminal subculture of drugs and gambling.

Groups such as the Coalition Against Trafficking in Women view female prostitution as subordinating female sex workers to pimps, brothel owners, and the male buyers of sex. The opponents of AI's proposal to decriminalize prostitution claim that this will lead to an increase in sex trafficking to satisfy the anticipated increased demand for sexual services of women. The only solution that will protect women is the elimination of the $99 billion global sex industry. The best approach to the eradication of prostitution, according to critics of AI's proposal, is the "Swedish model" (also followed in Norway and in France), which criminalizes customers and individuals who exploit sex workers rather than the sex workers themselves.

OBSCENITY

Until the eighteenth century, obscenity in England was punished before religious courts. In 1727, royal judges asserted jurisdiction over obscenity, asserting that possession of such material constituted an offense against the peace and weakened the "bonds of civil society, virtue, and morality."[42]

In *Roth v. United States*, the U.S. Supreme Court held that obscenity was not constitutionally protected speech or press within the First Amendment, reasoning that this form of expression is "utterly without redeeming social importance."[43] The lack of protection afforded to obscenity is based on several public policy considerations:

Protection of the Community. A community is entitled to protect itself against threats to the moral fabric of society.

Antisocial Conduct. Obscenity causes antisocial conduct.

Women. Obscenity degrades women.

Communication. Obscenity produces a sexual, rather than mental, response and is a form of sexual communication rather than the expression of ideas.

These assertions all have been challenged. For instance, the government *Report of the Commission on Obscenity and Pornography*, in 1970, concluded that exposure to explicit sexual materials does not play a significant role in causing delinquent or criminal behavior.

In *Miller v. California*, in 1973, the U.S. Supreme Court affirmed that obscene material is not protected by the First Amendment and established a three-part test for obscenity. Obscenity is defined as a description or representation of sexual conduct that, taken as a whole by the average person applying contemporary community standards, has the following three qualities[44]:

1. *Prurient Interest.* Appeals to the prurient interest in sex (an obsession with obscene, lewd, or immoral matters).

2. *Offensive.* Portrays sex in a patently offensive way.

3. *Value.* Applying a reasonable person standard, lacks serious literary, artistic, political, or scientific value when taken as a whole.

In *New York v. Ferber*, the U.S. Supreme Court held that **child pornography** could be prohibited despite the fact that the material did not satisfy the *Miller* standard. The Court upheld a New York law that prohibited the depiction of a child under sixteen years old in a "sexual performance," defined as engaging in actual or simulated sexual activity or the lewd display of the genitals. The sexual performance was considered criminal under the statute regardless of whether it possessed literary, artistic, political, or scientific value.[45]

It is illegal in every state to buy, sell, exhibit, produce, advertise, distribute, or possess with the intent to distribute obscene material or illegal child pornography. The offense of **lewdness** involves conduct that is obscene, such as willfully exposing the genitals of one person to another in a public place for the purpose of arousing or gratifying the sexual desire of either individual. **Indecent exposure** generally entails an act of public indecency, including sexual intercourse, exposure of the sexual organs, a lewd appearance in a state of partial or complete nudity, or a lewd caress or fondling of the body of another person. **Voyeurism** involves obtaining sexual gratification from viewing another individual's sex organs or sexual activities and typically is punished under what are termed "peeping Tom laws."

Several municipalities have expanded the definition of obscenity to include other forms of communication that are considered harmful. An Indianapolis ordinance, for instance, was ruled unconstitutional that prohibited the portrayal of women as sexual objects who enjoy pain or humiliation or who experience sexual pleasure in being raped or who are presented as sexual objects for domination or violation. The ordinance was ruled unconstitutional by the Seventh Circuit Court of Appeals, which held that Indianapolis was improperly penalizing speech based on the content of the message: Communication depicting women in the approved way was lawful no matter how sexually explicit, and speech portraying women in the unapproved way was unlawful whatever the literary or artistic value.[46]

You Decide

11.3 California Assembly Bill 1179 (2005), Cal. Civ. Code Ann. §§ 1746–1746.5, prohibits the sale or rental of "violent video games" to minors unless accompanied by an adult, and requires their packaging to be labeled "18." The act covers games "in which the range of options available to a player includes killing, maiming, dismembering, or sexually assaulting an image of a human being, if those acts are depicted" in a manner that "[a] reasonable person, considering the game as a whole, would find appeals to a deviant or morbid interest of minors," that is "patently offensive to prevailing standards in the community as to what is suitable for minors," and that "causes the game, as a whole, to lack serious literary, artistic, political, or scientific value for minors." Violation of the act is punishable by a civil fine of up to $1,000.

The video game and software industries brought a challenge to the act in the U.S. District Court for the Northern District of California. The district court concluded that the act violated the First Amendment and permanently enjoined its enforcement. The State of California appealed to the U.S. Supreme Court.

How would you decide the case? As a state legislator, would you vote in favor of this type of legislation? See *Brown v. Entertainment Merchants Association*, 564 U.S. ___ (2011).

You can find the answer at study.sagepub.com/lippmaness2e

CRIME IN THE NEWS

In 1989, Denver, Colorado, enacted an ordinance banning pit bulls from the city. The law was precipitated by dog attacks that resulted in the death of a five-year-old boy and the savage maiming of a pastor. Denver had experienced twenty such attacks over a five-year period. The Colorado legislature subsequently passed a law prohibiting counties and municipalities from enacting breed-specific bans on dogs. In December 2004, a Denver court ruled that Colorado lacked the authority to prevent the city from prohibiting any person from "owning, possessing, keeping, exercising control over, maintaining, harboring, or selling a Pit Bull in the City and County of Denver." A pit bull is defined in the ordinance as any dog that is an American pit bull terrier, an American Staffordshire terrier, a Staffordshire bull terrier, or any dog displaying the majority of the physical traits of any one or more of these breeds.

Animal control officers under the ordinance are authorized to confiscate pit bulls, and a determination then is made by a veterinarian as to whether the dog is one of the three "banned breeds." In the event that the animal is found to be a member of a banned breed, the owner is provided the opportunity to remove the dog from the city. A failure to remove the animal results in the dog being put to sleep. A second offense of possession results in automatic euthanasia. An owner who removes his or her dog must provide a statement listing the dog's new home. The penalty for harboring an illegal pit bull is a fine of up to $1,000 and a year in jail. The ordinance permits the transportation of a pit bull through Denver so long as the dog remains in a vehicle. Since 1989, opponents of the Denver ordinance estimate that roughly 1,100 pit bulls have been seized and put down. There reportedly have been no deaths in Denver from pit bulls since the prohibition went into effect. As for national statistics, between 2005 and 2015, pit bulls killed 232 individuals and rottweilers killed 41 individuals, and a majority of the victims were children.

Denver and Miami are the largest cities to ban pit bulls, and at one point nearly seven hundred cities and towns adopted similar bans or imposed restrictions on the owners of pit bulls, including liability insurance, muzzling dogs in public, keeping the dogs in pens when in the yard surrounding the home, the posting of warning signs, and even mandatory sterilization. Seventeen states have legislation that prohibits breed-specific bans. The legislation in most states focuses on a dog's behavior rather than on a dog's breed. The typical approach is represented by Michigan, which prohibits "dangerous dogs"; such an animal is defined as a dog that "bites or attacks a person, or a dog that bites or attacks and causes serious injury or death to another dog while the other dog is on the property or under the control of its owner." An exception is made for an attack against trespassers and persons who provoke or torment the animal, or in those instances in which the animal acts to protect an individual.

The Denver ordinance is based on the belief that pit bulls tend to be inherently aggressive toward other animals and children and inflict more severe injuries than other dogs. In addition, the breed is favored by gang members and drug dealers. Defenders of the breed claim that pit bulls are no more dangerous than other dogs and that most of the pit bulls that are impounded are completely harmless. Historically, various breeds have been victims of the same form of social hysteria that is being directed at pit bulls. Various studies have challenged the wisdom of the ban on pit bulls and conclude that it is irresponsible owners who present the problem rather than the breed. These owners will turn any dog they own into an aggressive animal. Pit bull advocates also argue that the breed often is misidentified and incorrectly blamed for an attack.

(Continued)

(Continued)

Some courts have struck down pit bull ordinances on the ground that the term *pit bull* "is vague and risks depriving owners of their pets without due process of law." The majority view, however, is that the regulation of pit bulls is a valid exercise of the state and local government's power to protect the public health and safety. A Kansas court found that pit bulls "possess a strongly developed 'kill instinct' not shared by other breeds of dogs," are "unique in their 'savageness and unpredictability,'" and are "twice as likely to cause multiple injuries as other breeds of dogs." See *Hearn v. City of Overland Park*, 772 P.2d 758 (Kan. 1989).

CRUELTY TO ANIMALS

In 2007, the issue of animal cruelty became a topic of public attention when Atlanta Falcons star quarterback Michael Vick was convicted and sentenced to twenty-three months in prison for violating a federal law prohibiting cruelty to animals. The crime of cruelty to animals is recognized as an offense against public order and decency. These laws were originally based on the belief that respect for animals helped to teach people to act with sensitivity and regard for their fellow citizens, particularly the most vulnerable members of human society. Today, laws against cruelty to animals also reflect the emotional attachment that people have toward their pets and other animals and the increasingly common belief that animals experience pleasure and pain and possess rights. Violence toward animals is also thought to encourage aggression toward human beings. Prior to 1990, only six states punished cruelty to animals as a felony. All fifty states now punish animal cruelty as a felony and have laws against dog fighting and cock fighting. The Animal Legal Defense Fund ranks the five states having the strongest anticruelty laws as Illinois, Maine, Michigan, Oregon, and California. The states considered to have the weakest anticruelty laws are Kentucky, North Dakota, Idaho, Mississippi, and Iowa.

The Animal Welfare Act of 1966[47] is a comprehensive federal law that regulates research, exhibition, transport, and treatment of animals by dealers. In 2010, in *United States v. Stevens*, the U.S. Supreme Court held that a congressional act prohibiting the creating, selling, or possessing of depictions of animal cruelty with the purpose of placing the depiction in "interstate commerce . . . for commercial gain" was in violation of First Amendment freedom of expression.[48]

There also is a long list of federal laws that protect all varieties of wildlife. For example, the Lacey Act prohibits interstate trafficking in wildlife and wildlife parts that have been taken in violation of a state, federal, foreign, or trial law or regulation.[49] Another example is the Migratory Bird Treaty Act that safeguards virtually all native North American birds, [50] and the Endangered Species Act protects species and populations of plants and animals that are in imminent danger of extinction. [51]

CASE ANALYSIS

In *People v. Upshaw*, the defendants argued that the evidence did not support the charge against them of inciting to riot and disorderly conduct.

Did Upshaw Incite a Riot?

People v. Upshaw, *741 N.Y.S.2d 664 (Crim. Ct. N.Y.C. 2002)*
Opinion by: Harrington, J.

Defendant argues that the accusatory instrument [indictment], which charges him and two codefendants with inciting to riot and disorderly conduct, is not facially sufficient and must be dismissed. Specifically, defendant argues that his actions, rather than criminal, were an exercise of his right to free speech under the First Amendment of the United States Constitution. . . . After reviewing the complaint, and after consideration of defendant's motion to dismiss and the People's opposition thereto, the court concludes that the accusatory instrument is facially sufficient. Therefore, and for the following reasons, defendant's motion is denied.

Penal Law section 240.08 provides that a person is guilty of inciting to riot "when he urges ten or more persons to engage in tumultuous and violent conduct of a kind likely to create public alarm." Although Penal Law section 240.08 does not expressly provide for the element of intent, courts have recognized that in order to pass constitutional muster, the incitement statute necessarily includes the "elements of 'intent' and 'clear and present danger' before one's freedom of speech may be abridged under the First Amendment." "Thus, the People must prove not only that defendant's conduct . . . created a clear and present danger of riotous behavior, but also that by such conduct he in fact intended a riot to ensue." The complaint contains the following narrative of defendant's alleged criminal conduct:

> Deponent [Police Officer Charles Carlstrom] states that he observed each defendant at [234 W. 42nd Street in the County and State of New York] yelling and stating in substance: IT'S GOOD THAT THE WORLD TRADE CENTER WAS BOMBED. MORE COPS AND FIREMEN SHOULD HAVE DIED. MORE BOMBS SHOULD HAVE DROPPED AND MORE PEOPLE SHOULD HAVE BEEN KILLED. WE'VE GOT SOMETHING FOR YOUR A----.

> Deponent states that a total of 5 defendants (Eric White, Reggie Upshaw, Steven Murdock, Jesse Atkinson and Kyle Jones) where [*sic*] yelling the above statements to a crowd of approximately 50 people. Deponent states that said people gathered around defendants and some of said people yelled back at defendants.

> Deponent states that defendants did approach people in the crowd and yell in their faces.

> Deponent further states that defendants were asked to disperse and refused to do so.

> Deponent states that defendants' conduct caused the crowd to gather and arguments to ensue.

Arguing that the complaint does not allege that he acted with the requisite intent to incite a riot,

defendant contends that the complaint alleges merely that he "spoke in praise of the assault on the World Trade Center and stated that worse should have happened," but does not allege that "defendant urged or encouraged people to commit acts of terrorism or treason." . . . Defendant analogizes his conduct to "the mere abstract teaching . . . of the moral propriety or even moral necessity for a resort to force and violence" in contrast to "preparing a group for violent action and steeling it to such action." In defendant's view, "the language attributed to defendant was an expression of a political nature, intended to spur debate and thought, not to create the type of public harm contemplated by the statute."

In analyzing whether the allegations in the complaint evince defendant's intent that his alleged conduct led to riotous behavior, and whether his alleged conduct created a clear and present danger of riotous behavior, it is necessary to consider defendant's words and deeds in the context in which he and his alleged accomplices spoke and acted. The alleged crime took place only days after one of the greatest catastrophes this nation has suffered—the overwhelming brunt of which was felt most keenly here in New York—and within sight of the massive smoke plume emanating from the still-smoldering mass grave site that had been the twin towers of the World Trade Center. It took place while many New Yorkers were grieving for the loss of loved ones or praying in hope that the missing might yet be found, and as New Yorkers, indeed, all Americans, held their collective breath at what, at the time, appeared to be the likelihood, if not the inevitability, of additional terrorist attacks. It was under these circumstances that defendant and his cohorts allegedly chose a crowded 42nd Street near Times Square as their venue not merely to engage in what any reasonable person would consider to be a vile and morally reprehensible diatribe, but to intentionally confront the gathering crowd, at point blank range, for the purpose of inciting riotous behavior. It is estimated that approximately 3,000 people died in the World Trade Center attack. By comparison, 2,403 Americans were killed in the attack on Pearl Harbor.

There can be no doubt that the words and deeds alleged in the complaint make out the elements of the crime of inciting to riot. According to the complaint, defendant and his accomplices used extremely inflammatory language calculated to cause unrest in the crowd; praising the tragic deaths of thousands of innocents at the hands of terrorists and wishing for even more carnage while the threat of further attacks loomed over the city cannot be considered "an expression of a political nature, intended to spur debate and thought, not to create the type of public harm contemplated by the statute" to use defendant's words. The talismanic phrase "freedom of speech" does not

(Continued)

(Continued)

cloak all utterances in legality. "It is one thing to say that the police cannot be used as an instrument for the suppression of unpopular views, and another to say that, when the speaker passes the bounds of argument or persuasion and undertakes incitement to riot, they are powerless to prevent a breach of the peace."

Viewed in context, defendant's words—IT'S GOOD THAT THE WORLD TRADE CENTER WAS BOMBED. MORE COPS AND FIREMEN SHOULD HAVE DIED. MORE BOMBS SHOULD HAVE DROPPED AND MORE PEOPLE SHOULD HAVE BEEN KILLED—were plainly intended to incite the crowd to violence, and not simply to express a point of view. But the allegations extend beyond mere words. It is further alleged that defendant accosted people in the crowd and shouted a threat—WE'VE GOT SOMETHING FOR YOUR A------ directly into the faces of some of the onlookers. It is also alleged that as the confrontation escalated, defendant and his accomplices refused police entreaties to disperse. This conduct went well beyond protected speech and firmly into the realm of criminal behavior. It was far more than "the mere abstract teaching . . . of the moral propriety or even moral necessity for a

resort to force and violence"; under the circumstances, it constituted the very real threat of violence itself.

All that is required under Penal Law section 240.08 . . . is that defendant urge ten or more persons to engage in tumultuous and violent conduct of a kind likely to create public harm. Angrily confronting and threatening a crowd of onlookers with the intent to stir the crowd to violence is sufficient; the object of that tumultuous or violent conduct is irrelevant so long as the conduct defendant urges is of a kind likely to cause public harm. . . .

Penal Law section 240.20 provides, in pertinent part, that a person is guilty of disorderly conduct "when, with intent to cause public inconvenience, annoyance, or alarm, or recklessly creating a risk thereof . . . he engages in fighting or in violent, tumultuous or threatening behavior." . . . Defendant's words and deeds as alleged in the complaint demonstrate his intent to cause public inconvenience, annoyance, or alarm, or recklessly create a risk thereof by engaging in tumultuous or threatening behavior. Therefore, defendant's request to dismiss both counts in the accusatory instrument is denied.

CHAPTER SUMMARY

Crimes against public order and morality have traditionally been viewed as of secondary importance. These misdemeanor offenses are disposed of in summary trials and carry modest punishments. Offenses such as disorderly conduct, however, constitute a significant percentage of arrests and prosecutions, and the treatment of these arrestees helps to shape perceptions of the criminal justice system.

Crimes against public order and morality were historically used to remove the unemployed and political agitators from cities and towns. Today, we are seeing a renewed emphasis on these offenses by municipalities. An increasing number of middle-class individuals are moving into urban areas and find themselves sharing their neighborhood with prostitutes, drug addicts, alcoholics, and gangs. The so-called broken windows theory reasons that the tolerance of small-scale, quality-of-life crimes leads to neighborhood deterioration and facilitates the growth of crime.

Individual disorderly conduct is directed at a broad range of conduct that risks or causes public inconvenience, annoyance, or alarm and risks causing

or does cause a breach of the peace. The Model Penal Code punishes engaging in fighting or threatening violent behavior; creating unreasonable noise, offensive utterances, or gestures; or creating a hazardous or physically offensive condition. A riot is group disorderly conduct and entails participating with others in tumultuous and violent conduct with the intent of causing a grave risk of public alarm.

The broken windows theory of crime, as you recall, is based on the belief that public indecencies or quality-of-life crimes lead to neighborhood deterioration and result in an increased incidence of crime. Two controversial quality-of-life crimes are vagrancy, defined in the common law as wandering the streets with no apparent means of earning a living, and loitering, a related offense that is defined at common law as standing in public with no apparent purpose. These broad statutes have historically been used against individuals based on their status as "undesirables." Vagrancy and loitering statutes have been found void for vagueness by the U.S. Supreme Court. Many states have responded by adopting the approach of the

MPC and punish individuals whose conduct warrants "alarm for the safety of persons or property in the vicinity." Municipal ordinances directed against the homeless and gangs have been challenged as void for vagueness, and laws against the homeless also have been attacked as punishing individuals based on their economic status. These legal actions have generally proven unsuccessful.

Crimes against public order and decency have been criticized as punishing "victimless crimes," or consensual offenses that the individuals involved do not view as harmful. Other commentators argue that the law is properly concerned with private morality and challenge the notion that these offenses against public order and decency do not result in harm to individuals and to society. A particular object of debate is the criminalization of prostitution or the exchange of sexual acts for money or some other item of value. Obscenity is another offense that is claimed to be a victimless crime, which some claim creates social harm. There is particular controversy concerning efforts to extend obscenity to include depictions and descriptions of violence, particularly when directed to children. Another growing area of concern is the protection of animals.

In the next chapter, we review three additional crimes against public order and morality: alcoholism, gambling, and drugs.

CHAPTER REVIEW QUESTIONS

1. List specific acts constituting disorderly conduct.
2. What is the difference between disorderly conduct and riot?
3. Distinguish between vagrancy and loitering.
4. What constitutional objections have been raised to vagrancy and loitering statutes?
5. What was the constitutional basis for the Supreme Court's holding Chicago's Gang Congregation Ordinance unconstitutional? Explain the reasoning of the Supreme Court.
6. What are the elements of the crime of prostitution?
7. How does the U.S. Supreme Court define obscenity?
8. Considering the descriptions of cases you read on homelessness and gangs, does the broken windows theory pose a threat to civil liberties? Support your answer with examples from the textbook.
9. Why do some commentators argue that the criminal law is overreaching?
10. Are prostitution and soliciting for prostitution victimless crimes?
11. Define the legal standard for obscenity and child pornography.
12. Should individuals be held criminally liable for cruelty to "wild" animals?

LEGAL TERMINOLOGY

adultery

breach of the peace

broken windows theory

child pornography

crimes against public order and morality

crimes against the quality of life

disorderly conduct

distracted driving

fornication

human trafficking

indecent exposure

keeping a place of prostitution

lewdness

living off prostitution

loitering

masturbation for hire

pandering

pimping

promoting prostitution

prostitution

public indecencies

riot

rout

solicitation for prostitution

unlawful assembly

vagrancy

voyeurism

CRIMINAL LAW ON THE WEB

Visit **study.sagepub.com/lippmaness2e** to access additional study tools including suggested answers to the You Decide questions, reprints of cases and statutes, online appendices, and more!

CRIMES AGAINST SOCIAL ORDER AND MORALITY

Alcoholism, Gambling, and Drug Offenses

Was the defendant guilty of possession of drug paraphernalia and driving while intoxicated?

[Moran] to be guilty must be shown to "knowingly use, or possess with purpose to use" drug paraphernalia in order to "ingest, inhale, or otherwise introduce into the human body, a controlled substance." Officer Landbert identified the pipe found in defendant's jean pocket at the police station as a marijuana pipe. Landbert in his 32 years as a police officer has made thousands of arrests of persons under the influence of drugs or alcohol . . . The city failed to establish that the pipe contained any drug residue, marijuana or otherwise.

Moran refused to take a field sobriety test at the scene. Officer Landbert testified that he smelled alcohol and detected defendant's slurred speech after he pulled him over. Landbert observed that defendant had an unsteady gait and he was swaying. . . . Landbert could see and smell that defendant's pants were soaked with urine. At the police station defendant refused both a Breathalyzer and intoxilyzer test. Officer Lukas, however, also smelled alcohol on defendant and observed his glassy, bloodshot eyes. From his twelve years' experience as a police officer, Lukas agreed with Landbert that defendant was under the influence of alcohol.

[Moran] testified that he had urinated in his clothes just before he was pulled over by Landbert, not because he was drunk, but because he has an on-going bladder problem and also explained that on the morning of the arrest he . . . went to a local bar where he met friends and had two or three beers. One of his friends bought him a whiskey, which he spilled on his clothes. (*Village of Newburgh Heights v. Moran*, 2005-Ohio-2610)

In this chapter, learn about alcohol and narcotics offenses.

Learning Objectives

1. Know the law on the possession of alcohol by juveniles and the law on selling, serving, and giving alcohol to juveniles.

2. Understand the law on public intoxication.

3. Define driving while intoxicated, driving under the influence, and driving with an unlawful blood alcohol level.

4. Know the different ways a police officer may establish that an individual is in violation of a law prohibiting driving under the influence of alcohol and driving with an unlawful blood alcohol level.

5. Appreciate the legal definition of gambling.

6. Know how the federal law and state laws schedule controlled substances and the various types of drug-related acts punishable under federal and state law.

7. Understand the development of the criminal regulation of marijuana.

8. Know the law on drug possession and possession with intent to deliver.

9. Understand the constitutional status of mandatory minimum sentences and the debate over mandatory minimum sentences.

10. Know the elements of the crime of possession of drug paraphernalia and why the possession of drug paraphernalia is a crime.

11. Understand assets forfeiture and the difference between civil and criminal assets forfeiture.

12. Know how drug courts differ from ordinary criminal courts.

There are three additional important crimes against morality and social order: alcoholism, gambling, and drugs. These criminal offenses at times are included within the category of "victimless crimes" because they purportedly do not affect others or significantly harm society. The criminal punishment of crimes like gambling also is criticized because of the inconsistency in enforcement. State-sponsored gambling in lotteries is accepted, although other forms of gambling are criminalized.

Should alcoholism, gambling, and drug abuse be considered victimless crimes? They can be addictive, lead to criminal behavior to support the addiction, disrupt and destroy families, and impose costs on society in terms of imprisonment and medical treatment, and black market sales of narcotics may be used to subsidize organized crime and gangs.

ALCOHOLISM

Alcohol is an accepted part of American life. It is used to help us relax, celebrate significant events, and connect with our friends. Alcohol, however, has a more menacing side; it may be addictive and abused and is associated with domestic abuse and violence.

Roughly 17.6 million American adults are addicted to alcohol or report that they drink to excess. Alcohol abuse in addition to threatening health is related to dangerous criminal behavior. As many as 25 million Americans report driving under the influence of alcohol, and in 2009, 11,839 individuals were killed in alcohol-related traffic accidents. Alcohol reportedly is involved in 40 percent of violent crimes and between 60 and 70 percent of domestic violence.[1]

Alcoholism and Juveniles

Minors are prohibited from possessing or purchasing alcoholic beverages in every state. It also is unlawful for an adult to sell, serve, or give alcohol to a juvenile. California Business and Professions Code Section 25662 prohibits "persons under 21 from possessing alcoholic beverages in any public place." The "minor in possession" law in California requires the following:

Age. You are under twenty-one.

Possession. You possess an alcoholic beverage.

Public place. You possess the alcohol in a public place: a store or restaurant or other area open to the public, or on any street or highway.

It also is a crime in California under Business and Professions Code Section 25658 to sell, furnish, give or cause to be sold, and furnish or give away any alcohol to a minor under 21 years of age, or for a licensed establishment knowingly to permit a person under twenty-one years of age to consume alcohol on the premises. This offense is punishable by a fine and/or community service. An individual may be subject to a prison term when a serious accident or injury results from a violation of this section.

States are free to establish their own drinking age. The federal government withholds a percentage of federal highway funds from states that do not establish a minimum drinking age of twenty-one years. Every state, as a result, has established the drinking age at age twenty-one although forty states have provided for exceptions with parental consent and for exemptions from the law for religious ceremonies and for educational purposes and in other instances.[2]

We previously discussed so-called *social host liability laws* (in Chapter 4). In Illinois, it is a crime punishable by up to one year in jail and a minimum fine of $500 to permit an underage person "on premises under your control" to consume alcohol under circumstances in which you should have known that he or she was consuming alcohol. If a serious injury or death occurs, the individual may be punished by up to three years in prison and a $25,000 fine.[3]

In 2008, one hundred university presidents called for a vigorous debate over whether the drinking age should be lowered to eighteen years of age. The university presidents contended that establishing the drinking age at twenty-one years discriminated against younger students, and that the law was regularly disregarded. Declaring alcohol illegal for students under twenty-one according to the college presidents encouraged binge drinking by younger students who were attracted to the "forbidden fruit" of alcohol. What is your view on lowering the drinking age?

Public Intoxication

Most states treat public intoxication as a misdemeanor. In practice, when individuals violate a **public intoxication** law, a police officer will take them into custody and release them once they are sober, or the officer may exercise his or her discretion and take the individual home.

Virginia Code Section 18-2-202 prohibits an individual from being drunk in public. An officer is not required to administer a Breathalyzer test before arresting an individual for public intoxication. A conviction may be based on the officer's testimony that the individual's behavior established that he or she was drunk in public. A person is "intoxicated" under Virginia law if he "has drunk enough alcoholic beverages to observably affect his manner, disposition, speech, muscular movement, general appearance or behavior." An arrest under Virginia law is required to be based on an individual's behavior, and neither an individual's appearance nor the fact that he or she "smells of alcohol" justifies his or her arrest.[4]

State statutes may punish more seriously public intoxication that poses a threat to the public. Indiana, for example, provides that it is a felony for an individual to be in public in a "state of intoxication" caused by "the person's use of alcohol or a controlled substance" if the person endangers his or her own life or the life of another person, breaches the peace or is in imminent danger of breaching the peace, or harasses, annoys, or alarms another person.[5]

California Penal Code Section 647(f) requires that for an individual to be held liable for public intoxication, he or she must be intentionally under the influence of alcohol and/or drugs in a public place and that the individual is "unable to exercise care for his or her own safety or the safety of others or the individual obstructed or prevented free use of a sidewalk or street."

California courts broadly interpret a "public place" and consider a broad range of locations outside the home to be a "public place." This includes restaurants, streets, sidewalks, stores, movie theaters, concerts, and an individual's presence in a car parked or moving on a public street.

The fact that you reek of alcohol does not satisfy the requirements of the California law. The defendant must be disoriented, sprawled out on the sidewalk, or aggressive. The officer's testimony is sufficient for a conviction, particularly where supported by the testimony of eyewitnesses. There is no requirement that the police subject individuals to a field sobriety test or Breathalyzer test to determine whether they are inebriated.

California also explicitly provides that a police officer may place individuals arrested for public intoxication in civil protective custody and detain them for seventy-two hours rather than arrest them for a criminal misdemeanor offense.[6]

The U.S. Supreme Court, in *Powell v. Texas*, confronted whether alcoholism is a disease and whether it constitutes cruel and unusual punishment to convict an individual for being intoxicated in public. In a 5-4 decision, the court majority held that Powell had been punished for being intoxicated in public rather than for the disease of alcoholism. The plurality opinion noted that Texas had "imposed upon appellant a criminal sanction for public behavior which may create substantial health and safety hazards both for appellant and for members of the general public, and which offends the moral and esthetic sensibilities of a large segment of the community. This seems a far cry from convicting one for being an addict, being a chronic alcoholic, being 'mentally ill, or [being] a leper.'"[7]

Driving and Alcoholism

An average of twelve thousand individuals are killed each year in drunk driving–related accidents. Over nine hundred thousand individuals are arrested for alcohol-related driving infractions; one-third of these individuals are repeat offenders. The classic offense for "driving and drinking" is **driving while intoxicated (DWI)**, which prohibits an individual from driving an automobile while intoxicated. In the 1970s, DWI was expanded to punish **driving under the influence (DUI)**, which punishes driving under the influence of liquor or narcotics. Individuals charged under these two types of statutes may challenge the charges on the grounds that despite their inebriated state, their driving was unaffected. States expanded their laws against DWI by adopting statutes prohibiting **driving with an unlawful blood alcohol level (DUBAL)**. DUBAL laws hold individuals liable for driving while their blood alcohol level is too high, despite the fact that their driving may be unaffected. Every state has gradually lowered the required blood alcohol level from 0.10 percent in the 1960s to 0.08 percent in the 1990s. States typically impose harsher punishment on individuals with a higher blood alcohol level typically between 0.15 and 0.20 percent. Keep in mind that an individual may be convicted of DWI or DUI even when tests determine that his or her blood alcohol content is below the level established in the state for DUBAL.[8]

There are two requirements to hold an individual criminally responsible for DUBAL.

1. *Driving.* You drove a vehicle.

2. *Blood alcohol content.* You drove with a blood alcohol content of 0.08 percent or more.

The police rely on various methods to determine whether an individual is DUBAL. Breathalyzer and blood tests are accepted as accurate as long as proper procedures are followed. The U.S. Supreme Court has upheld the constitutionality of **implied consent laws** that provide that individuals who obtain a driver's license impliedly have consented to the administration of a urine or blood test or Breathalyzer to determine their blood alcohol content. The Court further held that it does not violate the Fifth Amendment right against self-incrimination for a state to provide that a refusal to submit to a blood test under the implied consent law will result in suspension of an individual's driver's license and that a refusal to submit to a blood test may be introduced as evidence of the individual's guilt of DUBAL or other criminal offense. In some states, refusal to take a test to determine your blood alcohol content also may result in a fine and a brief jail term.[9] In 2013, in *Missouri v. McNeely*, the Supreme Court held that a nonconsensual drawing of blood ordinarily requires a warrant other than in emergency circumstances.[10] In 2016, the Supreme Court ruled that a warrant is required before subjecting an individual arrested for DWI to a blood test, although a warrant is not required for a breath test.

A DWI or DUI conviction may be based solely on the testimony of police officers or eyewitnesses. The question for the judge or jury is whether to believe the testimony of the police and eyewitnesses or whether to believe the testimony of the defendant. An Indiana appellate court noted that a conviction for DWI may be based on various types of evidence of impairment including the consumption of a significant amount of alcohol, slow reflexes, slurred speech, watery or bloodshot eyes, the odor of alcohol, unsteady balance, and the results of any tests.[11]

Another method relied on by the police to determine whether an individual is DUI is a field sobriety test administered in accordance with the guidelines of the National Highway Traffic Safety Administration (NHTSA). Another test used by the police to determine whether an individual is DUI is the horizontal gaze nystagmus (HGN) test, which measures the abnormal and involuntary movement of the eyes caused by alcohol.

What constitutes "driving an automobile"? May an individual be convicted of DUBAL if arrested in a parked or stationary vehicle? In *State v. Owen*, the defendant was sitting behind the wheel of an automobile that was stuck in a ditch and protested that because the car was not moving, he was not DUI. A Missouri appellate court held that an individual who is inebriated may be held liable for DUI, although unconscious or asleep, as long as the "key is in the ignition, the engine is running, and the person is sitting behind the steering wheel." There are decisions holding inebriated individuals criminally responsible whose hands are on the wheel of a car whose engine is not running or who are asleep in an automobile and within reach of the steering wheel.[12]

In *State v. Sims*, a police officer found Sims passed out or asleep behind the wheel of his vehicle located in a commercial parking lot. The keys were on the front passenger seat of the vehicle. While awakening Sims, the officer detected a strong odor of alcohol and observed that he had bloodshot, watery eyes. Sims was convicted based on the possibility that in the future that he would reach for the keys and drive the automobile while intoxicated. The New Mexico Supreme Court reversed Sims's conviction and stressed that a fact finder cannot simply assume or speculate that the individual in question might sometime in the future commence driving his or her vehicle and instead must establish that the defendant had the intent to drive so as to pose a danger to him- or herself or to the public. In this instance, the prosecution failed to prove that Sims used the vehicle other than as a nonmoving shelter. "It was pure speculation whether [Sims] would rouse himself and drive the vehicle. [Sims] could not be convicted for what he might have done.

The State had to prove beyond a reasonable doubt that defendant actually exercised physical control over the vehicle with the general intent to drive so as to endanger the public. Having failed to meet its burden, the State did not establish actual physical control." The New Mexico Supreme Court was concerned that broadly interpreting the conditions under which an individual is criminally liable for being in control of an automobile as in *State v. Owen* (e.g., whether the key is in the ignition and the sleeping defendant is behind the wheel) would encourage individuals to drive their vehicle while intoxicated rather than waiting to drive until they were sober. What factors do you believe should be considered in determining that the defendant posed the intent to drive the car?[13]

There also are cases finding inebriated individuals liable for DUBAL who are arrested outside their motor vehicle based on testimony that they were driving an automobile a short time before being arrested by the police. In *State v. Butler*, the defendant was found inebriated one hundred yards from his motorcycle with the key in the ignition. He was found to be in control of the motorcycle because he had removed the spark plug from the motorcycle and was walking toward the store to buy a new spark plug. The arresting officer found that the defendant reeked of alcohol, had slurred speech, and was unsteady on his feet. The Tennessee Supreme Court in affirming the defendant's conviction reasoned that "the only reason that the defendant's motorcycle was not operational at the time of his arrest was because he had just removed the sparkplug and flooded the engine. . . . [T]he defendant admitted to driving the motorcycle to [the store] shortly before being arrested. . . . [A] rational juror could have determined that the defendant's vehicle was either operable or reasonably capable of being rendered operable."[14]

States generally provide for a **mandatory minimum drug sentence** of several days, a fine, and brief license suspension for the first offense of DWI and impose increasingly harsh penalties for subsequent convictions. In California, a second offense may result in a jail sentence of up to one year, a fine of between $1,800 and $2,800, and a suspension of a driver's license for up to two years. The severity of the sentence will vary according to the circumstances of the offense, including whether the driver was involved in an accident, whether a child was in the vehicle, and whether the accident involved property damage. In several states, prosecutors are prohibited from plea bargaining a charge of DUI, and in other states, prosecutors may offer the defendant a plea to reckless driving.

In some states, including California, repeat offenders may have an "ignition lock" installed in their automobile. The lock prevents individuals with a blood alcohol level above a designated level from operating the car.

The National Highway System Designation Act of 1995 required states receiving federal highway funds to establish a 0.02 percent blood alcohol content as the standard for DUBAL for individuals under the age of twenty-one. This is a lower threshold than the 0.08 percent in states for individuals twenty-one years of age and older. An individual with the required blood alcohol content is considered to be DUBAL, and there is no obligation on the prosecution to establish impaired driving.

Individuals under twenty-one often are prohibited from driving with any measurable amount of blood alcohol. These so-called state **zero tolerance laws** are based on the fact that roughly one-third of the deaths of fifteen- to twenty-year-olds result from motor vehicle crashes, and about 35 percent of these fatalities are alcohol related. Drunk driving laws generally are applicable to individuals driving motorcycles and bikes but have not been extended to Segways.[15]

In virtually every state, an individual who is inebriated and causes an accident that results in death will be held liable for *vehicular manslaughter*.

Most state courts do not recognize that involuntary intoxication is a defense to drunk driving. This defense would impede the enforcement of DWI laws that are intended to "curb the senseless havoc and destruction caused by drunk driving" and "eliminate intoxicated drivers from the roadways."[16] Courts have refused to recognize other affirmative defenses to drunk driving on the grounds that it would open the door to defendants fabricating defenses. For example, courts have refused to recognize the insanity defense to a charge of drunk driving[17] and have refused to recognize the necessity defense to a charge of drunk driving.[18] In *State v. Squires*, the defendant drank so heavily at a bar that his inexperienced, seventeen-year-old nephew was required to drive the defendant home. The car stalled in the middle of the street, and Squires took control of the car and was arrested. The Vermont Supreme Court held that Squires had created the necessity by his excessive drinking and was not entitled to claim necessity.[19]

You Decide

12.1 Charles Franklin Rogers was intoxicated when two police officers found him asleep or passed out in the driver's seat of his Cadillac Escalade. The vehicle was parked outside an Elks Lodge at about 2 a.m. in Fayetteville, Arkansas. The engine was running with exhaust visible from the tailpipe; the headlights and taillights were on. It was a very cold night, well below freezing. Officers tapped on the window and awakened Rogers from sleep. His foot appeared to the officers to be on the brake pedal. Rogers turned the vehicle off and exited to speak to the officers. The officers testified that the vehicle keys were recovered from the front passenger area of the vehicle, although the officers could not recall the precise location. Rogers had been taken by a friend to the Elks Lodge where they listened to music and drank. Later in the evening, Rogers and his friend went to a bar where Rogers "drank too much." The friend drove Rogers back to the lodge where Rogers remote-started the Escalade. After his vehicle had warmed for a few minutes, he promised his friend that he would enter his Escalade and sleep until he was safe to drive. Rogers testified that once he entered his Escalade, the keys were never in the ignition but rather were on the floorboard.

The electronics technician who installed the remote start said that the remote start turns on the headlights and taillights and makes the auto's accessories such as the radio, heat, and air conditioning available. The technician explained that when in remote start an individual cannot drive the vehicle because the steering is locked and the gearshift is locked. "The only way to actually move the car is to put the keys into the ignition and turn the ignition to the run position, then brake and shift into gear." Arkansas Code Annotated Section 5-65-103(a) (Supp. 2005) provides that "[i]t is unlawful and punishable as provided in this act for any person who is intoxicated to operate or be in actual physical control of a motor vehicle."

Would you convict Rogers of DWI? See *Rogers v. State*, 224 S.W.3d 564 (Ark. 2006).

You can find the answer at study.sagepub.com/lippmaness2e

CRIMINAL LAW IN THE NEWS

On June 15, 2013, sixteen-year-old Ethan Couch and seven friends stole beer from a store and went to Couch's parents' house to party. Later that night, Couch and seven friends took a Ford F-350 owned by his father's company and headed for the store. Couch had a blood alcohol content of over 24 percent, three times the legal limit for an adult in Texas, and accelerated the Ford F-350 to seventy miles per hour in a forty-mph zone. The truck swerved off the road, killing four pedestrians, three of whom were assisting a stranded motorist. Two teenagers riding in the bed of the pickup were thrown from the vehicle. One of the young men, Sergio Molina, fourteen, suffered a severe brain injury and was paralyzed.

Couch's parents live in a wealthy suburb of Fort Worth, Texas, with a median income of $250,000. Couch pled guilty, and his lawyer at the sentencing hearing called psychologist G. Dick Miller to testify. Miller diagnosed Couch as suffering from "affluenza" or a diminished sense of responsibility associated with being the pampered child of wealthy parents who are too busy to properly parent their child. Miller explained that Couch "never learned to say that you're sorry if you hurt someone. If you hurt someone, you sent him money." Miller testified that Couch possessed an emotional age of twelve and that he never learned that "sometimes you don't get your way. He had the cars and he had the money. He had freedoms that no young man would be able to handle."

Prosecutors asked for the maximum sentence of twenty years in prison. They pointed out that a court had never before recognized the "affluenza" defense and that "affluenza" is not recognized as an illness by the American Psychiatric Association. Judge Jean Boyd decided against following the prosecutors' recommendation and sentenced Couch to ten years' probation and ordered Couch to receive treatment at a high-priced California drug facility where he was to have no contact with his parents. Couch's parents were to pay the cost of the treatment, which is estimated to be roughly $450,000 per year. Judge Boyd noted that it would be difficult for Couch to receive this type of high-caliber, intensive treatment in the underfunded Texas correctional system.

Defense attorneys explained that it was good social policy to sentence a young person to probation rather than to condemn him to prison and that the judge acted appropriately in giving Ethan a chance to rehabilitate himself. The prosecutor and families of the victims were outraged and asked whether a defendant from a low-income family would have received the same consideration if his or her lawyer pled that the defendant's crime was a product of the individual's impoverished background. The decision was a stark reminder that there was one standard of justice for the wealthy and another standard of justice for the poor. They also pointed out that it was possible that Ethan would serve as little as two years of the twenty-year sentence.

On the other hand, defenders of the sentence pointed out that the court had acted appropriately because the Texas juvenile justice system is built on the notion of rehabilitation rather than punishment of youthful offenders. One journalist for the *Dallas Observer* noted that "[b]ecause we condemn everybody else's kid to violent prisons, does that mean it is unjust to let any one kid go [outside the system]?"

Couch's parents reached a $2 million settlement with the family of Molina who was paralyzed in the crash. Five other families also are known to have reached financial confidential settlements. Judge Boyd after issuing the decision announced she would not run for reelection.

In December 2015, Couch and his mother fled to Mexico after a video surfaced showing Couch at a party with drunk and drinking friends although they were quickly arrested and returned to the United States. Couch, on reaching the age of eighteen, was transferred to adult court and as a result will be required to serve nearly two years in jail before his release. He will be on probation for ten years, and a violation of adult probation will carry a lengthy prison term. Do you agree with Judge Boyd's original sentence?

GAMBLING

Gambling generally is used to describe an activity that is prohibited under criminal law. **Gaming** refers to activity that has been legalized by existing law or that may be exempted from coverage of the criminal law. A card game among friends, for example, may be exempted from criminal statutes in some states.

The early American colonists brought games of chance with them that were popular in England, and there were few restrictions on gambling. Lotteries were used in the eighteenth and nineteenth centuries to raise revenues for universities and to support education. By the early twentieth century, gambling had become viewed as immoral and was driven underground. Unlawful gambling, along with the illegal sale of alcohol, became the cash cow for organized crime. In 1931, Nevada legalized most forms of gambling, and over the next thirty years, Las Vegas became known as the center of gambling in the United States. In 1977, New Jersey established legalized gambling in Atlantic City.

There are twenty-two states that allow commercial casinos in some form. The more than one thousand river-based, land-based, and racetrack commercial casinos and card rooms in these states produced a gross gaming revenue of $35.64 billion in 2011.[20]

Each state determines whether to allow gambling, what forms of gambling to permit, and who may gamble. States differ on whether to permit betting on horse races and dog races, allow card or table games, and permit slot machines and video poker and on where these forms of gambling may be located. Some states require a minimum age for gambling, and in other states, a minimum age is established for particular forms of gambling. In New Jersey, you can buy a lottery ticket and bet on horse racing at age eighteen although you must be twenty-one years of age to enter an Atlantic City casino. Every state allows gambling activities such as bingo games that benefit charities.

Native American tribes are legally entitled to establish casinos on tribal land. In 1979, the Florida Seminole tribe began sponsoring bingo games. Native American gaming is regulated by the federal Indian Gaming Regulatory Act of 1988, and jurisdiction over various aspects of Native American gaming is shared by the federal and state governments and the tribes. Profits may be used only for community welfare purposes. There are roughly 493 Native American–owned gaming enterprises in twenty-eight states, owned by 244 of the 565 federally recognized tribes that operate in twenty-eight of the fifty states. The annual revenue from all Indian gaming represents over 40 percent of casino gaming revenue in the United States.

New Hampshire established a state lottery in 1963, which marked the first time in the twentieth century that a state directly established a lottery. By 1999, thirty-seven states had established lotteries to raise money, and as of 2016, forty-four states plus the District of Columbia have lotteries.

In the last decade, Internet gambling became enormously popular. Delaware, New Jersey, and Nevada are the only states to have legalized Internet gambling, although several other states likely will provide for online gambling in the near future.

The American Gaming Association divides gaming into several categories:

- Card rooms
- Commercial casinos
- Charitable games
- Native American casinos
- Legal bookmaking on sports
- Lotteries
- Pari-mutuel wagering on racing

State Gambling Laws

States apply a dominant factor or predominance test to determine whether an activity constitutes gambling. An activity involves gambling if the element of luck is the dominant factor or predominates over skill. In *People v. Hua*, a New York City criminal court held that the Chinese tile game mah-jongg involves skills such as tactics, observation, and memory and does not constitute gambling. The court explained the legal test for determining whether a game constituted gambling[21]:

> While some games may involve both an element of skill and chance, if "the outcome depends in a material degree upon an element of chance," the game will be deemed a contest of chance. "The test of the character of the game is not whether it contains an element of chance or an element of skill, but which is the dominating element that determines the result of the game?" It follows then that wagering on the outcome of a game of skill is therefore not gambling as it falls outside the ambit of the statute. . . . "[G]ames of chess, checkers, billiards and bowling [are] held to be games of skill." Three card monte, when played fairly, has been characterized by some courts as a game of skill, while other courts have characterized three card monte and other similar type shell games as games of chance.

Most state statutes declare that it is a crime to possess gambling devices, and the devices are confiscated if the defendant is convicted of unlawful possession.

Social gambling between friends on card games is permitted under most state statutes. This generally is defined as a "social context" in which everyone participates in the activity and no one profits by conducting or sponsoring the game. Some states limit the amount of money that an individual may win in a single hand and require that the game be conducted in a residence or other "private place." All states allow nonprofit charitable organizations to raise money by sponsoring certain types of gambling activities. Another common exception is "drawings" conducted by stores in which the "winner" receives a prize. Virtually every state treats gambling as a misdemeanor, although several states treat subsequent arrests for gambling as felonies.[22]

Texas Penal Code Section 47.02 is an example of a state gambling statute. The Texas law prohibits a person from making a bet on the result of a game or contest or on the performance of a participant; making a bet on the result of a political nomination, appointment, or election; or betting for money or another thing of value on any game played with cards, dice, balls, or any other gambling device. It is a defense that

> (1) the actor engaged in gambling in a private place; (2) no person received any economic benefit other than personal winnings; and (3) except for the advantage of skill or luck, the risks of losing and the chances of winning were the same for all participants.

A South Carolina defendant in an unusual case was convicted for sponsoring weekly games of "Texas Hold'm." The State Supreme Court held that the statute punished wagering in the home on various games despite the fact that the games involved more skill than chance.[23]

Internet Gambling

The U.S. Congress has relied on its constitutional power to regulate interstate commerce to restrict gambling across state lines.

The Interstate Wire Act (1961) prohibits individuals engaged in the business of betting from knowingly using a wire (e.g., phone, computer) to transmit information relating to sports betting.[24]

In the 1990s, various individuals and commercial enterprises evaded the prohibition on gambling within the United States by locating outside U.S. territorial boundaries and relying on the Internet to communicate with individuals interested in betting on sports and other events. In 2006, Congress adopted the Unlawful Internet Gambling Enforcement Act (UIGEA), which prohibits gambling businesses from "knowingly accepting payments in connection with the participation of another person in a bet or wager that involves the use of the internet." UIGEA does not prohibit individuals from placing bets. In reaction to this law, various betting enterprises stopped accepting bets from U.S. customers.[25] In 2012, the Department of Justice brought criminal charges against several offshore Internet poker enterprises that continued to do business in the United States.

The most profound change in gambling has been the introduction of fantasy betting sites. UIGEA provides that "unlawful wagering" does not prohibit individuals from participating in fantasy sports that meet certain criteria.[26] Fantasy sports betting still must meet the legal standard for gaming under state law. Roughly forty-five states allow daily fantasy although five states define gambling to prohibit daily fantasy. Nevada has taken the position that all fantasy sports competitions constitute "gambling" under state law and require a gambling license.

Federal Gambling Laws

Congress has relied on the constitutional power to regulate interstate commerce to restrict gambling across state lines. There are a number of federal laws that address gambling:

Transportation of Gambling Devices Act (1951). Prohibits the interstate shipment of gambling devices such as slot machines to states where the betting is illegal.[27]

Interstate Transportation of Wagering Paraphernalia Act (1961). Prohibits the interstate shipment of gambling material to prevent the distribution of material used in gambling.[35]

Interstate Wire Act (1961). Prohibits individuals engaged in the business of betting from knowingly using a wire (e.g., phone, computer) to transmit information relating to sports betting.[29]

Travel Act (1961). Prohibits traveling in interstate or foreign commerce or using the mail or any facility in interstate or foreign commerce for purposes of promoting gambling.[28]

Wagering Paraphernalia Act (1961). Prohibits the interstate shipment of gambling material to states where gambling is illegal.[30]

Illegal Gambling Business Act (1970). As part of the Organized Crime Control Act, individuals are prohibited from financing, managing, supervising, directing, and owning large-scale gambling businesses that are in violation of state or local law.[31]

Interstate Horse Racing Act (1978). Congress regulates wagering on interstate horse racing.[32]

Professional and Amateur Sports Protection Act (1992). Prohibits state sports betting, with exemptions for certain states.[33]

Gambling Ship Act (1994). Prohibits the use of a ship as a gambling establishment.[34]

Unlawful Internet Gambling Enforcement Act (2006). Prohibits gambling businesses from "knowingly accepting payments in connection with the participation of another person in a bet or wager that involves the use of the internet." An exception is made for "fantasy sports."[36]

CONTROLLED SUBSTANCES

The "War on Drugs"

The United States has been waging an officially proclaimed "War on Drugs" for over forty years. President Richard Nixon, in issuing a declaration of war against drugs, characterized unlawful narcotics "public enemy number one." This campaign against unlawful drugs has been advanced by subsequent U.S. presidents. For example, President George H. W. Bush in 1989 called drug abuse the "most pressing problem facing the nation," a view shared by 64 percent of the population.

President Bill Clinton also endorsed tough antidrug policies and proclaimed a "One Strike and You're Out" policy for residents of federally assisted public housing. President George W. Bush, on first being elected president, declared that "this scourge [of drugs] will stop."[37]

The multiprong attack on drugs involves the detection, arrest, and disruption of drug smugglers and distribution networks; assistance to foreign countries in combating the cultivation and production of narcotics; treatment for drug addicts; and public education on the perils of narcotics abuse.

What has been the impact of the "War on Drugs"? The *National Drug Threat Assessment* (2011) drafted by the National Drug Intelligence Center of the U.S. Department of Justice estimates that the economic cost of illicit drug use to society is more than $193 billion per year as measured by crime, health, and lost productivity. Drug use among young people recently has increased after more than a decade of decline. Methamphetamine, ecstasy, marijuana, and heroin are easily available, and the supply of cocaine remains stable after declining in recent years. An estimated 8.7 percent of Americans age twelve or older are current "illicit drug users" (21.8 million people). Young people between the ages of eighteen and twenty-five represent the largest group of users of unlawful drugs. The two illicit drugs that attract the greatest number of users are marijuana and controlled prescription drugs (CPDs). Roughly seven million people are nonmedical users of CPDs. The number of prescription drug overdose deaths is greater than the number of overdose deaths from cocaine, heroin, and methamphetamine combined.

Transnational criminal organizations (TCOs) dominate criminal narcotic networks in the United States. The most powerful are seven Mexican cartels that sell heroin, marijuana, and methamphetamine. These cartels are active in over 1,200 American cities and generate billions of dollars in profit. The cartels are engaged in a violent competition for control of border crossing points from Mexico into the United States, and this violence at times spills over into adjoining U.S. states. Each cartel commands thousands of armed gunmen, and the competition for ascendancy has resulted in the death of over forty-seven thousand Mexican civilians and over three thousand police officers and soldiers in the last five years. The National Drug Intelligence Center concludes that the "threat posed by the trafficking and abuse of illicit drugs will not abate in the near term and may increase."[38]

The criminal law is a central component of the "War on Drugs." The criminal law is used to prosecute and to punish the abuse of unlawful and lawful drugs and to deter criminal activity.

The Evolution of American Antinarcotics Strategy

Drugs and chemicals are referred to as **controlled substances** because their manufacture, distribution, and possession are regulated by the government.

The common law did not address the use, sale, or possession of drugs. The most important early antinarcotics law in the United States was an 1875 San Francisco ordinance prohibiting the smoking of opium. This law was directed against a practice that was identified with Chinese immigrants and was based on an irrational fear that smoking of opium would spread throughout society and lead to a loosening of the moral fabric of the country. The San Francisco ordinance inspired various western states to incorporate similar statutes into their criminal codes.

You may be surprised to learn that until the early twentieth century, heroin, cocaine, and marijuana were lawfully available and were included in the ingredients of various over-the-counter medicines used to treat health problems ranging from headaches to coughs. There was concern over the addictive quality of these drugs, and in 1906, the U.S. Congress passed the Federal Food and Drugs Act to ensure that medications were properly labeled and consumers were informed about the side effects and dangers involved in consuming medications containing potentially addictive drugs. The Food and Drug Administration (FDA) was established in 1927 with responsibility for ensuring that medically important drugs were safe and accurately labeled.

The first federal criminal law punishing the nonmedical use of drugs was the Harrison Narcotics Tax Act of 1914. The law regulated opium, morphine, and cocaine and their derivatives. Congress drafted the law as a tax measure. Doctors, in return for paying a dollar, were authorized to prescribe these drugs. An individual who obtained narcotics outside of the health care system was subject to a criminal penalty of up to five years in prison and a $5,000 fine. In 1919, the U.S. Supreme Court held that the Harrison Act was a valid exercise of the federal government's authority to raise revenues.[39] That same year, the Court determined that prescribing drugs for narcotics addicts "maintained" rather than medically treated their drug habit. As a consequence, the Court held that doctors were not authorized under the act to prescribe drugs to narcotics addicts. The result of the decision was that narcotics addicts were "driven underground" and could obtain drugs only on the criminal black market.[40]

Marijuana or hemp was raised in the United States and initially was used as fiber for the manufacture of rope and as an ingredient of medicine. Marijuana (cannabis), in other parts of the world, was a source of recreation and relaxation, and by the twentieth century, marijuana had become an accepted part of the recreational drug culture in the United States. Following the repeal of the prohibition of alcohol in 1933, federal and state authorities turned their attention to curbing the use of marijuana. By 1937, forty-six states prohibited the growing, possession, use, and sale of cannabis. The Marijuana Tax Act of 1937 placed a tax of $100 an ounce on anyone who dealt commercially with cannabis, hemp, or marijuana. A failure to pay the tax was punishable by five years in prison and a $2,000 fine. An individual who paid the tax confronted the "catch-22" that he or she would be prosecuted for violation of state criminal laws prohibiting growing, possession, use, and/or sale of marijuana.

The attitude toward marijuana, cocaine, and heroin became increasingly punitive. The Boggs Act of 1951 and the Narcotics Control Act of 1956 imposed stringent mandatory sentences for possession of marijuana, heroin, and other drugs. Marijuana was viewed as a "gateway" drug that was the first step toward the use of more addictive narcotics. A first offense for marijuana possession and for possession of other prohibited narcotics was punished by a jail sentence of up to two years and a fine of $20,000. A first offense for the sale of an unlawful narcotic was punished by a jail sentence of up to five years. The Narcotics Control Act punished the sale of heroin to anyone under eighteen with the death penalty.

The 1960s were marked by the rise of the youth-oriented counterculture and the open embrace of marijuana and mind-altering drugs such as LSD. A popular slogan advocated that young people "turn on, tune in, and drop out." Congress responded by enacting the Comprehensive Drug Abuse Prevention and Control Act of 1970,[41] commonly known as the Controlled Substances Act. The act categorizes drugs within one of five schedules. The drugs considered to have the greatest negative impact on the mind and body and the potential for addiction are listed in Schedule I, and the least dangerous drugs are listed in Schedule III, Schedule IV, and Schedule V (see Table 12.1). The schedules are adjusted as new drugs are introduced. In 2000, the Date Rape Prevention Drug Act added several "date rape drugs" to Schedule I and to Schedule III. The Controlled Substances Act also established criminal penalties for possession, possession with intent to distribute, and the manufacture, sale, and distribution of Schedule I and Schedule II controlled substances. Criminal penalties in addition are provided for the possession and distribution without a prescription of Schedule III and Schedule IV drugs.

The next major federal law addressing controlled substances was the Anti–Drug Abuse Act of 1986. The act was a reaction to the death from a drug overdose of University of Maryland basketball star Len Bias, the panic over the epidemic of crack cocaine, and the fear that drug addicts were spreading AIDS. The bill introduced stiff mandatory minimum penalties for crack and powder cocaine. In 1988, the Anti–Drug Abuse Act was amended to authorize public housing authorities to evict tenants who allowed drug-related criminal activity on or near public housing and strengthened criminal sentences. The act also established a "drug-free America" as a policy goal and created the White House Office of National Drug Control Policy (ONDCP) headed by a "White House drug czar."

The Crime Control Act of 1990 and Violent Crime Control and Law Enforcement Act of 1994 increased the funds directed to state and local antinarcotics efforts, provided money for the drug testing of inmates and for drug courts, and further stiffened criminal penalties for repeat drug offenders. The 1998 Higher Education Act barred individuals convicted of drug possession from receiving federal student aid.

States share jurisdiction with the federal government over narcotics offenses. The next section provides an overview of state antinarcotics laws.

State Antidrug Laws

State drug laws generally follow the Uniform Controlled Substances Act, which was drafted in 1972 by the National Conference of Commissioners on Uniform State Laws. This is a group of experts

Table 12.1 Schedules of Controlled Substances Under the Controlled Substances Act

(1) Schedule I.
   • (A) The drug or other substance has a high potential for abuse.
   • (B) The drug or other substance has no currently accepted medical use in treatment in the United States.
   • (C) There is a lack of accepted safety for use of the drug or other substance under medical supervision. Only available for research.
   • (D) Includes heroin, LSD, ecstasy, peyote, marijuana, and hashish.

(2) Schedule II.
   • (A) The drug or other substance has a high potential for abuse.
   • (B) The drug or other substance has a currently accepted medical use in treatment in the United States or a currently accepted medical use with severe restrictions. Requires a nonrenewable prescription.
   • (C) Abuse of the drug or other substances may lead to severe psychological or physical dependence.
   • (D) Includes morphine, opium, codeine, cocaine, methamphetamine, PCP, and barbiturates.

(3) Schedule III.
   • (A) The drug or other substance has a potential for abuse less than the drugs or other substances in Schedules I and II.
   • (B) The drug or other substance has a currently accepted medical use in treatment in the United States. Requires a doctor's prescription and may be renewed.
   • (C) Abuse of the drug or other substance may lead to moderate or low physical dependence or high psychological dependence.
   • (D) Common antidiarrheals and cold medicine and pain relievers with low dosages of Schedule II substances such as opium and codeine. Anabolic steroids added in 1991.

(4) Schedule IV.
   • (A) The drug or other substance has a low potential for abuse relative to the drugs or other substances in Schedule III.
   • (B) The drug or other substance has a currently accepted medical use in treatment in the United States. Available by a prescription, which may be renewed.
   • (C) Abuse of the drug or other substance may lead to limited physical dependence or psychological dependence relative to the drugs or other substances in Schedule III.
   • (D) Depressants and mild tranquilizers: Valium, Librium, and Equanil and other depressants and mild tranquilizers and some stimulants.

(5) Schedule V.
   • (A) The drug or other substance has a low potential for abuse relative to the drugs or other substances in Schedule IV.
   • (B) The drug or other substance has a currently accepted medical use in treatment in the United States. May be purchased over the counter with identification and/or signature.
   • (C) Abuse of the drug or other substance may lead to limited physical dependence or psychological dependence relative to the drugs or other substances in Schedule IV.
   • (D) Includes cough medicines and antidiarrheals containing small amounts of opium, morphine, or codeine.

Source: 21 U.S.C. § 812 – Schedules of controlled substances.

who formulated a set of "model laws" intended to guide state legislatures in addressing public policy issues. The Uniform Controlled Substances Act adopts the organizational approach of the federal Comprehensive Drug Abuse Prevention and Control Act and divides drugs into five schedules based on the drugs' or other substances' potential for abuse and harm and medical value. State drug laws typically prohibit the following acts:

- *Prohibited Acts.* The manufacture, sale, and purchase of controlled substances or intent to sell or deliver a controlled substance. It is a crime to enter into a conspiracy with the intent to engage in any of these acts.
- *School Zones.* The sale, manufacture, and possession with the intent to sell or to deliver a controlled substance within one thousand feet of a school.
- *Prescriptions.* The purchase or possession with the intent to sell controlled substances that may not be legally conveyed absent a lawful prescription or license.
- *Children.* The sale of narcotics to juveniles or involvement of juveniles in the narcotics trade.
- *Drug Paraphernalia.* The possession, manufacture, delivery, or advertisement of drug paraphernalia.

The possession of narcotics and the possession of narcotics with the intent to sell are the drug offenses that account for most arrests.

Possession of Narcotics and Possession With Intent to Distribute Narcotics

Possession of a controlled substance is the most common drug offense. The federal Controlled Substances Act[42] requires that an individual "knowingly or intentionally possess the controlled substances." State criminal statutes incorporate the "knowingly" or "intentionally" *mens rea* requirement of federal law. Possession may be either *actual possession* or *constructive possession*. A person may exercise individual possession or *joint possession* over a controlled substance.

Establishing actual possession is relatively straightforward. An individual has actual possession when narcotics are found in the individual's physical possession or immediate physical presence. The prosecution to prove *actual possession* is required to establish that the defendant (1) knew of the presence of the "object," (2) exercised dominion and control over the object, and (3) had knowledge of the narcotic's "unlawful character." Dominion and control are established for purposes of actual possession if the drugs are in the individual's physical control or within reach. What of the intent requirement? The defendant is required to know only that the substance is an unlawful controlled substance and is not required to know the precise type of unlawful narcotic over which he or she is exercising "dominion and control." In *United States v. De La Torre*, the defendant conceded that he knew there was marijuana in his backpack, although he claimed that he was unaware that methamphetamines also were in his backpack. The Tenth Circuit Court of Appeals nonetheless affirmed the defendant's conviction for possession of methamphetamine. The court held that the prosecution can establish the *mens rea* for possession by establishing that the defendant knew that he possessed an unlawful substance, and that the prosecution is not required to establish that the defendant knew that he or she possessed a specific category of unlawful substance. The Tenth Circuit explained in *De La Torre* that

> [o]nce it is established that the defendant had the requisite guilty mind to possess some controlled substance within the universe of all controlled substances, it has established the *mens rea* necessary to establish the possession element with respect to any and all drugs the defendant actually possessed. . . . The Government is not required . . . to prove that the controlled substance the defendant actually possessed corresponds to the controlled substance the defendant believed he possessed.[43]

A defendant also may be held guilty who has constructive possession over a controlled substance. Constructive possession is established when a defendant who does not have physical possession over a controlled substance has "dominion and control" over the area in which the narcotics are found. An individual may share constructive possession with another individual who also exercises "dominion and control" over the area. In *State v. Harrison*, the defendant was arrested outside his apartment in which the police seized narcotics, large amounts of cash, and weapons and arrested the defendant's wife. He was convicted of constructive possession of a firearm while in the course of committing a drug offense, based on his control over the apartment.[44]

Constructive possession cases are particularly challenging for courts when there are multiple parties who have access to an automobile or to an apartment in which controlled substances are found. Mere presence in the car or house is not sufficient to convict a defendant of drug possession. Courts require evidence connecting the defendant to the controlled substance. The prosecution "must point to evidence of acts, statements, or conduct of the accused or other facts or circumstances which tend to show that the defendant was aware of both the presence and character of the substance and that it was subject to his dominion and control." A Minnesota appellate court, for example, overturned a defendant's conviction for possession of cocaine found in the pockets of pants seized in her bedroom. The court stressed that six people were in the defendant's house for an hour after she had left and there was "no . . . evidence linking [her] to the cocaine, such as fingerprints or DNA on the baggie containing the cocaine, or evidence that appellant had cocaine in her system or a history of using cocaine." The evidence did not "exclude the possibility that someone other than the defendant possessed the narcotics."[45]

The prosecution in these multiparty cases looks for an affirmative link between the defendant and the controlled substance. This might be a combination of evidence such as a fingerprint on a package, the individual's possession of a large amount of cash, whether the defendant has exclusive control over the area in which the narcotics are seized, the defendant's demeanor when confronted by the police, whether the defendant was in actual possession of drug paraphernalia or narcotics, and any incriminating statements made by the accused.[46]

Some state courts and the federal courts have held defendants liable for possession of small quantities of narcotics. The central question for most courts is whether the defendant knowingly possessed the small amount of illicit narcotics or whether the defendant was unaware of the small amount of illicit narcotics.[47] California, in contrast, limits liability to a "useable amount." The quantity of the drug must be sufficient to have a narcotic effect. The California Supreme Court held that "in penalizing a person who possesses a narcotic the Legislature proscribed possession of a substance that has a narcotic effect. . . . It did not refer to useless traces or residue of such substance. Hence, the possession of a minute crystalline residue of narcotic useless for either sale or consumption . . . does not constitute sufficient evidence in itself to sustain a conviction."[48] In *People v. Rubacalba*, the California Supreme Court held that one-tenth of a gram or one hundred milligrams of cocaine was a usable quantity. The court explained that the "quantity rule prohibits conviction only when the substance possessed simply cannot be used, such as when it is a blackened residue or a useless trace. It does not extend to a substance containing contraband, even if not pure, if the substance is in a form and quantity that can be used."[49]

The prosecution of drug traffickers or individuals who transport and/or sell narcotics is based on federal and state statutes punishing unlawful **possession with intent to distribute** a controlled substance. These laws make it a crime to possess a controlled substance with the intent to sell or transfer the narcotic. Federal law provides that "it shall be unlawful for any person knowingly or intentionally . . . to . . . possess with intent to manufacture, distribute, or dispense a controlled substance."[50] Similar text is incorporated into most state criminal codes. Actual delivery may be established by proof that the defendant sold or transferred narcotics to an undercover agent or that he or she is observed or is videoed selling or distributing narcotics.

Possession with intent to distribute narcotics requires that the prosecution establish that "the defendant knowingly and intentionally possessed the drug, and that he did so with the specific intent to distribute it." The question confronting a court in many instances is whether the defendant is in actual or constructive possession of the drugs with the intent to distribute or whether the defendant merely has the intent to possess the drugs.

The three factors listed below are relied on by courts in determining whether an individual possessed narcotics with the intent to distribute or possessed the narcotics for personal use.

1. *Quantity.* The defendant possesses more narcotics than are required by a single individual. A small amount of narcotics may not be determinative because the individual already may have sold most of the drugs in his or her possession.

2. *Value.* Addicts and recreational drug users typically cannot afford to possess a valuable cache of narcotics for personal use.

3. *Drug paraphernalia.* Items are discovered that are associated with an intent to distribute narcotics, such as a scale to weigh narcotics and packaging material.

In *State v. Smith*, a Louisiana appellate court affirmed the defendant's conviction for possession with intent to distribute the cocaine and heroin that was seized from clothes in his bedroom. The court noted that the defendant's intent to sell could be inferred from the presence of plastic baggies for packaging the narcotics; razor blades, scales, and measuring devices, all of which are used in preparing drugs for sale; and $1,330 in cash, most of which was in $20 bills. The court considered it important that these items were discovered in the defendant's bedroom rather than in the kitchen where many of these items ordinarily are stored. Other circumstantial evidence or evidence that, in totality, created an inference of an intent to sell included multiple cell phones and weapons that might be intended to be used to protect the cache of drugs. The court also found it significant that the defendant had a previous conviction for selling narcotics. The appellate court credited the testimony of a police officer "that nine grams of powder cocaine would cost about $350.00 or $400.00 and would be much more than the amount generally obtained by an addict for personal consumption." The officer also testified that there was an absence of items ordinarily employed for personal use such as "needles, spoons, metal objects, bottle caps, straws, a rolled up piece of paper, or a dollar bill, to ingest the drugs they obtain."[51]

In a Massachusetts case, an appellate court affirmed the defendant's conviction for possession with intent to sell narcotics based on the fact that the defendant was found with "three individually wrapped rocks of crack cocaine, had $312 in cash in his pocket, and carried no paraphernalia for ingesting the drugs. . . . [T]he defendant [when arrested] had been located in an area known for drug sales for at least an hour, and was in the company of an individual who conducted a drug transaction in his presence." The court concluded that "the inference of an intent to distribute . . . is both reasonable and possible."[52]

In contrast, an Ohio court found that a defendant had not been in possession of narcotics with intent to distribute where the defendant was in possession of three unwrapped rocks of crack cocaine weighing an ounce, where he was not in an area known for drug use, and where his mother testified that she had given him the several thousand dollars in his possession to hire a lawyer to represent him in another case.[53]

CRIMINAL LAW AND PUBLIC POLICY

Determinate sentences have the advantage of being predictable, definite, and uniform. On the other hand, this "one size fits all" approach may prevent judges from tailoring sentences to the circumstances of a specific case. A particularly controversial area of determinate sentencing is mandatory minimum drug offenses. In 1975, New York governor Nelson Rockefeller initiated the controversial "Rockefeller drug laws" that required that an individual convicted of selling two ounces of a narcotic substance or of possessing eight ounces of a narcotic substance receive a sentence of between eight and twenty years, regardless of the individual's criminal history. The New York model in which a judge must sentence a defendant to a minimum sentence was followed by other states. The federal government joined this trend and introduced mandatory minimum sentences in the Anti–Drug Abuse Act of 1986 and its 1988 amendments.

5-Year Mandatory Minimum	
Previous law	5 g crack/500 g powder cocaine
New law	28 g crack/500 g powder cocaine
10-Year Mandatory Minimum	
Previous law	50 g crack/5,000 g powder cocaine
New law	280 g crack/5,000 g powder cocaine

Fair Sentencing Act of 2010: Punishment Based on Type and Amount of Drugs in Possession	
Possession of 5 Grams of Crack Without the Intent to Distribute	
Previous law	5-year mandatory minimum
New law	No mandatory minimum

The most debated aspect of federal law is the punishment of an individual based on the type and amount of drugs in his or her possession, regardless of the individual's criminal history. Under the previous federal law, a conviction for possession with intent to distribute five grams of crack cocaine or five hundred grams of powder cocaine resulted in the same five-year sentence. Fifty grams of crack cocaine and five kilograms of powder cocaine triggered the same ten-year sentence. The Fair Sentencing Act of 2010 reduced the hundred-to-one ratio between crack and powder

(Continued)

(Continued)

cocaine to eighteen to one to trigger the five- and ten-year mandatory minimums.

The thinking behind the previous law was that crack is sold in small, relatively inexpensive amounts on the street and that the ease of access to crack leads to individuals becoming addicts who threaten the safety and welfare of communities. The profitability of the "crack trade" leads to street violence between street gangs competing for control of the drug trade. The law was criticized for resulting in the disproportionate arrest and imprisonment of African American gang members for lengthy terms while Caucasian sellers and users of powder cocaine received much less severe prison terms.

The sentencing reform law, as noted, reduces the hundred-to-one ratio to eighteen to one. This means that 28 grams of crack trigger a five-year mandatory minimum and 280 grams of crack trigger a ten-year mandatory minimum. The triggering weights for powder cocaine remain the same. The law also eliminated the previous five-year mandatory minimum for simple possession (without the intent to distribute) of five grams of crack cocaine by first-time offenders. Roughly twelve states continue to punish possession of crack cocaine with the same sentence as a greater amount of powder cocaine.

It is estimated that the new law will reduce sentences for crack-cocaine-related offenses by an average of twenty-seven months in prison and save the government $42 million during the next five years. The act took effect when President Barack Obama signed the law on August 3, 2010. Almost a year later, the new law was applied retroactively to allow thousands of individuals sentenced under the "old law" to petition a court to reduce their sentence. In June 2012, the Supreme Court held that new, more lenient penalty provisions apply to offenders who committed a crack cocaine offense before the law went into effect and are sentenced after the date that the law went into effect. The Court reasoned that sentencing these offenders under the old sentencing scheme would "seriously undermine . . . uniformity and proportionality in sentencing" (*Dorsey v. United States,* 132 S. Ct. 2321, 567 U.S. ___ [2012]).

The following quantities are punishable by five years in prison under federal law:

- 100 grams of heroin
- 500 grams of powder cocaine
- 28 grams of crack cocaine
- 100 kilograms of marijuana

The following quantities are punishable by ten years in prison under federal law:

- 1 kilogram of heroin
- 5 kilograms of powder cocaine
- 280 grams of crack cocaine
- 1,000 kilograms of marijuana

Congress softened the impact of the mandatory minimum drug sentences by providing that a judge may issue a lesser sentence in those instances in which prosecutors certify that a defendant has provided "substantial assistance" in convicting other drug offenders. There also is a safety valve that permits a reduced sentence for defendants determined by the judge to be low-level, nonviolent, first-time offenders.

Prosecutors argue that the mandatory minimum sentences are required to deter individuals from entering into the lucrative drug trade. The threat of a lengthy sentence also is necessary in order to encourage the cooperation of defendants. Prosecutors stress that individuals who are convicted and sentenced were fully aware of the consequences of their criminal actions.

These mandatory minimum laws nevertheless have come under attack by both conservative and liberal politicians, by the American Bar Association, and by the Judicial Conference, which is the organization of federal judges. An estimated twenty-seven states, including Maryland and Connecticut, have recently modified or are considering amending their mandatory minimum narcotics laws. New York also modified the Rockefeller drug laws in 2004 when Governor George Pataki signed the Drug Law Reform Act, and its legislators are contemplating abandoning determinate sentences for drug offenders. This trend is encouraged by studies that indicate that these laws have the following problems:

- *Inflexibility.* They fail to take into account the differences between defendants.
- *Plea Bargaining.* Drug kingpins are able to trade information for reduced sentences.
- *Prosecutorial Discretion.* Some prosecutors who object to the laws charge defendants with the possession of a lesser quantity of drugs to avoid the mandatory sentencing provisions.
- *Increase in Prison Population.* The laws are thought to be responsible for the growth of the state and federal prison population.

- *Disparate Effects.* A significant percentage of individuals sentenced under these laws are African Americans or Hispanics involved in street-level drug activity. The increase in the number of women who are incarcerated is attributed to the fact that females find themselves arrested for assisting their husbands or lovers who are involved in the drug trade.

In *Hutto v. Davis*, the U.S. Supreme Court upheld the constitutionality of mandatory minimum state drug laws. The Court reasoned that Hutto's forty-year prison sentence and $20,000 fine was not disproportionate to his conviction on two counts of possession with intent to distribute and the distribution of a total of nine ounces of marijuana with a street value of roughly $200. The Court held that the determination of the proper sentence for this offense was a matter that was appropriately determined by the Virginia legislature (*Hutto v. Davis*, 454 U.S. 370 [1982]).

A number of judges complain about mandatory minimum sentences. In 2012, now retired federal district court judge John Gleeson stated in *United States v. Dossie* that mandatory minimum sentences were intended to be used against high-level drug "masterminds" and "managers" and that prosecutors were abusing the law by asking judges to impose these harsh mandatory minimum sentences on low-level street dealers. Dossie was convicted as an "intermediary in four hand-to-hand crack sales, for which he made a total of about $140." Prosecutors asked for a "harsh" mandatory sentence because two of the sales were slightly beyond the twenty-eight-gram limit. Judge Gleeson explained that his "hands were tied" and that he was compelled to impose an "unjust" five-year prison term on Dossie. "Just as baseball is a game of inches," Judge Gleeson complained, "our drug-offense mandatory minimum provisions create a deadly serious game of grams" (*United States v. Dossie*, 851 F. Supp. 2d 478 [E.D.N.Y. 2012]).

President Obama indicated his concern for mandatory minimum sentences for drug offenses when in December 2013 he commuted the sentences of eight federal prisoners convicted of crack cocaine offenses. All of these individuals had served at least fifteen years in prison; six were sentenced to life imprisonment. The defendants had been sentenced under the hundred-to-one sentencing disparity between powder and crack cocaine, and President Obama noted that the inmates would have received significantly shorter sentences under current reformed drug laws and already would have completed their sentences. Clarence Aaron, for example, was sentenced to three life terms for a drug crime committed when he was twenty-two years old. Stephanie George received a life sentence in 1997 at age twenty-seven based on allowing her boyfriend to store crack in a box in her home.[54]

The Obama administration and states such as Texas, New York, Colorado, Michigan, and Arkansas have taken important steps to minimize the impact of mandatory minimum sentences on low-level, nonviolent drug offenders and on other nonviolent offenders. For example, in April 2014, Attorney General Eric Holder announced Clemency Project 2014 providing that nonviolent, low-level incarcerated felons who had served at least ten years and would have received a lesser sentence under current reformed federal laws would be considered for clemency. The primary beneficiaries are the roughly eight thousand drug offenders sentenced before Congress's 2010 reform of the punishment for crack cocaine offenses. President Obama has granted clemency to hundreds of federal offenders, most of whom were incarcerated for low-level, nonviolent narcotics offenses,[55] including a significant number in the last year of his presidency.[56]

What do you think about the argument that mandatory minimum sentences are so disproportionate and impose such hardship that jurors should refuse to convict defendants charged with quantities of narcotics carrying mandatory minimum sentences?[57]

You Decide  **12.2** Kody Farmer suffered from chronic back pain stemming from a work-related injury and underwent back surgery. Farmer, for roughly a decade, took a variety of different medications to relieve his pain including Ultram (a painkiller) and Soma (a muscle relaxer). Four days prior to his arrest for driving while intoxicated (DWI), Farmer also was prescribed Ambien to combat his insomnia. Farmer typically took the Ultram and Soma, both of which contain warning that they may induce drowsiness, before taking a shower in the morning and driving to work.

(Continued)

(Continued)

The Ultram and Ambien pills resemble one another. On the morning of Farmer's accident, his wife laid out his Ultram (and Soma) and Ambien on their microwave, but she separated the pills so that the appellant would take the Ambien at night because "both his doctor and his pharmacist recommended that he be within minutes of going to bed before taking Ambien." Following Farmer's arrest for DWI, Ambien was found in his bloodstream, and his wife testified that the Ambien she laid out for him in the morning was gone. Farmer appealed his conviction for DWI to the Texas Court of Criminal Appeals on the grounds that his conviction was based on an involuntary act because he did not recall taking the Ambien and did not intentionally take the Ambien.

Would you convict Farmer of DWI? See *Farmer v. State*, 411 S.W.3d 901 (Tex. Ct. of Crim. App. 2013).

You can find the answer at study.sagepub.com/lippmaness2e

In July 2014, the influential *New York Times* endorsed legalization of marijuana and pointed out that a majority of adults favor legalization and that there are considerable social costs associated with continuing to criminalize marijuana. For instance:

Arrests. From 2001 to 2010, there were 8.2 million marijuana arrests. Roughly nine out of ten were for possession. In 2010, there were 750,000 arrests involving marijuana, and in 2011, there were more arrests for marijuana than for all violent crimes.

Racial Disparity. Whites and African Americans use marijuana at comparable rates although African Americans are 3.7 times more likely to be arrested than whites.

Economics. The estimated cost of enforcing laws on marijuana possession is $3.6 billion.

Public Safety. Arresting individuals for marijuana does not remove dangerous individuals from society. Ninety percent of individuals imprisoned for marijuana possession have no history of violence. Marijuana arrests also contribute to prison overcrowding. Table 12.2 lists the punishment for federal marijuana offenses, and Table 12.3 lists the sentences for marijuana offenses in Florida.

Disabilities. Many marijuana arrests for possession are misdemeanors, and individuals are not imprisoned. A conviction, however, may result in the revocation of a professional license or suspension of a driver's license, and prevent an individual from obtaining a mortgage to buy a home or obtain a student loan.

The Obama administration responded to the *New York Times* by recognizing that there are credible concerns about "disproportionality [of sentencing] throughout our criminal justice system" and justifiable concerns about the classification of marijuana as a Schedule I offense. Marijuana, however, is "addictive and marijuana use has harmful consequences. . . . Addictive substances like alcohol and tobacco, which are legal and taxed, already result in much higher social costs than the revenue they generate." Consider, for example, the costs and public safety concerns that at present are created by drivers who are "high" on marijuana and the fact that some individuals will start with marijuana and transition to more powerful narcotics. Should marijuana be legalized? What is your view?

Marijuana

Marijuana is punished under both federal and state law. Roughly 760,000 arrests are made each year for the possession or the distribution of marijuana. This total constitutes roughly half of all arrests for the possession, sale, or manufacture of illicit drugs. Ninety-nine percent of prosecutions are under state law.

Roughly fifteen states and numerous cities have decriminalized the possession of small amounts of marijuana, and they punish the first offense for possession of small amounts of marijuana with a fine, much like a traffic ticket. One example of the **decriminalization of marijuana** is the Nebraska statute. First-offense possession is a civil infraction resulting in a citation rather than in an arrest, and it carries a $300 fine along with attendance at a drug education course. Second-offense possession of up to an ounce results in a $400 fine and up to five days in jail, and third-offense possession is punished by up to a week in jail and a $500 fine. In November 2012, voters in Detroit and in four other Michigan cities voted to decriminalize possession of small amounts of marijuana.

In 1991, a Florida appellate court held that a couple who had contracted AIDS as a result of a blood transfusion and who were arrested for marijuana possession were entitled to rely on the defense of medical necessity to justify their use of marijuana. "Jenks obviously did not intend to contract AIDS. Furthermore, the Jenks[es]' medical expert and physician testified that no drug or treatment is available that would effectively eliminate or diminish the Jenks[es]' nausea. Finally, the Jenks[es] established that if their nausea was not controlled, their lives were in danger." Critics of the decision viewed medical necessity as a "slippery slope," which ultimately would lead to the legalization of marijuana.

President George W. Bush directed the Department of Justice to bring criminal charges under the federal Controlled Substances Act against individuals and dispensaries involved in **medical marijuana**. In 2001, the Supreme Court provided support for federal prosecutions of individuals using medical marijuana when it held that the federal Controlled Substances Act does not recognize an exemption from criminal liability for marijuana possession based on medical necessity.[58]

Despite the U.S. Supreme Court decision, various states adopted medical marijuana laws. These states claimed that their state law authorizing individuals to use marijuana based on medical necessity took precedence over the federal prohibition on marijuana.

In 2005, in *Gonzales v. Raich*, the Supreme Court addressed the conflict between the California medical marijuana law that decriminalized marijuana and the federal prohibition on marijuana possession.[59]

California voters passed Proposition 215, the Compassionate Use Act of 1996, to ensure that "seriously ill" residents of California are able to obtain marijuana. The act provides an exemption from criminal prosecution for doctors who authorize patients to possess or cultivate marijuana for medical purposes. Angel Raich and Diane Monson, two California residents, suffer from severe medical disabilities. Their doctors found that marijuana is the only drug that is able to alleviate their pain and suffering. Raich's doctor went so far as to claim that Angel's pain is so intense that she may die if deprived of marijuana. Marijuana enables her to live a fairly normal life and to avoid being confined to a wheelchair. Monson cultivates her own marijuana, and Raich relies on two caregivers who provide her with California-grown marijuana at no cost.

Federal agents raided Monson's home and destroyed all six of her marijuana plants. Monson and Raich along with several doctors and patients asked the Supreme Court to rule on the federal government's refusal to exempt medical marijuana users from criminal prosecution and punishment. The U.S. Supreme Court held that the federal prohibition on the possession of marijuana would be undermined by exempting marijuana possession in California and other states from federal criminal enforcement. The Court explained that the cultivation of marijuana under California's medical marijuana law, although clearly a local activity, frustrated the federal government's effort to control the shipment of marijuana. This marijuana grown in California inevitably would find its way into interstate commerce, increase the nationwide supply, and drive down the price of the illegal drug. There was also a risk that completely healthy individuals in California would manage to be fraudulently certified by a doctor to be in need of medical marijuana. Three of the nine Supreme Court judges dissented from the majority opinion. Justice Sandra Day O'Connor observed that the majority judgment "stifle[s] an express choice by some States concerned for the lives and liberties of their people, to regulate medical marijuana differently."

Twenty-five states recognize medical marijuana. In October 2012, the Connecticut legislature voted for medical marijuana. Connecticut law provides that an individual who is qualified to possess marijuana and who is registered with the Department of Consumer Protection may possess "an amount of usable marijuana reasonably necessary to ensure . . . availability for . . . one month." Approved conditions include "[c]ancer, glaucoma, positive status for human immunodeficiency virus or acquired immune deficiency syndrome [HIV/AIDS], Parkinson's disease, multiple sclerosis, damage to the nervous tissue of the spinal cord with objective neurological indication of intractable spasticity, epilepsy, cachexia, wasting syndrome, Crohn's disease, posttraumatic stress disorder, or any medical condition, medical treatment or disease approved by the Department of Consumer Protection."

In November 2012, voters in Colorado and in Washington adopted ballot measures that resulted in these two jurisdictions becoming the first two states to legalize marijuana. Oregon voters rejected a similar referendum. It appears that the federal government will not enforce federal criminal laws against individuals in Colorado and in Washington whose cultivation, possession, or sale of marijuana is in compliance with state law.

Fifty-five percent of Colorado voters approved Amendment 64 legalizing the personal use of marijuana by individuals who are at least twenty-one years of age. The state legislature subsequently enacted regulations licensing the commercial production and sale of cannabis. Private possession of up to one ounce of marijuana is legal, and private cultivation of up to six marijuana plants is lawful. Individuals are free to transfer one ounce of marijuana so long as no money exchanges hands. Cannabis is prohibited from being smoked in public, and there are restrictions on driving while under the influence of marijuana. The sale of marijuana is strictly regulated, and consumers may purchase up to an ounce of "pot." Individuals who grow and traffic in marijuana in violation of Colorado law are subject to federal arrest and prosecution. Voters in Alaska, Oregon, and the District of Columbia in November 2014 overwhelmingly approved ballot measures legalizing marijuana for adults at least twenty-one years of age subject to restrictions that are similar to Colorado. Fifty-eight percent of individuals polled nationwide favor marijuana legalization as compared to 12 percent of individuals who favored marijuana legalization in 1969.

One interesting aspect of the regulation of marijuana involves the use of marijuana as a religious sacrament. In 2006, in *Gonzales v. O Centro Espirita*, the Supreme Court held that the government failed to demonstrate a "compelling interest" in prohibiting a religious group from drinking a ceremonial tea drink called hoasca, which contains DMT, a prohibited substance under Schedule I of the Controlled Substances Act. The Court rejected the government's argument that there could be no exemption from the requirements of the law for a religious group, based on the fact that Native Americans have been permitted to use peyote as a sacrament for the past thirty-five years.[60]

Table 12.2	Federal Marijuana Penalties
Possession	A first offense for possession of marijuana is punishable by up to one year in jail and a minimum fine of $1,000 for a first conviction. A second conviction results in a fifteen-day mandatory minimum sentence with a maximum of two years in prison and a fine of up to $2,500. Additional convictions carry a ninety-day mandatory minimum sentence and a maximum of up to three years in prison and a fine of up to $5,000.
Manufacture or distribution	Manufacture or distribution of less than fifty plants or fifty kilograms of marijuana is punishable by up to five years in prison and a fine of up to $250,000. The sentence for fifty to ninety-nine plants or fifty to ninety-nine kilograms is enhanced to up to twenty years in prison and a fine of up to $1 million. Manufacture or distribution of 100 to 999 plants or 100 to 999 kilograms carries a punishment of five to forty years in prison and a fine of $2 million to $5 million. The penalty for one thousand plants or one thousand kilograms or more is from ten years to life in prison and a fine of $4 million to $10 million.
Distribution to a minor	Distribution of more than five grams of marijuana to an individual under the age of twenty-one is punishable by twice the normal sentence. Distribution within one thousand feet of a school, playground, or public housing, or within one hundred feet of a youth center, public pool, or video arcade, also enhances the possible penalties.
Paraphernalia	The sale of paraphernalia is punishable by up to three years in prison.
Death penalty	The sentence of death can be imposed on a defendant who has been found guilty of manufacturing, importing, or distributing a controlled substance if the act was committed as part of a continuing criminal enterprise in those instances in which the defendant is a central leader; the quantity of the controlled substance is sixty thousand kilograms or more of a mixture or substance containing a detectable amount of marijuana, or sixty thousand or more marijuana plants; or the enterprise received more than $20 million in gross receipts during any twelve-month period of its existence.

Source: Federal Laws & Penalties, http://norml.org/laws/item/federal-penalties-2.

Table 12.3 Florida Marijuana Laws

Possession		Prison	Fine
20 grams or less	Misdemeanor	1 year	$ 1,000
More than 20 grams–25 pounds	Felony	5 years	$ 5,000
More than 25–less than 2,000 pounds	Felony	3*–15 years	$ 25,000
2,000–less than 10,000 pounds	Felony	7*–30 years	$ 50,000
10,000 pounds or more	Felony	15*–30 years	$200,000
Fewer than 25 plants	Felony	5 years	$ 5,000
25–300 plants	Felony	15 years	$ 10,000
300–2,000 plants	Felony	3*–15 years	$ 25,000
2,000–10,000 plants	Felony	7*–30 years	$ 50,000
Within 1,000 feet of a school, college, park, or other specified areas	Felony	15 years	$ 10,000
* Mandatory minimum sentence			
Sale			
20 grams or less without remuneration	Misdemeanor	1 year	$ 1,000
25 pounds or less	Felony	5 years	$ 5,000
More than 25–less than 2,000 pounds (or 300–2,000 plants)	Felony	3*–15 years	$ 25,000
2,000–less than 10,000 pounds (or 2,000–10,000 plants)	Felony	7*–30 years	$ 50,000
10,000 pounds or more	Felony	15*–30 years	$200,000
Within 1,000 feet of a school, college, park, or other specified areas	Felony	15 years	$ 10,000
* Mandatory minimum sentence			
Hash and Concentrates			
Possession of hashish or concentrates	Felony	5 years	$ 5,000
Selling, manufacturing, or delivering	Felony	5 years	$ 5,000
Paraphernalia			
Possession of paraphernalia	Misdemeanor	1 year	$ 1,000
Miscellaneous			
Conviction causes a driver's license suspension for a period of 1 year			

Crystal Meth

Homemade methamphetamine, popularly known as "crystal meth" or "crank," is the illicit "drug of choice" among a large number of young people. The highly addictive drug is manufactured with ingredients available over the counter. Individuals producing crystal meth nonetheless run a significant risk. The manufacture of the drug requires the use of highly unstable chemicals, which easily are ignited accidentally during the manufacturing process. The toxic nature of these chemicals when disposed of threatens the natural environment.

Crystal meth laboratories generally are located in rural areas and often are detected only as a result of an explosion, a fire, or environmental pollution. In 2005, Congress passed the Combat Methamphetamine Epidemic Act. The law regulates over-the-counter purchases of precursor chemicals for manufacturing crystal meth. The law makes several important contributions to combating crystal meth:

- *Penalties.* Penalties are increased for smuggling and selling methamphetamine.
- *Chemicals.* Precursor chemicals used to manufacture methamphetamine are required to be stored behind the counter in a locked display case, and a customer may buy only 3.6 grams per day and 9 grams per month. These chemicals ordinarily are found in cold and sinus products and in appetite suppressants. They include ephedrine, pseudoephedrine, and phenylpropanolamine.
- *Logbook.* Stores must keep a record of purchasers to prevent an individual from going from one store to another so as to purchase an unlimited amount of the chemicals.

The law punishes possession of both methamphetamine and paraphernalia used to ingest crystal meth.

PRESCRIPTION DRUGS

A major concern of both federal and state law is the abuse of prescription drugs, particularly painkillers. New Jersey law provides harsh penalties for the possession of prescription drugs not prescribed by a licensed health professional, the unlawful distribution of these drugs, the forgery of a prescription, acquiring prescription drugs by fraud or forgery, and the theft of blank prescription forms. An individual who is under the influence of a prescription drug that is unlawfully obtained is subject to a penalty of six months in prison and $1,000 in fines.[61]

Drug Paraphernalia

The federal **drug paraphernalia** statute, 21 U.S.C. § 863, prohibits the sale or offer for sale, shipment through interstate commerce, or importation or exportation of drug paraphernalia. A conviction is punishable by up to three years in prison, a fine, and forfeiture of paraphernalia. Drug paraphernalia includes "items" primarily intended or designed for the manufacture, processing, preparing, or concealing of narcotics and items primarily used in injecting, ingesting, or inhaling marijuana, cocaine, and hashish or another controlled substance.

State laws include provisions that are similar to the federal statute, and they also prohibit the possession of drug paraphernalia with the intent to use the "item" to ingest unlawful narcotics. The California Health and Safety Code, in part, provides that "[i]t is unlawful to possess an opium pipe or any device, contrivance, instrument, or paraphernalia used for unlawfully injecting or smoking . . . a controlled substance."[62]

Texas Health and Safety Code Section 481.125 provides that individuals may be charged with possession of drug paraphernalia if they knowingly or intentionally "possess an item that is used to plant, cultivate, grow, harvest, manufacture, compound, convert, produce, process, prepare, test, analyze, pack, repack, store, contain, inject, ingest, inhale, introduce into the body or conceal a controlled substance." The possession of drug paraphernalia with the intent that the item is to be used for ingesting illicit narcotics is punished with a fine not to exceed $500. Possessing, selling, or manufacturing paraphernalia knowing or intending that the paraphernalia is to be delivered or sold to another individual for use of illicit narcotics is punishable by up to one year and a fine not to exceed $4,000. Selling paraphernalia to a minor is a felony punishable by a mandatory minimum sentence of 180 days' imprisonment, a maximum of two years' imprisonment, and a fine not to exceed $10,000.

The justification for criminalizing paraphernalia is that it deters individuals from possessing or transferring devices required to ingest controlled substances. The prosecution to convict an individual for possession of paraphernalia is required to establish beyond a reasonable doubt that the individual intended to use the paraphernalia to ingest a controlled substance.[63]

Commentators criticize the criminalization of drug paraphernalia because most of these items and devices may be used in a legal fashion and pose a danger only when used to manufacture or to ingest controlled substances. Critics argue that it makes more sense to punish the actual possession of drugs rather than to punish devices that may be used to manufacture or to take narcotics. The prosecution also is able to "pile on the punishment" by holding a defendant liable for possession of narcotics as well as for possession of a hypodermic needle. Does it make sense for the law to punish possession of a pipe or cigarette rolling paper that may be lawfully used to smoke tobacco and also may be unlawfully used to smoke crack? Should the law be limited to criminalizing the sale of these items?

Another criticism of paraphernalia laws is that the definition of drug paraphernalia in criminal statutes in some instances is vague and does not always clearly inform individuals of the items and devices that are prohibited under the law. The Eighth Circuit Court of Appeals held that an ordinance that prohibits items "suitable to be used for smoking controlled substances" was "void for vagueness."[64] However, in *Hoffman Estates v. Flipside*, the U.S. Supreme Court discouraged these types of constitutional challenges to paraphernalia laws when the Court held that a local ordinance prohibiting merchants from selling drug "paraphernalia . . . designed or marketed for use with illegal cannabis or drugs" was not unconstitutionally "void for vagueness." The Court reasoned that a reasonable businessperson would know that the statute prohibited the sale of items such as a "roach clip, rolling paper, and pipe."[65]

Paraphernalia laws, nonetheless, continue to create uncertainty when a device may be used to ingest tobacco as well as narcotics. In *People v. Carreon*, Carreon was convicted of possession of marijuana and drug paraphernalia. The paraphernalia was a cigar loaded with cannabis. The Illinois appellate court acquitted the defendant on the grounds that the Illinois statute stated that drug paraphernalia did not include "[i]tems historically and customarily used in . . . ingesting or inhaling of tobacco, . . . tobacco pipes, and cigarette rolling papers." The court explained that "although sometimes used to ingest cannabis, cigars are historically and customarily used for the legal ingestion of tobacco. Accordingly, we hold that cigars are not included in the definition of drug paraphernalia under the Act, and defendant's conviction of possession of drug paraphernalia must be reversed."[66]

Individuals unlawfully involved with controlled substances, in addition to criminal punishment, risk the forfeiture of property.

Assets Forfeiture

The Comprehensive Drug Abuse Prevention and Control Act of 1970, 21 U.S.C. § 853, provides that an individual convicted of a federal narcotics offense punishable by at least a year of imprisonment shall forfeit property "derived from such violation, used to commit or to facilitate the commission of the violation along with any of the person's property intended to be used . . . to commit, or to facilitate" the commission of the narcotics offense. States all have forfeiture laws similar to the federal law.[67] Between 1989 and 2010, an estimated $12 billion in assets were seized by federal prosecutors.

Assets forfeiture has been criticized because the local police typically are allowed to retain a percentage of proceeds from the property that is forfeited and sold, along with a percentage of any cash that is seized. This so-called policing for profit, according to critics, provides an incentive for law enforcement to pursue property rather than criminal convictions and to engage in tactics like "reverse sting" operations in which undercover officers sell drugs to buyers whose property subsequently is seized. On the other hand, these proceeds financially help support law enforcement in a time of declining budgets, and they enable the local police to afford sophisticated technological equipment. Any money seized from individuals involved in financial crimes also is returned to the victims.

A forfeiture proceeding may be criminal or civil. In a *criminal forfeiture*, an individual convicted of a narcotics offense forfeits property associated with the offense for which he or she has been convicted. Criminal forfeiture is designed to further punish individuals guilty of a narcotics offense by preventing them from "benefitting from their own wrong." Keep in mind that criminal guilt requires guilt beyond a reasonable doubt, although forfeiture is based on the lower preponderance of the evidence standard. The same jury that determines guilt or innocence also determines whether property should be forfeited. Property subject to forfeiture includes narcotics, drug paraphernalia, money derived from drug transactions, and property purchased with the proceeds of drug transactions. A court may order the seizure of "substitute property" or property with a monetary value equal to the value of property that an individual has transferred or sold.

Civil forfeiture does not require a criminal charge or a criminal conviction, and it accounts for roughly 80 percent of forfeiture proceedings. The Supreme Court has held that civil forfeiture requires that the government provide an individual with notice of the property to be seized and that the individual is to be provided with a hearing in which the government must establish by a preponderance of the evidence that the property is linked to unlawful narcotics activity.[68]

In 2000, the U.S. Congress, concerned that individuals subjected to civil forfeiture lacked adequate protections, passed the Civil Asset Forfeiture Reform Act.[69] Although the act expands the number of offenses subject to civil forfeiture, a number of provisions make it more difficult for the government to seize property. The act, for example, establishes an "innocent owner defense" for individuals who are able to establish that they did know that the property to be seized was linked to unlawful activity or who took every effort to prevent the unlawful activity. For example, an individual's lack of knowledge that a home was purchased by his or her former spouse with money from an unlawful narcotics transaction would constitute a defense in a civil forfeiture proceeding.[70] Indigent defendants under the Reform Act are provided with legal representation, and the government is liable for damages in those instances in which the government is unsuccessful in forfeiting the property.

The U.S. Supreme Court held in *United States v. Ursery* that civil forfeitures do not constitute punishment and therefore do not raise an issue of double jeopardy.[71] The Court recently held that the government may not seize funds unconnected with criminal activity that a defendant requires in order to hire a lawyer.

The Supreme Court has upheld random drug testing as a method for detecting and for deterring drug use among public employees and high school students.

Drug Testing

The U.S. Supreme Court has approved the *drug testing* of government employees whose ingestion of narcotics may threaten the public safety and welfare. In 1989, in *Skinner v. Railway Labor Executives' Association*, the Court upheld the constitutionality of an alcohol and drug testing program established by the U.S. Federal Railroad Administration to prevent and to investigate accidents. The Court explained that the testing, which was conducted without probable cause or warrant or reasonable suspicion, was required in the interest of railroad safety.[72] *Skinner* was decided on the same day as *National Treasury Employees Union v. Von Raab*, which affirmed the constitutionality of a drug testing program established by the U.S. Customs Service as a condition of employment for individuals staffing positions involving drug interdiction or enforcement and for positions in which employees carry a firearm or handle "sensitive information."[73]

The Supreme Court also approved random drug testing programs in high schools. In *Vernonia School District 47J v. Acton*, the Court upheld the constitutionality of the random drug testing of athletes. The Court reasoned that athletes are subject to rules, regulations, and discipline and have less expectation of privacy than the average student and that there was a demonstrated need to test the athletes because they were the "leaders" of the drug culture in the school. A positive result for drugs led to suspension from athletic activities and did not result in a criminal arrest.[74] In *Board of Education of Independent School District No. 92 of Pottawatomie County v. Earls*, the Court extended drug testing to students involved in all competitive extracurricular activities.[75] The Supreme Court in *Safford Unified School District v. Redding* held that it was unconstitutional to "strip search" a student suspected of the unlawful possession of small amounts of a prescription drug.[76]

In most states, it is a crime to falsify a drug test. Texas Health and Safety Code Section 481.133 provides that "falsifying a drug test," or "possessing with intent to use any material for the falsification of a drug test," is punishable by up to 180 days imprisonment and a fine not to exceed $2,000.

Read *Board of Education of Independent School District No. 92 of Pottawatomie County v. Earls* and *Safford Unified School District v. Redding* on the study site: study.sagepub.com/lippmaness2e.

You Decide

12.3 The South Carolina Supreme Court in *Whitner v. State* was asked to decide whether the word *child* in Children's Code Section 20-7-50 includes viable fetuses. Cornelia Whitner pled guilty to criminal child neglect. Her baby was born with cocaine metabolites in its system because of Whitner's ingestion of crack cocaine during the third trimester of her pregnancy. She pled guilty and later appealed to the

> South Carolina Supreme Court. The relevant South Carolina statute is reprinted below.
>
> S.C. Code Ann. § 20-7-50 provides:
>
> Any person having the legal custody of any child or helpless person, who shall, without lawful excuse, refuse or neglect to provide . . . the proper care and attention for such child or helpless person, so that the life, health or comfort of such child or helpless person is endangered or is likely to be endangered, shall be guilty of a misdemeanor and shall be punished within the discretion of the circuit court.
>
> Would you hold Whitner guilty of child neglect? See *Whitner v. State*, 492 S.E.2d 777 (S.C. 1997).
>
> *You can find the answer at study.sagepub.com/lippmaness2e*

Drug Courts

In 1989, the first drug court was established in Miami, Florida. Drug courts subsequently have been established in all fifty states and in the District of Columbia. Over 2,600 drug courts are operating in the United States and in U.S. territories. The theory behind **drug courts** is that rather than sending nonviolent defendants charged with drug possession to prison, judges, defense attorneys, prosecutors, and court professionals should work together to establish goals and targets for defendants to achieve. Defendants' progress through the program is closely monitored and evaluated. Advocates of drug courts believe that treating an individual's addiction breaks the cycle of addicts who are imprisoned returning to crime to "feed their habit" once they are released from prison.

There are two approaches to drug courts. Under the *pretrial approach*, a defendant who is arrested for drug possession and who has not been convicted of a crime of violence in the past, with the agreement of the prosecutor, may be diverted from the conventional criminal justice process into the drug court program. Other courts adopt a *postadjudication approach* in which defendants plead guilty and then are eligible to enter the drug court program.

The defendant, under both the pretrial and postadjudication approaches, signs a contract to attend group meetings and counseling sessions, to submit to regular drug testing, to appear in court for periodic status hearings to review his or her progress, and to agree to work with job counselors in obtaining employment. Successful completion of the programs results in the dropping of the charges against the defendant. A defendant's failure to comply with the terms of the contract, which typically involves a commitment for a year, may result in additional counseling, treatment, or a brief period of incarceration. Serious or continuous violations of the terms of the contract result in a reinstatement of the charges against the defendant, criminal prosecution, and imprisonment.

An estimated 120,000 individuals participate in drug courts. Studies indicate that individuals in the drug court program have lower recidivism rates than individuals who are imprisoned for drug offenses and that drug court programs are less expensive than imprisonment.

Office of National Drug Control Policy

A cornerstone of the "War on Drugs" is the **Office of National Drug Control Policy (ONDCP)**, established by the Anti–Drug Abuse Act of 1988, 21 U.S.C. § 801. The ONDCP is part of the Executive Office of the President of the United States. The ONDCP directs the efforts of the various federal agencies concerned with narcotics, coordinates the state and national efforts to combat drugs, and sponsors national antinarcotics media campaigns. The goals of the ONDCP are to reduce illegal drug use and manufacturing, to combat domestic and international drug trafficking, to counter drug-related crime and violence, and to address drug-related health consequences. The ONDCP annually provides $10 billion in grants to domestic law enforcement, provides $9 billion for treatment, and spends roughly $4 billion to assist drug interdiction efforts at the U.S. borders.

The current national drug strategy places renewed emphasis on drug treatment as an alternative to incarceration and advocates lower sentences for minor drug crimes. Emphasis has been placed on combating prescription drug abuse among young people.[77]

The **Drug Enforcement Administration (DEA)**, established in 1973 by President Richard M. Nixon, is a "single unified command" that conducts and coordinates the national and international "War on Drugs." The DEA today has five thousand special agents posted across the globe with a budget of $3 billion. It is estimated that between 2005 and 2011, the DEA's drug seizures, destruction of drug processing facilities, and frustration of drug operations resulted in the loss of $19.3 billion in revenue for drug cartels.

CASE ANALYSIS

In *Boddie v. United States*, a District of Columbia appellate court was asked to determine whether the defendant was guilty of possession of unlawful narcotics within one thousand feet of a school with the intent to distribute the drugs.

Was Boddie Guilty of Intent to Distribute Drugs Within a Drug-Free Zone?

Boddie v. United States, 865 A.2d 544 (D.C. App. 2005)

Officer Croson, who was assigned to the vice unit, "received a telephone call from a reliable source." Officer Croson recognized the voice of an informant with whom he had worked previously around thirty times. The informant stated that a person "wearing a black leather jacket, blue jeans and a gray skull cap" "was holding and selling heroin in the park in the 300 block of K Street, in the Southeast quadrant of the District of Columbia." The informant "had observed the [person] selling the narcotics." About ten minutes after he received the call from the informant, Officer Croson and two other Metropolitan Police Department (MPD) officers arrived at the K Street location.

Upon his arrival . . . Officer Croson saw "eight to ten subjects standing in the courtyard," one of whom "match[ed] the description" given by the telephone informant. . . . Officer Croson followed Mr. Boddie into an alley, got out of his vehicle, and "stopped" him. The area in which Mr. Boddie was stopped is "a high drug area where [people] sell narcotics. . . ." A park in that area was known as "an open-air heroin market." Officer Croson asked whether Mr. Boddie "had anything on him." Mr. Boddie said "he had a stem on him." He also admitted that he had "a couple of bags on [him]." When the officer could not find any drugs in Mr. Boddie's pockets, he inquired whether Mr. Boddie had "anything in [his] pants." Mr. Boddie removed "a . . . plastic bag from his crotch area" and handed it to the officer. The bag contained 45 "green zip-lock[ ] bags with a white powder substance that field-tested positive for heroin." Mr. Boddie claimed that he was not selling heroin but used the drug. Mr. Boddie was placed under arrest.

Sergeant John Brennan, a thirty-one-year veteran of the Metropolitan Police Department, testified as an expert in the distribution, sale, and use of narcotics in the District of Columbia. He stated that 24 of the bags possessed by Mr. Boddie contained a 31 percent concentration, and the other 21 bags a 23 percent concentration, with respect to the purity of the heroin. This compared with the average street concentration of "between 15 and 20 percent" purity. The typical user would have only one to three bags on his or her person at a time. . . . Sgt. Brennan explained that a dealer might give a person bags of heroin to sell in exchange for part of the proceeds from the sales; or that a person might take the bags, sell most of them and keep one or two bags for personal use. He posed the question: "Would a user have 45 bags for personal use[?]" And, he answered his own question: "[N]o. Never in my 31 years on the police force have I ever seen that."

Section 33-547.1 specifically prohibits "possessing" with intent to distribute narcotics in a drug free zone . . . , whether or not the heroin market itself is in a drug free zone[ ]." . . . [I]t is clear that this provision requires that the *actus reus* must occur within 1,000 feet of a school. . . . Since the *actus reus* for this offense is possession, it follows that possession of the drugs, not the intended location for distribution, must be located within 1,000 of a school.

If we require proof of intent to distribute only within the school zone . . . the statute would exclude many cases where the presence of drugs, in fact, increased the risk of harm to students. In view of the danger that the mere presence of drugs near a school presents, the district courts' interpretation would provide an escape-hatch for a defendant when, as here, the government is unable to establish precisely where the drugs were meant to be distributed, thereby defeating the intent of Congress. In many such cases, school zone distribution may even be intended but proving this may be difficult. Certainly, the mere existence of a large quantity of drugs in an area increases the possibility of gang warfare and gunfire and other drug-related violence in that vicinity.

We hold that the government need only prove beyond a reasonable doubt that the defendant possessed a controlled substance within the drug-free zone, or within 1,000 feet of a school, with the intent to distribute it somewhere, not necessarily within the drug-free zone. Since the government's evidence here established beyond a reasonable doubt that Mr. Boddie possessed the 45 bags of heroin within the drug-free zone, or within 1,000 feet of the Van Ness Elementary School, with the intent to distribute them, the place where the police initially observed him is irrelevant.

CHAPTER SUMMARY

In this chapter, we have reviewed the essentials of three crimes against social order and morality: alcoholism, gambling, and drug offenses. Society has mixed views toward each of these offenses. States sponsor lotteries at the same time that they criminalize gambling.

Juveniles are criminally prohibited from possessing alcohol, and it is a crime to sell, furnish, or give alcohol to a juvenile. Individuals who are intoxicated in public are liable for the crime of public intoxication.

An individual also is prohibited from driving an automobile while intoxicated. In the 1970s, driving while intoxicated was expanded to punish driving under the influence of liquor or narcotics. Individuals may challenge these charges on the grounds that despite their inebriated state, their judgment and driving were not affected. States subsequently modified their statutes to prohibit "driving with an unlawful blood alcohol level." Every state has gradually lowered the required blood alcohol level from 0.10 percent in the 1960s to 0.08 percent in the 1990s. States often impose harsher punishment on individuals with a higher blood alcohol level, typically between 0.15 and 0.20 percent.

State gambling laws distinguish between gambling and lawful gaming. Gambling is defined as placing money on an activity in which luck predominates over skill in determining the outcome. Statutes typically exempt charitable activities and social gambling from the reach of their statutory law. Federal law regulates interstate gambling and Internet gambling across state lines.

The common law did not address the manufacture, use, sale, or possession of drugs. In 1970, Congress enacted the Comprehensive Drug Abuse Prevention and Control Act, commonly known as the Controlled Substances Act. The act categorizes drugs within one of five schedules. The drugs considered to have the greatest adverse impact on the mind and body and the potential for addiction are listed in Schedule I, and the least dangerous drugs are listed in Schedule III, Schedule IV, and Schedule V (see Table 12.1).

State drug laws generally are based on the provisions of the Uniform Controlled Substances Act, which was formulated in 1972 by the National Conference of Commissioners on Uniform State Laws, a group of experts who drafted a set of "model laws" intended to guide state legislatures in addressing public policy issues. The Uniform Controlled Substances Act adopts a framework that is similar to the federal Drug Abuse Prevention and Control Act.

The emphasis of the legal component of the "War on Drugs" is on (1) the prosecution of the possession of narcotics and possession with intent to deliver narcotics; (2) the prosecution of the manufacture, possession, and sale of drug paraphernalia; and (3) civil and criminal assets forfeiture. There is a movement toward diverting first-time offenders into drug courts rather than subjecting them to formal criminal prosecution and imprisonment. There continues to be a debate over the appropriate approach to marijuana.

CHAPTER REVIEW QUESTIONS

1. Are juveniles treated differently than adults in terms of alcohol?

2. Under what circumstances may a police officer arrest an individual for public intoxication?

3. What type of evidence is relied on to convict an individual of operating a motor vehicle while intoxicated?

4. How is gambling defined under state statutes? Are certain types of gambling exempt from punishment under state statutes?

5. What is the significance of the schedules of controlled substances under the Controlled Substances Act?

6. List the types of acts involving controlled substances that are punished under state statutes.

7. How does the crime of drug possession differ from the crime of possession with the intent to distribute narcotics?

8. Why is there disagreement over whether there should be mandatory minimum sentences for drug crime?

9. How has the approach to the criminal regulation of marijuana changed over time?

10. Outline the law on drug paraphernalia. Should the possession of drug paraphernalia be a crime?

11. What is the purpose of assets forfeiture? Distinguish between criminal and civil assets forfeiture.

12. How do drug courts differ from regular criminal courts?

13. What is the role of the Office of National Drug Control Policy and the Drug Enforcement Administration in the "War on Drugs"?

LEGAL TERMINOLOGY

assets forfeiture

controlled substances

decriminalization of marijuana

driving under the influence (DUI)

driving while intoxicated (DWI)

driving with an unlawful blood alcohol level (DUBAL)

drug courts

Drug Enforcement Administration (DEA)

drug paraphernalia

gambling

gaming

implied consent laws

mandatory minimum drug sentences

medical marijuana

Office of National Drug Control Policy (ONDCP)

possession with intent to distribute

public intoxication

zero tolerance laws

 CRIMINAL LAW ON THE WEB

Visit **study.sagepub.com/lippmaness2e** to access additional study tools including suggested answers to the You Decide questions, reprints of cases and statutes, online appendices, and more!

13 OFFENSES AGAINST PUBLIC ADMINISTRATION AND THE ADMINISTRATION OF JUSTICE

Was the appellant in contempt of court?

On July 14, 2006, Appellant attended her son's detention hearing in juvenile court. Based on the nature of the charges, the trial court ordered Appellant's son to be held in secure detention pending his arraignment and trial. The trial court also provisionally appointed the Public Defender to represent Appellant's son. Appellant became angry because she had hoped her son would be released into her custody and she wanted to hire a private attorney. After Appellant left the courtroom and the trial court began another juvenile hearing, the Assistant State Attorney asked to approach the bench on Appellant's son's case. He informed the judge that Appellant called the judge a "stupid b___" as she walked past counsel table and out of the courtroom. . . . Two other witnesses . . . also heard Appellant's remark. After giving Appellant an opportunity to show cause why she should not be held in contempt and to present any mitigating circumstances, the trial court found her in direct criminal contempt. (*Woodie v. Campbell*, 960 So.2d 877 [Fla. Dist. Ct. 2007])

In this chapter, learn about criminal contempt.

Learning Objectives

1. Know the three categories of crimes of official misconduct and the reason why it is important to punish the corrupt conduct of public officials.

2. Understand the elements of the crime of bribing a public official.

3. Appreciate the requirements for proving extortion and the differences between bribery and extortion.

4. Understand the elements of perjury and some of the rules of evidence involved in proving perjury.

5. Know acts constituting obstruction of justice.

6. Understand the circumstances in which an individual is entitled to resist an arrest.

7. Appreciate the elements of compounding a crime, and why this is a criminal offense.

8. Understand the intent and act requirements of the crime of escape.

9. Know the difference between civil and criminal contempt, between direct and indirect criminal contempt, and between judicial and legislative contempt. Understand the intent and act requirements for criminal contempt.

INTRODUCTION

Common law judges developed several crimes to ensure that the political and legal system were free of corruption and fraud. These offenses subsequently were incorporated into federal and state statutes in the United States. In this chapter, we look at these offenses against public administration and the administration of justice. Each of these offenses, whether committed by a private citizen or by a government official, is intended to ensure that the rule of law is followed:

Bribery

Extortion

Perjury

Subornation of perjury

Obstruction of justice

Resisting arrest

Compounding a crime

Escape

Contempt

OFFICIAL MISCONDUCT

Public officials are charged with upholding the law and with setting an example to be followed by society. The common law punished **official misconduct** in office by imprisonment or a fine and in some cases by removal from office and disqualification to hold office in the future. Official misconduct in office is defined as corrupt behavior by a government officer in the exercise of the duties of his or her official responsibilities. There are three broad categories of official misconduct:

1. *Malfeasance.* A wrongful act such as a police officer's abuse of a defendant to extract a confession, or a police officer's destruction of evidence.

2. *Misfeasance.* A lawful act undertaken in an unlawful manner. An example is a public official awarding a contract to a company in return for a bribe or a kickback.

3. *Nonfeasance.* The failure to fulfill a duty to act. For example, a mine inspector fails to report a company's violation of worker health and safety laws, or a health inspector fails to report unsanitary conditions in a restaurant.

These three types of acts are punished under various state and federal statutes. An individual charged with official misconduct must act "under the color of office" and with a "corrupt intent."

- *Color of Office.* The defendant must be acting in execution of the responsibilities of his or her official position. A prison official who physically abuses an inmate is acting in a criminal fashion as part of his or her responsibilities. A prison officer who gets in a bar fight after work is not acting "under color of law."
- *Corrupt Intent.* The defendant must act with the purposeful intent to deliberately violate his or her legal obligation.

Bribery, which is discussed in the next section, is one of the most damaging crimes against public administration and the administration of justice.

BRIBERY

In 2007, the *Corporate Crime Reporter* released a report on public corruption in the United States. The report found that an average of one thousand state public officials a year had been convicted for corruption over the twenty years included in the report. At the time of the report, three Connecticut mayors and the state treasurer had been sentenced to prison, and the governor's former deputy chief of staff had pled guilty to accepting gold coins in return for government contracts. Governor John Rowland admitted that firms with state contracts had provided him with a hot tub and cathedral ceilings in his home. As a result of this type of rampant corruption,

Connecticut, one of the cradles of American democracy, has been called one of the most corrupt states in the nation. Connecticut, however, is relatively "clean" compared to jurisdictions with the most criminal convictions per capita of state officials for corruption between 1976 and 2006: the District of Columbia, Louisiana, Mississippi, Kentucky, Alabama, Ohio, Illinois, Pennsylvania, Florida, New Jersey, and New York. In each of these jurisdictions, a number of public officials have been convicted of betraying the public trust by accepting or demanding money, campaign contributions, and other benefits in return for jobs, construction contracts, driver's licenses, and favorable judicial verdicts. The least corrupt states are Utah, Kansas, Minnesota, Iowa, and Oregon.

Federal officials are not immune from corruption. In 2010 alone, the Public Integrity Section of the U.S. Department of Justice reports that 422 federal officials were charged with crimes: 397 had been convicted, and 103 were awaiting trial. California congressman Randy "Duke" Cunningham, for example, was convicted of taking $2.4 million in bribes from defense contractors in return for assisting them to obtain contracts. Tom DeLay, Speaker of the House of Representatives, was forced to resign in 2006 after being indicted in Texas for money laundering; in 2010, he was convicted and sentenced to three years in prison and ten years' probation. DeLay's conviction was overturned on appeal. Members of DeLay's congressional staff also were implicated in the corrupt activities of lobbyist Jack A. Abramoff. In 2009, Louisiana congressman William Jefferson was convicted of bribery and sentenced to prison for taking over $400,000 from businesses in return for legislative favors.

The framers of the U.S. Constitution viewed public corruption as a significant problem. They were concerned that federal officials might be influenced by money or gifts to act in a way that did not serve the public interest. This would undermine respect for the government and breed public distrust. Article II, Section 4 provides that the president, vice president, and other federal officials may be removed from office for "Bribery" and for other "High Crimes and Misdemeanors." Other articles prohibit officeholders from accepting gifts or titles from foreign governments, bar members of Congress from taking a federal job after they voted to increase the compensation for the position, and prohibit the expenditure of federal funds without congressional authorization.[1]

The most widespread and frequently prosecuted state and federal official misconduct crime is the *bribery of a public official*. Why punish public bribery?

- *Public Interest.* Government officials are charged with acting in the interest of society rather than acting in the interest of individuals who offer a financial or other material benefit.
- *Public Confidence.* Corrupt behavior undermines confidence and trust in government.
- *Equality.* Corruption leads to dominance by the rich and powerful, and is contrary to the notion that every individual and interest group should have an equal voice in government. Government should be responsive to the majority of Americans rather than to the minority of millionaires.
- *Public Service.* Individuals should not use government employment to advance their own self-interest.

The common law crime of **bribery** originally was limited to offering money or an item of value to a judge in return for the judge's taking an official action such as acquitting a defendant of a criminal charge. Criminal liability was limited to the judge and gradually was extended to the individual offering the bribe. A second development was the expansion of bribery beyond judges to cover all public officials. The common law of bribery subsequently was transported to the United States.

Bribery today is committed by an individual who gives, offers, or promises a benefit to a public official as well as by a public official who demands, agrees to accept, or accepts a bribe. In other words, bribery involves two separate crimes—that is, it punishes giving as well as receiving a bribe, and requires an intent to influence or to be influenced in the carrying out of a public duty. Bribery does not require a mutual agreement between the individuals. If you offer money to a police officer with the intent that he or she not issue you a traffic ticket, you are guilty of the bribery of a public official, regardless of whether the officer agrees to accept the bribe.

The offense of offering a bribe to a public official requires that

- the accused wrongfully promised, offered, or gave money or an item of value to a public official;
- the public official occupied an official position or possessed official duties; and

- the money or item of value was promised, offered, or given with the intent to influence an official decision or action of the individual.

The offense of soliciting a bribe requires that

- the accused wrongfully asked, accepted, or received money or an item of value from a person or organization;
- the accused occupied an official position or exercised official duties; and
- the accused asked, accepted, or received money or an item of value with the intent to have his or her decision or action influenced with respect to this matter.

In *Page v. State*, Ernest Page, a member of the Orlando, Florida, city commission, was convicted for soliciting a bribe after Page blocked the proposal for a low-income housing project after the developer refused Page's demand that his firm be included as a partner in the development.[2]

The federal bribery statute punishes the offering of a bribe and separately punishes the taking of a bribe. Section 18 U.S.C. § 201(c)(1)(A) declares that it is a crime if an individual "directly or indirectly gives, offers, or promises anything of value to any public official, former public official, or person selected to be a public official, for or because of any official act performed or to be performed [or failure to act]." The bribery statute also punishes a public official who "directly or indirectly demands, seeks, receives, accepts, or agrees to receive or accept anything of value personally for or because of any official act performed or to be performed [or failure to act]."[3]

State bribery statutes generally follow the text of the federal statute. The Illinois statute provides that bribery involves the offer or promise of "property or personal advantage" to a "public officer" with the "intent to influence the performance of any act related to the employment or function of any public officer, . . . juror or witness." It also is a crime for a public official to "receive, keep or agree to accept" any "property or personal advantage . . . knowing that [it] was promised or tendered with the intent to cause him or her to influence . . . any act related to [his or her] employment or function" as a public officer.[4]

There are several points to keep in mind in the law of bribery[5]:

Public official. A public official is an individual who "occupies a position of public trust" with official federal or state responsibilities. An individual is not required to occupy a political office, but he or she may be performing a governmental function such as a juror, voter, adviser to a legislator, or president or member of a study commission.[6]

Benefit. Bribery involves a "benefit" or "thing of value." This is a subjective test; the question is whether the recipient views the inducement to be of "value." The Model Penal Code (MPC) states that a benefit means "gain or advantage, or anything regarded by the beneficiary as gain or advantage, including benefit to any other person."[7]

Official act. A bribe is required to be intended to influence an official act. An official act may involve an affirmative act such as a mayor awarding a business contract to a company to remove snow or a police officer's tearing up of a traffic ticket. An official act also may involve a failure to act, such as a mayor's decision not to open up the snow removal contract for competitive bidding by local businesses or a police officer's decision not to issue a ticket. In 2016, the U.S. Supreme Court overturned the conviction of Virginia governor Robert McDonnell and held that the normal services provided to a constituent, such as arranging for a meeting with a government official or making a phone call to gather information, do not constitute official policy action under the bribery statute.

Is it bribery to offer a benefit to a public official to perform an act that is "impossible" for the public official to perform? Is it bribery to pay a recently hired assistant prosecutor to drop the charges against a defendant under the mistaken belief that the assistant prosecutor has the authority to drop the charges? The MPC states that "it is no defense to a prosecution for bribery that a person whom the actor sought to influence was not qualified to act as desired 'whether because he had not yet assumed office, or lacked jurisdiction, or for any other reason.'"[8] The Florida bribery statute follows the MPC and provides that the prosecution is not required to prove that the public servant "was qualified to act in the desired way, or that he had assumed office, or . . . that he possessed jurisdiction over the matter, or that his official action was necessary to achieve the person's purposes."[9] The thinking behind this rule is that the essence of the crime of bribery is the intent to corrupt the government. In other words, in Florida, you can bribe a police officer with the intent that criminal charges are not brought by a prosecutor against you, although the police officer has no authority or power to affect a prosecutor's decision. There are a handful of states that take the opposite approach and recognize the impossibility defense to bribery.[10]

In *State v. Stanley*, Charles Stanley offered $500 to McCraw, a police officer, in return for McCraw's giving Stanley the arrest warrant for Raymond Patrick Weaver and Weaver's Breathalyzer report.[11] Stanley knew that without these documents, Weaver could not be successfully prosecuted. Half of the money was to be paid following the dismissal of the charges against Weaver. The warrant and Breathalyzer report already had been filed with the clerk of the court, and Weaver was in jail at the time that Stanley approached McCraw. Stanley claimed that the "custody and possession of the warrant and [B]reathalyzer report" were "beyond the control of Officer McCraw" and that he therefore could not be held liable for offering a bribe to "influence McCraw in the performance of an act or duty within the scope of his authority." The North Carolina Court of Appeals held that Stanley had attempted to influence McCraw's performance of his official responsibilities and was properly convicted of bribery. "The evidence in the case at hand tended to show that defendant attempted to induce McCraw to abandon his duty to aid in the prosecution of Weaver's case. . . . It is also the duty of a police officer to aid in the preservation of evidence against a defendant that he has arrested. The offer of money in return for the [B]reathalyzer report in this case was a clear attempt to deprive the court of essential evidence and, hence, was an offer to persuade McCraw to violate his duty to aid in preserving evidence." In other words, Stanley's intent to influence McCraw and the offer of a bribe were sufficient to convict Stanley despite the fact that McCraw had no access to the arrest warrant and Breathalyzer.

It also is not a requirement of the crime of bribery that the individual who is bribed is capable of accomplishing the desired result by himself or herself. A single member of the city council may not be able to control the votes of other members of the city council on whether to hire a firm to clean city buildings. It nonetheless still is bribery to pay money to influence the vote of a single member of the city council. The thinking is that individuals have the intent to skew the result of the city council voting in their favor, and the single member of the city council who is bribed may influence the votes of his or her colleagues.

Intent. The crime of bribery is complete the moment the bribe is offered with the required corrupt intent. You may be convicted of bribery although the public official did not accept the bribe, accepted the bribe and lacked intent to carry out the action, or possessed the required intent and failed to act. It also is no defense to bribery that the public official believed that the act was in the public interest and that he or she would have acted in the desired fashion without the bribe. Why? Bribery corrupts the government by promoting the self-interest of the individual offering the bribe rather than the public interest. A public official is guilty of bribery when he or she demands a bribe with the required intent, although you may have no intent to pay the bribe.

Bribery is a felony in the majority of states. Illinois punishes bribery as a felony punishable by two to three years with a maximum fine of $25,000, and Washington punishes public bribery with ten years in prison and a fine of $20,000.[12] Several states declare that it is a crime to fail to inform authorities about the offer of a bribe.

You may be asking yourself whether it is bribery to offer a campaign contribution to a law-maker in return for his or her support or opposition to gun control. The general answer is that this is not bribery because a campaign contribution is legal and is paid to advance the public interest rather than the individual's interest. Is this a satisfactory response?

Keep in mind that bribery is a separate crime from receiving an unlawful **gratuity,** which also is punished under the federal bribery statute. Bribery is payment with the intent to influence the public official to take a specific action. A gratuity is an unlawful payment made to reward a public official for action taken or that will be taken in the future. The gratuity is required to be a reward for a specific official act or acts, and money paid to create goodwill is not an unlawful gratuity. In *United States v. Sun Diamond Growers*, the Supreme Court overturned a conviction of a lobbying group for gifts to Secretary of Agriculture Michael Espy on the grounds that there was no showing that tickets to a tennis tournament and other benefits were connected to any of Espy's specific decisions.[13]

In 2013, nine sitting and former Philadelphia traffic court judges were accused of dismissing or reducing the severity of traffic charges in exchange for campaign contributions, car repairs, and gourmet food. Several of the judges have been sentenced to prison, and the corruption was so pervasive that the only solution was to abolish the traffic court..

Before we leave bribery, you should be aware of two types of nonpublic bribery that are punished under the federal criminal law—commercial bribery and sports bribery.

CRIMINAL LAW IN THE NEWS

In January 2016, Oklahoma police officer Daniel Holtzclaw was convicted on eighteen of thirty-six counts, including four counts of first-degree rape and four counts of forced oral sodomy, and was sentenced to 263 years in prison.

Thirteen witnesses ranging in age from seventeen to fifty-seven testified against Holtzclaw and described a pattern over the course of seven months in which he stopped African American women in one of Oklahoma City's poorest neighborhoods and upon discovering that they possessed criminal histories subjected them to sexual assaults ranging from groping to oral sodomy and rape. Holtzclaw apparently singled out these women because he believed they would conclude that no one would believe their claim of sexual abuse and for that reason they would be reluctant to file a complaint against him.

One victim asked, "Who are they going to believe?" . . . "It's my word against his . . . , he's a police officer. So I just left it alone and just prayed that I never saw this man again, run into him again, you know." Another woman stated, "I didn't think nobody was going to believe me anyway. And I'm a drug addict, so the only way I knew to handle it was to go and get high to try to block it out, to make it seem like it didn't happen."

A twenty-four-year-old woman testified that she was intoxicated when arrested by Holtzclaw and was handcuffed to a hospital bed to detox when he violated her. He allegedly continued to pursue her following her arrest and stalked her on social media.

A fifty-seven-year-old grandmother of twelve who neither was poor nor had a criminal record recounted that Holtzclaw pulled her over on a false charge of "swerving." He directed her to pull her pants down to her knees and shined a light on her privates. He

then ordered her into his squad car and forced her to perform oral sex. It was this victim's complaint to the police that led to the discovery of Holtzclaw's pattern of sexual abuse of women.

Holtzclaw, the son of a white police officer and a Japanese mother, was convicted by an all-white jury whose recommendation for a 263-year sentence was followed by the judge. A number of Holtzclaw's victims have filed a civil suit.

Holtzclaw was a former football player at Eastern Michigan University who first began sexually harassing individuals whom he stopped in December 2013. He was fired from the Oklahoma City police in January 2015 following an internal investigation. Oklahoma City police chief Bill Citty wrote in Holtzclaw's termination letter that his "offenses committed against women in our community constitute the greatest abuse of police authority I have witnessed in my 37 years as a member of this agency."

Sexual offenses are the third highest cause of termination of police officers behind unnecessary violence and financial crimes. The Associated Press obtained records from forty-one states and found that between 2009 and 2014 1,000 police officers were disciplined by decertification for sexually related activity. Decertification is an administrative process in which an officer's law enforcement license is revoked. Roughly 550 officers were decertified for sexual assault, including rape and sodomy, sexual shakedowns in which citizens were extorted into performing sexual favors to avoid arrest, or gratuitous pat-downs, and roughly 440 officers lost their badges for other sexual offenses, such as possessing child pornography and indecent exposure, sexting, or being a "peeping Tom." Was Holtzclaw a "bad apple," or was his behavior part of a larger pattern of behavior by the police?

COMMERCIAL BRIBERY

MPC Section 224.8 set forth the crime of **commercial bribery**, which has been incorporated into the criminal codes of a number of states. The theory behind commercial bribery is that an employee who accepts "money or anything of value" from a person other than his or her employer and uses his or her position to benefit the outside individual has betrayed the trust of his or her employer. California Penal Code Section 641.3(d)(3) requires that an employee solicit, accept, or agree to accept a benefit from an individual other than his or her employer and, in return, agree to work for the benefit of the outside individual. The benefit must have a value of more than $100, and the transaction must occur without the knowledge or consent of the employer. The jail term ranges from one year to as long as three years, depending on the amount of the bribe.

New Jersey law has a provision modeled on the MPC that punishes an "expert" who presents him- or herself as engaged in disinterested analysis who solicits, accepts, or agrees to accept "any benefit" to influence his or her decision.[14] This would punish disc jockeys in the 1950s "payola scandal" who accepted bribes to play the records produced by various record companies rather than play the most popular or deserving songs. Commercial bribery may be punished under the federal Travel Act when individuals travel in interstate commerce or use the mail or electronic communication to engage in commercial bribery.[15]

SPORTS BRIBERY

Several states have laws that specifically criminalize the offering of a bribe to influence a sporting event and additional laws punishing participants and referees who accept such bribes.

The New York **sports bribery** law reads as follows[16]:

A person is guilty of sports bribing when he:

1. Confers, or offers or agrees to confer, any benefit upon a sports participant with intent to influence him not to give his best efforts in a sports contest; or

2. Confers, or offers or agrees to confer, any benefit upon a sports official with intent to influence him to perform his duties improperly.

A person is guilty of sports bribe receiving when:

1. Being a sports participant, he solicits, accepts or agrees to accept any benefit from another person upon an agreement or understanding that he will thereby be influenced not to give his best efforts in a sports contest; or

2. Being a sports official, he solicits, accepts or agrees to accept any benefit from another person upon an agreement or understanding that he will perform his duties improperly.

Sports bribery also is punished under federal law in 18 U.S.C. § 224. This section reads as follows:

(a) Whoever carries into effect, attempts to carry into effect, or conspires with any other person to carry into effect any scheme in commerce to influence, in any way, by bribery any sporting contest, with knowledge that the purpose of such scheme is to influence by bribery that contest, shall be fined under this title, or imprisoned not more than 5 years, or both.

In 1995, two Arizona State basketball players along with various organized crime figures were arrested and convicted of involvement in a conspiracy to influence the outcome of games. In August 2012, three individuals pled guilty in federal court to paying bribes to a leading scorer on the University of San Diego basketball team to manipulate the score of the game. The individuals, after paying the bribe, would place bets on the outcome of the games or on the "point spread" between the two competing teams.

FOREIGN CORRUPT PRACTICES ACT

The **Foreign Corrupt Practices Act** addresses the bribery of foreign officials. The law declares that it is illegal for an individual or U.S. company to bribe a foreign official in order to cause that official to assist in obtaining or retaining business. The statute makes an exception for "facilitating payments" to speed or ensure the performance of a "routine governmental action," such as paying money to a foreign official to guarantee that an entry visa is quickly issued to a corporate employee. Between 1998 and 2010, 101 individuals and sixty-eight corporations were convicted of violating the Foreign Corrupt Practices Act. U.S. corporate officials, with some justification, claim that they are at a disadvantage in competing abroad against foreign corporations whose countries do not prohibit bribery of foreign officials.[17] Extortion as previously discussed may be directed at either a public official or a private citizen.

You Decide

13.1 Saad attempted to deliver $1,000 each to two police officers to obtain the return of $20,700 seized from him when he was arrested. A trial judge dismissed the bribery charges against Saad, reasoning that the police were legally obligated to return the money on the grounds that the "seizure had been unlawful" and that, as a result, Saad was entitled to return of the money. Was the trial court judge correct in dismissing the bribery charge? See *State v. Saad*, 429 So.2d 757 (Fla. App. 1983).

You can find the answer at study.sagepub.com/lippmaness2e

EXTORTION

The common law misdemeanor of extortion punished the unlawful collection of money by a government official. William Blackstone defined extortion as "an abuse of public justice, which consists in any officer's unlawful taking, by color of his office, from any man, any money or thing of value that is not due to him, or more than is due, or before it is due." The law of extortion was gradually expanded to punish the taking of property by a threat from a private individual as well as threat from public officials.

The federal extortion statute provides that "[w]hoever, being an officer, or employee of the United States or any department or agency thereof, or representing himself to be or assuming to act as such, under color or pretense of office or employment commits or attempts an act of extortion, shall be fined under this title or imprisoned not more than three years, or both; but if the amount so extorted or demanded does not exceed $1,000, he shall be fined under this title or imprisoned not more than one year, or both."[18] The federal blackmail statute focuses on a demand of money or other "valuable thing" in return for not reporting a violation of federal law. "Whoever, under a threat of informing, or as a consideration of not informing, against any violation of any law of the United States, demands or receives any money or other valuable thing" is punishable by imprisonment for more than one year and by a fine.[19] It also is unlawful to use the U.S. mail to demand a ransom.[20]

Extortion involving a public official may be contrasted with *bribery* involving a public official. Extortion involves a public official taking money, property, or anything of value from another through the threat of future violence or harm. In bribery, money or a valuable benefit is offered or provided to a public official in return for an official's action or inaction.

The next crime discussed, perjury, is intended to ensure that individuals' statements and testimony in the legal process or before other government institutions are honest and truthful.

PERJURY

The common law crime of **perjury** was developed to ensure that judicial proceedings are based on truthful testimony. Perjury punished a false oath in a judicial proceeding. False testimony was punished initially with death, and later with banishment or cutting out the tongue and with the forfeiture of property. By the eighteenth century, perjury was punished by imprisonment and with a fine and disqualification from testifying in future trials. The companion crime of "false swearing" was developed to punish false statements on documents; it subsequently was merged into the crime of perjury.[21]

The federal perjury statute, 18 U.S.C. § 1621, requires that the following elements must be established beyond a reasonable doubt in a perjury prosecution:

- *Oath.* The defendant testified under oath in a proceeding in which federal law requires that the testimony is under oath.
- *Administration of Oath.* The oath was administered by an individual legally qualified to administer the oath.

- *Proceedings*. The statement is made before courts, before grand juries, or in any other proceeding in which an oath is legally required, including congressional and agency proceedings.
- *False Statement*. The defendant made a false statement.
- *Material*. The statement was material to the case.
- *Intent*. The defendant acted with knowledge that the statement was untrue.

The perjury statute applies to statements under oath in legal proceedings and hearings before administrative agencies (e.g., immigration), as well as sworn statements on documents, such as a tax return. In 1989, the U.S. Congress passed a "false statement" law that applies to court proceedings and to grand juries that is intended to make it easier to establish perjury.[22] Section 1001 is the primary statute relied on to punish false statements to government agencies, including the FBI, whether given under oath or given without an oath:

Except as otherwise provided in this section, whoever in any matter within the jurisdiction of the executive, legislative, or judicial branch of the government of the United States, knowingly, and willfully

(1) falsifies, conceals, or covers up by any trick, scheme, or device a material fact;

(2) makes any materially false, fictitious, or fraudulent statement or representation;

(3) makes or uses any false writing or document knowing the same to contain any materially false, fictitious, or fraudulent statement or entry shall be fined under this title, imprisoned not more than 5 years or, if the offense involves international or domestic terrorism, . . . imprisoned not more than 8 years, or both. . . .

In this chapter, we primarily will be concerned with the perjury statute. State statutes punish perjury before state judicial and agency hearings and in sworn statements on documents. The California perjury law provides that a person is guilty of perjury who has taken an oath to testify truthfully before any "competent tribunal, officer, or person" and who "willfully states as true any material matter which he or she knows to be false."[23] New York divides perjury into degrees and treats perjury in a legal proceeding more seriously than perjury on a written instrument, such as a tax return.[24]

There are several additional points that are important in understanding the crime of perjury.

The prosecution must establish that the defendant took an oath to swear to tell the truth and intentionally or knowingly made a statement that is false. What of individuals who object to swearing an oath? The federal government and states allow individuals to make an "unsworn declaration" that a statement is true and accurate. The individual who makes an unsworn oath still may be prosecuted for perjury.

The next step for a prosecutor bringing a perjury charge is to establish beyond a reasonable doubt that the defendant's statement was false. A false response to a clear and understandable question constitutes perjury. What about an answer that avoids directly answering the question? The burden is on the lawyer to ask clear questions using understandable language and to follow up to clarify unclear or evasive answers.

In *Bronston v. United States*, Bronston was questioned under oath and asked "[d]o you have bank accounts in Swiss banks?" Bronston responded, "No sir." He then was asked "[h]ave you ever?" He responded under oath that his company "had an account there for about six months." Bronston later was indicted for perjury based on the fact that although he mentioned that the company had Swiss bank accounts, he failed to mention that in the past he also had Swiss bank accounts. The government claimed that Bronston's testimony, although "true," was intentionally "misleading" and "unresponsive" and was intended to give the impression that Bronston never had a personal Swiss bank account.[25]

The U.S. Supreme Court reversed Bronston's conviction and held that under the stress and strain of cross-examination, a witness may give answers that are not entirely clear and responsive. Congress did not intend to hold Bronston liable for perjury when the questioner could have asked him specifically whether he "ever had any personal Swiss bank accounts" and therefore clarify Bronston's response. A "no" answer to this follow-up question would have constituted perjury. The Supreme Court held that it is the responsibility of the questioner to "pin the witness down . . . it is the lawyer's responsibility to recognize the evasion and to bring the witness back to the mark, to flush out the whole truth with the tools of adversary examination." Do you agree with the Supreme Court's decision in *Bronston*?

Tammy Thomas, a former professional cyclist, was prosecuted for several counts of perjury during a grand jury investigation into the distribution of anabolic steroids and money laundering. Thomas answered "No" to the question, "Did you take anything that Patrick Arnold gave you?" Thomas contended her answer was literally true because she had bargained for and purchased steroids and the steroids were not "given" to her. The court held that both the prosecutor and Thomas reasonably understood that the term *gave* was being used as synonymous with *sell* and *buy*.[26]

What is the required intent for perjury? A false statement must be made with knowledge of its falsity. Some statutes also provide that the statement must be made with an intent to deceive. In practice, a defendant who knows that a statement is untrue likely made the statement with the intent to mislead.

A perjured statement is required to be "material" to the proceedings. The prosecution must demonstrate beyond a reasonable doubt that the statement was "capable of influencing the tribunal on the issue before it," or that the statement "has a natural tendency to influence, impede or dissuade [a grand jury] from pursuing its investigation." In other words, an immaterial statement is a statement that is not important to reaching a verdict. This is a broad standard, and courts rarely find that testimony is "immaterial."[27]

Several interesting aspects to proving perjury are discussed below.

Two-witness rule. The MPC adopts the common law **two-witness rule**, which also is followed by federal courts and most state courts in perjury prosecutions. The rule provides that a conviction for perjury is required to be based on the testimony of two witnesses or must be based on the testimony of one witness and supporting (corroborating) evidence such as a confession or a document. The reason for this rule is that courts want to avoid a "swearing contest" between a defendant who asserts that he or she was truthful and a witness who alleges that the defendant's statement was false.

Inconsistent statements. The federal false declaration statute and various state statutes provide that when a defendant has made **inconsistent statements** under oath within the period of the statute of limitations, the prosecution may establish falsity by offering both statements into evidence without specifying which of the two statements is false. The defendant may offer the defense that he or she genuinely believed at the time that each of the statements was true.[28]

Recantation. MPC Section 241.1(3), the federal false declaration statute, and various state statutes recognize the **recantation** defense as a bar to criminal prosecution. The defense applies when in the same "continuous" proceeding, an individual states that an earlier statement was false. The recantation must take place before the perjury "substantially affected the proceedings" and before it became manifest "that the falsification was or would be exposed." An individual is not entitled to the recantation defense who waits for the prosecution to raise the falsehood and then corrects the statement. The thinking behind the recantation defense is that it creates an incentive for defendants to correct false statements.[29]

The Legal Equation

Perjury = knowledge of false statement

+ made under oath

+ material to the proceedings.

You Decide **13.2** Charles Nickels, a Chicago police officer, was given a share of payoffs paid by illegal gambling interests and bar owners to Dawson, a former Chicago police officer, and to Cello, a suspended officer. In return, the gamblers were protected from arrest, and the taverns were able to disregard city regulations. Dawson and Cello made the payments in secrecy to Nickels and to sixteen other members of the police vice squad at a local hotel.

Nickels at trial denied that he received any money from any bar owner, tavern owner, or businessman who owned an establishment serving alcohol while on official duty as a Chicago police officer. He stated, "No sir, not for my duties." Nickels contended that his statements were "true." Did Nickels commit perjury? Apply the precedent in *Bronston v. United States* in deciding *Nickels*. See *United States v. Nickels*, 502 F.2d 1173 (7th Cir. 1974).

You can find the answer at study.sagepub.com/lippmaness2e

SUBORNATION OF PERJURY

The federal criminal code and state statutes punish **subornation of perjury**. Section 1622 provides that "[w]hoever procures another to commit any perjury is guilty of subornation of perjury, and shall be fined under this title or imprisoned not more than five years, or both." The prosecution must prove beyond a reasonable doubt that an individual intentionally induced another person to testify under oath knowing that the testimony constituted perjury. The crime is complete once an individual solicits another person to commit perjury.

Members of the "Q Street Gang" witnessed a fight between gang members Everett Allen and Pernell Gibson. After Allen was knocked to the ground, Julian Riley pulled out a gun and shot Gibson at point-blank range.

Linwood Davis was present at the gang shooting and was convicted for willfully procuring Sylvia Norris to commit perjury. Norris testified that Davis had told her to tell the grand jury he was with her when Gibson was shot although she knew it was not true. The prosecutor then asked Norris whether she knew that "when he was speaking to you, you understood that you were supposed to come to the grand jury and say something that wasn't true?" Norris stated that this was her understanding.

Allen told his girlfriend and the mother of his child, Rhonda Ford, who knew the identity of the killer, that she "should not tell the grand jury anything she knew about the shooting."

Allen was convicted of subornation of perjury. The court reasoned that "although Allen did not specifically instruct Ford to lie . . . he did order: 'Don't tell them nothing,' and Ford certainly understood that to mean she was not to tell the grand jury the truth concerning what Allen had told her about the shooter's identity." Ford followed Allen's orders and told authorities "nothing that incriminated Allen, and in doing so lied about what he had actually said." As a result, the appellate court reasoned that "the jury could reasonably infer that lying was the precise result intended by Allen." Several judges dissented from the decision and would have reversed Allen's conviction because Allen had instructed Ford to remain silent rather than instructing her not to tell the truth.[30]

Obstruction of justice, discussed in the next section, is another crime that is designed to prevent and to punish threats to the fair and objective administration of justice.

You Decide  **13.3** The lawyer testified that his client, Williams, mailed him an envelope from prison with the designation "legal mail." The envelope contained a letter to Williams's cousin, instructing him to testify that Williams had been involved in a marijuana deal on the day of the bank robbery with which he was charged and thus could not have participated in the robbery. The lawyer realized that Williams was involved in suborning perjury and turned the letter over to the government, withdrew as Williams's attorney, and agreed to testify against Williams at trial. Williams took the stand at trial and admitted that his purpose in writing the letter was to induce his cousin to "lie for him." Williams appealed his conviction and argued that the lawyer acted unethically in testifying against him and that the lawyer's testimony was responsible for his conviction. The Seventh Circuit Court of

(Continued)

(Continued)

Appeals upheld Williams's conviction. The court observed that Williams was involved in suborning perjury; that both Williams and his cousin would have committed perjury had they testified that Williams was involved in a drug deal at the time of robbery; and that the lawyer would have suborned perjury had he delivered the note to the cousin. Would you overturn Williams's conviction for suborning perjury based on the lawyer's alleged unethical behavior? See *United States v. Williams*, 698 F.3d 272 (7th Cir. 2012).

You can find the answer at study.sagepub.com/lippmaness2e

OBSTRUCTION OF JUSTICE

The common law supplemented bribery, extortion, and perjury with a fourth crime designed to protect the integrity of the justice system, **obstruction of justice**. MPC Section 242.1 includes a broad statute on obstruction of the administration of the law or other governmental function that provides that a person commits a misdemeanor "if he purposely obstructs, impairs or perverts the administration of law . . . by force, violence, physical interference or obstacle, breach of official duty, or any other unlawful act."

The central federal statute is 18 U.S.C. § 1503. The first two sections of the statute criminalize (1) individuals who by force or threat endeavor to influence a juror or judge or court officer and (2) injuring a juror, judge, or court officer. The third section is the "omnibus clause" and broadly punishes an individual who

corruptly or by threats or force, or by any threatening letter or communication, influences, obstructs, or impedes, or endeavors to influence, obstruct, or impede, the due administration of justice.

Other provisions prohibit bribing witnesses,[31] witness tampering,[32] the destruction of corporate financial records,[33] and corrupt persuasion, which involves interfering with an individual's testimony, the destruction of documents, and preventing communication with a federal official relating to the commission of a federal offense or parole.[34]

State statutes on obstruction of justice punish the same types of acts prohibited under federal statutes. The Illinois statute reads as follows[35]:

A person obstructs justice when, with intent to prevent the apprehension or obstruct the prosecution or defense of any person, he knowingly commits any of the following acts:

(a) Destroys, alters, conceals or disguises physical evidence, plants false evidence, furnishes false information; or

(b) Induces a witness having knowledge material to the subject at issue to leave the State or conceal himself; or

(c) Possessing knowledge material to the subject at issue, he leaves the State or conceals himself.

In an Illinois case, Jason Brake was pulled over for a driving offense, and the officer observed him stuff something into his mouth. Brake was transported to a hospital where his stomach was pumped and he expelled a bag of heroin. Brake, in addition to unlawful possession of narcotics, was convicted of obstruction of justice for concealing evidence. An appellate court explained that Brake's actions were intended to "destroy, alter, conceal or disguise physical evidence."[36]

As you might recall, in addition to statutes punishing obstruction of justice, most states have statutes punishing accessoryship after the fact, which declares it a crime to "prevent, hinder, or delay" the apprehension or prosecution of an individual who has committed a criminal offense.

Another related offense is **tampering with evidence**. An individual who knowingly and intentionally removes, alters, conceals, destroys, or otherwise tampers with evidence to be offered in a present or future official proceeding is guilty of tampering with evidence. In *People v. Danielak*, Danielak and the victim purchased heroin from Danielak's dealer. In the morning, Danielak discovered that the victim had died and rather than calling the authorities rang her boyfriend who told her that he would get rid of the body. Danielak's boyfriend abandoned the corpse by the side of the road. A Michigan appellate court concluded that the removal of the body with an intent to prevent the body from being used as evidence in a criminal trial constituted tampering with evidence.[37] An individual also may tamper with evidence by fabricating documents. In *People v. Kissner*, Kissner filed and swore a false affidavit that he was the former boyfriend of the daughter of the judge who presided over his criminal conviction and that he possibly fathered a child with the judge's daughter. As a result, Kissner argued that the judge should have disqualified himself from trial. Kissner was convicted of tampering with evidence for filing false information in an official proceeding. He also was convicted of attempted obstruction of justice for making an effort to thwart or to impede the administration of justice.[38]

State criminal statutes, in addition to prohibiting obstruction of justice, also impose a duty of citizens to assist law enforcement officers.

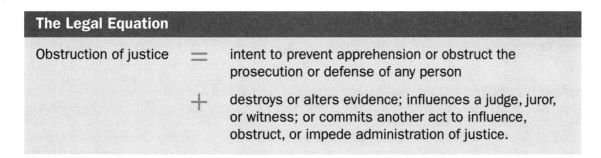

The Legal Equation

Obstruction of justice	$=$	intent to prevent apprehension or obstruct the prosecution or defense of any person
	$+$	destroys or alters evidence; influences a judge, juror, or witness; or commits another act to influence, obstruct, or impede administration of justice.

THE CITIZEN'S DUTY TO ASSIST LAW ENFORCEMENT

The common law custom of "hue and cry" requires all men to assist in the apprehension of offenders. In the thirteenth century, the English Parliament passed a law formally recognizing the practice of citizen assistance to law enforcement. Various municipal ordinances and state statutes impose a duty on citizens to assist law enforcement. An Ohio statute provides[39]:

> No person shall negligently fail or refuse to aid a law enforcement officer, when called upon for assistance in preventing or halting the commission of an offense, or in apprehending or detaining an offender, when such aid can be given without a substantial risk of physical harm to the person giving it.

In *State v. Floyd*, the Connecticut Supreme Court interpreted the requirements of a statute making it a misdemeanor for "any person to refuse to assist a peace officer or fireman authorized to command assistance in the execution of his duties." The court held that a peace officer could require civilian assistance only when "both demonstrable and necessary under all the circumstances."[40]

Statutes also punish the interference with the legal system by individuals who resist arrest.

RESISTING ARREST

The common law as discussed in Chapter 6 recognized the right of an individual to resist an unlawful arrest. This rule has been abandoned and today is recognized in only twelve states. Washington state law provides[41]:

> A person is guilty of resisting arrest if he or she intentionally prevents or attempts to prevent a peace officer from lawfully arresting him or her. . . . Resisting arrest is a misdemeanor.

An arrest requires that the officer physically seize an individual or that the officer reasonably communicate that the individual is under arrest. In an Ohio appellate court case, the suspect turned away from an officer and was convicted of resisting arrest. The court reversed the defendant's conviction on the grounds that the officer testified that he had not yet placed the suspect under arrest and as a result the suspect could not have reasonably understood that he was under arrest. The court held that the suspect "could not have resisted arrest if he did not know he was under arrest."[42]

The suspect must "hinder, impede, interrupt, or prevent an arrest." Some states provide that the intent requirement is satisfied by either intentional or reckless resistance.

Resisting arrest does not require the application of physical force. Knowing or intentionally fleeing from a law enforcement officer after the officer has by "visible or audible means . . . identified himself or herself and ordered the person to stop" has been held to constitute resisting arrest.[43] A suspect's pulling away from an arresting officer who grabbed the suspect's sleeve and the suspect's attempting to walk away from the officer was held to constitute recklessly or intentionally resisting arrest by an Ohio court. The appellate court also noted that "going limp" when an officer executes an arrest constitutes resisting arrest.[44] A defendant who grabbed the steering wheel to avoid being removed from his car was criminally liable for resisting arrest because he exerted the "strength and power of his bodily muscles" to counter the officer's efforts.[45]

An Arizona court held that kicking and biting a police officer implementing an arrest constitutes resisting arrest under a law that prohibits "intentionally preventing or attempting to prevent" an individual who he or she "has reason to know is a police officer" from executing an arrest by "using or threatening to use force or otherwise creating a substantial risk of injury."[46]

In *Williams v. State*, a Maryland court held that an offender who fled from the police and resisted the efforts of a citizen who was attempting to subdue him was guilty of resisting arrest. "All that must be shown is that a legal arrest was resisted by force. The necessary force may be employed against someone other than the police officer who is attempting to effectuate the arrest."[47]

As you may recall from the discussion of justification defenses, a police officer has the right to use reasonable force to subdue a suspect. A citizen possesses the right to employ reasonable force to resist the actions of an officer who employs excessive force in making an arrest. In *Shoultz v. State*, an Indiana appellate court determined that an officer used excessive force by spraying pepper spray in the suspect's eyes and hitting the suspect in the head and in the leg with a metal flashlight. The court found that Shoultz did not threaten the officer, did not make threatening gestures or touch the officer, and was not informed that he was under arrest for a misdemeanor, and that Evansville police procedures advise officers to avoid blows to the head unless absolutely necessary.[48]

In *State v. Ramsdell*, a Rhode Island court explained that citizens are afforded the right of self-defense against excessive force by the police because they otherwise have no way of protecting themselves against injury and would be limited to bringing a legal action after having suffered the injury.[49] In March 2012, the Indiana legislature passed a law recognizing that citizens possess the right of self-defense against police officers unlawfully entering their homes.

State statutes also declare that it is a crime to accept a payment or other benefit in return for agreeing not to cooperate in prosecuting a defendant for a crime.

The Legal Equation		
Resist arrest	=	intentionally
	+	prevents or attempts to prevent
	+	arrest.

COMPOUNDING A CRIME

Larceny at common law was a crime committed with alarming frequency and was difficult to solve. Thieves who were apprehended were subject to harsh punishment to deter the commission of acts of theft. The severity of the punishment made victims who were aware of the identity of the thief reluctant to pursue a criminal remedy. Victims instead sought to reach a private settlement with the thief. The acceptance of money or something of value in exchange for agreeing not to prosecute a felony was considered a "perversion of justice" and developed into the misdemeanor of **compounding a crime**. Liability is limited to the individual who agrees to accept or accepts payment in return for promising not to pursue the prosecution of the offense.

The Illinois compounding statute is a concise statement of the law of compounding a crime and reads as follows[50]:

(a) A person commits compounding a crime when he or she knowingly receives or offers to another any consideration for a promise not to prosecute or aid in the prosecution of an offender.

(b) Compounding a crime is a petty offense.

The offense of compounding a crime is based on several considerations:

- *Society.* A crime is an offense against society as well as the victim, and the victim should not impede the public interest in prosecuting criminal behavior.
- *Reporting Crime.* Individuals should be encouraged to report crimes to criminal justice officials who are authorized to make a judgment whether to pursue the prosecution.
- *Public Policy.* Economically advantaged offenders are not entitled to "buy" an exemption from criminal liability.

MPC Section 242.5 made significant changes to the common law crime of compounding a crime and has been adopted with various modifications by most states. The Colorado statute on compounding a crime generally follows the MPC. Compounding a crime in Colorado punishes an individual who accepts or agrees to accept money or a benefit of economic value in return for failing to pursue a prosecution or for failing to report the commission or suspected commission of any crime or for failing to provide information relating to a crime.[51]

A controversial part of the Colorado statute recognizes the defense that the benefit received by the defendant did not exceed the amount the defendant reasonably believed that he or she lost as a result of the crime. In other words, it is a defense to compounding a crime that the thief paid you the money to buy a new phone to replace the phone that was stolen. Is the Colorado provision consistent with the societal interest in prosecuting offenders?

The Colorado statute is summarized below:

(1) A person commits compounding who accepts or agrees to accept money, property, or any economic gain in return for:

(a) Failing to pursue prosecution of an offender; or

(b) Failing to report the commission or suspected commission of any crime or information relating to a crime.

(2) It is an affirmative defense that the benefit received by the defendant did not exceed an amount which the defendant reasonably believed to be due as restitution or indemnification for harm caused by the crime.

(3) Compounding is a class 3 misdemeanor punishable by up to six months in prison and a fine of between $50 and $750.

Defendants in Ohio are authorized to agree with a defendant to abandon a pending prosecution only in regard to theft and three fraud offenses. The Ohio law explicitly provides that such an agreement is not binding on a prosecutor.[52] The Georgia statute requires defendants who accept a benefit not to prosecute or aid in the prosecution of an individual to obtain approval of the court or of the prosecuting attorney.[53]

The New Mexico statute recognizes that the essence of the crime of compounding is "knowingly agreeing to take anything of value" in return for concealing a crime, withholding evidence, or failing to pursue a prosecution. In other words, the crime is complete when an agreement is reached to accept a payment in return for failing to cooperate with the criminal justice process. It is not a defense that the individual subsequently is prosecuted or that the prosecutor decided to drop the charges.[54]

The common law recognized the crime of **misprision of a felony**. An individual was liable who failed to report a felony or act of treason, despite the fact that the individual did not take an affirmative step to assist the offender. In practice, criminal prosecutions were directed against individuals who directly assisted an offender.

The federal criminal code continues to recognize the common law crime of misprision of a felony, although most states do not incorporate the offense into their criminal codes and instead rely on the crime of accessory after the fact. The elements of misprision of a felony in the U.S. Code are as follows[55]:

1. *Knowledge* a felony was committed;

2. *Failure to notify* the authorities of the crime;

3. Taking *affirmative steps* to conceal the crime, such as destruction of evidence.

The Legal Equation

Compounding a crime	=	knowingly
	+	receive or offer item of value
	+	in return for a promise not to prosecute or not to aid in prosecution.

ESCAPE

The common law recognized four different offenses involving flight from custody[56]:

1. *Escape.* A detainee's unlawful flight from confinement.

2. *Prison break.* A detainee's unlawful flight from confinement through the use of force.

3. *Rescue.* Assisting a detainee to unlawfully flee from confinement through the use of force.

4. *Negligent escape.* Negligently or recklessly allowing an individual to escape from confinement.

Modern statutes incorporate all of these offenses and punish **escape** more harshly when physical force is employed. MPC Section 242.6 provides that an individual is guilty of escape who fails to return to detention following a temporary leave. The code clarifies that "official detention" for purposes of escape means detention as a result of arrest or detention in a facility because of a criminal charge or criminal conviction or the fact that the individual detained is waiting for extradition to another jurisdiction or deportation to another country.

Federal law provides that an individual confined based on a felony charge or conviction who escapes "custody or confinement" shall be imprisoned not more than five years and fined or both.[57] It also is a federal crime to rescue, attempt to rescue, or aid and assist in an escape.[58] Federal law also prohibits an individual from fleeing across state lines to avoid arrest or confinement.[59]

State statutes punishing the crime of escape may impose differing lengths of punishment depending on whether the escapee was charged with or convicted of a misdemeanor or a felony, whether he or she employed force, or whether he or she was involved in a conspiratorial relationship with a correctional official or officer. Various states also impose criminal liability on correctional personnel who knowingly or recklessly permit an escape. The Pennsylvania statute on escape reads, in part, as follows[60]:

(a) Escape—A person commits an offense if he unlawfully removes himself from official detention or fails to return to official detention following temporary leave granted for a specific purpose or limited period.

(b) Permitting or facilitating escape—A public servant concerned in detention commits an offense if he knowingly or recklessly permits an escape. Any person who knowingly causes or facilitates an escape commits an offense . . .

(d) Grading—

(1) An offense under this section is a felony of the third degree [punishable by up to seven years] where:

(i) the actor was under arrest for or detained on a charge of felony or following conviction of crime;

(ii) the actor employs force, threat, deadly weapon or other dangerous instrumentality to effect the escape; or

(iii) a public servant concerned in detention of persons convicted of crime intentionally facilitates or permits an escape from a detention facility.

(2) Otherwise an offense under this section is a misdemeanor of the second degree [punishable by up to two years].

(e) Definition—As used in this section the phrase "official detention" means arrest, detention in any facility for custody of persons under charge or conviction of crime or alleged or found to be delinquent, detention for extradition or deportation, or any other detention for law enforcement purposes; but the phrase does not include supervision of probation or parole, or constraint incidental to release on bail.

Defenses to Prison Escape

As noted in Chapter 6, inmates threatened with physical assault have successfully invoked the defense of duress to excuse their escape. As you recall, in *People v. Unger*, Francis Unger was subjected to and threatened with sexual assault while he was incarcerated.[61] After he had escaped and was recaptured, the Illinois appellate court held that it was unrealistic to require that a prisoner wait to escape until the moment that he was being "immediately pursued by armed inmates." The court also determined that the correctional system was dominated by gangs that were too powerful to be controlled by prison officials. Under these circumstances, Unger was entitled to a jury instruction on duress because he may have reasonably believed that he had no alternative other than to escape, to be killed, or to suffer severe bodily harm.

Inmates relying on duress must establish that they did not use force or violence toward prison personnel or other innocent individuals in the escape and that they immediately contacted authorities once having reached a position of safety. *Unger* is only one of a number of cases that have recognized that inmates are entitled to rely on duress.[62] Do you believe that the judiciary acted correctly in recognizing Unger's claim of duress? Are you confident that he was "telling the truth"? What about his failure to "turn himself in" to correctional authorities?

In *United States v. Bailey*, the U.S. Supreme Court held that in order to be entitled to a jury instruction on duress or necessity as a defense to escape, the defendant must offer evidence justifying his or her "initial departure" as well as evidence "justifying his [or her] continued absence from custody."[63] An "indispensable element of such an offer is . . . a bona fide effort to surrender or return to custody as soon as the claimed duress or necessity had lost its coercive force." Escape is a "continuing offense," and an individual, although justified in escaping based on duress or necessity, may be held liable because he or she failed to turn him- or herself into authorities once the imminent and immediate threat was removed.

Court decisions recognizing the necessity or duress defense focus public attention on the inability of correctional officials to protect inmates from physical violence. There also is a developing trend for courts to recognize that an inmate may rely on a justification or excuse defense because of the need to seek medical care.[64]

Some courts recognize the defense that an individual who escaped was wrongfully incarcerated, although most courts do not recognize the defense of "self-help."

You Decide

13.4 After a conviction for bank robbery and commitment to prison, appellant was released to a "half-way house" in Seattle. He was restricted during furloughs to the limits of King County, Washington. Jones received a weekend pass, which required that he return by Sunday at midnight. He took a bus to Vancouver, Washington, 175 miles from Seattle, and committed a burglary on Saturday. He was arrested and detained, did not return to the halfway house, and was charged with escape. Was Jones guilty of the federal crime of escape under 18 U.S.C. § 751? See *United States v. Jones*, 569 F.2d 499 (9th Cir. 1978).

You can find the answer at study.sagepub.com/lippmaness2e

Read *People v. Lovercamp* and *State v. Horn* on the study site: study .sagepub.com/ lippmaness2e.

The Legal Equation

Escape = knowingly
\+ flee custody following arrest or detention.

CRIMINAL LAW AND PUBLIC POLICY

The common belief is that the U.S. Constitution provides protections that ensure that innocent individuals will be protected from wrongful criminal convictions. The criminal justice system is premised on the belief that it is better to let nine guilty persons go free than to convict one innocent individual. We have become increasingly aware that innocent individuals have been convicted and that these wrongful convictions pose a significant threat to the integrity of the criminal justice system. Exoneration is an official decision by a judge that an individual was wrongfully convicted or a decision by a governor or the president of the United States to pardon a defendant because he or she was wrongfully convicted.

The number of innocent individuals incarcerated is uncertain, although, according to the National Registry of Exonerations, between 1989 and 2012 there were a total of 872 non-DNA- and DNA-based exonerations. In 2015, there were a record number of exonerations, 26 of which were based on DNA and 123 of which were non-DNA exonerations. Fifty-eight of these exonerations involved individuals convicted of murder, two-thirds of whom were minorities; 47 were for narcotics offenses; and 12 involved individuals convicted of sexual offenses. Six of the exonerees were on death row when released from prison, and the exonerees served an average of fourteen and a half years in prison. Sixty-five of these individuals pled guilty, and the remainder were convicted at trial.

What accounts for these wrongful convictions?

Eyewitness Misidentification. Eyewitness misidentification is the leading cause of wrongful convictions and was a factor in 72 percent of the wrongful conviction cases. Individuals, in some instances, did not clearly observe the perpetrator and, in other instances, were influenced by "suggestions" from the police. Roughly 40 percent of these misidentifications were cross-racial identifications, which are particularly prone to misidentification.

False Confessions. False confessions account for roughly one-quarter of wrongful convictions. These confessions result from physical and emotional coercion and the youth or mental disability of the defendants.

Informants. Jailhouse informants contributed to wrongful convictions in roughly 18 percent of cases. Inmate-informants typically testified that they overheard the defendant disclosing details of a crime or admitting his or her guilt to the informant.

Inaccurate Forensic Science. Roughly 50 percent of wrongful convictions involve inaccurate forensic analysis of blood, fibers, or DNA. Other methods of analysis such as hair analysis, bite marks, firearm tool mark analysis, handwriting exemplars, and shoe print comparisons have not been fully perfected and often are inaccurate. In other instances, evidence is not accurately catalogued, misplaced or lost, or even fabricated. Forensic experts also may misrepresent the statistical significance of their analysis.

Defense attorneys, at times, lack the experience and expertise of prosecutors. They typically do not have the same resources as prosecutors and are not able to hire forensic experts or investigators.

Do you believe that there is a problem of wrongful convictions in the United States, or is the seriousness of the problem of wrongful convictions greatly exaggerated? Can we prevent wrongful convictions?

CONTEMPT

The English common law recognized the inherent authority of judges to hold an individual in contempt who interfered with the functioning of the court. An individual held in contempt of court is referred to as the **contemnor**. The U.S. Supreme Court has recognized that courts cannot function unless they have the authority to enforce orders and to punish individuals with contempt who disrupt the judicial proceedings.[65]

Courts exercise two types of contempt power, **civil contempt** and **criminal contempt**. Civil contempt is not part of criminal law, and we will focus most of our attention on criminal contempt. Keep in mind that the difference between civil and criminal contempt is not always crystal clear.

Civil contempt is disobedience to an order or direction of the judge by one of the litigants in a judicial proceeding. The contemnor may be jailed or fined or both by the judge until he or she obeys the order of the court. The purpose of the penalty is to coerce the individual to comply with the court order rather than to punish him or her. The judge, before ordering incarceration, is required to find that the individual is capable of complying with the order. An individual, for example, may not be incarcerated who lacks the money to pay the alimony or child support ordered by the court to be paid to his or her spouse.[66] In *Bernard v. Smith*, a Tennessee appellate court overturned Smith's contempt citation, noting that the trial court acknowledged in its final order that "[Smith] was not in a financial position to pay the entire amount of child support that he was ordered to pay. [T]he evidence was insufficient to prove that he had the ability to pay the amount ordered at that time and that his failure to pay was willful."[67]

One of the most well-known examples of the exercise of the contempt power involves Susan McDougal, who refused to answer questions put to her before a grand jury investigating allegations of corruption against President Bill Clinton resulting from his tenure as governor in Arkansas. In 1996, McDougal was incarcerated for eighteen months, and she spent eight months in solitary confinement at various federal correctional institutions.

Criminal contempt protects the efficient and effective functioning of the legal system and is directed against acts intended to impede or interfere with the justice process or that demonstrate a lack of respect for the court by denigrating, demeaning, or disregarding the judge. Congress and state legislative bodies also have the power to hold individuals in contempt of Congress and of the legislature.

The Judiciary Act of 1789, which established the federal judicial system, recognized that courts possessed the power of contempt. The modern federal contempt power is set forth in various statutes. The most important of these laws is 18 U.S.C. § 401, which grants the federal courts broad contempt powers:

A court of the United States shall have the power to punish by fine or imprisonment, at its discretion, such contempt of its authority, and none other, as

1. Misbehavior of any person in its presence or so near thereto as to obstruct the administration of justice;

2. Misbehavior of any of its officers in their official transactions;

3. Disobedience or resistance to its lawful writ, process, order, rule, decree, or command.

The U.S. Supreme Court noted that the federal contempt statute limits the contempt power of federal courts to ensuring "order and decorum in their presence"; to securing "faithfulness" on the part of court personnel, jurors, and prosecutions; and to the enforcement of "obedience to their lawful orders, judgments and processes."[68]

A defendant to be held liable for contempt must be shown, beyond a reasonable doubt, to have acted with an intentional or knowing criminal intent. In 1976, in *Commonwealth v. Washington*, the Pennsylvania Supreme Court overturned the contempt conviction of a defendant who overslept and failed to appear in court on time.[69] The court noted that "[u]nless the evidence establishes an intentional disobedience or an intentional neglect of the lawful process of the court, no contempt has been proven. Such is the case here." The Second Circuit Court of Appeals commented that to hold a defendant liable for contempt for "misbehavior" in the courtroom, "the contemnor's conduct must constitute misbehavior which rises to the level of an obstruction of and an imminent threat to the administration of justice, and it must be accompanied by the intention on the part of the contemnor to obstruct, disrupt, or interfere with the administration of justice."[70]

Va. Code Ann. § 18.2-456. Cases in which courts and judges may punish summarily for contempt

The courts and judges may issue attachments for contempt, and punish them summarily, only in the cases following:

(1) Misbehavior in the presence of the court, or so near thereto as to obstruct or interrupt the administration of justice;

(2) Violence, or threats of violence, to a judge or officer of the court, or to a juror, witness or party going to, attending or returning from the court, for or in respect of any act or proceeding had or to be had in such court;

(3) Vile, contemptuous or insulting language addressed to or published of a judge for or in respect of any act or proceeding had, or to be had, in such court, or like language used in his presence and intended for his hearing for or in respect of such act or proceeding;

(4) Misbehavior of an officer of the court in his official character;

(5) Disobedience or resistance of an officer of the court, juror, witness or other person to any lawful process, judgment, decree or order of the court.

Direct and Indirect Criminal Contempt

There are two forms of criminal contempt, direct criminal contempt and constructive criminal contempt.

Direct criminal contempt is committed in the immediate presence of the judge or court or sufficiently close to the court to impede or to interfere with the judicial process. Examples of direct criminal contempt are an insulting remark or physical assault on the judge, repeated disregard of a judge's direction to limit the length of an opening or closing statement or cross-examination of a witness, and disruptive behavior by a spectator. **Indirect criminal contempt** involves acts that occur outside the presence of the court that impede or interfere with the judicial process. An example is a lawyer who violates a "gag order" and holds a press conference with the media criticizing the judge. Jurors may be held in contempt for disregarding the judge's direction not to discuss the case among themselves or with their friends and family during the trial.

In *Davila v. State*, Davila uttered an expletive under his breath in the courtroom when learning that his trial was postponed.[71] The judge found Davila's actions "disrespectful to the court and that the comment obstructed or hindered the administration of justice." He was sentenced to six months in jail along with a fine. A Florida appellate court overturned Davila's conviction noting that Davila uttered a brief profanity that was not heard by the judge, his comment did not interrupt any proceeding, and it was "clear that the administration of justice was not hindered because the court moved on to the next case without hesitation." Criminal contempt "requires some willful act or omission calculated to hinder the orderly functions of the court." The provocation must never be "slight, doubtful, or of shifting interpretations. The occasion should be real and necessary." The U.S. Supreme Court, in *Eaton v. City of Tulsa*, noted that a "single usage of street vernacular, not directed at the judge or any officer of the court, cannot . . . support the conviction of criminal contempt. . . . [There must be] a likely threat to the administration of justice."[72]

The standards for contempt in a specific case nonetheless are not entirely clear. In *Greenberg v. United States*, a judge found lawyer Stanley Greenberg in contempt of court for continuing to object in a loud voice to the prosecutor's argument before the jury. Greenberg when ordered to be seated slammed his hand on the table in an angry manner, demanding a ruling from the court. Greenberg continued to object to the prosecutor's argument and subsequently was held in contempt for interrupting the court and disrupting the proceedings in an unethical manner. The Ninth Circuit Court of Appeals overturned Greenberg's conviction and explained that he "did not cause an obstruction of the judicial process sufficiently serious to justify a summary criminal contempt conviction. . . . Greenberg's loud voice and hand slamming during the heat of a long and hard fought trial, although annoying and not condoned by this court, do not constitute the type of 'exceptional circumstances' that pose an immediate threat to the judicial process, thereby justifying a summary criminal contempt conviction."[73]

There are different procedures for direct and indirect criminal contempt. Direct criminal contempt is committed in the presence of the court, and the contemnor may be immediately punished. The reasons that the judge may summarily punish the contemnor are that the acts occurred in the presence of the judge and the facts are clear. The judge is required to inform the individual of the allegations and provide him or her with the opportunity to demonstrate whether there is any reason why the court should not find that the individual's acts constitute contempt.

Indirect criminal contempt involves a formal legal process. The judge is required to prepare a written document setting forth the facts supporting the charge of criminal contempt and is to provide the individual with a reasonable time to prepare a defense. The contemnor is entitled to a jury trial if he or she is to be sentenced to more than six months in prison. The defendant in both indirect and direct contempt must be found guilty beyond a reasonable doubt.

Criminal Contempt and Criminal Law

There is disagreement whether contempt is a crime or an exercise of the judiciary's supervisory authority to ensure respect for the judicial process. Professors Perkins and Boyce state that there is little doubt that criminal contempt should be categorized as a crime. In *Bloom v. Illinois*, the U.S. Supreme Court stated that "[c]riminal contempt is a crime in the ordinary senses; it is a violation of the law, a public wrong which is punishable by fine or imprisonment or both."[74]

Various states have adopted contempt statutes categorizing different degrees of criminal contempt as either a misdemeanor or a felony. The New York contempt statutes categorize second-degree contempt as a misdemeanor punishable by up to one year in prison and describe first-degree and aggravated contempt as a felony.[75] Contempt in the second degree is a misdemeanor punishable by up to one year in prison and includes disorderly conduct committed in the immediate view and presence of the judge, loud and disruptive behavior directly interrupting the court's proceedings, and a refusal to be sworn in as a witness in a court proceeding. Contempt in the first degree is a felony punishable by between two and five years in prison and includes a knowing violation of an order of protection with the intent of placing or attempting to place a person for whose protection the order was issued in reasonable fear of physical injury or death, and harassing and menacing an individual for whom an order of protection was issued with the intention of placing the individual for whom the order was issued in reasonable fear of death or imminent serious physical injury. Aggravated contempt is a felony punishable by between two and seven years in prison and involves a second violation of an order of protection punishable under first-degree contempt.

Punishing Criminal Contempt

In *United States v. United Mine Workers of America*, the U.S. Supreme Court listed the factors that courts should consider in punishing criminal contempt: (1) the extent of the willful and deliberate defiance of the court's order, (2) the seriousness of the consequences of the contumacious behavior, (3) the necessity of effectively terminating the defendant's defiance as required by the public interest, and (4) the importance of deterring such acts in the future.[76]

In *State v. Geiger*, the Illinois Supreme Court noted that judges have the inherent power to punish with contempt conduct "calculated to impede, embarrass, or obstruct the court in its administration of justice or derogate from the court's authority or dignity, or to bring the administration of the law into disrepute."[77]

A judge, according to the Illinois court, does not possess unlimited discretion to punish contempt; a sentence for contempt may not be "grossly disproportionate." In *Geiger*, the Illinois Supreme Court found that the trial court's twenty-year sentence for contempt was "manifestly disproportionate to the nature of the offense and, therefore, unreasonably excessive." The Illinois court explained:

> Although defendant willfully and deliberately refused to testify, his refusal was based on his mistaken belief that he had a Fifth Amendment right to do so. . . . [D]efendant's refusal to testify might have been driven, in part, by the fact that, as a gang member, he feared retaliation. . . . [His] contemptuous conduct was nonviolent and he was not flagrantly disrespectful to the trial judge. . . . It should also be recognized that defendant's refusal to testify did not seriously hamper the State's ability to prosecute Hollins [his co-defendant].

Legislative Contempt

The power of the U.S. Congress and state legislatures to hold individuals in contempt is based on the authority of the English Crown to punish insults to the king or to his government with swift and certain retribution. The Parliament was considered part of the royal government and therefore was entitled to hold critics in contempt. The **legislative contempt** power includes the power to punish "disrespectful and disorderly" behavior as well as individuals who refuse a subpoena to testify or to submit documents. Individuals have a Fifth Amendment right against self-incrimination, and the legislature cannot require individuals to testify before a legislative committee if the answer would expose the individuals to legal liability.

Federal law authorizes Congress to hold individuals in contempt who intentionally refuse to testify or to produce documents. Contempt is a misdemeanor punishable by a fine of not more than $1,000 or less than $100 and imprisonment in jail for between one month and twelve months.[78] In 2012, the House of Representatives voted to hold U.S. Attorney General Eric Holder in contempt for failing to turn over documents to Congress; and in 2007, a Democratic-dominated Congress voted to hold White House officials liable for contempt based on a failure to cooperate in an investigation of the firing of several U.S. attorneys. State statutes provide that state legislatures and legislative committees possess the authority to hold individuals in contempt.

You Decide

13.5 Ali was charged with conspiracy to provide material support to al Shabaab, a Somali terrorist organization. Ali did not "rise" when the judge entered the courtroom. Ali, despite being advised to adhere to the rules of the court, disregarded the "all rise" command of the U.S. marshal in the courtroom. Ali explained that she was aware of the rules of court decorum and that she would continue to remain seated despite the imposition of sanctions because "rising" before the secular authority of the court violated her religious beliefs. Ali failed to stand on ten occasions during the first day of trial and subsequently was convicted of criminal contempt and was sentenced to five days to be served consecutively for each failure to stand. On the third day, Ali told the judge that she would respect the "all rise" call. The federal district court accepted that Ali's failure "to rise" reflected her sincerely held religious beliefs. The question was whether there is a compelling government interest in requiring Ali "to rise" and, if so, whether there is an alternative approach to maintaining order and security that does not infringe on Ali's religious beliefs. Should Ali be exempted from "rising" on the judge's entry into the courtroom? See *United States v. Ali*, Criminal No. 10-187(MJD) (D. Minn. 2012).

You can find the answer at study.sagepub.com/lippmaness2e

CASE ANALYSIS

In *Dobbs v. State*, the Texas Court of Appeals was asked to determine whether Dobbs resisted arrest.

Did Dobbs Resist Arrest?

Dobbs v. State, 434 S.W.3d 166 (Ct. Crim. App. Tex. 2014)

Atha Albert Dobbs, appellant, challenges the sufficiency of the evidence to sustain his conviction for resisting arrest with a deadly weapon. Tex. Penal Code § 38.03(a),(d).

In September 2010, appellant was living with his wife, Dawn, and her two daughters in Washington County when one of the daughters told Dawn that appellant had been sexually abusing her for several years. Dawn and her daughters moved out of the house the following day. Dawn contacted the police to report her daughter's allegations, and a warrant was issued for appellant's arrest.

Because Dawn had indicated to police that appellant might resist arrest or attempt to harm himself, five sheriff's deputies were dispatched to his house to carry out the warrant. Appellant saw the deputies approach the house through the kitchen window, and he retrieved a loaded pistol out of his gun cabinet. The deputies surrounded the house and could see inside through the windows. Two of the deputies went to the back of the house, two to the side, and one officer, Deputy Kokemoor, approached the front door. From his position, Kokemoor could see appellant walking toward the door with a gun in his hand. One officer shouted to the others that appellant was holding a gun. The officers drew their weapons, and Kokemoor ordered appellant to put down the gun. Appellant did not comply. Instead, he pointed the gun at his own temple. Although Kokemoor could not hear what appellant was saying, it appeared to him that appellant was repeatedly mouthing the words, "I'm going to kill myself."

Appellant then turned around and retreated deeper into the house. Kokemoor, believing that appellant was suicidal and not a threat to the officers, lowered his gun, pulled out his [T]aser, and entered the house. Upon realizing that Kokemoor had entered, appellant began to run into the living room, where the deputy shot him with the [T]aser. Appellant then fell to the floor, pinning one hand beneath himself while his other hand was still holding the gun. When appellant did not comply with Kokemoor's instruction to put his hands behind his back, the deputy tased appellant a second time and then kicked the gun out

of appellant's hand. Appellant was arrested and transported to jail.

Appellant was charged with continuous sexual abuse of a young child, aggravated sexual assault, and resisting arrest. The resisting-arrest offense was elevated from a misdemeanor to a third-degree felony because the State alleged that appellant had used a deadly weapon during commission of the offense. At trial, the jury was unable to reach a unanimous verdict on the continuous-sexual-abuse and aggravated-sexual-assault offenses.

However, the jury did find appellant guilty of resisting arrest with a deadly weapon, and it sentenced him to six years in prison and assessed an $8,000 fine.

The complete statutory elements of the offense of resisting arrest are that a person:

(1) "intentionally prevents or obstructs"

(2) "a person he knows is a peace officer or a person acting in a peace officer's presence and at his direction"

(3) "from effecting an arrest, search, or transportation of the actor or another"

(4) "by using force against the peace officer or another."

The offense is elevated from a Class A misdemeanor to a third-degree felony if "the actor uses a deadly weapon to resist the arrest or search." Applying these principles to the facts of this case, we conclude that the evidence is insufficient to sustain appellant's resisting-arrest conviction. Here, the record indicates that appellant at all times either held the gun at his side or pointed it at himself, and never at officers or anyone else. The record is devoid of any evidence to indicate that appellant threatened to use any kind of force against the officers, but instead shows that he threatened only to shoot himself. Kokemoor indicated in his testimony that he did not feel threatened by appellant at any point, and no evidence in the record suggests that appellant directed any threat to or against Kokemoor or any of the other officers.

(Continued)

(Continued)

It is true that appellant's conduct in displaying the gun in the presence of officers and refusing to put the gun down when ordered to do so could rationally be found to constitute a use of "force" within the meaning of the statute, but without an additional showing that the force was directed at or in opposition to the officers, he cannot reasonably be said to have used force "against" a peace officer. Furthermore, although appellant's refusal to put down the gun when ordered to do so had the likely effect of delaying his arrest, that refusal cannot reasonably be understood as constituting a use of force against the officer by virtue of its being opposed to the officer's goal of making an arrest. Likewise, appellant's efforts to manipulate the situation and intimidate officers for the purpose of delaying his arrest by threatening to shoot himself cannot reasonably be found to constitute a use of force against officers.

Because he did not use force "against" a peace officer within the meaning of the resisting-arrest statute, we hold that the evidence is insufficient to sustain appellant's conviction. We reverse the judgment of the court of appeals and render a judgment of acquittal.

Dissenting Opinion

The majority asserts that Appellant's actions were not "against" a peace officer because he never directed a threat toward the officers. I disagree with this conclusion, however, because I believe the threat was inherent in Appellant's actions and did not need to be expressly stated. When officers encounter a person threatening to kill himself, whether that person is an arrestee or not, they will work toward a resolution that leaves every individual involved safe and alive, including the officers. In an arrest situation, this would likely result in the arrest being delayed until officers could safely approach the arrestee.

This is particularly true where there is a dangerous or deadly weapon involved that needs to be secured for everyone's, including the officers', safety. Anytime someone is brandishing a weapon, there is a special danger. While a person may be threatening only himself, no one can read his thoughts or predict what he may do next. The dangerous weapon could be used against the individual or turned against other people at any moment. And if the individual did use the weapon only upon himself, there is still a danger of it causing great harm to the people around him. If, for example, a bullet passed all the way through someone's body and continued traveling, there could be grave repercussions for a bystander. The officers' goal would be to maintain everyone's safety, including both the defendant's and their own, and this goal is threatened once a weapon is used against any individual involved in the situation. Therefore, as demonstrated by this case, someone pointing a gun at his own head while officers are attempting to make an arrest is a use of force against those officers that obstructs them from effecting the arrest. Consequently, I believe that the evidence of the force used by Appellant was sufficient to convict him of resisting arrest with a deadly weapon.

Contrary to the majority's conclusion, Appellant used force "in opposition to" the officer. And because Appellant inherently threatened him, using a firearm to delay his arrest and gain control of the situation, a jury could reasonably conclude that he used force against the officer.

CHAPTER SUMMARY

This chapter covered offenses against public administration and the administration of justice that are designed to ensure that the legal system functions in a fair fashion.

Official misconduct in office is defined as corrupt behavior by a government officer in the exercise of the duties of his or her office in the exercise of his or her official responsibilities. This may entail malfeasance, misfeasance, or nonfeasance.

Bribery is the most frequently prosecuted federal and state crime involving official misconduct. Bribery involves two separate crimes and punishes giving as well as receiving a bribe and requires an intent to influence or to be influenced in carrying out a public duty. The crimes of commercial bribery and sports bribery also have been incorporated into the criminal codes of various states. The Foreign Corrupt Practices Act extends the concern with good government abroad and declares that it is illegal for an individual or a U.S. company to bribe a foreign official in order to cause that official to assist in obtaining or retaining business.

Extortion is the "taking of property by a present threat of future violence or present threat to circulate secret, embarrassing, or harmful information; threat of criminal charges; threat to take or withhold official government action; or threat to inflict economic harm and other harms listed in the state statute, with a specific intent to deprive a lawful possessor of money or property." The threat to disclose secret or embarrassing information is commonly referred to as the crime of blackmail.

An individual is guilty of perjury who has taken an oath to testify truthfully before any "competent tribunal, officer, or person" and who "willfully states as true any material matter that he or she knows to be false." The federal criminal code and state statutes punish subornation of perjury, which is procuring another to commit perjury.

An individual is guilty of obstruction of justice if he or she purposely obstructs, impairs, or perverts the administration of law by force, violence, physical interference or obstacle, breach of official duty, or any other unlawful act. Some state statutes list acts constituting obstruction of justice. A related crime is resisting arrest. A person is guilty of resisting arrest if he or she intentionally prevents or attempts to prevent a peace officer from lawfully arresting him or her.

A person commits compounding a crime when he or she knowingly receives or offers to another any consideration for a promise not to prosecute or to aid in the prosecution of an offender. Courts exercise two types of contempt: civil contempt and criminal contempt. The next chapter discusses crimes against the state.

CHAPTER REVIEW QUESTIONS

1. Define official misconduct. What types of acts constitute official misconduct?

2. What are the elements of the crime of bribery of a public official and of the crime of a public official's soliciting of a bribe?

3. Discuss commercial bribery and sports bribery.

4. What is the purpose of the Foreign Corrupt Practices Act?

5. How does bribery differ from extortion?

6. List the elements of the crime of perjury and of the crime of subornation of perjury.

7. What types of acts are involved in the crime of obstruction of justice?

8. What is required of citizens under statutes that impose a duty to assist law enforcement?

9. Discuss the types of acts that constitute the crime of resisting arrest.

10. Define the elements of the criminal offense of compounding a crime.

11. Discuss the crime of escape. What must an inmate charged with escape demonstrate in order to rely on the duress defense?

12. Distinguish criminal from civil contempt.

13. What is the difference between direct and indirect criminal contempt?

14. Discuss the factors a court considers in sentencing an individual for criminal contempt.

15. When may an individual be charged with legislative contempt?

LEGAL TERMINOLOGY

bribery

civil contempt

commercial bribery

compounding a crime

contemnor

criminal contempt

direct criminal contempt

escape

Foreign Corrupt Practices Act

gratuity

inconsistent statements

indirect criminal contempt

legislative contempt

misprision of a felony

obstruction of justice

official misconduct

perjury

recantation

resisting arrest

sports bribery

subornation of perjury

tampering with evidence

two-witness rule

CRIMINAL LAW ON THE WEB

Visit **study.sagepub.com/lippmaness2e** to access additional study tools including suggested answers to the You Decide questions, reprints of cases and statutes, online appendices, and more!

14 CRIMES AGAINST THE STATE

Was John Walker Lindh guilty of conspiracy to murder American soldiers, or did he engage in a lawful act of war?

While at the Dar ul-Anan Headquarters, Lindh agreed to receive additional and extensive military training at an al Qaeda training camp. He made this decision "knowing that America and its citizens were the enemies of Bin Laden and al-Qaeda and that a principal purpose of al-Qaeda was to fight and kill Americans." In late May or June 2001, Lindh traveled to a bin Laden guest house in Kandahar, Afghanistan, where he stayed for several days, and then traveled to the al Farooq training camp, "an al Qaeda facility located several hours west of Kandahar." He reported to the camp with approximately twenty other trainees, mostly Saudis, and remained there throughout June and July. During this period, he participated fully in the camp's training activities, despite being told early in his stay that "Bin Laden had sent forth some fifty people to carry out twenty suicide terrorist operations against the United States and Israel." As part of his al Qaeda training, Lindh participated in "terrorist training courses in, among other things, weapons, orientating, navigation, explosives and battlefield combat." This training included the use of "shoulder weapons, pistols, and rocket-propelled grenades, and the construction of Molotov cocktails." During his stay at al Farooq, Lindh met personally with bin Laden, "who thanked him and other trainees for taking part in jihad." He also met with a senior al Qaeda official, Abu Mohammad Al-Masri, who inquired whether Lindh was interested in traveling outside Afghanistan to conduct operations against the United States and Israel. Lindh declined Al-Masri's offer in favor of going to the front lines to fight. It is specifically alleged that Lindh swore allegiance to jihad in June or July 2001. (*United States v. Lindh*, 212 F.Supp.2d 541 [E.D. Va. 2002])

In this chapter, learn about U.S. counterterrorism laws.

Learning Objectives

1. Understand the law of treason and evidentiary requirements to prove treason.

2. Know the act and intent requirements for sedition and for seditious conspiracy.

3. Understand the intent and act standards required to prove sabotage.

4. Know the elements of the crime of espionage.

5. Understand the difference between domestic and international terrorism, and terrorism transcending international borders.

6. Know the types of acts that are punished criminally under federal terrorism statutes.

7. Understand combat immunity and its importance for the war on terror.

8. Know the purpose of immigration law and the types of violations of immigration law that are punished criminally.

9. Understand the development and functioning of international criminal law.

INTRODUCTION

The American colonists adopted a constitutional system intended to guard against the excesses of governmental power. However, the colonists also appreciated the need to prevent and to punish domestic threats to the government.

A significant percentage of the Europeans who settled in the American colonies were fleeing religious or political persecution and understandably developed a suspicion of government. This distrust was enhanced by the colonists' unhappy experiences with the often-repressive policies of the British authorities. There was almost uniform agreement to build the new American democracy on a foundation of strong limits on official authority along with a commitment to individual freedom. The colonists were also reluctant to adopt the type of harsh legislation that had been used by English monarchs to stifle dissent and criticism. Nevertheless, there was the reality that the United States confronted a threat from European countries eager to acquire additional territory in North America. A number of Americans and most Canadians also continued to harbor deep loyalties to England. This dictated that the United States put various laws in place to protect the government and people from attack. In this chapter, we examine these **crimes against the state**:

- *Treason.* Involvement in an attack on the United States.
- *Sedition.* A written or verbal communication intended to create disaffection, hatred, or contempt toward the U.S. government.
- *Sabotage.* Destruction of national defense materials.
- *Espionage.* Conveying information to a foreign government with the intent of injuring the United States.

Recent events have also led to the development of various counterterrorism laws, including the punishment of materially assisting terrorism. In reading about these counterterrorism offenses, you will see that these statutes are modern and updated versions of laws against treason, sedition, sabotage, and espionage.

In the last portion of the chapter, we examine immigration and immigration crimes that challenge the ability of the United States to control its borders and to determine who lives and works in the country.

TREASON

English royalty prosecuted and convicted critics of the monarchy for **treason**. Monarchs intentionally avoided writing down the requirements of treason in a statute in order to permit the crime to be applied against all varieties of critics. Parliament was finally able to mobilize enough power in 1352 to limit the power of the king and to force Edward III to agree to a Declaration Which Offenses Shall Be Adjudged Treason.

British officials in the American colonies applied the law on treason against rebellious servants and government critics, who typically were punished by "drawing and hanging." The drafters of the U.S. Constitution harbored bitter memories of the abusive use of the law on treason against critics of the colonial regime. At the same time, the drafters of the U.S. Constitution were conscious of the need to protect the newly independent American states against the threat posed by individuals whose loyalty remained with England and against European states that desired to expand their territorial presence in North America.

How could these various concerns be balanced against one another? The decision was made for the Constitution to clearly set forth the definition of treason, the proof necessary to establish the offense, and the appropriate punishment. James Madison explained in the *Federalist Papers* No. 43 that as "new-fangled and artificial treasons have been the great engines by which violent factions . . . have usually wreaked their . . . malignity on each other, the convention have, with great judgment, opposed a barrier to this peculiar danger, by inserting a constitutional definition of the crime." Article III, Section 3 of the U.S. Constitution provides that treason against the United States "shall consist only in levying War against them, or in adhering to their Enemies giving them Aid and Comfort. No Person shall be convicted of Treason unless on the Testimony of two Witnesses to the same overt Act or on Confession in open Court." Congress is also constitutionally prohibited from adopting the policy practiced in England of extending penalties beyond the individual offender to members of his or her family.

In summary, the United States adopted a law against treason while clearly limiting the definition of the offense in the Constitution.

Criminal Act and Criminal Intent

Treason is the only crime defined in the U.S. Constitution. Treason against the United States is a federal crime and may not be prosecuted by the states. Various states, such as California, prohibit treason against the state government.

The Constitution limits the *actus reus* of treason to individuals engaged in armed opposition to the government or in providing aid and comfort to the enemy:

- Levying war against the United States.
- Giving aid and comfort to the enemy.

Supreme Court Justice Robert Jackson, in *Cramer v. United States*, clarified that levying war consists of taking up arms and that giving aid and comfort involves concrete and tangible assistance.[1] Justice Jackson stressed that a citizen may "intellectually or emotionally" favor the enemy or may "harbor sympathies or convictions disloyal" to the United States, but absent the required *actus reus*, there is no treason. He explained that an individual gives aid and comfort to the enemy by such acts as fomenting strikes in defense plants, charging exorbitant prices for essential armaments, providing arms to the enemy, or engaging in countless other acts that "impair our cohesion and diminish our strength." In a treason prosecution of sailors who seized, equipped, and armed a ship with the intent of attacking the federal government, Supreme Court Justice Joseph Fields observed that treason may be directed to the overthrow of the U.S. government throughout the country or only in certain states or in selected localities.[2] There is also no requirement that the enemy be shown to have benefited by the assistance provided by the accused.

The Constitution requires that treason be clearly established by the prosecution. This protects individuals against convictions based on passion, prejudice, or false testimony.

- Two witnesses must testify that the defendant committed the same overt act of treason, or
- the accused must make a confession in open court.

The *mens rea* of treason is an "intent to betray" the United States. Justice Jackson observed that "if there is no intent to betray there is no treason." Proof of the defendant's treasonous intent is not limited to the testimony of two witnesses. The required intent may be established by the testimony of a number of witnesses concerning the defendant's statements or behavior. Do not confuse motive with intent. An act that clearly assists and is intended to assist the enemy is treason, despite the fact that the defendant may be motivated by profit, anger, or personal opposition to war rather than by a belief in the justice of the enemy's cause.

In *Cramer*, Justice Jackson cautioned that treason is "one of the most intricate of crimes" and that the U.S. Constitution "gives a superficial appearance of clarity and simplicity which proves illusory when it is put to practical application. . . . The little clause is packed with controversy and difficulty."

Prosecuting Treason

The United States has brought only a handful of prosecutions for treason, and most offenders have had their death sentences modified or have received full pardons from the president. Courts have also been vigilant in ensuring that the rights of defendants are protected. Justice Jackson observed that the United States has "managed to do without treason prosecutions to a degree that probably would be impossible except [where] a people was singularly confident of external security and internal stability."

Cramer v. United States, in 1945, is the most important treason case decided by the U.S. Supreme Court. A team of eight German saboteurs was transported across the Atlantic in two submarines and secretly put ashore in New York and Florida with the intent of engaging in acts of sabotage designed to impede the U.S. war effort and to undermine morale. Saboteurs Werner Thiel and Edward Kerling contacted a former friend of Thiel's in New York, Anthony Cramer. Cramer was subsequently charged and convicted of treason. His conviction was based on the testimony of two FBI agents who alleged that the three suspects drank together and engaged in long and intense conversation. The U.S. Supreme Court reversed Cramer's conviction based on the government's failure to establish an overt act that provided aid and comfort to the enemy. There was no indication that Cramer provided aid and comfort to the enemy by providing information; by securing food, shelter, or supplies; or by offering encouragement or advice. In summary, "without the use of some imagination it is difficult to perceive any advantage which this meeting afforded to Thiel and Kerling as enemies or how it strengthened Germany or weakened the United States in any way whatever."

In *D'Aquino v. United States*, D'Aquino, a U.S. citizen, was convicted of giving aid and comfort to the enemy during World War II by working as a radio broadcaster for the Japanese government. The Court of Appeals for the Ninth Circuit rejected her duress defense. The court held that an individual may not claim immunity from prosecution based on a claim of mental fear of possible future action and that "the citizen owing allegiance to the United States must manifest a determination to resist commands and orders until such time as he [or she] is faced with the alternative of immediate injury or death."[3]

The Legal Equation

Treason	=	Overt act of levying war against the United States or giving aid and comfort to the enemies of the United States
	+	intent to betray the United States
	+	two witnesses to an overt act of levying war or giving aid or comfort or confession in open court.

SEDITION

Sedition at English common law was any communication intended or likely to bring about hatred, contempt, or disaffection with the king, the constitution, or the government. This agitation could be accomplished by **seditious speech** or **seditious libel** (writing). Sedition was punishable by imprisonment, fine, or pillory. In *The Case of the Seven Bishops* in 1688, English Justice Allybone pronounced that "[n]o man can take upon him to write against the actual exercise of the government . . . be what he writes true or false. . . . It is the business of the government to manage . . . the government; it is the business of subjects to mind their own properties and interests." Sedition was gradually expanded to include any and all criticism of the king or the government and the advocacy of reform of the government or church, as well as inciting discontent or promoting hostility between various economic and social classes.

During the debates over the U.S. Constitution, various speakers predicted that the effort to restrict the definition of treason would prove a "tempest in a teapot" because the government would merely resort to other laws to punish critics. This seemed borne out in 1798, when Congress passed the Alien and Sedition Acts. These laws punished any person writing or stating anything "false, scandalous and malicious" against the government, president, or Congress with the "intent to defame" or to bring any of these parties into "disrepute" or to "excite . . . the hatred of the . . . people of the United States, or to stir up sedition." The law differed from the common law in that the statute recognized truth as a defense. An individual convicted of sedition under the act was subject to a maximum punishment of two years in prison and by a fine of no more than $2,000. Although the law was defended as an effort to combat subversives who sought to sow the seeds of revolutionary violence, in fact it was used to persecute political opponents of the government. For instance, a member of Congress from Vermont was sentenced to four months in prison for writing that President John Adams should be committed to a mental institution.

The modern version of the Alien and Sedition Acts is Section 2383 in Title 18 of the U.S. Code. This statute punishes an individual who "incites, sets on foot, assists, or engages in any rebellion or insurrection against the authority of the United States or the laws thereof or gives aid or comfort thereto." This is punished by imprisonment for up to ten years, a fine, or both. An individual convicted of rebellion or insurrection under this law is prohibited from holding any federal office. Note that Section 2383 prohibits incitement to sedition or criminal action against the United States or against a particular law.

The U.S. Code, in Section 2384, punishes **seditious conspiracy**. This statute is directed at the use of force against the government, the use of force to prevent the execution of any law, or the use of force to interfere with governmental property and has been employed by prosecutors in recent years in terrorist prosecutions.

> If two or more persons in any state, territory, or in any place subject to the jurisdiction of the United States, conspire to overthrow, put down, or to destroy by force the government of the United States, or to levy war against them, or to oppose by force the authority thereof, or by force to prevent, hinder or delay the execution of any law of the United States, or by force to seize, take, or possess any property of the United States contrary to the authority thereof, they shall be fined . . . or imprisoned not more than twenty years or both.

In 1940, Congress adopted the Smith Act, which declared that it was a crime to conspire to teach or advocate the forcible overthrow of the U.S. government or to be a member of a group that advocated the overthrow of the government. In *Dennis v. United States* in 1951, the Supreme Court upheld the constitutionality of this statute and affirmed the convictions of twelve leaders of the Communist Party.[4] The Supreme Court reconsidered the wisdom of this ruling in *Yates v. United States*.[5] The Court held that the "Smith Act does not denounce advocacy in the sense of preaching abstractly the forcible overthrow of the Government. . . . [T]he Smith Act reaches only advocacy of action for the overthrow of government by force and violence. The essential distinction is that those to whom the advocacy is addressed must be urged to do something, now or in the future, rather than merely to believe in something."

The Legal Equation

Sedition	=	Intentionally
	+	inciting action or acting to overthrow, destroy, oppose by force, or resist
	+	the government of the United States or any law.

SABOTAGE

Sabotage is the willful injury, destruction, contamination, or infection of any war material, war premises, or war utilities with the intent of injuring, interfering, or obstructing the United States or an allied country during a war or national emergency. Sabotage is punishable by imprisonment for not more than thirty years, a fine, or both.[6]

> Whoever, when the United States is at war, or in times of national emergency as declared by the President or by Congress, with the intent to injure, interfere with, or obstruct the United States or any associate nation in preparing for or carrying on the war or defense activities, or with reason to believe that his act may injure, interfere with, or obstruct the United States or any associate nation in preparing for or carrying on the war or defense activities, willfully injures, destroys, contaminates or infects, or attempts to so injure, destroy, contaminate or infect any war material, war premises, or war utilities shall be fined under this title or imprisoned not more than thirty years, or both.

Sabotage may also be committed in peacetime against defense material, premises, or utilities.[7]

Whoever, with intent to injure, interfere with, or obstruct the national defense of the United States, willfully injures, destroys, contaminates or infects, or attempts to so injure, destroy, contaminate or infect any national-defense material, national-defense premises, or national-defense utilities, shall be fined under this title or imprisoned not more than 20 years, or both, and, if death results to any person, shall be imprisoned for any term of years or for life.

Other provisions punish the injury or destruction of harbors, premises, or utilities (e.g., transportation, water, power, electricity) and the production of defective national defense materials.[8]

Courts have held that sabotage requires a specific intent or purpose to damage the national defense of the United States. A defendant injuring property that he or she does not realize is part of the military defense may rely on the defense that although he or she intentionally damaged the property, there was a lack of a specific intent to injure the national defense. Several courts have taken the position that a knowledge standard satisfies the *mens rea* for sabotage. These judges reason that a defendant should be assumed to know that the destruction of defense material is practically certain to interfere with the national defense.

In *United States v. Kabat*, the defendants broke through a fence surrounding a missile silo in Missouri and used a jackhammer to slightly damage cables and chip a hundred-ton lid covering the silo.[9] The defendants were motivated by a desire to protest nuclear weapons and to educate the public concerning the mass destruction that would result from nuclear war. They hung banners and spray-painted slogans that called attention to the fact that these weapons made the world less rather than more safe and were contrary to biblical teachings. Did the high-minded defendants who were motivated by a desire to save the planet from nuclear destruction possess a specific intent to injure, interfere with, or damage the national defense? The Eighth Circuit Court of Appeals ruled that the defendants' "intent to injure, interfere with or obstruct the national defense" was clear from their antinuclear statements and travel to Missouri for the specific purpose of damaging the missile silo. The damage to the silo clearly "interfered" with the defense of the United States, and to "allow citizens who thought they could further U.S. security to act on their theories at will could make it impossible for this country to maintain a coherent defense system." The issue remains whether the defendants intended to damage the national defense.

In contrast, in *United States v. Walli*, the defendants cut through four layers of fencing in a facility in Oak Ridge, Tennessee, where the government stored enriched uranium for nuclear weapons. They spray-painted antiwar slogans, hung banners, splashed blood, sang hymns, and recited a message. The Sixth Circuit Court of Appeals reversed the defendants' conviction for sabotage. "The defendants' actions in this case had zero effect, at the time of their actions or anytime afterwards, on the nation's ability to wage war or defend against attack. Those actions were wrongful, to be sure, and the defendants have convictions for destruction of government property as a result of them. But the government did not prove the defendants guilty of sabotage. . . . That is not to say, of course, that there is nothing a defendant could do at Y-12 [National Security Complex] that would constitute sabotage. . . . If a defendant blew up a building used to manufacture components for nuclear weapons, for example, and thereby prevented the timely replacement of weapons in the nation's arsenal, the government surely could demonstrate an adverse effect on the nation's ability to attack or defend—and, more to the point, that the defendant knew that his actions were practically certain to have that effect."[10]

The Legal Equation

Sabotage	=	Intentionally or knowingly
	+	injuring, interfering with, obstructing, destroying, contaminating, infecting, or defectively producing
	+	national defense materials, premises, utilities, or activities (in times of war, national emergency, or peace).

ESPIONAGE

The U.S. Code prohibits **espionage** or spying. The statute punishes espionage and espionage during war as separate offenses.[11]

> Whoever, with intent or reason to believe that it is to be used to the injury of the United States or to the advantage of a foreign nation, communicates, delivers, or transmits, or attempts to communicate, deliver, or transmit, to any foreign government . . . faction or party or military or naval force within a foreign country . . . or to any representative or citizen thereof either directly or indirectly any document, writing, code book, signal book, sketch, photograph, photographic negative, blueprint, plan, map, model, note, instrument, appliance, or information relating to the national defense, shall be punished by death or by imprisonment for any term of years or for life, except that the sentence of death shall not be imposed unless [the jury or judge determines that the offense resulted in] the death of an agent of the United States . . . or directly concerned nuclear weaponry, military spacecraft or satellites, early warning systems, or other means of defense or retaliation against large-scale attack; war plans; communications intelligence or cryptographic information; or any other major weapons system or element of defense strategy.

Espionage in wartime is also defined in federal statutes.

> Whoever, in time of war, with intent that the same shall be communicated to the enemy, collects, records, publishes, or communicates, or attempts to elicit any information with respect to the movement, numbers, description, condition, or disposition of any of the Armed Forces, ships, aircraft, or war materials of the United States, or with respect to the plans or conduct, or supposed plans or conduct of any naval or military operations, or with respect to any works or measures undertaken for or connected with, or intended for the fortification or defense of any place, or any other information relating to the public defense, which might be useful to the enemy, shall be punished by death or by imprisonment for any term of years or for life.

One of the most active areas of criminal activity in the new global economy is the theft by foreign governments of trade secrets from U.S. corporations. This may range from the formula for a new anticancer drug to the code for a computer program. Individuals involved in "industrial espionage" are subject to prosecution under the Economic Espionage Act of 1996.

In *Gorin v. United States*, the U.S. Supreme Court ruled that espionage during peacetime requires that the government establish that an individual acted in "bad faith" with the intent to injure the United States or to advantage a foreign nation.[12] The foreign government that receives the information may be a friend or foe of the United States, because a country allied with the United States today may prove to be its enemy tomorrow. The majority in *Gorin* held that "evil which the statute punishes is the obtaining or furnishing of this guarded information, either to our hurt or another's gain." Material that is stolen from U.S. military files concerning British troop strength and armed preparedness may not directly harm the United States but may assist or advantage another country in protecting itself against the British and may constitute espionage.

Note that espionage during wartime is easier for the prosecution to prove and requires the establishment of an intent to communicate information to the enemy along with a clear act toward the accomplishment of this goal.

National defense information that has not yet been officially released to the public but that has been reported by the press or generally referred to in government publications may be the subject of espionage because the government has not made the decision to release the specific details. Stealing plans for the design of a nuclear bomb in U.S. defense files would be espionage, despite the fact that the broad outlines of the design are available on the Internet.

Information subject to espionage is not limited to the specific types of materials listed in the statutes. Under the espionage law, national defense is broadly interpreted to mean any information relating to the military and naval establishments and national preparation for war.

There have been six major indictments for violation of the Espionage Act. In a recent prosecution, in July 2013, Chelsea Elizabeth Manning, twenty-nine, a U.S. solider, was convicted of violating the Espionage Act and other criminal statutes after disclosing nearly three-quarters of a million classified or unclassified-but-sensitive military and diplomatic documents. Manning was sentenced to thirty-five years in prison, with the possibility of parole after eight years, and dishonorable discharge from the military.

The Legal Equation		
Espionage	=	Communicating, delivering, transmitting, or attempting to communicate, deliver, or transmit information
	+	to a foreign government, faction, or military
	+	purposely to injure or with reason to believe that material will injure the United States or will be used to advantage a foreign nation.
Espionage during wartime	=	Collecting, recording, publishing, communicating, or attempting to elicit information relating to national defense that might be useful to the enemy
	+	with intent to communicate to the enemy
	+	during time of war.

TERRORISM

The bombing of the Alfred P. Murrah federal building in Oklahoma City on April 19, 1995, and the attack on the United States on September 11, 2001, combined to push Congress to act to prohibit and to punish terrorism. Keep in mind that most acts of terrorism within the United States are prosecuted as ordinary murders, arson, kidnappings, and bombings rather than as acts of terrorism.

The central provisions of the U.S. law on terrorism are found in Title 18 of the U.S. Code, Chapter 113B, "Terrorism." These statutes have been amended and strengthened by the Antiterrorism and Effective Death Penalty Act (1996) and the Uniting and Strengthening America by Providing Appropriate Tools Required to Intercept and Obstruct Terrorism Act (2001), better known as the USA Patriot Act.

Definition of Terrorism

Various federal statutes use the term *terrorism* or *terrorist*. For instance, it is a crime to materially aid a terrorist or foreign terrorist organization. What is terrorism? Federal law divides terrorism into **international terrorism** and **domestic terrorism**.

International terrorism is distinguished by the fact that it occurs outside the United States. Both international and domestic terrorism are intended to intimidate or coerce the American population or are intended to influence or affect the public policy of the United States. We have several tragic examples, including the August 7, 1998, bombing of the U.S. embassies in Kenya (killing 213 and injuring more than 4,500) and Tanzania (killing 11 and injuring 85) and the attack on a U.S. Navy warship, the USS *Cole*, in Yemen on October 12, 2000 (killing 17 U.S. sailors). Other clear examples are the acts of violence intended to force the United States to withdraw troops from Iraq. International terrorism is defined as

> violent acts or acts dangerous to human life that primarily occur outside the United States, would be criminal if committed in the United States, and appear to be intended to either intimidate or coerce a civilian population; or influence the policy of a government by intimidation or coercion; or affect the conduct of a government through mass destruction, assassination, or kidnapping.

Domestic terrorism is defined in the same fashion with the exception that it occurs "primarily within the territorial jurisdiction of the United States" rather than "outside the United States." Note that terrorism is defined in terms of the intent of the offender rather than by the target of the attack.

The U.S. Code defines the **federal crime of terrorism** as an offense "calculated to influence or affect the conduct of government by intimidation or coercion, or to retaliate against government conduct" that involves a violation of a long list of violent and dangerous federal offenses.[13] Chapter 113B of the U.S. Code provides for several specific terrorist crimes that are discussed in the following sections.

Terrorism Outside the United States

Section 2332 of the U.S. Code punishes various crimes against nationals of the United States that occur outside the United States. The killing of a U.S. national outside the United States is punishable by imprisonment for a term of years or death as well as a fine. Voluntary manslaughter is subject to ten years' imprisonment along with a fine, and involuntary manslaughter is punished by a fine or imprisonment of not more than three years, or both. A conspiracy to kill a U.S. national is punished by up to life imprisonment as well as a fine, and a conspiracy leading to an attempt is subject to imprisonment for up to twenty years in prison as well as a fine. Physical violence with the intent to cause serious bodily injury to a U.S. national and physical violence that results in serious bodily injury are both subject to a fine as well as to imprisonment by up to ten years. The U.S. assertion of the right to prosecute and punish criminal acts that occur outside U.S. territory is termed **extraterritorial jurisdiction**.[14]

Terrorism Transcending National Boundaries

U.S. law punishes as a felony acts of terrorism that occur within the United States but that are connected to foreign countries. Offenses involving conduct occurring both outside and within the United States are termed **terrorism transcending national boundaries**. In other words, the fact that conspirators meet in another country and plan to attack a U.S. city would not remove the crime from the jurisdiction of the United States. Prime examples are the September 11, 2001, attacks on the World Trade Center and Pentagon, which were planned, directed, and funded from outside the United States. This statute permits the United States to prosecute individuals living in Afghanistan, England, Germany, Spain, and other countries who were involved in the 9/11 conspiracy. Federal law also provides that criminal attacks against U.S. agencies, embassies, or property abroad or in the air or at sea, or against property owned by the U.S. government or by a U.S. citizen, are considered to have taken place within U.S. territory and are punishable by the United States.

Three crimes of violence are included within the statute on terrorism that transcends national boundaries:

1. *Crimes Against the Person.* Killing, kidnapping, maiming, or committing an assault resulting in serious bodily injury or assault with a dangerous weapon against an individual within the United States.

2. *Crimes Against Property Harming the Person.* Acts that create a substantial risk of serious bodily injury by destroying or damaging any structure, real estate, or object within the United States.

3. *Inchoate Offenses.* Threats, attempts, and conspiracies to commit either of these two offenses and accessories after the fact.

The offenses under this provision must meet one of several conditions. These include the following:

- *Federal Official.* The victim or intended victim is the U.S. government, a member of the uniformed services, or any official, officer, employee, or agent of the legislative, executive, or judicial branches or of any department or agency of the United States.
- *Property.* The building, vehicle, real estate, or object is owned or leased by the United States or a U.S. citizen.

- *Territory.* The offense is committed within the territorial sea or U.S. airspace.
- *Interstate Commerce.* The offense makes use of the mail or any facility in interstate or foreign commerce.

Penalties include capital punishment for a crime resulting in death, life imprisonment for the crime of kidnapping, thirty-five years for maiming, thirty years for aggravated assault, and twenty-five years for damaging property.[15]

Weapons of Mass Destruction

The use, threat, attempt, or conspiracy to use a weapon of mass destruction is punishable by imprisonment for a term of years or life and, in the event of death, by life imprisonment.

The statute on weapons of mass destruction, 18 U.S.C. § 2332a, declares that it is a crime when such a weapon is used outside the United States against a U.S. resident or citizen, within the United States against any person so as to affect commerce, or within or outside the United States against property that is owned, leased, or used by the federal government. It is also an offense to threaten, attempt to use, or conspire to use a weapon of mass destruction. A **weapon of mass destruction** is defined as follows:

- Toxic or poisonous chemical weapons that are designed or intended to cause death or serious bodily injury (poison gas).
- Weapons involving biological agents (smallpox).
- Weapons releasing radiation or radioactivity at a level dangerous to human life (nuclear material).
- Explosive bombs, grenades, rockets, missiles, and mines.

Possession of a biological or toxic weapon or delivery system that cannot be justified by a peaceful purpose is subject to imprisonment for up to ten years, a fine, or both.[16] In April 2005, Zacarias Moussaoui, while denying involvement in the September 11, 2001, attacks against the Pentagon and World Trade Center, pled guilty to conspiring to use an airplane as a "weapon of mass destruction" to attack the White House.

Mass Transportation Systems

Subways, buses, and trains are some of the most vulnerable and potentially damaging terrorist targets. In 1995, a chemical gas attack on a subway train in Tokyo resulted in twelve deaths and more than five thousand injuries. Federal law provides that it is a crime to willfully wreck, derail, set fire to, or disable a mass transportation vehicle or ferry or to damage or impair the operation of a signal or control system. It is also a federal crime to cause the death or serious bodily injury of an employee or passenger on a mass transportation vehicle. Other provisions prohibit using a weapon of mass destruction against a mass transportation system. These offenses are punishable by a fine and as much as twenty years in prison. An aggravated offense punishable by up to life in prison results when the mass transportation vehicle or ferry is carrying one or more passengers or the offense results in the death of any person. The destruction of aircraft and air piracy are subject to punishment under separate provisions of the U.S. Code. Air piracy is defined in Title 49, Section 46502, as "seizing or exercising control" over an aircraft by force, violence, threat of force or violence, or any form of intimidation with a wrongful intent.[17]

Harboring or Concealing Terrorists

It is a crime to harbor or conceal a person who an individual knows or has reasonable grounds to believe has committed or is about to commit various terrorist offenses or crimes posing a serious and widespread danger. Harboring a terrorist is subject to ten years in prison and to a fine.[18]

Material Support for Terrorism

The offense of providing **material support to a terrorist** is defined in the U.S. Code as providing material support or resources or concealing or disguising the nature, location, source, or ownership of material support or resources, knowing or intending that they are to be used in preparation for or in carrying out various terrorist acts or acts of violence or in the preparation of, concealment of, or escape from such crimes. This is punishable by imprisonment for no more than fifteen years, a fine, or both. In the event that death results, the accused is subject to imprisonment for a term of years or capital punishment.

There is a separate offense of knowingly providing **material support to a foreign terrorist organization** or an attempt or conspiracy to do so. This is also subject to imprisonment for up to fifteen years, a fine, or both. The death of a victim may result in imprisonment for up to life. Material support or resources in support of terrorism include money, financial services, housing, training, expert advice or assistance, personnel, safe houses, false documentation, communication equipment, facilities, weapons, lethal substances, explosives, transportation, and other "physical assets." Medical and religious materials are exempt from the prohibition on material support.[19] The U.S. Secretary of State is charged with determining whether a group is a foreign terrorist organization.[20]

These two statutes are the primary laws relied on by prosecutors in terrorist prosecutions in the United States. Prosecutors explain that the material support statutes are central in combating terrorism because hard-core terrorists rely on the support provided by individuals willing to provide financial resources, passports, expertise in computer technology, weapons, and information. These laws also have been relied on by the government to prosecute individuals for "providing personnel to terrorist organizations" who have traveled abroad to undergo terrorist training. The material support statutes have the advantage of permitting the arrest of individuals before terrorist plots are carried out. Critics caution that the material support provisions may be used to prosecute individuals who do not pose a threat. For instance, defendants in a New York case who had attended a terrorist training camp abroad and who had not been involved with terrorist activities after returning to the United States pled guilty to providing material support. It is also argued that these statutes are broadly written and that individuals may be criminally prosecuted who have merely donated money to a hospital or school in the Middle East run by a group labeled as terrorist.

In 2010, in *Holder v. Humanitarian Law Project*, the U.S. Supreme Court addressed the constitutional status of the material support statute.[21] The U.S. Secretary of State designated the Kurdistan Workers' Party (PKK) and the Liberation Tigers of Tamil Eelam (LTTE) as "foreign terrorist organizations." Two U.S. citizens and six domestic organizations claimed that they wished to provide support for the lawful and nonviolent humanitarian and political activities of the PKK and LTTE and that applying the material support law to prevent them from doing so violated their First Amendment rights. The plaintiffs explained that they wanted to provide "training" and "expert advice or assistance" to members of the PKK on how to seek humanitarian financial support from various international institutions such as the United Nations and how to use international law to peacefully resolve disputes. They also wished to engage in political advocacy promoting the cause of Kurds living in Turkey and Tamils living in Sri Lanka. The plaintiffs expressed the fear that "such advocacy might be regarded as 'material support' in the form of providing 'personnel' or 'expert advice or services.'"

The Supreme Court first held that the intent requirement of the material support statute is satisfied by knowledge of the "organization's connection to terrorism" and that the government is not required to establish that a defendant possessed the "specific intent to further the organization's terrorist activities."

The Court decided that terms like *training, expert advice or assistance, service*, and *personnel* provided fair notice to a person of ordinary intelligence of "what is prohibited." Further, the Court ruled that those terms are not "so standardless" that they authorize or encourage "seriously discriminatory enforcement." The plaintiffs undoubtedly were aware that activities in which they seek to engage "readily fall within the scope of the terms 'training' and 'expert advice or assistance.'"

The most significant part of the decision in *Holder* addresses whether the material support statute, as applied to plaintiffs, violates the freedom of speech guaranteed by the First Amendment. The Court clarified that the material support statute does not prohibit "independent advocacy" on behalf of a terrorist organization. Individuals are free to "say anything they wish on any topic." The material support statute is "carefully drawn to cover only a narrow category of speech . . . under the direction of, or in coordination with foreign groups that the speaker knows to be terrorist organizations."

Read *Holder v. Humanitarian Law Project* and *United States v. Bell* on the study site: study .sagepub.com/ lippmaness2e.

The Court explained that nonviolent or humanitarian material support intended to promote peaceable lawful conduct can further violent terrorists in "multiple ways." Terrorist organizations often conceal their violent activities behind what appears to be lawful activity. Advocacy by outside groups working under the guidance or with the cooperation of a terrorist group may promote the organization's legitimacy as a responsible political organization, which helps the organization to recruit members and raise funds. Money that is raised for medical assistance or refugee support releases the organization's other funds to support terrorism. Terrorist organizations may use the skills they learned in peaceful negotiation for "lulling opponents into complacency and ultimately preparing for renewed attacks." The Supreme Court in *Holder* made the important point that humanitarian assistance to a terrorist organization allowed the organization to devote funds to violent terrorism that formerly were used for humanitarian purposes. Counterterrorism prosecutions in federal courts of late have focused on the prosecution of individuals who have attempted to travel to the Middle East to fight on behalf of the Islamic State (ISIS).[22]

The Legal Equation

Material support to terrorists	=	Providing material support to a terrorist or concealing or disguising the nature, location, source, or ownership of material
	+	knowing or intending that support or resources are used in preparation for or in carrying out various terrorist acts.
Material support to foreign terrorist organizations	=	Providing material support to a foreign terrorist organization
	+	knowingly providing material support.

CRIMINAL LAW IN THE NEWS

Dzhokhar Tsarnaev, "Jahar" to his friends, was a popular high school student who liked wrestling, soccer, and hip-hop; enjoyed marijuana; and followed popular television programs like *The Walking Dead* and *Game of Thrones*. On April 15, 2013, nineteen-year-old Jahar and his twenty-six-year-old brother Tamerlan positioned two pressure cooker homemade bombs at the finish line of the Boston Marathon. The marathon is held each year on Patriots' Day, a long-standing citywide celebration. The bombs exploded as the runners approached, killing three persons, including an eight-year-old child, and injuring 264 others, a number of whom sustained life-altering injuries. As you read about the Tsarnaev brothers, do not forget about the pain and suffering of the victims.

As the investigation centered on the Tsarnaev brothers, they fled and encountered and killed Sean Collier, a Massachusetts Institute of Technology police officer; and they stole an SUV, kidnapped the driver, and

when cornered by the police engaged in a shoot-out in which Tamerlan was killed. Jahar escaped in the SUV and took refuge in a dry-docked motorboat. Roughly eighteen hours later, Jahar found himself surrounded by police and surrendered to FBI negotiators. Jahar before being apprehended scrawled a message in the boat that "the U.S. . . . is killing our innocent civilians . . . I can't stand to see such evil go unpunished. . . . We Muslims are one body, you hurt one, you hurt us all. . . . F__ America." He allegedly also referred to the victims of the Boston bombings as "collateral damage" who deserved their fate because of the Muslims killed by the United States across the globe. Jahar also allegedly wrote that he did not mourn for his brother who now was a martyr in paradise.

Jahar pled not guilty to thirty counts, seventeen of which carried a potential death penalty. The central count charged him with using and conspiring to use a weapon of mass destruction that resulted in death.

Media reports indicate that Jahar told the FBI that following the Boston bombing along with his brother he had planned to drive to New York City to launch a second attack in Times Square. Investigators failed to find direct links between the Tsarnaev brothers and foreign terrorist groups although there is substantial evidence that they were inspired by online jihadist videos and postings.

A police investigation later connected Tamerlan to a triple homicide that took place on the tenth anniversary of the September 11, 2001, attacks on the World Trade Center and Pentagon.

An estimated twenty-five terrorist plots by homegrown terrorists had been foiled prior to the attack launched by the Tsarnaev brothers. The brothers' attack was the first large-scale domestic terrorist attack that had proven successful since the September 11 attacks. Experts on terrorism continue to speculate on why Jahar, whose extremist views undoubtedly are shared by other young Americans, decided to translate these views into a deadly attack.

Tamerlan already was a teenager when his family emigrated to the United States, and his speech was heavily accented. He abandoned his aspirations to be an Olympic boxer when he was disqualified from competition for taunting an opponent. Tamerlan fit the profile of a frustrated young migrant who is angered by the downward trajectory of his life in America and who finds comfort in religious fundamentalism. Zubeidat, Tamerlan's mother, who herself had become increasingly religious, encouraged Tamerlan to abandon his life in the "fast lane" and to turn to Islam. He became increasingly intolerant and militant, and at one point Tamerlan was arrested for domestic battery against his girlfriend who alleged that he pressured her to convert to Islam and to dress modestly. Tamerlan's outspoken condemnation of fellow Muslims in the mosque and his online interest in al Qaeda led to his being placed on U.S. and Russian terrorist watch lists. At one point, he traveled to Dagestan in an effort to join the Islamic resistance to the Russians. Married with a child, Tamerlan found himself unemployed and on public assistance and on the verge of being forced to vacate his apartment in Cambridge, Massachusetts.

Jahar, on the other hand, was a formidable high school wrestler and popular with his peers at Cambridge Rindge and Latin high school in Cambridge, Massachusetts. He was a volunteer in the "Best Buddies" program, became a U.S. citizen on September 11, 2012, and earned a $2,500 scholarship to the University of Massachusetts at Dartmouth.

His friends described Jahar as "superchill," "smooth," "cool," and "always joking" and cannot recall him ever referring to his Islamic faith. He seemed to fit right into the diverse, politically progressive world of Cambridge. Jahar's tweets were the typical teenage mixture of immature observations and occasional philosophical reflections and were more concerned with wrestling and smoking marijuana than with Islam and politics.

Jahar's calm and controlled exterior was briefly broken on only one occasion when he proclaimed his anger over Americans' equation of Islam with terrorism. He argued that jihadist terrorism was justified because of the violence of U.S. foreign policy and tweeted that 9/11 was an "inside job."

Jahar beneath the surface was percolating with anger and frustration. Anzor, his father, was a lawyer who after arriving in the United States worked as a mechanic for $10 an hour and regularly erupted in anger. His frustration over the growing Americanization of his daughters Ailina and Bella led him to force them into arranged marriages. Anzor, depressed over his inability to support his family and opposed to Zubeidat's growing fundamentalism, returned to Russia. He divorced and later reconciled with Zubeidat who fled Boston after being arrested for shoplifting.

Jahar, although earning strong grades in high school, was disappointed over the fact that the elite private Boston colleges were beyond his financial means. He abandoned his aspiration of studying engineering after flunking most of his university classes. Jahar found himself heavily in debt from college and made money by selling marijuana.

Jahar created a Facebook page that describes his worldview as divided between "Islam" and a "career and money" and posted links to Islamic fighters. Jahar tweeted that the Prophet Muhammad was his role model and proclaimed "never underestimate the rebel with a cause."

In early February, Tamerlan drove to New Hampshire and purchased forty-eight mortars containing approximately eight pounds of low-explosive powder. He also bought nine-millimeter handguns along with two hundred rounds of ammunition. Jahar began downloading al Qaeda military manuals including an article on "Make a Bomb in the Kitchen of Your Mom," which offered detailed instructions on how to construct a pressure cooker explosive.

On April 15, 2013, Jahar, wearing his high school wrestling jacket, ignited the bomb at the finish line of the Boston Marathon. Was the bombing a political statement or a product of personal frustrations? Why did Jahar bomb the Boston Marathon? In May 2015, a Boston jury determined that Jahar should receive the death penalty. Do you agree with the verdict?

Combat Immunity

American John Walker Lindh, the so-called American Taliban, was captured by U.S. forces in Afghanistan and subsequently pled guilty to supplying services to the Taliban (the Islamic fundamentalist ruling party of Afghanistan) and of carrying an explosive during the commission of a felony. Lindh's lawyer made various arguments on his behalf, including **combat immunity**. This is the contention that, as a member of the Afghan military, Lindh was immune from criminal prosecution for acts of lawful combat undertaken in the defense of Afghanistan against the United States. The U.S. government, however, contended that Lindh was not entitled to the status of a legal combatant and that his acts on behalf of the Taliban regime in Afghanistan were unlawful criminal offenses rather than acts of lawful warfare. The standard for determining whether an individual is a lawful or unlawful combatant is set forth in the **Geneva Convention of 1949**. The Geneva Convention is an international treaty regulating the law of war that the United States has signed and recognizes as part of U.S. law.

The Geneva Convention Relative to the Treatment of Prisoners of War sets forth four criteria an organization must meet for its members to qualify for lawful combatant status:

1. The organization must be commanded by a person responsible for his subordinates;
2. The organization's members must have a fixed distinctive emblem or uniform recognizable at a distance;
3. The organization's members must carry arms openly; and
4. The organization's members must conduct their operations in accordance with the laws and customs of war.

A federal district court concluded that Lindh did not qualify as a lawful combatant. The Taliban lacked a coherent command structure; wore no distinctive, recognizable insignia; and, although they carried arms openly, failed to observe the laws and customs of war by targeting civilians.[23]

State Terrorism Statutes

Virtually every state has a terrorism statute to cover criminal acts that do not fall within federal jurisdiction. Consider the "beltway sniper" case from Virginia, *Muhammad v. Commonwealth*.[24] The two defendants killed at least ten individuals as they traveled from Maryland and the District of Columbia through Virginia. Muhammad was sentenced to death and appealed his conviction to the Virginia Supreme Court.

An act of terrorism under Virginia law is an "act of violence . . . committed with the intent to (i) intimidate the civilian population at large or (ii) influence the conduct or activities of the government of the United States, a state, or locality through intimidation." An "act of violence" includes a list of aggravated felonies including murder, voluntary manslaughter, mob-related felonies, malicious assault or bodily wounding, robbery, carjacking, sexual assault, and arson.

The jury sentenced Muhammad to two death sentences based on his terrorist killings. The Virginia Supreme Court held that the provisions of the statute provided sufficient notice to ordinary individuals to understand "what conduct they prohibit and do not authorize" and that the law did not impose "arbitrary and discriminatory enforcement." *Intimidate* has been defined in various cases to mean "putting in fear," and *population at large* requires a "more pervasive intimidation of the community rather than a narrowly defined group of people. . . . We do not believe that a person of ordinary intelligence would fail to understand this phrase."

CRIMINAL LAW AND PUBLIC POLICY

On June 5 and June 6, 2014, British newspaper the *Guardian* and the *Washington Post* disclosed that an anonymous source had leaked classified information that the U.S. government was requiring large telecommunications providers to turn the telephone numbers dialed by Americans over to the National Security

Agency (NSA), the U.S. agency charged with gathering foreign electronic intelligence. On June 9, the *Guardian* released a video interview with Edward Snowden, the individual responsible for leaking the information. The thirty-three-year-old Snowden was a former CIA and NSA contractor. After fleeing the United States and being denied asylum in Hong Kong and unsuccessfully seeking asylum in several other countries, Snowden received temporary asylum for three years in Russia.

Little is known about Snowden's background. He reportedly never received a high school diploma and briefly attended a community college. There is little doubt that he had a strong interest and aptitude for computers and maintained an active online presence. In 2004, Snowden, whose father was a veteran of the Coast Guard, joined the military in the aftermath of 9/11 and enlisted in a program that fast-tracked him into the Special Forces.

Snowden's slight build and various physical limitations made him an unlikely candidate for the Special Forces. In the summer of 2005, he was discharged from the Army after allegedly breaking both his legs. Snowden spent the next several months as an IT security specialist at the University of Maryland Center for Advanced Study of Languages, a joint enterprise with the U.S. government.

In 2007–2008, Snowden worked in Geneva, Switzerland, as a contractor for the CIA maintaining network security. He later claimed that he grew disillusioned with the agency, and in 2009, Snowden terminated his relationship with the CIA, perhaps in response to an investigation into his attempt to access classified files.

Snowden next was hired by Dell as a contractor engaged in computer analysis for the NSA. He was sent to Japan, which fulfilled a longtime interest in Japanese culture and language. At some point, Snowden was certified as an "Ethical Hacker" employed by the NSA to counteract efforts to penetrate the agency's computer system. Snowden subsequently was transferred to Hawaii to work at the NSA's regional cryptological center.

A central event in shaping Snowden's attitudes toward U.S. security services was his inadvertent discovery of a report that provided a detailed account of the Bush administration's warrantless wiretapping of both Americans and foreigners following 9/11. His sense of alienation was heightened in March 2013 when James Clapper, the director of national intelligence, denied before a congressional committee that the NSA had been collecting data on U.S. citizens, a claim that Snowden knew to be false.

Snowden next took a job with the technology consulting firm Booz Allen Hamilton (BAH), which like Dell contracted to work with the NSA. Snowden worked as a professional hacker charged with detecting vulnerabilities in U.S. technology that might be exploited by foreign countries. Snowden's responsibilities allowed him access to top-secret Internet programs and provided him with the opportunity to illicitly transfer data onto a thumb drive that he transmitted to journalists whom he trusted at the *Guardian* and *Washington Post*.

The information leaked by Snowden to journalists revealed that since 2006 the NSA had engaged the bulk collection of the domestic and foreign telephone numbers dialed by Americans. This secret "metadata" program called PRISM was based on bulk search warrants issued every three months by the Foreign Intelligence Surveillance Court (FISC) that directed nine Internet providers to turn records of the phone numbers dialed by every American over to the government. Once an individual was specifically singled out for additional investigation, the NSA followed a "three hops rule," analyzing all phone calls made by the target and all phone calls made by individuals called by the target, as well as all phone calls made by the individuals they called. This might be followed by a search warrant allowing the government to monitor the content of an individual's phone calls and e-mails.

Snowden believed that the government's bulk collection and storage for five years of all the numbers dialed by Americans without any basis to suspect that U.S. citizens or residents were agents of a foreign power or were engaged in criminal activity violated the Fourth Amendment prohibition on unreasonable searches and seizures and violated the privacy of U.S. citizens. Studies concluded that the collection of the numbers dialed by an individual could reveal virtually every aspect of an individual's life. Snowden argued that the U.S. public was entitled to be informed that the phone numbers they dialed were being monitored, and explained that his goal in revealing large amounts of information to selected journalists was to spark a worldwide discussion on privacy and on the state surveillance of individuals across the globe.

A special review committee appointed by President Obama concluded that the "metadata" program had not been proven essential to detecting terrorist plots and the information obtained through the "metadata" program could have been obtained by relying on the traditional search warrant procedure.

The disclosure of PRISM led President Obama to propose reforms in the program.

Congress after an extended debate adopted the USA Freedom Act, which provided that phone providers retain metadata rather than turning the data over to the government. The NSA may obtain access to these records only by obtaining a warrant from the FISC.

The U.S. government has charged Snowden with espionage, and government officials labeled him a coward for fleeing rather than remaining in the United States and assuming responsibility for his actions.

(Continued)

(Continued)

Critics asked how Snowden could portray himself as a defender of liberty and human rights and yet seek asylum in a repressive regime like Russia. Some high-ranking intelligence officials claim that Snowden's disclosures have made the United States less safe and have placed Americans at risk.

Polls indicated that the majority of Americans view Snowden as a whistle-blower rather than a traitor. Absent his unlawful leaking of information, the "metadata" program would not have been revealed. Snowden's revelations led to the disclosure of other surveillance programs, such as the Post Office's extensive monitoring of the mail sent and received by Americans and the Obama administration's approval of the warrantless search for suspicious addresses or computer codes that might be linked to malicious hackers regardless of whether they were affiliated with a foreign government.

The journalistic community recognized Snowden's contribution to public awareness of government surveillance by awarding him the Ridenhour Award for "truth telling," and the journalists who worked with him also were the recipients of prestigious awards for their reporting. Should Snowden be permitted to return to the United States and plead guilty to a minor criminal violation?

IMMIGRATION

Immigration law regulates the entry of individuals into the United States, the length of their stay, whether they may work or attend school, the treatment of individuals who are in the United States unlawfully, and the process by which individuals can become legally naturalized citizens. Immigration law protects the border of the United States and the sovereign right of the United States to control who may enter and who may remain in the country. The United States is known as a "nation of immigrants," and underlying U.S. immigration policy is the widespread recognition that immigrants have made substantial contributions to U.S. society.

In 2012, in *Arizona v. United States*, the U.S. Supreme Court affirmed that immigration is the responsibility of the federal government with a limited state role.[25] The Court held that three provisions of the Arizona law SB 1070 were preempted by the federal Immigration Reform and Control Act (IRCA). Allowing state legislation would interfere with the ability of the federal government to set a uniform immigration policy.

The United States historically favored immigration from Europe and limited immigration and citizenship for nonwhites and for individuals who were considered to possess an immoral character. This restrictive policy changed with the Immigration and Nationality Act of 1952 (INA).[26] The act eliminated restrictions on Asian immigration and naturalization but continued a quota system introduced in the early twentieth century based on country of origin. The act also created quotas for individuals with special skills and opened the door to reuniting families. The INA, which continues to provide the foundation of U.S. immigration law, also created the Immigration and Naturalization Service (INS) to enforce the law.

The 1986 IRCA, also known as the Simpson-Mazzoli Act, obligated employers to check their employees' immigration status, imposed criminal penalties on employers who hired undocumented workers, and provided an amnesty for immigrants who unlawfully entered the United States before January 1, 1982.[27]

The Immigration Marriage Fraud Amendments of 1986 sought to limit "sham marriages" by placing restrictions on the ability of individuals to marry to obtain citizenship.[28] The Immigration Act of 1990 attempted to equalize immigration from various countries by establishing "diversity visas" for regions that, in the previous year, had not received a fair portion of immigration.[29]

The Illegal Immigration Reform and Immigrant Responsibility Act of 1996 (IIRIRA) addresses a broad range of areas.[30] One important focus is on immigration-related offenses such as alien smuggling, the creation of fraudulent documents, and the deportation of aliens who commit criminal offenses.

In 2003, the INS was subsumed in the newly created Department of Homeland Security (DHS). The Bush administration's intent was to combine a number of agencies into the new department in order to increase cooperation in responding to domestic terrorism, natural disasters, and other emergencies and to promote the sharing of intelligence. Most of the responsibilities of the INS were divided between three services of the DHS. Customs and Border Protection has assumed the INS's border patrol duties; Citizenship and Immigration Services now is responsible for the INS's naturalization, asylum, and permanent residence functions; and Immigration and Customs Enforcement handles the INS's deportation, intelligence, and investigatory functions.

In 2007, Congress voted to build roughly seven hundred miles (1,100 km) of fencing along the United States–Mexico border to fortify those portions of the border not already protected.

Roughly forty million migrants have been legally admitted into the United States since 2000. There are approximately two million residents in the United States who have been admitted to work or to attend school. Individuals can enter the United States from Mexico or Canada to shop or to visit friends as long as they possess certain documents. Immigration enforcement at the border, airports, and seaports involves ensuring that individuals do not enter the United States without the required documents or enter the United States with forged documents (see Table 14.1). Estimates are that there are roughly eleven million individuals in the United States without legally required documentation. Many of these individuals have lived and worked in the United States for a lengthy period of time. Immigration reform is intended to legalize the status of these individuals and of their families.

Deferred Action for Childhood Arrivals (DACA) was implemented by the Obama administration in June 2012 and allows undocumented immigrants who entered the country before their sixteenth birthday and before June 2007 to receive a renewable two-year work permit and exemption from deportation. DACA does not provide a path to citizenship. In November 2014, President Obama once again bypassed the U.S. Congress and implemented Deferred Action for Parents of Americans (DAPA), which provides temporary residence and work privileges to the parents of lawful residents and U.S. citizens. The Fifth Circuit Court of Appeals issued an injunction blocking enforcement of DAPA as well as an expansion of DACA pending a trial on the constitutionality of President Obama's executive order. In 2016, the U.S. Supreme Court divided 4-to-4 on the case, which had the effect of upholding the injunction and returning the case to the lower court for trial.

Violations of Immigration Law

The relevant immigration laws are compiled in the U.S. Code. According to the DHS, some of the most frequently violated provisions of federal immigration law include those listed below. Individuals violating these provisions are subject to fines and, in some instances, to criminal penalties and to deportation from the United States back to their country of origin:

- Making, altering, or using counterfeit immigration documents.
- Assisting or encouraging aliens to come to the United States unlawfully in violation of the law.
- Harboring an illegal alien.
- Knowingly employing aliens who do not have permission to work in the United States.
- Failing to depart the United States when ordered removed (deported).
- Attempting to enter the United States by misrepresenting (lying about) material facts.
- Entering into a marriage to circumvent the immigration laws.
- Entering or attempting to enter the United States without permission after having been removed (deported).
- Assisting an alien to enter the United States for prostitution or other immoral purposes.

State Laws

A number of U.S. cities and towns have declared themselves to be "sanctuary cities." The police and other city workers in these cities and towns are instructed to overlook the presence of undocumented individuals whom they encounter. A larger number of cities and counties participate in the "Secure Communities" program and notify federal law enforcement when they apprehend individuals who are unlawfully present in the United States. Critics assert that the program results in individuals who do not pose a danger being turned over to federal authorities and deported.

There is a strong backlash against immigrants. Forty-five state legislatures in 2012 considered restrictions on undocumented individuals. Courts have struck down many of the most restrictive measures as unconstitutional based on the fact that immigration is a federal rather than a state concern.

Table 14.1   Selected Provisions of U.S. Immigration Law

8 U.S.C. § 1324

(a)   Criminal penalties for harboring an undocumented individual

(1)

(A)   Any person who—

(i)   knowing that a person is an alien, brings to or attempts to bring to the United States in any manner whatsoever such person at a place other than a designated port of entry . . . or

(ii)   remains in the United States in violation of law, transports, or moves or attempts to transport or move such alien within the United States by means of transportation or otherwise, in furtherance of such violation of law;

(iii) knowing or in reckless disregard of the fact that an alien has come to, entered, or remains in the United States in violation of law, conceals, harbors, or shields from detection, or attempts to conceal, harbor, or shield from detection, such alien in any place, including any building or any means of transportation;

(iv) encourages or induces an alien to come to, enter, or reside in the United States, knowing or in reckless disregard of the fact that such coming to, entry, or residence is or will be in violation of law; or

(v)

(I)   engages in any conspiracy to commit any of the preceding acts, or

(II)   aids or abets the commission of any of the preceding acts,

shall be punished as provided in subparagraph (B).

(B)   A person who violates subparagraph (A) shall, for each alien in respect to whom such a violation occurs—

(i)   in the case of a violation of subparagraph (A)(i) or (v)(I) or in the case of a violation of subparagraph (A)(ii), (iii), or (iv) in which the offense was done for the purpose of commercial advantage or private financial gain, be fined . . . [and/or] imprisoned not more than 10 years, or both;

(ii)   in the case of a violation of subparagraph (A)(ii), (iii), (iv), or (v)(II), be fined . . . [and/or] imprisoned not more than 5 years, or both;

(iii) in the case of a violation of subparagraph (A)(i), (ii), (iii), (iv), or (v) during and in relation to which the person causes serious bodily injury to . . . or places in jeopardy the life of, any person, be fined [and] imprisoned not more than 20 years, or both; and

(iv) in the case of a violation of subparagraph (A)(i), (ii), (iii), (iv), or (v) resulting in the death of any person, be punished by death or imprisoned for any term of years or for life, fined . . . or both.

8 U.S.C. § 1324C

(e)   Criminal penalties for failure to disclose role as document preparer

(1)   Whoever, . . . knowingly and willfully fails to disclose, conceals, or covers up the fact that they have, on behalf of any person and for a fee or other remuneration, prepared or assisted in preparing an application which was falsely made . . . for immigration benefits, shall be fined . . . imprisoned for not more than 5 years, or both, and prohibited from preparing or assisting in preparing, whether or not for a fee or other remuneration, any other such application.

(2)   Whoever, having been convicted of a violation of paragraph (1), knowingly and willfully prepares or assists in preparing an application for immigration benefits . . . shall be fined in accordance with title 18, imprisoned for not more than 15 years, or both, and prohibited from preparing or assisting in preparing any other such application.

8 U.S.C. § 1253

(a)   Penalty for failure to depart

(1)   In general

Any alien against whom a final order of removal is outstanding . . . who—

(A) willfully fails or refuses to depart from the United States within a period of 90 days from the date of the final order of removal . . . ,

    (B) willfully fails or refuses to make timely application in good faith for travel or other documents necessary to the alien's departure,

    (C) connives or conspires, or takes any other action, designed to prevent or hamper or with the purpose of preventing or hampering the alien's departure pursuant to such, or

    (D) willfully fails or refuses to present himself or herself for removal at the time and place required by the Attorney General pursuant to such order, shall be fined . . . or imprisoned not more than four years. . . .

8 U.S.C. § 1325

(c) Marriage fraud

Any individual who knowingly enters into a marriage for the purpose of evading any provision of the immigration laws shall be imprisoned for not more than 5 years, or fined not more than $250,000, or both.

8 U.S.C. § 1227

  (i) Crimes of moral turpitude. Any alien who—

    (I) is convicted of a crime involving moral turpitude committed within five years (or 10 years in the case of an alien provided lawful permanent resident status) and

    (II) is convicted of a crime for which a sentence of one year or longer may be imposed, is deportable.

  (ii) Multiple criminal convictions. Any alien who at any time after admission is convicted of two or more crimes involving moral turpitude, not arising out of a single scheme of criminal misconduct, regardless of whether confined therefore and regardless of whether the convictions were in a single trial, is deportable.

  (iii) Aggravated felony. Any alien who is convicted of an aggravated felony at any time after admission is deportable.

  (iv) High speed flight. Any alien who is convicted of a violation (relating to high speed flight from an immigration checkpoint) is deportable.

  (v) Failure to register as a sex offender . . . is deportable. . . .

(B) Controlled substances

  (i) Conviction. Any alien who at any time after admission has been convicted of a violation of (or a conspiracy or attempt to violate) any law or regulation of a State, the United States, or a foreign country relating to a controlled . . . other than a single offense involving possession for one's own use of 30 grams or less of marijuana, is deportable.

  (ii) Drug abusers and addicts. Any alien who is, or at any time after admission has been, a drug abuser or addict is deportable.

(C) Certain firearm offenses

  Any alien who at any time after admission is convicted under any law of purchasing, selling, offering for sale, exchanging, using, owning, possessing, or carrying, or of attempting or conspiring to purchase, sell, offer for sale, exchange, use, own, possess, or carry, any weapon, part, or accessory which is a firearm or destructive device . . . is deportable.

(E) Crimes of domestic violence, stalking, or violation of protection order, crimes against children and

  (i) Any alien who at any time after admission is convicted of a crime of domestic violence, a crime of stalking, or a crime of child abuse, child neglect, or child abandonment is deportable. . . .

INTERNATIONAL CRIMINAL LAW

The origins of **international criminal law** can be traced to the prosecution of Nazi war criminals at Nuremberg in 1944. The international community subsequently agreed to a number of treaties that addressed crimes that are so serious that they are considered to be the concern of all nations and peoples. These treaties prohibit and punish acts such as genocide, torture, war crimes, and terrorism. A majority of countries in the world have signed these treaties and have incorporated the provisions into their domestic criminal codes.

International crimes typically are committed by individuals acting on behalf of the government. The exception, of course, is terrorism, which in most cases is committed by "non-state actors." Prosecutors in countries in which regimes carry out international crimes are reluctant or frightened to indict government officials for crimes, even after the officials have left office. As a result, the perpetrators of international crimes, in many instances, have not been brought to the bar of justice.

The international community periodically has convened tribunals to prosecute and to punish government leaders who have carried out international crimes and who otherwise would have gone unpunished. In 1993, the United Nations established criminal tribunals to hear cases arising from genocide and war crimes in Rwanda and in Yugoslavia. The most significant step occurred in 2001 with the formation of the International Criminal Court (ICC). This court has jurisdiction over serious international crimes and comprises judges from countries that have joined the court. The United States, although a leading nation in the movement to prosecute and punish international crimes, is not a member of the ICC.

The United States, as part of its international obligation to punish international crimes, has claimed jurisdiction over international offenses committed outside its territorial boundaries and has brought offenders to trial before U.S. domestic courts. The United States, for example, has prosecuted pirates for attacks on European and U.S. ships off the coast of the African country of Somalia.

CASE ANALYSIS

In *United States v. Mohammed Zaki Amawi*, a U.S. district court reviewed the defendant's conviction for conspiring to provide material support to overseas terrorism, conspiring to kill and maim Americans overseas, unlawful distribution of information relating to making a "bomb vest," and unlawfully distributing an Arabic language "Explosives Cookbook."

Was the Defendant Guilty of Terrorism?

United States v. Mohammed Zaki Amawi, 579 F. Supp. 2d 923 (N.D. Ohio 2008)

The government charged that the defendant [Mohammed Zaki Amawi] agreed with Marwan El-Hindi and Wassim Mazloum to provide material support for terrorism and kill and maim Americans overseas. Much of the government's evidence—especially evidence of the conspiratorial agreement and certain acts undertaken in furtherance of that agreement—was obtained by an undercover informant, Darren Griffin.

The F.B.I. hired Griffin, a former D.E.A. undercover informant, to go into the Toledo community to try to uncover terroristic plots and activities. He became active in a Toledo, Ohio, mosque attended by the defendants. Prior to Griffin's activities, the defendants were not acquainted with one another, though they may have been aware that [the others] were members of the mosque. Griffin, a former U.S. Army Special Forces soldier, held himself out to be a radical convert to Islam. He talked about the need for *jihad* and to resist the American campaign in Iraq and American policies elsewhere. He promoted himself as being able to provide *jihadist* training.

The defendants succumbed to his efforts to encourage them to agree to obtain training with the prospect of either going to Iraq to fight with the insurgents against American forces or themselves becoming trainers of others for the same purpose. To some extent, some training was given to those who went to a firing range and shot pistols.

In addition, the government proved other actions directly related to the desire to become trained *jihadists*. Among these were watching and discussing *jihadist* videos showing . . . snipers shooting soldiers, installation and detonation of improvised explosive devices and suicide bombings. Other videos promoted Islamic *jihad* against America.

"[A]fter viewing the evidence in the light most favorable to the prosecution" and giving the government the benefit of all reasonable inferences, I am persuaded that a "rational trier of fact could have found the essential elements of the crime beyond a reasonable doubt."

Conspiracy to Kill or Maim Americans Overseas and Provide Material Support to Terrorism

The defendant acknowledges his own interest in, and discussion with his codefendants about combat training, security, and defense tactics. Those discussions, he contends, did not encompass a "plan or agreement with them to acquire or implement any such training in a particular location, at a particular time or to kill and maim anyone in particular."

That doesn't matter. . . . What matters is that the government's evidence sufficed to enable the jury to find beyond a reasonable doubt that the defendant intended to acquire and use martial training to engage in *jihad* in Iraq against American forces, and, ultimately, to kill, or try to kill American military personnel.

An example of this intent comes from evidence of the defendant's efforts, via contact with someone in Syria, to obtain the explosive Astrolite. . . . The government's proof showed, in other words, that the defendant's interest in being trained was not limited to defending himself from possible acts of violence. It also showed that he was doing more than simply getting together with like-minded individuals to talk about common interests, such as political views or religious beliefs.

A keystone in the evidentiary construct was Griffin's video of a meeting between the defendant, El-Hindi and Mazloum on February 16, 2005. The film secretly created by Griffin showed that the defendants agreed with objectives and actions being discussed between the three of them and Griffin. Those objectives included recruiting others, maintaining security, initially acquiring small arms training, creating a "cell," the need for money, manpower and weapons in Iraq, and the need according specifically to Amawi, "to know explosives these days" as the best way for "making damage." To be sure, as the defendant points out, this was the only occasion when all three codefendants met with one another. A single encounter suffices to create a conspiracy.

In any event, the record showed numerous contacts by Amawi separately with El-Hindi and Mazloum. Between July, 2004, and February, 2006, Amawi spoke by telephone with El-Hindi twenty-two times and Mazloum twenty-one times. In addition, he met separately with each on several occasions.

In sum, there was enough evidence to enable the jury to find beyond a reasonable doubt that the defendant conspired with the other defendants to provide material support to terrorism and kill and maim Americans overseas.

Distribution of Bomb Vest Video

The defendant found and downloaded the bomb vest video from the Internet. Accompanied by Arabic commentary, the video showed how to place ball bearings, or ball bearing-type objects, into an explosive compound, install a detonator, and enfold everything into a vest to be worn by a suicide bomber. The video also showed the effects of detonating the bomb vest. It was, in essence, similar to a "how to" demonstration that one might see on a cooking channel or a home improvement show. As the demonstration was proceeding, Amawi translated the Arabic commentary for Griffin.

Count Three charged the defendant with having unlawfully distributed the bomb vest video by showing it to Griffin. Showing the video sufficed to establish distribution.

The government also had to prove the defendant intended that the information be used for an activity that constituted a federal crime of violence. The jury could reasonably conclude beyond a reasonable doubt that Amawi showed the video to Griffin intending that Griffin, the former Special Forces solider, would use the information from the video either to make similar bombs or teach others how to do so.

Distribution of the "Explosives Cookbook"

The government charged the defendant with also having unlawfully distributed materials relating to explosives intending that it be used to commit a federal crime when he transferred an Arabic-language manual on explosives to Griffin.

Amawi copied the manual onto a compact disc along with other materials and gave the CD to Griffin. This sufficed to prove distribution of the manual.

The defendant contends, *inter alia*, that there is no evidence that Griffin, whose knowledge of Arabic is rudimentary, could or did undertake to read the manual, or that he was even aware that it was included

(Continued)

(Continued)

on the disc and what it contained. Thus, according to Amawi, he could not have intended for Griffin to use the information in the manual to commit a federal crime of violence—a crucial element in this charge.

Griffin's ability on his own to understand the material doesn't matter. Nor does the fact that he and Amawi did not discuss the manual and its contents. I am persuaded that, under all the circumstances, as presented by the totality of the evidence in the case, Amawi gave the manual to Griffin intending and expecting that at some point it would be used and useful in the commission of a crime of violence.

The jury could reasonably conclude beyond a reasonable doubt that Amawi, himself fluent in Arabic, gave the explosives manual to Griffin in anticipation that Griffin would use the manual during his training of Amawi and the other defendants. Whether ultimately translated for Griffin by Amawi or someone else, the manual, the jury reasonably could find, had been given to Griffin to enable him to make its information available to Amawi and others, and thereby facilitate their actions against Americans in Iraq.

Whether Griffin could, acting solely on his own, have used the manual for those purposes doesn't matter. Thanks to Amawi, he had the material in his possession, and would have been able, had he been so inclined, to put it to the uses to which Amawi—by its transfer, if nothing else—wanted it to be put. Griffin had held himself out to be able and willing to train Amawi and others in terroristic tactics. There would have been no reason to give Griffin the manual—or show him the bomb vest video for that matter—except to facilitate the training that Amawi and his codefendants anticipated receiving and enabling them, in due course, to create, deploy and detonate explosive devices.

CHAPTER SUMMARY

The founding figures of the United States were fearful of a strong centralized government, and they provided protections for individual freedom and liberty. Nevertheless, they appreciated that there was a need to protect the government from foreign and domestic attack and accordingly incorporated a provision on treason into the Constitution. This was augmented by congressional enactments punishing sedition, sabotage, and espionage. In recent years, the United States has adopted laws intended to combat global terrorism.

Treason is defined in Article III, Section 3 of the U.S. Constitution. Treason requires an overt act of either levying war against the United States or providing aid and comfort to an enemy of the United States. The accused must be shown to have possessed the intent to betray the United States. The Constitution requires two witnesses or a confession in open court to an act of treason.

Sedition at English common law constituted a communication intended or likely to bring about hatred, contempt, or disaffection with the king, the constitution, or the government. This was broadly defined to include any criticism of the king and of English royalty. U.S. courts have ruled that the punishment of seditious speech and libel may conflict with the First Amendment right to freedom of expression. As a result, judges have limited the punishment of seditious expression to the urging of the necessity or duty of taking action to forcibly overthrow the government. A seditious conspiracy requires an agreement to take immediate action.

Sabotage is the willful injury, destruction, contamination, or infection of war materials, premises, or utilities with the intent to injure, interfere with, or obstruct the United States or an allied nation in preparing for or carrying on war. Sabotage may also be committed in peacetime and requires that the damage to property is carried out with the intent to injure, interfere with, or obstruct the national defense of the United States.

An individual is guilty of espionage who communicates, delivers, or transmits information relating to the national defense to a foreign nation or force within a foreign nation with the purpose of injuring the United States or with reason to believe that it will injure the United States or advantage a foreign nation. Espionage in wartime involves collecting, recording, publishing, communicating, or attempting to elicit such information with the intent of communicating this information to the enemy.

The U.S. Code, Title 18, Chapter 113B, punishes various terrorist crimes. This has been strengthened by the Antiterrorism and Effective Death Penalty Act of 1996 and by the USA PATRIOT Act (2001). Terrorism is divided into international and domestic terrorism. International terrorism is defined as violent acts or acts dangerous to human life that occur outside the United States; domestic terrorism is defined as violent acts or acts dangerous to human life that occur inside the United States. Terrorist acts transcending national boundaries are coordinated across national boundaries.

Terrorist acts require the intent to either intimidate or coerce a civilian population, to influence the policy of a government by intimidation or coercion, or to affect the conduct of a government by mass destruction, assassination, or kidnapping. The U.S. government has primarily relied on the prohibition against material assistance to terrorists and to terrorist organizations in order to prevent and punish terrorist designs before they are executed. This law has proven to be a powerful tool to deny terrorists the resources they require to carry out attacks. Federal law also punishes terrorist crimes involving attacks on mass transit systems and the use of weapons of mass destruction and prohibits the harboring or concealing of terrorists. The United States does not consider terrorists to be lawful combatants, and they are not viewed as prisoners of war under the Geneva Convention by U.S. authorities. Virtually every state has adopted a terrorism statute.

Most terrorist offenses are based on the foundation offenses of treason, sedition, sabotage, and espionage.

Immigration law is intended to protect the sovereign authority of the United States to control individuals who enter and who reside in the territorial boundaries of the country.

CHAPTER REVIEW QUESTIONS

1. Treason is the only crime defined in the U.S. Constitution. What is treason? What type of evidence is required to establish treason?

2. Define sedition. Distinguish seditious speech from seditious libel. What constitutes a seditious conspiracy?

3. What is sabotage? Distinguish between sabotage and sabotage during wartime.

4. Explain the difference between espionage and espionage during wartime.

5. How do the definitions of international and domestic terrorism differ?

6. List some of the terrorist crimes set forth in the U.S. Code.

7. Define and discuss combat immunity.

8. What is the purpose of immigration law? Give some examples of violations of immigration law that are punished criminally.

LEGAL TERMINOLOGY

combat immunity

crimes against the state

Deferred Action for Childhood Arrivals (DACA)

domestic terrorism

espionage

extraterritorial jurisdiction

federal crime of terrorism

Geneva Convention of 1949

immigration law

international criminal law

international terrorism

material support to a foreign terrorist organization

material support to a terrorist

sabotage

sedition

seditious conspiracy

seditious libel

seditious speech

terrorism transcending national boundaries

treason

weapons of mass destruction

CRIMINAL LAW ON THE WEB

Visit **study.sagepub.com/lippmaness2e** to access additional study tools including suggested answers to the You Decide questions, reprints of cases and statutes, online appendices, and more!

Notes

CHAPTER 1

1. Ala. Code § 13-12-5; Fla. Stat. § 823.12; R.I. Gen. Laws §§ 11-12-1–3; Wyo. Stat. §§ 6-9-301(a), 6-9-202; La. Rev. Stat. § 14:67.13.
2. Henry M. Hart Jr., "The Aims of the Criminal Law," *Law and Contemporary Problems* 23, no. 3 (1958): 401–441.
3. *In re Winship*, 397 U.S. 358 (1972).
4. William Blackstone, *Commentaries on the Laws of England*, vol. 4 (Chicago, IL: University of Chicago Press, 1979), p. 5.
5. *Kansas v. Hendricks*, 521 U.S. 346 (1997).
6. Tex. Penal Code Ann. § 1.02.
7. N.Y. Penal Law § 1.05.
8. Jerome Hall, *General Principles of Criminal Law*, 2nd ed. (Indianapolis, IN: Bobbs-Merrill, 1960), p. 18.
9. Wayne R. LaFave, *Criminal Law*, 3rd ed. (St. Paul, MN: West, 2000), p. 8.
10. Fla. Stat. §§ 796.045.
11. LaFave, *Criminal Law*, pp. 70–71.
12. *Commonwealth v. Mochan*, 110 A.2d 788 (Pa. Super. Ct. 1955).
13. Lawrence M. Friedman, *Crime and Punishment in American History* (New York, NY: Basic Books, 1994), pp. 64–65.
14. Fla. Stat. § §775.01–775.02.
15. Cal. Penal Code § 2-24-6.
16. Utah Code § 76-105.
17. LaFave, *Criminal Law*, pp. 72–73.
18. *Keeler v. Superior Court*, 470 P.2d 617 (Cal. 1970).
19. *Kovacs v. Cooper*, 336 U.S. 77 (1949).
20. *Village of Belle Terre v. Boraas*, 416 U.S. 1 (1974).
21. Joshua Dressler, *Understanding Criminal Law*, 3rd ed. (New York, NY: Lexis, 2001), p. 31.
22. *Arizona v. United States*, 567 U.S. ___ (2012).
23. *United States v. Lopez*, 514 U.S. 549 (1995).
24. *United States v. Jones*, 529 U.S. 848 (2000).
25. *Oregon v. Gonzalez*, 546 U.S. 243 (2006).
26. *Texas v. Johnson*, 491 U.S. 1 (1989).

CHAPTER 2

1. Joshua Dressler, *Understanding Criminal Law*, 3rd ed. (New York, NY: Lexis, 2001), p. 39.
2. *United States v. Lovett*, 328 U.S. 303 (1946).
3. *United States v. Brown*, 381 U.S. 437 (1965).
4. Alexander Hamilton, "The Federalist No. 84," in A. Hamilton, J. Madison, and J. Jay, *The Federalist Papers* (New York, NY: New American Library, 1961), p. 512.
5. *Calder v. Bull*, 3 U.S. 386 (1798).
6. *Carmell v. Texas*, 529 U.S. 513 (2000).
7. *Stogner v. California*, 539 U.S. 607 (2003).
8. *Grayned v. Rockford*, 408 U.S. 104 (1972).
9. *Coates v. Cincinnati*, 402 U.S. 611 (1971).
10. *Kolender v. Lawson*, 461 U.S. 352 (1983).
11. *Coates*, 402 U.S. at 611.
12. *Coates*, 402 U.S. at 611.
13. *Papachristou v. Jacksonville*, 405 U.S. 156 (1971).
14. *Nebraska v. Metzger*, 319 N.W.2d 459 (Neb. 1982).
15. *Bolling v. Sharpe*, 347 U.S. 497 (1954).
16. *Buck v. Bell*, 274 U.S. 200 (1927).
17. *Brown v. Board of Education*, 374 U.S. 483 (1954).
18. *McGowan v. Maryland*, 366 U.S. 420 (1961).
19. *Westbrook v. Alaska*, 2003 WL 1732398 (Alaska App. 2003).
20. *Strauder v. West Virginia*, 100 U.S. 303 (1879).
21. *McLaughlin v. Florida*, 379 U.S. 184 (1964).
22. *Loving v. Virginia*, 388 U.S. 1 (1967).
23. *United States v. Virginia*, 518 U.S. 515 (1996).
24. *Michael M. v. Superior Court*, 450 U.S. 464 (1981).
25. *United States v. Windsor*, 570 U.S. __ (2013).
26. *Obergefell v. Hodges*, 576 U.S. __ (2015).
27. Erwin Chemerinsky, *Constitutional Law, Principles and Politics*, 2nd ed. (New York, NY: Aspen, 2002), p. 472.
28. *Barron v. Mayor & City Council of Baltimore*, 32 U.S. [7 Pet.] 243, 247, 250 (1833).
29. *Scott v. Sandford*, 60 U.S. [19 How.] 393 (1857).
30. *Gitlow v. New York*, 268 U.S. 652 (1925).
31. Thomas I. Emerson, *The System of Freedom of Expression* (New York, NY: Vintage Books, 1970), pp. 6–7.
32. *Terminiello v. Chicago*, 337 U.S. 1 (1949).
33. *Chaplinsky v. New Hampshire*, 315 U.S. 568 (1942).
34. *Feiner v. New York*, 340 U.S. 315 (1951).
35. *Terminiello*, 337 U.S. at 1.
36. *Brandenburg v. Ohio*, 395 U.S. 444 (1969).
37. *Watts v. United States*, 394 U.S. 705 (1969).
38. *Elonis v. United States*, 575 U.S. ___ (2015).
39. *Jacobellis v. Ohio*, 378 U.S. 184 (1974).
40. *Miller v. California*, 413 U.S. 15 (1973).
41. *New York v. Ferber*, 458 U.S. 747 (1982).
42. *New York Times v. Sullivan*, 376 U.S. 254 (1964).
43. *Gertz v. Welch*, 418 U.S. 323 (1974).
44. *West Virginia v. Barnette*, 319 U.S. 624 (1943).
45. *United States v. Stevens*, 559 U.S. 460 (2010).

46. *Broadrick v. Oklahoma*, 413 U.S. 601 (1973).
47. *New York v. Ferber*, 458 U.S. at 747.
48. *Tinker v. Des Moines Independent Community School District*, 393 U.S. 503 (1969).
49. *Wooley v. Maynard*, 430 U.S. 705 (1977).
50. *Texas v. Johnson*, 491 U.S. 397 (1989).
51. *United States v. Eichman*, 496 U.S. 310 (1990).
52. *R.A.V. v. St. Paul*, 505 U.S. 377 (1992).
53. *Wisconsin v. Mitchell*, 508 U.S. 476 (1993).
54. *Virginia v. Black*, 538 U.S. 343 (2003).
55. *DeJonge v. Oregon*, 299 U.S. 353 (1937).
56. *Grayned*, 408 U.S. at 104.
57. *Employment Division v. Smith*, 494 U.S. 872 (1990).
58. *Reynolds v. United States*, 98 U.S. [8 Otto] 145 (1878).
59. *Church of the Lukumi Babalu Aye, Inc. v. Hialeah*, 508 U.S. 520 (1993).
60. *Walker v. Superior Court*, 763 P.2d 852 (Cal. 1988).
61. *Holt v. Hobbs*, 574 U.S. ___ (2015).
62. Samuel D. Warren and Louis D. Brandeis, "The Right to Privacy," *Harvard Law Review* 4, no. 5 (1890): 1–23.
63. *Pavesich v. New England Life Ins. Co.*, 50 S.E. 68 (Ga. 1905).
64. *Griswold v. Connecticut*, 381 U.S. 479 (1965).
65. Arthur R. Miller, *The Assault on Privacy* (Ann Arbor: University of Michigan Press, 1971).
66. *Olmstead v. United States*, 277 U.S. 438 (1928).
67. *Bowers v. Hardwick*, 478 U.S. 186 (1986).
68. *Lawrence v. Texas*, 539 U.S. 558 (2003).
69. *Katz v. United States*, 389 U.S. 347 (1967).
70. *United States v. Jones*, 565 U.S. ___ (2012).
71. *Riley v. California*, 573 U.S. ___ (2014).
72. *Kyllo v. United States*, 533 U.S. 27 (2001).
73. *United States v. Miller*, 307 U.S. 174 (1939).
74. *District of Columbia v. Heller*, 554 U.S. 570 (2008).
75. *McDonald v. Chicago*, 561 U.S. 742 (2010).
76. *Moore v. Madigan*, 702 F.3d 933 (7th Cir. 2013).
77. *Caetano v. Massachusetts*, 577 U.S. ___ (2015).
78. Wayne R. LaFave, *Criminal Law*, 3rd ed. (St. Paul, MN: West), p. 189.
79. *Trop v. Dulles*, 356 U.S. 86 (1958).
80. *In re Kemmler*, 136 U.S. 36 (1890).
81. *Louisiana ex rel. Francis v. Resweber*, 329 U.S. 459 (1947).
82. *Baze v. Rees*, 553 U.S. 35 (2008).
83. *Brown v. Plata*, 563 U.S. 493 (2011).
84. *Furman v. Georgia*, 408 U.S. 238 (1973).
85. *Gregg v. Georgia*, 428 U.S. 153 (1976).
86. *Ring v. United States*, 536 U.S. 584 (2002).
87. *Hurst v. Florida*, 577 U.S. ___ (2016).
88. *Coker v. Georgia*, 433 U.S. 584 (1977).
89. *Kennedy v. Louisiana*, 554 U.S. 407 (2008).
90. *Atkins v. Virginia*, 536 U.S. 34 (2000).
91. *Enmund v. Florida*, 458 U.S. 782 (1982).
92. *Thompson v. Oklahoma*, 487 U.S. 815 (1988).
93. *Roper v. Simmons*, 543 U.S. 551 (2005).
94. *Graham v. Florida*, 560 U.S. 48 (2010).
95. *Miller v. Alabama*, 567 U.S. ___ (2012).
96. *Montgomery v. Louisiana*, 577 U.S. ___ (2016).
97. *Lockyer v. Andrade*, 538 U.S. 63 (2003).
98. *Ewing v. California*, 538 U.S. 11 (2003).
99. *Robinson v. California*, 370 U.S. 660 (1962).
100. Erica Goode, "Solitary Confinement: Punished for Life," *The New York Times* (August 3, 2015), http://www.nytimes.com/2015/08/04/health/solitary-confinement-mental-illness.html?_r=0

CHAPTER 3

1. Cal. Penal Code § 20 (1999).
2. Ind. Code § 35-41-2-1 (1993).
3. *McClain v. State*, 678 N.E.2d 104 (Ind. 1997).
4. Joshua Dressler, *Understanding Criminal Law*, 3rd ed. (New York, NY: Lexis, 2001), p. 208.
5. Wayne R. LaFave, *Criminal Law*, 3rd ed. (St. Paul, MN: West, 2000), p. 208.
6. *State v. Tippetts*, 45 P.3d 455 (Ore. 2011).
7. *People v. Decina*, 138 N.E. 799 (N.Y. 1956).
8. A. Roger Ekirch, "Violence in the Land of Sleep," *The New York Times* (March 23, 2010), http://opinionator.blogs.nytimes.com/2010/03/23/violence-in-the-land-of-sleep/
9. *Wheeler v. Goodman*, 306 F. Supp. 58 (W.D.N.C. 1969).
10. *Robinson v. California*, 370 U.S. 600 (1962).
11. *Powell v. Texas*, 392 U.S. 514 (1968).
12. *People v. Beardsley*, 113 N.W. 1128, 1132 (Mich. 1907).
13. *Buch v. Amory Manufacturing*, 44 A. 809, 810 (N.H. 1897).
14. *Kuntz v. Montana Thirteenth Judicial District*, 995 P.2d 951 (Mont. 1999).
15. Dressler, *Understanding Criminal Law*, pp. 96–99.
16. *Hughes v. State*, 719 S.W.2d 560 (Tex. Ct. App. 1986).
17. *State v. Mally*, 366 P.2d 868 (Mont. 1961).
18. *Craig v. State*, 155 A.2d 684 (Md. 1959).
19. *Commonwealth v. Pestinikas*, 617 A.2d 1339 (Pa. Super. 1992).
20. *People v. Oliver*, 285 Cal. Rptr. 138 (Cal. App. 1989).
21. *People v. Burton*, 788 N.E.2d 220 (Ill. App. 2003).
22. Arnold H. Loewy, *Criminal Law in a Nutshell*, 4th ed. (St. Paul, MN: West, 2003), pp. 235–236.
23. Dressler, *Understanding Criminal Law*, pp. 92–93.
24. LaFave, *Criminal Law*, pp. 211–213.
25. *State v. Cashen*, 666 N.W.2d 566 (Iowa 2003).
26. *United States v. Jewell*, 534 F.2d 697 (9th Cir. 1976).
27. *Morissette v. United States*, 342 U.S. 246 (1952).
28. Oliver Wendell Holmes Jr., *The Common Law*, ed. Mark Howe (Boston, MA: Little Brown, 1963), p. 7.
29. *Dennis v. United States*, 341 U.S. 494 (1951).
30. *United States v. U.S. Gypsum Company*, 438 U.S. 422 (1978).
31. *People v. Conley*, 543 N.E.2d 138 (Ill. App. 1989).
32. *People v. Nowack*, 614 N.W.2d 78 (Mich. 2000).
33. *Alvarado v. State*, 704 S.W.2d 36 (Tex. Crim. App. 1986).
34. *United States v. Bailey*, 444 U.S. 394 (1980).
35. Dressler, *Understanding Criminal Law*, p. 137.
36. *State v. Sanborn*, 2012 N.J. Super. Unpub. LEXIS 993 No. A-1418-10T1 (Superior Ct. 2012).
37. *State v. Fuelling*, 145 S.W.3d 464 (Mo. App. 2004).
38. *Durkovitz v. State*, 771 S.W.2d 12 (Tex. App. 1989).
39. State v. Williams, 235 S.W.2nd 745 (Tx. Ct. Crim. App. 2007).
40. *State v. Jones*, 151 S.W.3d 494 (Tenn. 2004).
41. *People v. Stanfield*, 44 A.D. 780 (NY. App. 1974).
42. *State v. Harmon*, 516 A.2d 1047 (N.J. 1986).
43. *State v. Robles*, 623 P.2d 1245 (Ariz. App. 1981).
44. *Regina v. Saunders & Archer*, (1575) 75 Eng. Rep. 706.
45. *People v. Scott*, 927 P.2d 288 (Cal. 1996).
46. *Morissette v. United States*, 342 U.S. at 246.
47. *Morissette*, 342 U.S. at 246.

48. *Staples v. United States*, 511 U.S. 600 (1964).
49. *People v. Janes*, 836 N.W.2d 883 (Mich. App. 2013).
50. *Cooper v. People*, 973 P.2d 1234 (Colo. 1999).
51. Cal. Penal Code § 20 (1999).
52. *United States v. Main*, 113 F.3d 1046 (9th Cir. 1997).
53. Dressler, *Understanding Criminal Law*, p. 191.
54. *People v. Armitage*, 239 Cal. Rptr. 515 (Cal. App. 1987).
55. *People v. Schmies*, 51 Cal. Rptr.2d 185 (Cal. App. 1996).
56. *People v. Saavedra-Rodriguez*, 971 P.2d 223 (Colo. 1998).

CHAPTER 4

1. Rollin M. Perkins and Ronald N. Boyce, *Criminal Law*, 3rd ed. (Mineola, NY: Foundation Press, 1982), pp. 730–732.
2. Joshua Dressler, *Understanding Criminal Law*, 3rd ed. (New York, NY: Lexis, 2000), p. 461.
3. *Wilcox v. Jeffery*, (1951) 1 All E.R. 464.
4. *Brown v. Mississippi*, 864 So. 2d 1009 (Miss. Ct. App. 2004).
5. *State v. Mendez*, 2003 Tenn. Crim. App. LEXIS 790.
6. *State v. Phillips*, 76 S.W.3d 1 (Tenn. Crim. App. 2001).
7. *State v. Anderson*, 702 So.2d 2 (La. 1997).
8. *State v. Walden*, 293 S.E.2d 780 (N.C. 1982).
9. *United States v. Peoni*, 100 F.2d 401 (2nd Cir. 1938).
10. *State v. Barker*, 442 S.W.3d 165 (Mo. App. 2014).
11. *United States v. Fountain*, 768 F.2d 790 (7th Cir. 1985).
12. *State v. Linscott*, 520 A.2d 1067 (Me. 1987).
13. *Wilson-Bey v. United States*, 903 A.2d 818 (D.C. 2006) (en banc).
14. *Browne v. People*, 55 V.I. 931 (2011).
15. *State v. Thomas*, 556 N.E.2d 721 (Ill. App. 1998).
16. *State v. Jordan*, 590 S.E.2d 424 (N.C. App. 2004).
17. Fla. Stat. § 777.03(1)(b).
18. Richard G. Singer and John Q. La Fond, *Criminal Law Examples and Explanations*, 2nd ed. (New York, NY: Aspen, 2001), p. 108.
19. *People v. Travers*, 52 Cal. App. 3d 111 (1975).
20. Wayne R. LaFave, *Criminal Law*, 3rd ed. (St. Paul, MN: West, 2000), p. 264.

CHAPTER 5

1. George Fletcher, *Rethinking Criminal Law* (New York, NY: Oxford University Press, 2000), pp. 131–132.
2. Joshua Dressler, *Understanding Criminal Law*, 3rd ed. (New York, NY: Lexis, 2001), pp. 373–374.
3. *People v. Miller*, 42 P.2d 308 (Cal. 1935).
4. Jerome Hall, *General Principles of Criminal Law*, 2nd ed. (Indianapolis, IN: Bobbs-Merrill, 1960), p. 559.
5. Hall, *General Principles of Criminal Law*, p. 560.
6. *Rex v. Scofield*, (1784) Caldecott 397.
7. *Rex v. Higgins*, (1801) 2 East 5.
8. Dressler, *Understanding Criminal Law*, p. 375.
9. Dressler, *Understanding Criminal Law*, pp. 384–385.
10. *People v. Gentry*, 510 N.E.2d 963 (Ill. App. 1987).
11. American Law Institute, *Model Penal Code and Commentaries*, vol. 11, pt. 1 (Philadelphia, PA: American Law Institute, 1985), p. 305.
12. *People v. Rizzo*, 158 N.E.2d 888 (N.Y. 1927).
13. *Commonwealth v. Gilliam*, 417 A.2d 1203 (Pa. Super. 1980).
14. Cal. Penal Code § 466.
15. Hall, *General Principles of Criminal Law*, p. 595.
16. *Attorney General v. Sillem*, (1863) 159 Eng. Rep. 178.
17. Colo. Rev. Stat. § 18-1-201.
18. *State v. Damms*, 100 N.W.2d 592 (Wis. 1960).
19. *State v. Glass*, 87 P.3d 302 (Idaho Ct. App. 2003).
20. *People v. Dlugash*, 363 N.E.2d 1155 (N.Y. 1977).
21. *People v. Staples*, 85 Cal. Rptr. 589 (Cal. App. 1970).
22. Wayne R. LaFave, *Criminal Law*, 3rd ed. (St. Paul, MN: West, 2000), pp. 561–564.
23. American Law Institute, *Model Penal Code and Commentaries*, pp. 358–362.
24. *Commonwealth v. Bursell*, 678 N.E.2d 143 (Mass. 1997).
25. *State v. Otto*, 629 P.2d 646 (Idaho 1981).
26. *State v. Butler*, 35 P. 1093 (Wash. 1894).
27. *People v. Smith*, 806 N.E.2d 1262 (Ill. App. 2004).
28. *State v. Cotton*, 790 P.2d 1050 (N.M. 1990).
29. Fla. Stat. § 777.04(3).
30. Ill. Comp. Stat. § 8-2.
31. LaFave, *Criminal Law*, pp. 612–614.
32. *Krulewitch v. United States*, 336 U.S. 440 (1949).
33. *Commonwealth v. Azim*, 459 A.2d 1244 (Pa. Super. 1983).
34. *United States v. Brown*, 776 F.2d 397 (2nd Cir. 1985).
35. *Hyde v. United States*, 225 U.S. 347 (1912).
36. *Yates v. United States*, 354 U.S. 298 (1957).
37. *Cline v. State*, 319 S.W.2d 227 (Tenn. 1958).
38. Rollin M. Perkins and Ronald N. Boyce, *Criminal Law*, 3rd ed. (Mineola, NY: Foundation Press, 1982), pp. 685–687.
39. LaFave, *Criminal Law*, pp. 592–593.
40. *Direct Sales Co. v. United States*, 319 U.S. 703 (1943).
41. *United States v. Falcone*, 311 U.S. 205 (1940).
42. *People v. Lauria*, 59 Cal. Rptr. 628 (Cal. App. 1967).
43. *Pinkerton v. United States*, 328 U.S. 640 (1946).
44. American Law Institute, *Model Penal Code and Commentaries*, pp. 305–307.
45. *People v. McGee*, 399 N.E.2d 1177 (N.Y. 1979).
46. *Morrison v. California*, 291 U.S. 82 (1934).
47. Dressler, *Understanding Criminal Law*, pp. 439–440.
48. American Law Institute, *Model Penal Code and Commentaries*, p. 399.
49. *State v. Pacheco*, 882 P.2d 183 (Wash. 1994).
50. Richard G. Singer and John Q. La Fond, *Criminal Law Examples and Explanations*, 2nd ed. (New York, NY: Aspen, 2001), p. 287.
51. *United States v. Bruno*, 105 F.2d 921 (2d Cir.), *rev'd on other grounds*, 308 U.S. 287 (1939).
52. *Kotteakos v. United States*, 328 U.S. 750 (1946).
53. *Rex v. Jones*, 110 Eng. Rep. 485 (1832).
54. *State v. Burnham*, 15 N.H. 296 (1844).
55. *People v. Fisher*, 14 Wend. 2 (N.Y. 1835).
56. *Shaw v. Director of Public Prosecutions*, A.C. 220 (1962).
57. *Musser v. Utah*, 333 U.S. 95 (1948).
58. 18 U.S.C. § 371.
59. *Pinkerton v. United States*, 328 U.S. at 640.
60. Dressler, *Understanding Criminal Law*, pp. 455–456.
61. *Gebardi v. United States*, 287 U.S. 112 (1932).
62. *Harrison v. United States*, 7 F.2d 259 (2nd Cir. 1925).
63. LaFave, *Criminal Law*, pp. 569–573.
64. 18 U.S.C. §§ 1961–1963.

CHAPTER 6

1. *In re Winship*, 397 U.S. 358 (1970).
2. *Jackson v. Virginia*, 443 U.S. 307 (1979).
3. *Commonwealth v. Webster*, 59 Mass. 295 (1850).
4. *Wardius v. Oregon*, 412 U.S. 470 (1973).
5. Joshua Dressler, *Understanding Criminal Law,* 3rd ed. (New York, NY: Lexis, 2001), pp. 63–65.
6. Wayne R. LaFave, *Criminal Law* (St. Paul, MN: West, 2000), p. 54.
7. Richard G. Singer and John Q. La Fond, *Criminal Law Examples and Explanations,* 2nd ed. (New York, NY: Aspen, 2001), p. 374.
8. George P. Fletcher, *Rethinking Criminal Law* (New York, NY: Oxford University Press, 2000), p. 759.
9. Dressler, *Understanding Criminal Law,* p. 205.
10. Dressler, *Understanding Criminal Law,* pp. 206–209.
11. Singer and La Fond, *Criminal Law Examples and Explanations,* pp. 386–388.
12. Rollin M. Perkins and Ronald N. Boyce, *Criminal Law,* 3rd ed. (Mineola, NY: Foundation Press, 1982), pp. 950–951.
13. Jerome Hall, *General Principles of Criminal Law,* 2nd ed. (Indianapolis, IN: Bobbs-Merrill, 1960), p. 475.
14. Perkins and Boyce, *Criminal Law,* pp. 958–959.
15. Arnold H. Loewy, *Criminal Law in a Nutshell,* 4th ed. (St. Paul, MN: West, 2003), p. 165.
16. *State v. Crenshaw*, 659 P.2d 488 (Wn. 1983).
17. Dressler, *Understanding Criminal Law,* p. 349.
18. Ibid.
19. *United States v. Lyons*, 731 F.2d 243 (5th Cir. 1984).
20. *State v. Pike*, 49 N.H. 399 (1869).
21. *Durham v. United States*, 214 F.2d 862 (D.C. Cir. 1954).
22. *United States v. Brawner*, 471 F.2d 969 (D.C. Cir. 1972).
23. 18 U.S.C. § 17(b).
24. *United States v. Duran*, 96 F.3d 1495 (D.C. Cir. 1996).
25. LaFave, *Criminal Law,* pp. 374–377.
26. *United States v. Amos*, 803 F.2d 419 (8th Cir. 1986); *United States v. Freeman*, 804 F.2d 1574 (11th Cir. 1986).
27. Dressler, *Understanding Criminal Law,* pp. 361–371.
28. Cal. Penal Code §§ 25–29.
29. *Montana v. Egelhoff*, 518 U.S. 37 (1996).
30. *People v. Hood*, 1 Cal.3d 444 (Cal. 1969).
31. Markus D. Dubber, *Criminal Law: Model Penal Code* (New York, NY: Foundation Press, 2002), pp. 84–90.
32. Jerome Hall, *General Principles of Criminal Law,* p. 545.
33. *State v. Cameron*, 514 A.2d 1302 (N.J. 1986).
34. *Montana v. Egelhoff*, 518 U.S. at 44.
35. *City of Minneapolis v. Altimus*, 238 N.W.2d 851 (Minn. 1976).
36. Wis. Stat. Ann. §939.42.
37. *Brazill v. State*, 845 So.2d 282 (Fla. Dist. Ct. App. 2003).
38. *Tate v. State*, 967 So.2d 214 (Fla. Dist. Ct. App. 4th Dist. 2007).
39. Perkins and Boyce, *Criminal Law,* pp. 936–938.
40. LaFave, *Criminal Law,* pp. 426–429.
41. LaFave, *Criminal Law,* pp. 429–430.
42. *Kent v. United States*, 383 U.S. 541 (1966).
43. LaFave, *Criminal Law,* pp. 476–479.
44. *State v. Salin*, No. 0302016999, 2003 Del. Ct. C.P.
45. Dressler, *Understanding Criminal Law,* p. 287.
46. Hall, *General Principles of Criminal Law,* p. 438.
47. *Lynch v. D.P.P.*, [1975] A.C. 417.
48. *People v. Unger*, 338 N.E.2d 442 (Ill. App. Ct. 1975).
49. *United States v. Moreno*, 102 F.3d 994 (9th Cir. 1994).
50. *Commonwealth v. Appleby*, 402 N.E.2d 1051 (Mass. 1980).
51. *State v. Brown*, 364 A.2d 27 (N.J. Super. Ct. Law Div. 1976).
52. *People v. Lenti*, 253 N.Y.S.2d 9 (N.Y. Co. Ct. 1964).
53. LaFave, *Criminal Law,* pp. 432–433.
54. LaFave, *Criminal Law,* pp. 441–443.
55. LaFave, *Criminal Law,* pp. 442–443.
56. Singer and La Fond, *Criminal Law Examples and Explanations,* p. 83.
57. *Lambert v. California*, 355 U.S. 335 (1957).
58. *Cheek v. United States*, 498 U.S. 192 (1991).
59. *Cox v. Louisiana*, 379 U.S. 536 (1965).
60. LaFave, *Principles of Criminal Law,* pp. 433–434.
61. LaFave, *Principles of Criminal Law,* p. 434.
62. William Blackstone, *Commentaries on the Laws of England,* vol. 4 (Chicago, IL: Chicago University Press, 1979), pp. 183–187.
63. *Brown v. United States*, 256 U.S. 335 (1921).
64. *Vigil v. People*, 353 P.2d 82 (Colo. 1960).
65. Dressler, *Understanding Criminal Law,* pp. 222–223.
66. *Harshaw v. State*, 39 S.W.3d 753 (Ark. 2001).
67. *People v. Goetz*, 497 N.E.2d 41 (N.Y. 1986).
68. *State v. Schroeder*, 261 N.W. 2d 759 (Neb. 1978).
69. *State v. Norman*, 366 S.E.2d 586 (N.C. Ct. App. 1988).
70. *State v. Norman*, 378 S.E.2d 8 (N.C. 1989).
71. *State v. Richardson*, 525 N.W.2d 378 (Wis. Ct. App. 1994).
72. Cal. Evid. Code § 1107 (a).
73. Mo. Rev. Stat. § 563.33.
74. *State v. Jones*, 850 P.2d 495 (Wash. 1993).
75. Wis. Stat. § 939.48.
76. *State v. DeJesus*, 481 A.2d 127 (Conn. 1984).
77. Dressler, *Understanding Criminal Law,* p. 227.
78. Dressler, *Understanding Criminal Law,* pp. 228–229.
79. *State v. Gartland*, 694 A.2d 564 (N.J. 1997).
80. *State v. Harden*, 69 S.E.2d 628 (W.Va. 2009).
81. Fletcher, *Rethinking Criminal Law,* p. 869.
82. *People v. Eatman*, 91 N.E.2d 387 (Ill. 1957).
83. Dressler, *Understanding Criminal Law,* pp. 263–265.
84. Colo. Rev. Stat. § 18-1-704.5.
85. *State v. Anderson*, 972 P.2d 32 (Okla. Crim. App. 1998).
86. Dressler, *Understanding Criminal Law,* p. 263.
87. *Tennessee v. Garner*, 471 U.S. 1 (1985).
88. *Scott v. Harris*, 550 U.S. 374 (2007); *Plumhoff v. Rickard*, 572 U.S. ___ (2012); *Mullenix v. Luna*, 577 U.S. ___ (2015).
89. *John Bad Elk v. United States*, 177 U.S. 529 (1900).
90. *United States v. Di Re*, 332 U.S. 581 (1948).
91. *State v. King*, 149 So.2d 482 (Miss. 1963).
92. Loewy, *Criminal Law in a Nutshell,* pp. 82–83.
93. *Commonwealth v. French*, 611 A.2d 175 (Pa. 1992).
94. *Sorrells v. United States*, 387 U.S. 435 (1932).
95. *Sherman v. United States*, 356 U.S. 369 (1958).
96. *Sherman v. United States*, 356 U.S. at 369.
97. LaFave, *Criminal Law,* p. 464.
98. *United States v. Fusko*, 869 F.2d 1048 (7th Cir. 1989).
99. LaFave, *Criminal Law,* p. 458.

100. *Sherman v. United States*, 456 U.S. at 382–383.
101. *Mathews v. United States*, 485 U.S. 58 (1988).
102. Alan Dershowitz, *Abuse Excuse and Other Cop-Outs, Sob Stories, and Erosions of Responsibility* (Boston, MA: Little, Brown, 1994), p. 3.
103. Fletcher, *Rethinking Criminal Law*, pp. 801–802.
104. *Millard v. State*, 261 A.2d 227 (Md. Ct. Spec. App. 1970).
105. Dershowitz, *Abuse Excuse*, pp. 54–55.
106. *People v. Molina*, 202 Cal. App. 3d 1168 (Cal. Ct. App. 1988).
107. *Commonwealth v. Garabedian*, 503 N.E.2d 1290 (Mass. 1987).
108. *State v. Phipps*, 883 S.W.2d 138 (Tenn. Ct. App. 1994).
109. Deborah Goldklang, "Post Traumatic Stress Disorder and Black Rage: Clinical Validity, Criminal Responsibility," *Virginia Journal of Social Policy & Law* 5 (1997): 213–243.
110. Wally Owens, "*State v. Osby*, The Urban Survival Defense," *American Journal of Criminal Law 22* (1995): 21.
111. Patricia J. Falk, "Novel Theories of Criminal Defense Based Upon the Toxicity of the Social Environment: Urban Psychosis, Television Intoxication, and Black Rage," *North Carolina Law Review 74* (1996): 731.
112. *United States v. Alexander*, 471 F.2d 923 (D.C. Cir. 1972).
113. *State v. Jerrett*, 307 S.E.2d 339 (N.C. 1983).
114. Doriane Lambelet Coleman, "Individualizing Justice Through Multiculturalism: The Liberals' Dilemma," *Columbia Law Review 96* (1996): 1093, 1150.
115. *State v. Kargar*, 679 A.2d 81 (Me. 1996).

CHAPTER 7

1. *Gregg v. Georgia*, 428 U.S. 153 (1976).
2. *Coker v. Georgia*, 433 U.S. 584 (1977).
3. George P. Fletcher, *Rethinking Criminal Law* (New York, NY: Oxford University Press, 2000), p. 236.
4. Nev. Rev. Stat. § 200.020.
5. Kans. Stat. §21-3405.
6. 18 U.S.C. §§ 1114, 1116.
7. N.M. Stat. §30-2-1.
8. *State v. Myers*, 81 A.2d 710 (N.J. 1951).
9. Utah Code Ann. § 76-5-291.
10. *State v. Schrader*, 302 S.E.2d 70 (W.Va. 1982).
11. *State v. Bingham*, 719 P.2d 109 (Wash. 1986).
12. *State v. Forrest*, 362 S.E.2d 252 (N.C. 1987).
13. Va. Code Ann. § 18.2-31.
14. Fla. Stat. § 921.141.
15. *Owen v. State*, 862 So.2d 687 (Fla. 2000).
16. Wash. Rev. Code § 9A.32.050.
17. Idaho Code Ann. § 18-4003.
18. La. Rev. Stat. Ann. § 14.30.1.
19. Ark. Code Ann. § 5-10-103.
20. *Midgett v. State*, 729 S.W.2d 410 (Ark. 1987).
21. *Alston v. State*, 643 A.2d 468 (Md. Ct. Spec. App. 1994).
22. *Commonwealth v. Malone*, 47 A.2d 445 (Pa. 1946).
23. Cal. Penal Code § 188.
24. *State v. Doub*, 95 P.3d 116 (Kan. App. 2004).
25. *Commonwealth v. Malone*, 47 A.2d at 445.
26. *Banks v. State*, 211 S.W. 217 (Tex. 1919).
27. *Alston v. State*, 643 A.2d at 468.
28. *State v. Davidson*, 987 P.2d 335 (Kan. 1999).
29. *People v. Stamp*, 82 Cal. Rptr. 598 (Cal. Ct. App. 1969).
30. *People v. Fuller*, 150 Cal. Rptr. 515 (Cal. Ct. App. 1978).
31. *Regina v. Serne*, 16 Cox C.C. 311 (1887).
32. *Enmund v. Florida*, 458 U.S. 782 (1982).
33. Va. Code Ann. § 18.2-32.
34. Mo. Rev. Stat. § 565.021.
35. *People v. Burroughs*, 678 P.2d 894 (Cal. 1984).
36. *Allen v. State*, 690 So.2d 1332 (Fla. 2d Dist. Ct. App. 1998).
37. *Lester v. State*, 737 So.2d 1149 (Fla.2d. Dist. Ct. App. 1999).
38. *Parker v. State*, 570 So.2d 1048 (Fla. 1st Dist. Ct. App. 1990).
39. *Campbell v. State*, 444 A.2d 1034 (Md. 1982).
40. *Commonwealth v. Campbell*, 87 Mass. (7 Allen) 541 (1963).
41. *Kinchion v. State*, 81 P.3d 681 (Okla. Crim. App. 2003).
42. Oliver Wendell Holmes Jr., *The Common Law* (New York, NY: Dover Press, 1991), pp. 57–58.
43. *State v. Gounagias*, 153 P. 9 (Wash. 1901).
44. *Keeler v. Superior Court*, 470 P.2d 617 (Cal. 1970).
45. Cal. Penal Code § 187(a).
46. *State v. Lamy*, 158 N.H. 511 (2009).
47. *Commonwealth v. Cass*, 467 N.E.2d 1324 (Mass. 1984).
48. *Roe v. Wade*, 410 U.S. 113 (1973).
49. *People v. Davis*, 872 P.2d 591 (Cal. 1994).
50. 18 U.S.C. § 1841; 10 U.S.C. § 919a.
51. *Kilmon v. State*, 905 A.2d 306 (Md. 2006).
52. *Whitner v. South Carolina*, 492 S.E.2d 777 (1995).
53. *State v. Fierro*, 603 P.2d 74 (Ariz. 1979).
54. *State v. Rogers*, 992 S.W.3d 393 (Tenn. 1999), aff'd 532 U.S. 451 (2001).
55. *Commonwealth v. Casanova*, 708 N.E.2d 86 (Mass. 1999).
56. Cal. Penal Code § 194.
57. Wayne R. LaFave, *Criminal Law*, 3rd ed. (St. Paul, MN: West, 2000), p. 18.

CHAPTER 8

1. Ga. Code Ann. § 16-5-22.
2. American Law Institute, Model Penal Code and Commentaries, § 211.1(1)(a)(b).
3. 720 Ill. Comp. Stat. 5/12-1.
4. Ga. Code Ann. § 16-5-23.1.
5. Cal. Penal Code § 242.
6. Minn. Stat. § 609.226.
7. *State v. Sherer*, 60 P.3d 1010 (Mont. 2002).
8. *State v. Humphries*, 586 P.2d 130 (Wash. Ct. App. 1978).
9. Ga. Code Ann. § 16-5-23.1.
10. Ga. Code Ann. § 16-5-24.
11. 720 Ill. Comp. Stat. 5/12-4.
12. S.D. Codified Laws § 22-18-1-3.
13. Fla. Stat. 784.045(2)(b).
14. Minn. Stat. § 609.228.
15. Cal. Penal Code §§ 243.2, 243.25, 243.3, 243.65.
16. 720 Ill. Comp. Stat. 5/12-21.

17. *United States v. Mullett,* 767 F.3d 585 (2014).
18. Mass. Gen. Laws ch. 265, § 15A.
19. *State v. Basting,* 572 N.W.2d 281 (Minn. 1997).
20. *State v. Davis,* 540 N.W.2d 88 (Minn. App. 1995).
21. *State v. Mings,* 289 N.W.2d 497 (Minn. 1980).
22. *State v. Coauette,* 601 N.W.2d 443 (Minn. App. 1999).
23. Cal. Penal Code § 203.
24. Cal. Penal Code § 206.
25. Ga. Code Ann. § 16-5-20.
26. Cal. Penal Code § 240.
27. 720 Ill. Comp. Stat. 5/12-1.
28. Cal. Penal Code § 241.3.
29. Ohio Rev. Code Ann. § 2903.22.
30. Wayne R. LaFave, *Criminal Law,* 3rd ed. (St. Paul, MN: West, 2000), pp. 376–377.
31. *Wilson v. State,* 53 Ga. 205 (1874).
32. Ga. Code Ann. § 16-5-21.
33. 720 Ill. Comp. Stat. 5/12-2.
34. 720 Ill. Comp. Stat. 5/12-2-5.
35. S.D. Codified Laws § 22-18-1.
36. Centers for Disease Control and Prevention, *National Intimate Partner and Sexual Violence Survey* (2010), http://www.cdc.gov/ViolencePrevention/pdf/NISVS_FactSheet-a.pdf
37. 720 ILCS 5/12-7.3.
38. 720 ILCS 5/12-7.5.
39. LaFave, *Criminal Law,* p. 787.
40. *Coker v. Georgia,* 433 U.S. 584 (1977).
41. *Kennedy v. Louisiana,* 433 U.S. 407 (2008).
42. *State v. Smith,* 436 A.2d 38 (N.J. 1981).
43. National Center for Victims of Crime, *Acquaintance Rape Fact Sheet* (1998), http://www.wistv.com/Global/story.asp?s=273237&clienttype=printable
44. Susan Estrich, *Real Rape* (Cambridge, MA: Harvard University Press, 1987).
45. Roni Caryn Rabin, "Men Struggle for Rape Awareness," *The New York Times* (January 23, 2012), http://www.nytimes.com/2012/01/24/health/as-victims-men-struggle-for-rape-awareness.html?pagewanted=all&_r=0
46. LaFave, *Criminal Law,* p. 762.
47. *State of New Jersey in the Interest of M.T.S.,* 609 A.2d 1266 (N.J. 1992).
48. William Blackstone, *Commentaries on the Laws of England,* vol. 4 (Chicago: University of Chicago Press, 1979), p. 215.
49. LaFave, *Criminal Law,* p. 755.
50. Blackstone, *Commentaries on the Laws of England,* p. 213.
51. *State v. Rusk,* 434 A.2d 720 (Md. 1981).
52. *Brown v. State,* 106 N.W. 536 (Wis. 1906).
53. *State v. Schuster,* 282 S.W.3d 553 (Mo. 1955).
54. LaFave, *Criminal Law,* pp. 773–774.
55. LaFave, *Criminal Law,* pp. 775–777.
56. *People v. Minkowski,* 23 Cal. Rptr. 92 (Cal. Ct. App. 1962).
57. *Boro v. Superior Court,* 210 Cal. Rptr. 92 (Cal. Ct. App. 1985).
58. American Law Institute, *Model Penal Code and Commentaries,* vol. 1, pt. 2 (Philadelphia, PA: American Law Institute, 1980), pp. 305–306.
59. LaFave, *Criminal Law,* p. 744.
60. LaFave, *Criminal Law,* pp. 780–781.
61. *People v. Banks,* 552 N.E.2d 131 (N.Y. 1996).
62. 13 V.S.A §§3252, 3253.
63. Ind. Code Ann. § 35-42-4-1.
64. *Stogner v. California,* 539 U.S. 607 (2003).
65. *Smith v. Doe,* 538 U.S. 84 (2003).
66. *In the Interest of J.B., et al.,* No. J-44A-G-2014 (Pa. Dec. 29, 2014).
67. American Law Institute, *Model Penal Code and Commentaries,* p. 346.
68. Cal. Penal Code § 263.
69. *State v. Kidwell,* 556 P.2d 20 (Ariz. Ct. App. 1976).
70. LaFave, *Criminal Law,* pp. 762–764.
71. *Commonwealth v. Berkowitz,* 609 A.2d 1338 (Pa. Super. Ct. 1992), aff'd, 641 A.2d 1161 (Pa. 1994).
72. Cal. Penal Code § 261.
73. Mich. Comp. Laws § 750.520(b)(1)(e).
74. *Commonwealth v. Mlinarich,* 542 A.2d 1335 (Pa. 1988).
75. *In the Interest of M.T.S.,* 609 A.2d 1266 (N.J. 1992).
76. Joshua Dressler, *Understanding Criminal Law,* 3rd ed. (New York, NY: Lexis, 2001), p. 533.
77. Cal. Penal Code § 261.
78. Texas Penal Code § 22.011.
79. *Commonwealth v. Mlinarich,* 542 A.2d at 1335.
80. *People v. Mayberry,* 542 P.2d 1337 (Cal. 1997).
81. *Tyson v. State,* 619 N.E.2d 276 (Ind. Ct. App. 1993).
82. LaFave, *Criminal Law,* p. 778.
83. LaFave, *Criminal Law,* pp. 778–779.
84. Ill. Comp. Stat. 5/12-14 (a)(2).
85. *People v. John Z.,* 60 P.3d 183 (Cal. 2003).
86. *People v. Abbott,* 19 Wend. 192 (N.Y. 1838).
87. *State v. Colbath,* 540 A.2d 1212 (N.H. 1988).
88. *People v. Wilhelm,* 476 N.W.2d 753 (Mich. Ct. App. 1991).
89. *State v. Marks,* 647 P.2d 1292 (Kan. 1982).
90. *State v. Obeta,* 796 N.W.2d 282 (Minn. 2011).
91. *People v. Shreck,* 22 P.3d 68 (Colo. 2001).
92. *State v. Obeta,* 796 N.W.2d at 282.
93. *Henson v. Indiana,* 535 N.E.2d 1189 (Ind. 1989).
94. Cal. Penal Code §§ 243.4(e), 243.4(e)(6)(J).
95. Cal. Penal Code § 273.5.
96. Ind. Code §§ 34-26-5-1, 34-6-2-44.8.
97. 18 U.S.C. § 116.
98. *People v. Chessman,* 238 P.2d 1001 (Cal. 1951).
99. *People v. Daniels,* 71 Cal.2d 1119 (1969).
100. *Faison v. State,* 399 So. 2d 19 (Dist. Ct. Fla. 1981).
101. *People v. Aguilar,* 16 Cal. Rptr.3d 231 (Cal. Ct. App. 2004).
102. *People v. Majors,* 92 P.3d 360 (Cal. 2004).
103. 720 ILCS 5/10-5.
104. *People v. Hampton,* 212 Ill. App. 10656U.
105. Idaho Code Ann. §§ 18-2901, 18-2902.
106. Ark. Code Ann. § 5-11-104.
107. *People v. Cohoon,* 42 N.E.2d 969 (Ill. App. Ct. 1942).
108. *McKendree v. Christy,* 172 N.E.2d 380 (Ill. App. Ct. 1961).
109. Rollin M. Perkins and Ronald N. Boyce, *Criminal Law,* 3rd ed. (Mineola, NY: Foundation Press, 1982), p. 224.
110. Wis. Stat. §940.31.
111. Ala. Code § 13A-6-41.
112. *Cole v. State,* 942 So.2d 1010 (Fla. Dist. Ct. 2006).

CHAPTER 9

1. *People v. Hoban,* 88 N.E. 806, 807 (Ill. 1909).
2. *Anon. v. The Sheriff of London,* Year Book 13 Edw. IV f.9, p 1.5 (1473).
3. Joshua Dressler, *Understanding Criminal Law,* 3rd ed. (New York, NY: Lexis, 2001), pp. 550–551.
4. Rollin M. Perkins and Ronald N. Boyce, *Criminal Law,* 3rd ed. (Mineola, NY: Foundation Press, 1982), p. 298.
5. Dressler, *Understanding Criminal Law,* p. 550.
6. Dressler, *Understanding Criminal Law,* p. 553.
7. Dressler, *Understanding Criminal Law,* p. 554.
8. *Wilkinson v. State,* 60 So.2d 786 (Miss. 1952).
9. *Smith v. State,* 74 S.E. 1093 (Ga. 1912).
10. Tex. Code § 31.03.
11. Cal. Penal Code §§ 484–502.9.
12. Wayne R. LaFave, *Criminal Law,* 3rd ed. (St. Paul, MN: West, 2000), p. 813.
13. S.C. Code Ann. § 16-13-30.
14. Tex. Code § 31.03.
15. Pa. Cons. Stat. § 3903(c)(1)-(3).
16. Cal. Penal Code § 487.
17. *People v. Gasparik,* 420 N.E.2d 40 (N.Y. 1978).
18. *Rex v. Bazeley,* 2 Leach 835, 168 Eng. Rep. 517 (1799).
19. *Batin v. State,* 38 P.3d 990 (Nev. 2002).
20. *United States v. Alvarez,* 567 U.S. __ (2012).
21. Tex. Code § 31.02.
22. LaFave, *Criminal Law,* p. 850.
23. Perkins and Boyce, *Criminal Law,* pp. 343–344.
24. Cal. Penal Code § 211.
25. *People v. Braverman,* 173 N.E. 55 (Ill. 1930).
26. LaFave, *Criminal Law,* pp. 869–870.
27. Fla. Stat. § 812.13.
28. American Law Institute, *Model Penal Code and Commentaries,* vol. 1, pt. 11 (Philadelphia, PA: American Law Institute, 1980), p. 104.
29. Fla. Stat. § 812.13.
30. Cal. Penal Code § 215.
31. N.J. Stat. Ann. § 2C:15-1.
32. Va. Code Ann. § 18.2-58.1.
33. Fla. Stat. § 812.133.
34. William Blackstone, *Commentaries on the Laws of England,* vol. 4 (Chicago, IL: University of Chicago Press, 1979), p. 141.
35. Mich. Comp. Laws §§ 750.213–214.
36. N.Y. Penal Law § 155.05.
37. *State v. Crone,* 545 N.W.2d 267 (Iowa 1996).
38. *State v. Harrington,* 260 A.2d 692 (Vt. 1969).
39. American Law Institute, *Model Penal Code and Commentaries,* p. 67.
40. Blackstone, *Commentaries on the Laws of England,* p. 223.
41. *Taylor v. United States,* 495 U.S. 575 (1990).
42. *State v. Miller,* 954 P.2d 925 (Wash. Ct. App. 1998).
43. *State v. Roberts,* 2004 Wash. App. LEXIS 255 (Wash. Ct. App. 2004).
44. *Sears v. State,* 713 P.2d 1218 (Alaska Ct. App. 1986).
45. *Dixon v. State,* 855 So. 2d 1245 (Fla. Dist. Ct. App. 2003).
46. *Stowell v. People,* 90 P.2d 520 (Colo. 1939).
47. 720 Ill. Comp. Stat. 5/19-1(a).
48. *State v. Wentz,* 68 P.3d 282 (Wash. 2003).
49. Cal. Penal Code § 459.
50. 18 Pa. Cons. Stat. § 3502(d).
51. *Ellyson v. State,* 603 N.E.2d 1369 (Ind. Ct. App. 1992).
52. LaFave, *Criminal Law,* p. 890.
53. *Jewell v. State,* 672 N.E. 417 (Ind. App. 1996).
54. 18 Pa. Cons. Stat. § 3502(d).
55. Cal. Penal Code § 464.
56. Ariz. Rev. Stat. Ann. § 13-1506–1508.
57. Idaho Code Ann. § 18-1406.
58. 18 Pa. Cons. Stat. § 3502.
59. *State v. Stinton,* 89 P.3d 717 (Wash. Ct. App. 2004).
60. *Williams v. State,* 600 N.E.2d 962 (Ind. Ct. App. 1993).
61. N.J. Stat. Ann. § 2C:17-lb.
62. Fla. Stat. § 806.01(1).
63. 720 Ill. Comp. Stat. 5/201.1.
64. Fla. Stat. § 806.01(2).
65. Rev. Code Wash. 9A.48.030.
66. Rev. Code Wash. 9A.20.021.
67. Cal. Penal Code §§ 451–452.

CHAPTER 10

1. Edwin H. Sutherland, *White Collar Crime: The Uncut Version* (New Haven, CT: Yale University Press, 1983), p. 7.
2. *New York Cent. & H.R.R. Co. v. United States,* 212 U.S. 481 (1909).
3. *United States v. Dotterweich,* 320 U.S. 277 (1943).
4. *United States v. Park,* 421 U.S. 658 (1971).
5. *United States v. Dotterweich,* 320 U.S. at 281.
6. *People v. Travers,* 52 Cal.App.3d 111 (1975).
7. Wayne R. LaFave, *Criminal Law,* 3rd ed. (St. Paul, MN: West, 2000), p. 275.
8. LaFave, *Criminal Law,* pp. 275–276.
9. *United States v. Allegheny Bottling Company,* 695 F. Supp. 856 (E.D. Va. 1988), aff'd 870 F.2d 655 (4th Cir. 1989).
10. *Commonwealth v. Penn Valley Resorts, Inc.,* 494 A.2d 1139 (Pa. Super. 1985).
11. Ellen S. Podgor and Jerold Israel, *White Collar Crime in a Nutshell,* 3rd ed. (St. Paul, MN: West, 1997), pp. 205–216.
12. 29 U.S.C. § 651.
13. 29 U.S.C. § 666.
14. David Barstow, "U.S. Rarely Seeks Charges for Deaths in Workplace," *The New York Times* (December 22, 2003).
15. *People v. O'Neil,* 550 N.E.2d 1090 (Ill. App. 1990).
16. *People v. Pymm,* 565 N.E.2d 1 (N.Y. 1990).
17. 18 U.S.C. §§ 1348–1350.
18. *Diamond v. Oreamuno,* 248 N.E.2d 910 (N.Y. 1969).
19. *United States v. O'Hagan,* 521 U.S. 642 (1998).
20. 18 U.S.C. § 1343.
21. 18 U.S.C. § 371.
22. *United States v. Duff,* 336 F. Supp. 3d 852 (N.D. Ill. 2004).
23. *United States v. Jenkins,* 943 F.2d 167 (2nd Cir. 1991).
24. *United States v. Goodman,* 945 F.2d 125 (6th Cir. 1991).
25. 18 U.S.C. § 1347.
26. *United States v. Baldwin,* 277 F. Supp. 2d 67 (D.D.C. 2003).
27. *United States v. Lucien,* 347 F.3d 45 (2nd Cir. 2003).
28. *United States v. Miles,* 360 F.3d 472 (5th Cir. 2004).

29. *United States v. Franklin-El,* 554 F.3d 903 (10th Cir. 2009).
30. *Northern Pacific Railroad Co. v. United States,* 356 U.S. 1 (1958).
31. 15 U.S.C. § 1.
32. *United States v. Azzarelli Construction Co. and John F. Azzarelli,* 612 F.2d 292 (7th Cir. 1979).
33. *United States v. Allegheny Bottling Co.,* 695 F. Supp. 856 (E.D. Va. 1988).
34. Utah Code §§ 7606-1101–1104.
35. *Flores-Figueroa v. United States,* 556 U.S. 646 (2009).
36. *City of Liberal Kansas v. Vargas,* 24 P.3d 155 (Kan. App. 2000).
37. *United States v. Johnson,* 971 F.2d 562 (10th Cir. 1998).
38. *United States v. Jackson,* 935 F.2d 832 (7th Cir. 1991).
39. 31 U.S.C. §§ 5313, 5322, 5324.
40. *Ratzlaf v. United States,* 510 U.S. 135 (1994).
41. 26 U.S.C. § 7201.
42. 26 U.S.C. § 7202.
43. 26 U.S.C. § 7206.
44. 26 U.S.C. § 7203.
45. 26 U.S.C. § 7206.
46. *Cheek v. United States,* 498 U.S. 192 (1991).
47. *Lund v. Commonwealth,* 232 S.E.2d 745 (Va. 1977).
48. *People v. Puesan,* 973 N.Y.S.2d 121 (N.Y. App. Div., 2013).
49. 18 U.S.C. § 1030(a)(6)(A)(B).
50. 18 U.S.C. §1030(a)(7).
51. 18 U.S.C. § 1030(a)(5)(A).
52. 18 U.S.C. § 1030(a)(2).
53. 15 U.S.C. §§ 7701–7713.
54. Marcella Bombardieri, "Aaron Swartz and MIT: The Inside Story," *The Boston Globe* (March 29, 2014), https://www.bostonglobe.com/metro/2014/03/29/the-inside-story-mit-and-aaron-swartz/YvJZ5P6VHaPJusReuaN7SI/story.html.
55. 17 U.S.C. § 302(a).
56. 17 U.S.C. § 506.
57. 17 U.S.C. § 107.
58. 17 U.S.C. § 2319.
59. 18 U.S.C. § 2318.
60. 17 U.S.C. § 506; 18 U.S.C. § 2319.
61. 18 U.S.C. § 2320.
62. 18 U.S.C. §§ 1831–1832.
63. 18 U.S.C. §§ 1961–1963.
64. *United States v. Robertson,* 514 U.S. 669 (1995).
65. *United States v. Local 560 of the International Brotherhood of Teamsters,* 780 F.2d 267 (3rd Cir. 1985).
66. *United States v. Thompson,* 685 F. 993 (6th Cir. 1982).

CHAPTER 11

1. William Blackstone, *Commentaries on the Laws of England,* vol. 4 (Chicago, IL: University of Chicago Press, 1969), pp. 142–152.
2. Wis. Stat. § 947.01.
3. ILCS CS 5/26-1.
4. Ariz. Rev. Stat. § 13-2904.
5. *State v. McCarthy,* 659 N.W.2d 808 (Minn. App. 2003).
6. *People v. Barron,* 808 N.E.2d 1051 (Ill. App. 2004).
7. *State v. A.S.,* 626 N.W.2d 712 (Wis. 2001).
8. American Law Institute, *Model Penal Code and Commentaries,* vol. 3, pt. 2 (Philadelphia, PA: American Law Institute, 1985), pp. 313–314.
9. *Cole v. Arkansas,* 338 U.S. 345 (1949).
10. N.Y. Penal Law §§ 240.05, 240.06.
11. N.Y. Penal Law §§ 240.10, 240.15.
12. Ohio Laws § 2817.04.
13. *J.B.A. v. State,* 2004 Utah App. 450 (2004).
14. *Atwater v. Lago Vista,* 532 U.S. 318 (2000).
15. George I. Kelling and James Q. Wilson, "Broken Windows," *The Atlantic* (March 1982), http://www.theatlantic.com/magazine/archive/1982/03/broken-windows/304465/.
16. American Law Institute, *Model Penal Code and Commentaries,* p. 385.
17. American Law Institute, *Model Penal Code and Commentaries,* pp. 385–386.
18. *Mayor of the City of New York v. Miln,* 36 U.S. 102 (1837).
19. *Edwards v. California,* 314 U.S. 160 (1941).
20. *Papachristou v. City of Jacksonville,* 405 U.S. 156 (1972).
21. *Kolender v. Lawson,* 461 U.S. 352 (1983).
22. *Pottinger v. City of Miami,* 810 F. Supp. 1551 (S.D. Fla. 1992).
23. *Joyce v. City and County of San Francisco,* 846 F. Supp. 843 (N.D. Cal. 1994).
24. *Loper v. New York City Police Dept.,* 999 F.2d 699 (2nd Cir. 1993).
25. *Gresham v. Peterson,* 225 F.2d 899 (7th Cir. 2000).
26. 740 ILCS 147/1.
27. *Gallo v. Acuna,* 929 P.2d 596 (Cal. 1997).
28. *City of Chicago v. Morales,* 527 U.S. 41 (1999).
29. Municipal Code of the City of Chicago, 8-4-105, 8-4-017.
30. Norval Morris and Gordon Hawkins, *The Honest Politician's Guide to Crime Control* (Chicago, IL: University of Chicago Press, 1969).
31. Patrick Devlin, *The Enforcement of Morals* (New York, NY: Oxford University Press, 1965).
32. *People v. James,* 98 Misc.2d 755 (Crim. Ct. N.Y.C. 1979).
33. Ga. Code § 16–6-9.
34. Pa. Cons. Stat. § 5902(a).
35. Cal. Penal Code § 653.22.
36. *Banks v. State* 975 N.E.2d 854 (Ind. Ct. App. 2012).
37. Pa. Cons. Stat. § 5902(e.2).
38. 18 U.S.C. § 2421.
39. *Cleveland v. United States,* 329 U.S. 67 (1946).
40. Ga. Cons. Stat. § 16–6-13(b).
41. *City of Milwaukee v. Burnette,* 637 N.W.3d 447 (Wis. App. 2001).
42. *Rex v. Curl,* 93 Eng. Rep. 849 (K.B. 1727).
43. *Roth v. United States,* 354 U.S. 476 (1957).
44. *Miller v. California,* 413 U.S. 15 (1973).
45. *New York v. Ferber,* 458 U.S. 747 (1982).
46. *American Booksellers Ass'n v. Hudnut,* 771 F.3d 323 (7th Cir. 1985).
47. 7 U.S.C. § 2137.
48. *United States v. Stevens,* 559 U.S. 460 (2010).
49. 16 U.S.C. §§ 3371–3378.
50. 16 U.S.C. §§ 703–712.
51. 16 U.S.C. §§ 1531–1543.

CHAPTER 12

1. Buddy T., "Domestic Abuse and Alcohol: Some Doubt the Role Alcohol Plays," *VeryWell* (September 27, 2015), https://www.verywell.com/domestic-abuse-and-alcohol-62643.
2. 23 U.S.C. § 158.
3. 740 ILCS 58/1.
4. Va. Code § 4.1-100.
5. IC 7.1-5-1-3.
6. Cal. Penal Law § 647(f).
7. *Powell v. Texas*, 392 U.S. 514 (1968).
8. *Foster v. State*, 2012 Ark. App. 640 (2012).
9. *Mackey v. Montrym*, 443 U.S. 1 (1979); *South Dakota v. Neville*, 459 U.S. 553 (1983).
10. *Missouri v. McNeely*, 569 U.S. ___ (2013).
11. *Millard v. State*, Ind. App. Unpub. LEXIS 1422 (Ind. App. 2012).
12. *State v. Owen*, 2012 Mo. App. LEXIS 1399 (2012).
13. *State v. Sims*, 48 N.M. 330 (N.M. 2010).
14. *State v. Butler*, 108 S.W.3d 845 (Tenn. 2003).
15. *State v. Greenman*, 148 S.W.3d 347 (Minn. App. 2013).
16. *State v. Hammond*, 571 A.2d 940 (N.J. 1990).
17. *State v. Inglis*, 698 A.2d 1290 (Law Div. N.J. 1997).
18. *State v. Romano*, 809 A.2d 158 (Super. Ct. N.J. 2012).
19. *State v. Squires*, 519 A.2d 1154 (Vt. 1986).
20. American Gaming Association, *State of the States* (January 1, 2012), https://www.americangaming.org/research/reports/state-states-12.
21. *People v. Hua*, 885 N.Y.S.2d 380 (Crim. Ct. N.Y.C. 2009).
22. Fla. Stat. §§ 849.231–849.232.
23. *Town of Mount Pleasant v. Chimento*, 737 S.E.2d 830 (S.C. 2013).
24. 18 U.S.C. § 1084.
25. 31 U.S.C. §§ 5361–5366.
26. 31 U.S.C. § 5361.
27. 15 U.S.C. § 1171.
28. 22 U.S.C. § 2121.
29. 18 U.S.C. § 1084.
30. 15 U.S.C. § 1953.
31. 18 U.S.C. § 1955.
32. 15 U.S.C. § 3001.
33. 18 U.S.C. § 178.
34. 18 U.S.C. § 1081.
35. 15 U.S.C. § 1953.
36. 31 U.S.C. § 5361.
37. Michelle Alexander, *The New Jim Crow Mass Incarceration in the Age of Colorblindness* (New York, NY: New Press, 2010), pp. 47–57.
38. National Drug Intelligence Center, *National Drug Threat Assessment* (2011), http://www.justice.gov/archive/ndic/topics/ndtas.htm.
39. *United States v. Doremus*, 249 U.S. 86 (1919).
40. *Webb v. United States*, 249 U.S. 96 (1919).
41. 12 U.S.C. § 801.
42. 21 U.S.C. § 841(a)(1).
43. *United States v. De La Torre*, 599 F.3d 1198 (10th Cir. 2010).
44. *State v. Harrison*, 818 A.2d 487 (N.J. App. 2003).
45. *State v. Christensen*, 2012 Minn. App. Unpub. LEXIS 1133.
46. *State v. Webb*, 648 N.W.2d 72 (Iowa 2002).
47. *Fabricant v. Henry*, 35 F.3d 570 (9th Cir. 1994); *Beeler v. State*, 807 N.E.2d 789 (Ind. App. 2004).
48. *People v. Leal*, 64 Cal. 2d 504 (1966).
49. *People v. Rubacalba*, 6 Cal. 4th 62 (1993).
50. 21 U.S.C. § 841(a).
51. *State v. Smith*, La. App. LEXIS 1608 (2012).
52. *Commonwealth v. Stephens*, 2012 Mass. App. LEXIS 280 (2012).
53. *State v. Smith*, 2011-Ohio-6466.
54. Charlie Savage, "Obama Curbs Sentences of 8 in Crack Cases," *The New York Times* (December 20, 2013).
55. Sari Horowitz and Ann E. Marinow, "President Obama Grants Early Release to 61 More Federal Drug Offenders," *The Washington Post* (March 30, 2016), https://www.washingtonpost.com/world/national-security/president-obama-grants-early-release-to-61-more-federal-drug-offenders/2016/03/30/7256bb60-f683-11e5-8b23-538270a1ca31_story.html.
56. Julie Hirschfeld and Peter Baker, "In 'Fairness,' Obama Commutes Sentences for 95, Mostly Drug Offenders," *The New York Times* (December 18, 2015).
57. *Ravin v. State*, 537 P.2d 494 (Alaska, 1975).
58. *United States v. Oakland Cannabis Buyers Cooperative*, 532 U.S. 483 (2001).
59. *Gonzales v. Raich*, 545 U.S. 1 (2005).
60. *Gonzales v. O Centro Espirita*, 546 U.S. 418 (2006).
61. N.J.S.A. 2C: 21-1; N.J.S.A. 2C: 35-1; N.J.S.A. 2C: 35-21; N.J.S.A. 2C: 35-10.5.
62. California Health and Safety Code § 11364.
63. *United States v. Janus Industries*, 48 F.3d 1548 (10th Cir. 1988).
64. *Geiger v. City of Eagan*, 618 F.2d 26 (8th Cir. 1980).
65. *Hoffman Estates v. Flipside*, 455 U.S. 489 (1982).
66. *People v. Carreon*, 2012 Ill.App.2d 100391.
67. RCW § 69.50.505.
68. *United States v. Good Real Property*, 510 U.S. 43 (1993).
69. 18 U.S.C. § 983.
70. *United States v. Good Real Property*, 510 U.S. at 43.
71. *United States v. Ursery*, 518 U.S. 267 (1996).
72. *Skinner v. Railway Labor Executives' Association*, 489 U.S. 602 (1989).
73. *National Treasury Employees Union v. Von Raab*, 489 U.S. 656 (1989).
74. *Vernonia School District 47J v. Acton*, 525 U.S. 646 (1995).
75. *Board of Education of Independent School District No. 92 of Pottawatomie County v. Earls*, 536 U.S. 822 (2002).
76. *Safford Unified School District v. Redding*, 557 U.S. 364 (2009).
77. 21 U.S.C. § 829.

CHAPTER 13

1. Art. 1, § 9, cl. 8; Art. 1, § 6, cl. 2; Art. I, § 9, cl. 7.
2. *Page v. State*, 980 So. 2d 528 (Fla. App. Ct. 2008).
3. 18 U.S.C. § 201(c)(1)(B).
4. 720 ILCS 5/33-1.
5. Rollin M. Perkins and Ronald N. Boyce, *Criminal Law*, 3rd ed. (Mineola, NY: Foundation Press, 1982), pp. 528–538.

6. Model Penal Code § 240(8).

7. Model Penal Code § 240.0 (1).

8. American Law Institute, *Model Penal Code and Commentaries*, Part 11, § 240-§ 251.4 (Philadelphia, PA: American Law Institute, 1980), p. 37.

9. Fla. Stat. § 838.015(2).

10. *State v. Bowling*, 427 P.2d 928 (Ariz. App. 1967).

11. *State v. Stanley*, 200 S.E.2d 223 (N.C. 1973).

12. 720 Il.CS 5/33-1; 9A.68.010 RCW.

13. *United States v. Sun Diamond Growers*, 526 U.S. 398 (1999).

14. N.J. Stat. § 2C:21-10.

15. 18 U.S.C. §1952(b); *United States v. Welch*, 327 F.3d 1081 (10th Cir. 2003).

16. N.Y. Penal Law §§ 180.35, 180.45.

17. 5 U.S.C. § 78dd-1.

18. 18 U.S.C. § 872.

19. 18 U.S.C. § 873.

20. 18 U.S.C. § 876.

21. 18 U.S.C. § 876.

22. 18 U.S.C. § 1623.

23. Cal. Penal Code § 118.

24. N.Y. Penal Law §§ 210.10, 210.15.

25. *Bronston v. United States*, 409 U.S. 352 (1973).

26. *United States v. Thomas*, No. 08-10450 (9th Cir. 2010).

27. *United States v. Gremillion*, 464 F.2d 90 (5th Cir. 1972).

28. 18 U.S.C. § 1623(c).

29. *United States v. Fornaro*, 894 F.2d 58 (2nd Cir. 1990).

30. *Riley v. United States*, 647 A.2d 1165 (D.C. 1994).

31. 18 U.S.C. § 1510.

32. 18 U.S.C. § 1512.

33. 18 U.S.C. § 1520.

34. 18 U.S.C. § 1512(b)(1).

35. 720 ILCS 5/31-4.

36. *People v. Brake*, 783 N.E.2d 1084 (Ill. App. 2003).

37. *People v. Danielak*, 2012 Mich. App. LEXIS 2285.

38. *People v. Kissner*, 292 Mich. App. 26 (2011).

39. Ohio Rev. Code Ann. § 2921.23 (a).

40. *State v. Floyd*, 584 A.2d 115 (Conn. 1991).

41. § 9A76.040 RCW.

42. *In re B.M.*, 2012 Ohio 6221.

43. *Patterson v. State*, 973 N.E.2d 1266 (Ind. App. 2012).

44. *State v. Kornilov*, 2012 Ohio 6218.

45. *State v. Miller*, 172 S.W.3d 838 (Mo. App. Ct. 2005).

46. *State v. Herrin*, 2012 Ariz. App. Unpub. LEXIS 975.

47. *Williams v. State*, 2012 Md. App. LEXIS 147 (Ct. Spec. App. 2012).

48. *Shoultz v. State*, 735 N.E.2d 818 (Ind. App. 2000).

49. *State v. Ramsdell*, 285 A.2d 399 (R.I. 1971).

50. 72 ILCS /32-1.

51. Col. Stat. §18-8-108.

52. ORC § 292.21.

53. Ga. Code Ann. § 16-10-90.

54. N.M. Stat. Ann. § 30-22-6.

55. 18 U.S.C. § 4.

56. Perkins and Boyce, *Criminal Law*, pp. 560–571.

57. 18 U.S.C. § 751.

58. 18 U.S.C. § 752.

59. 18 U.S.C. § 1073.

60. Pa. Cons. Stat. § 5121.

61. *People v. Unger*, 338 N.E. 2d 442 (Ill. App. 1975).

62. *State v. Pichon*, 811 P.2d 517 (Kan. App. 1991).

63. *United States v. Bailey*, 444 U.S. 394 (1980).

64. *People v. Martin*, 298 N.W.2d 900 (Mich. App. 1980).

65. *Shillitani v. United States*, 384 U.S. 364 (1966).

66. Perkins and Boyce, *Criminal Law*, pp. 591–592.

67. *Bernard v. Smith*, 2012 Tenn. App. LEXIS 711.

68. *Ex parte Robinson*, 86 U.S. 505 (1873).

69. *Commonwealth v. Washington*, 353 A.2d 806 (Pa. 1976).

70. *In re Williams*, 509 F.2d 949 (2nd Cir. 1975).

71. *Davila v. State*, 75 So.3d 192 (Fla. 2011).

72. *Eaton v. City of Tulsa*, 415 U.S. 697 (1974).

73. *Greenberg v. United States*, 849 F.2d 1251 (1987).

74. *Bloom v. Illinois*, 391 U.S. 194 (1968).

75. N.Y. Penal Law §§ 215.50–215.52.

76. *United States v. United Mine Workers of America*, 330 U.S. 258 (1947).

77. *State v. Geiger*, 978 N.E.2d 1061 (Ill. 2012).

78. 2 U.S.C. § 192.

CHAPTER 14

1. *Cramer v. United States*, 325 U.S. 1 (1945).

2. *United States v. Greathouse*, 26 F. Cas. 18 (C.C.N.D. Cal. 1863) (No. 15,254).

3. *D'Aquino v. United States*, 192 F.2d 338 (9th Cir. 1951).

4. *Dennis v. United States*, 341 U.S. 494 (1951).

5. *Yates v. United States*, 354 U.S. 298 (1957).

6. 18 U.S.C. § 2153.

7. 18 U.S.C. § 2155.

8. 18 U.S.C. §§ 2152, 2156.

9. *United States v. Kabat*, 797 F.2d 580 (8th Cir. 1986).

10. *United States v. Walli*, 785 F.3d 1986 (6th Cir. 2015).

11. 18 U.S.C. § 794.

12. *Gorin v. United States*, 312 U.S. 19 (1941).

13. 18 U.S.C. § 2332(b)(g)(3)–(5).

14. 18 U.S.C. § 2332.

15. 18 U.S.C. § 2332(b).

16. 18 U.S.C. § 175.

17. 49 U.S.C. § 46502.

18. 18 U.S.C. § 2339.

19. 18 U.S.C. §§ 2339A, 2339B.

20. 8 U.S.C. § 1189(a)(1).

21. *Holder v. Humanitarian Law Project*, 561 U.S. 1 (2010).

22. *United States v. Bell*, 81 F.SUPP. 3d 1301 (D.C. M.D. Fla. 2015).

23. *United States v. Lindh*, 212 F. Supp. 2d 541 (E.D. Va. 2002).

24. *Muhammad v. Commonwealth*, 619 S.E.2d 16 (Va. 2005).

25. *Arizona v. United States*, 567 U.S. ___ (2012).

26. Pub. Law No. 82-414, 66 Stat. 163.

27. Pub. Law No. 99-603, 100 Stat. 3359.

28. 8 U.S.C. § 1325(c).

29. Pub. Law No. 101-649, 104 Stat. 4978.

30. Pub. Law No. 104-208, 110 Stat. 3009.

Glossary

abandonment: an individual who completely and voluntarily renounces his or her criminal purpose is not liable for an attempt. Abandonment as a result of outside or extraneous factors does not constitute a defense.

abuse excuse: criminal defenses that involve a claim of lack of criminal responsibility based on past abuse or experiences.

access device fraud: fraud involving the theft of a personal identification number (PIN) or other identifying information used to access money.

accessories: parties responsible for the separate and lesser offense of assisting a criminal offender to avoid apprehension, prosecution, or conviction.

accessories after the fact: individuals liable for assisting an offender to avoid arrest, prosecution, or punishment.

accessories before the fact: individuals under the common law who assist an individual prior to the commission of a crime and who are not present at the scene of the crime.

accomplices: parties liable as principles before and during the commission of a crime.

acquaintance rape: rape between two individuals who know one another.

actual possession: an object within an individual's immediate physical control or on his or her person.

*actus reus***:** a criminal act, the physical or external component of a crime.

adultery: having sexual intercourse and living with a person who is married.

affirmative defenses: the burden of production, and in most cases the burden of persuasion, is on the defendant.

agency theory of felony murder: a felon is liable for a murder committed by a co-felon.

aggravated assault: an assault committed with a dangerous or deadly weapon or with the intent to threaten or to commit rape or another serious crime.

aggravated battery: a felony that typically requires serious bodily injury, the use of a dangerous or deadly weapon, or the intent to kill, rape, or seriously harm.

aggravated rape: a rape that is more harshly punished based on the use of force, injury to the victim, or the fact that the perpetrator is a stranger or other factors.

aggravated sexual assault: a sexual assault committed under circumstances deserving of a more severe punishment.

aggravating factors: factors that permit the application of the death penalty under a capital murder statute, including an offender's prior record, nature of the offense, and identity of the victim.

aggressor: individuals initiating a physical confrontation are not entitled to self-defense unless they retreat.

alibi: a defense that an accused has been somewhere else at the time of the crime.

alter ego rule: an individual intervening in defense of others possesses the rights of the person he or she is assisting.

American bystander rule: no legal duty to assist or to rescue an individual in danger.

American rule for resistance to an unlawful arrest: an individual may not resist an illegal arrest.

appellant: the individual appealing.

appellate courts: intermediate or supreme courts of appeals.

appellee: the party against whom an appeal is filed.

arson: willful and malicious burning of the dwelling of another. Modified by statute to encompass any building or structure.

assault and battery: battery is the application of force to another person. An assault may be committed either by attempting to commit a battery or by intentionally placing another in fear of a battery.

assets forfeiture: seizure pursuant to a court order of the "fruits" of illegal narcotics transactions (along with certain other crimes) or of material that was used to engage in such activity.

attempt: an intent or purpose to commit a crime, an act or acts toward the commission of the crime, and a failure to commit the crime.

attendant circumstances: the conditions or context required for a crime.

bench trial: trial before a judge without a jury.

bilateral: a conspiratorial agreement requires at least two persons with the intent to enter into the agreement who possess the intent to achieve a common criminal objective.

bill of attainder: a legislative act directed against an individual or group of individuals imposing punishment without trial.

Bill of Rights: first ten amendments to the U.S. Constitution.

binding authority: a decision that establishes a precedent.

blackmail: the taking of property through the threat to disclose secret or embarrassing information.

brain death test: the irreversible function of all brain functions is the point at which an individual is legally dead.

breach of the peace: acts that disturb or tend to disturb the tranquility of citizens.

bribery: giving, offering, or promising a benefit as well as demanding, agreeing to accept, or accepting a benefit. In other words, bribery involves

two separate crimes—that is, it punishes giving as well as receiving a bribe, and requires an intent to influence or to be influenced in the carrying out of a public duty. Bribery does not require a mutual agreement between the individuals.

brief: a written legal argument submitted to an appellate court.

broken windows theory: a failure to prevent and punish misdemeanor offenses causes major crimes.

burden of persuasion: responsibility to convince the fact finder, usually beyond a reasonable doubt.

burden of production: responsibility to produce sufficient evidence for the fact finder to consider the merits of a claim.

burglary: breaking and entry of a dwelling at night with an intent to commit a felony therein. Modified by statute to cover an illegal entry into any structure with a criminal intent.

capital felony: punishable by the death penalty or by life imprisonment in states without the death penalty.

capital murder: heinous, atrocious, and cruel killing of another. This is punishable by the death penalty or life imprisonment and in noncapital punishment states by life imprisonment. Also referred to in some states as aggravated murder.

carjacking: the taking of a motor vehicle in the possession of another from his or her person or immediate presence by force against his or her will.

case-in-chief: the prosecution's phase of the trial.

Castle Doctrine: individuals have no obligation to retreat inside their home.

causation: there must be a connection between an act and the resulting prohibited harm.

cause in fact: the defendant must be shown to be the "but for" cause of the harm or injury.

certiorari: a writ or order issued by the U.S. Supreme Court assuming jurisdiction over an appeal. Four judges must vote to review a case.

chain conspiracy: a conspiracy in which individuals are linked in a vertical chain to achieve a criminal objective.

child abduction: "an offense that requires the state to prove that the defendant 'intentionally lure[d] or attempt[ed] to lure a child under the age of 16 into a motor vehicle . . . without the consent of the parent . . . of the child for other than a lawful purpose.'"

child pornography: a juvenile engaged in actual or simulated sexual activity or in the lewd display of genitals.

choice of evils: the defense of necessity in which an individual commits a crime to avoid an imminent and greater social harm or evil.

civil commitment: a procedure for detaining psychologically troubled individuals.

civil contempt: disobedience to an order or direction of the judge by one of the litigants in a judicial proceeding.

civil law: protects the individual rather than societal interest.

code jurisdiction: acts or omissions only are punishable that are contained in state criminal code.

coincidental intervening act: a defendant's criminal act results in the victim being at a particular place at a particular time and being impacted by an independent intervening act. The defendant is responsible for foreseeable coincidental intervening acts.

collateral attack: a challenge to a conviction filed following the exhaustion of direct appeals.

combat immunity: individuals meeting standards set forth in the Geneva Convention are to be treated as prisoners of war when apprehended.

commercial bribery: accepting "money or anything of value" from a person other than one's employer and using one's position to benefit the outside individual.

common law crimes: crimes developed by the common law judges in England and supplemented by acts of Parliament and decrees issued by the king.

common law states: the common law may be applied where the legislature has not acted.

competence to stand trial: a defendant is competent to stand trial who is able to intelligently assist his or her attorney and to follow and understand the trial.

complete attempt: an individual takes every act required to commit a crime and fails to succeed.

compounding a crime: knowingly receiving or offering an item of value in return for a promise not to prosecute or not to aid in prosecution.

computer crime: crimes involving the computer, including unauthorized access to computers and computer programs and networks, modification or destruction of data and programs, and the sending of mass unsolicited messages and messages intended to trick and deceive.

concurrence: a criminal intent must trigger and coincide with a criminal act.

concurrent jurisdiction: joint authority of courts of different jurisdictions. Typically refers to joint authority of federal and state courts over a legal matter.

concurring opinion: an opinion by a judge supporting a majority or dissenting opinion, typically based on other grounds.

conspiracy: an agreement to commit a crime. Various state statutes require an overt act in furtherance of this purpose.

constitutional democracy: a constitutional system that limits the powers of the government.

constructive intent: individuals who act in a gross and wantonly reckless fashion are considered to intend the natural consequences of their actions and are guilty of a willful and intentional battery or homicide.

constructive possession: an individual who retains legal possession over property that is not within his or her actual control.

contemnor: an individual held in contempt of court.

contraband: material that is unlawful to possess or to manufacture.

controlled substances: drugs and chemicals whose manufacture, distribution, and possession are regulated by the government.

cooling of blood: the point at which an individual who has been provoked no longer is acting in response to an act of provocation.

copyright: a federal law providing that only the "creator" of an intellectual work is free to license the rights to his or her

product to other individuals, and that he or she is protected for life plus seventy years.

corporate liability: the imposition of vicarious liability on a corporate officer or corporation.

corporate murder: a killing for which a business enterprise is held criminally liable.

corpus delicti: a "body of crime" or "substance of the crime."

corroboration: at common law a rape victim's complaint was required to be supported by evidence that confirms the victim's testimony.

courts of general jurisdiction: state courts that hear serious criminal and civil cases. In some states, these courts have jurisdiction over criminal appeals from courts of limited jurisdiction.

courts of limited jurisdiction: courts with jurisdiction over a narrow range of cases. Typically refers to state courts that prosecute misdemeanors and certain felonies and hear traffic offenses, set bail, and conduct preliminary hearings. These local courts are commonly called municipal courts, police courts, or magistrates' courts.

courts of original jurisdiction: the court in which a prosecution originates.

crime: conduct that if shown to have taken place will result in a formal and solemn pronouncement of the moral condemnation of the community.

crimes against public order and morality: offenses that threaten public peace, quiet, and tranquility.

crimes against state: treason, sedition, sabotage, espionage, and terrorism and other offenses intended to harm the government.

crimes against the quality of life: misdemeanor offenses that diminish the sense of safety and security in a neighborhood.

crimes of cause and result: the intent to achieve a specific result.

criminal attempt: comprises three elements: (1) an intent or purpose to commit a crime, (2) an act or acts toward the commission of the crime, and (3) a failure to complete the crime.

criminal contempt: acts intended to impede or interfere with the justice process or that demonstrate a lack of respect for the court by denigrating, demeaning, or disregarding the judge.

criminal homicide: all homicides that are neither justified nor excused.

criminal mischief: damage or destruction of tangible property.

criminal procedure: investigation and detection of crime by the police and the procedures used at trial.

criminal trespass: unauthorized entry or remaining on the land or premises of another.

custody: temporary and limited right to control property.

cybercrime: crime committed through the use of a computer.

cyberstalking: stalking on the computer.

dangerous weapon battery: an aggravated battery under state statutes in which a dangerous weapon is used to inflict serious bodily harm.

deadly force: use of physical force or a weapon likely to cause death or serious bodily harm.

decriminalization of marijuana: reduction in criminal classification of the possession of small amounts of marijuana, which typically are subject to a small fine.

defendant: individual charged with a criminal offense.

Deferred Action for Childhood Arrivals (DACA): a law implemented by the Obama administration in June 2012 that allows undocumented immigrants who entered the country before their sixteenth birthday and before June 2007 to receive a renewable two-year work permit and exemption from deportation but does not provide a path to citizenship.

defiant trespass: entering or remaining on the property of another after receiving notice that an individual's presence is without the consent of the owner.

depraved heart murder: killing as a result of extreme recklessness and wanton unconcern and indifference to human life with malice aforethought.

derivative liability: the guilt of a party to a crime based on the criminal acts of the primary party.

diminished capacity: an excuse defense in which the defendant claims an incapacity to form the required criminal intent for the crime and should be held liable for a lesser crime.

direct criminal contempt: an insulting remark or physical assault on the judge, repeated disregard of a judge's direction to limit the length of an opening or closing statement or cross-examination of a witness, or disruptive behavior by a spectator committed in the immediate presence of the judge or court or sufficiently close to the court to impede or to interfere with the judicial process.

disclose or abstain doctrine: the obligation either to make corporate information public or to refrain from trading in the corporation's stock.

discretionary appeal: a court is not obligated to hear an appeal.

disorderly conduct: intentionally or knowingly causing or risking public inconvenience, annoyance, or alarm.

dissenting opinion: an opinion by a judge disagreeing with the majority of a multijudge court.

distracted driving: driving while doing acts that may divert an individual's attention.

domestic battery: aggravated felony battery of a spouse, a former spouse, or the mother or father of the assailant's child that results in a "traumatic condition."

domestic terrorism: a violent or dangerous act occurring within the United States intended to intimidate or coerce the civilian population or to influence government policy by intimidation or coercion or to affect the conduct of a government by mass destruction, assassination, or kidnapping.

domestic violence: violent crimes committed against any member of a household.

driving under the influence (DUI): driving while under the influence of liquor or narcotics.

driving while intoxicated (DWI): driving an automobile while intoxicated.

driving with an unlawful blood alcohol level (DUBAL): driving while one's blood alcohol level is too high, despite the fact that one's driving may be unaffected.

drug courts: courts in which, rather than sending nonviolent defendants charged with drug

possession to prison, judges, defense attorneys, prosecutors, and court professionals work together to establish goals and targets for defendants to achieve.

Drug Enforcement Administration (DEA): a "single unified command" established in 1973 by President Richard M. Nixon that conducts and coordinates the national and international war on drugs.

drug paraphernalia: items primarily intended or designed for the manufacture, processing, preparing, or concealing of narcotics and items primarily used in injecting, ingesting, and inhaling marijuana, cocaine, and hashish or other controlled substances.

dual sovereignty: sharing of power between federal and state governments. Each has different interests that permit both a state and a federal prosecution for the same crime.

Due Process Clause: the Fifth and Fourteenth Amendments to the U.S. Constitution guarantee individuals due process of law. The Fourteenth Amendment Due Process Clause incorporates most of the protections of the Bill of Rights.

duress: a crime is excused when committed to avoid what is reasonably believed to be the imminent infliction of serious physical harm or death.

Durham product test: a defendant's unlawful act is the product of a mental disease or defect.

duty to intervene: the legal obligation to act.

earnest resistance: a standard of resistance to rape under the common law.

Eighth Amendment: an amendment to the U.S. Constitution that prohibits cruel and unusual punishment.

embezzlement: the fraudulent conversion of the property of another by an individual in lawful possession.

en banc: a case before a judicial panel comprising all judges on a federal court of appeals. Literally translated as the "entire court."

English rule for resistance to an unlawful arrest: an individual may use reasonable force to resist an illegal arrest.

entrapment: defense based on governmental inducement of an otherwise innocent defendant to commit a defense (subjective test) or based on governmental conduct that falls below accepted standards and would cause an innocent individual to commit a criminal offense (objective test).

environmental crimes: crimes that damage the natural environment, including harm to the air, water, land, and natural resources.

equal protection: the Fifth and Fourteenth Amendments to the U.S. Constitution guarantee individuals equal protection of the law.

escape: knowingly fleeing custody following arrest or detention.

espionage: delivering information to a foreign government with the intent or reason to believe that it is to be used to injure the United States or to advantage a foreign government.

European bystander rule: a rule in Europe imposing a legal duty on individuals to assist those in peril.

ex post facto law: a law declaring an act criminal following the commission of the act.

excusable homicide: individuals are relieved of criminal liability based on lack of criminal intent. This includes insanity, infancy, and intoxication.

excuses: defenses in which defendants admit wrongful conduct while claiming a lack of legal responsibility based on a lack of a criminal intent or the involuntary nature of their acts.

extortion: the taking of property from another by threat of future violence or action, such as circulating secret or embarrassing information, threat of a criminal charge, or threat to inflict economic harm.

extraneous factor: a circumstance that is not created by a defendant that prevents the completion of a criminal act.

extraterritorial jurisdiction: prosecuting crimes outside of a country's national boundaries.

extrinsic force: an act of force beyond the effort required to accomplish penetration.

factual impossibility: a criminal act is prevented from being completed because of an extraneous factor.

false imprisonment: intentional and unlawful confinement or restraint of another person.

false pretenses: obtaining title and possession of property of another by a knowingly false representation of a present or past material fact with an intent to defraud that causes an individual to pass title.

federal crime of terrorism: one or more violent federal offenses calculated to influence or affect the conduct of government by intimidation or coercion, or to retaliate against government conduct.

federal criminal code: federal criminal statutes.

felony: crime punishable by death or by imprisonment for more than one year.

felony murder: a killing committed during the commission of a felony.

fiduciary relationship: a duty of care owed by a corporate official to the stockholders in a corporation.

fighting words: insulting words causing a breach of the peace.

First Amendment: an amendment to the U.S. Constitution that protects freedom of expression, assembly, and free exercise of religion.

first-degree murder: intentional and premeditated murder with malice aforethought.

first impression: a legal issue before a court with no existing precedent on which to rely.

fleeing felon rule: the common law rule permitting deadly force against a felon fleeing the police.

fleeting possession: temporary dominion and control over an object and typically not considered possession for purposes of criminal liability.

Foreign Corrupt Practices Act: established that it is illegal for an individual or company to bribe a foreign official in order to gain assistance in obtaining or retaining business.

forgery: creating a false legal document or the material modification of an existing document with the intent to deceive or to defraud others.

fornication: an unmarried person who has voluntary sexual intercourse with another individual.

Fourteenth Amendment: an amendment to the U.S. Constitution passed in 1868 to provide equal rights and opportunity for newly freed African American slaves. The Fourteenth Amendment incorporates most of the provisions of the Bill of Rights and extends these protections to the states.

Fourth Amendment: an amendment to the U.S. Constitution that protects individuals against unreasonable searches and seizures.

fraud: an intentional and knowing misrepresentation of a material (important) fact intended to induce another person to hand over money or property.

fraud in inducement: misrepresentation in regard to the purpose or benefits of a sexual relationship does not constitute rape.

fraud in the *factum*: misrepresentation in regard to the act to which an individual consents constitutes rape.

gambling: activity that is prohibited under criminal law. The element of luck typically is required to predominate over the element of skill.

gaming: activity that has been legalized by existing law or that may be exempted from coverage of the criminal law.

***Gebardi* rule:** an individual who is excluded from liability under a criminal statute may not be held legally liable as a conspirator to violate the law.

general intent: an intent to commit an *actus reus*.

Geneva Convention of 1949: international treaty on the law of war providing standards for lawful combatant status.

***Gerstein* hearing:** hearing to determine whether police possessed probable cause for an arrest.

Good Samaritan laws: legislation requiring individuals to assist an individual in peril.

grading: the categorization of homicide in accordance with the "moral blameworthiness" of the perpetrator.

grand larceny: a serious larceny, determined by the value of the property that is taken.

gratuity: an unlawful payment made to reward a public official for action taken or that will be taken in the future.

gross misdemeanor: punishable by between six and twelve months in prison.

guilty but mentally ill (GBMI): the defendant found to be guilty and mentally ill at the time of the criminal offense. The defendant is provided with psychiatric care while incarcerated. This is distinguished from a verdict of not guilty by reason of insanity (NGRI).

hate speech: speech that denigrates, humiliates, and attacks individuals on account of race, religion, ethnicity, nationality, gender, sexual preference, or other personal characteristics and preferences.

health care fraud: fraud in which health care providers or consumers knowingly and willfully execute or attempt to execute a scheme involving false statements intended to obtain, keep, or qualify for benefits or to increase benefits under a federal health care program.

heat of passion: acting in response to adequate provocation.

human trafficking: providing or obtaining the labor of another through threat of serious harm or restraint or trafficking in persons who are to be subjected to slavery or forced labor.

identity theft: stealing of an individual's personal identifying information.

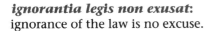

ignorantia legis non exusat: ignorance of the law is no excuse.

immigration law: protects the border of the United States and the sovereign right of the United States to control who may enter and who may remain in the country.

imperfect self-defense: an honest but unreasonable belief in the justifiability of self-defense that results in a conviction for manslaughter rather than murder.

implied consent laws: laws that provide that individuals who obtain a driver's license impliedly have consented to the administration of a urine or blood test or Breathalyzer to determine their blood alcohol content.

inchoate crimes: attempts, conspiracy, and solicitation. Each requires a specific purpose to accomplish a criminal objective and an act in furtherance of the intent. These offenses are punished to the same extent or to a lesser extent than the target crime.

incitement to violent action: words provoking individuals to breach the peace.

incomplete attempt: an individual abandons or is prevented from completing an attempt due to an extraneous or intervening factor.

inconsistent statements: divergent statements made under oath within the period of the statute of limitations, in which the prosecution may establish falsity by offering both statements into evidence without specifying which of the two statements is false. The defendant may offer the defense that he or she genuinely believed at the time that each of the statements was true.

incorporation: the Due Process Clause of the Fourteenth Amendment to the U.S.

Constitution is interpreted to include most of the rights contained in the first eight amendments and extends these protections to the states.

indecent exposure: an act of public indecency.

indictment: an accusation of criminal activity returned by a grand jury.

indirect criminal contempt: acts that occur outside the presence of the court that impede or interfere with the judicial process.

infamous crimes: deserving of shame or disgrace.

infancy: at common law there was an irrebuttable presumption that children under seven lack criminal intent. In the case of children over seven and under fourteen there was a rebuttable presumption of a lack of capacity to form a criminal intent. Individuals over fourteen were considered to possess the same capacity as an adult.

information: a document signed by a prosecutor charging an individual with a crime.

infraction: punishable by a fine.

inherent impossibility: an act that is incapable of achieving the desired result.

insanity defense: a legal excuse based on a mental disease or defect.

Insanity Defense Reform Act of 1984: law passed by the U.S. Congress making it more difficult to establish legal insanity in federal courts following the jury verdict that John Hinckley was not guilty by reason of insanity for the attempted assassination of President Ronald Reagan.

insider trading: use of confidential corporate information to buy or sell stocks.

intangible property: property that represents something of value such as checks, money orders, credit card numbers, car titles, and deeds demonstrating ownership of property.

intellectual property: the content of books, films, artistic works, musical scores, and other "products of the mind."

intent-to-do-serious-bodily-harm murder: a killing committed with the purpose of causing serious physical injury.

intermediate appellate courts: courts between municipal courts and the Supreme Court.

intermediate level of scrutiny: classifications based on gender must be factually related to differences based on gender and must be substantially related to the achievement of a valid state objective.

international criminal law: treaties agreed to by the international community that addresses crimes that are so serious that they are considered to be the concern of all nations and peoples. These treaties prohibit and punish acts such as genocide, torture, war crimes, and terrorism.

international terrorism: a violent or dangerous act occurring outside the United States intended to intimidate or coerce the civilian population or to influence government policy by intimidation or coercion or to affect the conduct of a government by mass destruction, assassination, or kidnapping.

Interstate Commerce Clause: constitutional power of the U.S. Congress to regulate commerce among the states.

intervening cause: a cause that occurs between the defendant's criminal act and a social harm.

intervention in defense of others: the privilege to exercise self-defense on behalf of an individual in peril.

intrinsic force: the amount of force required to achieve penetration.

involuntary act: unconscious act or automatism.

involuntary intoxication: a defense to criminal offenses where the defendant meets the standard for mental illness in the state.

involuntary manslaughter: killing of another as a result of gross negligence or recklessness or during the commission of an unlawful act.

irresistible impulse test: mental disease causes the defendant to lose the ability to choose between right and wrong and to avoid engaging in criminal acts.

joint possession: several individuals exercise dominion and control over an object.

justifiable homicide: murder is justified under the circumstances. This includes self-defense, police use of deadly force, and the death penalty.

justification: a defense based on the circumstances of a criminal act.

keeping a place of prostitution: the crime of using a building for prostitution.

kidnapping: the unlawful, nonconsensual, intentional, and forcible asportation of an individual.

knowingly: awareness that conduct is practically certain to cause a result or awareness that circumstances exist.

larceny: trespassory taking and carrying away of the personal property of another with the intent to permanently deprive the individual of possession of the property.

larceny by trick: obtaining possession by a misrepresentation.

legal impossibility: the defense that an individual's act does not constitute a crime as a matter of law.

legislative contempt: the power to punish "disrespectful and disorderly" behavior as well as individuals who refuse a subpoena to testify or to submit documents.

lewdness: willful exposing of the genitals of one person to another in a public place for purposes of sexual arousal or gratification.

libel: a civil action for words that harm an individual's reputation.

living off prostitution: being knowingly supported in whole or in substantial part by the proceeds of prostitution.

loitering: standing in public with no apparent purpose.

magistrate: a lawyer who serves an eight-year term in a U.S. district court who issues search warrants, conducts preliminary hearings, and rules on pretrial motions.

mail fraud: knowing and intentional participation in a scheme or artifice intended to obtain money or property through the use of the mail to execute the scheme.

majority opinion: the decision of a majority of the judges on a multiple-judge panel.

make my day laws: statutes that authorize any degree of force against a trespasser who uses or threatens to use even slight force against the occupant of a home.

mala in se: crimes that are inherently evil.

mala prohibita: crimes that are not inherently evil.

malice aforethought: an intent to kill with ill will and hatred. This may be express or implied.

mandatory minimum drug sentences: the legislature requires judges to sentence an offender to a minimum sentence, regardless of mitigating factors. Prison sentences may be reduced by good-time credits while incarcerated.

manslaughter: killing of another without malice aforethought and without excuse or justification.

masturbation for hire: crime of stimulating the genitals of another.

material support to a foreign terrorist organization: providing material support or resources to a foreign terrorist organization or attempt or conspiracy to do so.

material support to a terrorist: providing support or resources or concealing the nature, location, source, or ownership of material support or resources knowing or intending that the material is to be used in terrorist acts.

mayhem: depriving another individual of a member of his or her body or disfiguring or rendering it useless.

medical marijuana: marijuana allowed under state law for use based on medical necessity.

mens rea: the mental element of a crime.

mere presence rule: an individual's presence at the scene of a crime generally does not satisfy the *actus reus* requirement for accomplice liability.

minimum level of scrutiny test: law presumed constitutional so long as reasonably related to a valid state purpose.

misappropriation doctrine: using inside information to trade on the stock market.

misdemeanor: punishable by less than a year in prison.

misdemeanor manslaughter: killing during the course of a misdemeanor punished as involuntary manslaughter.

misprision of a felony: knowledge a felony was committed; failure to notify the authorities of the crime; and taking affirmative steps to conceal the crime, such as destruction of evidence.

mistake of fact: defense based on mistake of fact that negates a specific criminal intent or knowledge or purpose.

mistake of law: an error of law, with isolated exceptions, is not a defense.

mitigating circumstances: factors that may reduce or moderate the sentence of a defendant convicted at trial.

***M'Naghten* test:** a disease or defect of the mind that results in an individual not knowing what he or she was doing was right or wrong or not knowing what he or she was doing.

Model Penal Code: an influential criminal code drafted by prominent academics, practitioners, and judges affiliated with the American Law Institute to encourage state legislatures to adopt a uniform approach to the criminal law.

money laundering: financial transaction involving proceeds or property derived from unlawful activity.

motive: the underlying reason that explains or inspires an individual to act.

murder: killing of another with malice aforethought and without excuse or justification.

natural and probable consequences doctrine: a person encouraging or facilitating the commission of a crime will be held liable as an accomplice for the crime he or she aided and abetted as well as for crimes that are the natural and probable outcome of the criminal conduct.

necessity defense: a criminal act is justified when undertaken to prevent an imminent, immediate, and greater harm.

negligent manslaughter: negligent manslaughter arises when an individual commits an act that he or she is unaware creates a high degree of risk of human injury or death under circumstances in which a reasonable person would have been aware of the threat.

negligently: a failure to be aware of a substantial and unjustifiable risk that constitutes a gross deviation from the standard of care that a reasonable person would observe in the actor's situation.

nolo contendere: a plea that has the legal effect of a plea of guilty, which does not constitute an admission of guilt in proceedings outside of the immediate trial.

nondeadly force: use of physical force or a weapon that is not likely to cause death or serious injury.

***nullum crimen sine lege, nulla poena sine lege*:** no crime without law, no punishment without law.

objective test for intervention in defense of others: a person intervening in defense of others may intervene where a reasonable person would believe a person is in need of assistance.

obscenity: description or representation of sexual conduct that, taken as a whole, by the average person, applying contemporary community standards, appeals to the prurient interest in sex. Sex is portrayed in a patently offensive way and lacks serious literary, artistic, political, or scientific value when taken as a whole.

obstruction of justice: purposely obstructing, impairing, or perverting the administration of justice by force, violence, physical interference, obstacle, breach of official duty, or any other unlawful act or attempts to undertake these acts.

Occupational Safety and Health Act (OSHA): a federal law protecting workplace safety.

Office of National Drug Control Policy (ONDCP): part of the Executive Office of the President of the United States, established by the Anti–Drug Abuse Act of 1988, that directs the efforts of the various federal agencies concerned with narcotics, coordinates the state and national efforts to combat drugs, and sponsors national antinarcotics media campaigns.

official misconduct: corrupt behavior by a government officer in the exercise of the duties of his or her official responsibilities that may entail malfeasance, misfeasance, or nonfeasance.

omission: failure to act or to intervene to assist another.

original jurisdiction: the first court to hear a case.

overbreadth: a statute that is unconstitutionally broad and punishes both unprotected speech or conduct and protected speech or conduct.

overt act: an overt act in furtherance of an agreement is required under most modern conspiracy statutes.

pandering: encouraging and inducing another to remain a prostitute.

parental responsibility laws: statutory rule that parents are responsible for the criminal acts of their children.

parties to a crime: individuals liable for assisting another to commit a crime.

per curiam: an opinion of an entire court without any single judge being identified as the author.

perfect self-defense: an honest and reasonable belief that constitutes a complete defense to a criminal charge.

perjury: knowledge of a false statement made under oath and material to the proceedings.

persuasive authority: a decision that a court may consult to assist in a judgment that does not constitute binding authority.

petit larceny: a minor larceny, typically involving the taking of property valued at less than a designated monetary amount.

petitioner: an individual filing a collateral attack on a verdict following the exhaustion of direct appeals.

petty misdemeanor: punishable by less than six months in prison.

physical proximity test: an act constituting an attempt must be physically proximate to the completion of the crime.

pimping: procuring a prostitute for another.

***Pinkerton* doctrine:** a conspirator is liable for all criminal acts taken in furtherance of the conspiracy.

plurality opinion: a judicial opinion that represents the views of the largest number of judges on court, although short of a majority. The plurality opinion is typically combined with a concurring opinion to constitute the court majority.

plurality requirement: a conspiracy requires an agreement between two or more parties.

police power: duty to protect the well-being and tranquility of the community.

possession: physical control over property with the ability to freely use and to enjoy the property.

possession with intent to distribute: possession of a controlled substance with the intent to sell or transfer the narcotic.

precedent: a judicial opinion that controls the decision of a court presented with the same issue. A court may conclude that a precedent does not fully fit the case it is adjudicating and distinguish the case before it from the existing precedent.

preemption doctrine: federal law is superior to state law in areas reserved to the national government.

premeditation and deliberation: the standard for first-degree murder involving planning and reflecting on a killing. Premeditation may occur instantaneously.

preparation: acts taken to prepare for committing a crime.

presumption of innocence: an individual is presumed to be not guilty, and the burden is on the government to establish guilt.

principals in the first degree: common law term for the actual perpetrators of a crime.

principals in the second degree: common law term for individuals who are present at the crime scene and assist in the crime.

privacy: the constitutional right to be free from unjustified governmental intrusion into the sphere of personal autonomy.

promoting prostitution: aiding or abetting prostitution.

prompt complaint: a rape victim at common law was required to lodge an immediate report of a rape.

prosecutrix: the victim or complainant in a rape prosecution.

prostitution: soliciting or engaging in sexual activity in exchange for money or other consideration.

proximate cause: the legally responsible cause of a criminal harm and that may involve policy considerations.

proximate cause theory of felony murder: a felon is liable for all foreseeable results of the felony.

public indecencies: public drunkenness, vagrancy, loitering, panhandling, graffiti, and urinating and sleeping in public.

public intoxication: being drunk in public, a misdemeanor offense.

public welfare offenses: regulatory offenses carrying fines that typically do not require a criminal intent.

pump and dump: spreading false information about a company to drive up the stock price.

purposely: a conscious intent to cause a particular result.

rape shield laws: the prosecution may not introduce evidence relating to the victim's sexual relations with individuals other than the accused and may not introduce evidence pertaining to the victim's reputation for chastity.

rape trauma syndrome: a psychological and medical condition common among victims of rape.

rational basis test: a law is presumed valid so long as it is reasonably related to a valid state purpose.

reasonable person: the ideal type of the balanced and fair individual.

reasonable resistance: resistance to rape that is objectively reasonable under the circumstances.

rebuttal: the defense case at trial.

recantation: occurs when, in the same "continuous" proceeding, an individual states that an earlier statement is false. The recantation must take place before the perjury "substantially affected the proceedings" and before it became manifest "that the falsification was or would be exposed."

receiving stolen property: receiving stolen property knowing it to be stolen with the intent to permanently deprive the owner of the property.

reception statute: a state receives the common law as an unwritten part of a state's criminal law.

recklessly: conscious disregard of a substantial and unjustifiable risk that constitutes a gross deviation from the standard of conduct that a law-abiding person would observe in the defendant's situation.

recklessness: an individual is personally aware that his or her conduct creates a substantial risk of death or serious bodily harm.

resist to the utmost: at common law a rape victim was required to demonstrate a determined resistance to the rape.

resisting arrest: knowingly or intentionally fleeing from a law enforcement officer after the officer has by "visible or audible means . . . identified himself or herself and ordered the person to stop."

respondent: an individual against whom a collateral attack is directed.

responsive intervening act: a defendant's criminal act leads to an act undertaken by the victim in reaction to the threat. An unforeseeable and abnormal responsive act limits the defendant's criminal liability.

result crime: requires that the act cause a very specific harm and requires a specific intent.

retreat: withdrawal from a conflict while indicating a desire to avoid a confrontation.

retreat to the wall: obligation to withdraw as fully as possible before resorting to self-defense.

RICO: Title IX of the Organized Crime Control Act of 1970, the Racketeer Influenced and Corrupt Organizations Act, enacted to counter the infiltration of legitimate businesses engaged in interstate commerce by organized crime.

riot: group disorderly conduct by three or more persons.

robbery: the taking of the personal property from an individual's person or presence by violence or intimidation.

Romeo and Juliet laws: laws that recognize that young people will engage in sexual experimentation and that statutory rape should not be a crime where the parties are roughly the same age, or it should be punished less severely.

rout: three or more persons take steps toward the creation of a riot.

rule of four: four Supreme Court justices are required to vote to hear a case.

rule of legality: an individual may not be punished for an act that was not clearly condemned in a statute prior to the time that the individual committed the act.

sabotage: during a time of war or national emergency, the willful injury to war material or premises or utilities with the intent to injure, interfere with, or obstruct the United States or any associate nation in preparing for or carrying out the war or defense activities. During peacetime, sabotage requires an intent to injure, interfere with, or obstruct the national defense of the United States.

Sarbanes-Oxley Act: a securities fraud statute that requires corporate executive officers to certify that corporate financial statements are accurate.

Second Amendment: an amendment to the U.S. Constitution that protects the right of individuals to "keep and bear ams."

second-degree murder: intentional killing of another with malice aforethought.

sedition: any communication intended or likely to bring about hatred, contempt, or disaffection with the constitution or the government.

seditious conspiracy: an agreement to overthrow or destroy a government by force.

seditious libel: writing intended or likely to bring about hatred, contempt, or dissatisfaction with the constitution or the government.

seditious speech: verbal communications intended or likely to bring about hatred, contempt, or disaffection with the constitution or the government.

self-defense: a justification defense that recognizes the right of an individual to defend him- or herself against an armed attack.

sexual assault: assault that involves compelling another person to participate in a sexual act without consent, by threatening or coercing the other person, by placing the other person in fear of imminent bodily injury, by substantially impairing the ability of the other person through drugs or intoxicants without his or her knowledge or against his or her will, or when the victim is below a statutorily designated age and the perpetrator is above a statutorily designated age.

sexual battery: "touching against the will of the person touched" for the "specific purpose of sexual arousal, sexual gratification or sexual abuse."

Sherman Antitrust Act of 1890: criminal punishment of contracts, combinations, and conspiracies in restraint of interstate commerce.

simulation: creation with intent to defraud of false objects, such as antique furniture.

social host liability laws: liability for serving or providing alcohol to minors in the event of an accident or injury.

solicitation: a written or spoken statement in which an individual intentionally advises, requests, counsels, commands, hires, encourages, or incites another person to commit a crime with the purpose that the other individual commit the crime.

solicitation for prostitution: requesting another person to engage in an act of prostitution.

specific intent: a mental determination to accomplish a specific result.

sports bribery: offering of a bribe to influence a sporting event or accepting such bribes.

stalking: following another person or placing another person under surveillance, creating a reasonable fear of immediate or future bodily harm.

stand your ground rule: no requirement to retreat.

stare decisis: precedent.

status: a "characteristic" or a "condition" or "state of being." The rule is that you may not be criminally punished for "who you are"; you may be held liable only for "what you do."

status offense: offense based on personal characteristics or condition rather than conduct that constitutes cruel and unusual punishment.

statutory rape: strict liability offense of intercourse with an underage individual.

strict liability offense: a crime that does not require a criminal intent.

strict scrutiny test: the state has the burden of demonstrating that a law employing a racial or ethnic classification is strictly necessary to accomplish a valid objective.

subornation of perjury: intentionally inducing another person to testify under oath knowing that the testimony constituted perjury. The crime is complete once an individual solicits another person to commit perjury.

substantial capacity test: a person is not responsible for criminal conduct, if at the time of such conduct, as a result of mental disease or defect, he or she lacks substantial capacity.

substantial step test: the Model Penal Code approach to determining attempt. There must be a clear step toward the commission of a crime that is not required to be immediately proximate to the crime itself. The act must be committed under circumstances strongly corroborative of an intent to commit a crime.

substantive criminal law: specific crimes and defenses and general principles.

Supremacy Clause: the clause in the U.S. Constitution that provides that federal laws take precedence over state laws.

symbolic speech: conduct may be protected under the First Amendment where there is an intent to convey a particularized message and there is a strong likelihood that the message will be understood by observers.

tactical retreat: an individual withdraws from a conflict while intending to continue the physical conflict.

tampering with evidence: knowingly and intentionally removing, altering, concealing, or destroying evidence to be offered in a present or future official proceeding.

tangible property: physical property including personal property and real property. Distinguished from intangible property.

terrorism transcending national boundaries: terrorism occurring partly within and partly outside of the United States.

theft statutes: states have adopted consolidated laws punishing larceny, embezzlement, and false pretenses.

tippees: individuals who receive insider information.

tippers: individuals who provide insider information.

tort: civil action for injury to an individual or to his or her property.

torture: inflicting great bodily injury upon another person with the intent to cause cruel or extreme pain and suffering for the purpose of revenge, extortion, or persuasion, or for any sadistic purpose.

trade secret: confidential information that a business relies on for a competitive advantage.

trademark: a specific word, phrase, symbol, or logo used to label a commercial product and to distinguish the product from competitors.

transferred intent: the intent to harm one individual is transferred to another.

Travel Act: interstate or foreign travel or use of the mail or of a facility in interstate or international commerce with the intent to distribute the proceeds of any specified unlawful activity or violence or to promote a specified unlawful activity and thereafter to commit or attempt to commit a crime.

treason: levying war or giving aid and comfort to the enemy.

trial *de novo*: a new trial before an appellate court.

trial transcript: the written record of trial proceedings.

true man: an individual without fault who is able to rely on self-defense.

true threat: threat of bodily harm directed against an individual or a group of individuals.

two-witness rule: rule providing that a conviction for perjury is required to be based on the testimony of two witnesses or must be based on the testimony of one witness and supporting (corroborating) evidence such as a confession or a document.

unilateral: an individual with the intent to enter into a conspiratorial agreement is guilty regardless of the intent of the other party.

unlawful assembly: a gathering of at least three individuals for the purpose of engaging or preparing to engage in conduct likely to cause public alarm.

uttering: circulating or using a forged document.

vagrancy: wandering the street with no apparent means of earning a living.

vehicular manslaughter: killing resulting from the grossly negligent operation of a motor vehicle or resulting from driving while intoxicated (DWI).

vicarious liability: holding an individual or corporation liable for a crime committed by another based on the nature of the relationship between the parties.

violation: a minor crime punishable by a fine and not subject to imprisonment. Also called an infraction.

void for vagueness: a law violates due process that fails to clearly inform individuals of what acts are prohibited and/or fails to establish clear standards for the police.

voluntary intoxication: defendant not held liable for an offense involving "knowledge or purpose." Increasingly not recognized as a defense.

voluntary manslaughter: instantaneous killing of another in the heat of passion in response to adequate provocation without a "cooling of blood."

voyeurism: obtaining sexual gratification from viewing another individual's sex organs or sexual activities.

weapons of mass destruction: toxic or poisonous chemical weapons, weapons involving biological agents, or weapons releasing radiation or radioactivity at a level dangerous to human life or explosive bombs.

Wharton's Rule: an agreement by two persons to engage in a criminal act that requires the involvement of two persons cannot constitute a conspiracy.

wheel conspiracy: a conspiracy in which a single individual or individuals serve as a hub that is connected to various individuals or spokes.

white-collar crime: crimes committed by an individual of high status in the course of his or her occupation. The U.S. Justice Department defines white-collar crime as an illegal act that employs deceit and concealment rather than the application of force to obtain money, property, or service or to avoid the payment or loss of money or to secure a business or professional advantage.

willful blindness: knowledge is imputed to individuals who consciously avoid awareness in order to avoid criminal responsibility.

wire fraud: knowing and intentional participation in a scheme or artifice intended to obtain money or property through the use of interstate wire communication.

withdrawal in good faith: individuals involved in a fight may gain the right of self-defense by clearly communicating that they are retreating from the struggle.

withdrawal of consent: an individual who initially consents to sexual penetration may change his or her mind.

year-and-a-day rule: common law requirement that is being abandoned by many states that limits liability for homicide to a year and a day.

zero tolerance laws: traffic laws prohibiting individuals under twenty-one from driving with any measurable amount of blood alcohol.

Case Index

Subject Index

About the Author

Matthew Lippman is Professor Emeritus at the University of Illinois at Chicago (UIC) and has taught criminal law and criminal procedure in the Department of Criminology, Law, and Justice for more than twenty-five years. He has also taught courses on civil liberties, law and society, and terrorism and teaches international criminal law at John Marshall Law School in Chicago. He earned a doctorate in political science from Northwestern University and a Master of Laws from Harvard Law School, and is a member of the Pennsylvania Bar. He has been voted by the graduating seniors at UIC to receive the Silver Circle Award for outstanding teaching on six separate occasions and has also received the UIC Flame Award from the University of Illinois Alumni Association, as well as the Excellence in Teaching Award, Teaching Recognition (Portfolio) Award, and Honors College Fellow of the Year Award. The university chapter of Alpha Phi Sigma, the criminal justice honors society, named him "criminal justice professor of the year" on three occasions. In 2008, he was recognized as College of Liberal Arts and Sciences Master Teacher. He was honored by the College of Liberal Arts and Sciences, which named him Commencement Marshal at the May 2012 graduation. Professor Lippman is also recognized in *Who's Who Among America's Teachers*.

Professor Lippman is author of one hundred articles and two coauthored books. These publications focus on criminal law and criminal procedure, international human rights, and comparative law. He also is author of four other SAGE volumes, *Contemporary Criminal Law: Concepts, Cases, and Controversies* (4th ed., 2016); *Criminal Procedure* (3rd ed., 2017); *Law and Society* (2015); and *Criminal Evidence* (2016). His work is cited in hundreds of academic publications and by domestic and international courts and organizations. He has also served on legal teams appearing before the International Court of Justice in The Hague, has testified as an expert witness on international law before numerous state and federal courts, and has consulted with both private organizations and branches of the U.S. government. Professor Lippman regularly appears as a radio and television commentator and is frequently quoted in leading newspapers. He has served in every major administrative position in the Department of Criminology, Law, and Justice including Department Head, Director of Undergraduate Studies, and Director of Graduate Studies.